Marketing of High-Technology Products and Innovations

Jakki Mohr

University of Montana

Prentice
Hall

Upper Saddle River, New Jersey 07458

Library of Congress Cataloging-in-Publication Data

Mohr, Jakki J.
 Marketing of high-technology products and innovations / Jakki Mohr.
  p. cm.
 Includes bibliographical references and index.
 ISBN 0-13-013606-9
 1. High technology industries—Marketing. I. Title.

 HC79.H53 M64 2001
 620'.0068'8—dc21

                    00-063700

Vice President/Editorial Director: James Boyd
Senior Editor: Whitney Blake
Assistant Editor: Anthony Palmiotto
Media Project Manager: Cindy Harford
Senior Marketing Manager: Shannon Moore
Production/Manufacturing Manager: Gail Steier de Acevedo
Production Coordinator: Maureen Wilson
Senior Prepress/Manufacturing Manager: Vincent Scelta
Manufacturing Buyer: Natacha St. Hill Moore
Cover Design: Bruce Kenselaar
Cover Art/Photo: Tommy Borah
Composition: Omegatype Typography

10 9 8 7 6 5 4 3 2 1
ISBN 0-13-013606-9

This book is dedicated to my grandmothers, Elda Berg, Verna Sipple, and Gertrude Mohr, who in the past years have given me an appreciation of the fragility of life, and the need to live it wisely.

To the people who see the possibilities,
and who, sometimes with courage, sometimes with faith and hope—
but always with effort, perseverance, and energy
(despite self-doubt)—
strive to make the possible become reality.

Dreams can come true.

Contents

Preface

Marketing high-technology products and innovations is not the same as marketing more traditional products and services. For example, the marketing of a familiar product, such as Coca-Cola, is very different than marketing products with which customers are unfamiliar, such as new computer hardware, software such as a Pentium chip or customer relationship management software, or even a new computer video game. Customers' fear, uncertainty, and doubt about how to use and attain the full benefits of using the product contribute to the need for different marketing considerations. In addition, the competitive environment found in high-tech industries is different than that found in more traditional contexts: Often, innovations are introduced by industry outsiders that industry incumbents are not aware of. Yet another factor contributing to high-tech marketing challenges is the velocity of change: Due to technological breakthroughs, products change so rapidly that standard marketing concepts may not be sufficient.

While a standard approach to marketing, such as the "four Ps" of marketing (product, price, place, and promotion) is still relevant, the standard approaches must be modified to account for the inherent uncertainty in high-tech environments. My primary aim in this book is to provide a framework for making marketing decisions in a high-tech environment. Using a framework to manage the marketing decision-making process will foster greater understanding of the common characteristics in high-tech environments and help manage the riskiness of marketing in a high-tech context.

Based on theories and research from both academics and industry experts (including both venerable hallmarks in the writings on high-tech marketing and more recent articles), the concepts covered in this text represent best practices in the field of high-tech marketing. Although high-tech marketing is an emerging field of study (and because of this, some believe it would be hard to identify right or wrong answers about how to market high-technology products and services), I believe that using the frameworks developed in this book will help high-tech firms to maximize their odds of success. Naturally, as in any emerging field, there will be some tools and concepts that may challenge one's own ideas and beliefs. I encourage readers to draw on the material that is useful and incorporate their own experience and insights.

I use examples from a wide variety of industries and technologies to illustrate the marketing tools and concepts covered in the book. This variety not only captures the richness of the high-tech environment, but also proves the utility of the frameworks and gives the reader experience in applying the frameworks to diverse situations. Some of the industries and contexts covered include telecommunications, information technology (hardware and software), biotechnology, and consumer electronics such as high-definition TV and digital videodisks.

The Internet is an important context in which the frameworks are applied. This book is the first to provide a systematic approach, grounded in relevant theories and empirical research, of marketing on the Internet. Each chapter applies the pertinent concepts to e-commerce and marketing on the Internet.

Marketing does not occur in isolation in any firm but rather is cross-functional in nature. This book brings together marketing with other business disciplines (for example, research-and-development, legal, and management and strategy) to offer insights on how marketing is inter-related and dependent on interactions with other disciplines. Issues for both small and big business will be addressed. The book provides a balance between conceptual discussions and examples, small and big business, products and services, and consumer and business-to-business marketing contexts.

Who Should Read This Book

The book will prove useful in a variety of venues, including

- Upper-level undergraduate and graduate courses on the marketing of high technology and innovation
- Technology institutes, engineering management programs, biotechnology centers, and telecommunications programs
- Executive education courses
- Managers in high-tech firms
- Training programs in high-tech firms
- Technology incubators

Pedagogical Intent

The book is written as a twelve-chapter handbook. Chapter 1 begins with an introduction to high-technology products and industries, offering a definition of high technology based on common characteristics found in empirical research: market, technological, and competitive uncertainty. Chapter 1 also introduces the notion that high-tech marketing strategies must be tailored to the type of innovation (incremental or radical). This notion is carried through subsequent chapters.

Chapters 2 through 4 address issues related to strategy and corporate culture in high-tech firms: core competencies/core rigidities, organizational learning, a culture of innovation, product champions, venture capital funding, relationship marketing, market orientation, and R&D–marketing interactions. Coverage of these issues lays a foundation for marketing effectiveness.

Chapters 5 and 6 address marketing research tools and customer behavior considerations, respectively. One of the particularly challenging aspects of high-tech marketing is understanding customers and markets. Topical coverage in Chapter 5 includes empathic design, lead users, quality function deployment, competitive intelligence gathering, and forecasting. Customer considerations in Chapter 6 include customer decision making for high-tech products, and how marketing to early adopters must be different than marketing to late adopters. This chapter draws heavily on the work of Geoffrey Moore (*Crossing the Chasm* and *Inside the Tornado*).

Chapters 7–10 provide coverage of the 4 Ps of marketing: product, place, price, and promotion:

- Chapter 7, Product Development and Management Issues in High-Tech Markets, begins with the framework of the use of a technology map to guide product development. Pertinent considerations include decisions about technology transfer and licensing, product platforms and derivatives, protection of intellectual property, and so forth.
- Chapter 8, Distribution Channels and Supply Chain Management in High-Tech Markets, provides a framework for making distribution decisions. Focus is given to the use of the Internet as a new channel, and the need to manage the transition and resulting conflict.
- Chapter 9, Pricing Considerations in High-Tech Markets, provides a framework for pricing decisions, with heavy emphasis given to the need to be customer-oriented in managing this element of the marketing mix. Moreover, in light of the rapid price declines in many high-tech industries (the most extreme of which is a price of $0 for many digital products available on the Internet), focused attention is given to strategies used to generate profits in light of the "technology paradox" (how to make money when the price of product is declining rapidly).
- Chapter 10, Advertising and Promotion in High-Tech Markets: Tools to Build and Maintain Customer Relationships, emphasizes the importance of using advertising and promotion tools to develop a strong brand name (as one mechanism to allay customer anxiety), the need to manage product preannouncements, and communication tools used in managing customer relationships.

Chapter 11 focuses exclusively on e-commerce and Internet marketing. Using the case of Charles Schwab's successful foray into the world of on-line brokering, the chapter discusses issues unique to marketing and managing business on the Internet.

Chapter 12, Realizing the Promise of Technology, concludes with regulatory and ethical considerations high-tech marketers face.

The book's flexibility lets it be used in several ways. First, it can be used as the primary textbook in a full-semester course on the marketing of high technology and innovation. In addition to covering the material in the text, instructors can add cases, semester projects, class presentations, and industry speakers for a very full semester. The companion Instructor's Manual provides suggestions for cases, as well as ideas for semester projects that have worked well in the class I teach. The Instructor's Manual will also provide Powerpoint slides for class lecture and answers to end-of-chapter discussion questions. Instructors and students will also have access to a text Web site, providing updates and current events on a timely basis.

Second, the book can also be used for classes of less than a full semester in duration. The twelve-chapter format makes the material accessible in a compressed time period.

Third, in addition to being used as a stand-alone text in a full-semester course, the book can also be used as a companion text for other courses, including

- The management of technology and innovation
- Business-to-business marketing
- New-product development
- Internet marketing and e-commerce
- Marketing management

A Caveat: What This Book Is Not

First, this book is not meant to be the only marketing reference that a high-tech marketer relies on. Rather than addressing marketing fundamentals, the book's primary focus is on the unique characteristics of the high-tech environment and the challenges those characteristics pose for marketing. This is not to say that standard marketing concepts should not be used; hence, a book of marketing fundamentals should be used as a reference as well.

Second, this book is not focused specifically on Internet marketing nor on the use of technology for marketing purposes. Although Internet and e-commerce applications are woven throughout, Chapter 11 deals specifically with Internet issues, interested readers are referred to other sources for more thorough coverage of the background and issues in Internet marketing.

Third, although this book addresses new-product development, it draws very selectively from that literature and research. For readers interested in a more thorough overview of issues and the process of new-product development, a new-product development/management book should also be referenced.

Fourth, many high-tech marketing tools and concepts relate to business-to-business marketing, or the selling of high-tech products and services to other businesses, be they users of the product, manufacturers who incorporate the product, say, computer chips, into their own products, or resellers of the product. Cultivating relationships can be a critical component in such business-to-business relationships, and interested readers are referred to the several recent books on this topic.

Finally, this book is focused primarily on the marketing of technology and innovation. There are related books on the management of technology and innovation that might also be useful complements.

Special Features

- *End-of-Chapter Discussion Questions.* The discussion questions at the end of each chapter are designed to assess the reader's knowledge of the material covered, offer additional opportunities to apply the chapter's concepts, and allow students to generate additional insights about the concepts.
- *Technology Tidbits.* Each chapter includes a one- or two-paragraph summary about cool, cutting-edge technology of which the average person is unaware, to stimulate thoughts and knowledge about radical innovations coming down the pike.
- *Technology Expert's View from the Trenches.* Each chapter has one or two technology experts sharing their views about specific issues pertinent to each chapter. These are insights from people working in the field in a variety of high-tech positions. For example, Keith Flaugh, IBM's director of pricing, offers his insights in the pricing chapter; Tami Syverson, competitive intelligence analyst at Sun Microsystems, offers her insights in the market research chapter; Judy Mohr, patent agent for biotech products, offers her insights in Chapter 7 on protection of intellectual property. Other experts include Mike McDonough, senior vice president of sales and marketing, GTE Wireless; Jack Trautman, general manager, Hewlett-Packard's Bristol Division; Jennifer Longstaff, technical marketing, Xilinx; and Greg Simon, CEO, Simon Strategies (consulting group for government policy on high tech), to name a few.

- *Web site.* The text will have a password-protected companion Web site for use by instructors. The site will feature current events articles and assignments on a chapter-by-chapter basis, a chat room for instructors to share resources and pedagogical information, and updated and current information on available cases and resources (such as recommended readings from the trade press for books and related information). Links to useful related Web sites will also be provided for each chapter.
- *Instructor's Manual.* The Instructor's Manual will feature answers to the end-of-chapter discussion questions, PowerPoint slides for each chapter, suggested course projects and student assignments, suggested films, and case recommendations on a chapter-by-chapter basis.

Conclusion

High-tech products and services are introduced in turbulent, chaotic environments, where the odds of success are often difficult to ascertain at best and stacked against success at worst. This book is designed to provide frameworks for systematic decision making about marketing in high-tech environments. In doing so, it offers insights about how marketing tools and techniques must be adapted and modified for high-technology products and services. The text highlights possible pitfalls, mitigating factors, and the how-to's of successful high-tech marketing.

ACKNOWLEDGMENTS

I've come to appreciate that, although the author's name is listed on the front of a book, it is only through the efforts of many people that a book actually is completed.

This book would never have left the ground were it not for the enthusiastic encouragement from my colleagues in marketing, including Ajay Kohli, Arvind Sahay, Jim Simpson, Joe Cannon, Sanjit Sengupta, Ely Dahan, and Shikhar Sarin, to name only a few. In addition, the energy and commitment exhibited by the team at Prentice Hall, Larry Armstrong, Gabrielle Dudnyk, Whitney Blake, Bruce Kaplan, Shannon Moore, and Maureen Wilson, were also inspirational at the outset of this project and through its development.

Although these people were instrumental in getting the project off the ground, my early mentors in high-tech marketing infused in me a passion for the subject. Tom Kelly, my high-tech marketing professor at Colorado State University (and a Hewlett-Packard executive), and Jack Trautman (also a Hewlett-Packard executive) were early influences on my view of the field.

I've also had much helpful assistance along the way in compiling information and just keeping me organized. I'd like to thank the following students who offered me dedicated assistance: Tahnee Beartusk, Tom Disburg, and Thomas Lundell. The majority of the artwork in the text is due to the fine efforts of Laurie Toomey, who worked tirelessly to get my figures correct. I'd also like the thank the students in my fall 1999 High-Tech Marketing class for "piloting" early drafts of the chapters. In addition to providing a wonderful, supportive environment, they provided useful feedback and helped me to see where the materials were simply not clear enough. This book is also the product of the supportiveness of my dean, Larry Gianchetta; department chair, Nader Shooshtari; and colleagues at the University of Montana.

One of the special features of this book—the Technology Expert's View from the Trenches—exists solely because of the generosity of the experts and their companies. I appreciate the many willing contributions of my dear friends, and friends of friends, who have written excellent contributions in their "Technology Experts" boxes throughout the text. I'd like to give a special thanks to my sister, Judy Mohr, for her willingness to work with me to develop a prototype for these contributions. Another of the special features—the Technology Tidbits—exists because of the conscientiousness and willing support of product managers whom I contacted out of the blue. They graciously provided critiques of the summaries of their technologies and were prompt in providing pictures.

The monumental task of writing a book had me despairing early in the project, and I'd like to thank Philip Cateora, not only for his encouragement but also for his mentoring on the process. Useful insights and support were also forthcoming from Gil Churchill, Mary Fischer, Charles Goeldner, Michael Solomon, and Gary Porter. I would also like to thank the following reviewers: Don Bacon, University of Denver; Joseph Cannon, Colorado State University; William Moor, Arizona State University; Andrew Sage, George Mason University; Shikhar Sarin, Rensselaer Polytechnic Institute; Sanjit Sengupta, San Francisco State University; James Simpson, University of Alabama–Huntsville; Jack Swasy, American University; and Kathy Winsted, Pace University.

Finally, and most importantly, I sincerely thank my husband, Steve Zellmer, and young children, Willie and Claire, for their unflagging understanding of the many long weekends and many late nights that I was away.

About the Author

Dr. Mohr is the Ron and Judy Paige Faculty Fellow and an associate professor of marketing at the University of Montana–Missoula. Prior to joining the University of Montana in the fall of 1997, Dr. Mohr was an assistant professor at the University of Colorado–Boulder (1989–1997), where she earned both the Frascona Teaching Excellence Award (1992) and the Susan Wright Research Award (1995). Before beginning her academic career, she worked in Silicon Valley in the advertising area for both Hewlett-Packard's Personal Computer Group and TeleVideo Systems. She received her B.B.A. from Boise State University (1982), her M.S. in marketing from Colorado State University (1984), and her Ph.D. in marketing from the University of Wisconsin–Madison (1989).

Dr. Mohr's research has been published in the *Journal of Marketing,* the *Strategic Management Journal,* the *Journal of Public Policy and Marketing,* the *Journal of Retailing,* the *Journal of High Technology Management Research, Marketing Management,* and *Computer Reseller News.*

Dr. Mohr's interests lie primarily in the area of marketing of high-technology products and services, spanning a broad range of technologies including but not limited to the Internet and e-commerce. She teaches courses in the marketing of high-technology products and services, business-to-business marketing, electronic commerce and Internet marketing, and marketing management.

Her early research focuses on organizational communication between partners in strategic alliances/partnerships and between distribution channel members. In addition, she studies the use of proprietary information in high-technology marketing, and marketing communications budget allocation decisions.

CHAPTER 1

Introduction to High Technology

oday's global economy is, to a large extent, driven by technological innovation. Advances in microchip technology are finding applications across a wide range of industries, well beyond traditional computer applications. For example, computer chips are being used in everyday household appliances such as toasters, and even being implanted in pets and farm animals for identification and health monitoring. The field of biotechnology has taken off and is spawning innovations not only in medical applications but also in waste cleanup and crop biology. The advances in crop biology are one reason that chemical giants such as Monsanto Company, Dow Chemical, and DuPont are acquiring or investing heavily in food-technology firms, including seed and soybean companies such as Pioneer Hi-Bred International Inc., and forming partnerships with grain- and meat-processing companies such as Cargill and ConAgra Inc.[1]

The list of even basic industries that technology is changing is vast and includes automobiles, oil and gas, and consumer foods. Although some might believe that these industries are more low tech than high tech, innovations are revolutionizing them. The traditional mechanical engineering used in automobile design is migrating to electrical engineering. The auto industry has coined a new term, *mechatronics,* to describe this combination of mechanical and electrical principles.[2] And Hewlett-Packard, a strong player in the computer industry, has recently spun off a division in Loveland, Colorado, to deal exclusively with the Big Three automakers in Detroit to address innovations in this area. The oil industry is closer to a high-tech industry than to the commodity business it once was, now driven by companies that lead in the key technologies that drive down the costs of exploration and production.[3] Even consumer products companies, such as Procter & Gamble, are driven by technology. Procter & Gamble filed 16,000 patents in 1995[4] and introduced such biotech innovations as olestra, the fat substitute. Clearly, technological innovations are revolutionizing many industries, creating a high-tech environment very similar in flavor and feel to more standard high-tech industries of computers, telecommunications, and so on.

As these examples indicate, the scope of high-technology applications is no longer limited to computers, telecommunications, or consumer electronics—the "traditional" high-tech industries; it encompasses a broad cross section of industries in today's business economy. Indeed, during the 1993 to 1996 time frame, the high-tech sector contributed 27% of the growth in gross domestic product, compared with 14% for residential housing and only 4% for the auto sector. In 1996, a stunning 33% of GDP growth came from information technology industries alone,[5] and information technology (including computers, software, and telecommunications) is the leader in the continued growth of the New Economy.[6] Internet-based transactions are exploding, from $150 billion in 1999 to $330 billion in 2000 to predictions of $660 billion in 2001.[7] Some argue that the impact of the technology sector on the economy means that new tools and indicators for economic forecasting are required; additional detail on the New Economy is provided in Box 1-1, "The New Business Cycle."

The New Business Cycle

Rather than being inversely related, the New Economy exhibits the unique combination of faster growth and lower inflation rates at the same time. The U.S. economy has been able to sustain high rates of growth for an extended period—nearly 4% growth since 1994 (with the resulting low unemployment rates)—and, at the same time, keep inflation at a low level (roughly 2% in 1999). At no other time have high growth rates been coupled with low inflation rates. At its extreme, economic growth has actually propelled prices lower!

Many believe that the New Economy's basis on massive investments in information technology has enhanced the stability of business operations (smoothing inventories and orders), improved communications, and, as a result, yielded huge increases in productivity. Moreover, improvements in e-commerce provide efficiencies in business operations that will further fuel productivity enhancements. The substitution of knowledge and information for physical assets (or the conversion of "atoms" to "bits") has reduced costs and enabled radically new ways of doing business.

Moreover, despite strong demand and rising wages for high-tech workers, inflationary pressures are counteracted by constantly falling prices for computers and communications equipment. And, unlike traditional industries (in which productivity growth would slow as factories hit their capacity limits, prices would rise, and create a turnaround), high-tech products require a big up-front investment, but then the cost of production is relatively low. Hence, rising demand drives average costs down, making it possible to charge lower prices and boost demand even further. As a result, some economists believe that the boom–bust cycle of the past is now history.

How large is the role of high tech in the New Economy? High-tech (computer, software, and communications) industries grew at a pace far exceeding the rest of the economy during the period from 1993 to 1996. In 1996, U.S. consumers and businesses spent $282 billion on information technology hardware alone, making it larger than any of the traditionally cyclical sectors such as autos and construction—that's 17% more than purchases of new cars and 49% more than new homes. Indeed, high tech has grown to be such a large chunk of the economy that there's a feedback loop to the rest of the economy. When high tech expands, more workers earn more dollars to finance the purchases of new cars, homes, and so forth. One study showed that each Microsoft job created 6.7 new jobs in the state of Washington, compared to 3.8 new jobs created by every new opening at the Boeing Company.

As another indicator of the importance of technology, some $600 billion was spent worldwide to battle the Y2K bug. To cope with the situation, companies in a variety of industries diverted productive resources (people) to fixing it, to the tune of $119 billion in lost economic output between 1998 and 2001, while management consulting and accounting firms added 200,000 new workers to advise clients on Y2K.[a] Although very few problems arising from the Y2K bug were encountered, the benefits of the investments in new technology provided a solid foundation for new on-line systems for e-commerce, cleaning outdated equipment and modernizing business processes.[b]

The large role of high tech in the economy calls into question the use of traditional cyclical indicators, such as housing starts, auto sales, or inflation. Rather, the new business cycle is tied to the health of the high-tech sector. Yet, government statistics fail to capture the productivity-enhancing effects of digital technology, and accounting records generally find it hard to capture the effects of knowledge.[c]

But high tech can be more volatile than the automobile industry, with the biggest swings driven by new technologies in a spiral effect. If the new-product pipeline slows, demand can fall sharply. (On the flip side, a hot new technology can send sales skyrocketing.) If profits drop sharply, many high-tech companies have to curtail new-product development. As the pace of technological change slows, buyers have less reason to upgrade immediately, dampening demand even more. Information technology is now the single largest line item in many corporate capital budgets, which makes it a tempting target for cost cutting if the product cycle slows. And, unlike cars, consumers do not really need a new computer, buying a new model only if they can afford it.

Moreover, some predict a huge shake-out in the dot.com world, with as many as 90% of existing dot.coms either out of business, purchased, or merged in 2000.[d] (However, others believe that the efficiencies offered by the Internet constitute a permanent economic shift.) This will be particularly painful because, as stated by former Fed Chairman Paul Volcker,

> The fate of the world economy is now totally dependent on the growth of the U.S. economy, which is dependent on the stock market, whose growth is dependent on about 50 stocks, half of which have never reported any earnings.[e]

A slowdown could have repercussions on the whole economy. So, the downside to the major role of high tech is that the economy is vulnerable to a high-tech slowdown in a way that was never true before.[f] And, regardless of the impact,

> the industrial economy will persist as far into the third millennium as anyone can see, just as the agricultural economy persisted through the Industrial Age and remains vital today. But, there's little doubt that much of today's economic dogma will account for an ever-shrinking proportion of economy activity.[g]

---

[a] Mandel, Michael (1998), "Zap! How the Year 2000 Bug Will Hurt the Economy" *Business Week,* March 2, pp. 93–97.

[b] Stepanek, Marcia (2000), "The Y2K Bug Repellent Wasn't a Waste," *Business Week,* January 17, p. 35; Starkman, Dean and Danielle Stessa (1999), "Debugging Yields Corporate America Unexpected Benefits," *Wall Street Journal,* p. A10.

[c] Stewart, Thomas (1998), "Real Assets, Unreal Reporting: Why Generally Accepted Accounting Principles Do an Unacceptable Job of Accounting for the Principal Activities of Knowledge-Intensive Companies," *Business Week,* July 6, pp. 207–208.

[d] James, Dana (2000), "Are You Ready for the Coming Dot-Com Crash?" *Marketing News,* January 31, pp. 11, 15.

[e] "Numbers," (2000), *Business 2.0,* February, p. 252.

[f] Richards, Bill (1998), "'Silicon Forest' Worries, Is This Goodbye Mr. Chips?" *Wall Street Journal,* October 26, p. B1.

[g] Petzinger, Thomas, Jr. (2000), "So Long Supply and Demand," *Wall Street Journal,* January 1, p. R31.

Sources: Petzinger, Thomas, Jr. (2000), "So Long Supply and Demand," *Wall Street Journal,* January 1, p. R31; "Industry Outlook," (2000), *Business Week,* January 10, pp. 84–146; Mandel, Michael (2000), "The New Economy," *Business Week,* January 31, pp. 73–91; Mandel, Michael (1997), "The New Business Cycle," *Business Week,* March 31, pp. 58–68.

Given the increasing role of technological developments in our economy, categorizing particular industries as low or high tech may not be as easy as one would expect. Simply drawing a continuum ranging from low-tech industries on the one end to high-tech industries on the other and placing industries on the continuum based on common perceptions might, in fact, be misleading. Agriculture, heavy industry (steel mills, etc.), and services might not be as low tech as some might believe. The next section details various approaches to defining *high technology*.

DEFINING *HIGH TECH*

If high tech is permeating even basic industries, just what is high tech? Is it an industry that produces technology? Or is it one that intensively uses technology? Just what is technology? *Technology* is the stock of relevant knowledge that allows new techniques to be derived and includes both product and process know-how.[8] *Product technology* covers the ideas embodied in the product and its constituent components. *Process technology* encompasses the ideas involved in the manufacture of a product. Box 1-2 on the British Broadcasting Corporation's definition of technology provides an interesting perspective.

BOX 1-2

British Broadcasting Corporation's Definition of Technology

The word *technology* usually conveys images of computers, laser beams, robots, and complex gadgets. Or, depending upon one's interests, it might conjure up thoughts of a camera, or a car, or state-of-the-art keyhole surgery. Regardless of one's specific thoughts, chances are it's something new. Technology generally means cutting edge.

The word technology comes from the Greek word *techne,* meaning art or craft, which implies a set of crafts, techniques, or a collection of methods that can be used for building, manufacturing, or producing. This definition can be broadened to mean "that which humans use to control their environment" or "the ways that people bring nature under control." The funny thing is that although the word technology comes from Greece, it wasn't part of the Greek vocabulary. In fact, the word didn't even exist until the nineteenth century. So, even though technology has been around ever since people inhabited the earth, it's only actually been called technology for the last hundred years.

People have used technology for thousands of years. The history of technology, then, is a study of the ways people have survived and prospered in the natural world. During the Stone Age, the phrase *cutting edge* really did mean a cutting edge!

In modern times, technology is also seen as the application of science, where a scientist conducts research, develops theories, and writes a journal article, and then the scientist or someone else may commercialize the science into something useful.

Source: Adapted from BBC Online, "Reinventing the Wheel." Available: www.bbc.co.uk/education/archive/wheel.

If technology is useful know-how, what, then, is *high* technology? There are nearly as many definitions of high tech as there are people studying it. For example, one definition defines high-technology industries as

> [those] engaged in the design, development, and introduction of new products and/or innovative manufacturing processes through the systematic application of scientific and technical knowledge.[9]

This section overviews various governmental definitions of high technology, as well as definitions found in research on high-technology marketing.

Government Definitions of High Technology

Most government definitions of high technology classify industries as high tech based on certain criteria such as the number of technical employees, the amount of research and development outlays, or the number of patents filed in a given industry. For example, the U.S. Bureau of Labor Statistics classified industries based on their proportion of R&D employment.[10] Thirty R&D-intensive industries—those with 50% higher R&D employment than the average proportion for all industries surveyed (Level I)—were identified; another 10 R&D-moderate (Level II) industries were identified, or those whose proportion of R&D employment was at least equal to the average proportion for all industries (but less than 50%). These 40 industries are shown in Table 1-1; they include both manufacturing and service industries, as well as defense and civilian industries.

The Organisation for Economic Cooperation and Development (OECD) uses a similar definition, defining high tech in terms of the ratio of R&D expenditures to value added of a particular industry.[11] The National Science Foundation examines the R&D intensity, or R&D spending-to-net-sales ratios.[12]

However, definitions based on these specific criteria do have shortcomings. The range of technical innovation in industries classified by the Bureau of Labor Statistics as R&D intensive is extremely wide,[13] including some industries whose products are modified only incrementally (e.g., cigarettes) and in which new technological breakthroughs have not been seen in years. The classification may include industries in which most output is standardized and produced in large volume by relatively unskilled workers. These industries have a proportion of scientific or engineering workers high enough to make them R&D intensive or moderate, but the bulk of this talent may be used to alter incrementally the characteristics of established products in slowly growing, advertising-intensive markets.[14] One example would be the cigarette industry. Part of the reason for this ostensible misclassification stems from the underlying basis: the number of employees engaged in R&D.

Moreover, this classification may exclude the development of new products or processes by skilled workers in an industry whose score on R&D employment does not qualify it for high-tech status. For example, in one R&D center funded by the textile industry (generally not considered a high-tech industry), engineers and computer scientists are working to automate the design, cutting, and fitting of garments for retail customers. This project uses the latest in laser and computer technology.[15]

Finally, many low-cost manufacturers of electronic computers (SIC 3571) now use mass-produced components assembled in highly routine settings with minimal engineering and

TABLE I-I	High-Technology Industry Employment, Total and by Level, 1989	
SIC code	*Industry*	*Percent Research and Development Employment*
	Total	100.00
	Level I industries[a]	**86.5**
131	Crude petroleum and natural gas operations	1.9
211	Cigarettes	.4
281	Industrial inorganic chemicals	1.3
282	Plastics materials and synthetics	1.8
283	Drugs	2.3
284	Soap, cleaners, and toilet goods	1.6
285	Paints and allied products	.6
286	Industrial organic chemicals	1.5
287	Agricultural chemicals	.5
289	Miscellaneous chemical products	1.0
291	Petroleum refining	1.2
299	Miscellaneous petroleum and coal products	.1
335	Nonferrous rolling and drawing	1.8
355	Special industry machinery	1.6
357	Computer and office equipment	4.5
362	Electrical industrial apparatus	1.8
366	Communications equipment	2.7
367	Electronic components and accessories	6.1
371	Motor vehicles and equipment	8.5
372	Aircraft and parts	7.1
376	Guided missiles, space vehicles, parts	1.9
381	Search and navigation equipment	3.0
382	Measuring and controlling devices	3.3
384	Medical instruments and supplies	2.4
386	Photographic equipment and supplies	1.0
737	Computer and data-processing services	7.3
871	Engineering and architectural services	7.7
873	Research and testing services	5.3
874	Management and public relations	5.8
899	Services, n.e.c.[b]	.4
	Level II industries	**13.4**
229	Miscellaneous textile goods	.5
261	Pulp mills	.2
267	Miscellaneous converted paper products	2.4
348	Ordnance and accessories, n.e.c.[b]	.8
351	Engines and turbines	.9
356	General industrial machinery	2.4
359	Industrial machines, n.e.c.[b]	3.2
365	Household audio and video equipment	.9
369	Miscellaneous electrical equipment and supplies	1.7
379	Miscellaneous transportation equipment	.5

[a] See text for definition of Level I and Level II industries.

[b] n.e.c. = not elsewhere classified.

Source: Hadlock, Paul, Daniel Hecker, and Joseph Gannon (1991), "High Technology Employment: Another View," *Monthly Labor Review*, July, pp. 26–30.

scientific input. Even within the semiconductor industry, high-volume chip manufacturing can involve high capital-to-labor ratios and relatively low scientific labor requirements.[16] Although such industries are generally classified as high tech, the innovations at this stage of the industry development may be fairly incremental.

As these examples, as well as the others noted at the outset of this chapter, show, the effects of technological change can be seen in almost every industry. Hence, rather than taking an industry-based approach to defining high tech, some advocate a definition based on common underlying characteristics. This approach is found in research on the marketing of high-technology products and innovations.

Defining High Tech in Terms of Common Characteristics

As shown in Figure 1-1, another view of high technology is based on common characteristics that all high-technology industries share,[17] most notably, market uncertainty, technology uncertainty, and competitive volatility.[18]

FIGURE 1-1 Characterizing High-Tech Marketing Environments

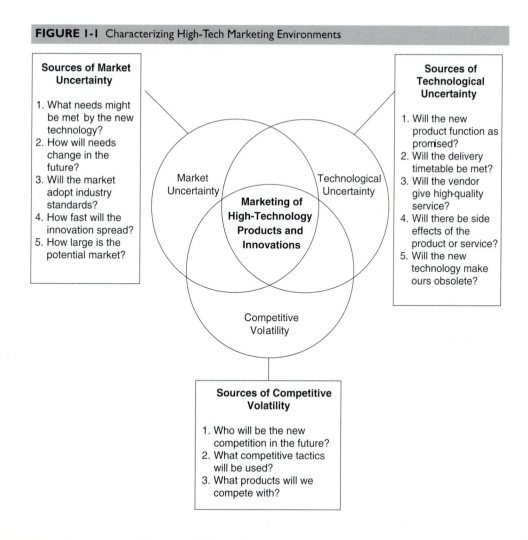

Sources of Market Uncertainty

1. What needs might be met by the new technology?
2. How will needs change in the future?
3. Will the market adopt industry standards?
4. How fast will the innovation spread?
5. How large is the potential market?

Market Uncertainty

Marketing of High-Technology Products and Innovations

Technological Uncertainty

Sources of Technological Uncertainty

1. Will the new product function as promised?
2. Will the delivery timetable be met?
3. Will the vendor give high-quality service?
4. Will there be side effects of the product or service?
5. Will the new technology make ours obsolete?

Competitive Volatility

Sources of Competitive Volatility

1. Who will be the new competition in the future?
2. What competitive tactics will be used?
3. What products will we compete with?

Market Uncertainty   Market uncertainty refers to ambiguity about the type and extent of customer needs that can be satisfied by a particular technology.[19] There are five sources of market uncertainty.

Market uncertainty arises, first and foremost, from consumer fear, uncertainty, and doubt (or the FUD factor[20]) about what needs or problems the new technology will address, as well as how well it will meet those needs. Anxiety about these factors means that customers may delay adopting new innovations, require a high degree of education and information about the new innovation, and need postpurchase reassurance and reinforcement to assuage any lingering doubt. For example, when a business decides to automate its sales force with computers, employees are bound to have some apprehension about learning new skills, wondering if the new mode of working will be better than the old one, and so forth. Hence, marketers must take steps to allay such apprehension both before and after the sale.

Second, customer needs may change rapidly, and in an unpredictable fashion, in high-tech environments. For example, customers today may want to treat their illnesses with a particular medical regimen but next year may desire a completely different approach to the same health problems. Such uncertainties make satisfying consumer needs a moving target.

Third, customer anxiety is perpetuated by the lack of a clear standard for new innovations in a market. For example, the market for digital videodiscs (DVDs)—a product similar to audio CDs that stores entire movies and can also be used in place of CD-ROMs on high-end PCs—has been plagued by a problem with standards. In the United States, an alliance that includes Circuit City stores, Matsushita Electric, Thomson, and several film studios is pushing a format called Divx, which stands for "digital video express." These disks will be only partly compatible with DVD. Toshiba, DVD's largest advocate, says it is not worried.[21] However, questions about the dominant design of the future will hamper customer adoption, as consumers delay purchase to minimize the odds of making a "wrong" choice. (Remember the Beta–VHS fiasco?)

One important role of high-tech marketing is to recognize the market uncertainty customers face in adoption decisions of new technology. Coalescing disparate product development efforts around common standards can help reduce the perceived risk for customers in terms of making a bad choice. Reducing fear and uncertainty can help serve as a catalyst for adoptions. Moreover, setting standards in an industry is intimately related to the product development process and involvement of business partners. If a firm chooses to use a unique or proprietary system in its product development, that is a very different process (with very different consequences) than choosing to develop a system based on open standards available to multiple players in an industry. For example, some have argued that Apple's decision to retain a proprietary operating system rather than collaborating on development of an open standard was a key downfall in its strategy. Having a common industry standard allows the various players in an industry to collaborate on developing the complementary infrastructure required for products to perform. As another example, cellular phone signals can be either digital (PCS devices) or analog. However, not all regions of the country can broadcast both types of signals. Hence, customers who adopted one technology could not use it in all areas. The lack of a standard for transmission has further perpetuated consumer fear, uncertainty, and doubt and slowed adoption of the new technology.

Fourth, due in large part to the prior three factors, uncertainty exists among both consumers and manufacturers over how fast the innovation will spread. For example, Figure 1-2 shows that 10 years after color TVs were introduced, only 3% of U.S. households

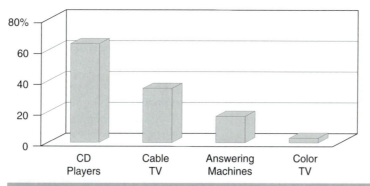

FIGURE 1-2 Technology Adoption (percentage of households 10 years after introduction)

Sources: Adapted from data from Consumer Electronics Association, Electronic Industries Alliance, National Cable TV Association, and Encyclopedia Britannica.

had purchased one. In many cases, the market for high-tech innovations is slower to materialize than most would predict.[22]

Finally, uncertainty over how fast the innovation will spread contributes to an inability for manufacturers to estimate the size of the market. Obviously, market forecasts are crucial for cash flow planning, production planning, and staffing. However, the other sources of market uncertainty contribute to the very real possibility of error in forecasting. For example, in 1988, Zenith forecast that in the year 1992, 66,000 high-definition televisions would be sold (10% of all TV sales), reaching 790,000 (100% of all TVs sold would be HDTV) by the year 1997.[23] However, not until January 1998 were the first HDTV sets sold and broadcasts aired—with a forecast of 100,000 units for 1998.[24]

Indeed, Geoffrey Moore[25] refers to the "chasm" that high-tech products must cross in appealing to a mainstream market. When radically new innovations appear in the marketplace, they appeal to "visionaries" in the market (or innovators and early adopters), who are willing to adopt the new technology despite the often high price tag such items carry. For example, the earliest adopters of electric cars in California paid nearly 25% more to lease their cars than did people who leased a year later. These visionaries were willing to make do with the higher price and hassles that can accompany being an early adopter. For early adopters of electric cars, the "hassle factor" came in the limited number of stations that were capable of recharging batteries and the limited mileage range (90 miles between charges). For software adopters, the hassle factor might come in glitches and incompatibilities with other system components. The visionaries are willing to accept such inconveniences for the psychological and substantive benefits they do receive.

However, such benefits are not sufficient for the majority of the market to adopt new technology. Typically, pragmatists comprise the majority of the market, and they require a different set of benefits and inducements to adopt. The chasm represents the gulf between two distinct marketplaces for technology products. Visionaries are quick to appreciate the new development, but the pragmatists need more hand-holding. The transition between these two markets can be rocky at best, with many high-tech firms never crossing the chasm. Many high-tech firms find it hard to abandon their "techie" roots and talk to this group in customer-friendly terms. The inability to predict whether, and the degree to which, the mainstream market will adopt the product—and the rate of such adoption—given the presence of the chasm, makes it extremely difficult for manufacturers to estimate the size of the market.

In summary, market uncertainty arises from not knowing what customers want from the new technology, how their needs and desires will change, and how that uncertainty affects market development and size.

Technological Uncertainty   **Technological uncertainty** is "not knowing whether the technology—or the company providing it—can deliver on its promise to meet specific needs."[26] Five factors give rise to technological uncertainty. The first comes from questions about whether the new innovation will function as promised. For example, when new cancer drugs are introduced, patients have anxiety about whether they will actually be cured. As another example, the new on-line brokerage firms, the "guinea pigs of the Internet age" on the bleeding edge of technology,[27] have faced major disabling computer glitches. After embarrassing failures early on (1997), the major on-line brokerages beefed up their Internet connections and added more computers to handle more transactions. But the crucial software (known as "middleware") knitting the Internet servers that display Web pages and the back-office computers that process the trades was vulnerable. Coupled with the inability to forecast the volume of trades that would occur, even better testing might not have revealed the problems.

The second source of technological uncertainty relates to the timetable for availability of the new product. In high-tech industries, product development commonly takes longer than expected, causing headaches for both customers and firms. For example, Storage Technology Corporation (STK), a manufacturer of tape backup systems for computer data, announced a new technology to back up massive amounts of data on tape library systems, with the code name Iceberg. However, the product was delayed so long that a competitor beat STK to market, the company nearly went bankrupt, and customers who had delayed purchase of backup systems in anticipation of this new technology were extremely frustrated.

Third, technological uncertainty arises from concerns about the supplier of the new technology: If a customer has problems, will the supplier provide prompt, effective service? When (if?) a technician arrives, will the problem even be "fixable"?

Fourth, the very real concern over unanticipated consequences or side effects also creates technological uncertainty. For example, many companies invested in information technology with the expectation that such investments would make their businesses more productive. However, years later, people question whether there is a productivity boost from investments in information technology—or whether, in the continued efforts to keep current with software upgrades, the use of computers for personal activities (such as e-mail and Internet surfing) actually results in a productivity decrement.[28]

Finally, in high-tech markets, technological uncertainty exists because one is never certain just how long the new technology will be viable—before an even newer development makes it obsolete. As a new technology is introduced, its performance capacity improves slowly and then, because of heavy R&D efforts, improves tremendously, before reaching its performance limits. For example, some people predict that future improvements in microchip performance are limited by the use of semiconductor technology. Japan's Ministry of International Trade and Industry has sponsored a $30 million research program focused on technologies that could replace conventional semiconductors. These technologies are based on quantum physics and neural networks, rather than on electrical engineering. In the tape backup market, some are predicting that lasers and optic devices may make developments in tape media obsolete.

Competitive Volatility   A third characteristic that underlies high-tech markets is competitive volatility. **Competitive volatility** refers to changes in the competitive landscape: which firms are one's competitors, their product offerings, the tools they use to compete. There are three sources of competitive volatility.

First, uncertainty over which firms will be new competitors in the future makes it difficult for firms to understand high-tech markets. Indeed, the majority of the time, new technologies are commercialized by companies *outside* the threatened industry.[29] These new players are viewed as disruptive and frequently dismissed by incumbents.

Second, new competitors that come from outside existing industry boundaries often bring their own set of competitive tactics, tactics with which existing industry incumbents may be unfamiliar. However, these new players end up rewriting the "rules of the game," so to speak, and changing the face of the industry for all players.[30] The most recent example of this type of volatility is the emergence of the "dot.com" players, which have revolutionized the consumer retail business. Amazon.com, Travelocity.com, and etoys.com, among others, were totally unknown to retail booksellers, airlines and travel agents, and toy stores just a few short years ago.

Third, new competition often arises in the form of product form competition, or new ways to satisfy customer needs and problems. One of the big sources of uncertainty that personal computer manufacturers face in 2000 are the new "information appliances" that can be used to access the Internet. Hewlett-Packard decided to hedge its bets, and focus on both PCs and information appliances simultaneously.[31]

As another example of competitive volatility, witness the Internet browser market that was introduced by industry outsider Netscape and how Microsoft scrambled to play catch-up. Rather than using the idea that all stand-alone personal computers would have their own operating system and software, Netscape's idea was to have all software available in an open architecture, available to all to simply download from the Internet. This was a radical departure from Microsoft's definition of an operating system that would be sold and licensed based on fees.

Innovations by both new entrants and incumbents can render obsolete older technologies, and hence, the mortality rate of businesses in high-tech industries can be high, further contributing to competitive volatility. Ongoing industry leadership hinges on the notion of *creative destruction*. Paradoxically, a firm must proactively work to develop the next best technology, which is likely to destroy the basis of its current success and make its sunk investments in the prior technology obsolete. However, if the firm does not commercialize a new technology, rivals will surely do so. Even with successful products, rather than being overly focused on experience curve effects and economies of scale in production, firms should instead strive to develop even better technologies.

Figure 1-1 shows how the marketing of high-technology products and innovations occurs at the intersection of these three variables: market uncertainty, technological uncertainty, and competitive volatility. Although one of three characteristics may exist, or even a combination of two of the three, if all three factors do not exist simultaneously, then the uniqueness that such an environment poses for marketers will be less pronounced.

So, for example, in the case of a decision involving customer anxiety (say, a high-involvement–low-tech decision such as which home to purchase), if buyers aren't also simultaneously considering a radically new way of meeting their needs, then it wouldn't be characterized as high tech. Similarly, customer needs may change rapidly in some areas (such as clothing styles, music, etc.), in which new styles and preferences may make obsolete older ones (technological uncertainty). However, although fads may indicate rapid change in an industry, such purchase decisions generally do not include both (1) a high degree of anxiety and (2) totally new ways of meeting customer needs. Finally, although competitive turbulence may be present in many industries (e.g., restaurants in college towns), the issue in a high-tech environment is whether the new competitors offer a radically new way of meeting customer needs. These situations highlight the fact that the *intersection* of these three characteristics typifies a high-tech marketing environment.

Additional Characteristics Common to High-Tech Markets Additional features that are common to technology markets include the following:[32]

- *Unit-one costs.* **Unit-one costs** refer to the fact that the cost of producing the first unit is very high relative to the costs of reproduction. This type of cost structure is likely to exist when know-how, or knowledge embedded in the design of the product, represents a substantial portion of the value of the products and services. For example, the costs of pressing and distributing a CD-ROM are trivial compared to the cost of hiring programmers and content specialists to develop the code recorded on it.
- *Demand-side increasing returns.* Also called network externalities, or a bandwagon effect, **demand-side increasing returns** exist when the value of the product increases as more users adopt it. In other words, the utility received from an innovation is a function of the number of users; the inflection point is where the utility or value of the innovation increases rapidly because a critical mass of users has adopted it. Examples include the telephone, portals on the Internet, and so forth: The first telephone was worthless, the second made the first more valuable, and so on.

  This concept runs contrary to basic rules of supply and demand, which suggest that increases in supply devalue products. However, products used in networks increase in unit value as the supply increases. This explains, in part, why some firms are willing to give their products away for free.
- *Tradeability problems.* When underlying know-how represents a substantial portion of the value of the products and services in question, buyer–seller exchanges are effectively transformed into intellectual property transactions. So, **tradeability problems** occur when it is difficult to value the knowledge, especially when it is tacit and resides in people and organizational routines.
- *Knowledge spillovers.* **Knowledge spillovers** exist when synergies in the creation and distribution of know-how further enrich a related stock of knowledge. Simply, every innovation creates the opportunity for a greater number of innovations. For example, it was once projected that the Human Genome Project (used to map all human genes) would take at least 40 years, but it took only a fraction of that time, due to knowledge building on knowledge.[33]

  These spillovers create increasing returns in the development of related technologies, resulting in modularity in components and subsystems. Such modularity gives users more choice over time, based on compatibility and common standards.

Even when an industry is subject to market, technological, and competitive uncertainty, innovations are a question of degree and occur at different levels in the supply chain. The next section explores where the innovations occur across a supply chain.

A SUPPLY CHAIN PERSPECTIVE ON TECHNOLOGY

A supply chain depicts the flow of product from producer to consumer. A sample supply chain—albeit a simplistic one—for the automotive industry is shown in Figure 1-3. Customers who buy cars—both consumers for personal household consumption as well as businesses who need fleets for salespeople, company cars, and so forth—purchase cars from car dealers (either with a physical location or on the Internet). Car dealers replenish their inventories from the car manufacturers. To produce the cars, manufacturers must either make or buy all the requisite components: glass, metal, tires, electrical assemblies, drivetrains, and so forth, as well as production equipment (i.e., CAD–CAM systems for car design, etc.).

In many cases, technological innovations occur at the supplier level in the supply chain, rather than in the product (i.e., cars) itself. For example, a major innovation in the auto industry was the electric car. This innovation required major changes in the car's design and componentry. Batteries, wiring, and the frame all had to be reworked. Each of these changes occurred at levels in the supply chain rather distant from the end user, who is still using the same mode of transportation—a car—despite the innovation.

To be sure, innovations can occur in the nature of the product itself; for example, maybe for commuting in the year 2050, we'll be using jetpacks to propel ourselves through the air. (Or, as this chapter's Technology Tidbit predicts, we might have flying cars!) However, more often than not, innovations occur at higher levels in the supply chain, affecting the design, componentry, and production processes of the product, rather than revolutionizing the nature of the product itself. Other examples of the prevalence and predominance of technological innovations occurring at higher levels in the supply chain can be found across many industries, both high and low tech:

- In the oil industry: Major innovations have occurred in exploration and extraction that have revolutionized that industry.
- In the computer industry: Major innovations have occurred in the chips that power the computers.
- In the food industry: The fat substitute olestra is an ingredient that can be used in many foods, such as potato chips and ice cream.
- In hairstyling: Stylists can use 3-D images to view what a particular style would look like on a specific client prior to the cut.

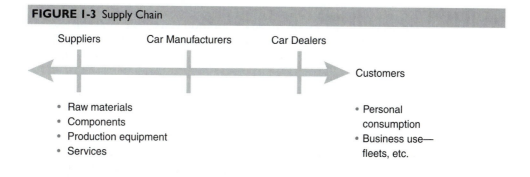

FIGURE I-3 Supply Chain

Suppliers   Car Manufacturers   Car Dealers

Customers

- Raw materials
- Components
- Production equipment
- Services

- Personal consumption
- Business use—fleets, etc.

Dream Machine

THOMAS LUNDELL

Have you ever found yourself stuck in a traffic jam thinking, "If only my car could lift from the ground and fly away"? Well, with the M400 Skycar, you can. The M400 can take off from your backyard and fly at 350 mph, racing over the heads of land-bound commuters stuck in traffic below.

Photograph reprinted with the permission of Moller International, Davis, California

The M400 takes off using the thrust of four sets of shrouded, ducted fans. It is quieter and less dangerous than a helicopter, and the user-friendly control system makes flying the M400 about as easy as driving a car. Once in the air, you log on to a satellite tracking system and the Skycar flies by itself to your destination of choice.

Paul Moller, inventor of the Skycar, believes that we are about five years from large-scale controlled airways. But if you have one million dollars to spend today, you don't have to wait five years. You can throw condescending looks on your stuck coworkers by rush hour tomorrow morning.

Source: McCosh, Dan (2000), "Dream Machine: M400 Skycar," *Popular Science,* February 28, www.popsci.com/scitech/features/skycar/index.html; Waldman, Peter (1999), "Great Idea . . . If It Flies," *Wall Street Journal,* June 24, pp. B1, B4.

The idea of a supply chain reinforces why many believe that the Internet companies likely to be most successful over the long term are those that provide the hardware and software to power Web sites. Using the analogy of the gold rush, it was the people who sold the pans and shovels, and provided infrastructure, who got rich.

Many innovations occur at levels in the supply chain that are removed from end users. Hence, one cannot assume that an industry is *not* high tech simply because the products don't change much at the end-use level. Has the way in which we gas up our cars changed due to the innovations in oil exploration and extraction? Not really. Do we use our computers differently because they have a new chip design? Not typically. A supply chain can be a useful tool to help understand and define high tech in broader terms than just the nature of the products we use.

Clearly, some innovations are more significant in terms of the nature of the breakthrough represented. The next section explores the various types and patterns innovations can take.

A CONTINUUM OF INNOVATIONS

As shown in Figure 1-4, innovative developments can be placed on a continuum rang-ing from radical, breakthrough developments on the one hand to more incremental, modest developments on the other.

Radical/Breakthrough Innovations   Radical innovations are "so different that they can-not be compared to any existing practices or perceptions. They employ new technologies and create new markets. Breakthroughs are conceptual shifts that make history."[34] In stan-dard marketing parlance, they are discontinuous innovations. Others refer to breakthrough innovations as revolutionary,[35] and they are developed in "supply-side" markets.[36] Supply-side markets are characterized by innovation-driven practice, in which a company's goal is to achieve profitable commercial applications for laboratory output; R&D is the prime mover behind marketing efforts, and specific commercial applications or targets are con-sidered only after the innovation is developed. For these reasons, these markets are some-times referred to as "technology-push" situations.

Most radical innovations are typically developed by R&D groups (in companies, in universities, in research laboratories) who often haven't specifically thought about a par-ticular commercial market application during the development process. For example, Tim Berners-Lee, a software engineer, assembled a network of interconnected comput-ers to share and distribute information easily and cheaply in 1980, well before Marc An-dreessen developed a Web browser.[37] In the United States, the Internet emerged as an outgrowth of the need for the U.S. military computer system to survive a Soviet nuclear attack.[38] These innovations were created independently of the vision of the uses they would serve. In the words of Amgen's CEO, Gordon Binder,

> Conventional wisdom says listen to the market. Most pharmaceuticals compa-nies, and quite a few biotech ones as well, are basically market-driven. They see that large numbers of people have a particular disease and decide to do something about it.[39]

FIGURE 1-4 Continuum of Innovations

Incremental ⟷ Radical

- Extension of existing product or process
- Product characteristics well defined
- Competitive advantage on low-cost production
- Often developed in response to specific market need
- "Demand-side" market
- Customer pull

- New technology creates new market
- R&D invention in the lab
- Superior functional performance over "old" technology
- Specific market opportunity or need of only secondary concern
- "Supply-side" market
- Technology push

However, rather than start with the disease and work back to the science, Amgen does the opposite. It takes brilliant science and finds a unique use for it. The company's immune booster, for instance, helps keep the side effects of chemotherapy from killing cancer patients. And a collaborative arrangement with a professor at Rockefeller University discovered a gene that may yield new treatments for obesity.

In other cases, radical innovations are developed as a new way to meet an existing need, or in response to the identification of an emerging need. Regardless of whether the innovation originates from "pure" science or in response to a need, the new technology then creates a new market for itself. Competitive advantage for a breakthrough technology is based on the superior functional performance that the new innovation has to offer over existing methods or products.

Likening it to the invention of the printing press, some see the Internet as a radical innovation. By breaking the monopoly that the rich and the churches had on information, the invention of the Gutenberg printing press in the fifteenth century revolutionized religion, government, science, and the global distribution of wealth. The Internet's abilities to decentralize information, allow interaction between people on a global level, and redistribute wealth seem similar in scope and magnitude to the printing press.[40]

Incremental Innovations　**Incremental innovations,** on the other hand, are continuations of existing methods or practices and may involve extension of products already on the market; they are "evolutionary" as opposed to "revolutionary." Both suppliers and customers have a clear conceptualization of the products and what they can do. Existing products are sufficiently close substitutes.[41] Incremental innovations occur in "demand-side" markets,[42] in which product characteristics are well defined and customers can articulate their needs. In contrast to the view of the Internet as a radical innovation, some see it as an evolutionary innovation, "part of a continuum of technologies that drop the cost and improve the distribution of information," comparable to the impact of television.[43]

In an industrial context (manufacturing applications), incremental innovations may be developed by producers of a mature product who have achieved high volume in their production process.[44] Hence, economies of scale may be very important, and pricing may be based on experience curve effects (costs decline by a fixed and known amount every time accumulated volume doubles) that arise from economies of scale and learning curves. Often, because of the importance of scale economies to these firms, innovations may take the form of production *process innovations,* which lower the costs of production. Competitive advantage is frequently based on low-cost production. Firms whose bread-and-butter business comes from a specific product find that they may be less flexible to radical change and are vulnerable to obsolescence.

Some believe that marketing strategy for innovations is complicated by the fact that innovating firms might view an innovation as a breakthrough, whereas customers might view it as incremental (or vice versa). The unique problems this discrepancy in perceptions can cause are explored in Box 1-3, "Supplier's and Customer's Different Perceptions of Innovation."

It would be overly simplistic to say that high-tech industries are characterized solely by breakthrough innovations. Clearly, many high-tech markets develop incremental innovations. For example, in the area of software, Windows 98 was more of an incremental than a breakthrough innovation. It is vitally important that high-tech marketers be aware of the two different types of innovations, because they have very different implications.

BOX 1-3

Supplier's and Customer's Different Perceptions of Innovation

Figure 1-5 highlights the four possibilities that can occur when considering both the supplier's and customer's perceptions of the innovativeness of a new product. Obviously, when both parties' perceptions match, the path to marketing is fairly clear—as long as marketers understand that each type of innovation needs to be managed differently, as explained in the chapter. However, when a firm views an innovation as incremental but customers see the innovation as a breakthrough (or vice versa), mistakes can happen.

1. *Shadow products* are developed in the shadow of other, more central products and are not the central thrust of a firm's efforts. An example is the Post-It note at 3M Company, which was developed out of a manager's desire to keep a bookmark from falling out of his hymnbook.

    Such innovations appear at the outset to offer a marginal contribution, and very few companies pay attention to marketing them proactively. Hence, such products tend to be marketed within the structure of the existing organization (existing brand manager, sales manager, and manufacturing line). Market segmentation and channel section, if anchored to existing solutions, are typically wrong, presenting a marketing mistake.

    The real market might be with new customers in new segments. Imagination and creativity may identify new problems the innovation could solve. Shadowed projects lack urgency and attention, which further undermines their potential odds of success.

2. *Delusionary products* are innovations where the suppliers have grandiose visions for the product but their customers do not share the same euphoria. These might be the typical "lab" projects, wherein the technical team views the innovation as the "next best thing since sliced bread" but consumers simply don't understand it or

FIGURE 1-5 Supplier versus Customer Perceptions of Innovation

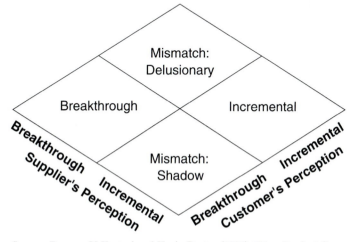

Source: Rangan, V. Kasturi and Kevin Bartus (1995), "New Product Commercialization: Common Mistakes," in *Business Marketing Strategy,* V. K. Rangan et al. (eds.), Chicago: Irwin. Reprinted with permission of McGraw-Hill Companies.

don't agree that it is so great. For example, some predict that high-definition television may be a "yawner" for the consumer. After all, who wants to watch what many perceive as bad TV programming in higher resolution with better sound quality?

In such a situation, rather than marketing the product as a major innovation, a "new and improved" positioning strategy might be a better option—with the pricing, advertising, and distribution of an incremental extension. To position such products as a revolutionary new category, rather than to position against existing solutions, would be a mistake.

Source: Rangan, V. Kasturi and Kevin Bartus (1995), "New Product Commercialization: Common Mistakes," in *Business Marketing Strategy,* V. K. Rangan et al. (eds.), Chicago: Irwin, pp. 63–75.

Implications of Different Types of Innovations: A Contingency Model for High-Tech Marketing

Knowledge of the different types of innovations has important implications for how marketing is conducted. "Market planning that explicitly recognizes and accounts for the strategic distinction between market-driven and innovation-driven research goes a long way toward yielding better corporate performance."[45] In other words, the two types of innovation must be managed differently.[46] For example, cross-functional teams must be staffed with people having the right kind of skills and perspectives. Short-term, results-oriented line people would be best matched to incremental innovation and be mismatched on a breakthrough project. Visionaries who question the value of a new product concept might hamper an incremental innovation.[47]

By appropriately matching marketing tools to each distinct type of innovation, the odds of success in the market are enhanced. This means that the appropriate marketing strategy is *contingent upon* the type of innovation. Figure 1-6 provides a picture of how **contingency theory** works.

Many implications arise from the difference between breakthrough and incremental innovation. Four specific implications are explored here, and additional ones are provided in Box 1-4, "Managing Radical Innovations in Large Established Firms." First, the nature of the interaction between research and development groups and marketing departments depends on the type of innovation. Because technological prowess is key in supply-driven markets, the role of R&D is critical. Research and development is likely to give direction to marketing people in seeking commercial applications for technological

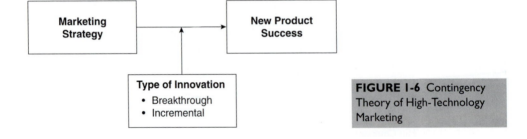

FIGURE 1-6 Contingency Theory of High-Technology Marketing

BOX 1-4

Managing Radical Innovations in Large Established Firms

GINA COLARELLI O'CONNOR
Lally School of Management and Technology,
Rensselaer Polytechnic Institute,
Troy, New York

During the 1980s and early 1990s, U.S. and European firms were competitively challenged in many industries. U.S. firms took a beating in memory chips, office and factory automation, consumer electronics, and automobile manufacturing. These behemoth companies were routinely outmaneuvered by new competitors from other corners of the earth. Kodak watched as videotape camcorders reduced its home movie business to cinders. Xerox's lock on the photocopier business was broken by Canon, Sharp, and others. Consumer electronics products made by Motorola, Zenith, and RCA were largely displaced by better, cheaper, faster versions offered by Sony, Panasonic, and Toshiba. On the automotive front, Toyota, Honda, and Nissan expanded their inroads in the North American market, winning virtually every kudos for quality and reliability. Effective incremental innovation and dramatic improvements in operating efficiency were the two keys to success of these new leaders.

In response, U.S. firms increased their competencies in managing the development of incremental innovation in existing products and processes, with an emphasis on cost competitiveness and quality improvements. Extensive study of incremental innovation by both business managers and academic researchers led to a variety of prescriptions for improvement: six sigma quality in manufacturing, concurrent engineering, just-in-time inventory management, and stage-gate management systems for managing the new product development process. These prescriptions were widely adopted and helped many American companies gain their competitive positions in the world marketplace.

All of these prescriptions are based on the fundamental premise that the firm understands its market's needs and wants and is able to leverage its current technological base to fulfill those needs quickly, cheaply, and reliably. All aspects of the product development project are managed simultaneously by a team comprised of representatives from every function in the business: engineering, production, marketing, cost accounting, and, often, suppliers and customers. Having all constituents present on the team, the argument goes, ensures that decisions are not made with tunnel vision (i.e., that products are not conceived of that cannot be designed) or that products are not designed that cannot be manufactured, etc. This is the world of incremental innovation.

Managers' attention to incremental innovation, however, came at a price. It diminished the focus and capacity of America's largest companies to engage in truly *breakthrough* innovation, which offers the promise of growth through whole new lines of business and the development of new markets. Central R&D labs, traditionally the source of radical innovation ideas, were redirected to serve the immediate needs of business units. Those business units, always under pressure to maximize short-term financial performance, were reluctant to invest in high-risk, long-term projects. The consequences can be disastrous, as Polaroid has now found. Its business is built on film, but film is being quickly replaced with digital imaging technologies that Po-laroid considers far afield from its competency base.

In this case and many others like it, the message is clear: to remain successful over the long haul, firms must be adept at managing both incremental and radical innovation. It turns out that the processes firms have adopted so well for incremental innovation are not only *not applicable* but may be *detrimental* to the management of radical innovation, as illustrated in Table 1-2 and Table 1-3.

It is obvious that the challenges to managing these two types of innovation differ widely and call for different tools, organizational structures, processes, evaluative criteria, and skills. The firm's challenge is to be able to manage both simultaneously, because both are needed for the long-term health of the organization.

TABLE 1-2 Managerial Challenges in Radical versus Incremental Innovation

Management Issue	Incremental Innovation	Radical Innovation
Time frame of development	Short term—6 months to 2 years.	Long term—often 10 years or more.
Trajectory	A linear and continuous path from concept development to commercialization following designated phases and gates.	The path is marked by numerous discontinuities that must be bridged, due to the high levels of uncertainty in the technology, market, organizational, and resource arenas. The process is sporadic, with many starts and stops, hibernations and revivals. Trajectory changes in response to unanticipated events, outcomes, and discoveries.
Idea generation and opportunity recognition	Occur at the front end, often with customer involvement.	Occur sporadically throughout the life cycle, often in response to discontinuities (funding, personnel, technical, market) in the project trajectory.

Management Issue	*Incremental Innovation*	*Radical Innovation*
Evaluation process	Follows a formal, approved process with known go–kill reviews and clear evaluative criteria.	The formal process is treated with disdain. Financially based evaluative criteria, such as internal rate of return and net present value, are clearly too hard to predict because of high levels of uncertainty. Project participants often make up "pie in the sky" numbers to try to obtain funding and rely heavily on currying favor with senior management to gain protection.
Business case	A complete and detailed plan can be developed at the beginning of the process because of the relatively low uncertainty.	The business model evolves through discovery-based technical and market learning, and likewise the business plan becomes a working document that evolves as uncertainty is reduced.
The players	Representatives from each functional area form the team. Each team member has a clearly specified responsibility within his or her area of expertise.	Key players come and go during the early life of the project. Many are part of the informal network that grows up around a radical innovation project. Key players tend to be cross-functional individuals and have expertise in a singular area.
Resources and competencies	The project team has all the competencies required to complete the process. The project is subject to the standard budget allocation process.	Creativity and skill in resource and competency acquisition—from a variety of internal and external sources—are critical to the survival and success of the project.
Business unit involvement	The relevant business unit is involved from the beginning and, in most cases, stimulated the project.	In many cases, it is unclear at the outset which business unit is appropriate for commercializing the project. When an appropriate SBU is obvious, problems with cannibalizing cash cow products make receptivity to the innovation troublesome in some cases. In other cases, entirely new SBUs must be created.

TABLE I-3 Market Issues: Radical versus Incremental Innovations

Market Issues	Incremental Innovation	Radical Innovation
Objectives	Clear objectives, usually expressed in terms of • Market share by a certain time • Product positioning relative to competitive brands • Targeted segments	Broadly stated objectives about solving a previously unsolved problem or about beginning a new platform • Timing unclear • Little direct competition • Appropriate segmentation schemes not known
Role of competition	• Breathing down our necks • Causing a short window of opportunity • Important efforts to differentiate the product	• Typically not a major role in early phase • Competitors not known
Earliest critical issues	• Speed to market	• Will the technology work?
Market learning methods	• Features versus cost trade-offs done through customer surveys	• New alliance/customer partners help validate concept value through early prototypes
Senior management role	• Management clear about the importance of this project to the firm	• Management among those who must be convinced through demonstration of the technology or testimonials by outsiders
Role of SBU	• SBU and sales force impatient to launch the product	• SBU and sales force often resist an innovation seen as cannibalizing their business
Role of customers	• Key customers identified—usually long-held accounts • Possibly suggested the product idea	• Appropriate application areas not clear • Early potential users not known, and likely unfamiliar to the firm

Source: Leifer, Richard, Christopher M. McDermott, Gina Colarelli O'Connor, Lois Peters, Mark Rice, and Robert W. Veryzer, Jr. (2000), *Radical Innovation: How Mature Companies Can Outsmart Upstarts,* Cambridge, MA: Harvard Business School Press.

advances. A critical issue is the original market that the firm chooses to pursue. The role of marketing is to identify markets.[48]

A second implication relates to the type of market research tools that are appropriately used. Gathering market research data on breakthrough products can be difficult. Often the customer doesn't understand the new technology. It can be difficult to articulate performance criteria for the product.[49] For example, if a person has never used jet propulsion for transportation, how will he or she specify what is good performance? Hence, the value of customer feedback through standard marketing research can be questionable. But the voice of the customer remains vitally important; more commonly, qualitative research is used to guide breakthrough product developments.

Or, in situations where the customer might understand the technology, as in the case of lead users who face a need well before the majority of other customers in a market do, the users themselves may be the innovators.[50] For example, Eric von Hippel finds that in many manufacturing processes, the manufacturers who face a particular problem in the production process innovate a solution themselves. An example he cites is Lockheed Martin, which pioneered a new machining technique to speed the removal of titanium metal by up to 20 times with a new face-milling tool that shears rather than chips the metal. The tool was later introduced commercially and expanded to other applications including stainless steels and other hard-to-cut alloys.

A third implication relates to the role of advertising. For breakthrough products, once a viable commercial market is identified, marketers must educate customers, stimulating primary demand for the product class as a whole. Finally, with respect to pricing, because the breakthrough technology may offer a significant advantage over the former mode of doing things, customers may be willing to pay a premium for the new technology.

In contrast to the four implications above for radical innovations, R&D–marketing interaction, market research tools, advertising, and pricing must be managed differently for incremental innovations. For more incremental innovations, the role of marketing is critical. In these situations, customers can play a major role in product development. They can confidently articulate their desires and preferences. In such cases, firms can use standard marketing research tools to identify customer needs, passing the information to R&D, which then develops the appropriate innovations to satisfy those needs. Marketing takes a lead role in such cases. It is more common in incremental innovation to see more standard management controls and formal planning groups.[51] Advertising typically stimulates selective demand, building preference for the firm's specific brand or product. Pricing is more competitive.

It is important to note that the resource allocations of a firm should match the long-term financial attractiveness of the project. Some breakthrough projects might not have a large market potential to start with. And many incremental innovations may absolutely require a major investment (i.e., if a firm's product is hopelessly out of date in a very large market). Hence, marketers should not confuse the nature of the innovation with potential payoff and wrongly assume that breakthrough innovations will have a large payoff![52]

DOES MARKETING NEED TO BE DIFFERENT FOR HIGH-TECHNOLOGY PRODUCTS AND INNOVATIONS?

In light of this discussion, it is clear that the nature of the marketing must be tailored to the type of innovation. But is high-tech marketing all that different from its low-tech counterpart? Or, will standard marketing tools suffice for high-tech markets? Are high-tech marketing disasters caused by the use of a standard marketing approach, when a unique set of tools is necessary to handle the market, technological, and competitive uncertainties? Or, are high-tech marketing disasters merely the result of flawed execution of basic marketing?[53]

Given the high degree of uncertainty, the margin for error for high-tech marketers is likely smaller than for conventional markets. In that sense, high-tech firms must execute basic marketing principles flawlessly.[54] For example, selecting a receptive target market, being able to communicate clearly the benefits the innovation offers relative to other solutions, having an effective/efficient distribution channel, and using solid relationship-building skills cannot be ignored—or overlooked—by high-tech marketers. Because of the importance of following a basic marketing plan in conceptualizing and implementing marketing strategy for any product, be it high or low tech, the Appendix to this chapter presents an outline to follow in developing a basic marketing plan.

However, it is all too common that small high-tech start-ups lack marketing expertise or relegate the role of marketing to second-class status (i.e., beneath the role of engineering/R&D) in the organization. Technical people often have a hard time becoming market focused. Cross-functional collaboration between engineers and marketers is a necessity but extremely difficult to implement well. Further complicating the issue is the fact that many people hired to do "marketing" lack an understanding of how to market in high-tech industries. These organizational realities, as well as the level of market, technological, and competitive uncertainties, mean that although a standard approach to marketing, such as the four Ps (product, price, place, and promotion), is still relevant, the standard approaches must be modified to account for the inherent uncertainty in high-tech environments.[55]

Framework for Making High-Technology Marketing Decisions

This book's primary aim is to provide a framework for making marketing decisions in a high-tech environment. Using a framework to manage the marketing decision-making process will foster greater understanding of the common characteristics in high-tech environments and help manage the riskiness of marketing in a high-tech context.

Figure 1-7 provides the conceptual framework used for making high-technology marketing decisions. On the left side of the figure are the internal considerations that a firm must address and understand as the foundation to effective marketing. The management of high-tech firms has some unique considerations compared to management of traditional companies. Larger high-tech firms that begin to function as a corporate bureaucracy can struggle with how to remain innovative (the "liability of bigness"). Smaller high-tech firms wrestle with how to move from a technology-driven, engineering mind-set to a market focus (the "liability of smallness"). For both sizes of firms, the dynamics between R&D and marketing are paramount. Moreover, whereas all marketing is premised upon relationships, the management of relationships and strategic alliances in high-tech industries requires special considerations. For example, strategic alliances often necessitate collaboration with competitors, where protection of intellectual property is even more important than in more traditional strategic alliances—particularly when the innovative firms are collaborating on cutting-edge research.[56] Hence, Chapters 2 through 4 address issues related to strategy and corporate culture in high-tech firms: core competencies/core rigidities, venture capital funding, market orientation, relationship marketing, and R&D–marketing interactions. Coverage of these issues lays a foundation for marketing effectiveness.

On the right side of the figure are the customer considerations. One of the particularly challenging aspects of high-tech marketing is understanding customers and markets. For example, in conducting marketing research in high-tech industries, users often cannot articulate their needs very clearly because they simply cannot envision what the technology can do or how it can benefit them. In addition, conducting marketing research to forecast the size of the market can be extremely difficult. Research tools used in high-tech markets, such as empathic design and lead users, quality function deployment, competitive intelligence gathering, and forecasting, are explored in Chapter 5.

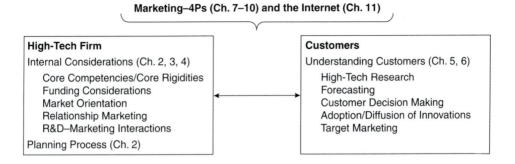

FIGURE I-7 Framework for High-Tech Marketing Decisions

Chapter 6 addresses customer behavior considerations, including customer decision making for high-tech products, issues associated with adoption and diffusion of innovation unique to high-tech markets, and how marketing to early adopters must be different than marketing to late adopters. This chapter draws heavily on the work of Geoffrey Moore (*Crossing the Chasm* and *Inside the Tornado*).

The link between the firm and its customers is enacted through the marketing mix. Chapters 7 to 10 provide coverage of the four elements (4 Ps) of marketing: product, place, price, and promotion.

Product Product development and management may not follow standard marketing practice. For example, some argue that the use of the product life cycle to manage products in high-tech markets is flawed; competitive volatility means that products may never reach maturity.[57] Market uncertainty means that the progression from introduction to growth may be greatly disrupted—some call this "the chasm."[58] Hence, Chapter 7, "Product Development and Management Issues in High-Tech Markets," begins with the framework of a technology map to guide product development. Pertinent considerations include decisions about technology transfer and licensing, product platforms and derivatives, protection of intellectual property, and so forth.

Place Decisions about the role of distribution channels and management of relationships along the supply chain in high-tech markets can be very complicated. For example, consider the case of Intel. When Intel develops chip upgrades, this implies that customers will forgo buying a new computer and buy a replacement chip instead. But such a strategy has the strong possibility of alienating Intel's largest customers—the computer manufacturers who buy the majority of Intel's chips. Hence, it is important that marketers consider the impact of their decisions on all members of the supply chain. In addition, the role of channel members in selling technology is crucial. One study[59] cites two revealing statistics:

- Seventy-seven percent of computer purchasers who visit a dealer do not have a specific brand in mind; 90% of those customers purchase a brand recommended by the dealer.
- Of the 23% of computer purchasers who do have a specific brand in mind, 53% of them switch to an alternative brand recommended by the dealer.

Hence, the role of channel members in selling technology can be very powerful. Chapter 8, "Distribution Channels and Supply Chain Management in High-Tech Markets," provides a framework for making distribution decisions. Focus is given to the use of the Internet as a new channel and the need to manage the transition and resulting conflict.

Price Standard pricing practices can be very misleading in high-tech markets. For example, pricing based on experience curve effects—where costs decline by a fixed and predictable amount every time accumulated volume doubles—is simply not feasible. Competitive volatility means that the firm may never see large volumes on any given product. In addition, in order to survive, high-tech firms must constantly introduce new innovations that obsolete their current product line; this means that firms who rely on economies of scale and production costs as a source of competitive advantage are likely doomed.[60] Instead, high-tech marketers follow a tenet called the technology paradox in pricing.[61] This means that firms may find it more profitable to price products low—even free!—and make a return on upgrades, service, complementary products, and so forth. Chapter 9, "Pricing Considerations in High-Tech Markets," provides a framework for pricing decisions, with heavy emphasis given to the need to be customer oriented in managing this element of the marketing mix. Moreover, in light of the rapid price declines in many high-tech industries (the most extreme of which is a price of $0 for many digital products available for free on the Internet), focused attention is given to strategies used to generate profits in light of the technology paradox (how to survive when the price of product is declining rapidly).

Promotion Communicating with customers via advertising and promotion for high-tech products can be difficult. "Preannouncing"[62] is a useful strategy to persuade customers to delay purchase until the new technology is available, but there are issues of timing: When does a firm announce that it is working on a revolutionary new technology? Although preannouncements can be used in both high-tech and more traditional marketing contexts, their effects may be more pronounced in a high-tech environment for several reasons.

First, given the uncertainty and fears of obsolescence that customers face, preannouncements may encourage customers to forgo a current-generation technology in anticipation of the future one. Some refer to such behavior as "leapfrogging." Second, technological uncertainty implies ambiguity in the delivery timetable. There are many examples of high-tech products being months, if not years, behind promised delivery dates. Indeed, in the software arena, such preannounced products are referred to as "vaporware," products that are never produced. Third, when preannouncements are used, issues of intent arise. In fact, in cases investigated by the Justice Department, if a firm's intent in using preannouncements is specifically to discourage customers from buying a competitor's product, anticompetitive penalties may be applied. Hence, firms in the high-tech arena have strong reasons to use preannouncements but must be especially cautious in doing so. It logically follows, therefore, that future high-tech marketers must have an understanding of such issues.

In addition to understanding issues surrounding preannouncement communication strategies, high-tech marketers must also effectively use marketing communications to allay customer fear, uncertainty, and doubt. High-tech marketers are turning to one strategy used frequently by consumer goods marketers: the use of communications to build a strong brand name. A strong brand is a heuristic that is used by consumers to reduce perceived risk. Strong brand names in the high-tech arena "stand as a beacon in the confusing and quickly changing world of technology . . . they offer reassurance about a purchase that is fraught with confusion and anxiety."[63] In technology arenas where products change rapidly, the brand can be more important than in packaged goods industries where a product is more understandable because it has stayed the same for a long time. Microsoft, Intel, Hewlett-Packard, and even 3-Com are using strong brand strategies, in part to assuage consumer anxiety.

To be sure, advertising and promotion strategies used to allay consumer anxiety in a high-tech context may also be used in more traditional marketing contexts. The critical points of distinction are that

1. It is a difficult cultural shift for people in technology-oriented firms to become marketing or customer oriented. Even Microsoft still sees itself as "doing technology for technology's sake rather than based on customer needs."[64]
2. The combination of customer, technological, and competitive uncertainty surrounding high-tech purchases implies more riskiness for consumers, and hence, the need for a strategy to reduce such riskiness.

Future high-tech marketers must understand how these more traditional marketing tools are especially crucial in their environment, despite the lack of a customer focus in many high-tech firms. Hence, among other topics, Chapter 10, "Advertising and Promotion in High-Tech Markets: Tools to Build and Maintain Customer Relationships," emphasizes the importance of using advertising and promotion tools to develop a strong brand name (as one mechanism to allay customer anxiety), the need to manage product preannouncements, and communication tools used in managing customer relationships.

Although not one of the 4 Ps of marketing, the new abilities offered via the Internet to interact with customers and its vital role in serving both high-tech firms and customers warrant special attention. Indeed, a book on the marketing of high-technology products and innovations would not be complete without some coverage of how the Internet is revolutionizing the face of marketing. Hence, Chapter 11 focuses exclusively on e-commerce and Internet marketing. Using the case of Charles Schwab's successful foray into the world of on-line brokering, the chapter discusses issues unique to marketing on the Internet and managing business on the Net.

Chapter 12, "Realizing the Promise of Technology," concludes with regulatory and ethical considerations high-tech marketers face. Despite the Justice Department's investigations of Microsoft and Intel, there is a heated debate about whether antitrust is even relevant in today's high-tech era.[65]

In light of the high degree of market, technological, and competitive uncertainties surrounding high-tech products and markets, the need for effective marketing in high-tech industries is paramount. High-tech products and services are introduced in turbulent, chaotic environments, in which the odds of success are often difficult to ascertain at best and stacked against success at worst. This book is designed to provide frameworks for systematic decision making about marketing in high-tech environments. In doing so, it offers insights about how marketing tools and techniques must be adapted and modified for high-technology products and services. Effective high-tech marketing includes a blend of marketing fundamentals and the unique tools explored in this book. The text highlights possible pitfalls, mitigating factors, and the how-tos of successful high-tech marketing. The poem in Box 1-5 provides a flavor of these unique tools. Before leaving this opening chapter, readers may be wondering about specific job opportunities in high-tech industries.

BOX 1-5

Ode on a Grecian Scuzzi[a] Interface

M. PATHIC AND D. SIGN
(With Apologies to Keats)

THOU chip of silicon, oh please some answers can you give?
Was your birth deemed radical or just derivative?
Will your purchase price afford us not an economic care?
Or will we sell you at a loss to increase market share?

The techies want to dress you up with all the functions they can cite
But if you do what you do well, I'm sure you will delight.
The mix of FUD and FIT for you should have this implication
That better products are derived from cross-functional collaboration.

Will you cross successfully the high-tech market chasm?
Or will we drop you down the drain when we get a panic spasm?
Oh chip of silicon, just one more answer can you give?
Is as a high-tech marketer a decent way to live?

---

[a] Scuzzi is a technical term for Small Computer Systems Interface (SCSI).
Source: Written by Scott MacDonald, MBA, University of Montana.

JOB OPPORTUNITIES IN HIGH TECH

Due to the differing definitions of high tech, employment statistics vary. A 1997 article in *Business Week* identified 9 million workers in the core high-tech industries of computers, software, and communications; ancillary management consulting work; and programmers, technicians, and the like in the rest of the economy.[66] This figure is very similar to the 8.8 million high-tech employees counted in 1996 by the Bureau of Labor Statistics in R&D-intensive industries.[67] More recently, the high growth rates found in information technology sectors, including a projected increase of 22% in sales of networking equipment, a 21% increase in the number of U.S. wireless communications customers, and a doubling of Internet-related commerce,[68] are harbingers of strong hiring in those industries. The American Electronics Association identified 152,203 technology companies in the United States in 1999, 74% more than in 1990, and an increase of 617,000 new jobs since 1994.[69] Indeed, the competition for hiring qualified people has been quite intense. Salaries in high tech continue to be high, with increases higher than most industries (due to a shortage of qualified workers).[70]

However, high-tech employment opportunities are not evenly spread across all high-tech sectors. Box 1-6, "Employment Changes and Opportunities in R&D-Intensive Industries, 1988 to 1996," highlights some of the specifics of these numbers, showing real opportunities in high-tech service industries.

High-tech marketing can include a variety of positions and job titles, including product management, sales, advertising, and research, to name a few. For those with a technical background, product marketing or account management can be a career path out of the lab, if so desired. Many MBA programs report high demand for students with a

---

Employment Changes and Opportunities in R&D-Intensive Industries, 1988 to 1996

Many hoped that revolutions in microelectronics, genetics, aeronautics, physics, and materials sciences would create an engine for high-tech employment that could make up for the permanent loss of jobs in heavily unionized sectors of U.S. manufacturing. However, the data from 1988 to 1996 simply do not bear that out. As Table 1-4 shows, during the eight-year time frame, total employment in R&D-intensive industries increased by about 5%, compared to 13.7% growth in total nonfarm employment.

One reason for the relatively small increase in high-tech employment was that R&D-intensive *manufacturing* industries lost almost 600,000 jobs, or more than 10% of the workers employed in that sector, as of January 1988. This loss was felt most severely in the defense-dependent industries, whereas civilian manufacturing was relatively stable. In addition, the industry that many regard as having begun the high-tech revolution of the 1980s—computer and office equipment—experienced the largest net employment decline (97,700 jobs) among civilian R&D-intensive industries. The sad irony of this last statistic is that the labor-saving processes developed by R&D-intensive industries have caused these structural changes. For example, computing power has continually increased over the last two decades, while the price of that power has decreased. This has lowered the cost of automating design and manufacturing processes, which has reduced the number of workers required at any output level—even while demand for computers has continued to grow. The trend is likely to continue. The BLS reports that between 1994 and 2005, annual output in the computer industry will rise by 7.3%, but employment levels will fall by an annual rate of 2.6%.

However, R&D-intensive *services*—management and public relations, computer and data processing, engineering and architectural, and research and testing services—gained nearly 46% in total employment. Competitive pressure in the computing industry that forces producers to sell products at or below cost in order to boost sales of complementary goods and services with higher profit margins—such as software and technical services—gives impetus to the shift to services. The automotive, medical instruments, and drug manufacturing industries also increased their employment significantly.

Source: Luker, William and Donald Lyons (1997), "Employment Shifts in High-Technology Industries, 1988–1996," *Monthly Labor Review,* June, pp. 12–25.

TABLE I-4 Employment Changes (in thousands) in R&D-Intensive Industries, 1988–1996

SIC Code	Industry	January 1988	January 1996	Net Change	Percent Change
874	Management and public relations	482.3	859.0	376.7	78.1
737	Computer and data-processing services	656.7	1,139.1	482.4	73.5
873	Research and testing services	470.4	562.6	92.2	19.6
384	Medical instruments and supplies	225.2	264.9	39.7	17.6
283	Drugs	222.2	255.4	33.2	14.9
871	Engineering and architectural services	708.2	813.0	104.8	14.8
355	Special-industry machinery	154.4	177.0	22.6	14.6
371	Motor vehicles and equipment	835.0	949.2	114.2	13.7
286	Industrial organic chemicals	143.6	146.9	3.3	2.3
287	Agricultural chemicals	51.0	52.1	1.1	2.2
367	Electronic components and accessories	608.6	608.9	.3	.0
284	Soap, cleaners, and toilet goods	153.4	149.7	–3.7	–2.4
366	Communications equipment	272.9	263.0	–9.9	–3.6
335	Nonferrous rolling and drawing	179.0	167.3	–11.7	–6.5
289	Miscellaneous chemical products	99.5	90.6	–8.9	–8.9
282	Plastics materials and synthetics	173.4	155.5	–17.9	–10.3
382	Measuring and controlling devices	318.7	284.7	–34.0	–10.7
362	Electrical industrial apparatus	178.1	159.0	–19.1	–10.7
285	Paints and allied products	62.2	55.3	–6.9	–11.1
281	Industrial inorganic chemicals	133.0	116.4	–16.6	–12.5
291	Petroleum refining	123.4	99.7	–23.7	–19.2
357	Computer and office equipment	455.0	357.3	–97.7	–21.5
386	Photographic equipment and supplies	109.8	84.7	–25.1	–22.9
131	Crude petroleum and natural gas operations	198.1	143.2	–54.9	–27.7
211	Cigarettes	40.6	28.2	–12.4	–30.5
372	Aircraft and parts	682.2	446.9	–235.3	–34.5
381	Search and navigation equipment	325.4	153.0	–172.4	–53.0
376	Guided missiles, space vehicles, and parts	211.6	93.4	–118.2	–55.9
	All R&D-intensive employment	8,273.9	8,676.0	402.1	4.9
	R&D-intensive manufacturing	5,758.2	5,159.1	–599.1	–10.4
	R&D-intensive durables	4,555.9	4,009.3	–546.6	–12.0
	R&D-intensive nondurables	1,202.3	1,149.8	–52.5	–4.4
	Defense-related R&D-intensive manufacturing	1,219.2	693.3	–525.9	–43.1
	Civilian R&D-intensive manufacturing	4,166.6	4,112.2	–54.4	–1.3
	R&D-intensive services	2,317.6	3,373.7	1,056.1	45.6
	R&D-intensive mining	198.1	143.2	–54.9	–27.7

technical undergraduate degree combined with a Masters of Business Administration degree. The many on-line job sites have no paucity of marketing jobs in high-tech companies.

For individuals with nontechnical backgrounds (say liberal arts or business majors), it is still possible to find a high-tech job, despite the lack of technical training. As cited by a 1997 *Wall Street Journal* article, "examples abound of nontechnical folk thriving at high-tech companies."[71] For example, it is possible to get jobs in marketing communications (advertising and promotion, public relations, trade show management) or marketing research without a technical background. And sales and management experience is a great asset because "it implies that, unlike most techies, the candidate understands how to communicate with fellow humans, including customers."[72] To find employment in a high-tech company without technical experience, a *Wall Street Journal* article offers the following suggestions:[73]

- Get in the door any way you can. Work as a temporary worker or an intern, for example. Once in the door, expand your duties. Take on additional projects; volunteer to work on teams.
- Read industry trade publications; experiment with products; attend meetings.
- Work for a high-tech firm's customer or supplier to learn the industry and make contacts.
- Find a company that will provide training on technology. For example, Arthur Andersen's management consulting group has been known to hire liberal arts majors because they know how to think critically.

It is also important to subscribe to computer and trade magazines so that one understands the jargon and industry issues. Last, but not least, it would be very helpful to understand high-tech marketing and the unique demands high-tech marketers face. Becoming acquainted with the strategies and tools presented in this text would be a step in that direction.

Summary

This chapter has provided an introduction to high-technology marketing. In addition to providing an in-depth examination of the various ways to define high-tech industries and companies, it has also shown that many innovations frequently occur at levels in the supply chain far removed from the end user. The chapter also showed that innovations are a question of degree, ranging from incremental to radical. In order to be effective, marketing strategies must be tailored to the type of innovation. This notion of matching marketing to the type of innovation is known as the contingency theory of successful high-tech marketing, which will be a common theme running throughout this book. Finally, the chapter concluded with an examination of job opportunities in high-tech markets.

Discussion Questions

1. What are the pros and cons of the various definitions of high tech? Of these definitions, which do you think is the most useful? Why? Based on that definition, draw a continuum of low- versus high-tech industries.
2. What three characteristics are common to high-tech industries? Provide examples of each of the specific dimensions of the characteristics.

3. Define and give an example of each of the following: unit-one costs, demand-side increasing returns, tradeability problems, and knowledge spillovers.
4. Think of some examples in which low-tech industries have been transformed by high-tech innovations. Where in the supply chain have these innovations originated?
5. How are radical innovations different from incremental innovations? Provide examples of the two types of innovations.
6. What is a contingency theory of new product success? What marketing tools are appropriately used for incremental innovations? What marketing tools are appropriately used for radical innovations?
7. Does high-tech marketing need to be different from marketing of traditional products? Why? How?

Glossary

Competitive volatility. Refers to rapid changes in the competitive landscape: which firms are one's competitors, their product offerings, the tools they use to compete.

Contingency theory. The effects of one set of variables on another (say, marketing variables on new product success) depend on yet a third variable (say, type of innovation).

Demand-side increasing returns. Also called network externalities or a bandwagon effect; when the value of the product increases as more users adopt it. In other words, the utility received from an innovation is a function of the number of users.

Incremental innovation. Continuations of existing methods or practices; may involve extension of products already on the market.

Knowledge spillovers. When synergies in the creation and distribution of know-how further enrich a related stock of knowledge, which creates increasing returns in the development of related technologies.

Market uncertainty. Ambiguity about the type and extent of customer needs that can be satisfied by a particular technology, arising from consumer fear, uncertainty, and doubt about the needs or problems the new technology will address and meet.

Radical innovation. Breakthrough innovation that cannot be compared with any existing practices or perceptions; technology is so new that it creates a new product class.

Technological uncertainty. Skepticism about whether the technology will function as promised or be available when expected by the company providing it.

Tradeability problems. When underlying know-how represents a substantial portion of the value of the products and services, it is difficult to value the knowledge, especially when it is tacit and resides in people and organizational routines.

Unit-one costs. The cost of producing the first unit is very high relative to the costs of reproduction; this type of cost structure is likely to exist when know-how, or knowledge embedded in the design of the product, represents a substantial portion of the value of the products and services.

Endnotes

1. Kilman, Scott (1998), "If Fat-Free Pork Is Your Idea of Savory, It's a Bright Future," *Wall Street Journal,* January 29, p. A1.
2. Frost & Sullivan (1997), "Mechatronics for Automobiles Is the Buzzword When It Comes to Electronic Control Modules," www.frost.com/ verify/press/transportation/pr556218.htm.
3. McWilliams, Gary (1997), "Technology Is What's Driving This Business," *Business Week,* November 3, pp. 146–148.
4. Morris, Betsy (1996), "The Brand's the Thing," *Fortune,* March 4, pp. 73–86.
5. Mandel, Michael (1997), "The New Business Cycle," *Business Week,* March 31, pp. 58–68.

For additional information on high-tech industry forecasts, see *Business Week* (2000), "Industry Outlook," January 10, pp. 84–146.

6. "Industry Outlook," (2000), *Business Week,* January 10, pp. 84–146; Mandel, Michael (2000), "The New Economy," *Business Week,* January 31, pp. 73–91.

7. "Industry Outlook," (2000), *Business Week,* January 10, pp. 84–87.

8. Capon, Noel and Rashi Glazer (1987), "Marketing and Technology: A Strategic Coalignment," *Journal of Marketing,* 51 (July), pp. 1–14.

9. *Technology, Innovation, and Regional Economic Development* (1982), Washington, DC: U.S. Congress, Office of Technology Assessment, September 9.

10. Hadlock, Paul, Daniel Hecker, and Joseph Gannon (1991), "High Technology Employment: Another View," *Monthly Labor Review,* July, pp. 26–30.

11. Hatzichronoglou, Thomas (1997), "Revision of the High-Technology Sector and Product Classification," OECD STI working paper.

12. *Science and Engineering Indicators* (1996), National Science Foundation, chapters 4 and 6.

13. Luker, William and Donald Lyons (1997), "Employment Shifts in High-Technology Industries, 1988–1996," *Monthly Labor Review,* June, pp. 12–25.

14. Luker, William and Donald Lyons (1997), "Employment Shifts in High-Technology Industries, 1988–1996," *Monthly Labor Review,* June, pp. 12–25.

15. Lipkin, Richard (1996), "Fit for a King," *Science News,* May 18, pp. 316–317.

16. Luker, William and Donald Lyons (1997), "Employment Shifts in High-Technology Industries, 1988–1996," *Monthly Labor Review,* June, pp. 12–25.

17. Moriarty, Rowland and Thomas Kosnik (1989), "High-Tech Marketing: Concepts, Continuity, and Change," *Sloan Management Review,* 30 (Summer), pp. 7–17.

18. See also Gardner, David (1990), "Are High Technology Products Really Different?" Faculty working paper case #90-1706, University of Illinois at Urbana-Champaign.

19. Moriarty, Rowland and Thomas Kosnik (1989), "High-Tech Marketing: Concepts, Continuity, and Change," *Sloan Management Review,* 30 (Summer), pp. 7–17; Moriarty, Rowland and Thomas Kosnik (1987), "High-Tech vs. Low-Tech Marketing: Where's the Beef?" Harvard Business School, case #9-588-012.

20. Moore, Geoffrey (1991), *Crossing the Chasm, Marketing and Selling Technology Products to Mainstream Customers,* New York: HarperCollins.

21. Moffett, Sebastian (1998), "Mixed Signals on DVDs," *Business Week,* January 12, p. 89.

22. Moore, Geoffrey (1991), *Crossing the Chasm, Marketing and Selling Technology Products to Mainstream Customers,* New York: HarperCollins.

23. Sultan, Fareena (1990), "Zenith: Marketing Research for High Definition Television," Harvard Business School, case #9-591-025.

24. Pope, Kyle and Evan Ramstad (1998), "HDTV Sets: Too Pricy, Too Late?" *Wall Street Journal,* January 7, p. B1.

25. Moore, Geoffrey (1991), *Crossing the Chasm, Marketing and Selling Technology Products to Mainstream Customers,* New York: HarperCollins.

26. Moriarty, Rowland and Thomas Kosnik (1989), "High-Tech Marketing: Concepts, Continuity, and Change," *Sloan Management Review,* 30 (Summer), pp. 7–17.

27. Thurm, Scott (1999), "For Frazzled Online Brokers, Technology Is the Problem," *Wall Street Journal,* March 4, p. B6.

28. Siegel, Matt (1998), "Do Computers Slow Us Down?" *Fortune,* March 30, pp. 34, 38; Landauer, Thomas (1995), *The Trouble with Computers: Usefulness, Usability, and Productivity,* Cambridge, MA: MIT Press.

29. Cooper, Arnold and Dan Schendel (1976), "Strategic Responses to Technological Threats," *Business Horizons,* February, pp. 61–69.

30. Hamel, Gary (1997), "Killer Strategies That Make Shareholders Rich," *Fortune,* June 23, pp. 70–84.

31. Burrows, Peter (2000), "Computers and Chips," *Business Week,* January 10, pp. 92–93.

32. John, George, Allen Weiss, and Shantanu Dutta (1999), "Marketing in Technology Intensive Markets: Towards a Conceptual Framework," *Journal of Marketing,* 63 (Special Issue), pp. 78–91.

33. Mandel, Michael (2000), "The New Economy," *Business Week,* January 31, pp. 73–91.

34. Rangan, V. Kasturi and Kevin Bartus (1995), "New Product Commercialization: Common Mistakes," in *Business Marketing Strategy,* V. K. Rangan et al. (eds.), Chicago: Irwin, p. 66.

35. Abernathy, W. and J. Utterback (1978), "Patterns of Industrial Innovation," *Technology Review,* June–July, pp. 41–47.

36. Shanklin, William and John Ryans (1984), "Organizing for High-Tech Marketing," *Harvard Business Review,* 62 (November–December), pp. 164–171.

37. Maney, Kevin (1999), "The Net Effect: Evolution or Revolution?" *USA Today,* August 8, p. B2.

38. Gross, Neil and Peter Coy with Otis Port (1995), "The Technology Paradox," *Business Week,* March 6, pp. 76–84.

39. Hamel, Gary (1997), "Killer Strategies That Make Shareholders Rich," *Fortune,* June 23, pp. 70–84.

40. Maney, Kevin (1999), "The Net Effect: Evolution or Revolution?" *USA Today,* August 8, p. B2.

41. Rangan, V. Kasturi and Kevin Bartus (1995), "New Product Commercialization: Common Mistakes," in *Business Marketing Strategy,* V. K. Rangan et al. (eds.), Chicago: Irwin, pp. 63–75.

42. Shanklin, William and John Ryans (1984), "Organizing for High-Tech Marketing," *Harvard Business Review,* 62 (November–December), pp. 164–171.

43. Maney, Kevin (1999), "The Net Effect: Evolution or Revolution?" *USA Today,* August 8, p. B2.

44. Abernathy, W. and J. Utterback (1978), "Patterns of Industrial Innovation," *Technology Review,* June–July, pp. 41–47.

45. Shanklin, William and John Ryans (1984), "Organizing for High-Tech Marketing," *Harvard Business Review,* 62 (November–December), p. 167.

46. Rangan, V. Kasturi and Kevin Bartus (1995), "New Product Commercialization: Common Mistakes," in *Business Marketing Strategy,* V. K. Rangan et al. (eds.), Chicago: Irwin, pp. 63–75.

47. Rangan, V. Kasturi and Kevin Bartus (1995), "New Product Commercialization: Common Mistakes," in *Business Marketing Strategy,* V. K. Rangan et al. (eds.), Chicago: Irwin, pp. 63–75.

48. Shanklin, William and John Ryans (1984), "Organizing for High-Tech Marketing," *Harvard*

49. Abernathy, W. and J. Utterback (1978), "Patterns of Industrial Innovation," *Technology Review,* June–July, pp. 41–47.

50. von Hippel, Eric (1986), "Lead Users: A Source of Novel Product Concepts," *Management Science,* July, pp. 791–805.

51. Abernathy, W. and J. Utterback (1978), "Patterns of Industrial Innovation," *Technology Review,* June–July, pp. 41–47.

52. Rangan, V. Kasturi and Kevin Bartus (1995), "New Product Commercialization: Common Mistakes," in *Business Marketing Strategy,* V. K. Rangan et al. (eds.), Chicago: Irwin, pp. 63–75.

53. Moriarty, Rowland and Thomas Kosnik (1987), "High-Tech vs. Low-Tech Marketing: Where's the Beef?" Harvard Business School, case #9-588-012, p. 18.

54. Moriarty, Rowland and Thomas Kosnik (1987), "High-Tech vs. Low-Tech Marketing: Where's the Beef?" Harvard Business School, case #9-588-012.

55. See also Gardner, David (1990), "A Strategic Approach to High Technology Marketing," Faculty working paper #90-1707, University of Illinois, Urbana-Champaign.

56. Hamel, G., Y. Doz, and C. K. Prahalad (1989), "Collaborate with Your Competitors—And Win," *Harvard Business Review,* January–February, pp. 133–139.

57. Shanklin, William and John Ryans (1987), *Essentials of Marketing High Technology,* Lexington, MA: DC Heath.

58. Moore, Geoffrey (1991), *Crossing the Chasm, Marketing and Selling Technology Products to Mainstream Customers,* New York: Harper-Collins.

59. "How Technology Sells," (1997), Dataquest, Gartner Group, and CMP Channel Group, CMP Publications, Jericho, NY.

60. Shanklin, William and John Ryans (1987), *Essentials of Marketing High Technology,* Lexington, MA: DC Heath.

61. Gross, Neil and Peter Coy with Otis Port (1995), "The Technology Paradox," *Business Week,* March 6, pp. 76–84.

62. Eliashberg, J. and T. Robertson (1988), "New Product Preannouncing Behavior: A Market Signaling Study," *Journal of Marketing Research,* 25 (August), pp. 282–292.

63. Morris, Betsy (1996), "The Brand's the Thing," *Fortune,* March 4, p. 82.

64. Moeller, Michael (1999), "Remaking Microsoft," *Business Week,* May 17, pp. 106–114 (p. 112).

65. Murray, Alan (1997), "Antitrust Isn't Obsolete in an Era of High-Tech," *Wall Street Journal,* November 10, p. A1.

66. Mandel, Michael (1997), "The New Business Cycle," *Business Week,* March 31, pp. 58–68.

67. Luker, William and Donald Lyons (1997), "Employment Shifts in High-Technology Industries, 1988–1996," *Monthly Labor Review,* June, pp. 12–25.

68. "Industry Outlook," (2000), *Business Week,* January 10, pp. 84–87.

69. Fisher, Anne (1999), "Job Hunting in Tech Land," *Business Week,* April 12, p. 172.

70. Heckman, James (1998), "Marketers Making $$$ in High-Tech," *Marketing News,* November 23, pp. 1, 20.

71. Lancaster, Hal (1997), "You Can Get a Job in a High-Tech Firm with Low-Tech Skills," *Wall Street Journal,* February 4, p. B1.

72. Fisher, Anne (1999), "Job Hunting in Tech Land," *Business Week,* April 12, p. 172.

73. Lancaster, Hal (1997), "You Can Get a Job in a High-Tech Firm with Low-Tech Skills," *Wall Street Journal,* February 4, p. B1.

APPENDIX

Outline for a Marketing Plan

The purpose of this section is to present an outline of the steps to be systematically considered and developed in the course of a marketing plan. Supporting detail can be found in any basic marketing textbook.

SITUATION ANALYSIS

I. *Internal Concerns*   Unique to the company (or organization, profit or nonprofit) and include resources, skills, competencies, people, culture, finances, brand reputation. Purpose of addressing internal concerns is to identify strengths and weaknesses of the firm.

II. *External Concerns*   Affect all players in the environment, across a broad range of industries and companies. Purpose of addressing external concerns is to identify opportunities and threats.

   A. Sociocultural: changes in societal values and beliefs
   B. Demographic: changes in demographic patterns in society
   C. Competitive: brand versus product form (selective versus primary demand)
   D. Economic: macro-economic patterns

   E. Natural Resources
   F. Technology

Summary of the situation analysis is SWOT analysis: summary of key strengths, weaknesses, opportunities, and threats.

III. *Customers*
   A. Consumer Behavior
      1. Who is likely to be predisposed to buy?
      2. How do they buy?
      3. Why do they buy?
   B. Segmentation: Create meaningful groups of customers who are similar on some important dimensions.
      1. Heavy versus light users: 20% of a firm's customers are likely to generate 80% of its volume. Who are the heavy users?
      2. Usage situation: People's reasons for buying may vary by the situation or occasion in which the product will be used.
      3. Benefit segmentation: People's reasons for buying may vary depending on the particular benefits a person is seeking.

4. Psychographics: People's underlying values and lifestyles, and activities, interests, and opinions are likely to make them predisposed to buy certain products for certain reasons.
5. Demographics: Differences in people's ages, gender, socioeconomic status, geographic location, and so forth, are related to how and why people buy different products. Note, however, that because people of similar demographic groups may exhibit very different purchasing patterns, demographics are often the least powerful basis of segmentation.

C. Select target market(s) on the basis of size of the segment (in terms of sales volume), growth rate in the segment, competitive intensity in the segment, and the firm's strengths and core competencies in ability to serve the needs of the segment.

D. Positioning: Customer's perceptions of how product compares to competitors on important dimensions.

IV. *Set Objectives*
A. Quantitative: sales, share, penetration, usage
B. Qualitative: positioning

V. *Marketing Mix (4 Ps)*
A. Product–Service Decisions: Include new product development processes, decisions about what to sell and what features to include, branding strategies, packaging decisions, warranty, and ancillary services.
B. Price Decisions: Include decisions about what to charge for specific products, features, or services, as well as discount structures and payment plans.
C. Place (Distribution) Decisions: Decisions regarding the locations at which product or service is made available to customer, and the channel members that offer it.
D. Promotion Decisions
1. Advertising strategies, regarding both the message content in ads and media used to communicate the message. May include direct media.
2. Sales promotion strategies, regarding any short-term incentives for both trade members and consumers (coupons, rebates, premiums, etc.).
3. Public relations and publicity strategies, regarding the generation of news articles, community relations, event sponsorships, and goodwill.
4. Personal selling/trade shows.

VI. *Relationship Marketing* Attempts to develop long-term relationships with customers to ensure lifetime value. Relationship marketing is based on win–win solutions to customers' needs and actively solicits feedback in order to tailor strategies to individual customer needs. This approach may entail sacrificing short-term profits for long-term gains.

VII. *Budgeting Methods, Evaluation, Audits* Develop budgets to implement the marketing plan, as well as ways to assess the effectiveness of the marketing strategies, to ensure feedback into future marketing plan development.

CHAPTER 2

Strategy and Corporate Culture in High-Tech Firms

Many large firms struggle mightily with the task of creating really new products that change the competitive landscape of a given industry. The characteristics of large firms (bureaucratic, focused on economies of scale, and so forth)—characteristics that are useful for developing incremental innovations—can seriously inhibit these firms' ability to develop breakthrough products. It is no small wonder that one of the hottest consulting areas in the 1990s was how to develop a culture of innovativeness in Corporate America. Indeed, the Management Roundtable sponsors a conference called Achieving Market Leadership with Breakthrough Products, for which participants pay a $1,895 fee for the two-day session. Some of the topics include specific ways in which firms can overcome ingrained corporate obstacles to create truly new products. Often, the creation and discovery of really new products are based on a deep understanding of customers in such a way that the new products that are developed change the rules of competition. Such innovation can create radically new products that put the firm on top of a whole new business category.

At the same time that many large firms struggle with becoming more innovative and nimble, many small firms struggle with their own unique marketing problems. Small firms often are created on the basis of the superior technology they can bring to a marketplace. The roots of such firms are often found in their founders' sophisticated technical leadership. The technical orientation is a necessary ingredient for success, but not the only ingredient. Many such firms die for a variety of reasons. Some lack access to vital resources including funding and management expertise. Others find it difficult to blend their technical insights with marketing sophistication. Technical leaders often do not recognize that market savvy is a key ingredient for success. Such a difficulty is further exacerbated by the sense that technical people have the innate ability to be marketers as well as technical gurus. These beliefs often prove to be fatal flaws.

Moreover, in many large and small technology-driven firms, a perceived status differential exists between the technical folks and marketers (with marketers coming out on the short end of the stick). This perceived difference in many firms translates into a systemic bias that minimizes the contributions marketers make to the firm, diminishes their voices, and downplays the information they bring to the table. Such perceptions detract from the close R&D–marketing interaction that must occur for successful marketing programs.

Moreover, the marketing of high-technology products requires a discussion of strategic market planning. Because many managers in technology-intensive industries can be overwhelmed with the complexities they face, an overview of strategic market planning tailored to this demanding environment is imperative.

The purpose of Chapters 2, 3, and 4 is to discuss some of these basic issues all high-tech firms face, be they large or small. As shown in the organizing framework in Figure 2-1,

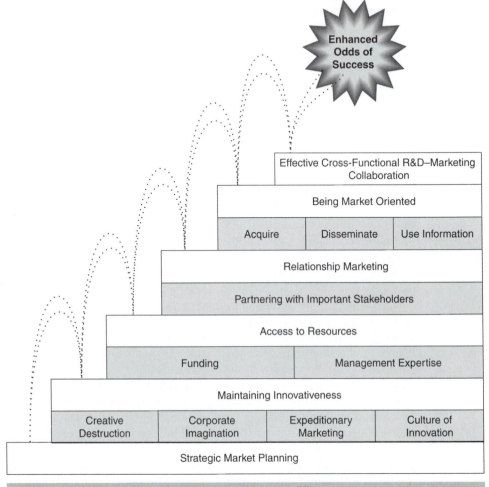

FIGURE 2-1 Building Blocks of High-Technology Marketing Effectiveness

these issues represent the building blocks that enhance the odds of marketing success. Moreover, these issues provide the foundation for later topics, which assume that the high-tech firm is willing to assess its firm's capabilities with respect to each of these issues in a genuine, wholehearted manner.

By the end of these chapters, you should

- Understand the strategic market planning process in technology-intensive industries
- Understand the need for and barriers to corporate innovativeness, as well as the strategies firms are implementing to become more innovative
- Understand the liabilities small high-tech firms face in being successful
- Understand the role of relationship marketing in high-tech firms
- Understand what it means to be market driven and customer oriented
- Identify the barriers to being market driven
- Understand the value of and barriers to collaborative R&D–marketing interaction

STRATEGIC MARKET PLANNING IN HIGH-TECH COMPANIES

Effective high-technology marketing requires a discussion of strategic market planning.[1] The fundamental issues are

- Do traditional marketing planning processes work in a high-tech environment?
- Are the characteristics of the context described in Chapter 1 (market uncertainty, technological uncertainty, and competitive volatility) amenable to traditional strategic market planning processes?

The tendency is to answer the above questions with a *No.* Many managers in technology-intensive situations are simply overwhelmed by the complexities they face and, sadly enough, confront these complexities with strategic market planning processes more complex and unmanageable than the situations themselves. Current planning processes can tie up enormous amounts of management time with extensive analysis, documentation, and a lack of cross-functional involvement. The processes produce plans that are quickly obsolete in the face of competitive actions and reactions.

Confronted with complexity, strategic market planning processes must become simpler, faster, iterative, opportunity-based, team-based, and functionally integrated. Market planning and strategic action must be closely coupled. Rather than reinventing the wheel, the responsive planning approach found in a book titled *Winning Market Leadership— In Technology-Driven Businesses* can be used. This approach, outlined in Box 2-1, provides a systematic and highly integrated process for evaluating market opportunities and for developing strategies to win market leadership, focusing on the key issues and tough choices faced by executives in these very demanding technology-intensive markets. Most of the examples in the book are drawn from the experiences of large, multinational, high-technology companies, such as Intel, Compaq, Hewlett-Packard, Glaxo-Wellcome, and General Electric.

THE LIABILITY OF BIGNESS: HOW TO MAINTAIN INNOVATIVENESS IN ESTABLISHED COMPANIES

Core Competencies/Core Rigidities

Core competencies refer to the set of skills at which a company excels. Such competencies can be identified based on their three underlying characteristics.

- Core skills and capabilities are extremely difficult for competitors to imitate, because they are *embedded* deeply in the organization's routines, procedures, and people.
- True core competencies are significantly related to the benefits a customer receives in using a product.
- Core competencies allow a firm to access a wide variety of very disparate market opportunities.[2]

In the high-tech arena, Hewlett-Packard serves as a good example of leveraging core competencies. One of Hewlett-Packard's core competencies is in the area of transferring digital images to paper with superior quality (clarity, detail, and color). This core competency was exhibited in its resounding success in the laser printer business. While other companies also made laser printers, HP's superior technology and production skills made

BOX 2-1

Winning Market Leadership

DON BARCLAY AND ADRIAN RYANS
University of Western Ontario, London, Ontario

The integrated Winning Market Leadership strategic market planning process is pictured and outlined in Figure 2-2.

1. Define the Business Arena

The first step in the planning process is to identify the broad business arena the firm will be targeting. Each arena of opportunity should be given a business definition along four major dimensions:

- Potential customer segments that could be served
- Potential applications or functionality that could be provided to these customers

FIGURE 2-2 Strategic Market Planning Process

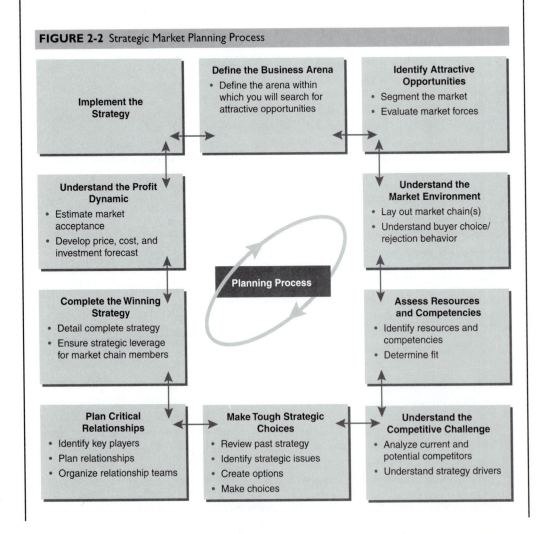

- Possible technologies and capabilities that could be used to create the applications or functionality
- Possible role for the organization in providing the value to the customer versus the roles of others in the market chain

2. Identify Attractive Opportunities

Sometimes an opportunity will present itself—a current customer will bring a new need to the firm's attention, or the organization's scientists or engineers may have a technological breakthrough. Other times, a firm may be actively searching for new opportunities if its current ones are not meeting revenue or earnings targets. Whatever the case, one needs to acquire an in-depth understanding of the opportunities in the arena selected.

An important early step in identifying attractive opportunities involves thoroughly segmenting the market. This starts the development of an in-depth understanding of the applications or functionality customers require, the technologies that might be used to deliver the applications, and the value added required from the market chain involved.

Then, the firm must determine the potential profitability of serving particular market segments. If the market and competitive forces are so negative that no company serving this market segment is likely to be profitable, then this market segment might be eliminated from further consideration—or maybe not. Management might think it can see a way to change a segment's dynamics or feel that, for strategic reasons, it has to have a presence in the segment. For example, in 1996, Sony clearly felt that the potential convergence of the home computer and home entertainment markets made it essential that it develop a strong presence in the home computer market. In conducting this analysis,

watch for market segments that may allow the firm to drive the market by adopting a radically different strategy. Such opportunities arise when major discontinuities occur in a market, such as a technology breakthrough or deregulation.

Once the planning team has identified opportunities that look attractive, it can then take these opportunities, either individually or as a group, through the next three steps of the process.

3. Understand the Market Environment

In order to understand the market environment, the firm must lay out the actual and potential market chains that could supply the targeted end users with the proposed product or service. This visual representation, extending from major suppliers of raw materials through to distribution channels, is one to which the planning team will return often.

Develop an appreciation of buyer behavior in the potential target segments. If customers' needs are being met by other suppliers, determine what will influence the target customers to switch to the new product your firm offers.

The firm will also need to understand the market chain, the members' buying criteria, and the likely buying process they will go through. Major barriers to adopting the proposed product or service may surface, resulting in this opportunity being dropped.

4. Assess Resources and Competencies

After looking at the external marketplace, assess the available internal resources (including financial resources, technology platforms, intellectual capital, manufacturing capacity, and brand equity) and capabilities (including skills and knowledge). Again, the internal situation may be such that the firm decides to abandon the opportunity.

5. Understand the Competitive Challenge

Although a competitive analysis is a key part of the analysis of the external environment, it is best done after reviewing the business's resources and capabilities—you are always in a better position to assess competitors if you have carefully looked at your own position first. Any competitive analysis has two fundamental purposes:

- To determine if winning a profitable position in a particular market opportunity is likely
- To develop the strategy and tactics that will allow the firm to achieve that winning position

To conduct the competitive analysis, first identify the actual, potential, and indirect competitors the organization will face. The indirect competitors are simply the companies that use a different technology to meet the same functional need of the customer. If the planning team did a good job of its market forces analysis when it was assessing the opportunity's attractiveness, this step should be straightforward.

Next, determine how each competitor competes, its current and likely future performance, and what drivers underlie its business strategies. Changes in key executives, such as a new CEO, can signal that a major shift in strategy is imminent. For example, when George Fisher became Eastman Kodak's CEO in 1993, he sold all of Kodak's businesses that were unrelated to imaging, and placed Kodak's embryonic digital imaging businesses in a business unit separate from its traditional silver-halide photography businesses.

As a final step in a competitive analysis, consider the implications for the opportunity being evaluated. What is this competitor likely to do next? What are this competitor's areas of weakness or vulnerability that the firm could exploit? How is this competitor likely to react if you do X, Y, or Z?

6. Make Tough Strategic Choices

For each individual opportunity, two common strategic issues arise. The first addresses winning and involves selecting the best strategy for taking advantage of the opportunity. Based on the analysis that the planning team has done, can it develop a strategy that will allow the organization to achieve a leadership position in the opportunity? The second issue involves deciding whether or not this is an opportunity that should be pursued. What will it be worth to win? Is the market opportunity attractive enough, and is the strategy powerful enough to generate a level of profitability that will meet the firm's financial targets? Or if not, are there compelling reasons to proceed?

When one considers the entire portfolio of opportunities, strategic issues often arise as to how well the opportunities fit with each other—do synergies exist within the portfolio, such as leveraging on a common technology or market chain? Another consideration is whether the strategies for the various opportunities are reasonably consistent. For example, a strategy based on product leadership for one product line is unlikely to be workable with a strategy of cost leadership for a related line.

Perhaps the most challenging aspect of any strategic thinking process is making the hard choices among the opportunities. Any good planning process should select the few truly attractive opportunities, concentrate the resources on these opportunities, and develop a leadership position in them.

7. Plan Critical Relationships

In many technology-intensive industries, developing and managing the relationships between one's organization and the market chain are crucial for success. In addition, important relationships may need to be developed with individuals or organizations outside the market chain—perhaps a company with a complementary product or service that will enhance the firm's offering.

8. Complete the Winning Strategy

To complete the winning strategy, attend to pricing and marketing communications. Both activities can help create the economic incentive for others in the market chain to work with you rather than with your competitors. The strategy must allow all key players in the market chain to achieve their business and personal objectives by working with your firm.

9. Understand the Profit Dynamic

A more refined profitability analysis is possible now with a detailed understanding of the complete marketing strategy and the associated costs. Develop a detailed financial model for each opportunity that has reached this stage in the planning process. This analysis may suggest modifications to the strategy that may enhance the opportunity's overall profitability.

10. Implement the Strategy

Finally, the firm is ready to implement the strategic market plan. No matter how good a strategy is, ineffectively implementing it will ensure failure. One way to ensure it is done right is to have the people who will play key roles in the implementation heavily involved in—and committed to—the strategy. They will then contribute to the strategy's development, understand the rationale for particular choices, and be able to make the many minor adjustments in strategy needed as the theory behind the strategy hits the shifting reality of the marketplace.

Strategic market planning requires the ideas and energy from all of a company's major functional units. As the plan comes together, finalize the supporting functional strategies in such areas as R&D, purchasing, manufacturing, and logistics.

Source: Adapted with permission by Donald W. Barclay and Adrian B. Ryans from Adrian B. Ryans, Roger A. More, Donald W. Barclay, and Terry H. Deutscher, *Winning Market Leadership,* Toronto, ON: John Wiley & Sons, 2000.

the high quality very difficult to imitate. Moreover, the skill in transferring digital images to paper in a high-quality fashion was significantly related to the benefits customers were seeking in printing their computer images. Hewlett-Packard has leveraged this core competency into a very different market: HP has entered the digital photography business with a digital photography package consisting of a camera, scanner, and printer. The digital photography business taps into essentially the same skills and capabilities that made HP successful in the laser printer business: transferring high-quality images to paper.[3]

Figure 2-3 shows a diagram of core competencies, using the analogy of a tree,[4] applying the analogy to Honda. The branches or canopy of the tree represents the widely different product markets to which the core competencies have provided access. In Honda's case, this would be the end markets in which it competes: small cars, snowblowers,

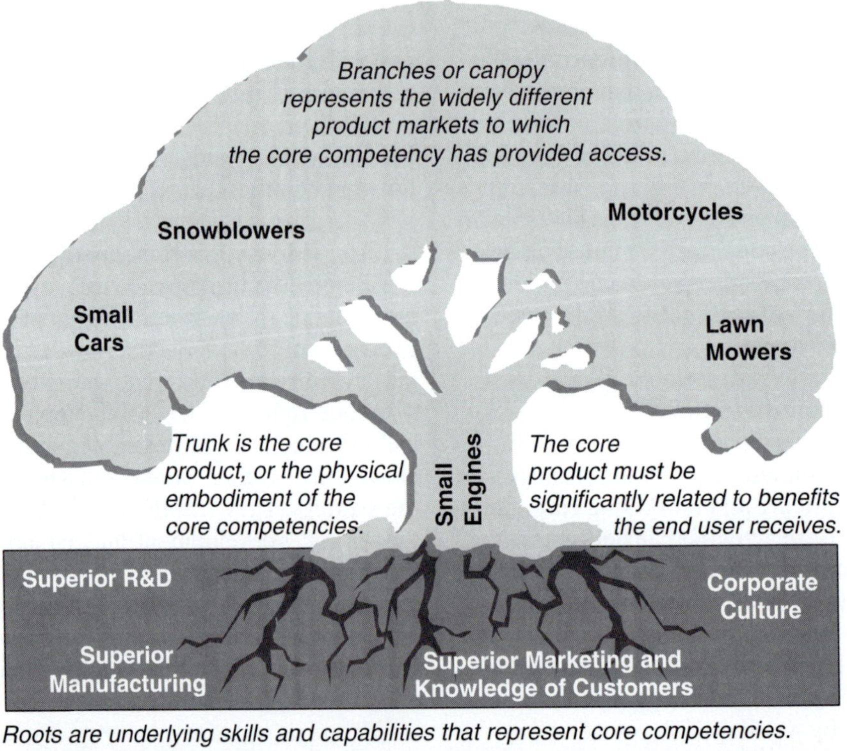

Branches or canopy
represents the widely different
product markets to which
the core competency has provided access.

Motorcycles

Snowblowers

**Small
Cars**

**Lawn
Mowers**

*Trunk is the core
product, or the physical
embodiment of the
core competencies.*

**Small
Engines**

*The core
product must be
significantly related to benefits
the end user receives.*

Superior R&D

**Corporate
Culture**

**Superior
Manufacturing**

**Superior Marketing and
Knowledge of Customers**

Roots are underlying skills and capabilities that represent core competencies.

FIGURE 2-3 Core Competencies for the Example of Honda

Source: Adapted from Prahalad, C. K. and Gary Hamel (1990), "The Core Competence of the Corporation," *Harvard Business Review,* May–June, pp. 79–91.

motorcycles, and lawn mowers, to name a few. The trunk represents the core product, or the physical embodiment of the core competencies. The core product must be significantly related to the benefits the end user receives. The roots of the tree represent the underlying skills and capabilities that form the basis of the core competencies. In this case, Honda's superior research and development, manufacturing techniques, marketing and knowledge of customers, and its corporate culture give rise to its success in small engine technology.

Using a core competencies approach to resource allocations can result in decisions that may seem to defy conventional logic. For example, a basic, underlying business tenet is that firms evaluate possible investments in new projects on criteria such as return on investment or payback period. However, using a core competency model of strategy, firms' investments may often defy the use of traditional criteria. One of the best examples might be found in a non-high-tech setting. Wal-Mart decided that to achieve its mission of delivering high-quality brand name products at the cheapest prices possible, it had to have a superior logistics and distribution infrastructure. Based on this underlying mission, Wal-Mart invested to achieve core competency in distribution by purchasing satellites, trucks, warehousing, and other assets needed to implement its unique cross-docking system. Wal-Mart made these investments at a time when many other companies were outsourcing these same functions, based on more traditional investment criteria. However, by taking a more sophisticated view of the strengths such investments would provide, Wal-Mart made investments that might have failed traditional ROI criteria, investments which allowed it to achieve nonimitable skills that have delivered its basic mission.

Although core competencies are an essential ingredient for success, they might also become **core rigidities** and possibly hinder new-product development. For example, new-product ideas built on familiar skills and capabilities are more likely to be embraced by a firm than those built on unfamiliar technologies. However, when market conditions are changing—for example, when new technologies are being developed by other firms in the industry—it may be important for a firm to examine closely the viability of a new technology. But ingrained routines, procedures, preferences for information sources, and existing views of the market—all of which can be related to underlying core competencies—can become barriers to a realistic assessment of new market opportunities. In such a situation, core competencies can become core rigidities, which strangle a firm's ability to act on novel information.[5]

Core rigidities are straitjackets that inhibit a firm from being innovative and can include

- Cultural norms in the firm
- Preferences for existing technology and routines
- Status hierarchies that give preference to, say, technical engineers over marketers

It is understandable that the cultural norms, technologies, routines, and company leaders' beliefs are valued, because they are the basis for the success many companies enjoy. At some point, however, such skills, values, and routines may not be as well suited to the changing business environment and necessitate reexamination and change themselves. Firms that are able to reevaluate such skills and capabilities on a regular basis, and update and modify them as needed, are not as burdened with rigidities as other firms may be.

For example, in the 1920s, New York–based oil-service company Schlumberger virtually established the oil-service industry by using electrical resistance to detect oil deep underground.[6] Recently, however, competition has developed something called smart wells, which challenge Schlumberger's most profitable business, Wireline and Testing. Schlumberger is losing its technological lead and has proved poorly prepared to meet customers' demands. It seems like past financial performance has created a sense of invincibility, which has resulted in underperformance and lack of innovation. In this case, its core competencies in one set of technologies may have prevented it from recognizing opportunities existing outside of its skill set.

So, how can a firm avoid falling prey to core rigidities? In addition to other ideas and insights presented throughout this text, firms in high-tech industries can use the following tools and techniques.

Creative Destruction   "No one is more blind than he who does not wish to see." Sometimes referred to as the "incumbent's curse,"[7] firms with an established advantage in a market are often blind to the possibilities of new innovations. For example, leadership in typewriting and word processing passed from Remington to Underwood to IBM to Wang and now to Microsoft. Never once did the leader at a particular stage pioneer the next stage. The same could be true of innovations on the Internet.

Firms must recognize that products in high-tech environments typically sustain only a finite spell at the technological frontier before being made obsolete by better products.

TECHNOLOGY TIDBIT

Scientists Working to Perfect Pond Scum as Car Fuel

THOMAS LUNDELL

What good could possibly come out of the filthy scum that gathers in ponds around the world? Well, according to scientists, it might fuel your car 20 years from now.

Two separate research teams have discovered how to alter the process of photosynthesis in the common green algae that flock in pond scum to produce hydrogen.

Many experts believe hydrogen power fuel cells will fuel cars and home generators in the future. The fuel cells combine hydrogen and oxygen to produce electricity, with water as the by-product instead of monoxide and other pollutants. Maybe this means that Evian and Exxon will merge and market bottled fuel residue? Who knows what the future will bring.

Source: Borenstein, Seth (2000), "Scientists Working to Perfect Pond Scum as Car Fuel," *The Missoulian,* February 23.

Given this reality, firms must proactively attempt to develop that next-generation technology—despite the fact that such developments may make obsolete its sunk investments in the prior technology and render any economies of scale and experience curve advantages useless. This notion of constantly innovating to develop the next-generation technology, despite the potential drawbacks of doing so, is known as **creative destruction.**[8]

The paradox of such a model of competition is that the firm itself must work to find the next best technology, which is likely to destroy the basis of its current success. The reason for such a model is that if the firm does not commercialize a new technology, rivals will surely do so. Hence, firms must not hold back a new technology that makes its existing products obsolete. Even with successful products, firms should not be too enamored with the technology that forms the basis of that success, but instead strive to develop even better technologies.[9] Indeed, ongoing industry leadership hinges upon creative destruction.

An example is Microsoft's continued desire to ride the wave of the success of its operating systems software (Windows 95, 98, etc.). However, when rivals Netscape (first) and Sun Microsystems (second) introduced new technologies (Internet browsers and Java scripts, respectively), Microsoft had to make a major turnaround in strategy to participate in these technologies[10]—even though they may radically change the world of desktop computing and, at the extreme, render proprietary operating systems obsolete. Rather than information being accessed by desktop computers, these technologies allow consumers to access information via a range of consumer electronic devices and "information appliances" that don't require the Windows operating system.

An additional example is found in the Internet realm. Companies whose past successes have been based heavily in a brick-and-mortar world with tangible distribution channels are finding that to compete with dot.com start-ups, they must offer sales through an Internet channel. Yet, doing so undermines the very basis for their success. However, this is the nature of creative destruction: If the company itself does not offer customers the access avenues they desire, a competitor surely will. More ties to the Internet will be developed later in this chapter.

Recent research on radical product innovation demonstrates that it is not size per se that contributes to the lack of innovativeness in firms (i.e., the **liability of bigness**); rather, it is the extent to which a firm is prepared to reduce the value of its past investments or is willing to cannibalize.[11] Willingness to cannibalize overlooks the sunk-cost fallacy, or the influence of expenditures that have been made in the past, expenditures that rationally should not be taken into account for decisions about the future. In the context of radical product innovation, willingness to cannibalize has positive effects.

Corporate Imagination   Another tool that can be used to overcome the liability of core rigidities and the inertia inherent in corporate bureaucracies is to attempt to develop what is known as **corporate imagination,**[12] creativity, and even playfulness. It is important for established organizations to replenish their stock of ideas continuously. For many innovative firms, a key measure of success is the percent of revenue derived from recently released products.

Corporate imagination requires the ability to create a vision of the future that consists of markets that do not yet exist and is based on a horizon not confined by the boundaries of the current business. As shown in Table 2-1, creative corporate imagination includes four important elements.

1. *Overturn price–performance assumptions.* Many established firms spend their time making incremental improvements to existing technologies. This is understandable, because existing customers want performance improvements in the products they are using. However, incremental improvements to existing technologies are based on improving performance on existing standards. Alternatively, really new products are more likely to be based on entirely different performance assumptions.

One tool that helps firms understand how to overturn such price–performance issues is the **technology life cycle.** The technology life cycle refers to improvements in product performance relative to the investments in effort in a particular technology.[13] As Figure 2-4 shows, as a new technology is introduced, its performance capacity improves slowly and then, because of heavy R&D efforts, improves rapidly, before reaching its performance limits. When a newer technology is introduced, the two technologies will compete with each other for a time period, until the new technology eventually supercedes the former.

TABLE 2-1   Four Elements of Corporate Imagination

1   Overturn price–performance assumptions, using the tool of technology life cycle curves.
2   Escape the tyranny of the served market.
3   Use new sources of ideas for innovative product concepts.
4   Get out in front of customers: Lead them where they want to go before they themselves know it.

Source: Hamel, Gary and C. K. Prahalad (1991), "Corporate Imagination and Expeditionary Marketing," *Harvard Business Review,* July–August, pp. 81–92.

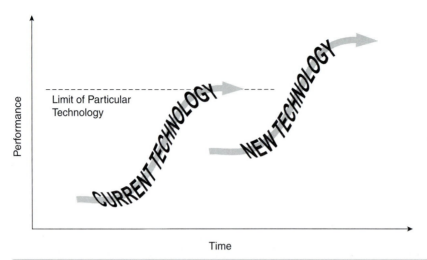

FIGURE 2-4 Technology Life Cycles

For example, advances in semiconductor speed and processing power, relative to price, have been formalized in **Moore's Law,** which states that semiconductor performance doubles every 18 months, with no increase in price. Stated differently, every 18 months or so, improvements in technology cut price in half for the same level of performance. However, some predict that future improvements in microchip performance are limited by the use of semiconductor technology and that Moore's Law is reaching its natural limit. In that sense, further investments in enhancing semiconductor performance may result in only incremental improvements in technology, improvements that may have reached a plateau. This possibility is one reason that Japan's Ministry of International Trade and Industry has sponsored a $30 million research program focused on technologies that could replace conventional semiconductors. These technologies are based on quantum physics and neural networks rather than on electrical engineering. Although such research is at a preliminary stage, and the nascent performance of these new technologies is unclear, the technologies hold the possibility of obsoleting semiconductors as we know them today.

Unfortunately, the majority of the time, new technologies are commercialized by companies *outside* the threatened industry,[14] suggesting that it is difficult for industry incumbents to be imaginative in envisioning new technologies. Established firms must realize that all products have performance limits; as an existing technology approaches its limit, it becomes more expensive to make improvements. Therefore, firms must look to develop new technologies.

However, many established firms try to hedge their bets with new technology. At worst, they do not strive to develop new technology. At best, they invest both in improving the current-generation technology and developing new technology. For example, a company may try to make investments to make its manufacturing facility more efficient in producing the current-generation technology. Yet, being the low-cost producer of an obsolete product is not worth much.[15]

Moreover, established firms tend to underestimate the firms introducing new technologies, either because such firms are small or the new technology appears crude. Because of all these reasons, technology substitutes can creep up slowly on established firms and then explode in terms of market performance. This was definitely true of the Internet, where much of the development was initiated by companies unknown to the major computer industry market players. Hence, established firms must aggressively pursue new technologies early on.[16]

How can a firm recognize when a current-generation technology is in danger of obsolescence? The technology life cycle curve demonstrates that one can't rely solely on economic signals: Based on incremental improvements, the revenue of the current technology can reach a peak even after the new technology is introduced. Hence, relying on economic signals may result in the firm moving too late into the new technology, and the competition will have established a stronghold. Underlying technology life cycles, based on diminishing performance returns to increasing investments in current-generation technology, is the crucial indicator.[17]

2. *Escape the tyranny of the served market.*[18] Firms have both expertise in matching their product offering to a particular market segment and a competitive advantage with customers in that segment. Established firms have a vested interest in maintaining their "bread-and-butter" line in major segments. Hence, they tend to develop more incremental innovations for these existing customers. The tyranny of the served market refers to the tendency for firms to focus very specifically on solving customers' needs with a current technology. Such a myopic focus obscures the possibility that customer needs may change over time and may be solved in radically different ways.

For example, in the Internet world, a firm's best customers may be the last to embrace a disruptive technology because it doesn't provide the service and performance they prefer. Those who embrace it first are typically the customers a company pays least attention to, and the innovation creeps up like a stealth attack.[19]

The tyranny of the served market is one of the main reasons that new innovations are typically introduced by firms that are new to the market or industry outsiders/newcomers. And, these newcomers frequently alter the rules of the game, jumping to a new technology life cycle with new price–performance ratios. Corporate imagination requires that firms look for market opportunities across or between the areas of a firm's competence.

3. *Use new sources of ideas for innovative product concepts.* Many large firms are familiar with standard approaches to market analysis that are often premised on existing market boundaries. For example, most large firms have used the standard marketing research techniques of running focus groups, administering surveys, using conjoint analysis to help decide the optimal combination of attributes for new products, and so forth. However, corporate imagination requires firms to rely on different types of marketing research to open new doors of opportunity. These marketing research techniques, especially useful in a high-tech marketing context, include ethnographic observation ("empathic design") and lead users. These tools are discussed in Chapter 5, "Marketing Research in High-Tech Markets."

4. *Get out in front of customers.* The fourth aspect of corporate imagination is to actually lead customers where they want to go before customers themselves know it. The ability to be a market leader, based on envisioning the future, requires profound insights that are not saddled with existing rules and procedures. Technical wizardry must be based on understanding customer needs for it to be successful. To be in front of customers

requires multidisciplinary product teams and procedures to inform those closest to the customers about emerging technological possibilities.

Firms can be innovative in both product development and how they approach their business strategies. As a parallel example to innovativeness in product development, Box 2-2, "Innovativeness in Corporate Strategy," provides information on how to be innovative in developing new business strategies.

An implicit assumption in these "lessons" of corporate imagination is that a firm should be a market pioneer to be successful. The large literature base on first-mover advantages accruing to market pioneers shows mixed benefits. The key highlights from this literature are summarized in Box 2-3, "Market Pioneering Advantages and Risks."

Each of these aspects of corporate imagination leads to another important element of not letting core competencies become core rigidities: expeditionary marketing.

Expeditionary Marketing   Because creating markets ahead of competitors is so risky—sometimes the hoped-for market does not develop at all, or if it does, it emerges more slowly than expected—companies must use strategies to minimize the risks. Successful new products include the right combination of functionality, price, and performance targeted to the correct market. There are two ways to improve the success ratio.

One way is to try to improve the odds on each individual product introduction, or to improve the "hit" rate. To have a successful new product launch, a company tries to gather as much information as possible to tailor the product as needed in terms of functionality, price, and performance, so that when it is delivered to the market, the odds of a successful hit are as high as possible.

The other route to success is to try many "mini-introductions" in quick succession and, by learning from each foray into the marketplace, to incorporate that learning into each successive "time at bat," such that over time, the firm has accumulated loyal customers and higher market share. This strategy is known as **expeditionary marketing.**[20] The issue here is not to improve the hit rate but to increase the number of times at bat in the market. The underlying strategy is based on learning: The firm wants to learn about the marketplace and customer needs by placing many small bets in the marketplace. These low-cost, fast-paced incursions allow the firm to learn and recalibrate its offerings each time, such that the combination of speed and learning enhances the odds of success.

Which of the two ways do most companies focus their attention on? Most companies focus their attention on the first way. Through careful market research, competitive analysis, and the use of stage-gate procedures that specify the hurdles a new idea must overcome at each stage of development, they try to maximize the odds of success. However, such a strategy is very time-consuming, and in high-tech markets, the accuracy of the information can be sketchy at best. Moreover, by the time the product is introduced to the market, the marketplace (customer needs and competitors) may have changed. Indeed, this approach might be characterized as "Ready. Aim. Aim. Aim."[21]

Hence, in high-tech markets, it may make more sense to undertake a series of fast-paced market incursions—expeditionary marketing. Such a strategy has several advantages. First, it allows the company to learn more accurately, through successive approximations, about what customer needs are. Second, through fast-paced market incursions, it maximizes the odds that the product actually delivered to the market meets customers' needs. Fast-paced incursions imply that the time-to-market cycle is faster,

BOX 2-2

Innovativeness in Corporate Strategy

Innovative breakthroughs can be found not only in products, but in processes and management practices as well. Although the focus of this book is primarily on high-tech products and services, it would be an oversight not to address how a firm can be innovative in its business strategies as a way to gain competitive advantage. Recent writings on this topic highlight the fact that firms that are able to sustain a high rate of growth do so by radically changing the basis of competition in their industries to create new wealth.

The idea of being innovative in their approach to strategy is vital for today's firms. Digitalization, deregulation, globalization, and new economic business models are profoundly changing the industrial landscape. Indeed, unless today's established corporations learn to reinvent themselves and their industries, new wealth will be created by newcomers. For example, between 1986 and 1996, just 17 companies of the *Fortune* 1,000 grew total shareholder return by 35% or more per year. Although quality concerns, cost awareness, time to market, and process improvements are vital, they are no longer a source of large gains. These tools and the resulting incremental improvements in strategy will keep profits from eroding and prolong the usefulness of current business strategies, but they won't create new wealth.

Importantly, firms focused on creating new wealth do not measure their success in terms of short-term shareholder return. Rather, they look at the company's share of total amount of new wealth that has been generated in an industry. This can be done by comparing a company's current share of the total market capitalization of its relevant competitive domain with its share a

decade ago. For example, in 1988, Gap's share of market capitalization within the broad retailing domain amounted to 1.2%, but by early 1997, it had risen to 4.6%; the Limited's share dropped from 4.7% to 2.5%. These statistics can also reveal that a company with a healthy return on invested capital may actually be losing "share of wealth." It would be unwise for a company to be content with a 10% growth rate and a positive return on investment while new competitors capture the majority of new wealth generated in a particular industry.

To create new wealth, companies must learn how to unleash the spirit of "strategy innovation," the idea of creating a revolution within their own companies. What does it take to identify killer strategies? It is really no different than what it takes to develop breakthrough innovations: Take risks, break the rules, be a maverick. Hamel offers the following insights:

- Rather than focusing on industry analysis as the key to strategy formulation, firms that create new wealth and play by new rules recognize that industry boundaries in today's environment are fluid rather than static. Hence, innovative firms do not focus their analysis on existing industry boundaries.

- Nor do firms with innovative strategies focus on direct competitors. With new business models, it is difficult to distinguish competitors from collaborators, suppliers from buyers. Rivalry is no longer easy to identify, and it is hard to know who is friend and who is foe. It is vital to look at product form competition and partners as potential competitors.

- Strategy formulation must recognize that today's business boundaries (in addition to industry boundaries) are fluid. With the rise of contract workers, outsourcing, and supply relationships, the firm no longer has control of all its critical assets.

A good strategy creation process is a deeply embedded skill; it is a way to understand what is going on in an industry, turn it on its head, and envision new opportunities. And it is based on the paradoxical notion that one can make serendipity happen. How?[a]

- Bring new voices into the strategy formulation dialogue. "Companies miss the future not because they are fat or lazy but because they are blind."[b] Many companies are unequipped to see where the future is coming from and lack the lens to know that. So bringing new voices into the process, outside of the company's normal comfort zone, can provide new vision.

- Bring new connections between new voices, across boundaries of function, technology, hierarchy, business, and geography. Such new conversations can offer a rich web of insights.

- Offer new perspectives, based on a new vantage point in viewing the business. Rather than based on analysis and number crunching, often innovative strategies emerge from novel experiences that yield novel insights.

- Exude passion for discovery and novelty, which engenders an emotional attachment of employees who are committed enough

to reduce the time between an idea and its implementation.

- Be willing to experiment. With innovative strategies, the end target may be known, but the route to it may be unknown. The best way to approach such a situation is to be willing to move in the right direction, and to refine strategy and process as the firm learns from its experiments. Although such a notion is an anathema to efficiency, it is a must in redefining radical business strategies.

What companies have followed this model in pursuit of "killer strategies"? WorldCom saw there was more than one way to be a telephone company. By offering the customer not only long distance but also local and Internet services, it broke out of the pack and became a powerhouse in the U.S. telecommunications industry. Intel chose not to follow the conventional wisdom that it pays to extend a product's shelf life. It keeps making its own chips obsolete with better designs and showed that with an effective advertising campaign, one can "brand" a component within another product. Other companies, such as Amgen, Oracle, and Iomega, to name a few, have all shown their willingness to look from the outside in and, in doing so, create new rules in established industries.

---

[a] See also Ryans, Adrian, Roger More, Donald Barclay, and Terry Deutscher (2000), *Winning Market Leadership— In Technology-Intensive Businesses,* Toronto: John Wiley, a book on strategy creation in technology-intensive industries.

[b] Hamel, Gary (1997), "Killer Strategies That Make Shareholders Rich," *Fortune,* June 23, p. 80.

Source: Hamel, Gary (1997), "Killer Strategies That Make Shareholders Rich," *Fortune,* June 23, pp. 70–84.

and therefore, the odds of the customers' needs changing in that time period are lower. Under such a model, what counts the most is not being right the first time, but how quickly a company can learn and modify its product offerings, based on its accumulated experience in the marketplace.[22]

As an example, Storage Technology Corporation (STK), maker of tape backup systems for large data installations (such as banks, insurance companies, etc.), uses the model

Market Pioneering Advantages and Risks

Should a firm speed the time-to-market cycle and attempt to be the market pioneer? Many studies report that pioneers have a strong first-mover advantage in the marketplace, including higher market share and stronger differential advantage. Yet, one can also find many examples of later entrants having a stronger advantage than the market pioneer. By allowing competitors to enter the market first, later entrants do not have the market development costs that a pioneer faces in terms of educating customers about the new technology. In addition, later entrants can introduce a product with a higher performance level or a better price–quality ratio.

Advantages.   What are the arguments in support of being a market pioneer?[a] First movers are thought to have competitive advantages due to entry barriers established by their market entry. Such entry barriers include economies of scale, experience effects, reputational effects, technological leadership, and buyer switching costs. These barriers can lengthen the lead time between a firm's head start and the response by followers. During the time when there is no competition, the first mover is, by definition, a monopolist who can gain higher profits than in a competitive marketplace. In addition, even after competitors enter, the first mover has the established market position, which allows it to retain a dominant market share and higher margins than later entrants. First movers are also able to "skim off" early adopters, whereas later entrants are left with potential customers who are less predisposed to purchasing new products.

Moreover, if customers know little about the importance of product attri-

butes or their ideal combinations, a first mover can influence how attributes are valued and define the ideal attribute combination to its advantage. The first mover becomes a prototype against which all other entrants are judged, making it harder for later entrants to make competitive inroads. First movers have a higher degree of consumer awareness, which lowers perceived risk and information costs.

For example, the Internet is not a world that tolerates caution or deliberation. In a medium where brand-name recognition is everything, losing the first-mover advantage can be a handicap. Barnes & Noble was blindsided by Amazon.com. And despite its huge expenditures and massive advertising since then, Barnes & Noble remains barely more than one-tenth of Amazon's size on-line.[b]

Are these arguments so compelling, and the research findings so supportive, that the pioneering advantage is automatically conferred? Not necessarily. A close examination of the literature shows that for a firm to definitively establish a pioneering advantage, it must have certain competencies and capabilities, including technological foresight, perceptive market research, skillful product and process development capabilities, marketing acumen, and possibly even luck. Being a market pioneer *per se* does not directly produce enduring competitive advantage. Indeed, it also comes with distinct risks.

Disadvantages.   In their study of the personal digital assistant (PDA) industry, Bayus, Jain, and Rao[c] found that speeding a product to market is not always a good idea. Firms must evaluate trade-offs among time to market, product performance, and development costs. Pioneers face huge development costs against a high degree of market uncertainty. Some say that in high-technology industries, one can tell the technology pioneers by the arrows in their backs. The true leaders often say they are not on the cutting edge, but on the bleeding edge! Often, the firms who take a more measured pace in approaching the market will be the ones reaping the rewards.[d]

How should marketing managers in a high-tech firm decide whether to pioneer the market? The success of a pioneering strategy depends on how well a firm understands the market (both the market size and market needs) and how well it understands its competitors' strengths and weaknesses. For example, in the PDA market, Apple overestimated the potential market size and underestimated the product performance desired by the market. In the PDA market, later entrants were more profitable. They entered the market with higher performance products targeted to more narrow target markets.

Late movers can overcome pioneers in at least two ways:[e]

1. A late mover can identify a superior but overlooked product position, undercut the pioneer on prices, or outadvertise/outdistribute the pioneer, thereby beating it at its own game.

2. A late mover can innovate either superior products or strategies that change the rules of the game. In particular, *innovative* late entrants, relative to pioneers, grow faster and have higher market potential. Moreover, innovative late entrants slow the pioneer's growth and reduce its marketing spending effectiveness.

This research suggests that by reshaping the category, late entrants can redefine the game in such a way that benefits the late mover and disadvantages the pioneer. So, for any given firm, the question of whether early or late entry is more advantageous depends on the firm's particular characteristics.

---

[a] Kerin, Roger A., P. Rajan Varadarajan, and Robert A. Peterson (1992), "First-Mover Advantage: A Synthesis, Conceptual Framework, and Research Propositions," *Journal of Marketing,* 56 (October), pp. 33–52.

[b] Byrnes, Nanette and Paul Judge (1999), "Internet Anxiety," *Business Week,* June 28, pp. 79–88.

[c] Bayus, Barry L., Sanjay Jain, and Ambar G. Rao (1997), "Too Little, Too Early: Introduction Timing and New Product Performance in the Personal Digital Assistant Industry," *Journal of Marketing Research,* 34 (February), pp. 50–63.

[d] Sager, Ira (1999), "Go Ahead, Farm Out Those Jobs," *Business Week e.biz,* March 22, p. EB35.

[e] Shankar, Venkates, Gregory S. Carpenter, and Lakshman Krishnamurthi (1998), "Late Mover Advantage: How Innovative Late Entrants Outsell Pioneers," *Journal of Marketing Research,* 35 (February), pp. 57–70; see also Zhang, Shi and Arthur B. Markman (1998), "Overcoming the Early Entrant Advantage: The Role of Alignable and Nonalignable Differences," *Journal of Marketing Research,* 35 (November), pp. 413–426.

---

depicted in Figure 2-5. The idea is that, rather than introducing the most advanced model possible based on a new technology (model 3), STK attempts to introduce in rapid succession a series of models based on the new technology.

In addition to speeding the cycle time to market (via techniques such as concurrent engineering, etc.), another important aspect of expeditionary marketing is the notion of organizational learning. Box 2-4, "Market Learning Processes," addresses the learning aspect in more detail.

Nurture a Culture of Innovation   The final strategy discussed here for established companies to retain an innovative culture is to recognize the nature of innovation itself. By the

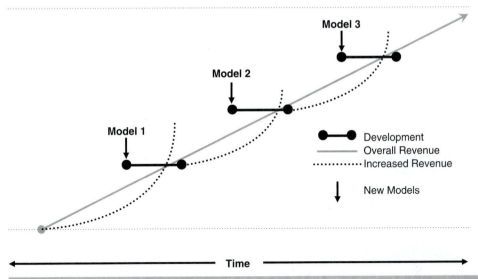

FIGURE 2-5 Expeditionary Marketing: Many Fast-Paced Incursions into the Market

Reprinted with the permission of Storage Technology Corporation, Louisville, Colorado.

time many firms are wrestling with a loss of innovativeness, they have become sluggish bureaucracies in which the new product development process is based on formal plans and procedures. The process is often rational and analytical and bears little resemblance to the nature of innovation, which is often tumultuous, nonlinear, and serendipitous.[23]

Rather than a stage-gate, step-by-step process through which new product ideas must pass, innovative activity in corporations might be better "managed" as an entrepreneurial process. Referred to variously as "autonomous strategic behavior,"[24] "emergent processes,"[25] or "intrapreneuring,"[26] the idea is to create an internal environment that fosters innovation and an entrepreneurial spirit. What characteristics does a firm exhibit if it wants to foster an innovative climate?

- The market need identified is one that diverges from (rather than converges on) the organization's concepts of strategy.
- The roles and responsibilities of the key players are poorly defined at the outset but become more formalized as the strategies evolve.
- Rather than a formal screen based on established administrative procedures, the screening process for the idea is done via an informal network that assesses technical and market merit.
- The communication between personnel tends to flow less along prescribed organizational decision-making channels and more through an informal network.
- Commitment to the idea emerges largely through the sponsorship efforts of a product champion.

Product champions.   Important to the success of any breakthrough innovation are **product champions,** or the people who create, define, or adopt an idea for an innovation and are willing to assume significant risk to make it happen.[27] Often referred to as iconoclasts, mavericks, or crusaders, these people break the rules, take risks, transform companies, and turn organizations upside down. They work tirelessly and lobby behind the

BOX 2-4

Market Learning Processes

CHRISTINE MOORMAN
Duke University

Many suggest that an organization's strongest assets are the abilities to use information and to learn. How does the use of information (and the level and impact of learning) affect new-product development in terms of speed, financial success, and innovation level of new products? What is the impact of organizational dynamics on the value that firms get from information use and learning activities? Christine Moorman and her colleagues' research points to four important conclusions.

1. *Competitive advantage is found, not in having information, but in using it.* Given the ubiquitous and public nature of information, organizations should emphasize improving the *use,* not acquisition, of information. Information acquisition and transmission activities do not alone impact new products. Rather, it is the use of information that has a positive impact on the profitability, creativity, and timing of new-product development. Therefore, high-tech marketing managers should focus on developing formal and informal organizational processes for encouraging managers to rely on the information that is available within the firm. This may involve changing the incentives to use information, developing work groups that process information informally, reducing the perceived costs, or showing the benefits of information use activities.

2. *Organizational and interpersonal dynamics have an important effect on the use of information.* For example, trust is a crucial factor in relationships between users and providers of market or product information in organizations. Trust encourages communication and commitment in the relationship, which makes information utilization possible. It is possible that trusting relationships may, over the long run, create problems of complacency, low innovation, and an unwillingness to share disconfirmatory information. Safeguards should be developed to mitigate these threats.

Differences in the impact of trust on information utilization depend on the specific nature of the organizational context. Trust has a stronger impact when the dyad

a. Involves a marketer–marketer relationship instead of a marketer–nonmarketer (e.g., high-tech product development manager) relationship

b. Is an interorganizational relationship (e.g., ventures between high-tech firms) as opposed to an intraorganizational relationship

These results suggest that high-tech marketing managers will need to consider how to reduce some of the barriers associated with interorganizational relationships and marketer–nonmarketer relationships. This may involve providing stronger signals of commitment to the relationship, such as incurring setup costs or low monitoring activities. It may also involve introducing legal mechanisms or interpersonal linkages into interorganizational relationships when competing firms involved in a venture may suffer reduced cooperation. The interpersonal relationships may be important because research indicates that strengthening or building strong trust-based relationships with firms among competitors (that have similar capabilities) increases knowledge transfer in the venture and has a positive impact on the speed and innovation level of the individual firm and venture's product development activities.

Within organizations, research shows that firms building commitment, loyalty, and trust among organizational members are the heaviest users of market information in the development of new products. Hence, the clan-like quality of a firm is important in determining information usage in new-product development.

3. *CAUTION: Information utilization activities are not a panacea and often have downside risks.* Information is not inherently valuable to performance. The idea that information does not have an unconditionally positive impact on performance runs counter to a great deal of popular press literature touting the "value of information." Research has tried to determine the right mix of conditions to maximize the impact of information utilization.

Specialized knowledge held by the marketing function in managing customer connections in the firm contributes to firm performance beyond that explained by a firm's general market orientation. High-tech firms should recognize and value marketing's contribution in providing knowledge and skills to manage the customer–product connection, the customer–service quality connection, and the customer–financial accountability connection.

Moreover, storing organizational information in a useful "organizational memory," although useful to financial performance, can hinder the innovativeness of new products. Indeed, an organizational memory with relatively homogeneous content based on a "shared vision" is useful for product innovation *only* when the firm operates in an environment with little turbulence. Given technological turbulence that most high-tech marketers face, a more varied or heterogeneous memory will be more useful for a firm seeking product innovation.

Finally, marketing knowledge and skills influence product innovation level and speed only when the firm has complementary technology knowledge and skills—a key part of all high-tech organizations. This again highlights the need to recognize and value the interplay of marketing knowledge and technological knowledge.

4. *New-product development is not always planned and controlled. Instead, it is often improvised and extemporaneous, which, in the right informational conditions, can benefit high-tech organizations.* Organizational improvisation refers to those times when firms plan and act at the same time. Thus, the more a firm composes an idea as it executes the idea, the more it is improvising as opposed to planning in advance. As with any form of organizational learning, improvisation does not have any inherent links to positive outcomes and may, on average, produce more harm than good. However, research indicates improvisation can enhance product design activities when there are

- High levels of organizational memory (i.e., high levels of knowledge and experience)
- Real-time information transfers among team members
- Flows of information into the team from the external environment

Therefore, the key to managing improvisation in a high-tech setting would appear to hinge on whether information flows can be managed to increase improvisation's effectiveness rate. Moreover, in a high-tech setting where turbulence is rampant, improvised actions are likely to be more common, making their management even more crucial to firm success.

Finally, research has shown that organizations actually develop organizational competencies related to improvisation. These competencies involve activities for producing effective improvisation and for harvesting valued improvisations.

scenes for organizational resources to help their ideas take off. The product champion is a person with drive, aggressiveness, political astuteness, technical competence, and market knowledge. Influential product champions can overcome firms' natural reluctance to cannibalize and motivate radical product innovations.[28]

Although product champions are found in both innovative and noninnovative companies, those in noninnovative companies wield less influence and are frustrated and demoralized. In successful companies, they have the power to make their ideas happen. Product champions in innovating firms wield substantially more influence than in less innovative firms. The reward systems and cultures promote the influence of product champions, and top management actively supports them.[29]

Additional characteristics.   Some additional characteristics are also important to foster a climate of innovation in large, established firms. First, people must be given time, incentives, and desire to be creative. Some companies, such as 3M, allocate a certain percentage of each employee's time that doesn't need to be accounted for by activity on a particular project. This allows people time to explore new ideas, and to create and discover possible inventions that they might not otherwise. Similarly, other companies give employees a financial stake in new inventions, whether through sharing of patent rights or through monetary payment for successful ideas.

Companies that foster a climate of innovativeness do not penalize people for ideas that don't work out. Such companies recognize that competing in high-tech markets carries with it the knowledge that not all products will be successful in the market. Tolerating risks and a certain number of mistakes is part of the entrepreneurial spirit. Indeed, learning from such ostensible "mistakes" may be the basis of the company's next new success.

Skunk works.   Because so many firms find it difficult to create an innovative climate, some advocate the isolation of new venture groups in a location removed from the normal corporate operations.[30] The thought is that when large, established companies develop new innovations, they do so *despite* the corporate system, not *because* of it.[31] Hence, in order to protect imaginative individuals from corporate orthodoxies, senior managers isolate them in new venture divisions, or corporate incubators, often at a remote site from the parent organization.

These new venture groups removed from the normal corporate operations are sometimes referred to as **skunk works.** The etymology of this term comes from the Skonk Works, an illicit distillery in the comic strip "Li'l Abner" by Al Capp, around 1974. Because illicit distilleries were bootleg operations, typically located in an isolated area with minimal formal oversight, the term has been adopted in organizational settings to refer to a usually small and often isolated department or facility (say, for research and development) that functions with minimal supervision or impediments from the normal corporate operating procedures.

Many firms have relied on skunk works operations to develop new lines of business. For example, IBM isolated its PC group in North Carolina, away from corporate headquarters in New York and away from any other established IBM locations. Dow Chemical also relies on skunk works for its new venture groups.

Despite the potential advantages of such isolation, some critics argue that trying to leverage corporate competencies into new businesses while at the same time protecting new ventures from the corporate culture is a contradiction in terms.[32] For an established company to become and remain innovative, it must allow individual creativity within the normal corporate operating procedures. A corporate culture that allows innovation to flourish shouldn't have to put up special protection mechanisms for it to happen. Indeed, Gary Hamel refers to such incubators as "orphanages" that isolate the creative conversations and make it hard for new ideas to emerge in the corporate hierarchy.[33]

So, the idea of isolating new product development groups from standard corporate procedures poses a dilemma. Ideally, it would probably be best if the corporation nourished innovation and did not need to have separate units to develop innovative ideas. On the other hand, if normal corporate operating procedures stifle creativity, a skunk works may be something of a temporary or "band-aid" solution; addressing the systemic reasons for the problem may be also necessary.

Applying Lessons of Innovativeness on the Internet

What can recent experiences in the world of Internet businesses tell us about the preceding "lessons"? As an application of the concepts in this chapter, it is instructive to examine companies' responses and forays into the on-line world of e-commerce.

On-line competitors pose huge threats to incumbents in established industries, because they change the rules of the game and operate under a radical new business model: fewer requirements for working capital, inherent speed and efficiency, and direct access to customers and suppliers. The obvious threat of this new business model is that of *extinction*.

> Companies that don't move fast to get in on the game risk having their lunch eaten by tiny rivals who may have barely existed just a few years ago. In industry after industry, fledgling Net companies have transformed the way business is done and snatched market share from their much bigger, established rivals.[34]

This is the nature of *competitive turbulence* in a high-tech environment. Companies that don't jump in despite the risks may be cut out altogether. The liability of bigness can be stifling. "Big companies are likely to be laggards at spotting fresh ways to do business—and equally ponderous at mobilizing to take advantage of those situations. For start-ups, the greatest strength may be an ability to react quickly to new opportunities."[35]

Despite the threat of extinction by newcomers, established competitors have a tendency to *underestimate their competition*. John Welch of General Electric initially derided Net stocks as "wampum," whereas IBM's Lou Gerstner said Net companies are "fireflies before the storm": They shine now but will eventually dim out.[36] Grocery industry executives' initial response to on-line grocery buying was, "Too expensive." They subsequently have learned that personalized delivery is something consumers are willing to pay for.[37] Indeed, each time the business model of retailing changed, a new group of leaders emerged, from the Woolworth's of Main Street in the 1950s to the Sears of the malls in the 1970s to the superstores of Wal-Mart and Costco in the 1990s.[38] Firms must recognize that innovations typically come from outside the industry.

Another risk is the potential *cannibalization* of a company's revenue stream. Going on-line requires that companies be willing to cannibalize their own core franchise, or engage in *creative destruction*. Often, the initial move to an on-line environment can result in a decrease in revenues, earnings, and stock prices. Indeed, the decision of how much an existing business should invest in the on-line world, with its huge up-front costs and only theoretical profits, is an anguishing decision. "In getting from A to C, B is hell," says Intel's VP of business development in discussing Internet investments. B is where revenues decline and profits go down, but there is no way for large companies to get to where they need to be in the future without going through this "valley of death."

Another aspect of being willing to engage in creative destruction is the willingness to risk upsetting partnerships with distributors and retailers. Conflict with existing sales channels has been identified as the biggest impediment to on-line selling.[39]

How else can the Internet world highlight examples of innovation? In the off-line world, where it is sometimes difficult to get rapid feedback when some part of the marketing mix isn't working, companies can be slow to learn from customers and slower to act on what they learn. However, in the on-line world, that changes. The Web lends itself to immediate customer feedback and rapid adjustment. Learning cycles are much shorter on-line than off-line. Companies that are quick to try, quick to learn, and quick to adapt will win. Those that learn fastest and keep learning will stay ahead. Zipping through the learning cycle creates positive feedback effects. The faster a company learns and adapts, the more customers it wins; the more customers it wins, the faster it can learn and adapt.[40] This learning process highlights the fact that effective Internet companies intuitively understand the notion of *expeditionary marketing.*

Indeed, until recently, being a market pioneer on the Web translated into huge advantages in site traffic and stock valuations. The Internet is all about speed, but to be fast necessarily implies that a company can't do it all. Rather, based on a *core competencies* model of strategic planning, companies have to outsource some (or many) aspects of getting on-line. Companies who can help others get on-line are seeing huge increases in volume.[41] Designing, hosting, maintaining the site, handling e-mail, and logistics and distribution can stretch many firms well beyond their capabilities. Insights on outsourcing are offered in the Technology Expert's View from the Trenches.

As a final example of the innovation concepts at work in the Internet arena, when Toys "R" Us decided to begin its on-line operations, it set up a separate unit in Northern California. The firm decided that being located in corporate headquarters would slow it down and hinder its innovativeness.[42] This is the classic setup of a *skunk works.*

Although large companies do have a number of liabilities in an on-line environment, and need a number of strategies to cope, they also have some important advantages. Household brand names, larger budgets, and tested leadership each provide resources that many smaller companies do not have.[43] Issues related to the liability of smallness are addressed next.

THE LIABILITY OF SMALLNESS: RESOURCES

Although they would rarely, if ever, be accused of not being innovative or nimble enough, small high-tech start-ups face their own set of unique difficulties. Probably one of the most salient concerns is the ability to fund the budding company prior to the time that real sales volume materializes.

For example, Gary Schneider devoted his life to the development and marketing of software that will help small farmers in optimizing their crop selection, an idea he got while studying agriculture and engineering at the University of Arizona.[44] After a decade of refining his idea, Gary finally set up his company, called AgDecision, in 1996 to commercialize his concept. To conserve cash, Gary acted as his own patent counsel, relied on his wife for help with marketing and administration, and drew no salary. He traveled

Wam!Net: Riding the Trend Toward Outsourcing

DENICE Y. GIBSON

Senior Vice President of Marketing, Development, Operations,
and Customer Support, Wam!Net, Minneapolis, Minnesota

During the previous decade, the Internet has transformed the way businesses define themselves, with its superior ability to maintain one-to-one customer relationships. In light of this, companies must step back and re-examine their business strategies. Whoever owns the customer is king. We at Wam!Net have understood for years that being a customer-centric organization is critical to future success and survival. The Internet has provided the means to deliver on that promise.

As companies rethink their business strategies, they need to focus on serving their customers. Flexibility, speed, and being seen as a global organization are key to serving customers. In order to achieve these traits, businesses will need to turn to outsourcing and partners to meet the demands of their customers. Outsourcing has altered the way enterprise (business-to-business) companies conduct their day-to-day practices.

In addressing the issue of outsourcing, the fundamental question a business must answer is: What is my core competency? Outsourcing services can improve the financials of an organization, lower its risks, and allow its capital to be invested in its core competency while maintaining customer relationships.

One of the earliest examples of a successful company utilizing the outsourcing strategy was Dell, who specialized in customer services and let other companies do the design, building, and shipping of its products. Another example is Amazon.com, which revolutionized the retail industry. By servicing customers directly, both Amazon.com and Dell maintain all of the customers' information. This ability to capture and manage the data is critical to maintain the customer relationship in the future.

In order to fulfill the needs of companies who have decided to outsource noncore services, the service sector of the market is growing rapidly. A services company specializes in one aspect of a business—whether it is infrastructure, payroll, accounts receivable, or a call center. These service organizations can develop greater knowledge about their area of expertise. Service companies can invest more in software, training, and expertise and offer that service to a broad group of companies.

Outsourcing companies effectively leverage an organization by providing in-depth knowledge in one area. Service companies develop their own core competency. By becoming the best in their class, service companies provide an excellent opportunity for knowledge workers to continue to expand their specialty, as people want to work for the best company in their field. This attraction helps service companies continue to innovate, providing better services.

Companies like Wam!Net are an outsourcing option for all industries. We provide a digital IP infrastructure for transport and storage of digital data. This is our core competency. We are a worldwide e-business services provider. We excel at managing this infrastructure by removing the burden and costs from our partners. When a company relies on another party to deliver key functionality to them, strategic partnerships are formed.

Wam!Net must provide excellent customer management to our partners. Our services are transparent to the end users. We must proactively manage these relationships. One of the reasons for the success of Wam!Net is that our services are horizontal, allowing all industries to consume the outsourced services. We must maintain our focus on e-services to our customers so that they, in return, can move aggressively toward their own core competencies and maintain their competitive advantage in the e-business space.

E-business will become the dominant way we will do business. The Internet has enabled customers to connect to a company's Web site in order to track and receive information about an order—e-service. How do brick and mortar companies handle this challenge? Using e-service does not mean that face-to-face or voice-to-voice contact with the customer goes away; rather, e-businesses are finding the opposite is true. Customers demand a highly efficient call center to support the self-service channel that successful e-businesses provide.

Customers today do not care about the underlying organizational structure or what technologies a firm uses to run its business. Customers care about how well a business services their needs. Becoming an e-business company is something organizations no longer have the option to ignore. Rather, a company must decide what it would like to do first in achieving its goals in an on-line environment.

---

extensively on consulting jobs to make money. While looking for investors, Gary and his wife were selling the product one at a time through networking and conventions. Recently, Gary made a cold call on a major crop insurer in Council Bluffs, Iowa: American Agrisurance. A senior researcher at the company found Gary's product very interesting and is considering making investments to finance further development of the software.

Absent independent wealth or wealthy family and friends, many high-tech entrepreneurs seek funding from venture capitalists (VCs). One area where the United States excels is the ability to fund innovative companies at an early stage. U.S. venture capital spending doubled to more than $40 billion in 1999.[45] And, according to a study by the Harvard Business School, a dollar of venture capital produces three to five times more patents than a dollar of research and development spending.

Venture Capital Funding[46]

Even though venture capitalists always have played an important role in the American economy, their importance increased considerably in the late 1990s. The growth of the economy has become more reliant on the innovative and entrepreneurial spirit of small,

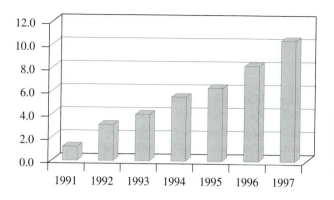

FIGURE 2-6 Money Inflow Capital Raised by U.S. Venture Funds (in $ billions)

Source: National Venture Capital Association 1997 Annual Report.

often high-tech, companies in need of external financing. The increase in capital raised by U.S. venture funds between 1991 and 1997 is shown in Figure 2-6. In fact, jobs in venture-backed companies increased by an annual 40.7% between 1992 and 1996, while jobs in the *Fortune* 500 companies declined 2.5% per year during the same time.[47]

The average venture capitalist in the late 1990s had about 80% of his or her portfolio invested in technology.[48] Venture capitalists are so keen on investing in the high-tech sector because companies in that industry offer rapid growth potential and high anticipated returns on investment.[49] However, the high returns don't come without increased risk. It is quite possible that venture capitalists will lose money on 50% of their investments and break even on 25 percent. But if the remaining 25% increase in value by 10 to 15 times, the overall portfolio will turn out successful. Hence, it is necessary for venture capitalists to invest in a variety of companies in order to spread risk.[50]

Companies usually need venture capital in early stages in the life cycle, when they begin to commercialize their innovations. At this stage, internally generated cash flows aren't enough to sustain growth, and banks fear the risk of issuing new loans because high-tech companies usually don't own much traditional collateral. Therefore, most emerging high-tech companies have to approach a venture capitalist.

So what is venture capital and what do venture capitalists do? Simply put, venture capital is money invested in rapidly growing emerging and start-up companies.[51] The capital is provided by venture capitalists, who usually spend their days meeting with industry leaders, meeting with other venture capitalists, listening to proposals from excited entrepreneurs, and pondering the future of technology.[52]

There are two types of venture capitalists: formal and informal. Formal venture capitalists are professional investors, such as venture capital firms and some banks. These investors often look for companies that have moved beyond the infant stage, where risks are the highest. Informal venture capitalists are usually referred to as "angels." They are probably called angels not only because of their salvaging qualities but also because they are so hard to find.[53]

Angels are usually part of an informal network of investors, who hear about promising start-ups through acquaintances or friends of friends. However, angels have recently started to act more like professional institutions. They have pooled resources, built explicit networks, and when investing they demand nothing less than a formal venture capitalist; that is, they want a business plan, clear and precise goals, a large equity stake, and very often a seat on the board.[54]

When venture capitalists screen high-tech companies for investment opportunities, they look for four key factors: management, marketing, technology/product, and anticipated return on investment.[55] Venture capitalists don't merely invest in a superior software code or specific technological innovation. Rather, they invest in the talented people who can transform that technology into a profitable product.[56] Managers who fit this description are often referred to as "entrepreneurs in residence."

Malik Khan is a good example of an entrepreneur in residence. While working for Motorola's Network Systems Division as the vice president and general manager, Khan already knew he wanted to start his own business. He had a vague idea about the business being Internet related, but he didn't know exactly how. Khan decided to meet with Joseph McCullen, a general manager at OneLiberty Boston, who was impressed with Khan's résumé and his passionate craving to start his own business. McCullen offered Khan $250,000 per year to come up with an idea. After spending a month visiting Internet trade shows and consulting with market research firms, Khan came up with the idea to develop a server that could distribute Web applications quickly over the Internet. His company, K2 Net, was successful and attracted a total of $5.3 million in venture capital.[57]

After the venture capitalist has found a target company, he or she has to put a value on the proposed deal. Although the venture capitalist can get a rough estimate of the value just by looking at the forecasted financial statements, there are more refined ways. To get a range of estimates of the value of a small business, venture capitalists use several models—for example, the comparable company approach, the discounted earnings method, and the discounted cash flow model.[58] To a novice investor, the price of emerging high-tech companies seems low when compared to companies in more mature industries. However, the value of a firm or investment will vary inversely with its risk, and because investing in emerging high-tech companies can be very risky, prices are low. The price of the firm will also depend on the entrepreneur's own investment, the company's upside potential, whether additional funds will be needed in the future, and how easy it will be for the investor to exit the relationship. The Technology Expert's View from the Trenches is written by a venture capitalist in San Francisco, Charles Walker.

Other Resources

Small high-tech start-ups are in general need of assistance in getting their budding business off the ground. Technology incubators can be a nice resource for many small start-ups. A special kind of formal venture capitalist is the incubator. An incubator is a facility that offers start-up companies a variety of support services, including concrete help from experienced managers and access to office space shared by several other companies. The incubator concept has several benefits. For example, sharing office space allows entrepreneurs to swap ideas, and inexperienced entrepreneurs will have access to qualified consultants.[59] The U.S. federal government has a number of resources available to small businesses, as shown in the Appendix to this chapter. Another option for small high-tech start-ups facing resource constraints is to partner with other firms who offer complementary skills and resources. Strategic alliances and partnerships fall under the domain of relationship marketing, the topic of the next chapter.

Considerations in the Venture Capital Process

CHARLIE WALKER
Managing Partner, Access Technology Partners, L.P.
(in affiliation with Chase/H&Q Securities
and Chase Capital Partners), San Francisco, California

The challenge for an entrepreneur is to always understand his or her audience. Be it customers, employees, partners, or financing sources, each has its own unique set of needs. Nowhere does this apply more than in the area of raising money from venture capitalists.

During the late 1990s, the venture capital industry grew and matured into a permanent fixture in the U.S. capital markets. Long the province of professional money managers, venture capital has gone retail, and with that, an entirely new set of financing dynamics has arisen. Woe to those entrepreneurs who come to this game without understanding the changing rules.

The new dynamics contain elements of the traditional venture capital business, including such requirements as presenting a quality management team and scalability of the proposed business. Newly arising considerations relate to the time constraints being placed on venture capitalists, the readiness of the public markets to provide funding earlier in a business's life cycle, and the ever-shifting requirements of operating a public company—assuming the entrepreneur gets there.

But first, the traditional components: The single most important consideration for obtaining venture capital is the *qual-ity of the management team.* Rare is the deal that obtains professional financing (as opposed to the "aunts and uncles network" or "angel financing") without a management team that has a proven track record of starting and scaling a business or division. Not that prior success is necessary; often a failure helps season a team. Given the time constraints of the industry, however, venture capitalists much prefer situations that are well managed, for the simple reason that they have all learned how draining (emotionally and financially) poorly managed companies can be. Therefore, having "walked the talk" is a powerfully important ingredient in attracting risk capital. Throw in a healthy degree of self-promotion, to insure ongoing access to capital and customers, and one begins to have the makings of an attractive venture deal.

Scalability of the business plan is also important in generating financial returns. Because most venture capitalists are measured on *how fast* they make money, in addition to *how much* they make (summarized mathematically by a deal's "IRR," or Internal Rate of Return, projections), it helps to propose a business that can grow very rapidly. "Making money while you sleep" is an oft-quoted phrase in the venture capital world. Notably, this is not a reference to 24-hour trading in the public markets, but rather to business models that are capable of generating revenues 'round the clock. Businesses that do not require large numbers of people are ideal examples of this proposition.

Newly emerging considerations include the importance of a *compelling-yet-simple financing pitch,* or "elevator pitch," to rapidly explain your proposal. (The reference to an elevator is intended to limit one's proposition to that amount of time it takes to ride an elevator!) With the ascendancy of venture capital and entrepreneurial activity in America, the industry is awash with business proposals. Time management is critically important, forcing venture capitalists to have the attention span of a gnat! Be quick and to the point, provide compelling reasons (financially *and* intellectually) to focus your audience, and cover all the bases. What are those bases? Whatever is relevant to your underlying business. On this point, *you* get to make the rules.

Do not characterize the raising of money as a waste of your time. Venture capitalists have the view that the business of raising money is critically important (after all, it *is* their line of work!), and these people will add more value to the underlying enterprise than most anything else you can do during the entire life cycle of the business. And, in a sense, they are correct. Done properly, a financing can elevate the valuation of a business more rapidly in the span of three months than the underlying business can in three years. Therefore, treat the process with the respect it deserves.

Be an expert in the venture capitalist's business. Concepts don't sell a financing—although they help; expertise of management does. Know your industry, thoroughly, and be prepared to explain *exactly* how you will deal with all the expected challenges, particularly in the capital markets. Provide confidence to the financier.

And, because new financing options are always emerging, become an expert in financing alternatives that will be available to you as you grow the business, beyond simply assuming the business can "go public." Matters of lease financing, secondary offerings, subordinated debt, and strategic investors can all provide the financial leverage that will further fuel returns for the early investors.

Finally, quite apart from the venture capital industry, understand that ultimately, the venture capitalist will cash out, and you will end up wanting and/or needing to still operate a business. What the entrepreneur needs to understand is that (s)he needs to propose a business that will endure far beyond the venture capital life cycle. Oddly enough, the more irrelevant venture capitalist money seems in the context of the business' overall life cycle, the more attractive the proposition becomes to a venture capitalist. In the final analysis, everyone wants to be associated, however briefly, with enduring companies!

Summary

This chapter, as the first of three chapters on considerations internal to the firm that affect high-tech marketing success, has addressed three broad topics. First, it has addressed the strategic planning process in high-tech firms. Second, it has addressed the need for large firms to remain nimble and innovative and to not allow their core competencies to become core rigidities. Strategies and techniques for maintaining innovativeness include

- Being willing to engage in creative destruction

- Having corporate imagination (using technology life cycles to jump to next-generation technology, escaping the tyranny of served markets, using new sources of ideas, and leading customers before they themselves know where they want to go)
- Engaging in expeditionary marketing by making many quick incursions into the market in order to apply learning to successive versions of the product
- Maintaining a culture of innovation (allowing product champions to flourish, giving time and incentives to innovate, using skunk works if necessary)

Third, the chapter addressed the issue of resources needed by small firms in order to establish a resource base. Venture capital funds, incubators, and government resources were discussed. In the continued exploration of the internal factors that affect marketing success, the next chapter looks at the role of establishing partnerships and alliances with key stakeholders.

Discussion Questions

1. Provide an overview of the strategic marketing planning process in high-tech firms. How does it differ from the traditional strategic planning process?
2. What are core competencies? Give an example of a firm's core competencies. Explain how your example stacks up on each of the criteria for a core competency.
3. Why is it hard for large firms to be innovative?
4. How can core competencies become core rigidities? Give an example.
5. What is creative destruction?
6. What are the four elements of corporate imagination?
7. What are technology life cycles? How can companies use them to be innovative? Give an example.
8. What is expeditionary marketing? What are the implications in terms of bringing products to market?
9. How does a firm nurture a culture of innovation?
10. What are skunk works? Do they make sense to you? Why or why not?
11. What are product champions? What are their characteristics? What are the pros and cons of taking on such a role?
12. What are the issues faced by small high-tech start-ups?

Glossary

Core competency.   Underlying skills and capabilities that give rise to a firm's source of competitive advantage. Typically based in embedded knowledge, which is hard to imitate.

Core rigidity.   Well-rehearsed skills and competencies that are so entrenched that they prevent a firm from seeing new ways of doing things; might include cultural norms giving status to engineers over marketers, preferences for existing technology, and so forth.

Corporate imagination.   A characteristic of a firm that allows its culture to exhibit creativity and playfulness, such that it (1) is willing to over-turn existing price–performance assumptions, (2) does not slavishly serve current markets, (3) uses new sources of ideas for innovative products, and (4) is willing to lead customers where they want to go.

Creative destruction.   The notion that in order to remain viable, a firm must be willing to destroy the basis of its current success. If a firm doesn't constantly innovate and reinvent itself, it will find its market share eroded by new competitors who are willing to do so.

Expeditionary marketing.   A strategy for new-product success based on trying many mini-introductions in quick succession and, by learning from each foray into the marketplace, incorporating that learning into each successive time at bat, such that over time, the firm has accumulated loyal customers and higher market share than firms that have fewer times at bat.

Liability of bigness.   Arises from the sense of inertia and unwieldiness of bureaucratic procedures that can be found in large organizations; can result in a lack of innovativeness and the inability to develop really new breakthrough products.

Moore's Law.   Every 18 months or so, improvements in technology double product performance at no increase in price. Stated a different way, every 18 months or so, improvements in technology cut price in half for the same level of performance.

Product champion.   A person who is so committed to a particular idea that he or she is willing to work tirelessly advocating the idea, to work outside normal channels to pursue it, and to bet future successes on the idea. Often, champions are iconoclasts, mavericks, risk takers.

Skunk works.   New venture teams that are isolated or removed from normal corporate operations in order to foster an innovative culture that allows the team to think out of the box.

Technology life cycles.   A graph depicting investments made in a particular technology relative to improvements in performance. Typically an S-shaped curve. Radical innovations "jump" technology life cycles and begin a new S-shaped curve.

Endnotes

1. Cooper, Lee (2000), "Strategic Marketing Planning for Radically New Products," *Journal of Marketing,* 64 (January), pp. 1–16; Eisenhardt, Kathleen and Shona Brown (1999), "Patching: Restitching Business Portfolios," *Harvard Business Review,* May–June, pp. 72–82.

2. Prahalad, C. K. and Gary Hamel (1990), "The Core Competence of the Corporation," *Harvard Business Review,* May–June, pp. 79–91.

3. Gomes, Lee (1997), "H-P to Unveil Digital Camera and Peripherals," *Wall Street Journal,* February 25, p. B7.

4. Prahalad, C. K. and Gary Hamel (1990), "The Core Competence of the Corporation," *Harvard Business Review* (May–June), pp. 79–91.

5. Leonard-Barton, Dorothy (1992), "Core Capabilities and Core Rigidities: A Paradox in Managing New Product Development," *Strategic Management Journal,* 13, pp. 111–125.

6. McWilliams, Gary (1999), "Schlumberger Digs Deeper," *Business Week,* July 27, pp. 48–49.

7. Chandy, Rajesh and Gerard Tellis (1999), "The Incumbent's Curse? Incumbency, Size, and Radical Product Innovation," working paper, University of Houston.

8. Schumpeter, Joseph (1942), *Capitalism, Socialism and Democracy,* New York: Harper & Row.

9. Shanklin, William and John Ryans (1987), *Essentials of Marketing High Technology,* Lexington, MA: DC Heath.

10. Moeller, Michael (1999), "E-Commerce May Be One Race Microsoft Can't Win," *Business Week,* March 22. Available at www. businessweek. com.

11. Chandy, Rajesh K. and Gerard J. Tellis (1998), "Organizing for Radical Product Innovation: The Overlooked Role of Willingness to Cannibalize," *Journal of Marketing Research,* 35 (November), pp. 474–487.

12. Hamel, Gary and C. K. Prahalad (1991), "Corporate Imagination and Expeditionary Marketing," *Harvard Business Review,* July–August, pp. 81–92.

13. Shanklin, William and John Ryans (1987), *Essentials of Marketing High Technology,* Lexington, MA: DC Heath.

14. Cooper, Arnold and Dan Schendel (1976), "Strategic Responses to Technological Threats," *Business Horizons,* February, pp. 61–69.

15. Shanklin, William and John Ryans (1987), *Essentials of Marketing High Technology,* Lexington, MA: DC Heath.

16. Shanklin, William and John Ryans (1987), *Essentials of Marketing High Technology,* chapter 7, Lexington, MA: DC Heath.

17. Shanklin, William and John Ryans (1987), *Essentials of Marketing High Technology,* chapter 7, Lexington, MA: DC Heath.

18. Leonard-Barton, Dorothy, Edith Wilson, and John Doyle (1995), "Commercializing Technology: Understanding User Needs," in *Business Marketing Strategy,* V. K. Rangan et al. (eds.), Chicago: Irwin, pp. 281–305.

19. Byrnes, Nanette and Paul Judge (1999), "Internet Anxiety," *Business Week,* June 28, pp. 79–88.

20. Hamel, Gary and C. K. Prahalad (1991), "Corporate Imagination and Expeditionary Marketing," *Harvard Business Review,* July–August, pp. 81–92.

21. MacDonald, Elizabeth and Joann Lublin (1998), "In the Debris of a Failed Merger: Trade Secrets," *Wall Street Journal,* March 10, p. B1.

22. See also the notion of waste in Gross, Neil and Peter Coy with Otis Port (1995), "The Technology Paradox," *Business Week,* March 6, pp. 76–84.

23. Quinn, James (1985), "Managing Innovation: Controlled Chaos," *Harvard Business Review,* 63 (May–June), pp. 73–85.

24. Burgelman, Robert (1983), "Corporate Entrepreneurship and Strategic Management: Insights from a Process Study," *Management Science,* 29 (December), pp. 1349–1364.

25. Hutt, Michael, Peter Reingen, and John Ronchetto, Jr. (1988), "Tracing Emergent Processes in Marketing Strategy Formulation," *Journal of Marketing,* 52 (January), pp. 4–19.

26. Pinchot, Gifford (2000), *Intrapreneuring: Why You Don't Have to Leave the Corporation to Become an Entrepreneur,* San Francisco, CA: Berrett-Koehler Publishing.

27. Maidique, Modesto (1980), "Entrepreneurs, Champions, and Technological Innovations," *Sloan Management Review,* 21 (Spring), pp. 59–70; see also Howell, Jane (1990), "Champions of Technological Innovation," *Administrative Science Quarterly,* 35 (June), pp. 317–341.

28. Chandy, Rajesh K. and Gerard J. Tellis (1998), "Organizing for Radical Product Innovation: The Overlooked Role of Willingness to Cannibalize," *Journal of Marketing Research,* 35 (November), pp. 474–487.

29. Chandy, Rajesh K. and Gerard J. Tellis (1998), "Organizing for Radical Product Innovation: The Overlooked Role of Willingness to Can-

nibalize," *Journal of Marketing Research,* 35 (November), pp. 474–487.

30. Tabrizi, Behnam and Rick Walleigh (1997), "Defining Next-Generation Products: An Inside Look," *Harvard Business Review,* November–December, pp. 116–124.

31. Hamel, Gary and C. K. Prahalad (1991), "Corporate Imagination and Expeditionary Marketing," *Harvard Business Review,* July–August, pp. 81–92.

32. Hamel, Gary and C. K. Prahalad (1991), "Corporate Imagination and Expeditionary Marketing," *Harvard Business Review,* July–August, pp. 81–92.

33. Hamel, Gary (1997), "Killer Strategies That Make Shareholders Rich," *Fortune,* June 23, pp. 70–84.

34. Byrnes, Nanette and Paul Judge (1999), "Internet Anxiety," *Business Week,* June 28, p. 84.

35. Anders, George (1999), "Buying Frenzy," *Wall Street Journal,* July 12, pp. R6, R10.

36. Byrnes, Nanette and Paul Judge (1999), "Internet Anxiety," *Business Week,* June 28, p. 84.

37. Hamel, Gary and Jeff Sampler (1998), "The e-Corporation," *Fortune,* December 7, pp. 80–92.

38. Hamel, Gary and Jeff Sampler (1998), "The e-Corporation," *Fortune,* December 7, pp. 80–92.

39. Hof, Robert (1998), "The Click Here Economy," *Business Week,* June 22, pp. 122–128.

40. Hamel, Gary and Jeff Sampler (1998), "The e-Corporation," *Fortune,* December 7, pp. 80–92.

41. Sager, Ira (1999), "Go Ahead, Farm Out Those Jobs," *Business Week e.biz,* March 22, p. EB35.

42. Byrnes, Nanette and Paul Judge (1999), "Internet Anxiety," *Business Week,* June 28, p. 84.

43. Sager, Ira (1999), "Go Ahead, Farm Out Those Jobs," *Business Week e.biz,* March 22, p. EB35.

44. "Selling a 'Killer App' Is a Far Tougher Job Than Dreaming It Up," (1998), *Wall Street Journal,* April 13, p. B1.

45. Mandel, Michael (2000), "The New Economy," *Business Week,* January 31, pp. 73–91.

46. This section was contributed by Thomas Lundell, MBA, University of Montana.

47. Ivey, Mike (1999), "Exactly What Is Venture Capital?" *The Capital Times,* June 26, p. 1A.

48. Evanson, David R. (1999), "Capital Questions," *Entrepreneur Magazine,* October. Retrieved October 25 from the World Wide Web: www.entrepreneurmag.com/resource/raising-money.hts.

49. Ivey, Mike (1999), "Exactly What Is Venture Capital?" *The Capital Times,* June 26, p. 1A.
50. Ivey, Mike (1999), "Exactly What Is Venture Capital?" *The Capital Times,* June 26, p. 1A.
51. Ivey, Mike (1999), "Exactly What Is Venture Capital?" *The Capital Times,* June 26, p. 1A.
52. Warner, Melanie (1998), "The New Way to Start Up in Silicon Valley," *Fortune,* March 2, pp. 168–174.
53. Neu, Clyde W. (ed.) (1993), *Proceedings of a Seminar on Venture Capital Financing,* University of Montana: Missoula, MT, p. 93.
54. Gruner, Stephanie (1998), "The Trouble with Angels," *Inc.,* February 1.
55. Neu, Clyde W. (ed.) (1993), *Proceedings of a Seminar on Venture Capital Financing,* University of Montana: Missoula, MT, p. 139.
56. Warner, Melanie (1998), "The New Way to Start Up in Silicon Valley," *Fortune,* March 2, pp. 168–174.
57. Useem, Jerry (1997), "Help Wanted: Smart CEOs. No Ideas Necessary," *Inc.,* March 1.
58. Neu, Clyde W. (ed.) (1993), *Proceedings of a Seminar on Venture Capital Financing,* University of Montana: Missoula, MT, p. 153.
59. Bransten, Lisa (1999), "Seeking More High-Tech Home Runs," *Wall Street Journal Interactive,* October 15. Available at http:interactive.wsj.com.

Recommended Readings

Expeditionary Marketing

Lynn, G., J. Morone, and A. Paulson (1996), "Marketing and Discontinuous Innovation: The Probe and Learn Process," *California Management Review,* 38 (3), pp. 8–37.

Management of Innovation

Academy of Management Review (1996), Vol. 21 (4) was a special issue on the management of innovation and included 12 articles on the topic.

Brown, Shona and Kathleen Eisenhardt (1998), *Competing on the Edge: Strategy as Structured Chaos,* Boston: Harvard Business School Press.

Eisenhardt, Kathleen and Shona Brown (1999), "Patching: Restitching Business Portfolios in Dynamic Markets," *Harvard Business Review,* 77 (May), pp. 72–82.

Grove, Andrew (1996), *Only the Paranoid Survive,* New York: Currency/Doubleday.

Hamel, Gary (2000), *Leading the Revolution,* Boston: Harvard Business School Press.

von Hippel, Eric (1988), *The Sources of Innovation,* New York: Oxford University Press.

Kao, John (1997), *Jamming: The Art and Discipline of Business Creativity,* Scranton, PA: Harper Business.

Leonard, Dorothy and Walter Swap (1999), *When Sparks Fly,* Boston: Harvard Business School Press.

Levy, Nino (1998), *Managing High Technology and Innovation,* Upper Saddle River, NJ: Prentice Hall.

Markides, Constantinos (1999), *All the Right Moves: A Guide to Crafting Breakthrough Strategy,* Cambridge, MA: Harvard Business School Press.

Moss, Rosabeth Kanter (ed.) (1997), *Innovation: Breakthrough Thinking at 3M, DuPont, GE, Pfizer, and Rubbermaid,* Scranton, PA: Harper Business.

Sharma, Anurag (1999), "Central Dilemmas of Managing Innovation in Large Firms," *California Management Review,* 41 (Spring), pp. 147–157.

Innovativeness in Strategy Formulation

Christensen, Clayton M. (1997), "Making Strategy: Learning by Doing," *Harvard Business Review,* November–December, pp. 141–156.

Hamel, Gary (1997), "Turning Your Business Upside Down," *Fortune,* June 23, pp. 87–88.

Hammer, Michael and Steven A. Stanton (1997), "Smart Managing: The Power of Reflection," *Fortune,* November 24, pp. 291–296.

Markides, Constantinos (1999), *All the Right Moves: A Guide to Crafting Breakthrough Strategy,* Cambridge, MA: Harvard Business School Press.

Normann, Richard and Rafael Ramirez (1993), "From Value Chain to Value Constellation: Designing Interactive Strategy," *Harvard Business Review,* July–August, pp. 65–77.

Speed in Cycle Time

Datar, Srikant, et al. (1997), "Advantages of Time-Based New Product Development in a Fast-Cycle Industry," *Journal of Marketing Research,* 34 (February), pp. 36–49.

Eisenhardt, Kathleen (1989), "Making Fast Strategic Decisions in High-Velocity Environments," *Academy of Management Journal, 32* (3), pp. 543–576.

Eisenhardt, Kathleen M. and Shona L. Brown (1998), "Time Pacing: Competing in Markets That Won't Stand Still," *Harvard Business Review,* March–April, pp. 59–69.

Gates, Bill (1999), *Business @ the Speed of Thought,* New York: Warner Books.

Griffin, Abbie (1997), "The Effect of Project and Process Characteristics on Product Development Cycle Time," *Journal of Marketing Research,* 34 (February), pp. 24–35.

Ittner, Christopher D. and David F. Larcker (1997), "Product Development Cycle Time and Organizational Performance," *Journal of Marketing Research,* 34 (February), pp. 13–23.

Karlsson, C. and Par Ahlstrom (1999), "Technological Level and Product Development Cycle Time," *Journal of Product Innovation Management,* 16 (July), pp. 352–362.

Lambert, Denis and Stanley Slater (1999), "First, Fast, and On Time: The Path to Success. Or Is It?" *Journal of Product Innovation Management,* 16 (September), pp. 427–438.

Yoffie, David and Michael Cusumano (1998), "Judo Strategy: The Competitive Dynamics of Internet Time," *Harvard Business Review,* January–February, pp. 70–81.

APPENDIX
Government Assistance for Small Business Start-Ups

MARK PETERS
Director, Montana Export Assistance Center,
Department of Commerce, Missoula, Montana

Small businesses looking to develop new ventures and markets have many options for assistance, both public and private. The U.S. government offers programs for the development of new technologies and for market entry support for exporting. However, there are limitations to the quality and quantity of support that can be expected from government institutions.

At a basic level, start-ups may want to get in touch with the Senior Corp of Retired Executives (SCORE), a volunteer group available to counsel budding entrepreneurs (www.score.org). The volunteers are identified by the Small Business Administration (SBA), and there are local SCORE chapters throughout the country. The nature of the expertise available may be geographic-specific, so high-tech start-ups may find this service more valuable if they are based in areas with a plethora of high-tech businesses. The SBA also offers loan guarantee programs that may be useful for a new business (www.sba.gov).

For a start-up or a firm looking into new technologies, the National Lab system and NASA have programs to transition technologies from pure science into the marketplace. NASA has a partnership with many universities and state economic development agencies to commercialize technology developed in the space program. Many local Small Business Development Centers (SBDCs) can assist in locating such programs. Alternatively, an entrepreneur can call a state university (say, Montana State University's Tech-Link partnership with NASA at techlink.msu. montana.edu) or a national lab (say Los Alamos at www.lanl.gov) to see what technology transfer programs are available through specific labs.

For those firms that are looking to international markets, the U.S. Department of Commerce has multiple tools for identifying markets and finding partners. First, the U.S. government has commercial sections in most U.S. embassies around the world. These offices, along with a network of export assistance centers and offices throughout the United States, are available to provide counseling, market intelligence, and contacts. Indeed, the staff in these offices will help a firm develop a customized strategy to export to a particular country by identifying possible partners and trade events. Moreover, the Commerce Department conducts an annual analysis for U.S. products in export markets. These reports are made available via the Internet. Being listed on the on-line trade show maintained by the Department of Commerce (www.e-expousa.doc.gov) is also possible. In addition to market intelligence,

the commercial sections employ locals who are experts in targeted industries. These trade experts have the ability to identify potential partners and introduce U.S. firms. Using the introduction by the embassy can expedite the search process and add a prestige factor that can be critical in gaining access to some countries. Each of these services can be found at the U.S. Department of Commerce's Commercial Service's Web site: www.usatrade.gov.

When a firm sells products overseas, a critical issue for high-tech products is knowing what standards and certification are necessary for different countries. The National Institutes of Standards and Technology (www.NIST.gov) compiles and maintains such information for marketers and others.

Although many government programs can provide excellent support and access, an entrepreneur must realize that, many times, the staff at government agencies have not been in the private sector. This means that they may have a tendency to work on their own timeline rather than the businessperson's and may tend to think that more information is better. So, a businessperson should actively manage and clarify the requirements when seeking government assistance.

CHAPTER 3

Relationship Marketing: Partnerships and Alliances

Relationship marketing refers to the formation of long-term relationships with customers and other business partners, which yield mutually satisfying win–win results. In high-tech fields, several forces exist that necessitate the use of partnerships and alliances. Because the time-to-market cycle is short and development costs and risks are high, firms can find it faster and more cost efficient to develop products jointly than alone. For example, GM and Toyota have teamed up in the development of alternative fuel vehicles. They believe that the race to produce a viable alternative-technology auto will be a battle "not of individual auto makers, but of corporate—and often transcontinental—alliances."[1]

Moreover, the need to bring a complete, end-to-end solution to the market may mean that partners are needed to develop different aspects of the product. For example, in the development of enterprise resource planning (ERP) software—which companies use to integrate and improve the various business functions such as manufacturing, sales, finance, human resources, supply chain management, and customer relationship management—the major players have found that they need to partner in order to offer customers a complete solution. A leading provider of this software, SAP AG (Germany) works with a host of other companies to round out its offering in order to provide customers an integrated set of features.

This chapter explores important issues in the formation and management of such relationships, which are vital to success in high-tech markets.

PARTNERSHIPS AND ALLIANCES

Types of Partnerships

The synergies of partnering can lead to both parties becoming more competitive through a win–win situation, possibly even strengthening both companies against outsiders. For example, scientists and research executives at most of the large pharmaceutical companies believe that open access to a map of genetic breakthroughs will be central in the way drugs are developed and tested in the future. They have formed a nonprofit venture in which the usually highly competitive companies are working together to build the biological blueprint for all human life. This new venture will also collaborate with competing biotech companies, which currently lead the race in genetic mapping. The idea is to store valuable data in a public database to which drug companies, academic researchers, and biotech firms will all have free and equal access. Executives at the major drug companies realize that progress would be much slower if every company had to create its own map—especially given the lead the biotech companies hold.[2] The Technology Tidbit explores this mapping technology a bit further.

A wide variety of different types of partnerships can be formed at all levels of the supply chain, as shown in Figure 3-1.[3]

Vertical Partnerships Firms may form **vertical partnerships** with members at other levels in the supply chain (either suppliers, distribution channel members, or customers). Relationships with *suppliers* are often formed to gain efficiencies in accessing parts and materials. Collaborative relationships that are built around common procedures and intensive information sharing mean that the supplier's operations can be more closely fitted to the customer's needs. Moreover, early supplier involvement (ESI) is also useful in developing innovations in supplies that can help differentiate the customer's product in downstream markets. For example, a firm may choose to form partnerships with key suppliers whose skills and experiences complement its strengths to develop next-generation technology. Chip manufacturers and computer manufacturers are working together to develop next-generation computers. Because chips are a supply used in computers, this is an example of a supplier–OEM,* or vertical, relationship.

TECHNOLOGY TIDBIT

Mapping the Human Genome

Identifying the sequence of the human genome, the molecular "letters" that make up the genetic code embedded in our DNA, will allow scientists to know how each human gene works and how it can malfunction, design sensitive diagnostic tests, find the genetic roots of diseases, customize medicines to each individual's unique genetic makeup, and possibly even replace defective genes with normal ones. For example, based on genome segments already available, the British pharmaceutical company Glaxo Wellcome has identified groups of genes involved in Alzheimer's disease and is working on a drug to counteract them.

Scientists were taking two very different approaches to this mapping effort. The federal government broke DNA samples into segments about 150 million letters long (the overall genome has about 3.4 billion letters), which were then subdivided into segments of about 6,000 letters each, to be read by sequencing machines. In the final step, the pieces were to be reassembled in their original order on the chromosomes.

Beating the federal genome project's original deadline by a half decade, a private company, Celera Genomics of Rockville, Maryland, took a more radical approach, smashing the DNA into millions of pieces, then feeding each into high-speed robotic sequencers. Although all of the pieces were read by March 27, 2000, reassembly (about 3 to 6 weeks), figuring out where the letters fall in our 100,000 genes, and understanding what each gene does is a long-term project.

Source: Lemonick, Michael (2000), "Victory for Venter," *Time,* April 17, p. 71.

---

*OEM stands for original equipment manufacturer. OEMs are firms that buy components from suppliers, which are then used in the product the OEM makes. Often, the supplier's product, say the chip, is not identified by the supplier's brand, but by the OEM's brand. For example, with the exception of Intel, most computers are not identified by the brand of chip inside them, but by the computer brand name.

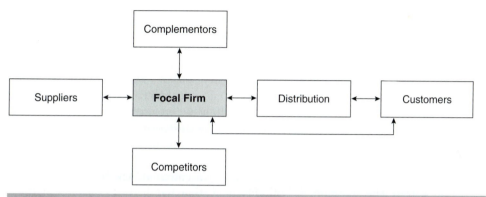

FIGURE 3-1 Possible Alliance Partners Along the Supply Chain

Relationships with *channel members* are used to gain efficiency and effectiveness in accessing downstream markets. For example, collaborative relationships with channel members provide both a source of competitive advantage that can be used in more effectively implementing marketing programs and a conduit of market information back to the manufacturer. Relationships with channel intermediaries are discussed in Chapter 8.

Another source of important relationships referenced in discussions of relationship marketing are relationships with *customers,* be they end users of the product or business customers who use the product in their businesses. Close, long-term relationships with customers are vital in many types of markets and particularly in high-tech markets. Because of the need to rely on customers for beta-test sites and ideas for innovations, firms that have close relationships with customers have a strong source of market-based information. Moreover, a focus on establishing long-term relationships with each customer is more likely to produce a long-term revenue stream from that customer, capturing the lifetime value of a customer's purchases in a particular product category. Customer relationships are discussed in detail in a later section of this chapter.

Horizontal Partnerships   In the high-technology arena, a common type of relationship is with a company at the same level of the value chain. **Horizontal alliances** are created with either competing firms or firms that provide jointly used, complementary products. These relationships provide customers a product that delivers a complete, integrated solution. Such alliances are also referred to as **complementary alliances,** and the members are referred to as *complementors*.[4] For example, in 1997, Hewlett-Packard and Kodak jointly decided to pursue the digital photography market. The alliance relied on Kodak's thermal dye transfer process to produce prints on HP's printers. Similarly, IBM has a series of relationships with software vendors in order to develop software for particular industry applications. This form of horizontal partnering (because both firms are producers of some good that, in turn, is resold to customers or channel intermediaries) is not necessarily between direct competitors.

Competing firms may choose to join forces to develop next-generation technology, to define standards for new technologies, to provide market access in an area that one firm lacks, or to be a stronger force against a larger competitor. **Competitive collaboration** between firms is also a form of horizontal alliance, because these firms typically compete at the same level of the supply chain. Another name given for this type of collaboration is *co-opetition*,[5] whereby firms compete in some arenas and collaborate in others. For example, in the mid-1980s, when the U.S. semiconductor industry was in danger of losing its competitive edge to Japanese competitors, a variety of firms in the industry decided to join forces to develop a next-generation semiconductor.[6] In 1987, SEMATECH (the Semiconductor Manufacturing Technology Consortium) was founded, as described in Box 3-1.

Indeed, to stimulate more collaboration between competing firms in the hopes of generating innovation and enhancing the competitiveness of U.S. businesses, traditional antitrust laws have been eased in the past few decades to allow more forms of collaboration. For example, the **National Cooperative Research Act** (1984) promotes research and development, encourages innovation, and stimulates trade. The act applies to R&D activities up to and including the testing of prototypes. This act was expanded in 1993 with the **National Cooperative Production Amendment,** which allowed joint production as well. The amendment excludes marketing and distribution agreements, except for the products manufactured by the venture, and also excludes the use of existing facilities by the joint venture.

The nexus of relationships formed may be quite complex, with the same players serving as suppliers in some arenas, complementors in others, and competitors in still others. For example, in the enterprise resource planning software market, key players include Oracle and SAP. Oracle builds databases, which are the core of all ERP systems. SAP is a customer of Oracle, cooperating to bundle Oracle databases into its applications, and it simultaneously competes with Oracle in the ERP market. In a similar vein, Oracle competes aggressively with Microsoft in the database market; Microsoft offers its SQL Server with 75% of Oracles's functionality at 25% of the price.[7] But Oracle must cooperate with Microsoft to ensure that its software works well with Microsoft's NT operating system. AMR's President Tony Friscia states:

> One side of Oracle considers Microsoft the enemy, and the other side considers SAP the enemy. The side that considers Microsoft the enemy needs a relationship with SAP, and the side that considers SAP the enemy needs a relationship with Microsoft.[8]

Reasons for Partnering

In general, partnerships are formed to provide one firm access to resources and skills that, if it had to develop in isolation, would be costly in terms of either money or time. So, by partnering, firms are able to gain access to such resources and skills in a timely, more cost-efficient manner. Cisco has methodically built its company by strategically investing in other companies whose technology rounds out its product line. For example, Cisco recognized that it needed fiber optic expertise and initially partnered with (and then bought) Cerent, a company whose products make it cheaper to move voice and data over fiber optic lines.

Another important reason for collaborating with competing firms is to *define standards for new technologies.* The GM–Toyota partnership—to share research into battery-powered electric, fuel-cell-powered electric, and hybrid vehicles—was formed partly in the hopes that through sheer combined size, they would be able to set technical standards regarding what fuel the industry will use for fuel cells. The special case of collaborating to set standards, because of its vital importance in stimulating market growth and overcoming customer anxiety about making a bad choice, is discussed in detail in Box 3-2.

BOX 3-1

SEMATECH,
an Example of Competitive Collaboration
in Product Development

The U.S. semiconductor industry had traditionally conformed to the neoclassical ideal of free market competition. This competitive ethos made cooperation across organizational boundaries very difficult. Moreover, proprietary standards were a powerful competitive weapon in the semiconductor industry. Disputes over proprietary standards led to long, drawn-out battles in court. In industries with rapidly changing technologies, proprietary standards create an intense level of competition fueled by the law of increasing returns: The "firstest with the mostest" gets farther and farther ahead.

However, market analysts predicted that by 1993, the U.S. market share, once at 85 percent, would shrink to 20 percent. Given the superordinate threat posed by Japanese competitors, U.S. semiconductor firms decided to join forces. In 1987, the Semiconductor Manufacturing Technology Consortium (SEMATECH) of U.S. semiconductor manufacturers and the U.S. government was jointly founded by 14 firms that then accounted for 80% of the semiconductor manufacturing industry (including Digital Equipment, IBM, Intel, NCR, Texas Instruments, National Semiconductor, Advanced Micro Devices, and LSI Logic, to name a few). Its mission was to provide the U.S. semiconductor industry the capability of achieving a world-leadership manufacturing position by the mid-1990s. The U.S. industry had to do two things to remain competitive: Increase the number of usable chips that could be manufactured from each wafer of silicon, and make each chip capable of doing more. Through SEMATECH, firms could pool resources in the fight to recover market share from Japanese companies.

SEMATECH's main cited achievements have been in finding ways to pack features onto chips by reducing the width of the circuit lines etched on chips. Eleven of the original 14 member companies and the U.S. government agreed to extend their membership in SEMATECH for a second 5-year period and committed themselves to new and expanded goals. Their continued commitment to SEMATECH indicated that they believed SEMATECH had achieved something worth their investments. As Craig Barrett of Intel said, "I judge SEMATECH by results. The organization set out to recover market share from Japan; five years later, market share has been recovered. At Intel we call that a results-oriented, successful project." SEMATECH is novel in that it offers insight into how cooperation can arise and persist in a highly competitive industry.

Source: Browning, Larry D., Janice M. Beyer, and Judy C. Shetler (1995), "Building Cooperation in a Competitive Industry: SEMATECH and the Semiconductor Industry" (Special Research Forum: Intra- and Interorganizational Cooperation), *Academy of Management Journal,* 38 (February), pp. 113–139.

BOX 3-2

Collaborating to Set Industry Standards

WHY ARE STANDARDS IMPORTANT?

Industry-wide standards result in a common, underlying architecture for products offered by different firms in the market. As a result, *customers gain compatibility* across the various components of a product—say, across hardware and software—and across product choices in an industry—say, across different types of computers. Because the complementary products share a common interface, the customers' hardware and software interface seamlessly. For example, in the cellular telecommunications industry, compatibility allows base stations, switches, and handsets to work with each other across service areas.

Compatibility, achieved when many different companies produce their offerings based on a common set of design principles, increases the value a customer receives from owning a product. First, standards reduce customer fear, uncertainty, and doubt about which technology to purchase. This can be particularly helpful when the value of the product to the customer increases as more customers adopt products based on the same technology (demand-side increasing returns). As a result, the more customers that adopt products sharing a common, underlying technological standard, the greater the value each of them receives. Second, the availability of complementary products is largely determined by the installed base of the given product. For example, software developers are more willing to write applications programs around technology platforms that have wider penetration in the market. Third, standards ensure a greater

availability of complementary products. The greater the availability of complementary products, the greater the value a customer derives from the base product.

Each of these factors works in a self-reinforcing manner. A larger installed base leads to greater availability of complementary products, which increases the value of the product to the customer, which in turn increases demand for that product by others, which translates into a larger installed base.

Different technologies are often incompatible, and thus, the first company to have its technology widely adopted may well set the technology standard for all. Indeed, the originator of a new technology has a clear advantage: The first product on the market is the standard. However, when competitors come on the scene, they may have developed alternative technologies and, with the right advantages (say, in product, production, or marketing), may flood the market with their own products.[a]

So, the more successful a firm is at getting its technology accepted as a standard, the more successful it will become in the future. This self-reinforcing cycle exists even when the emerging technological standard is inferior to other designs.

One of the earliest examples of a market cleaving to an inferior technology is the QWERTY format for typewriter keyboards, which gets its name from the first six characters on the upper left side of the keyboard. Because the type bars in the typewriters of the 1860s had a tendency to jam when keys were struck in rapid succession, it was necessary to separate letters that frequently appeared next to each other in common words. In other words, the QWERTY design was deliberately created to slow down typing speed. By the 1890s, better engineering had alleviated the problem of clashing type bars, and a new keyboard format that enabled faster typing was developed. However, these superior keyboards did not do well in the market; typists were so comfortable with the QWERTY design that attempts to use a new design seemed cumbersome to them. As a result, QWERTY is still the standard, even today.

The logical conclusion from the self-reinforcing nature of standards is that a critical success factor in industries where demand-side increasing returns exist is *how quickly a firm can grow its installed base of customers using its design.* Some lawyers argue that dominant technology suppliers, such as Intel and Microsoft, have become *de facto* monopolies because their products are so widely used as the basis for the industry standard.[b] The combined standard is referred to as the "Wintel" (Windows–Intel) duopoly. These two products are critical to the success of many of their customers—companies such as IBM, Compaq, HP, and others. As a result, legal experts call such products "essential facilities"[c] as uneven access to such products may be a basis for unfair competition and, hence, antitrust suits.

WHAT STRATEGIES CAN A FIRM USE FOR SETTING AN INDUSTRY STANDARD?

Four main strategies a firm can use to set an industry standard are discussed here,[d] the first two of which specifically relate to partnerships.

1. Licensing and OEM agreements.   By licensing its technological design to others,

a firm can help to grow the market quickly using that design. A spin-off of this strategy is for a firm to sell subcomponents on an OEM basis to other companies that compete in the same market. For example, Matsushita licensed its VHS format to Hitachi, Sharp, Mitsubishi, and Philips NV, who produced their own VHS-format videocassette recorders and tapes. In addition, Matsushita also provided to GE, RCA, and Zenith, on an OEM basis, the components needed to assemble their companies' equipment. (Note that this OEM strategy is consistent with the core competencies model presented in Chapter 2, in which a company should strive to maximize its market share of the core product used by other companies in the industry.)

The licensing strategy ensures a wide initial distribution for the technology, which helps to build the installed base. In addition, this strategy co-opts competitors that might have had the capabilities to produce their own competing technology. It also limits the number of technologically incompatible product choices that customers face, reducing their confusion and doubt and hastening market acceptance. For example, Philips NV's decision to license the VHS format from Matsushita eliminated its push into a different VCR format (the V2000). Licensing also signals to suppliers of complementary products the possibility of a larger installed base, providing an incentive for them to pursue development.

The main drawbacks of a licensing strategy are that

- Licensees may attempt to alter the technology and avoid paying licensing fees or royalties.

- By increasing the number of suppliers in the market, the original developer loses a possible monopoly position, having to share revenues derived from the market with its licensees. Moreover, competition may result in lower prices in the market (lowering profits for the original developer as well).

2. Strategic alliances. By entering into a cooperative agreement with one or more actual or potential competitors, firms can jointly sponsor development of a particular technological standard. For example, during the development of the digital audio technology used in compact disc players, at least four companies were pursuing incompatible designs. Although Philips NV was closest to commercialization, it worried about the issue of compatibility. So it partnered with Sony to cooperate on the commercialization of the first compact disc system. Philips NV contributed a superior basic design and Sony provided the error correction system. This alliance threw momentum behind the Philips–Sony standard, and 18 months prior to product introduction, over 30 firms had signed agreements to license the Philips–Sony technology.

Again, strategic alliances help to ensure a wide initial distribution for the technology, they can co-opt competitors, and they help to build positive expectations for the market demand, inducing other companies to develop complementary products. Alliances can help reduce confusion in the marketplace and build momentum behind the jointly sponsored standard, persuading potential competitors to commit to the standard. A particularly compelling advantage of this strategy for standards development is the fact that alliances may be able to produce a superior technology by combining the best aspects of two companies' know-how, which can also increase the probability of the joint development becoming the industry standard.

Of course, the risk exists that a partner might appropriate the firm's know-how in an opportunistic fashion. This risk might be mitigated by crafting terms to structure and manage the alliance in such a way that provides a disincentive for doing so. For example, by structuring the alliance as a joint venture, in which each company has a stake, each party then has a credible commitment to avoid undermining the alliance. Alternatively, the alliance might be structured in such a way that, after the standard has been developed, each party might be free to go its own way with regard to future extensions of the technology.

3. Product diversification. Because customers are hesitant to adopt a new technology unless complementary products from which its value is derived are available, firms may choose to diversify into developing the complementary products. This is the situation faced when no installed base of customers for the new technology exists, which means that suppliers of complementary products have no incentive to develop. Given this chicken-and-egg situation, a firm just may have to produce the complementary products whose wide availability is crucial to the success of a new technology. For example, Matsushita had its in-house record label, MCA, develop an extended offering of digital compact cassette (DCC) recordable audiotapes in order to jump-start the adoption of its DCC technology. Similarly, Philips issued a wide selection of prerecorded DCC tapes under its in-house PolyGram Records label when it introduced its DCC digital audio recording equipment in 1992. In addition to providing the impetus in the market to start an increasing-returns process, this strategy allows the company to realize revenue from not only the sales of the base product but also the sales of the complementary products.

The downside risks to this strategy can be significant, however. If the company is starting the development of complementary products from scratch, it can entail a significant capital commitment, as well as possibly straying from its core competencies. If the technology fails to become the standard, the costs of failure are that much greater.

4. Aggressive product positioning. Positioning to maximize the installed base of customers relies on penetration pricing, product proliferation, and wide distribution. *Penetration pricing,* including pricing below current costs, makes sense in high-tech markets with demand-side increasing returns. This is why, for example, cellular phone companies are willing to give handsets away for free, why Internet companies are providing free PCs, and why companies such as Sega charge a mere pittance for the base station to their games. In each case, the company plans to grow the installed base in order to establish the company's product as the standard in the market. Moreover, in these cases, the companies try to recoup the base product's costs in sales of the complementary products (phone services, Internet access, or the games themselves). *Product proliferation* attempts to serve as many customers as is feasible by developing a product offering to appeal to different segments in the market. Finally, *wide distribution* can help to build the initial market base for a new technology and ensure its place as the market standard. Companies can gain distribution by raising expectations in the market regarding the likely success of the new standard, by participating in alliances, and by

licensing the technology. Each of these will signal to the distribution channel the clout that is behind the new technology. Aggressive positioning requires considerable investments in production capacity, product development, and market share building, all of which are sunk costs if the strategy fails.

Some believe that this latter strategy was the reason behind the failure of the DCC technology. Although DCC technology would replace cassette tapes (which are based on analog technology) in much the same way that CDs and CD players have replaced analog record players and albums, customers were confused over the benefits of the digital recording technology. Philips did not mention the fact that the DCC tape decks would play both existing analog and new digital tapes and did not highlight the benefits of the new recording technology. Moreover, the initial market price of $900 to $1,200 per DCC tape player was very high. Consumers were also worried about the presence of another, incompatible digital recording standard, Sony's minidisc system, and so adopted a wait-and-see attitude. Retailers were unable to move their initial inventory of DCC players and tapes and are wary about trying again. Philips's initial offer was limited to home entertainment centers and did not include portable players or car players. This lack of proliferation further limited the potential installed base.

WHICH STRATEGY MAKES SENSE?

The question of which of these four strategies to use in growing an installed base in hopes of coalescing customers and competitors around a particular standard depends upon the barriers to imitation, a firm's skills and resources, the capabilities of its competitors, and the supply of complementary products available in the market. *Barriers to imitation* might be found in patents or copyright protections, for example. In terms of *skills and resources,* obviously, technological skills alone are insufficient for establishing a technology as a standard; the firm must also have manufacturing and marketing capabilities, as well as financial resources and a strong reputation. The *existence of capable competitors* puts a premium on the firm's ability to build an installed base of customers rapidly, despite the risks. So, licensing or alliances might be particularly attractive. Finally, if no *potential suppliers of complementary products* will respond rapidly to the firm's introduction of a new technology, then the firm may have no choice but to diversify into complementary products.

Given consideration of these factors, a firm has four distinct options:

1. Aggressive sole provider. A firm should establish itself as the sole supplier of a standard-defining technology, avoiding licensing agreements and alliances, developing key complementary products if needed, and adopting an aggressive positioning strategy when

- Barriers to imitation are high.
- The firm possesses required skills and resources to establish the technology as the standard.
- There is an absence of capable competitors who might develop their own, possibly superior technology.

2. Passive multiple licensing. Licensing the technology to all comers and letting the licensees build the market for the technology makes sense when

- Barriers to imitation are low.
- The firm lacks requisite skills and resources for market development.
- There are many capable competitors.

For example, Dolby has adopted this strategy, licensing its high-fidelity sound technology to all players in the audio player market. Its low licensing fee has prevented competitors from developing a superior technology. Despite the low licensing fee, the large market volume provides Dolby a good revenue base.

3. Aggressive multiple licensing. This strategy involves licensing to as many firms as possible to build momentum for a standard, while at the same time adopting an aggressive positioning strategy in order to become the dominant supplier of the technology. So, while a firm is trying to persuade rivals to adopt its technology (building market expectations that it will become the standard and providing the incentive for development of complementary products) and facilitate their entry into the market, it also tries to preempt its licensees in the marketplace through aggressive positioning. This strategy makes sense when

- The firm has the needed skills and resources to establish its technology as the standard.
- Barriers to imitation are low.
- There are many capable competitors.

4. Selective partnering. In this strategy, the firm partners with one or a few other companies in order to jointly develop the firm's technology as a new industry standard. This makes sense when there are

- High barriers to imitation
- A lack of critical resources and skills
- Capable competitors who could develop a competing technology

For example, when IBM was developing the first personal computer, it partnered with Microsoft and Intel. IBM lacked an operating system for the PC, and the operating system was dependent upon the chip. (Note the risk in this approach, in that Microsoft seized industry leadership from IBM as a result of this alliance.)

---

[a] Ford, David and Chris Ryan (1981), "Taking Technology to Market," *Harvard Business Review,* 59 (March–April), pp. 117–126.

[b] Takahashi, Dean and Jon Auerbach (1997), "Digital Files Antitrust Suit Against Intel," *Wall Street Journal,* July 24, p. B5.

[c] Gundlach, Gregory and Paul Bloom (1993), "The 'Essential Facility' Doctrine: Legal Limits and Antitrust Considerations," *Journal of Public Policy and Marketing,* 12 (Fall), pp. 156–177.

[d] Note that this discussion does not address the use of government intervention, standards-setting bodies such as the International Standards Organization, or trade associations' attempts to establish an industry standard.

Source: Except where noted, this section is drawn from Hill, Charles (1997), "Establishing a Standard: Competitive Strategy and Technological Standards in Winner-Take-All Industries," *Academy of Management Executive,* 11 (May), pp. 7–25.

Partnerships and alliances are frequently prescribed as the panacea for success, the *modus operandi* for a successful business model in today's business environment. However, despite the many reasons for partnering, as summarized in Table 3-1, the prescription to partner overlooks the reality that the overwhelming majority of partnerships fail

TABLE 3-1 Reasons, Risks, and Success Factors for Partnering	
Reasons to Partner	Access resources and skills
	Gain cost efficiencies
	Speed time to market
	Access new markets
	Develop innovations and new products
	Develop complementary products
	Define industry standards
	Gain market clout
Risks to Partnering	Loss of autonomy and control
	Loss of trade secrets
	Legal issues and antitrust concerns
	Failure to achieve objectives
Success Factors	Interdependence
	Appropriate governance structures
	Commitment
	Trust
	Communication
	Compatible cultures
	Integrative conflict resolution

to achieve the objectives set by at least one of the partners.[9] In addition to outright failure, many risks are inherent to partnering efforts. These inescapable realities of strategic alliances highlight the need to understand fully the risks as well as the factors that contribute to the potential success and viability of the partnership.

Risks Involved in Partnering

Although partnerships do provide the many benefits mentioned previously, firms face serious impediments to realizing those benefits. For starters, working in tandem with another organization increases the project's complexity. More serious is the *potential loss of autonomy and control* that accompanies a joint effort. In teaming with another firm, decisions must be made jointly, and the success of the project becomes, to some extent, dependent on the efforts of another. Sharing decision-making control is a very difficult hurdle for many firms in choosing to partner, and because some are never able to give up their autonomy, their partnerships fail (at worst) or do not function effectively (at best).

Some identify the *loss of trade secrets* as the least noticed, but potentially riskiest, aspect of alliances.[10] Although companies typically sign confidentiality agreements that ostensibly prevent partners from exploiting what they learn about each other, shared secrets are a hazard of the game. Many experts recommend that a firm never forget that a partner may be out to "disarm" the other. A quote from a business manager highlights this fact: "If they were really our partners, they wouldn't try to suck us dry of technology ideas they could use in their own product. Whatever they learn from us they are going to use against us worldwide."[11] Indeed, product managers cited the leakage of information as the greatest risk in joint product development.[12]

The potential leakage of information can lead to one partner learning skills and knowledge from the other. Partners may gain access to knowledge and know-how that can be very valuable. As Oracle notes, "The partners we catch up to in our core applications will cease to be useful partners." Although one wants to learn as much as possible from one's partners in order to maximize the effectiveness and efficiency of the partnership, one also must limit transparency and leakage of information in the partnership so as not to dilute the firms' sources of competitive advantage. The Appendix to this chapter explores more fully the issues involved in inter-firm learning.

Another risk that strategic alliances face is that of *legal issues and antitrust problems.*[13] Cooperative ventures may run afoul of U.S. antitrust laws, especially when they involve large firms. Public policy officials wrestle with finding an appropriate balance in the trade-offs between protecting consumer welfare and maintaining national competitiveness in an increasingly global market. On the one hand, collaborative ventures are necessary to compete globally. On the other hand, collaborative relationships can result in less competition in markets, potentially harming consumer welfare.

To help clarify its position, on October 1, 1999, the Federal Trade Commission, in consultation with the Justice Department, issued its Guidelines for Collaborations Among Competitors (www.ftc.gov/bc/guidelin.htm).[14] Any partnership that has the potential to directly or indirectly affect pricing is of great concern. Hence, partnerships that affect allocation of customers or supply in a market are likely to be carefully scrutinized because of the indirect impact on pricing. On the other hand, partnerships that arise because firms are unable to pursue projects alone, and which create some common good in the market, are likely to be encouraged. For example, costly research and development efforts are typically easily justified. Another factor involves the impact of the collaboration on market share. If, together, the partners will not control more than 20% of the market being affected, their partnership is unlikely to raise concerns.

Possibly the largest risk of any partnership is the reality that the overwhelming majority of *partnerships fails to achieve the objectives* set by at least one of the partners. Reasons for this failure can be attributed to a host of factors: incompatible cultures between the two firms, lack of attention and resources allocated to the ongoing management of the relationship, lack of trust in the other party's motives or ability to deliver its part of the agreement, and so forth. The risks involved highlight the need to understand the factors that contribute to the potential success and viability of the partnership.

Factors for Partnership Success

Effective partnerships are characterized by the existence of traits that are important in nearly all business relationships, but alliances show a greater amount or intensity of these characteristics.[15] Effective strategic alliances have been shown to exhibit the following characteristics.

Interdependence   To enhance the odds of partnership success, both parties must be dependent on the other for some resource that is important, valued, and hard to obtain elsewhere. Shared mutual dependencies form the basis for a give-and-take relationship in which both parties are equally motivated to ensure the success of the alliance. Uneven, or asymmetrical, dependence undermines the dual nature of the relationship, can lead to exploitation, and may leave one party more vulnerable than the other. Alliances with low levels of interdependence suffer from a lack of commitment and need.

A special case of interdependence arises with partners of very disparate sizes. Past research has shown that partnerships between relatively equally sized partners are more likely to be successful than those between partners of unequal size.[16] However, in the technology arena, one commonly finds small, new start-ups partnering with large industry behemoths. In a typical case, the small start-up has an exciting new technology whereas the large company brings needed resources, access to markets, and management and marketing expertise. When small companies partner with large companies, the risks can loom large and special attention should be paid to the governance structure of the relationship.

Governance Structure   Governance structures are the terms, conditions, systems, and processes used to manage the ongoing interactions between two companies. At a simple level, governance structures can be *unilateral* in nature, granting one party the authority to make decisions, or *bilateral* in nature, based on mutual expectations regarding behaviors and activities.

Generally, the governance structure should be matched to the level of risk in the partnership. When a partner has assets that are at risk, should the other party behave in an opportunistic fashion, or when uncertainty is high, it is important to have a governance structure that mitigates that risk. Governance structures that are based on "credible commitments," or mutual investments that both parties place in the relationship such that both are vulnerable should the partnership fail, are one way to achieve interdependence. Alternatively, a vulnerable partner could adopt an interfirm agreement that only loosely couples the organizations,[17] relying on a narrow marketing agreement or licensing agreement rather than a joint venture. However, these looser, arms-length relationships can compromise the ability of the partnership to function effectively. As a last resort, the more vulnerable party might either trust or rely on its partner's reputation as a governance strategy. However, this too can involve a gamble.

A governance structure that is based on bilateral norms including expectations for future interactions (commitment), acting in the best interests of the partnership (trust), and intensive information sharing (communication) can also provide a reasonable solution, as discussed in the next three factors.

Commitment   Commitment, or the desire to continue the relationship into the future, is an important element for strategic alliances to succeed. Partners who are committed to the relationship are less likely to take advantage of the other partner or to make decisions that may sabotage the long-run viability of the relationship. Commitment can be demonstrated by making investments in the relationship that are dedicated solely to that relationship. Importantly, commitment should arise from a positive feeling and regard for each other's contributions, rather than from feelings of desperation or economic necessity.[18] When the nature of commitment between partners is of the "have to be committed" variety (rather than because of a positive, voluntary desire), the impact on the alliance is negative.

Trust   Trust refers to the sense that the other partner will make decisions that serve the best interests of the partnership when one party is vulnerable and act honestly and benevolently. Trust is necessary for the partnership to succeed because it leads to more effective information sharing, a willingness to allocate scarce and sensitive resources to a shared effort, and the sense that both parties will benefit in the long run.

Communication   Effective communication in strategic alliances is absolutely critical to success. Effective communication is characterized by frequent sharing of information, even information that may be considered proprietary. Such communication flows bi-directionally, with both partners participating in the flow of information about their needs and potential problems. The quality of the communication, in terms of its credibility and reliability, is vital. Communication needs to be somewhat structured, with someone accountable for maintaining open lines of information. Informal, unplanned, and ad hoc interactions are also an important component of communication.

Compatible Corporate Cultures   Although two firms may have synergistic skills that could usefully be shared in a partnership, such synergies are difficult to realize if corporate cultures clash. For example, some suspect that one of the contributing factors to the demise of Taligent, the joint venture formed between IBM and Apple, was the very different cultures brought to the venture by the respective companies' employees. The IBMers were unaccustomed to working in an open and nonhierarchical environment, whereas Apple's people were equally uncomfortable in a more formal atmosphere. Conversely, John Chambers, CEO of Cisco, knows that a good fit is important. When Cisco partnered with Cerent, Cerent's sales team had a "high-octane" spirit similar to that of the Cisco sales force, and its offices were as utilitarian as Cisco's.

Integrative Conflict Resolution and Negotiation Techniques   In any relationship in which parties' outcomes are dependent to some extent on the actions and decisions of another, difficulties will arise. For example, SAP's relationships with its partners has been confrontational in some cases. The company has stated, "We will select a handful of partners to work with. If our partners cross us, we will crush them into the dust."[19] Similarly, Microsoft has exerted coercive (albeit indirect) pressure on even one of its largest, most important partners, Intel, by threatening to withhold Windows 95 if Intel's largest customers (computer makers) supported some of Intel's new-product development efforts that would undermine Microsoft's clout in the market.[20] In the Intel–Microsoft case, conflict arises because Intel focuses on innovating products that will persuade existing users to buy new hardware whereas Microsoft wants to sell products for existing machines.

Some level of conflict is likely functional, because it indicates that problems are being identified and addressed rather than being ignored. The ways in which such conflicts are addressed are more important than the sheer level of conflict in determining the alliance's future success. Parties must be willing to resolve conflict in a way that allows for both partners to have a stake in the outcome, addresses both partners' needs simultaneously, and is mutually beneficial to both. Although this may seem idealistic, many types of problem-solving techniques can be used to creatively identify solutions that do not result in a win–loss outcome, but rather win–win solutions.

In sum, the *spirit of cooperation,* identified in the traits mentioned, signals the likelihood of future success of partnerships and alliances. In the Technology Expert's View from the Trenches, IBM's Melissa Porter offers her insights on managing horizontal alliances.

The next section provides focused coverage on one type of vital relationship, relationships with customers.

CUSTOMER RELATIONSHIPS

Customer relationship marketing refers to the development of close, long-term relationships with customers that provide mutual benefits, or win–win solutions. Companies that believe in the philosophy of relationship marketing recognize the value of using marketing as a process of building long-term relationships with customers to keep them satisfied and to keep them coming back. Studies show that it is cheaper to keep current customers happy than to prospect for new ones.

A relationship marketing strategy may require that a firm be willing to sacrifice short-term profits for long-term gains. For example, Spencer Clark, a salesperson at Dynamic Solutions International, a Denver-based firm that integrates and customizes computer applications for business customers, has been known to recommend competitors' solutions for customers' needs. He justifies this by recognizing that his company's solutions are appropriate for a particular size of customer firm and that smaller firms can get their needs met with smaller-scale solutions. As a result, he is focused in the immediate term on generating a customer's trust, knowing that in the long term, as the customer grows, its computing needs will grow also. Customers who trust him are likely to turn to him first when their computing needs change. They trust that he will recommend an appropriate solution.

A philosophy of forging close, long-term customer relationships built on the spirit of loyalty, trust, commitment, and interdependence does yield benefits. However, attempting to build long-term relationships with *all* a firm's customers is not only unmanageable in many cases but also inconsistent with the reality that 20% of a firm's customers provide 80% of its revenues.

When Is Relationship Marketing Appropriate?

Despite the advantages of a relationship marketing strategy, it may not be appropriate under all circumstances. As shown in Table 3-2, Barbara Bund Jackson identifies two types of customers.[21]

TECHNOLOGY EXPERT'S VIEW FROM THE TRENCHES

The Art of Alliances

MELISSA PORTER
Channel Development Manager, Utility and Energy Services,
IBM Corporation, Oak Brook, Illinois

Alliance (*n*)
1. a bond or connection between parties or individuals
2. an association to further the common interests of the members
3. union by relationship in qualities

Companies today are finding that they cannot be all things to all people, so they are seeking out other companies to form alliances in order to combine strengths and to get leverage within a market segment. Working together as a team, each bringing to the partnership unique skills, abilities, and experiences, allows for a more powerful resource to meet the needs of mutual customers.

Forming and managing alliances is truly an art, not a science. Attempting to bring together different companies and to build a partnership that has lasting power has its challenges. Once a firm puts a stake in the ground to define the relationship and establishes principles to engage in the marketplace, effective partnerships should allow a firm to provide best-of-breed solutions to its customers. I often recommend a Crawl-Walk-Run strategy when first entering into an alliance . . . start slow and get some success in working together, and this will generate momentum leading to a more successful partnership.

One place where alliances can be particularly useful is in serving customers facing quickly changing environments. For example, utilities are being challenged by many issues in a rapidly deregulating marketplace all over the world. Faced with competitive market pressure to lower prices, and offer better service, and a mandate to open transmission lines for unrestricted access in energy trading, many utilities now require information technology solutions to help them compete successfully in a radically different, consumer-driven environment. By partnering with software vendors to develop these solutions, IBM is helping Utility and Energy Services customers all over the world to meet the challenge of change.

The complexity and dynamic nature of the marketplace do continually present barriers to both sides of an alliance. When discussing alliances, I sometimes use the term "coopetition," meaning that in certain instances we cooperate with our partners and at other times we compete. Enhancing cooperation between parties and offering a support structure will allow for a long-term and productive partnership.

IBM has addressed the need for strong relationships with its alliance partners by creating the Business Partner Charter. Originally announced in 1996, the charter was a new milestone in recognition of the importance of these partners. Within the charter was a message to partners and IBMers alike: that we were committed to a strong relationship with our business partners, many of them developing industry software applications, and that cooperation in delivering solutions would make each business stronger.

Each year at the Business Partner Executive Conference (now known as PartnerWorld) we review the status of key objectives of the charter and announce new programs and processes to further enhance these alliances. Since 1996, the percentage of IBM's revenue generated from business with its partners has greatly increased, and the partner firms report similar results as well.

IBM is now entering into a new range of strategic alliances that will couple applications from leading software firms with IBM's hardware, software, services, financing, and unmatched industry expertise to meet growing customer demand for end-to-end information technology solutions. As part of these alliances, independent software vendors (ISVs) will gain access to new customers and revenue opportunities through IBM's extensive marketing, sales, and solution resources. At the same time, ISVs will commit to increased use of IBM's leading hardware (server) platforms, middleware, and services.

Partnerships like these are truly

1. connections between parties that
2. further the common interests of members and
3. are seen as relationships in qualities!

The **lost-for-good customer** is the account that is either totally committed to the vendor or totally lost and committed to some other vendor. The idea is that, due to the high switching costs these customers face, if a company does not meet that customer's needs and the customer switches to a competitor, the account will be lost for good because it would be too costly for the customer to switch back again to the original supplier. These customers appropriately deserve intensive relationship-development efforts.

On the other hand, accounts that do not warrant intensive relationship-development efforts are referred to as **always-a-share customers.** This customer represents an account

TABLE 3-2   Relationship versus Transaction Marketing

	Transaction "Always-a-Share" ◄————————————————————►	Relationship "Lost-for-Good"
Customer Behavior		
Customer time horizon	*Short-term*	*Long-term*
Switching costs	*Low*	*High*
Customer system	*Modular*	*Integrated*
Buyer focus	*Product or person*	*Technology or vendor*
Marketing Implications		
Short-term tools	*Price, Advertising*	
Medium-term tools	*Personal selling*	
Long-term tools		*Product, Distribution*

Source: Adapted from Jackson, Barbara B. (1985), *Winning and Keeping Industrial Customers,* Lexington, MA: Lexington Books.

that has a lasting, but less intensive, tie to the vendor; views relationships with vendors as more interchangeable and short-term; and is focused on immediate benefits. Due in part to lower switching costs, these customers can share their patronage among several suppliers with little risk incurred. These customers do not warrant a relationship marketing approach. Given their focus on the short term, they are effectively served with **transaction marketing.**

A critical issue in determining whether customers fall more toward the lost-for-good or the always-a-share end of the continuum is switching costs.

The Role of Switching Costs   Switching costs make it costly or risky for a customer to switch to a competing vendor's products. Switching costs can arise from investments in equipment, procedures, or people that a customer has made. For example, to implement electronic data interchange between firms, the customer has to purchase dedicated equipment to link to the supplier's computer. As another example, switching on-line services means finding a new Internet service provider, loading new software, and creating a new e-mail address. Switching costs can also arise from the risk of making a poor choice. If a purchase is important to operations, if the brand is not well known, or if the product is complex, the customer's switching costs will be perceived as higher. A relationship marketing strategy makes sense only when customers face high switching costs. If a vendor were to follow a relationship marketing philosophy when customers face low switching costs, it may find itself using high-price marketing strategies and then losing customers to low-cost competitors.

Switching costs are also related to whether the customer has a highly modular system or a fully integrated system. Modular systems allow customers to combine pieces or parts from different vendors, mixing and matching them rather freely, and hence are less likely to benefit from a strong relationship marketing orientation.

Finally, switching costs are also related to whether the customer's purchase is wrapped around a particular technology (say, a Unix system) or a particular vendor (say, an IBM e-business solution). In these situations, customers tend to be more long-term focused and experience greater switching costs. On the other hand, firms that focus on a particular product or on a salesperson may not be as committed to a certain company. If they can buy a similar product from other vendors, or if the salesperson leaves to work elsewhere, that customer may move its account elsewhere.

Implications for Marketing: Match Marketing Tools to the Type of Account

Based on this model, the marketing tools used for different types of customer accounts should vary, depending on whether the customer is categorized as more relationship or transaction oriented. Tools with a short-term horizon are better matched to always-a-share customers, whereas tools with a longer-term horizon are better matched to lost-for-good customers. Tools that have a short-term horizon include price and advertising, both of which can be modified and adapted fairly readily. On the other hand, product and distribution decisions are more long-term commitments that cannot be changed as quickly. The use of the sales force is characterized as somewhere between short and long term. Importantly, the use of short-term tools alone cannot win long-term relationships. But overreliance on short-term tools can cause the loss of long-term accounts. The appropriate use of short-term tools is to support long-term tools in long-term relationships.

Firms can take actions to bind customers more closely to them. Procedures that help to link customers more closely to sellers or that rely on information exchanged between the two can create switching costs for customers and make them more dependent on the supplier. For example, one of the reasons that Amazon.com has been so successful in retaining its customers is that it knows as much as possible about its existing customers and makes it very hard for them to disengage.[22] By leveraging each exchange with a customer, the company is learning. For another company to catch up with this history would be difficult, and would require quite a bit of effort and time on the customer's part.

Effective relationship marketing efforts require a customer database, the purpose of which is the creation of an ongoing relationship with a set of customers who have an identifiable interest in a product and whose responses to promotional efforts become part of future communication attempts.[23] Such a database is interactive, allows solid measurement of the return on marketing investments, and can lead to opportunities to cross-sell customers. Through its relationship marketing efforts, Xerox earns 65% of its revenue in after-sales service and support.

Customer relationship management has important implications for pricing and advertising and promotions strategies, which are discussed in Chapters 9 and 10.

Summary

This chapter has explored the role of partnerships and alliances in high-tech markets. Because of the dynamic nature of the high-tech marketplace, most firms find that they cannot go it alone and must partner in some capacity to be effective in their marketing efforts. Understanding the range of partnerships available, the purposes each serves, and the risk factors as well as the success factors is necessary to managing partnerships effectively.

Moreover, the focus on customer relationships is consistent with the need to have a customer or market orientation, the focus of the next chapter.

Discussion Questions

1. What various types of partnerships may a firm form? Provide a current example of each. Draw a supply chain to demonstrate the nature of the relationship.
2. What is the National Cooperative Research Act and its amendment?
3. What are the various strategies a firm can take to form standards? Which strategy makes sense when?
4. What are the risks of partnering arrangements? How can each of these risks be mitigated?
5. Give an overview of some of the issues and perspectives regarding learning in inter-firm relationships.
6. What factors are associated with the success of strategic alliances?
7. What is customer relationship marketing? Does it make sense in all cases?
8. Enumerate and describe the various types of switching costs.
9. Compare and contrast relationship versus transaction marketing. Under what conditions is relationship marketing appropriate? What marketing tools are appropriate?
10. What actions can vendors take to link their customers to them more closely?
11. "Thought" question: How do the unique characteristics of the high-tech environment affect the desirability of and techniques used to build customer relationships?

Glossary

Always-a-share customer. A customer who has a lasting, but less intensive, tie to the vendor; views vendors as more interchangeable; and is focused on immediate benefits. Customers who have low switching costs and a short-term horizon on a particular solution can share their patronage among several suppliers with little risk incurred.

Competitive collaboration, co-opetition. When firms who typically compete in some segment in the marketplace join forces to collaborate on some aspect of their business, say new-product development. These firms typically compete at the same level of the supply chain.

Complementary alliances. When firms who make products that are jointly used team together in some aspect of their business, say new-product development. The members are referred to as *complementors*.

Horizontal alliances/partnerships. A relationship between firms at the same level of the value chain; may be competitors or firms that provide complementary products.

Lost-for-good customers. A customer who is either totally committed to the vendor or totally lost and committed to some other vendor. Due to the high switching costs these customers face, if a company does not meet that customer's needs and the customer switches to a competitor, the account will be lost for good because it would be too costly for the customer to switch back again to the original supplier.

National Cooperative Production Amendment (1993). Act to allow joint production of products. The amendment excludes marketing and distribution agreements, except for the products manufactured by the joint venture, and the use of existing facilities by the joint venture.

National Cooperative Research Act (1984). Act passed by the U.S. government to promote joint research and development, encourage innovation, and stimulate trade. The act applies to R&D activities up to and including the testing of prototypes.

Relationship marketing. The forming of close, long-term relationships with business partners to achieve win–win business solutions.

Switching costs. Costs incurred by a customer that make it costly or risky to switch to a competing vendor's products. Switching costs can arise from monetary (tangible) investments in equipment, procedures, or people that a customer has made, or from intangible feelings of risk or exposure.

Transaction marketing. Marketing focused on the immediate transaction at hand, without a view to forming a long-term relationship with a customer.

Vertical partnership. When firms who sell products to another firm at a different level of the value chain team up to collaborate on some aspect of their business strategy.

Endnotes

1. Ball, Jeffrey (1999), "To Define Future Car, GM, Toyota Say Bigger Is Better," *Wall Street Journal,* April 20, p. B4.
2. Langreth, Robert (1999), "DNA Dreams: Big Drug Firms Discuss Linking Up to Pursue Disease-Causing Genes, *Wall Street Journal,* March 4.
3. Morgan, Robert and Shelby D. Hunt (1994), "The Commitment–Trust Theory of Relationship Marketing," *Journal of Marketing,* 58 (July), pp. 20–38.
4. Brandenburger, Adam and Barry Nalebuff (1996), *Co-opetition,* New York: Currency/Doubleday.
5. Brandenburger, Adam and Barry Nalebuff (1996), *Co-opetition,* New York: Currency/Doubleday.
6. Browning, Larry D., Janice M. Beyer, and Judy C. Shetler (1995), "Building Cooperation in a Competitive Industry: SEMATECH and the Semiconductor Industry" (Special Research Forum: Intra- and Interorganizational Coop-

eration), *Academy of Management Journal,* 38 (February), pp. 113–139.

7. Kirkpatrick, David (1998), "The E-Ware War," *Fortune,* December 7, p. 102.

8. Kirkpatrick, David (1998), "The E-Ware War," *Fortune,* December 7, p. 102.

9. Mohr, Jakki and Robert Spekman (1994), "Characteristics of Partnership Success: Partnership Attributes, Communication Behavior, and Conflict Resolution Techniques," *Strategic Management Journal,* 15 (February), pp. 135–152.

10. MacDonald, Elizabeth and Joann Lublin (1998), "In the Debris of a Failed Merger: Trade Secrets," *Wall Street Journal,* March 10, p. B1.

11. Hamel, Gary (1991), "Competition for Competence and Inter-Partner Learning with International Strategic Alliances," *Strategic Management Journal,* 12, pp. 83–103 (quote p. 87).

12. Littler, Dale, Fiona Leverick, and Margaret Bruce (1995), "Factors Affecting the Process of Collaborative Product Development," *Journal of Product Innovation Management,* 12, pp. 16–32.

13. Mohr, Jakki, Gregory T. Gundlach, and Robert Spekman (1994), "Legal Ramifications of Strategic Alliances," *Marketing Management,* 3 (2), pp. 38–46; Gundlach, Greg and Jakki Mohr (1992), "Collaborative Relationships: Legal Limits and Antitrust Considerations," *Journal of Public Policy and Marketing,* 11 (November), pp. 101–114.

14. Brady, Diane (1999), "When Is Cozy Too Cozy?" *Business Week,* October 25, pp. 127–130.

15. Mohr, Jakki and Robert Spekman (1994), "Characteristics of Partnership Success: Partnership Attributes, Communication Behavior, and Conflict Resolution Techniques," *Strategic Management Journal,* 15 (February), pp. 135–152; Mohr, Jakki and Robert Spekman (1996), "Perfecting Partnerships," *Marketing Management,* 4 (Winter–Spring), pp. 34–43.

16. Bucklin, Louis P. and Sanjit Sengupta (1993), "Organizing Successful Co-Marketing Alliances," *Journal of Marketing,* 57 (April), pp. 32–46.

17. Dutta, Shantanu and Allen M. Weiss (1997), "The Relationship Between a Firm's Level of Technological Innovativeness and Its Pattern of Partnership Agreements," *Management Science,* 43 (March), pp. 343–356.

18. Kumar, Nirmalya, Jonathon Hibbard, and Louis Stern (1994), "The Nature and Consequences of Marketing Channel Intermediary Commitment," working paper #94-115, Cambridge, MA: Marketing Science Institute.

19. Kirkpatrick, David (1998), "The E-Ware War," *Fortune,* December 7, p. 102.

20. Takahashi, Dean (1998), "Microsoft–Intel Relationship Has Become Contentious," *Wall Street Journal,* September 25, pp. B1, B5.

21. Jackson, Barbara Bund (1985), "Build Customer Relationships That Last," *Harvard Business Review,* November–December, pp. 120–128.

22. Rosenspan, Alan (2000), "Internet Marketing 2001: A Direct Marketing Odyssey," *Direct Marketing,* 62 (July) pp. 52–55.

23. Solomon, Michael and Elnora Stuart (1999), *Marketing: Real People, Real Choices,* 2nd ed., Upper Saddle River, NJ: Prentice Hall.

Recommended Readings

Jackson, Barbara B. (1985), *Winning and Keeping Industrial Customers,* Lexington, MA: Lexington Books.

McKenna, Regis (1991), *Relationship Marketing: Successful Strategies for the Age of the Customer,* Reading, MA: Addison-Wesley.

McKenna, Regis (1997), *Real Time: Preparing for the Age of the Never Satisfied Customer,* Boston: Harvard Business School Press.

Peppers, Don and Martha Rogers (1997), *Enterprise One to One,* New York: Doubleday.

APPENDIX

Learning from Partners in Collaborative Relationships

Knowledge can be categorized in terms of its nature or properties. A common typology categorizes knowledge as either explicit or tacit.[1] *Explicit,* or *migratory, knowledge* can be written down, encoded, and explained. Examples include blueprints, technical specifications, product designs, steps in the manufacturing process, and so forth. Importantly, explicit knowledge is not veiled in organizational routines, practices, and culture. Because such knowledge is transparent—anyone with a comparable knowledge or skills base can understand and decipher it—some firms turn to patent protection and other forms of intellectual property rights (discussed in Chapter 7) for ownership.

On the other hand, *tacit knowledge* is unwritten know-how and "know-why" that is embedded in the organization's skills and routines. Tacit knowledge is less transparent than is explicit knowledge and has a "sticky" quality to it, making it difficult to learn and absorb. It can include a way of approaching and solving problems, imagination, continuous improvement techniques, or artisan-like skills.[2] The *embeddedness* of tacit know-how may arise from *causal ambiguity,*[3] in which the relationship between a firm's knowledge/actions and outcomes is highly uncertain.

For example, product/market knowledge tends to be explicit and more easily transferred than are skills in technology development, manufacturing, or continuous quality improvement techniques.[4] On the other hand, tacit knowledge forms the basis of core skills and competencies, which (1) are harder to share and imitate than is explicit knowledge due to their deeply embedded nature, but (2) present the greater value.

Learning from partners in strategic alliances has both an upside and a downside. On the one hand, interfirm learning can lead to a win–win situation, in which both parties improve their skills and performance in the marketplace. Further, learning about each other can make the partnership more successful and contribute to positive relationship dynamics. On the other hand, interfirm learning can involve the "deskilling" of a partner, whereby one party absorbs the proprietary information of its partner, ultimately leading to a situation in which the deskilled partner is no longer needed.

These two views of interfirm learning highlight its paradoxical nature. In painting the "rosy" picture of interfirm learning, cooperative, harmonious ties are viewed as indicators of an effective relationship; the focus is on the value that interfirm learning can offer to the learning organization. The risks involved in the sharing of tacit, embedded information that the partner is attempting to acquire or internalize by having a tightly knit partnership agreement are minimized or overlooked. On the other hand, the "risky" view of interfirm learning explicitly alerts managers to the potential seepage of information in tightly knit relationships in which the partner has an acquisition intent. Cooperative, harmonious relational ties are potentially problematic and signal that one partner may be naïve to the other's intent. Rather, less relational characteristics may be desirable. One implication of these risks, which runs directly counter to the implications of the more favorable view of interfirm learning, is that firms must not partner too closely and that they must guard against interpersonal ties that are too collegial.[5]

These two views of interfirm learning are not mutually exclusive, but rather, are complementary sides to the same coin. Hence, the real challenge is to manage the paradox through the use of tools that allow firms to maximize the upside potential of interfirm learning while limiting its downside risks. At the heart of the issue is the reality that two different parties come to the relationship with potentially conflicting goals and objectives. One party may be content with mere access to a partner's knowledge and skills, whereas the other desires acquisition and internalization of the partner's knowledge. Such a situation makes the less aggressive party vulnerable to the risk of the potential opportunism of its partner. In such a situation, how can the more vulnerable party protect itself? One key is the nature of the governance mechanisms, or the tools used to structure and manage the interfirm relationship.

To the extent that the most valuable knowledge is tacit—which is also the most difficult to transfer—firms have an incentive to structure the closest type of partnership agreement possible. Indeed, the only way to learn skills and competencies that are highly embedded in organizational routines is to partner closely.[6] Firms seeking to learn and internalize tacit knowledge must absorb it through an apprenticeship model of learning, which often entails collaborative agreements such as joint ventures and R&D consortia. Close collaborative agreements allow organizational routines to be examined and understood, in terms of what is done, why it is done, and how it is done. Because more tightly linked relationships face greater risks from interfirm learning, the higher the firm's technological innovativeness, the less likely it is to use more transparent types of partnering arrangements such as joint ventures and research and development agreements, compared to marketing and licensing agreements.[7]

Close interpersonal ties between the parties may be especially risky. The partner with the learning intent would potentially take advantage of the close interpersonal relationships, using them to gain access to crucial information that the more vulnerable partner might share unintentionally or unconsciously. Indeed, studies of leakages of proprietary information find that the most common ones occur through such unintentional sharing.[8]

In any case, an explicit trade-off must be made between the need to restrict information sharing and the risks of not doing so. Although ideally there would be a combination of both looser, more collaborative mechanisms as well as more rigid procedures, in reality this may be quite difficult for operating personnel to implement. Ultimately, the people involved will determine the success or failure of a plan to limit knowledge transfer, and hence, a governance strategy must be clear to them.

Notes

1. Badaracco, J. L., Jr. (1991), *The Knowledge Link,* Boston: Harvard Business School Press.
2. Lei, David T. (1997), "Competence-Building, Technology Fusion and Competitive Advantage: The Key Roles of Organizational Learning and Strategic Alliances," *International Journal of Technology Management,* 14 (2, 3, 4), pp. 208–237.
3. Reed, R. and R. De Fillippi (1990), "Causal Ambiguity, Barrier to Imitation, and Sustainable Competitive Advantage," *Academy of Management Review,* 15, pp. 88–102.
4. Hamel, Gary (1991), "Competition for Competence and Inter-Partner Learning with International Strategic Alliances," *Strategic Management Journal,* 12, pp. 83–103; Inkpen, Andrew C. and Paul W. Beamish (1997), "Knowledge, Bargaining Power, and the Instability of International Joint Ventures," *Academy of Management Review,* 22 (January), pp. 177–202.
5. Hamel, Gary, Yves Doz, and C. K. Prahalad (1989), "Collaborate with Your Competitors—And Win," *Harvard Business Review,* January–February, pp. 133–139; Dutta, Shantanu and Allen M. Weiss (1997), "The Relationship Between a Firm's Level of Technological Innovativeness and Its Pattern of Partnership Agreements," *Management Science,* 43 (March), pp. 343–356.
6. Badaracco, J. L., Jr. (1991), *The Knowledge Link,* Boston: Harvard Business School Press.

7. Dutta, Shantanu and Allen M. Weiss (1997), "The Relationship Between a Firm's Level of Technological Innovativeness and Its Pattern of Partnership Agreements," *Management Science,* 43 (March), pp. 343–356.

8. Mohr, Jakki (1996), "The Management and Control of Information in High-Technology Firms," *Journal of High-Technology Management Research,* 7 (Fall), pp. 245–268.

CHAPTER 4

Market Orientation and R&D–Marketing Interaction in High-Technology Firms

Probably one of the most daunting challenges in many high-tech firms is to bring a customer-oriented philosophy to the firm's operations. This challenge is particularly daunting because its necessity is significantly less obvious to a firm than is the need for funding and additional resources. High-tech start-ups usually begin with a great technological idea that offers improvements over existing ways of doing things. Whether this great technological idea is one that customers will actually embrace is a completely different issue. Think of the numerous examples of superior technology that never became the *de facto* standard in a marketplace:

- Apple computers
- Beta-format video machines
- Netscape browsers

The need for firms in high-tech industries to understand customers, to be customer oriented, and to be market-driven is vital. However, start-up firms often lack marketing knowledge and personnel and, indeed, may even be suspicious of marketing tactics. Yet, the need to have a strong marketing capability is actually most important for firms that are good technologically.[1] Marketing capability has a disproportionate positive effect on R&D productivity for firms with strong technical skills. The higher the technological strengths, the greater the impact of strong marketing capability on R&D productivity. To be sure, being technology- or customer-oriented is not an either/or situation; a firm can benefit from being both technology and customer oriented in uncertain markets. Research has compared the impact of a technology orientation versus a customer orientation on performance. In highly uncertain markets, a customer orientation (a set of beliefs that puts customers first) has a positive influence on the commercial performance of an innovation.[2]

Although the smaller firm typically lacks marketing personnel and, indeed, may even be suspicious of marketing tactics, the need to be market driven is vital *for small and large firms alike*. A large body of research and literature on developing a market orientation applies to firms in many industries, not solely those that are high tech. However, given the market and technological uncertainty present in high-tech markets, the need for a market orientation may be even stronger than in more traditional contexts.

This chapter covers of the basic underpinnings of what it means to be market oriented, along with the vital importance of collaborative interactions between marketing and R&D personnel.

WHAT IT MEANS TO BE MARKET ORIENTED[3]

As shown in Figure 4-1, a firm that is market oriented emphasizes the *gathering, dissemination,* and *utilization* of market intelligence as the basis for decision making.[4] Customer-oriented marketing activities are critical to gathering information to reduce overwhelming uncertainty over demand.

First, market-oriented firms gather a wide array of information from the market. Market intelligence includes information about current and future customer needs, as well as competitive information and trends in the marketplace. The acquisition of information can be done via consumer hot lines, trade shows, customer visits, competitive intelligence, or some of the more high-tech-oriented research tools discussed in Chapter 5.

Second, the market-oriented firm disseminates the information gathered throughout the company. The use of a marketing information database can be useful in making the information available in a centrally located manner. People across functions and divisions in the organization should share information with each other and have a dialogue about it. Indeed, information on all buying influences should permeate every corporate function.

Third, the market-oriented firm uses the information to make decisions. To the extent that these decisions are made interfunctionally and interdivisionally, it will ensure greater representation of the information and a closer connection to the market issues. Moreover, it implies that the people who will be involved in *implementing* the decisions are the ones actually involved in *making* the decisions—the idea being that if one is involved in making the decision, he or she will be more committed to implementing that decision.

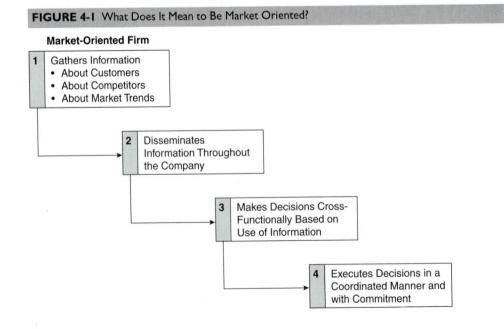

FIGURE 4-1 What Does It Mean to Be Market Oriented?

Finally, the market-oriented firm executes the decisions in a coordinated manner. Commitment to execution is necessary to successful implementation of a market orientation.

These, then, are the characteristics of firms that value and rely on information to guide strategic decision making. Distilled to its essence, a **customer** or **market orientation** simply means gathering, sharing, and using information about "the market" (customers, competitors, etc.) to make decisions. This philosophy of approaching decision making requires effective management of the knowledge that resides in different places within the firm. *Knowledge management* is an important process in becoming market oriented; it requires the proactive management of the firm's bases of knowledge and the effective use of that knowledge to enhance decision-making ability. Moreover, it requires the tearing down of walls and barriers between departments, functions, and individuals, both inside and outside the company, in order to better share and use information.[5] The Technology Expert's View from the Trenches in this section comes from a senior Hewlett-Packard executive who has worked with HP in its transition from being an engineering-driven firm to a more customer-oriented one.

Although the sharing of knowledge makes intuitive sense, it really represents a paradigm shift in the sources of competitive advantage within the firm. In the past, labor and capital were the primary determinants of firms' profits, but increasingly know-how is the profit engine. Yet, competitive advantage that resides in know-how is only as strong as the ability to share and use that knowledge across the organization's boundaries. Indeed, some say that effective knowledge management requires a boundaryless learning organization, which takes good ideas from disparate functions and uses them in many areas. However, freely sharing, and using, information is easier said than done.

Barriers to Being Market Oriented

It is all too easy in an organization to give mere lip service to being market oriented; organizational barriers can prevent the implementation of a market orientation. First, people often hoard information, having the sense that access to and control of information provide power and status within the organization. As a result, it logically follows that a very difficult part of knowledge management is to convince people to share information rather than to hoard knowledge to protect their standing in the organization.

Second, core rigidities may prevent market information from being utilized in decisions. As discussed in Chapter 2, core rigidities are straitjackets that inhibit a firm from being innovative and can include status hierarchies that give preference to, say, technical engineers over marketers. This preference often results in the disregard of information about users—unless it comes from someone with status in the organization.

For example, during the design of the Deskjet printer at Hewlett-Packard, marketers tested early prototypes in shopping malls to determine user response. They returned from their studies with a list of 21 changes they believed essential to the success of the product; however, the engineers accepted only 5. Unwilling to give up, the marketers persuaded the engineers to join them in the mall tests. After hearing the same feedback from the lips of users, that they had previously rejected, the product designers returned to their benches and incorporated the other 16 requested changes.[6] Unfortunately, because marketing personnel are often not a part of the distinctive competencies of technology-oriented firms, the information they bring to the design process goes unheeded—which can have very negative consequences.

TECHNOLOGY EXPERT'S VIEW FROM THE TRENCHES

What Does It Take to Become Customer Focused?

JACK TRAUTMAN
General Manager, Computer Peripherals Bristol Division,
Hewlett-Packard, Bristol, United Kingdom

The challenge in any high-tech organization is creating a customer-centered culture. On the surface, it sounds easy—listen to the customer and invent what the customer wants. In practice, it's a complex task to choose a target customer, accurately anticipate the target's exact needs, translate those needs into product features, and generate not only the right product but also the total customer experience that captures their money today and their loyalty tomorrow—and do it better than your competitors.

For a lot of high-tech start-ups, the founders are the customers. Their bright new ideas are spawned from their own user experiences. Through their engineering expertise, they solve their own problems with the products they invent, and in so doing, solve the same problem for all of their customers.

Such was the case in the early days of HP. Engineers developed test and measurement equipment for engineers. When they wanted to know what the customer wanted, they asked their fellow engineers. This "Next Bench Syndrome" served HP well for many years.

But then the business got more complex. HP diversified into computers, printers, and a host of other product types. Suddenly the customer was not sitting at the next bench. In the absence of real customers, engineers will still do their best to anticipate needs. But their instincts are more likely grounded in technical prowess than customer requirements. "I'll give them the most technically elegant solution, and surely they'll love it!" Maybe.

Enter marketing. Through market research, customer segmentation, competitive analysis, focus groups, a customer relationship management process, and a host of other techniques, a surrogate for the customer can be constructed. These are well-understood processes that can yield great results.

But an effective product marketing team is not enough to ensure success. It takes teamwork between marketing and engineering to truly bring the customer into the center of the product generation process. This teamwork comes through mutual respect, working together side by side, and an open sharing of ideas. Enlightened companies are co-locating product marketing and engineering teams beside each other to maximize interaction and a free-flowing exchange of ideas. Insights into ways to best satisfy customers will not occur in a "throw it over the wall" environment between marketing and engineering.

Finally, and most importantly, it takes management leadership to commit the entire organization to a customer-centered culture. Beyond marketing and engineering, every department and every person must embrace the total customer experience. Managers must be willing to invest in each employee to give them the tools and skills to get close to the customer. And then those managers must insist that every decision in the company be made with the customer in mind.

It's hard work to keep a focus on the customer. But the payoffs are big: increased customer satisfaction and loyalty, high employee motivation and morale, and increased shareholder value.

Other barriers that can prevent a firm from being market oriented are the tyranny of the current ("served") market (discussed previously in Chapter 2) and users' inability to envision new solutions that technology may have to offer.[7] Firms have a tendency to focus very specifically on solving customers' needs with a current technology. Such a myopic focus obscures the possibility that customer needs may change over time and may be solved in radically different ways. Although a market-oriented culture necessitates that a firm actually solicit information from, and listen to, customers, this can be hard to do when customers may not be able to articulate their needs clearly.

The Hidden Downside of a Market Orientation

Even if customers can articulate their needs, some argue that listening to customers may not always be the panacea that advocates of a market orientation indicate: Listening to customers too carefully can inhibit innovation, constraining it to ideas that customers can envision and articulate—which may lead to safe, but bland, offerings. A *Fortune* magazine article suggests that the obsessive devotion to listening to customers has gone too far and that in some cases, it's better to ignore the customer.[8] Why would this be?

First, problems may arise in listening to customers if they actually give market researchers bad information. For example, during a marketing research project, customers may say they love a new-product idea but then not buy the product when it comes out on the market. Spalding tried to market "pump baseball gloves" that tested well but just didn't do well in the marketplace. So, in some cases, marketers may need to ignore customers' assertions of what they want. Second, marketers may need to ignore feedback about what customers say they *don't* want. For example, some products that met with initial customer resistance included fax machines and overnight express delivery. In addition, people said they'd never give up their mainframe computers. A Motorola marketing executive has stated, "our biggest competitor isn't IBM or Sony. It's the way in which people currently do things."[9] So, in light of this concern, a key question becomes this: How can a firm be market driven and yet not be overly constrained by what customers say (or become a "feedback fanatic"[10])?

Overcoming Possible Pitfalls in Being Market Oriented   Although it sounds like an oxymoron, one way to be market oriented without being a market-orientation slave is to *ignore the customer.* One method of doing so is to judiciously ignore what customers say and, rather, watch what they do.[11] The best information can be gleaned through observation of what customers do under normal, natural conditions. Known as empathic design, this type of research is covered thoroughly in Chapter 5.

Second, it is important to match when a firm chooses to rely heavily on customer feedback to the type of innovation the firm is getting feedback on,[12] or in other words, to use the contingency model of marketing presented in Chapter 1. In the context of *incremental innovation,* relying on customer feedback is important and useful for fine-tuning a product. Customers are adept at providing useful information that can reinforce or refine existing technology. However, in the context of *radical or breakthrough innovations,* customers are less adept at providing useful information. Customers have natural "myopia,"[13] which means that, in gathering data from the market and customers, informants are bounded by their context or environment. They may not be aware of the latest trends in usage, and users cannot see the world through an innovator's eyes; they cannot know what solutions the technology may have to offer. Indeed, in advocating the use of customer observation to gather new insights, some high-tech marketing researchers believe that what customers *can't* tell you might be just what is needed to develop successful new products.[14]

Moreover, with the "tyranny of the served market," firms that focus too narrowly on their established customers may be constrained in the strategies and technologies they choose to pursue. For example, a firm's best customers may be those who are last to embrace a disruptive technology. In such a case, the people who embrace a new technology first are the ones a company pays the least attention to, and the innovation creeps up like a stealth attack.[15] For this reason, successful companies adopt a "future market focus."[16] Rather than being focused on current customers, innovative firms focus on future customers.

Customers who adopt a radical new technology are typically on the fringes of an established market or in an entirely new, emerging market. For example, in the early 1980s, the 5.25-inch disk drive technology was out of step with mainframe and minicomputer customer demands but was embraced by the emerging desktop personal computer marketplace.[17] Established disk drive firms did not fail because they were unable to develop innovative technologies. Rather, because established customers were uninterested in new technologies that didn't address their immediate needs, industry leaders did not allocate resources to the new technologies. This decision allowed new entrants to gain leadership in the new market.

"Ignoring the customer" may be difficult when statisticians and company conformists use reams of consumer research to stifle creative ideas. But a person who believes fervently in the value of an idea, say, a product champion, can overcome a sea of skeptics. To be a visionary takes faith in one's ideas and the resulting products, as well as a realistic time frame for perseverance. One shouldn't persevere so long that the signs of imminent failure are totally ignored. On the other hand, one wants to persevere long enough to give the invention a fair chance. A Compaq executive suggests that 12 to 18 months is a good time frame "to get a good read on whether what you're hearing is surmountable skepticism or a downright lack of market acceptance."[18] The Technology Tidbit highlights a product for which customers did not articulate a specific need.

For a firm to be truly market driven, these characteristics must be infused throughout the company, starting from the top down. If anything, these characteristics idealize a culture or philosophy that places very high value on market information. The acquisition, sharing, and dissemination of information require trust in coworkers and collaborative communication among them. In the high-tech arena, close collaboration between marketing personnel and R&D personnel is especially vital.

Precision Agriculture

THOMAS LUNDELL

Your great-great-grandfather probably thought that John Deere's all-steel plow was a great improvement in the 1830s. The plow did make effective plowing of the black prairie soils possible, and it lessened the animal power needed to turn the soil. When the settlers turned the wild, uncultivated, and virtually unoccupied land of North America into vast fields of crops and produce, they probably didn't grasp the notion of precision agriculture. Neither did they know that their heirs would use digital aerial photography to highlight and monitor soil patterns, drainage patterns, crop vigor, and crop stress. Yet, today's precision agriculture specialists (i.e., very so-phisticated farmers) hire companies like Positive Systems in Whitefish, Montana, to devise more efficient and cost-effective grid soil sampling strategies, evaluate drainage impacts, and measure performance using multispectral imagery.

The objective of the digital aerial photography is to correlate the Global Positioning Systems (GPS) and Geographic Information Systems (GIS) data that describe soil and yield characteristics identified *before* and *after* the growing season with imagery that can show the crop at various stages *during* the growing season. The goal is to understand not only what is going on in the fields, but why.

Source: "A Growing Industry, Digital Aerial Photography's Expanding Role in Precision Agriculture," *The Digital Flyer,* (1998), 3 (Summer), www.possys.com/digfly.

R&D–MARKETING INTERACTION

High-technology companies must effectively link research and development and marketing efforts in order to be successful.[19] Many studies highlight the importance of the nature of the interaction between R&D and marketing.[20] Firms in high-technology markets must excel at two things: the ability to come up with innovations constantly and the ability to commercialize these innovations into the kinds of products that capture customers' needs and preferences. Because one of marketing's tasks is to listen to the customer and come up with a pool of ideas, a strong marketing capability would imply that this pool of ideas is wider and, therefore, that the innovative technology can be applied to a wider range of industries. The voice that marketing brings to the innovation process must be joined with the knowledge that R&D brings.

Similar to the hurdles in becoming market oriented, high-tech firms face barriers to R&D–marketing integration. For example, the following are jokes made by engineers about marketing:[21]

- "Marketing Research: when marketing goes down to engineering to see what they're working on."
- "Marketing: what you do when your products aren't selling."

Because of its vital role in high-tech marketing success, this section provides supporting detail on R&D–marketing interactions. As shown in Figure 4-2, the nature of the cross-functional interaction must be effectively matched to the nature of the innovation (radical versus incremental). Second, firms must understand the barriers to interaction. Finally, ways to overcome barriers to interaction and, more specifically, how to enhance communication between marketing and engineering personnel are addressed.

Nature of R&D–Marketing Interaction: Breakthrough versus Incremental Innovations

Although the initial impetus for success in many high-tech firms comes from engineering breakthroughs, a successful transition to being market driven requires that input from marketing be both heard and responded to. Managing the R&D–marketing interface is vital for the firm to succeed as the market evolves from a supply-side, innovation-driven market to a demand-side, market-driven market.[22] Although R&D tends to play a stronger, more influential role in breakthrough products and marketing tends to play a greater role in more incremental products, for either R&D or marketing to overlook the vital perspective that the other brings to the table is a contributing factor to failure. Although cross-functional interaction is critical for both breakthrough and incremental products, consistent with the contingency model of marketing decision making, the nature of the interaction must be tailored to the type of innovation.

Research findings demonstrate that greater R&D–marketing integration in technical activities is required for *breakthrough products* than for incremental products.[23] Because the possibilities for the application of the new technology tend to be either nonobvious or very numerous, it can be difficult for engineering to proceed in isolation from market-related feedback. Hence, for breakthrough products, much of the early interface efforts between R&D and marketing should address what industry the company

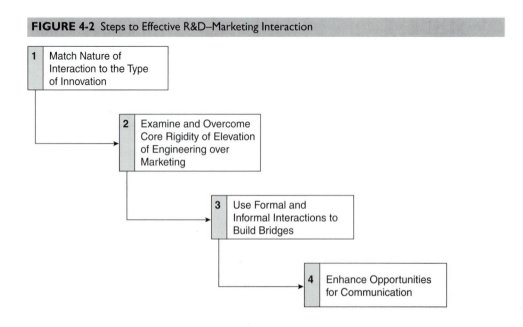

FIGURE 4-2 Steps to Effective R&D–Marketing Interaction

1. Match Nature of Interaction to the Type of Innovation

2. Examine and Overcome Core Rigidity of Elevation of Engineering over Marketing

3. Use Formal and Informal Interactions to Build Bridges

4. Enhance Opportunities for Communication

should compete in, what the conceivable market opportunities are, and what the market development priorities are.[24] The cross-functional interaction is helpful in determining desired product features and assessing engineering feasibility.

For *incremental innovations,* R&D again must actively participate in the market planning process, especially in setting objectives. R&D can ensure that marketing does not lose sight of R&D's vision for the product. Marketers can offer parameters for the engineers' efforts. Through give-and-take, the team members can agree on the target market, priorities, expectations, and timing. Moreover, R&D efforts don't end once selling beings; engineers should continue to help with brochures, research, pricing, sales promotion, trade shows, and customer visits. Research findings validate the importance of achieving R&D–marketing interaction for incremental innovations in the new-product development launch to establish the direction for commercialization, designing marketing plans, and implementing the launch.[25] Similarly, marketing should participate during the precommercialization period, bringing the voice of customer and marketplace into the development process.

Barriers to R&D–Marketing Collaboration

Despite the crucial need for effective R&D–marketing collaboration in high-tech product development, managing the reality of the interaction is very different.

One important barrier to R&D–marketing collaboration can be the corporate culture of a high-tech firm that respects and prefers engineering knowledge to marketing knowledge. This dominant engineering culture has been identified as a core rigidity in many high-tech firms.[26] High-level executives from firms with a dominant engineering culture typically come out of engineering; they are expected to develop a business orientation and understanding of customers as they advance. This type of technology-driven culture translates into a lack of regard and respect for marketing personnel. Obviously, it is very difficult for marketing personnel to be effective when the prevalent view is that "engineering does its thing and then marketing helps get it out the door."

The disdain for marketers also manifests itself in engineering taking on many tasks traditionally thought of as marketing, such as competitor analysis, product management, and so forth. The engineering culture further reinforces the dominant role of engineering and justifies not listening to marketing.[27] One of the most frequent reasons engineers give for not using market research or input from consumers is that "customers don't know what they want" or that "marketers don't know what they're talking about" (because they lack technical expertise). For example, "marketing wants everything right now at no cost—they have no concept of feasibility—they want a $5,000 Cadillac tomorrow."[28]

Even spatial dynamics contribute to the problem: Locating R&D and marketing in different parts of the building further contributes to the lack of collaboration. Yet, studies have found that increased R&D–marketing interaction increases the likelihood of a new-product development project's success.[29] In light of these barriers, how can R&D–marketing interaction be structured to enhance effectiveness?

Overcoming R&D–Marketing Barriers

Many firms specify a number of formal systems and processes by which marketing groups provide information to engineering groups.[30] For example, during specific review phases of the new-product development project, marketing offers input into the product requirements document and an understanding of the trade-offs involved in the myriad attributes being considered. In addition, during the annual planning process, marketing groups forecast revenue and profit for their market segments and indicate products and programs needed to achieve their goals. Finally, marketing communicates with engineering via the sales forecasting system.

Although these formal mechanisms exist for R&D–marketing interaction, they tend not to be the primary means by which such interaction occurs; indeed, they offer little in the way of marketing influence in the process. Such formal measures are often a chimera that gives the façade of R&D–marketing interaction but does little to make it productive.

In his study of a high-tech firm, John Workman[31] found that effective marketers also use the following methods to influence the product development process. Effective marketers

- Use informal networks and build bridges to engineering. They know the right people; they are in close physical and organizational proximity to engineering.
- Understand products and technology, which gives them credibility with engineers. Engineers "don't mind talking to marketers" if they know what they're talking about.
- Don't tell others what to do; rather, they ask questions, tell stories, and build consensus across groups.
- Form strategic coalitions that include high-level managers who push through changes that engineering resisted. However, there is a cost to this strategy, because it can alienate peers in engineering, so this option is the least preferred and should be saved for the most important issues.
- Recognize that it is the minor improvements to the new innovations that can be particularly important. "It's the 5% that's uninteresting to the engineering folks that can produce five times the levels of sales you would otherwise have."[32] In such a situation, effective marketers either undertake development themselves or turn to external partners to complete the work.

Even with these strategies, the reality still remains that marketing and R&D have very different world views, which can result in misunderstanding and conflicts in goals and solutions.[33] So, what factors affect the ability of the two groups to interact effectively? Most experts point to the need for enhanced communication.

Communication One commonly studied factor in enhancing R&D–marketing interaction is communication. Many argue that simply increasing the *frequency of interaction* between marketing and R&D will help improve the understanding and harmony between the two functions; increase their ability to cope with complex, dynamic environments; and lead to greater product success. Indeed, the use of market information provided by a marketing manager to nonmarketing managers (including not only R&D managers but also manufacturing and finance managers) requires a minimum threshold of interactions (approximately 125 interactions in a 3-month period).[34] However, too frequent communications can hurt perceptions of information quality (beyond 525 interactions in a 3-month period). Hence, increasing frequency of cross-functional communication may be warranted if the minimum threshold has not been reached, but increasing frequency may not always improve perceived quality and use of information.

This study[35] also found that when disseminated through *formal means* (those that are planned and verifiable), market information is used to a greater extent than when

disseminated through *informal channels.* Whereas informal channels, which are sponta-
neous and unplanned communication interactions, may provide greater openness and
clarification opportunities, formal interactions are more credible.

Additional findings show that when marketers perceive a greater frequency of
interaction, they also perceive more conflict with R&D personnel; however, that conflict doesn't necessarily result in a less effective relationship.[36] In fact, although many
studies have corroborated the need for close R&D–marketing interaction for new-
product development success, when relationships are too close, the desire to retain harmony precludes alternative viewpoints from emerging.[37] When such groupthink takes
over, adverse opinions are not expressed, and potential problems are not addressed,
resulting in lower product performance. A real question, then, is how to structure the
R&D–marketing collaboration for frequent interaction with the simultaneous ability to
challenge others' viewpoints. Having formalized roles within the group, with certain
members assigned the role of devil's advocate, may be helpful.

Other factors that affect the nature of the communication behaviors between marketing and R&D are discussed in Box 4-1 on information sharing norms and integration
of goals.

A Caveat   Each of these tools can help improve the flow of communication between
marketing and R&D. However, the nature of the communication must continue to be
solidly grounded in an *understanding of customer needs and wants.* As Figure 4-3 on "The
Rock Game" shows, marketing and engineering may think they are doing a good job of

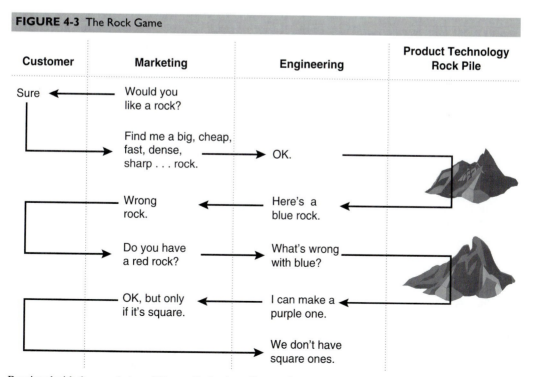

FIGURE 4-3 The Rock Game

Reprinted with the permission of Storage Technology Corporation, Louisville, Colorado.

BOX 4-1

Using Information Sharing Norms and Goal Integration to Increase R&D–Marketing Communication

Two factors that affect the nature of the communication behaviors between marketing and R&D are the presence of information sharing norms within the organization and the degree to which engineering goals are integrated with marketing goals (in which case the marketing manager's goal attainment depends on actions of the engineering counterpart and vice versa).

Information sharing norms indicate organizational expectations about the exchange of information between functions and can promote increased communication behaviors. However, the degree to which such norms really influence marketers' communication with engineering depends on on how strongly marketing managers identify with the marketing function. Marketing managers *who identify more strongly with the organization as a whole* (than with the marketing function) communicate more bidirectionally when information sharing norms are stressed.

Similarly, *integrated goals* suggest that the organization's needs are superordinate to the goals of the individual functional units and again can promote increased collaboration and cooperation. Marketing managers who *identify very strongly with the marketing function* are more likely to communicate more frequently and more bidirectionally when integrated goals are stressed. However, marketing managers who identify very strongly with their functional area of marketing also resort to coercion to ensure that the engineering contact comply with their functional perspective on organizational issues. In this case, integrated goals increase the coerciveness of influence attempts by high-functional-identification managers, because of their emphasis on functional solutions within the organization.

So, how should managers in high-tech firms use this information in facilitating R&D–marketing interaction? First, managers need to establish policies to encourage information sharing norms when marketing managers identify more strongly with the organization as a whole. Second, managers should set integrated goals for marketing and R&D when marketing managers identify more strongly with the marketing function specifically. Note, however, the increased risk of coercive influence attempts in this latter case.

Source: Fisher, Robert J., Elliot Maltz, and Bernard J. Jaworski (1997), "Enhancing Communication Between Marketing and Engineering: The Moderating Role of Relative Functional Identification," *Journal of Marketing,* 61 (3), pp. 54–70.

interacting, but in reality, they have not accurately captured or conveyed the customer's needs in the process.

As a case in point, a health care company recently adopted a new information system to manage customer records. This new information system included customized software from the vendor, which allowed the health care company to customize the screens and menus for its caseworkers, based on certain treatment criteria and standards. Unfortunately, in tailoring the software to its needs, the health care company encountered a series of bugs and other issues (i.e., security concerns), which required extensive rework on the part of the software vendor. In order to communicate their needs and concerns, the health care company personnel had talked to either the salesperson or a customer-support person, who, in turn, expressed the customer's concerns to the software engineers. The filtering and recommunicating of the customer's needs had resulted in several misunderstandings between the engineers and the customer. Despite this, the customer was not allowed to communicate directly with the software engineers. And why not? The reason given by the software vendor was that "its engineers' time was too costly to be spent in talking to customers"!

In summary, cross-functional integration between marketing and R&D is a key driver in diffusing market and customer knowledge among all members of a project team in high-tech firms. This integration ensures that an understanding of market needs, desires, and behavior in the early stages of development constitutes the foundation for technological applications—applications that are valued by customers. This diffusion of customer and market knowledge to the engineering team is enhanced by allowing them to have direct and repeated contact with customers and other outside sources of information—and, as discussed previously, having a strong connection between all internal departments and customers is part of a firm's market orientation. This section's Technology Expert's View from the Trenches is offered by Jennifer Longstaff, whose perspective is influenced by her background in both engineering and marketing.

TECHNOLOGY EXPERT'S VIEW FROM THE TRENCHES

Engineering–Marketing Collaboration

JENNIFER LONGSTAFF
MS Computer Science, MBA Technology and Innovation
Management, Technical Marketing Engineer,
Xilinx Inc., Boulder, Colorado

The relationship between engineering and marketing is often a source of conflict, even in the most cooperative, consensus-driven, proactive companies. In a market-driven, product-based company, *marketing's role* is typically to define a product based on input from customers and its knowledge of market needs. Marketing positions and delivers the finished product and then solicits customer feedback on how well the product has delivered needed solutions and has fared against competition. This feedback gets rolled into the next cycle of product definition as the product is improved. Marketing manages this cyclical process.

Engineering's role typically is to use the marketing definition and implement the product within a particular development time frame. Engineering must make it known to marketing whether marketing's product definitions are feasible and work with marketing to revise the product definitions if not.

Engineering and marketing communicate with each other throughout the definition and development process. Engineering suggests product design ideas based on implementation feasibility. Marketing monitors development progress, manages peripheral tasks (such as test plans, documentation, schedules), clarifies definition as needed throughout the development period, and ensures that the product being developed matches the definition.

Both groups feel a sense of "ownership" of the products, each taking pride in well-developed, useful products that meet customer needs. Marketing feels ownership much like an architect feels like a building is "my building, since I designed it." Engineering feels the same ownership, like a builder would feel it is "my building, since I built it." Each group feels that the product is *its own* product. While this joint-ownership feeling may promote a cooperative working relationship, it is also the root cause of conflict.

The reason problems occur in this process is *both groups begin to assume they can do the other's job better.*

Marketing makes assumptions as to the difficulty and feasibility of implementation. Marketing groups in high-tech companies are comprised of engineers as well, so when asking engineering for product features or enhancements, marketing believes it knows how difficult the development job is. Therefore, marketing often tells engineering how to develop its products and how long development should take.

Meanwhile, engineering personnel, working on a technical product, often feel that they are familiar enough with the customers (since the customers are engineers as well) that they can define the product better than marketing. In this case, engineering doesn't trust marketing, doesn't acknowledge any expertise from marketing, and doesn't acknowledge that marketing's job *is* to know the customers and the market. Engineers begin to ignore marketing's specifications, choosing instead to "go with their gut" and implement to their own designs.

Engineering also sees marketing as "taking all the glory for the product that engineering built." While this may be somewhat true, engineering doesn't appreciate that marketing also must take and respond to complaints from customers and the sales force. Since no products will be perfect, and all products will pale in comparison to some part of the competition in the fast-paced, ever-changing technical market, there are always complaints that marketing must address. Engineers often don't realize this aspect of marketing, since they don't interact directly with customers or the sales force.

How can this situation be improved? First of all, it's important for both groups to realize that the perpetuation of this conflict is a waste of time and a distraction from the product development work. This realization may be difficult, due to the potential for the conflict to become emotional, depending on the personalities involved.

Second, rather than make assumptions as to the difficulty of the engineering tasks it assigns, marketing would gain more engineering cooperation by prioritizing the tasks, using engineering input as to which ones are indeed more difficult or time-consuming. Although marketing drives the products, it is engineering that brings the marketing definition to fruition.

Marketing also needs to remember that engineering controls the situation during the product development cycle and give the engineers the information necessary for them to get the job finished. Marketing can also make engineering's job easier by taking on the administrative parts of the project, such as the management and coordination of testing, documentation, customer training, positioning, roll-out plans, and so on.

Third, it is not uncommon for personnel in a technology company to move between marketing and engineering groups. A savvy manager can determine which engineers would benefit from some experience in marketing and vice-versa, and might offer those employees an opportunity to move across groups. Even if only for one definition–development cycle, a rotation such as this will help the marketing–engineering conflict by giving employees a chance to see how the other side works!

Summary

This chapter has focused specifically on the final two building blocks in the organizational foundations for high-technology marketing effectiveness: being market oriented and having effective R&D–marketing interactions. These final two building blocks complement those established in the prior two chapters: relationship marketing (partnerships and alliances), access to resources, and maintaining innovativeness through creative destruction, corporate imagination, expeditionary marketing, and a culture of innovation.

Many of the topics addressed in these past three chapters deal with the organizational culture and processes for being innovative, for valuing market information, and for allowing that information to be shared cross-functionally. In that sense, the topics share the common tie of being housed within the firm itself.

Chapters 5 and 6 take a different perspective and more directly address issues related to customers: how marketers can gather information about customers, not only to develop successful products but also to forecast the market size for the new innovation, and issues customers face in adopting high-tech products. Figure 4-4 illustrates our continued movement across the high-tech marketing bridge.

Discussion Questions

1. What are the characteristics of a market-driven organization?
2. What are the advantages and pitfalls of being market oriented?
3. How does a firm balance when to listen to customers and when to ignore them?
4. Why is R&D–marketing interaction so important in high-tech firms?
5. What are the barriers to such interaction?
6. How are they overcome?

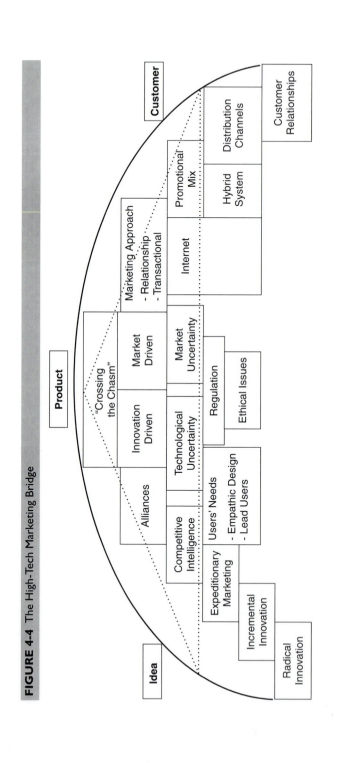

FIGURE 4-4 The High-Tech Marketing Bridge

Glossary

Customer/market orientation. A philosophy of doing business that emphasizes the shared gathering, dissemination, and utilization of market intelligence as the basis for decision making.

Endnotes

1. Dutta, Shantanu, Om Narasimhan, and Surendra Rajiv (1999), "Success in High-Technology Markets: Is Marketing Capability Critical?" *Marketing Science,* 18 (4), p. 547.
2. Gatignon, Hubert and Jean-Marc Xuereb (1997), "Strategic Orientation of the Firm and New Product Performance," *Journal of Marketing Research,* 34 (February), pp. 77–90.
3. Shapiro, Benson (1988), "What the Hell Is 'Market Oriented'?" *Harvard Business Review,* November–December, pp. 119–125.
4. Kohli, Ajay K. and Bernard J. Jaworski (1990), "Market Orientation: The Construct, Research Propositions, and Managerial Implications," *Journal of Marketing,* 54 (April), pp. 1–18.
5. McWilliams, Gary and Marcia Stepanek (1998), "Taming the Info Monster," *Business Week,* June 22, pp. 170–172.
6. This example is cited in Leonard-Barton, Dorothy (1992), "Core Capabilities and Core Rigidities: A Paradox in Managing New Product Development," *Strategic Management Journal,* 13, pp. 111–125.
7. Leonard-Barton, Dorothy, Edith Wilson, and John Doyle (1995), "Commercializing Technology: Understanding User Needs," in *Business Marketing Strategy,* V. K. Rangan et al. (eds.), Chicago: Irwin, pp. 281–305.
8. Martin, Justin (1995), "Ignore Your Customer," *Fortune,* May 1, pp. 121–126.
9. Martin, Justin (1995), "Ignore Your Customer," *Fortune,* May 1, p. 122.
10. Martin, Justin (1995), "Ignore Your Customer," *Fortune,* May 1, p. 121.
11. DeYoung, Garrett (1997), "Listen, Then Design," *Industry Week,* February 17, pp. 76–80; Martin, Justin (1995), "Ignore Your Customer," *Fortune,* May 1, pp. 121–126; Leonard-Barton, Dorothy, Edith Wilson, and John Doyle (1995), "Commercializing Technology: Understanding User Needs," in *Business Marketing Strategy,* V. K. Rangan et al. (eds.), Chicago: Irwin, pp. 281–305.
12. Christensen, Clayton and Joseph Bower (1995), "Customer Power, Strategic Investment, and the Failure of Leading Firms," *Strategic Management Journal,* 17, pp. 197–218.
13. Leonard-Barton, Dorothy, Edith Wilson, and John Doyle (1995), "Commercializing Technology: Understanding User Needs," in *Business Marketing Strategy,* V. K. Rangan et al. (eds.), Chicago: Irwin, pp. 281–305.
14. Leonard-Barton, Dorothy and Jeffrey F. Rayport (1997), "Spark Innovation Through Empathic Design," *Harvard Business Review,* November–December, pp. 102–113.
15. Byrnes, Nanette and Paul Judge (1999), "Internet Anxiety," *Business Week,* June 28, p. 84.
16. Chandy, Rajesh K. and Gerard J. Tellis (1998), "Organizing for Radical Product Innovation: The Overlooked Role of Willingness to Cannibalize," *Journal of Marketing Research,* 35 (November), pp. 474–487.
17. Christensen, Clayton and Joseph Bower (1995), "Customer Power, Strategic Investment, and the Failure of Leading Firms," *Strategic Management Journal,* 17, pp. 197–218.
18. Martin, Justin (1995), "Ignore Your Customer," *Fortune,* May 1, p. 124.
19. Song, X. Michael and Mark E. Parry (1997), "A Cross-National Comparative Study of New Product Development Processes: Japan and the United States," *Journal of Marketing,* 61 (2), pp. 1–18.
20. Griffin, Abbie and John Hauser (1996), "Integrating R&D and Marketing: A Review and Analysis of the Literature," *Journal of Product Innovation Management,* 13, pp. 191–215; Gupta, Ashok K., S. P. Raj, and David L. Wilemon (1986), "A Model for Studying R&D–Marketing Interface in the Product

Innovation Process," *Journal of Marketing,* 50 (April), pp. 7–17; Dutta, Shantanu, Om Narasimhan, and Surendra Rajiv (1999), "Success in High-Technology Markets: Is Marketing Capability Critical?" *Marketing Science,* 18 (4), p. 547.

21. Workman, John (1993), "Marketing's Limited Role in New Product Development in One Computer Systems Firm," *Journal of Marketing Research,* 30 (November), pp. 405–421.

22. Shanklin, William and John Ryans (1984), "Organizing for High-Tech Marketing," *Harvard Business Review,* 62 (November–December), pp. 164–171.

23. Song, X. Michael and JinHong Zie (1996), "The Effect of R&D–Manufacturing–Marketing Integration on New Product Performance in Japanese and U.S. Firms: A Contingency Perspective," report summary #96-117, Cambridge, MA: Marketing Science Institute.

24. Shanklin, William and John Ryans (1984), "Organizing for High-Tech Marketing," *Harvard Business Review,* 62 (November–December), pp. 164–171.

25. Song, X. Michael and JinHong Zie (1996), "The Effect of R&D–Manufacturing–Marketing Integration on New Product Performance in Japanese and U.S. Firms: A Contingency Perspective," report summary #96-117, Cambridge, MA: Marketing Science Institute.

26. Leonard-Barton, Dorothy (1992), "Core Capabilities and Core Rigidities: A Paradox in Managing New Product Development," *Strategic Management Journal,* 13, pp. 111–125.

27. Kunda, Gideon (1992), *Engineering Culture: Culture and Control in a High-Tech Organization,* Philadelphia: Temple University Press.

28. Workman, John (1993), "Marketing's Limited Role in New Product Development in One Computer Systems Firm," *Journal of Marketing Research,* 30 (November), pp. 405–421.

29. Ayers, Doug, Robert Dahlstrom, and Steven J. Skinner (1997), "An Exploratory Investiga-

tion of Organizational Antecedents to New Product Success," *Journal of Marketing Research,* 34 (February), pp. 107–116.

30. Workman, John (1993), "Marketing's Limited Role in New Product Development in One Computer Systems Firm," *Journal of Marketing Research,* 30 (November), pp. 405–421.

31. Workman, John (1993), "Marketing's Limited Role in New Product Development in One Computer Systems Firm," *Journal of Marketing Research,* 30 (November), pp. 405–421.

32. Workman, John (1993), "Marketing's Limited Role in New Product Development in One Computer Systems Firm," *Journal of Marketing Research,* 30 (November), p. 415.

33. Gupta, Ashok K., S. P. Raj, and David L. Wilemon (1986), "A Model for Studying R&D–Marketing Interface in the Product Innovation Process," *Journal of Marketing,* 50 (April), pp. 7–17; Griffin, Abbie and John R. Hauser (1992), "Patterns of Communication Among Marketing, Engineering and Manufacturing—A Comparison Between Two New Product Teams," *Management Science,* 38 (March), pp. 360–373.

34. Maltz, Elliot and Ajay K. Kohli (1996), "Market Intelligence Dissemination Across Functional Boundaries," *Journal of Marketing Research,* 33 (February), pp. 47–61.

35. Maltz, Elliot and Ajay K. Kohli (1996), "Market Intelligence Dissemination Across Functional Boundaries," *Journal of Marketing Research,* 33 (February), pp. 47–61.

36. Ruekert, Robert and Orville Walker (1987), "Interactions Between Marketing and R&D Departments in Implementing Different Strategies," *Strategic Management Journal,* 8, pp. 233–248.

37. Ayers, Doug, Robert Dahlstrom, and Steven J. Skinner (1997), "An Exploratory Investigation of Organizational Antecedents to New Product Success," *Journal of Marketing Research,* 34 (February), pp. 107–116.

Recommended Readings

Market Orientation

Day, George (1994), "The Capabilities of Market-Driven Organizations," *Journal of Marketing,* 58 (October), pp. 37–52.

Jaworski, B. and A. Kohli (1993), "Market Orientation: Antecedents and Consequences," *Journal of Marketing,* 57 (July), pp. 53–70.

Kohli, A. and B. Jaworski (1990), "Market Orientation: The Construct, Research Propositions, and Managerial Implications," *Journal of Marketing,* 54 (April), pp. 1–18.

McKenna, Regis (1991), "Marketing Is Everything," *Harvard Business Review,* January–February, pp. 65–79.

Narver, John C. and Stanley F. Slater (1990), "The Effect of a Market Orientation on Business Profitability," *Journal of Marketing,* 54 (October), pp. 20–35.

Slater, Stanley F. and John C. Narver (1993), "Product–Market Strategy and Performance: An Analysis of the Miles and Snow Strategy Types," *European Journal of Marketing,* 27 (10), pp. 33–51.

Slater, Stanley F. and John C. Narver (1994), "Market-Oriented Isn't Enough: Build a Learning Organization," report #94–101, Cambridge, MA: Marketing Science Institute.

Slater, Stanley F. and John C. Narver (1994), "Does Competitive Environment Moderate the Market Orientation–Performance Relationship?" *Journal of Marketing,* 58 (1), pp. 46–55.

Slater, Stanley F. and John C. Narver (1995), "Market Orientation and the Learning Organization," *Journal of Marketing,* 59 (3), pp. 63–74.

Slater, Stanley F. and John C. Narver (1998), "Customer-Led and Market-Oriented: Let's Not Confuse the Two," *Strategic Management Journal,* 19 (10), pp. 1001–1006.

R&D–Marketing Interaction

Gupta, Ashok K., S. P. Raj, and David Wilemon (1985), "The R&D–Marketing Interface in High-Tech Firms," *Journal of Product Innovation Management,* 2 (March), pp. 12–24.

Song, X. Michael and Mark E. Parry (1992), "The R&D–Marketing Interface in Japanese High-Technology Firms," *Journal of Product Innovation Management,* 9 (2), pp. 91–112.

Song, X. Michael and Mark E. Parry (1993), "R&D–Marketing Integration in Japanese High-Technology Firms: Hypothesis and Empirical Evidence," *Journal of Academy of Marketing Science,* 21 (2), pp. 125–133.

Olson, Eric M., Orville C. Walker, Jr., and Robert W. Ruekert (1995), "Organizing for Effective New Product Development: The Moderating Role of Product Innovativeness," *Journal of Marketing,* 59 (1), pp. 48–62.

Ruekert, Robert and Orville Walker (1987), "Marketing's Interaction with Other Functional Units: A Conceptual Framework and Empirical Evidence," *Journal of Marketing,* 51 (January), pp. 1–19.

CHAPTER 5

Marketing Research in High-Tech Markets

As we've seen in the prior chapters, technology marketers face a paradox. On the one hand, customers find it difficult to articulate what their specific needs are; on the other hand, high-tech firms must keep a finger on the pulse of the market in order to enhance their odds of success. Winning high-tech firms do not first develop new products and then worry later about how to market them; and taking calculated risks does not mean ignoring customers. High-tech firms must incorporate information about customers into the product development process, despite the inherent difficulties and the all-too-common tendency to overlook them.

For example, in the on-line arena, Amazon.com built its site with the visitor experience in mind. However, because site features are easily copied, Amazon's ability to innovate is based on identifying novel ways to deal with customers and leapfrog its competitors. "We ask customers what they want," says Jeff Bezos, CEO.[1] Amazon.com encourages feedback, sorts through purchase histories to identify customer preferences, conducts focus groups, and collects information in ways that don't impose on customers. Because of this superior customer knowledge, even if other sites offer better prices, customers tend not to switch. As one customer says, in a useful analogy: "I'm happily married, so it doesn't matter how cute the guys are I meet."[2] Other Internet companies, such as REI.com, use customer feedback to make sites easier to use or to add new features.

Ultimately, what separates companies is the kind of information they collect on customers and from whom they collect it.[3] Hence, this chapter focuses on gathering information in high-tech markets. High-tech marketing research tools, including empathic design and lead users, are addressed, as is quality function deployment, a tool to link customer input to product design. Moreover, a look at the gathering of competitive intelligence in high-tech markets is provided. Finally, effective forecasting in high-tech markets is paramount to making good decisions. This chapter begins with insights on the market research process from Bonnie Pinkerton, future product manager at Hewlett-Packard.

GATHERING INFORMATION: HIGH-TECH MARKETING RESEARCH TOOLS

High-tech environments are fraught with change and uncertainty. Customers have difficulty envisioning how technology can meet their needs. They aren't aware of what new technologies are available or how those technologies might be used to solve current problems. They might not even be aware of the needs they have. Moreover, in this environment, firms must accelerate the product development process, closing the time between

Using Market Research to Drive Successful Innovative Products

BONNIE PINKERTON
Future Product Manager, Hewlett-Packard, Loveland, Colorado

Ever wonder how *new* products are created? What about *new product categories* that don't exist today? These are very relevant questions to Future Product Managers who work with technologies that *replace* existing products, or radical innovations. Examples of radical innovations include digital cameras, portable CD music players, or microwave ovens when they were first introduced. In all these examples, there existed a "current" product that satisfied the customer need for such things as capturing memories, listening to music, or cooking food.

Gathering customer feedback is a very important step in all phases of the product development cycle, but how can it be applied to products that don't exist? Hewlett-Packard faced this challenge in 1995 when it researched the digital photography market. HP saw a market opportunity in digitally capturing and printing high-resolution images that could compete with the traditional silver-halide photography market. To start, HP had to ask

- Who is the customer?
- What would the user like to do?
- What problems would digital photography solve?

These are critical questions to answer during the investigation phase of product development.

HP set out to learn what customers liked and disliked about the traditional silver-halide photography process through a number of focus groups. These focus groups provided valuable insights about ease-of-use, quality, photo storage and retrieval, getting the "right" picture, red-eye, etc. Could digital photography improve the traditional photography process through offering benefits that customers valued? Solving customer frustrations would accelerate the adoption of a new technology.

Another step in the research process involved enlisting the help of "thought leaders"—individuals who are recognized as experts in a particular field. Individuals with backgrounds in computing, photography, anthropology, and psychology were brought together in a moderated session to give their perspectives. This provided HP insights into understanding trends, market readiness, and when certain existing technology constraints (examples here included camera resolution, costs, etc.) would be resolved. Insights were also gained about the role that photography plays in society.

Cross-functional design teams were also involved in additional thought-provoking "ideation" sessions. This phase of work built on the knowledge gained from the previous customer focus groups and thought-leader insights. Through creative exercises, "out-of-the-box" ideas and concepts were generated. These ideas were captured through real-time artist renditions, and a series of early product concepts were generated. Using customer needs as the basis for sorting and prioritizing concepts, the concepts were screened, and the remaining ideas were developed in more detail, keeping in mind design feasibility, cost, and schedule. The most promising concepts were then presented to customers at a series of focus groups.

To gain valuable customer input on future "new" products, consumers need to envision the future. A video may be created to take people into the future—it should show how a task would be done in the future, the product, etc. Mocked-up products, artist's drawings, and examples of product output are also very useful tools. The more realistic the "props," the better a focus group is able to respond to research needs, particularly when it involves a radical change from today's product. Customer feedback on product concepts will also help

"flush out" musts versus wants in a new product definition.

Often, as a result of focus group feedback, real-time product concepts are created and tested in future focus groups. For this reason, it is very important that the cross-functional team participate in observing the focus groups and listen to customers discuss their likes, dislikes, and needs.

The techniques described above have been used in numerous investigations where a disruptive technology, or radical innovation, is involved. The challenge for consumer products, like digital cameras, will continue to be the speed at which a group is able to execute the process, synthesize the information, and then make critical product development decisions.

idea to market introduction. Successful firms in high-tech markets collect useful information to guide decisions.

As Figure 5-1 shows, research methods must be aligned with the type of innovation being developed.[4] This is consistent with the contingency theory of high-technology marketing. For incremental innovations, new-product developments are in alignment with the current market. Customer needs are generally known, and traditional marketing research can help companies understand such needs. Indeed, traditional marketing research techniques are most effective when a product or service is well understood by customers, or when the customer is familiar with possible solutions because of related experience in other contexts. Traditional marketing research techniques such as focus groups, surveys, conjoint analysis, and multidimensional scaling can be useful to match new-product characteristics with customer demand. Readers interested in these standard marketing research tools may consult one of the many excellent resources available.[5]

However, standard marketing research tools typically don't address new uses or new attributes and are less effective when customers are unfamiliar with the product being researched. Hence, for breakthrough products or for markets with rapid change, standard marketing research techniques might not provide useful information. In the extreme, where technical solutions precede customer needs, market research might consist largely of guided intuition. Industry experts may be helpful, and the creation of different future scenarios can be used to guide decision making based on intuition.[6]

In the midrange (between incremental and radical innovation), two very useful techniques are empathic design and lead users.

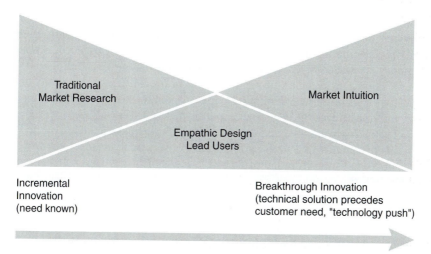

Traditional
Market Research

Market Intuition

Empathic Design
Lead Users

Incremental
Innovation
(need known)

Breakthrough Innovation
(technical solution precedes
customer need, "technology push")

FIGURE 5-1 Aligning Market Research with the Type of Innovation

Source: Adapted from Leonard-Barton, Dorothy, Edith Wilson, and John Doyle (1995), "Commercializing Technology: Understanding User Needs," in *Business Marketing Strategy*, V. K. Rangan et al. (eds.), Chicago: Irwin, pp. 281–305. Reprinted with permission of the McGraw-Hill Companies.

Empathic Design

Being market oriented in high-tech markets means that observation of customers (what they do) is often more useful in developing novel insights than is asking customers more direct questions (what they say). **Empathic design** is a research technique based on the idea that users may not be able to articulate their needs clearly. It focuses on understanding user needs through empathy with the user world, rather than from users' direct articulation of their needs.[7] For example, users may have developed "workarounds"— modifications to usage situations that are inconvenient yet so habitual that users are not even conscious of them. Or customers may not be able to envision the ways new technology could be used. Based in anthropology and ethnography, empathic design allows the marketer to develop a deep understanding of the current user environment, to extrapolate the evolution of that environment into the future, and to imagine the future need that technology can satisfy.[8]

Insights from Empathic Design   Observation of customers can provide illuminating insights when customers find it difficult to articulate their needs. For example, observations of customers using the product allow marketers to identify[9]

- *Triggers of use.* These are the circumstances that prompt people to use a product or service. For example, when Hewlett-Packard watched customers using its personal digital assistants (PDAs), it found that what it thought was the key reason people used PDAs—to use spreadsheet software—was strongly augmented by using the product for personal organizing functions.

- *How users cope with imperfect work environments and unarticulated user needs.* For example, when engineers from a manufacturer of lab equipment visited a customer, they noticed the equipment emitted an unpleasant smell when being used for certain uses. Customers were so accustomed to the smell that they had never mentioned it. In response, the company added a venting hood to its product line, which actually became a compelling sales point when comparing the product to those of competitors.

  As another example of the use of empathic design to show how users cope with imperfect work environments and unarticulated needs, the design team of the Power Tool Division at Ingersoll-Rand used customer observation to improve the designs of its products. Upon visiting factories where the tools were used, the design team found that half the people using wrenches on an auto assembly line were women, who typically have smaller hands than men. The women found it difficult to grasp the tools properly. As a result, the team developed a two-size variable-grip wrench that was made even easier to hold by using rubberized plastic. An unexpected bonus was that the wrench was a big hit in Japan, where hands generally are smaller than in the United States.[10]
- *Different usage situations.* When Intuit's developers observed customers using their Quicken software, they found that many small business owners were using Quicken to keep their books, an important market that Intuit has since targeted more specifically.
- *Customization of products of which marketers are unaware.* For example, in studying consumers' use of beepers and cell phones, researchers observed individuals giving special beeper codes to friends to screen out undesired calls. Based on this observation, companies have creatively implemented the filtering capability on cell phones.
- *The importance of intangible attributes that even customers may not articulate.* These include smell, feel, and so forth, which frequently aren't addressed in traditional surveys.

Empathic design techniques exploit a company's existing technological capabilities in the widest sense of the term. Company observers carry the knowledge of what is possible for the company to do. When that knowledge is combined with what customers need, existing organizational capabilities can be redirected toward new markets. A note of caution: Empathic design techniques do not replace market research; rather, they contribute to the flow of ideas that warrant additional testing before committing to the project.[11]

Process to Conduct Empathic Design Leonard-Barton and Rayport[12] offer a five-step process to conducting empathic design.

1. *Observation.* At the first step of undertaking an empathic design study, researchers should clarify the following:
   - *Who should be observed?* Although "customers" is a logical answer, often non-customers, customers of customers, or a group of individuals who collectively perform a task may provide useful information.
   - *Who should do the observing?* Differences in perception and background lead different people to notice very different details when observing the same situation. Hence, it is best to use a small cross-disciplinary team to conduct observational studies. Members should be open-minded and curious and understand the value of observation. For this reason, hiring trained ethnographers to assist in the study is useful. Moreover, as we learned in the prior chapter, those who know the capabilities of a particular technology are often *not* the ones who are in contact with the customer

(who knows what needs to be done). Hence, the process of conducting empathic design requires cross-functional collaboration between marketing and R&D.

- *What behavior should be observed?* It is important to observe the "subjects" in as normal an environment as possible. Although some believe that observation changes people's behavior (which is probably unavoidable), some alternatives to observation are experiments in highly artificial lab settings or focus groups, both of which also have limitations. The idea here is to gather new kinds of insights that other research techniques cannot.

2. *Capture the data.* At the second step of the empathic design process, researchers need to establish how to record the information. Most data from empathic design projects are gathered from visual, auditory, and sensory cues. Hence, photographs and videographs can be useful tools that capture information lost in verbal descriptions, such as spatial arrangements.

    Whereas standard research techniques may rely on a sequence of questioning, empathic design asks very few questions other than to explore, in a very open-ended fashion, why people are doing things. Researchers may want to know what problems the user is encountering in the course of the observed activity.

3. *Reflection and analysis.* At the third step, the different team members and other colleagues review the team's observations contained in the captured data. The purpose is to identify all of the customers' possible problems and needs.

4. *Brainstorm for solutions.* At the fourth step, brainstorming is used to transform observations into ideas for solutions.

5. *Develop prototypes of possible solutions.* At the fifth step, researchers need to consider more concretely how possible solutions might be implemented. The more radical an innovation, the harder it is to understand how it should look and function. Researchers can stimulate useful communication by creating some prototype of the idea. Such prototypes, because of their concreteness, can clarify the concept for the development team, allow insights from others who weren't on the team, and stimulate reaction and discussion with potential customers. Simulations and role playing can be useful prototypes when a tangible representation of the product cannot be made.

Increasingly, high-tech firms, such as Hewlett-Packard, IBM, Motorola, and Xerox, are using empathic design to augment their traditional marketing research practices. They are hiring social scientists, anthropologists, and psychologists to help them figure out how people use products. By observing customers at work, the research technique helps to close the gap between what people say they do and what they really do. Ethnographers tend to study relatively few subjects, chosen with great care, looking for big insights rather than statistical data.

Example[13] How does Intel learn about how customers work and use electronic equipment? How does the knowledge it learns help Intel design more effective products in the future? Intel has hired an eight-person team of "design ethnographers" who go to customer sites to observe customers at work. Their goal is to learn about how customers work and use tools that they can then use to help Intel design more effective products in the future.

At first, the corporate culture within Intel—particularly the R&D folks—did not take the ethnographers seriously. Indeed, their presence was an acknowledgment that the personal computer had shortcomings, and in the Intel culture, that acknowledgment put them at odds with most other employees. But the success rate when technical engineers design what they think other people want is only 20%, says Intel chairman, Andy Grove. For example, Grove believes that Intel wouldn't have sunk millions of dollars into its Proshare videophone, introduced by Intel in the early 1990s, if it had done more ethnographic research. The quality of the video was slow, jerky, and not synchronized with the sound. However, Intel loved the phone because it required significant computing power, based on the underlying microprocessors. Yet consumers hated it, because the out-of-sync video resulted in miscues when people nodded or shook their heads.

So, Intel has used empathic design in a variety of industries and with different customer groups to gain new insights. For example, its design team has spent time observing people working in the salmon industry off the coast of Alaska. The team was trying to understand how technology, such as satellite-guided locators instead of helicopters to monitor fishing boats, would help. Other insights have come from observing business owners. In observing their often harried schedules, the design team learned that businesspeople need a tool that can capture all the messages and phone numbers they write down on Post-It notes, such as an electronic organizer that recognizes handwriting.

Does the nature of being observed change people's behavior? The Intel team finds that most people love to be observed and eventually lower their guard when they are being studied by the researchers. And ethnographic researchers are masters at getting people to feel at ease under observation. For example, one of the Intel team members has spent hundreds of hours with teenagers in their bedrooms, using videotapes to catalog their behaviors and belongings, from dirty laundry to posters. His goal is to find out more about how they live and what technology they might find useful. Some of his insights: Teens should be able to send pictures to each other instantaneously, over phone lines to computers and into flat-display bedside picture frames. They also need handheld computers that allow them to communicate schedule changes to their parents when they're out and about.

The bottom line is that what a user does with a product, rather than what the product can do, ultimately drives its success.

The process of using empathic design tools is very similar in flavor to the notion of customer visits. A **customer visit program,** or a systematic program of visiting customers with a cross-functional team to understand customer needs, when implemented correctly, can also lead to significant insights and benefits for high-tech marketers. Box 5-1 provides some additional insights on a customer visit program.

Lead Users

Another research technique helpful in high-tech environments is the lead user process.[14] Used to generate ideas for breakthrough innovations, the lead user process collects information about both needs and solutions from the leading edges of a company's target market and from markets that face similar problems in a more extreme form. The types of customers that tend to innovate are **lead users**—customers that are well ahead of market trends and have needs that go far beyond those of the average user.[15] Lead users may face needs months or years before the bulk of the marketplace and, as such, are positioned to benefit significantly by obtaining solutions to those needs now. In some cases, lead users may have even developed a solution to their needs that marketers can then

Customer Visit Programs

The idea of using customer visits for market research has developed in response to the challenges faced by managers in many industries. Customer visits are more than a tool to groom customer relationships; they offer a variety of benefits, including the following:

- *Face-to-face communication.* Development of new-to-the-world products benefits from the unique capacity of personal communication to facilitate the transfer of complex, ambiguous, and novel information.

- *Field research.* Doing research at the customer's place of business allows personnel to see the product in use, talk to actual users of the product, and gain a better understanding of the product's role in the customer's total operation.

- *Firsthand knowledge.* Everyone believes his or her own eyes and ears first. When key players hear about problems and needs from the most credible source—the customers—responsiveness is enhanced.

- *Interactive conversation.* The ability to clarify, follow up, switch gears, and address surprising and unexpected insights provides depth to interactions.

- *Inclusion of multiple decision makers.* Many technology products are purchased by groups of people, and customer visits allow all of the players' various needs and desires to be addressed.

To realize these advantages, customer visits are much more than merely talking to people. Good customer visit programs can reveal new pieces of information that may have a direct impact on products or services offered to customers. How should customer visits be structured to maximize the benefits?

1. Get engineers in front of customers. It is vital that cross-functional teams participate in the customer visit program. Relying solely on marketing personnel to conduct customer visits makes cross-functional collaboration unlikely, and marketing may lack credibility with key technical people. The people who participate in the visits must be the ones who will use the information. Teams should include, at a minimum, an engineer, a product-marketing representative, and the account manager. For cross-functional teams to work smoothly in customer visits, good teamwork must exist between engineering and marketing.

Successful customer visit programs are part of the corporate culture and are enthusiastically embraced by the technical team. R&D managers who say, "Go see the customers yourself," or "Take the project team out to visit customers" are vital to communicating the appropriate attitude. Having only marketers go out to visit customers does not substitute for a commitment on the part of the entire organization to understand customers. Finally, having only high-level executives on customer visits makes other company personnel question the degree to which a customer focus is real or just window dressing.

2. Visit different kinds of customers. Ideally teams should visit multiple customers to get more than just an idiosyncratic reading on customer needs. The common tendency in customer visit programs is to visit only national accounts. Although visiting national accounts may result in increasing satisfaction with these accounts, market share may shrink if the firm falls into the trap of developing products that exactly suit an ever-smaller number of customers. Often the freshest perspectives and greatest surprises come from atypical sources, such as competitors' customers, global customers, lost leads, lead users, distribution channel members, or "internal" customers of the firm's own field staff. Customer councils are another important source of information. They are typically designed to get feedback and share perspectives and to build stronger customer relationships. They offer the potential of synergy through group action.

3. Get out of the conference room. Because customers often don't realize and cannot vocalize specific needs, it is important to listen and observe what they do. This is especially important for companies that tend to invite customers to their own premises. When a firm hosts its customers' visits on the premises, the visits tend to take place in the company's visit center. Such a policy may cut costs and save time in the customer visit program, but it puts the customers in a passive role; the company is typically showcasing its products and giving VIP treatment to customers.

4. Take every opportunity to ask questions. Customer visit programs are useful not only for new-product development ideas but also for customer satisfaction studies, identification of new market segments, and a myriad of other issues. Interesting questions to ask include

- If you could change any one thing about this product, what would it be?
- What aspects of your business are keeping you awake at night?
- What things do we do particularly well or poorly, relative to our competition?
- What things do we do particularly well or poorly, relative to your expectations?

5. Conduct programmatic visits. A systematic approach including between 15 and 40 visits will yield a depth of understanding and illumination that can go well beyond what a few scattered visits can offer. It is important to coordinate the visits so that customers are not confused and irritated by a series of haphazard visits from different divisions and levels in the firm. Promptly log and review customer visits in a central database. Reviewing all profiles that are kept in a central database allows the firm to spot trends, define segments, identify problems, and glimpse opportunities.

Sources: McQuarrie, Edward (1995), "Taking a Road Trip," *Marketing Management,* 3 (Spring), pp. 9–21; McQuarrie, Edward (1993), *Customer Visits: Building a Better Market Focus,* Beverly Hills, CA: Sage Publications.

commercialize for other users. Figure 5-2 shows where lead users exist, relative to the broader target market. Research on lead users[16] shows that many products are initially thought of, and even prototyped by, users rather than manufacturers. For example, Table 5-1 shows that across a variety of industries, the number of innovations conceived of by users is quite high.

Lead user problem solving may apply existing commercial products in ways not anticipated by their manufacturers. Or, lead users may have developed completely new products to solve their needs. For example, Lockheed Martin pioneered a new machining technique in the development of titanium aircraft; the innovation was later com-

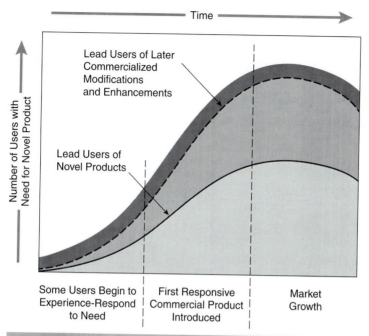

Time

Number of Users with
Need for Novel Product

Lead Users of Later
Commercialized
Modifications
and Enhancements

Lead Users of
Novel Products

Some Users Begin to
Experience-Respond
to Need

First Responsive
Commercial Product
Introduced

Market
Growth

FIGURE 5-2 Lead Users

A schematic of lead users' position in the life cycle of a novel product, process, or service. Lead users (1) encounter the need early and (2) expect high benefits from a responsive solution. (Higher expected benefits indicated by deeper shading.)

Source: von Hippel, Eric (1986), "Lead Users: A Source of Novel Product Concepts," *Management Science,* 32 (July), pp. 791–805.

mercialized by a machine tool operation that refined the Lockheed tool.[17] Other lead users may not have developed a solution but may simply be aware of the need. Experience with the problem is what makes the lead user's experience so valuable. The lead user process transforms the difficult job of creating breakthrough products into a systematic task of identifying lead users and learning from them. The development team actively attempts to track down promising lead users and adapt their ideas to its customers' needs.

Let's say an automobile company wanted to design an innovative braking system.[18] It might try to identify some users who had a strong need for better brakes—such as in auto racing teams or in an even more technologically advanced field in which users had even greater needs to stop quickly, such as in aerospace. In fact, because military aircraft must stop before reaching the end of the runway, antilock braking systems were first developed in the aerospace industry. The data from lead users consist of examining the solutions they have used to solve their problems.

Eric von Hippel advocates the use of a four-step process to incorporate lead users into marketing research. The process is conducted by a cross-disciplinary team that includes marketing and technical departments. The process can be time-consuming, with each step taking about four to six weeks, and the entire process four to six months.[19]

TABLE 5-1 Innovations Developed by Lead Users

	Percent of Products Developed By:		
	User	*Manufacturer*	*Other*
Computer industry	33%	67%	
Chemical industry	70	30	
Poltrusion-process machinery	85	15	
Scientific instrument with major functional improvements	82	18	
Semiconductor-electronic process equipment with major functional improvements	63	21	16%[a]
Electronic assembly	11	33	56[b]
Surface chemistry instruments with new functional capability	82	18	

[a] Joint user-manufacturer innovation

[b] Supplier innovations

Sources: Adapted from von Hippel, Eric (1986), "Lead Users: A Source of Novel Product Concepts," *Management Science,* 32 (July), pp. 791–805; and von Hippel, Eric, Stefan Thomke, and Mary Sonnack (1999), "Creating Breakthroughs at 3M," *Harvard Business Review,* September–October, pp. 47–57.

1. *Identify important market/technical trends.* Lead users are defined as being in advance of the market with respect to an important dimension, which is changing over time. Therefore, before one can identify lead users, one must identify the underlying trend on which these users have a leading position. "One cannot specify what the leading edge of a target market might be without first understanding the major trends in the heart of the market."[20]

The identification of trends is a standard part of most basic marketing courses. In the context of strategic planning, firms undertake an assessment of the external environment in which they operate, examining competitive, economic, regulatory, physical (natural), global, sociocultural, demographic, and technological opportunities and threats. For example, at 3M, the firm determined that a critical trend in the medical industry was the need to find inexpensive methods of infection control during surgery.

2. *Identify and question lead users.* Customers who are affected early on by significant trends often face product and process needs sooner than do others in a market. As such, they may be positioned to realize a relatively higher benefit from solutions to those needs than are others. In business-to-business markets, manufacturers typically have a better understanding of their key customers than may be possible in consumer markets. Hence, personal knowledge of customers may identify lead users, whereas surveys may be used to identify lead users in consumer goods industries. A very practical method for identifying lead users involves identifying those users who are actively innovating to solve problems present at the leading edge of a trend.

To track lead users down most efficiently, development teams may use telephone interviews to network their way into contact with experts on the leading edge of the target market.[21] People with a serious interest in any topic tend to know of others who may know even more than they do. Such people are research professionals, may have written articles on the topic, or have presented research at conferences. This networking can lead the team to the users at the front of the target market (as shown in Figure 5-2). It is also important to network to identify lead users in markets and fields that face similar problems, but in different and more extreme forms, as in the previous aerospace braking example.

It is important to note that lead users may not be within the firm's usual customer base; they may be customers of a competitor or outside the industry. Moreover, if lead users have already solved a problem, they may no longer articulate the solving of that need as an issue; hence, using a survey to identify them may be unproductive. In such a situation, the use of empathic design in the identification of lead users may be particularly wise.

A final issue in selecting and talking to lead users relates to their willingness to share information. The lead user project team should be up front about its company's commercial interest in the ideas being discussed. In a lead user study devoted to improving credit reporting services, a team found that at least two major users of such services had developed advanced on-line credit reporting processes. One of the users was unwilling to discuss details because the service was viewed as a significant source of competitive advantage. The other said, "we only developed this in the first place because we desperately needed it—we would be happy if you developed a similar service we could buy."[22] If a customer hesitates to talk, it is better to not pursue that interview due to the intellectual property concerns.

3. *Develop the breakthroughs.*   The team may begin this phase by hosting a workshop that includes several lead users who have a range of expertise, as well as a number of representatives from different areas of the company (marketing, engineering, manufacturing, etc.).[23] During the workshop, the group combines insights and experiences to provide ideas for the sponsoring company's needs.

Many users will participate simply for the intellectual challenge. Because they tend to come from other fields and industries, they generally are not concerned about loss of competitive advantage within their field. Moreover, by transferring their knowledge to a willing supplier (either voluntarily or on a licensing basis), they can continue to focus on their own core competencies and have an improved source of supply through transferring the innovation. On the other hand, lead users may not be willing to participate when the advantage they have gained is significant to their competitive position.

It is rare for a firm simply to adopt a lead user innovation "as is." Rather, information gained from a number of lead users and in-house developers leads to adaptations and modifications. The team may assess the business potential of ideas that emerge from the workshop and how they fit with the company's interests.

4. *Project the lead user data onto the larger market.*   One cannot assume that today's lead users are similar to the users who make up the major share of tomorrow's market. Firms must assess how lead user data will apply to more typical users rather than simply assume such data transfer in a straightforward fashion. Prototyping the solution and asking a sample of typical users to use it is one way to gather data to make the projection. Based on a determination of how the new concept fits the needs of a larger target market, the team will present its recommendations to senior managers. This presentation will include evidence about why customers would be willing to pay for the new products.

What are some of the benefits of the lead user process?[24] Ultimately, the lead user process allows a firm to gather and use information in a different way, which leads to new insights. In addition, because the process involves a cross-functional team from the organization, no one person feels like the lone ranger, pushing for change. The process brings cross-functional teams into close working relationship with leading-edge customers and other sources of expertise. But the lead user process is not a panacea for the difficulties in gathering research to develop breakthrough products. Without adequate corporate support, skilled teams, and needed time, the process may not succeed. A detailed example of how the lead user process works at 3M Corporation is addressed in Box 5-2.

In addition to using empathic design and the lead user process to understand customer needs and to innovate breakthrough solutions, high-tech firms must also make trade-offs among product specifications and product functionality in the product design process. A useful research tool that incorporates a customer orientation into design decisions is quality function deployment.

Quality Function Deployment

Quality function deployment (QFD) is an engineering tool that first identifies what the customer's requirements are (through customer visits, empathic design, etc.) and, second, maps those requirements onto the product design process.[25] The basic idea in quality function deployment is to use the voice of the customer in the new-product development process to ensure a tight correlation between customer needs and product specifications.[26] The process prioritizes and ensures that all design decisions take into account the importance of that design requirement from the customer's perspective. The ultimate outcome is a new product that provides superior value to the marketplace via a customer-informed design team. It requires close collaboration between marketing, engineers, and customers.

The implementation of QFD is a multistage process, including the following:[27]

- *Collect the voice of the customer.* Through customer visit programs or empathic design, identify customer needs, in the customers' own words, regarding the benefits they want the product to deliver. Roughly 10 to 12 customers will yield close to 80% or more of the customers' needs (assuming a relatively homogeneous market segment). These desired benefits and attributes can be weighted or prioritized to help the product development team in design trade-offs later (e.g., to trade off processing speed versus price, in the case of a computer chip).[28]
- *Collect customer perceptions of competitive products.* Surveys of customers can be used to assess how well current products fulfill customer needs. These data are an important component in identifying any gaps or opportunities in the market.
- *Transform customer insights into specific design requirements.* Sometimes called customer requirements deployment, the idea in this step is to identify the product attributes that will meet the customers' needs. It is important here to understand the interrelated nature of various attributes. For example, although customers may want more speed in processing, they may also want a lower price. This step is sometimes also referred to as *the house of quality,* or the planning approach that links customer requirements, competitive data, and design parameters.

The Lead User Process at Work: 3M Corporation

Examples of companies using the lead user process to improve their ability to match product development with customers' needs include Bose (maker of consumer electronics) and Cabletron (designer of fiber optic networks).[a] Another company, 3M Corporation, has relied on the lead user concept extensively.

3M EXAMPLE 1:
MEDICAL IMAGING

Step 1: Identify important market/technical trends. A team focused on medical imaging knew that a major trend was the development of capabilities to detect smaller and smaller features in medical images—very early stage tumors, for example. Its initial goal was to develop new ways to create better high-resolution images.

Step 2: Identify and question lead users. Through networking with research experts in the field, the team identified a few radiologists who were working on the most challenging medical problems. They discovered some lead users in radiology who had developed imaging innovations that were ahead of commercially available products.

Networking to other fields that were even further ahead in *any* important aspect of imaging led the team to specialists in pattern recognition and people working with images that show the fine detail in semiconductor chips. The lead users in pattern recognition were very valuable to the team. Military specialists relied on computerized pattern recognition in reconnaissance. These users had actually developed ways to enhance the resolution of the best images by adapting pattern recognition software. This discovery of the use of pattern recognition helped the development team refine its initial goal (developing new ways to create better high-resolution images) to finding enhanced methods for recognizing medically significant patterns in images, whether by better imaging or by other means.

Step 3: Develop the breakthroughs. In the course of a two-day lead user workshop, lead users with a variety of experiences were brought together: people on the leading edge of medical imaging, those who were ahead of the trend with ultra-high-resolution images, and experts on pattern recognition. Together, they created a solution that best suited the needs of the medical imaging marketplace and represented a breakthrough for the company.

3M EXAMPLE 2:
INFECTION CONTROL

Another 3M team was charged with developing a breakthrough product for the division's surgical drapes unit, which designs the material that prevents infections from spreading during surgery. Surgical drapes are thin, adhesive-backed plastic films that adhere to a patient's skin at the site of the surgical incision prior to surgery. Surgeons cut directly through these films during an operation. Drapes isolate the area being operated on from the most potential sources of infection: the rest of the patient's body, the operating table, and the members of the surgical team. But drapes don't cover catheters or tubes being inserted into the patient. The drapes' cost prohibited market entry into less developed countries.

Step 1: Identify important market/technical trends. In looking for a better type of disposable surgical draping, the team first had to learn about the causes and prevention of infections by reading research articles and interviewing experts in the field. Then, the team gathered information about important trends in infection control. During this process, the team realized it didn't know about the needs of surgeons in developing countries where infectious diseases are still major killers, so the team traveled to more hostile surgical environments to learn how people keep infections from spreading in those operating rooms. Some surgeons combated infections by using cheap antibiotics as a substitute for more expensive measures. The team saw a coming crisis with the doctors' reliance on antibiotics: Bacteria would become resistant to the drugs.

Step 2: Identify and communicate with lead users. The team networked to find the innovators at the leading edge of the trend toward much cheaper, more effective infection control. As is usually the case, some of the most valuable lead users turned up in surprising places. For example, specialists at leading veterinary hospitals were able to keep infection rates very low, despite facing difficult conditions and time constraints. As one vet said, "Our patients are covered with hair, they don't bathe, and they don't have medical insurance, so the infection controls we use can't cost much."

Another surprising source of ideas was from Hollywood: Makeup artists in Hollywood are experts in applying materials that don't irritate the skin and are easy to remove. Because infection control materials can be applied to the skin, those attributes were very important.

Step 3: Develop the breakthroughs. During the lead user workshop, the participants were invited to brainstorm about revolutionary ideas for low-cost infection control. The outcome of this session were the following ideas:

- An economy line of surgical drapes, made with existing 3M technology, targeted to the increasingly cost-conscious medical world.

- A "skin doctor" line of handheld devices to layer antimicrobial substances onto a patient's skin during an operation and to vacuum up blood and other liquids during surgery; this line again would be developed from existing 3M technology and would offer a new infection prevention tool.

- An "armor" line to coat catheters and tubes with antimicrobial protection, created with existing 3M technology; this line could open up major new markets outside surface infections, including bloodborne, urinary tract, and respiratory infections.

- A revolutionary approach to infection control based on the idea that some people enter the hospital with a greater risk of contracting infections—for example, those suffering from malnutrition or diabetes. Rather than providing every patient the same degree of infection prevention from the same basic drapes, this approach worked on a different philosophy. Through "upstream" containment of infection, treatment before people went to surgery, doctors could reduce the likelihood of these higher-risk patients contracting disease during an operation. This approach, however, would require 3M to radically change its strategy in the market and require new competencies, products, and services. After much debate, 3M decided to fund a "discovery center"

service to develop and diffuse the new approach to infection control, and the product lines needed to deploy it are being developed.

[a] DeYoung, Garrett (1997), "Listen, Then Design," *Industry Week,* February 17, pp. 76–80.
Source: von Hippel, Eric, Stefan Thomke, and Mary Sonnack (1999), "Creating Breakthroughs at 3M," *Harvard Business Review,* September–October, pp. 47–57.

Kano Diagram   At the heart of the process lies one of the key tools in QFD, the Kano concept (or Kano dimensions/diagram). The **Kano concept** (Figure 5-3) provides a graphical representation of the nature of the relationship between the presence of certain product attributes and customer satisfaction or dissatisfaction.

The graph in Figure 5-3 shows three types of attributes. Attributes that are linearly related to customer satisfaction are deemed *one-dimensional quality* attributes; increasing the performance of these attributes leads to a linear increase in satisfaction. These attributes are typically known and voiced by the customer. For example, in a laptop computer, lengthening the life of the battery would probably lead to a predictable increase in satisfaction.

The two other types of attributes have nonlinear relationships with satisfaction. *Must-be quality* attributes must be present in order for the customer to be satisfied. Although the *absence* of the attribute is exponentially related to levels of *dis*satisfaction, increasing the level of that attribute does not increase customer satisfaction with

FIGURE 5-3 The Kano Concept

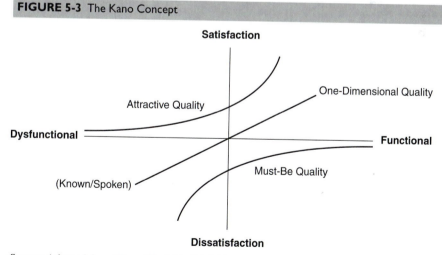

Source: Adapted from Kano, Noriaki, Shinichi Tsuji, Nobuhiko Seraku, and Fumio Takerhashi (1984), "Miryokuteki Hinshitsu to Atarimae Hinshitsu (Attractive Quality to Must-Be Quality)," Japanese Society for Quality Control.

the product. Moreover, these attributes are so essential to product functionality that they may not be explicitly voiced by the customer. For example, in the laptop industry, the computer must be fairly immune to bumps and roughness in handling. If the computer failed upon booting every time the laptop received rough handling, customers would be horribly dissatisfied. On the other hand, allocating significant resources to improve the degree of roughness the laptop can handle likely would not appreciably increase the satisfaction of most laptop users.

The final type of attributes, also exhibiting a nonlinear relationship with satisfaction, is *attractive quality* attributes, or those that exhibit an exponential relationship with satisfaction. When the attribute is lacking, the customer is not dissatisfied, but the presence of the attribute leads to an extremely favorable reaction. These attributes delight the customer and provide the wow factor in the product usage experience. Often, customers cannot articulate these attributes, and hence, they must be discovered through some of the techniques mentioned earlier (empathic design and lead users). In the laptop example, the wow factor might be found in the presence of a laptop that is decompressable into a pocket size for carrying but expands upon opening. Many experts in product innovation believe that firms that know how to identify those attributes that delight the customer are destined for success.

Rather than culminating in a specific design solution, the QFD process reveals friction points in the design process. It allows the product development team to develop a common understanding of the design issues and trade-offs, bases resolution of those trade-offs in customer needs, and enhances the collaborative processes between marketing, manufacturing, and engineering.[29] One study found that using QFD reduces design time by 40% and design costs by 60%, while enhancing design quality.[30] There are many seminars offered on this process and research firms that can provide expertise in implementing it. Interested readers are referred to additional reading.[31]

QFD and TQM　QFD emerged from the total quality management (TQM) movement in manufacturing and has become closely linked with the notion of market orientation. The total quality management paradigm is originally based on the notion of using the process to create value for customers. Value creation requires excellence in four key areas:[32]

1. *Customer excellence.* Knowing what customers require and delighting them with attractive quality are the hallmarks of customer excellence.

2. *Cycle time excellence.* Shortening a firm's time to market is vital in creating value. When cycle times run longer than expected, cost overruns occur. More importantly, however, when cycle times run longer than expected, the loss of market share contributes even more than do cost overruns to a decline in profitability. Although being fast to market is a necessary condition for excellence, it is not, in and of itself, sufficient: The firm must have the ability to hit customer requirements accurately. Because customer needs and expectations are a rapidly moving target in high-tech markets, faster cycle time also ensures a higher correlation with quality—as defined by the customer.

Recall the notion of expeditionary marketing: By undertaking a series of low-cost, fast-paced incursions into the market, the firm learns about customer needs and recalibrates its offerings each time; the combination of speed and learning enhances the odds of success. One of the key factors that affects cycle time is *complexity* in the product's features and functionality. As Figure 5-4 shows, in striving to get to the market quickly, firms

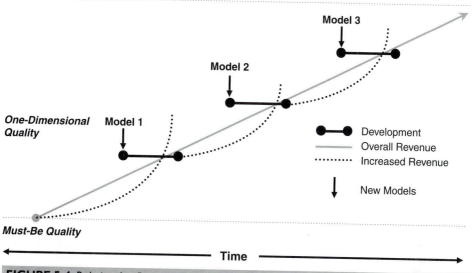

FIGURE 5-4 Relationship Between Entries in the Market and Quality

Reprinted with the permission of Storage Technology Corporation, Louisville, Colorado.

may initially develop a product with a relatively basic combination of attributes, such that the attributes exceed the must-be quality level and are in the desired one-dimensional quality space. As the firm brings additional versions of the product to market, it adds additional features, approaching the attractive quality threshold. Guy Kawasaki refers to this as Rule #2 for revolutionaries: "Don't worry, be crappy."[33] Although he uses fairly inflammatory rhetoric, what he means is that it is sometimes acceptable to strive not for perfection but for the minimum level of market acceptability with the first generation of a radical new product. This message does not mean that companies can introduce products that overlook key attributes in customer choice (which would fall below acceptable quality). Rather, it means they must be quick to market with an acceptable level of quality.

Although this prescription might sound counterintuitive, it makes good business sense for at least two reasons. First, many high-tech firms have failed because, in their striving to attain a complicated combination of product attributes—many of which require design time, testing, and debugging well beyond what was initially projected—either customer needs have changed or competitors have beat them to the market with similar products or products that serve the customers' needs in a different way. Storage Technology encountered this situation in its lengthy development of one of its radical innovations in data storage devices. Delays in technological development due to the high level of complexity resulted in a competitor beating it to market.

Second, many high-tech customers are faced with switching costs; as a result, there is an installed base of customers for later upgrades and versions. For example, Internet-based companies are finding that sites have a sticky quality to them; customers are willing to stay with a site that is based on the site's knowledge of customers' preferences and past purchase histories. Hence, a firm should work incrementally on features and functionality, guided closely by marketing input. Firms must ensure that their first foray in the market is quick and at least must-be quality; over time, additional product extensions can strive for attractive quality.

A final thought on cycle time excellence: Firms that focus on cycle time must realize that merely getting the product to market quickly is not enough. The real cycle time that matters is the time to market acceptance.[34] To hasten the time to market acceptance, involving customers early in the development process with a continuous dialogue is vital. New technologies make this more and more feasible.

3. *Cost excellence.* Cost excellence is found in providing customer value at minimum cost. Supply partnerships are one useful way to work on cost issues. Although many firms in the past focused on downsizing as a way to cut costs, downsizing can also cause decreases in customer value. Downsizing does not inherently lead to customer value unless the assets are somehow added back to enhance value.

4. *Cultural excellence.* Cultural excellence refers to the alignment of individual and organizational goals to respond to business conditions; organizational goals must be supported in order to capitalize on opportunities in the marketplace. A culture of innovation, discussed in Chapter 2, is one way to achieve cultural excellence. Engineering and marketing must also be integrated to focus on customer value.

In addition to gathering information on customers, firms must also gather information on competitors.

GATHERING COMPETITIVE INTELLIGENCE

Competitive intelligence is information about competitors: who they are, their products, their marketing strategies, and likely responses to the marketing strategies of other firms in the market. Effective competitive intelligence provides better knowledge of the market, customers, and competitors; quicker response time; and superior strategy based on identification of threats and opportunities.[35] Competitive intelligence provides firms with an early warning system to ward off disasters. Indeed, "the essence of smart competitive management is an action that preceded its obvious time."[36]

For competitive intelligence programs to work, they must affect the mind-set and decisions of the people whose actions most significantly affect the bottom line—namely, top management. Moreover, effective competitive intelligence programs are much more than mere passive watching of the market (i.e., competitive monitoring); rather, firms that are skilled at reading signals from the market actually develop a core competency in understanding the competition. To do so, they must find it safe to challenge the status quo, to bring an outside perspective, and to be unconventional.

For example, in 1985 Motorola launched a study of Japanese business strategies in Europe. At that time, Motorola-Europe executives saw no signs of a thrust by Japan into Europe. The lack of such entry did not seem to fit the character of their Japanese rivals. So, through a strategic gathering of competitive intelligence, Motorola discovered that the Japanese planned to double their capital investments, going after the European semiconductor market. As a result, Motorola changed strategy, sought joint ventures with European partners, and held off the Japanese.[37]

It can be difficult to gather competitive intelligence in high-tech markets. Sometimes, one doesn't think to look outside the industry for competition. However, Chapter 2 highlighted the fact that industry newcomers often pioneer breakthrough technology. This fact highlights the importance of monitoring related industries for competitive moves.

The Web has had a radical effect on the way marketers get the business intelligence they need.[38] Useful Web sites for gathering competitive intelligence are listed in Table 5-2. To leverage their power to communicate with prospective customers, employees, and other stakeholders, companies post plenty of information on their sites. Some of this information can be available to anyone who seeks it, making it possible to gather more information on competitors than ever, including

- Customer and client lists
- Detailed product and pricing information, as well as product specifications and technical data
- Specifics about business goals and strategies
- New-product plans and R&D efforts
- Extensive company job postings that shine a spotlight on new business emphases
- Details about manufacturing processes and quality-control efforts
- Company organizational structures and biographical information about managers
- Comprehensive information about business locations, distributors, and service centers
- Information about partnerships and alliances

The Deja news service (www.dejanews.com) shows job notices posted on specific Usenet groups, including details about hardware and software with which applicants must be familiar. The geographical nature of such postings can also yield insights into possible expansions. Another Web service, Company Sleuth (www.companysleuth.com), allows one to select up to 10 publicly traded companies to track. Each morning, it reports to the e-mail address specified any activities on those companies, including stock trades, trademark registrations, patent applications, and so forth.

Interestingly, cultural differences exist between countries in the views of intelligence. In the United States, intelligence is often associated with the military, with related

TABLE 5-2   Useful Web Sites for Competitive Intelligence

Society of Competitive Intelligence Professionals	www.scip.org
Fuld & Co.	www.fuld.com
Hoover's Online	www.hoovers.com
Farcast	www.farcast.com
Individual Inc.	www.individual.com
Deja News	www.dejanews.com
Newsworks	www.newsworks.com
Newsbot	www.newsbot.com
Newstracker	nt.excite.com
Companies Online	www.companiesonline.com
SEC's EDGAR file	www.sec.gov/cgi-bin/srch-edgar
Company Sleuth	www.companysleuth.com

connotations of covert activity and secrecy. In other countries, say Japan, for example, social networks of intelligence transfer are an integral part of society. And in Israel, the vast majority of top executives once served in the military. Given other countries' greater receptivity to and acceptance of intelligence-gathering activities, U.S. companies can probably learn some useful lessons about treating competitive intelligence activities more strategically.

Tami Syverson, competitive intelligence analyst at Sun Microsystems, provides insight about her position in this section's Technology Expert's View from the Trenches.

The flipside of *gathering* competitive intelligence is *sending* competitive signals. Indeed, some firms proactively attempt to send signals to competitors in the marketplace via a variety of mechanisms.[39] For example, preannouncing of products, or the announcement of a firm's intention to release a product in the future, is commonly used (and is covered in Chapter 10 on communications) and can preempt competitors by postponing customers' buying decisions. Firms can send competitive signals by sharing information with industry contacts, customers, or distributors; the information will eventually be disseminated to others.

Moreover, firms have been known to deliberately release several different stories to the marketplace, so as to confuse competitors. As stated by one manager:

> [We try to] keep competitors off guard as to what our "specs" really look like, when we are going to announce, and what the price is going to be. We always have three or four stories out in the marketplace, so people really don't know which is the right one, until we formally announce something.[40]

Hence, firms must carefully scrutinize the competitive information they receive from the marketplace and attempt to gauge its accuracy.

In addition to researching customers and competitors, high-tech firms are faced with the daunting prospect of forecasting demand for new products.

FORECASTING CUSTOMER DEMAND[41]

Forecasting future sales of high-tech products is difficult for many reasons. Quantitative methods typically rely on historical data, but for radically new products, there are no historical data. Moreover, data obtained through traditional techniques are of dubious value, because it is difficult for customers to articulate their preferences and expectations when they have no basis for understanding the new technology.

Although gathering information regarding customers in high-tech markets is difficult, the issue of developing a specific sales forecast is often akin to looking into a crystal ball. The "crystal ball" technique to develop forecasts for high-tech products is imprecise at best and flat-out wrong at worst. "Managers know little about predicting new-product sales, and nothing about the takeoff."[42] For example,[43]

- In reacting to the addition of audio technology to silent movies (circa 1927), Harry M. Warner said, "Who the hell wants to hear actors talk?"
- His later colleague, Darryl Zanuck, head of 20th Century Fox Films in 1946, predicted that "Television won't be able to hold on to any market it captures after the first six months. People will soon get tired of staring at a plywood box every night."
- More recently, Ken Olsen, president and founder of the DEC Corporation, said in 1977, "There is little reason for any individual to have a computer in their home."

TECHNOLOGY EXPERT'S VIEW FROM THE TRENCHES

A Day in the Life of a Competitive Analyst

TAMI SYVERSON
Competitive Analyst, Sun Microsystems, Boulder, Colorado

The Competitive Intelligence (CI) Team functions as a service organization within the corporation. The goal of a CI Team is to provide market research and competitive intelligence on the industry, both proactively and upon request by the internal customer base consisting of product managers, directors, sales force, public relations, and executive management. Information is provided to assist the development of materials such as product plans, marketing/sales literature, strategic plans, business cases, RFPs (requests for proposals), press releases, and presentations.

Taking a look at daily events will shed light on how the CI Team helps the organization gain a competitive advantage via awareness of the market and the competitive landscape. A typical day starts with a couple of hours of reading trade journals and on-line news subscriptions to remain current on the competitive moves and evolving industry trends. An integral service provided to people within the organization is keeping them alerted of current news events. Press releases are a good source of product announcements, service offerings, and pricing. A second source can be a competitor's Web site. On any given day, a major competitor can announce a new product that may compete directly or indirectly. Notification must be made internally, followed by an analysis of the effect on market positioning. A competitive comeback may be necessary so the sales force can respond to customer questions and concerns. This involves working with personnel in public relations, product management, and other areas of the organization.

Later in the day, a noon lunch meeting with a product manager uncovers a research inquiry. A new product is in development and the marketing manager needs an overview of the competition for the marketing plan. In order to correctly position the service/product within the marketplace, it is important to identify the correct price, complete offering, features, channel of distribution, and messaging.

Typically, most research requests can be categorized into the following three areas:

- Market trends and statistics
- Competitive offerings
- End user wants and needs

Some answers can be found in secondary research. In the event primary research is needed, the project may be outsourced to a market research company. At this time, the CI Team will manage the custom study. Industry analysts are integral to gathering competitive information, as they have insights that may not otherwise be found via standard research efforts. They track daily the industry and market events in their areas of expertise (i.e., computer hardware, software, etc.).

Conducting competitive research is not always easy; there will be challenges along the way. A few challenges to watch out for in this new era of information technology include business rules that are constantly changing, limited information, and new, unknown competitors.

When rolling out new products or services, often there are no set parameters to follow. It is difficult to find market trends and statistics on new innovations. Part of the challenge involves predicting the future. Just when you understand the competition, the market changes. New competitors land on the scene so quickly that your radar screen may not be fixed on them. It is important to widen the range to include competitors not previously thought of that can meet your customers' needs.

News breaks all day—don't miss it! A discontinuous innovation can radically change the competition and the way you do business. Staying abreast of the competitive landscape allows you to answer questions that arise from your customer base. It is impossible to know all the answers, but the key is to know where to find solutions.

Last words of warning: Beware of "Web-myopia," a nearsighted focus on Internet research. There are so many sources available beyond the Internet, but it may become difficult to refocus your energy.

An effective competitive analyst manages relationships and information carefully. Focus on building and maintaining good relations with internal and external contacts, as they will be a significant source of information. When gathering and analyzing information, be sure to integrate market research tools and techniques.

Note: The information presented here represents the opinions of the author and not those of Sun Microsystems, Inc.

High-tech marketers must not be daunted by the challenge. Tools are available to help them address the important issue of forecasting. And because the task is fraught with uncertainty and many sources of error, using a systematic process to develop the forecast is more important than ever.

Forecasting Methods Forecasting tools can be categorized into quantitative and qualitative tools.[44] Basic quantitative tools include moving averages, exponential smoothing, and regression analysis. As noted previously, because of their reliance on historical data—which are often nonexistent in a new high-tech marketplace—quantitative tools may not be available in high-tech markets. Qualitative forecasting methods, such as the Delphi and morphological methods, may be more applicable. Readers interested in these traditional forecasting tools can use one of the many excellent resources available.[45]

The *Delphi method* is probably the most common qualitative method. In this technique, a panel of experts is convened and asked to address specific questions, such as when a new product will gain widespread acceptance. These experts are purposefully kept separate, so that their judgments will not be influenced by social pressures or group influences. The answers to initial questions are sent back to the participants, who are asked to refine their own judgments and to comment on the predictions of the others, in an attempt to find a consensus. Anonymity among the panel members allows for open debate.[46]

Although this method does have limitations, including lack of reliability assessment and potential sensitivity to the experts selected, such limitations also apply— possibly even more so—to other subjective estimates. Selection of the experts also warrants careful attention. Experts from the industry in general, including lead users, can offer their knowledge as a useful benchmark against the estimates generated internally by a firm.

Another useful forecasting tool in high-tech markets relies on *analogous data* to make inferences about the new technology.[47] The basic idea is to use data about another product currently on the market, or one that existed at an earlier time, to forecast a new product's expected growth pattern. For example, in forecasting sales of high-definition TV (HDTV) equipment, forecasts can be based on the history of similar consumer products, such as color TVs or videocassette recorders. In selecting the analogous product, it is critical to establish a logical connection between the two. For example, do the two products serve a similar need or share other important characteristics? One also must take into consideration environmental factors and market conditions that may uniquely affect the new product's growth pattern. Then, based on the sales pattern for the analogous product, the use of intuitive judgment traces the expected pattern of sales for the new product.

This technique is valid only to the extent that the analogy holds true. The degree to which the analogy is appropriate depends on the logical connection between the products involved. For example, in forecasting the demand for personal digital assistants (also known as handheld computers), possible analogous products might include personal computers and cell phones.[48] The degree to which these analogous products are logically connected to handheld computers depends on similarities in the attributes of importance to the consumer in making purchase decisions and in the business factors that contribute to product success. Important attributes include technical support, ease of use, and product form/design considerations. Critical business factors include distribution considerations, brand-name considerations, and model options. Based on consideration of these factor, Handspring, Inc. (Mountain View, Calif.), concluded that both products served as useful benchmarks but neither alone was entirely appropriately analogous.

Additional techniques might also be useful in making forecasts for high-technology products. The *information acceleration (IA)* technique relies on a virtual representation of a new product to assist in product development and forecasting.[49] Such representations are more vivid and realistic than are traditional concept descriptions and less expensive than relying on actual prototypes. Hence, they provide a useful middle ground between traditional concept descriptions and actual physical prototypes. Feedback from customers is obtained through the use of the virtual representation of the new-product idea.

In addition, merely creating a virtual representation yields several other benefits. First, to simulate a future environment, the design team must agree on the implications of that future environment. This forces the team to carefully define the target group of customers and the core product benefits early in the process. Other issues that are brought to the fore are

- The requisite infrastructure required for product usage (e.g., recharging stations for electric vehicles)
- Technology requirements for future generations of the innovation (e.g., new battery technology for electric vehicles)
- Competitive forecasting of new market entrants
- Available alternatives to the new technology (e.g., hybrid electric vehicles that combine gas power with electric)

To simulate one product, the team must plan for the entire product line (including vans, two seaters, sedans, etc.) and cannibalization of existing products.

Other Considerations in Forecasting   Whichever forecast method or combination of methods is used, the forecaster must ensure that bias does not enter into the forecast due to personal or organizational desires of success for the technology. Stakeholders in a new technology often inflate predictions of its future success, and "since their bullish statements of technical potential are often misleadingly packaged as precise market forecasts, unwary businesses and investors often suffer."[50] Herb Brody suggests that marketing researchers can avoid bias by studying a new technology's potential buyers, who have less of a stake in its success. However, this is typically not done due to the fact that the group of potential customers can be difficult to reach, making accurate market research expensive and time-consuming.[51]

Another problem with forecasting new technologies is the "cross-competition of current technologies with new technologies serving the same market."[52] Although Chapter 2 addressed the "incumbent's curse," in which existing firms downplay the competitive threat posed by new technologies, new start-ups also suffer from their own curse: that of overenthusiasm. In developing a forecast for a new technology, managers must consider the entrenched market position of the incumbents. The main advantage of incumbent technologies is that they already have developed markets with established distribution channels and loyal consumers. Also, they have proven production processes and higher production volumes. All of these factors allow established technologies to be marketed with a cost leadership strategy, pushing prices downward and helping them maintain and even increase market share.[53] To avoid forecasting inaccuracies due to this problem, forecasters must fully consider the advantages of the established technologies and, at a minimum, temper their enthusiasm for the success of the innovation while adjusting their predictions of how quickly the new technology will overtake the existing technology.

Many times, decision makers are less than confident in the prepared forecast for a certain technology, and this lack of confidence can sometimes lead to indecisiveness or bad decisions. Although forecasting demand for new technologies is difficult, it is often critical to provide information to decision makers. Forecasters should keep in mind that the success of the forecast is not based on whether it comes true, but on the quality of information provided to the decision makers who are the end users of the forecast.

The Technology Tidbit focuses on breakthrough technologies in curing AIDS.

Protecting Against the AIDS Infection:
Prevention Is Worth a Pound of Cure

THOMAS LUNDELL

Despite all the benefits drugs can offer in treating an existing infection, the best approach is to prevent infection in the first place. And the best and most cost-effective means to prevent infection is through vaccination (think of smallpox, polio, and measles, for example).

Used with the permission of the Montana Biotechnology Center, University of Montana, Missoula, Montana.

More than 40 vaccines aimed at preventing HIV infection are currently being tested in human volunteers. Many of these are aimed at the envelope protein on the surface of the virus and have been shown in cell culture to prevent HIV infection by lab strains of the virus.

However, the effectiveness of these vaccines may be compromised by two problems:

- The variability of the virus (ongoing mutations make a vaccine effective against one subtype useless against another)
- The general failure of the vaccine to elicit antibodies that are capable of preventing infections even in cell culture by strains of the virus that infect people (versus the lab strains)

Since 1993, when these failures were first discovered, the burden of vaccine efforts has focused on overcoming these problems.

Jack Nunberg and his colleagues at the Montana Biotechnology Center at the University of Montana set out to see if they could expose the critical workings of the viral envelope protein, the protein that allows the virus to bind to and infect cells. The team allowed the protein to begin to interact with cell receptors. During this process, hidden areas of the protein become exposed for a very short period of time, usually not long enough for the immune system to respond to it. But by using formaldehyde to "freeze" the process—and the partially unfolded envelope protein—Nunberg's team managed to capture the transient intermediate forms of the protein.

Two major breakthroughs came out of this process. First, by eliciting antibodies that could actually block infection of patient viruses (versus lab viruses), their discovery gave real hope that an HIV vaccine was truly possible. Moreover, because they targeted the actual functioning of the protein (versus the resting form of envelope protein), they were able to block a wide range of HIV subtypes (since all envelope proteins function in the same way even if they have genetic differences). Their findings: When the antibodies developed by the immune system were mixed in cell culture with virus taken from infected humans, they neutralized 23 out of 24 different strains of HIV from around the world.

> Although much work remains to pursue these intriguing findings and to translate them into a vaccine that can be manufactured and safely tested in people, Jack Nunberg's findings (by targeting the intermediate structures rather than the resting protein) point out a new way of thinking about vaccine development.
>
> *Source:* Reuters (1999), "Frozen HIV May Aid Vaccine," ABCnews.com (January 14), www.abcnews.go.com/sections/living/DailyNews/aids_vaccine990114.html.

Summary

A key point to take away from this chapter is the overwhelming need to diligently and assiduously gather information from the marketplace. In addition to collecting information on competitors, high-tech marketers must work with customers—to understand them, to have an ongoing dialogue with them, to study them, and to incorporate their needs into the product development and marketing process. High-tech firms sometimes end up with baffled, frustrated, and unhappy customers, which is itself a threat to the health of the high-tech economy. Technical people find that, much of the time, users don't know what they want; and when they do know, they all want something different. Despite that, users are the customers; developers should delight the customers and be responsive to their needs and anticipate them in designs.[54]

The next chapter takes another step toward understanding customers and explores issues related to customer adoption decisions for high-technology products.

Discussion Questions

1. Using contingency theory from Chapter 1, identify how marketing research techniques must be matched to the type of innovation to ensure greater success and insight.
2. What is empathic design? What insights can it generate? What are the steps in the process?
3. How are customer visits similar to and different from empathic design?
4. Who are lead users? What are the four steps in the process of using lead users in marketing research?
5. What is QFD? How does a Kano concept add insights into customer needs? What are the four characteristics necessary for QFD?
6. What are some of the complicating factors in gathering competitive intelligence in high-tech markets?
7. What are some useful tools for forecasting in high-tech markets?

Glossary

Customer visit program. A systematic program of visiting customers by a cross-functional team to understand the customers' needs, how they use products, and their environment.

Empathic design. A research technique based on understanding user needs through observation of the customer, rather than through traditional questioning methods (focus groups, surveys).

Kano concept. A graphical representation of the nature of the relationship between the presence of certain product attributes and customer satisfaction or dissatisfaction. "Must-be quality" attributes are those that, if absent, cause an exponential decrease in satisfaction. "Attractive quality" attributes are those that delight the customer; when present, there is an exponential increase in satisfaction.

Lead users. Customers who face needs months or years before the bulk of the marketplace and are positioned to benefit significantly by obtaining solutions to those needs now. In some cases, lead users may have even developed a solution to their needs that marketers can then commercialize for other users.

Quality function deployment (QFD). An engineering tool to identify customer requirements and map those requirements onto the product design process.

Endnotes

1. Brown, Eryn (1999), "9 Ways to Win on the Web," *Fortune,* May 24, pp. 112–124.
2. Brown, Eryn (1999), "9 Ways to Win on the Web," *Fortune,* May 24, pp. 112–124.
3. von Hippel, Eric, Stefan Thomke, and Mary Sonnack (1999), "Creating Breakthroughs at 3M," *Harvard Business Review,* September–October, pp. 47–57.
4. Leonard-Barton, Dorothy, Edith Wilson, and John Doyle (1995), "Commercializing Technology: Understanding User Needs," in *Business Marketing Strategy,* V. K. Rangan et al. (eds.), Chicago: Irwin, pp. 281–305.
5. Churchill, Gilbert (1999), *Marketing Research: Methodological Foundations,* Fort Worth, TX: Harcourt Brace College Publishers.
6. Leonard-Barton, Dorothy, Edith Wilson, and John Doyle (1995), "Commercializing Technology: Understanding User Needs," in *Business Marketing Strategy,* V. K. Rangan et al. (eds.), Chicago: Irwin, pp. 281–305.
7. Leonard-Barton, Dorothy, Edith Wilson, and John Doyle (1995), "Commercializing Technology: Understanding User Needs," in *Business Marketing Strategy,* V. K. Rangan et al. (eds.), Chicago: Irwin, pp. 281–305.
8. Leonard-Barton, Dorothy and Jeffrey F. Rayport (1997), "Spark Innovation Through Empathic Design," *Harvard Business Review,* November–December, pp. 102–113.
9. Leonard-Barton, Dorothy and Jeffrey F. Rayport (1997), "Spark Innovation Through Empathic Design," *Harvard Business Review,* November–December, pp. 102–113.
10. Nussbaum, Bruce (1993), "Hot Products," *Business Week,* June 7, pp. 54–57.
11. Leonard-Barton, Dorothy and Jeffrey F. Rayport (1997), "Spark Innovation Through Empathic Design," *Harvard Business Review,* November–December, pp. 102–113.
12. Leonard-Barton, Dorothy and Jeffrey F. Rayport (1997), "Spark Innovation Through Empathic Design," *Harvard Business Review,* November–December, pp. 102–113.
13. Takahashi, Dean (1998), "Doing Fieldwork in the High-Tech Jungle," *Wall Street Journal,* October 27, pp. B1, B22.
14. von Hippel, Eric (1986), "Lead Users: A Source of Novel Product Concepts," *Management Science,* 32 (July), pp. 791–805; von Hippel, Eric, Stefan Thomke, and Mary Sonnack (1999), "Creating Breakthroughs at 3M," *Harvard Business Review,* September–October, pp. 47–57; Urban, Glen L. and Eric von Hippel (1988), "Lead User Analyses for the Development of New Industrial Products," *Management Science,* 34 (May), pp. 569–582.
15. von Hippel, Eric, Stefan Thomke, and Mary Sonnack (1999), "Creating Breakthroughs at 3M," *Harvard Business Review,* September–October, pp. 47–57.
16. von Hippel, Eric (1978), "Users as Innovators," *Technology Review,* 80 (January), pp. 3–11.
17. von Hippel, Eric (1986), "Lead Users: A Source of Novel Product Concepts," *Management Science,* 32 (July), pp. 791–805.
18. von Hippel, Eric, Stefan Thomke, and Mary Sonnack (1999), "Creating Breakthroughs at 3M," *Harvard Business Review,* September–October, pp. 47–57.
19. von Hippel, Eric, Stefan Thomke, and Mary Sonnack (1999), "Creating Breakthroughs at

3M," *Harvard Business Review,* September–October, pp. 47–57.

20. von Hippel, Eric, Stefan Thomke, and Mary Sonnack (1999), "Creating Breakthroughs at 3M," *Harvard Business Review,* September–October, p. 53.

21. von Hippel, Eric, Stefan Thomke, and Mary Sonnack (1999), "Creating Breakthroughs at 3M," *Harvard Business Review,* September–October, pp. 47–57.

22. von Hippel, Eric, Stefan Thomke, and Mary Sonnack (1999), "Creating Breakthroughs at 3M," *Harvard Business Review,* September–October, pp. 47–57.

23. 3M asks respondents first to sign an agreement granting 3M intellectual property rights for any ideas resulting from the workshop.

24. von Hippel, Eric, Stefan Thomke, and Mary Sonnack (1999), "Creating Breakthroughs at 3M," *Harvard Business Review,* September–October, pp. 47–57.

25. Center for Quality Management (1995), *Concept Engineering,* Cambridge, MA.

26. Griffin, Abbie and John R. Hauser (1993), "The Voice of the Customer," *Marketing Science,* 12 (Winter), pp. 1–27; Hauser, John R. and Don Clausing (1988), "The House of Quality," *Harvard Business Review,* 66 (May–June), pp. 63–73.

27. Center for Quality Management (1995), *Concept Engineering,* Cambridge, MA.

28. Another way to determine the value customers place on various features, attributes, or benefits, to better understand possible trade-offs, is conjoint analysis. Conjoint analysis breaks customers' preference of an overall product concept into its various attributes or components. Then, if one of the attributes changes, researchers can estimate the impact of that change alone. The following sources contrast this research technique with the simpler notion of *concept testing* and explain conjoint analysis in great clarity and detail: Moore, William (1992), "Conjoint Analysis," in E. Pessemier, *Product Planning and Management: Designing and Delivering Value,* New York: McGraw-Hill, Inc.; and Dolan, Robert (1999), "Analyzing Consumer Preferences," *Harvard Business Review,* reprint #9-599-112.

29. Griffin, Abbie and John Hauser (1992), "Patterns of Communication Among Marketing, Engineering, and Manufacturing: A Comparison Between Two New Product Teams," *Management Science,* 38 (March), pp. 360–373.

30. Hauser, John R. and Don Clausing (1988), "The House of Quality," *Harvard Business Review,* 66 (May–June), pp. 63–73.

31. Clark, Kim and Steven Wheelwright (1992), *Managing New Product and Process Development,* New York: Free Press.

32. Much of this material draws on the insights of Don Kleinschnitz, chief quality officer and vice president of corporate quality, Storage Technology Corporation.

33. Kawasaki, Guy and Michele Moreno (1999), *Rules for Revolutionaries,* New York: Harper Business.

34. McKenna, Regis (1995), "Real-Time Marketing," *Harvard Business Review,* July–August, pp. 87–95.

35. Gilad, Ben (1995), "Competitive Intelligence: What Has Gone Wrong," *Across the Board,* October, pp. 32–36.

36. Gilad, Ben (1995), "Competitive Intelligence: What Has Gone Wrong," *Across the Board,* October, pp. 32–36.

37. Gilad, Ben (1995), "Competitive Intelligence: What Has Gone Wrong," *Across the Board,* October, pp. 32–36.

38. Yovivich, B. G. (1997), "Browsers Get Peek at Rivals' Secrets," *Marketing News,* November 10, pp. 1, 6; Graef, Jean (1996), "Using the Internet for Competitive Intelligence," *CIO Magazine,* www.cio.com/CIO/arch_0695_cicolumn.html; Bort, Julie (1996), "Watching Rivals on the Net," *Denver Post,* February 16, p. C1.

39. Mohr, Jakki (1996), "The Management and Control of Information in High-Technology Firms," *Journal of High-Technology Management Research,* 7 (Fall), pp. 245–268.

40. Mohr, Jakki (1996), "The Management and Control of Information in High-Technology Firms," *Journal of High-Technology Management Research,* 7 (Fall), pp. 245–268.

41. This section was written in conjunction with information compiled by Tom Disburg.

42. "Will It Fly," (1998), *Wall Street Journal,* March 19, p. A1.

43. These next examples came from a presentation by Rajesh Chandy, professor of marketing, University of Houston.

44. Levary, Reuven R. and Dongchui Han (1995), "Choosing a Technological Forecasting Method," *Industrial Management,* 37 (January–February), p. 14.

45. Makridakis, S., S. C. Wheelwright, and V. E. McGee (1997), *Forecasting: Methods and Applications,* New York: John Wiley (comprehensive and detailed); Kress, G. and John Snyder (1994), *Forecasting and Market Analysis Techniques,* Westport, CT: Greenwood Publishing Group.

46. Lee, S., J. Krajewski, and Larry P. Ritzman (1998), *Operations Management, Strategy and Analysis,* 5th ed., Reading, MA: Addison-Wesley-Longman, p. 501.

47. Weiss, Allen (1999), *Hitchhiker's Guide to Forecasting,* available at www.marketingprofs.com.

48. This example is based on a presentation by Donna Dubinsky, CEO of Handspring Technologies, to the American Marketing Association Summer Educators' Conference, San Francisco, August 1999.

49. Urban, Glen, John Hauser, William Qualls, Bruce Weinberg, Jonathan Bohlmann, and Roberta Chicos (1997), "Information Acceleration: Validation and Lessons from the Field," *Journal of Marketing Research,* 34 (February), pp. 143–153.

50. Brody, Herb (1991), "Great Expectations: Why Technology Predictions Go Awry," *Technology Review,* 94 (July), p. 38.

51. Brody, Herb (1991), "Great Expectations: Why Technology Predictions Go Awry," *Technology Review,* 94 (July), p. 38.

52. Stevenson, Mirek J. (1998), "Advantages of Incumbent Technologies," *Electronic News,* 44 (July 20), p. 8.

53. Stevenson, Mirek J. (1998), "Advantages of Incumbent Technologies," *Electronic News,* 44 (July 20), p. 8.

54. Wildstrom, Stephen (1998), "They're Mad as Hell Out There," *Business Week,* October 19, p. 32.

Recommended Readings

Lead User Process

von Hippel, Eric (1988), *The Sources of Innovation,* New York: Oxford University Press.

Gathering Information on Customers

Barabba, Vincent and Gerald Zaltman (1991), *Hearing the Voice of the Market: Competitive Advantage Through Creative Use of Market Information,* Boston: Harvard Business School Press.

Griffin, Abbie and John Hauser (1992), "The Voice of the Customer," report #92-106, Cambridge, MA: Marketing Science Institute.

Guillart, Francis and Frederick Sturdivant (1994), "Spend a Day in the Life of Your Customer," *Harvard Business Review,* January–February, pp. 116–125.

CHAPTER 6

Understanding High-Tech Customers

Business Week states,

> As the $280 million consumer market for technology soars, companies that sell stuff ranging from cellular phones and computers to software and Internet services have some surprising blind spots about who their customers are and what motivates them.[1]

In order to develop effective marketing strategies, firms must have a solid understanding of how and why customers make purchase decisions for high-technology products and innovations. For example, take the case of a large company deciding to purchase enterprise resource planning (ERP) software to help manage and integrate a variety of different business functions and applications.[2] Some of the key vendors in the ERP software market include J. D. Edwards, Baan, Oracle, PeopleSoft, SAP, i2 Technologies, Siebel Systems, Aspect Development, Calico Systems, and Trilogy Software. *Front-office products* are designed both to help companies find and sell to customers and to automate and track data related to sales force management, marketing, and customers. For example, Siebel Systems's programs close the loop between sales, marketing, and customer service. *Back-office solutions* are designed to handle functions that do not interface with customers: functions such as supply chain management, accounting and finance, and so forth.

Effectively implementing enterprise resource planning requires a company to eliminate its stovepipe mentality, which keeps each functional area isolated from the others. Where different functional areas operate autonomously, goals may not be well integrated. For example, salespeople might have been rewarded on volume, operations personnel on cost of products and conformance to specifications, and so forth. The success of ERP planning hinges on integrating and collaborating across functions, such that each is working toward common goals.

Moreover, these programs are not cheap. To install an ERP system in a *Fortune* 500 company may cost $30 million in license fees and $200 million in consulting, plus investments in computers and networks. Issues such as application interfaces, compatibility ("plug and play"), interoperability between disparate systems, scalability across the enterprise, and linking new and legacy applications in an enterprise-wide system must be addressed. The time line can take three years or more. The suppliers of these software programs must have an intimate understanding of their customers' operations, concerns, and decision processes in order to market their products effectively.

Firms must look at at least three critical issues in assessing the motivations of customers to buy their products, as shown in the organizing framework in Figure 6-1. Marketing must be tailored to address these issues:

- What affects customers' purchase decisions? What motivates them to buy (or not)?
- Who is likely to buy? Are there categories of customers who are predisposed to adopt an innovation earlier than others? How can technology markets be segmented?
- What affects the timing of customers' purchase decisions? Are they likely to postpone purchases or bypass new generations of technology in anticipation of better options coming in the near future?

As an initial step in understanding the customer behavior of technology buyers, basic models of consumer behavior (business to consumer, or B-to-C) and organizational buyer behavior (business to business, or B-to-B) can be useful. However, a growing number of companies have found that when it comes to high-tech products and services, conventional consumer behavior models "don't go far enough."[3] Unlike soup or soda, technology products are complex and evolve rapidly. As a result, because consumers behave differently when they buy technology, marketers must go beyond demographics and buying patterns and capture how people really use technology day to day and how they feel about it.[4,5]

The next sections address an understanding of customers based on their technology-related behaviors. The chapter begins with a brief overview of the factors that affect customers' adoption decisions. These factors are derived from the traditional adoption and diffusion of innovation model. A discussion follows of the different categories of customers, also derived from the traditional adoption and diffusion of innovation model. The chapter continues with adaptations to marketing, based on the notion of a "chasm" between early-market adopters and later-market customers. Then a look at segmenting markets presents a process to identify attractive, viable target market opportunities in high-tech markets. The final topic covers the complications in high-tech customer decision making that arise from customers' desire to avoid obsolescence.

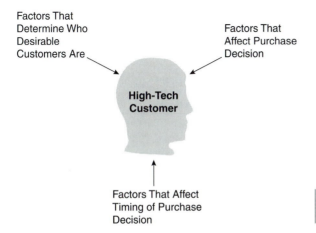

Factors That
Determine Who
Desirable
Customers Are

Factors That
Affect Purchase
Decision

**High-Tech
Customer**

Factors That Affect
Timing of Purchase
Decision

FIGURE 6-1 Understanding
High-Tech Customers

CUSTOMER PURCHASE DECISIONS

Factors Affecting Customer Purchase Decisions

From a customer's perspective, making the decision to adopt a new technology is a high-risk, anxiety-provoking one. The sources of market and technological uncertainty mean that customers are worried about making a bad decision, about switching costs involved, about training needs, and so forth. Understanding the factors that affect customers' purchase decisions is vital. Based on Everett Rogers's work on the adoption and diffusion of innovation,[6] the critical characteristics that influence a customer's potential adoption of a new innovation are shown in Table 6-1 and discussed here. High-tech marketers must be able to articulate their vision of how their product fares on each of these factors.

1. *Relative advantage.* Relative advantage refers to the benefits of adopting the new technology compared to the costs. In addition to the price of buying the new technology, the ambiguity of high-tech products can lead to emotional worry, a type of psychic cost. The customer will have fear, uncertainty, and doubt about (a) whether the technology will deliver the ostensible benefits and (b) whether the customer will have the skills and capabilities to realize those benefits.

Many high-tech entrepreneurs believe that their invention is the Holy Grail, a better mousetrap, and the next best thing to sliced bread, all rolled into one. However, the factor of relative advantage suggests that it is not sufficient for the inventor to believe that he or she truly has a better product; the improvements must be readily perceived by the customer *and* be worth the monetary and other costs of adoption.

As an example, some question whether high-definition TV (HDTV) really provides a perceived relative advantage to the large majority of consumers. Initially, the relative advantage was discussed in terms of the higher resolution that the digital format provided. The cost of initial sets was in the $2,000 to $3,000 range. Consumers asked themselves whether they needed to see their favorite shows in higher resolution for such a

---

TABLE 6-1   Five Factors Affecting Customer Purchase Decisions

1. Relative advantage	The benefits of adopting the new technology compared to the costs
2. Compatibility	The extent to which adopting and using the innovation is based on existing ways of doing things and standard cultural norms
3. Complexity	How difficult the new product is to use
4. Ability to Communicate Product Benefits	The ease and clarity with which the benefits of owning and using the new product can be communicated to prospective customers
5. Observability	How observable the benefits are to the consumer using the new product, and how easily other customers can observe the benefits being received by a customer who has already adopted the product

high price tag, relative to standard sets. When this concern was coupled with the reality that TV broadcasters were sending only a portion of their programming in the new digital format, the relative advantage to consumers just wasn't apparent.

2. *Compatibility.* Compatibility refers to the extent to which customers will have to learn new behaviors to adopt and use the innovation. Compatibility with existing ways of doing things, and with cultural norms, can hasten adoption and diffusion of innovation. Products that are incompatible with standard ways of doing things require more time in getting up to speed and require more education from the marketer. Especially in high-tech markets, the issue of compatibility arises in terms of offering interfaces to legacy systems (e.g., between new desktop computers and older mainframes in which data are stored) and in terms of compatibility with complementary products (say, between HDTV and programming content).

3. *Complexity.* Complexity refers to how difficult the new product is to use. Very complex products have slower adoption and diffusion rates compared to those that are less complex. Obviously, many new high-tech products are complex. Marketers should ask themselves how they can simplify their products and whether the level of complexity is absolutely necessary, in terms of customer requirements.

4. *Ability to communicate product benefits.* The likelihood of customer purchase is influenced by the ease with which the product benefits can be communicated to prospective customers. There are two issues pertinent to high-tech marketers here. First, for many high-tech products, the benefits are difficult to convey to customers. With the HDTV example, what does higher-quality resolution really mean in terms of benefit to the customer?

Second, many high-tech marketers tend to talk in technical terms when communicating about the product. Such communication typically focuses on product features and specifications, rather than the real benefit the customer will receive. For example, in 1999 new computer chips operated in the 650 megahertz (MHz) range, operated with a bus interface (i.e., data transfer speed) in megabits per second (mbps), and offered exciting possibilities in terms of the operating capacity. But what did all this mean to a customer? Simply, it meant speed. However, from a customer's perspective, what did the increase from 600 MHz to 650 MHz provide? The answer for most customers' uses was "not much." The increase in speed provided only negligible improvements to most of their existing applications.[7]

5. *Observability.* Observability refers to, first, how observable the benefits are to the consumer using the new product and, second, how easily other customers can observe the benefits being received by a customer who has already adopted the product. Is the increased resolution of the HDTV really noticeable to the average TV viewer? Does the crisper picture really stand out compared to traditional sets? Moreover, can other customers observe the benefits that a user of the new technology gets? For products that are used in a *public* manner and for which the *benefits are clearly observable,* the likelihood of purchase is greater.

These factors must be assessed by inventors of new products in order to understand just how quickly their product might take off in the marketplace. Although the factors sound deceptively simple, they pose crucial barriers that high-tech marketers must overcome. They must educate buyers to overcome the "FUD" factor (fear, uncertainty, and doubt) and highlight benefits. Because breakthrough products don't connect easily with buyers' existing expectations, traditional approaches to marketing, which assume customers understand the usefulness of the product and know how to evaluate its features, are often insufficient.

For example,[8] the potential for WebTV, a Web-surfing device for TVs, seemed huge in 1996. Internet use was exploding and nearly every U.S. household had a television, creating a large installed base. WebTV relied on a traditional marketing program that included heavy advertising and dealer training. Through research, the company realized that its target customers didn't understand the device or, even more generally, what the Internet could do for them. Moreover, salespeople at retail didn't devote sufficient time explaining the product to customers and gravitated toward easier-to-sell items such as TVs and VCRs, which customers understood. So, an education initiative was launched in May 1997, featuring infomercials in which customers explained the benefits of the Internet overall and WebTV in particular. WebTV hookups increased sevenfold in one year. This example highlights the need to understand the factors that will affect customer adoption and to educate customers in ways that may be very different than traditional marketing methods.

Insight about the factors can be gained by involving customers in the new-product development process and by involving innovative customers who might be early adopters in evaluating new-product ideas. If a new idea does not fly well with innovators, it should raise a red flag. Even if the new idea does fly with innovators, it still doesn't guarantee success. However, without excited innovators, a new product rarely survives.

In assessing the rate of adoption and diffusion of innovation, inventors must take the perspective of the majority of the possible users of the product and not be biased by their own familiarity and ease with using technology. Nor should they be blindsided by the excitement and ease with which early adopters might use the product.

How quick was the adoption rate of some new products? Ten years after their initial introduction, compact discs had been adopted by 64% of U.S. households, cable TV had been adopted by 35%, answering machines, only 15%, and color TVs, only 3%. Clearly, in these and many other cases, the mainstream market for technologically oriented products materialized much more slowly than many would have predicted. On the other hand, some innovations take off quickly. In three years, the Internet developed into a trading center of 90 million people. In contrast, it took radio 30 years to reach 60 million users, and TV 15 years. "Never has a technology caught fire so fast."[9]

It is vital to understand which customers might be the first to embrace a new technology. In the case of the Internet, a company's best customers might be the last to embrace it if it poses a disruption in their current routines and procedures or because the Internet might not provide the service and performance such customers prefer. On the other hand, if a company ignores the people who embrace the Internet first, the innovation can creep up like a stealth attack.[10] Moreover, although an early market for a product might exist, innovators are usually not representative of "typical" customers. Therefore, it is vitally important to understand the different categories of consumers in terms of their likelihood of early adoption and what contributes to the disconnect between the early adopters of new technology and the reluctance of the mainstream market.

Categories of Adopters[11]

The categories of adopters discussed in traditional adoption and diffusion models include innovators, early adopters, early majority, late majority, and laggards. Although these traditional categories may be applied in high-tech markets, Geoffrey Moore has adapted this theory to apply to the business purchase of high-technology computing products in business markets. His adaptation is shown in Figure 6-2; a summary description of each of the categories is also shown.

Innovators   The early market for high-tech products is comprised of *technology enthusiasts*, people who appreciate technology for its own sake and are motivated by the idea of being a change agent in their reference group. They are willing to tolerate initial glitches and problems that may accompany any innovation just coming to market and are willing to develop makeshift solutions to such problems. Geoffrey Moore believes that the enthusiasts want low pricing in return for alpha and beta testing new products. In the computer industry, often these technology enthusiasts work closely with the company's technical people to troubleshoot problems. Although not much revenue may come from this group, it is key to accessing the next group.

Early Adopters   The next category, the early adopters, are *visionaries* in their market. They are looking to adopt and use new technology to achieve a *revolutionary* breakthrough to gain dramatic competitive advantage in their industries. These people are attracted by high-risk, high-reward projects, and because they envision great gains in competitive advantage from adopting new technology, they are not very price sensitive. Customers in the early market typically demand personalized solutions and quick-response, highly-qualified sales and support. Competition is typically between product categories (e.g., between DVDs and CDs) at the primary demand level. Communication between possible customer adopters cuts across industry and professional boundaries.

As an example of this early market in the electric car industry, the earliest adopters of electric cars in California paid nearly 25% more to lease their cars than did people who leased a year later. These visionaries were willing to make do with the higher price and hassles that accompanied being an early adopter. For early adopters of electric cars, the "hassle factors" came in the few stations that were capable of recharging batteries and the limited mileage range (90 miles between charges). The visionaries were willing to accept such inconveniences for the psychological and substantive benefits they received.[12]

Early Majority   The next group, moving into the mainstream market, are the *pragmatists* or the early majority. Rather than looking for revolutionary changes, this group is motivated by *evolutionary* changes to gain productivity enhancements in their firms. They are averse to disruptions in their operations and, as such, want proven applications, reliable service, and results.

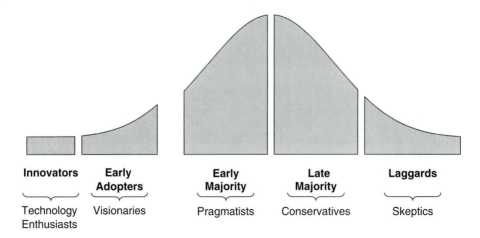

Innovators	**Early Adopters**	**Early Majority**	**Late Majority**	**Laggards**
Technology Enthusiasts	Visionaries	Pragmatists	Conservatives	Skeptics

Descriptions of Customer Categories[a]

Innovators	People who are fundamentally committed to new technology on the grounds that, sooner or later, it is bound to improve our lives. Moreover, they take pleasure in mastering its intricacies, just fiddling with it, and they love to get their hands on the latest and greatest innovations. Thus they are typically the first customers for anything that is truly brand-new.
Early Adopters	The first constituency who can and will bring real money to the table. They help to publicize the new innovations, which helps give them a necessary boost to succeed in the early market.
Early Majority	These people make the bulk of all technology infrastructure purchases. They do not love technology for its own sake. They believe in evolutionary, not revolutionary, products and innovations.
Late Majority	These customers are pessimistic about their ability to gain any value from technology investments and undertake them only under duress, typically because the remaining alternative is to let the rest of the world pass them by. They are price sensitive, highly skeptical, and very demanding.
Laggards	Not so much potential customers as ever-present critics. As such, the goal of high-tech marketing is not to sell to them but, rather, to sell around them.

FIGURE 6-2 The Categories of Adopters

[a] Contributed by Jacob Hachmeister, University of Montana, Missoula, MT.

Source: Adapted from Moore, Geoffrey A. (1991), The Product Adoption Curve in *Crossing the Chasm, Marketing and Selling Technology Products to Mainstream Customers,* New York: HarperCollins. Copyright © 1991 by Geoffrey A. Moore. Reprinted by permission of Harper-Collins Publishers Inc.

Pragmatists generally want to reduce risk in the adoption of the new technology and therefore follow three principles:[13]

1. "When it is time to move, let us all move together." This causes the landslide of demand.
2. "When we pick the vendor to lead us to the new paradigm, let us all pick the same one." This obviously determines which firm will become the market leader.
3. "Once the transition starts, the sooner we get it over with, the better." This is why this stage occurs very rapidly.

From a marketing perspective, these people are not likely to buy a new high-tech solution without a reference from a trusted colleague. A trusted colleague to a pragmatist is—who else?—another pragmatist, not a visionary or enthusiast who has a different view of technology. Obviously, this need for a reference from a pragmatist poses a real catch-22 to selling to this group: how to get just one pragmatist to buy, when the first won't buy without another pragmatist's reference. Yet, pragmatists are the bulwark of the mainstream market.

Late Majority   The late majority *conservatives* are risk averse and technology shy; they are very price sensitive and need completely preassembled, bulletproof solutions. They are motivated to buy technology just to stay even with the competition and often rely on a single, trusted adviser to help them make sense of technology.

Laggards   Finally, laggards are technology *skeptics* who want only to maintain the status quo. They tend not to believe that technology can enhance productivity and are likely to block new technology purchases. The only way they might buy is if they believe that all their other alternatives are worse and that the cost justification is absolutely solid.

The categories of adopters fall into a normal, bell-shaped curve. Although under most circumstances, a firm would likely target the innovators in a new-product launch, in some cases it might be more worthwhile to target the majority directly instead of the innovators. Firms will find it worthwhile to target the majority[14]

- When word-of-mouth effects are low
- In consumer products industries (versus business-to-business situations)
- When there is a low ratio of innovators to majority users
- When profit margins decline slowly with time
- The longer the time period for market acceptance of a new products

Each category of adopters has unique characteristics. Moore symbolizes the degree of these differences as gaps between each group in the marketplace. These gaps represent potential difficulty that any group will have in accepting a new product if it is presented in the same way as it was to the group to its immediate left. Each of the gaps represents an opportunity for marketing to lose momentum, to miss the transition to the next segment, and never to gain market leadership, which comes from selling to a mainstream market. The differences between the early market (innovators/early adopters) and the mainstream market (early majority) are more pronounced than differences between the other categories, and hence they warrant special attention.

Crossing the Chasm[15]

The largest gap between categories of adopters is between the early market (innovators/early adopters) and the mainstream market (early majority, late majority, and laggards). This deep and dividing schism is the most formidable and unforgiving transition in the adoption and diffusion process. The **chasm** is the gulf between the visionaries (early adopters) and the pragmatists (early majority, mainstream market) and derives from critical differences between the two. Visionaries see pragmatists as pedestrian, whereas pragmatists think visionaries are dangerous. Visionaries will think and spend big, whereas pragmatists are prudent and want to stay within the confines of reasonable expectations and budgets. Visionaries want to be first in bringing new ideas to the market, but pragmatists want to go slow and steady. The chasm arises because the early market is saturated but the mainstream market is not yet ready to adopt. Hence, there is no one to sell to.

What contributes to this chasm, and how can it be overcome? The nature of a firm's marketing strategy in selling to visionaries is very different than the marketing that is required to be successful with pragmatists. Many firms do not understand this and are unable to make the necessary shift in strategies to be successful.

Early-Market Strategies: Marketing to the Visionaries   As mentioned previously, visionaries require customized products and technical support. Because such customization for several visionaries can pull a firm in multiple market directions, they can be a costly group of customers to support. However, for a new high-tech start-up, sales to these visionaries represent the initial cash flows to the firm. Hence, given the demand from visionaries and need for cash flows, there is much pressure both to support their customization needs and to release products early to these customers. Just as customization can pull the firm in multiple market directions at a steep cost, early release of a product can backfire if it has not been adequately tested.

The goal of the marketer's firm at this point is to establish its reputation. In new high-tech start-ups, this time of selling to the early market is exciting and energizing. The product is often the focus; engineering and R&D folks play a critical role, and brilliance and vision are embraced. Firms try to develop the *best possible* technology for the market they pursue.

The Chasm   The bloom falls off the rose, however, when the firm takes on more visionaries than it can handle, given the high degree of customization and support they expect. No pragmatists are yet willing to buy, presumably because there is no credible reference for them. Hence, revenue growth tapers off or even declines. The goal of the high-tech marketer should be to minimize the time in the chasm. The longer the firm spends in the chasm, the more likely it is that it will never get out.

One implication of the chasm relates to relationships with venture capitalists and investors. Lack of knowledge of the existence of the chasm can create a crisis. Key personnel become disillusioned and management becomes discredited. Investors may pull out at the very time that more financing is necessary to get the product to the mainstream market. The ultimate demise of early-market success stories might be explained by the existence of this chasm.

The chasm in the Internet arena is often found after a company has made a decision to add an on-line sales channel—many times to the detriment of existing distribution channels. As a result, sales may actually decline in the short term after adding the on-line channel. As stated by Intel's VP of business development in discussing Internet investments, "In getting from point A to point C, B is hell." B is where revenues decline and profits go down, but there is simply no way for large companies to get to where they need to be in the future without going through it.[16] Because of this chasm, brick-and-mortar companies struggle with the issue of how much to invest in this still-emerging medium with huge up-front costs and only theoretical profits. It can be an especially anguishing decision for established companies who must show earnings growth quarter after quarter.

Marketing to the Pragmatists   In contrast to marketing to the visionaries, who are willing to tolerate some incompleteness in the product and will fill in the required "blanks," marketing to the mainstream market requires that the vendor assume total responsibility for system integration. This need demands the development of a *complete, end-to-end solution* for the customer's needs, or the **whole product.** Identifying the whole product requires an exhaustive analysis of what it takes to fulfill the reasons the customer is buying. Asking what else the customer will need, from a systems perspective, makes apparent possible switching costs and exposure. For example, in the computer industry, the whole product includes hardware, software, peripherals, interfaces and connectivity, installation and training, and service and support. In electronic business, the whole product includes Web site design, hosting of the site on a server, connection to the Internet, security, financial transactions, and, depending upon the purpose, customer relationship management.

The job of the firm in the chasm is to either develop or partner with firms to provide the whole solution to the initial customers in the mainstream market. Rather than developing the "best possible solution," the goal here is to develop the *best solution possible.* Yet, this is a very different skill set than that required to succeed in the early market. Now, the R&D team, rather than basing development on engineering solutions, must work closely with partners and allies on a project-oriented approach. For many, this is much less exciting than the pursuit of technological brilliance and requires painstaking work on compatibility, standards, and so forth. Moreover, this period may require that engineers go to customer sites to observe them in action. Customer service is a critical component of crossing the chasm.

Another crucial strategy in crossing the chasm and speaking to the needs of the mainstream market is simplifying, rather than adding additional features. Gadget makers tend to make new models bigger and more complicated—but not necessarily better— right at the time the mainstream market would buy if they were more user friendly. For example, Microsoft's Internet Explorer 5.0 did a good job of *not* focusing on dramatic breakthroughs. Rather, it focused on "thoughtful little advances that make using the Web simpler for average, nontechnical folks."[17] Similarly, the Palm III, introduced in 1998, recognized that the real growth in its sales would come from the explosion of third-party software and accessories that enhanced its abilities to link up with corporate networks.[18] And rather than clogging its new handheld device with useless extras, 3Com kept Palm III simple.[19] Because the developers took an evolutionary rather than revolutionary view, and because the Palm III is even easier to synchronize with a PC compared with the prior Palms, they followed the high-tech model perfectly. The Technology Tidbit provides a bit more about some of the new uses of handheld computers.

Infrared Sharing: The New Geeky Handshake

THOMAS LUNDELL

Who needs business cards and Rolodexes? In fact, who even needs pen and paper? Today it is all about beaming information. Users of 3Com's Palm Computing series or Handspring's Visor can swap address books and send memos at the touch of a button. A television ad for Palm Computing even shows romantic possibilities with beaming: A woman on a train locks eyes with a man on a different train the next track over. Just as they are about to take off in different directions, she takes her computer out and beams her phone number to him.

Although beaming has great courting functions, the most common use of this technology is probably exchanging business cards. The beamed information can be stored automatically in the computers' address books and pulled up at any time. In Japan, beaming is altering the way businesspersons interact. Swapping business cards has always been a part of a cordial greeting. Nowadays, users of handheld devices are "beaming and bowing."

Source: Srinivasan, Kalpana (2000), "Infrared Sharing: The New Geeky Handshake," *Popular Science* (retrieved February 28 from the World Wide Web: www.popsci.com/electronics/features/geekshake).

Communication between pragmatic customers in the mainstream market tends to be vertical, or within industry and professional boundaries (rather than horizontal, across industry boundaries, as in the early market). Competition is between vendors within a single category of solutions or product offerings. Indeed, pragmatists will want to see a competitor's proposal and product offering before making a decision. Competition, to the pragmatist, is actually a sign of legitimacy for the new technology. Customers typically demand some sort of industry standard to minimize their perceived risk. The vendor goal at this point is to bring in revenue.

Firms that succeed in the mainstream market have complemented their initially strong competencies in technological development with equally strong competencies in partnering and collaborative skills. Partners often drive further expansion, and so the firm's ability to interact with partners becomes a limit on growth. For example, although Intel's new Pentium III chip offered "only a very modest speed improvement—at most 10%—over existing chips,"[20] to really take advantage of the improved speed, Intel had to work closely with software developers to get Pentium III–enhanced products to market quickly. Partnering requires critical skills that were discussed earlier in Chapter 3.

SAP, maker of enterprise resource planning (ERP) software, did an excellent job of identifying what a whole product solution would look like and creating a series of partnerships to develop the whole product. SAP developed a "solution map" for each of 17 vertical markets, including automotive, media, oil and gas, and utilities, to name a few. The maps break down every function in each industry, specifying where SAP's software already offers a solution, where products from partner software developers are required, and where SAP will fill in gaps later. In essence, its solution map functions as a technology map for SAP, corresponding closely to the steps and needs of high-tech product development. Moreover, in terms of partnerships, SAP readily recognized that it needed the smaller developers, but the smaller developers were somewhat hesitant to partner; they wondered how long their investment in developing their own company's products based around an SAP product would be viable, or whether SAP would ultimately enter that market too. So, to entice small developers to partner, SAP had, to some extent, to guarantee that it would not enter the partner's space in a two- to three-year time frame. (Despite this, SAP sometimes did not honor that conditional "guarantee" and jettisoned its partners. For example, in working with i2, SAP announced it would enter i2's lucrative business of supply chain software, and the partnership died.) The challenge for the smaller developers was to partner with key market players (such as SAP, Oracle, or PeopleSoft) as a seal of approval in order even to be considered a viable option by large *Fortune* 500 customers (the pragmatists in the mainstream market). The smaller developers had to show *Fortune* 500 companies how well their products worked with the companies' existing ERP installations.

Partnerships generally revolve around the issues of power.[21] In the early market (enthusiasts and visionaries), power belongs to the technology providers and the systems integrators (firms that bring different suppliers' products together to create one integrated solution for a customer's needs). These market players (technology providers and systems integrators) make the decisions about whom to bring into the process as partners. In crossing the chasm and approaching the early mainstream pragmatists, the power is centralized in the hands of the company that has effectively picked the target customer, understands why they buy, and designed the whole product. In the pragmatist market, the market leader and its partners have the power. In later markets (mainstream conservatives), power is vested in the distribution channels or companies that provide superior distribution of product.

Marketing to Conservatives   Finally, for continued success in the mainstream market, the high-tech firm will also need to reach out to the conservative market. This requires making the product even simpler, cheaper, and more reliable and convenient, and possibly splitting the product line into simpler components. From an engineering perspective, this is the anathema of good engineering work. Rather than adding more interesting features and cool wow factors, engineers should actually do the opposite. Because this is so foreign to product development in high-tech firms, many high-tech companies leave the conservatives' money on the table.

In summary, crossing the chasm requires a different type of marketing than the marketing strategies used in the early market. The whole product is the critical success factor in crossing the chasm and reaching out to the mainstream market, yet bringing the whole product together is expensive and time-consuming. Until high-tech firms have established themselves in the mainstream market, they have not established staying power. How to succeed when the mainstream market takes off is addressed in Geoffrey Moore's second book, *Inside the Tornado,*[22] briefly summarized in Box 6-1.

The high-tech firm must make a decision about what one key market segment to put its resources behind and focus its efforts there. Going after too many market segments at once results in spreading its resources too thin and not building a strong reputation within that segment.

Inside the Tornado

What is a tornado? It is a whirling mael-strom that starts as a rather inconsequential storm but feeds on itself, getting larger in size, until it spins out of control into a violent, destructive, funnel-shaped whirl-wind. Geoffrey Moore likens the dramatic growth and development in mainstream high-tech markets to a tornado. This eye-popping growth results in companies such as Compaq having a revenue growth from zero to $1 billion in less than five years or Atari, which in a six-year span doubled in size every year, causing revenues to grow from $50 million to $1.6 billion.

The exponential growth in a high-tech market most often comes after a company has successfully crossed the chasm be-tween the early market (technology en-thusiasts and visionaries) and finds itself effectively marketing to the mainstream, pragmatist market. In marketing to the pragmatist market, a company finds three distinct phases:

1. The Bowling Alley. The *bowling alley* is a period during which the new product gains acceptance from niches within the mainstream market but has yet to achieve general, widespread adoption. Sales during this period are driven by compelling cus-tomer needs and the willingness of vendors to craft niche-specific whole products. Each niche is analogous to a bowling pin: some-thing that can be knocked over in itself but can also help knock over one or more ad-ditional pins. The goal is to progress from niche to niche, finding new applications to leverage the whole product and develop momentum. In the bowling alley, the firm must have business expertise in the vertical markets it is going after. Bowling alley suc-cesses help tornadoes to start because they

validate the underlying product architec-tures. During this phase, the market is typi-cally not large enough to support multiple industry players. The successful firm will es-tablish itself as the dominant market leader. One of the best ways to become the market leader is to follow a "whole product" strat-egy and partner extensively to create the *de facto* standard in the market.

2. The Tornado. The *tornado* is a period of mass-market adoption when the general marketplace switches over to the new tech-nology. It is driven by the development of a "killer app," or an application of the tech-nology that is based on a universal infra-structure, is appealing to a mass market, and is commoditizable.

The massive number of new customers entering the market in a rapid time period swamps the existing system of supply. During this stage, companies have a huge opportunity to develop their distribution channels. In fact, when companies hit this stage of the cycle, they need to focus on op-erational excellence: getting their products out to the consumers through streamlining the creation, distribution, installation, and adoption of their whole product. This is typically best done by beefing up internal systems so as to handle the high-volume workload.

An important caveat during the tor-nado: Do not bet on preventing a tornado. If a market leader begins to develop, even if it is not your company, it is important to switch efforts to follow the emerging leader.

Competing effectively in the tornado requires effective partnering skills. Moore looks at a number of the issues that must be addressed, one of the most important of which is: How do you dance with the

market leader, "a gorilla," in a tornado and come away in one piece? The answer is to sustain only enough ongoing innovation to stay out of the market leader's reach. In other words, don't try to pass the market leader by creating the next big thing. Do enough to remain stable, but not so much that the gorilla feels threatened—or it will crush you!

3. Main Street. *Main street* refers to the third period of the early majority/pragmatist market, when the tremendous growth in the market stabilizes. This period of after-market development is when the base infrastructure for the product's underlying technology has been deployed and the goal now is to flush out its potential. Rather than focusing on generating sales from new customers, companies must sell extensions of their products to their current customer base to be competitive. Overall, it is important to emphasize operational excellence and customer intimacy, rather than product leadership.

Source: Moore, Geoffrey (1995), *Inside the Tornado,* New York: Harper Business.
  Portions of this review were contributed by Jacob Hachmeister, University of Montana.

THE CHOICE OF CUSTOMER: SEGMENTING MARKETS AND SELECTING TARGET MARKETS

One of the most important issues with which high-tech firms wrestle is the choice of an initial target market to pursue with their promising new technologies. Yet, the choices that seem obvious in hindsight are rarely clear at the time of the decision. For example, Intel cofounder Gordon Moore rejected a proposal in the 1970s for a home computer built around an early microprocessor. He didn't see anything useful in it, so he never gave it another thought. In a list of possible uses for its 386 chip (written before the IBM PC), Intel omitted the personal computer, thinking instead of industrial automation, transaction processing, and telecommunications.[23]

The idea behind segmenting markets and selecting a target is to identify group(s) of customers who share similar needs and consumer behavior characteristics and who are responsive to the firm's offering. Directing marketing efforts toward a specific target is both more effective and more efficient than loosely attempting to reach as many customers as possible in the hopes that some of them might be interested and respond.

As shown in Table 6-2, market segmentation includes four steps.

TABLE 6-2 Steps in the Segmentation Process

1 Divide the market into groups, based on variables that meaningfully distinguish between customers' needs, choices, and buying habits.
2 Describe the customer's profile within each segment.
3 Evaluate the attractiveness of the various segments and select a target market.
4 Position the product within the segment selected.

1. *Divide possible customers into groups,* based on important characteristics that distinguish between customer groups in terms of the choices they make and the reasons they buy. For consumers, the traditional bases of segmentation include

- Demographic variables, such as age, income, gender, occupation, and so forth
- Geographic variables, such as geographic location, rural versus urban, and so forth
- Psychographic variables, or consumers' values and beliefs that affect their lifestyles and, hence, purchasing behavior, such as an orientation toward a healthy lifestyle or being technologically current or environmentally friendly
- Behavioral variables related to the customer's behavior with respect to the specific product category, such as
  - Frequency/volume of usage of a product (i.e., heavy versus light users)
  - The benefits desired in a product (i.e., ease of use)
  - The usage occasion (such as use for work versus home)

For businesses, traditional segmentation variables, such as SIC (Standard Industrial Classification) codes, firm size, and corporate culture, can be useful variables.

2. *Profile the customers in each segment* by describing a "typical" customer within each segment. A study compiled by technology consultant Forrester Research Inc., in conjunction with NPD Group, provides an example of steps 1 and 2.[24] This study identified 10 key consumer segments based on traditional demographics combined with technology-related behaviors. Dubbed "Technographics," the study polled 131,000 consumers about their motivations, buying habits, and financial ability to purchase technology products. The 10 segments are described in Figure 6-3.

FIGURE 6-3 Tech Customers: Segments and Descriptions

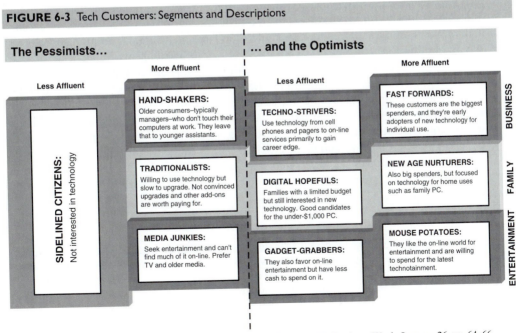

Source: Adapted from Judge, Paul (1998), "Are Tech Buyers Different?" *Business Week,* January 26, pp. 64–66.

The insights offered by the Technographics segments are changing the way technology companies make, sell, and deliver products. For example, consider two couples:

- Cindy and Gary Williams, ages 46 and 44, respectively, from Tulsa, Oklahoma. Cindy is an administrative secretary for a health-maintenance organization; her husband is a maintenance supervisor. They have two sons, ages 11 and 12. They have one PC they bought three years ago and have no Internet connections. They are considering an upgrade because their sons want speedier games than their sluggish machine can play.

Their family status and income are two traditional signposts that would highlight them as promising technology buyers. However, Forrester Research claims those factors are misleading and any technology company pitching products to the Williamses would likely be wasting its money. Its Technographics study pegs the Williams as *Traditionalists*— family-oriented buyers who are relatively well off but remain unconvinced that upgrades or other new technogadgets are worth buying. The key factor in their profile is the three-year age of their PC, making it ancient by tech standards. Traditionalists wait a long time before upgrading, making them not a very fertile part of the technology market.

- Carol and Robyn Linder, ages 46 and 53, respectively, from Milwaukee, Wisconsin. Carol is a customer service manager for Ameritech and her husband is a CPA; they have three school-age children, two pagers, and three PCs. Robyn spends time online for work.

Although similar to the Williams family in income and family status, the Linders are classified as *Fast Forwards,* using computers and other gadgets for job, family, and individual pursuits. So technology companies would find it desirable to target them.

Similarly, cable TV giant TCI knows that speed and performance were important to early users of cable modems, but that is not necessarily what will appeal to new types of buyers. Rather, kid-friendly Internet marketing targeted to family-oriented *New Age Nurturers*—the group focused on technology for home uses—or *Mouse Potatoes*—the group that likes entertainment-related technology—would be more successful.[25]

Research that focuses specifically on high-tech buyers can provide insights that more traditional segmentation variables may not. Other research firms that specialize in technology-related buyer issues are Odyssey Research (San Francisco), Yankelovich partners' Cyber Citizen, and SRI Consulting, Inc.

3. *Evaluate and select a target market.* After identifying meaningful segments in the market and understanding the customers within each of those segments, the third step in the segmentation process requires that the firm evaluate the attractiveness of the various segments in order to help narrow its choice of which to pursue. Four important criteria on which to evaluate each segment follow:

- *Size.* Estimates of the potential sales volume within each segment are needed in order to identify segments that are large in size. Don't make the mistake of basing size estimates on the number of customers *per se*, because it is their purchase volume that counts. Segments with fewer people may have larger dollar purchases. For example, the 80–20 rule says that 80% of the sales in any one category are typically purchased by only 20% of the customers.
- *Growth.* Estimates of the growth rates of various segments are also needed to help evaluate possible attractiveness. Segments that are growing in size are attractive for

at least two reasons. First, the growth means that the firm will be able to capitalize on customers' needs and grow with the market. Second, the growth means that, rather than stealing customers away from other firms, firms can capture new customers coming into the market.

- *Level of competition.* Estimates of the level of competitive intensity within each segment help a firm to identify how costly it may be to pursue that segment. High numbers of competitors or even a few powerfully entrenched competitors can pose formidable risks to a new firm. The issue is not so much "Is the new firm's technology better?" but how hard these competitors will work to defend their existing base of customers.

- *Capabilities of firm to serve the needs of that segment.* Finally, firms must take a good hard look at their core competencies and strengths to determine if they have the capabilities to serve the needs of a particular segment. Although partnering can augment some deficiencies, the reality is that customers will look to firms that offer the right set of skills to address their needs.

Geoffrey Moore refers to the selection of a target market as the identification of a **beachhead,** or a single target market from which to pursue the mainstream market.[26] The idea of a beachhead is that it will provide meaningful leadership to adjacent segments. If one uses a bowling pin analogy, the beachhead should be the lead pin; adjacent segments would be the pins immediately behind the beachhead. These adjacent segments can be "knocked off" more easily because of word-of-mouth relationships between customers in the two segments or similarities in whole product needs. Indeed, the definition of the whole product should be done within the confines of a single target market. Moreover, the segment should be capturable in a short period of time and provide entry to broader markets.

A good beachhead requires that customers have a single, compelling, "must have" reason to buy that maps fairly closely on to the capabilities of the firm. A variety of compelling reasons to buy, and their relative attractiveness to different categories of adopters, include the following:

- Purchase of the new technology provides the customer a dramatic competitive advantage in a previously unavailable domain in a critical market. This reason-to-buy is difficult to quantify in terms of costs/benefits, which, although appealing to the visionary, is unpalatable to pragmatists and conservatives.

- Purchase of the new technology radically improves productivity on an already well-understood critical success factor, and there is no other alternative to achieving a comparable result. This reason has the greatest appeal to a pragmatist, because the cost savings in terms of a better return on resource expenditures can be quantified, typically in terms of incremental dollars.

- Purchase of the new technology visibly, verifiably, and significantly reduces current total overall operating costs. This reason will have the greatest appeal to a conservative because of the hard dollar savings. However, the risk factors surrounding the new technology are still too high for conservatives to take a chance, and the surrounding infrastructure may not be sufficiently developed.

Moore believes that only the second reason represents a good choice for crossing the chasm, because it speaks directly to the pragmatist's concerns to generate incremental revenues from technology investments. The issue is whether the firm's capabilities offer this compelling reason for the customer.

For example, the digital networking firm Wam!Net, based in Minneapolis, provides a digital document delivery service to businesses. It identified the publishing industry as a strong beachhead. Customers such as Time Warner use thousands of suppliers to print their materials, and providing digital delivery improves both the quality and the speed of the process. Purchase of the new technology radically improved productivity on already well-understood critical success factors (quality and speed), and there were no other alternatives to achieving a comparable result. The cost savings could be quantified fairly easily. Wam!Net has identified adjacent segments with similar needs and positive spillover (word of mouth) effects in the entertainment industries.

Many high-tech firms make the mistake of attempting to pursue too many market segments at the outset. They are enthusiastic about the potential their innovation can offer to many different types of segments and are unwilling to limit their potential market opportunities. They also want to hedge their bets against selecting the wrong segment and so pursue several. However, most firms simply do not have the resources to be effective in multiple segments. They end up spreading their resources too thinly to be effective in any of the segments and, as a result, fail. A firm must be ruthless in its paring of its opportunities. Indeed, success in just one segment can be the catalyst required to succeed in other segments.

4. *Position the product within the segment.* The fourth and final step of the segmentation process is to create a meaningful market position for the new technology. A market position is the *image* of the product in the *eyes of the customer, relative to competitors,* on critical attributes of importance. There are several important aspects of this definition.

First, a market position is based on customers' perceptions. After all, customers will be making the decision to purchase (or not purchase) the new technology, and what matters is what they believe about the new technology. Whether the firm thinks the customers' perceptions are wrong is totally irrelevant. The issue is for the firm to use communications with customers to effectively create the market position the firm desires.

Second, a market position is always relative to competitors. Many new high-tech firms believe that they have no competition. Their innovation is so radical that no other firm provides anything remotely similar. Although this may be technically true, the customer's reality is that there are always other options (i.e., competition). The customer can choose to do things the old way or even do nothing. This is why positioning of the product is generally achieved by focusing on how the new technology fits within existing market categories by referencing the older technology that is being displaced (i.e., product form competition).

It is tough to be successful marketing a product that violates the categorical scheme of the marketplace, which creates confusion both among consumers and in the retail channel.[27] If positioned as something that is totally new, retailers will not know (a) if it is something that their store should carry or (b) which department to put the product in. As a result, consumers will not know where to find the product. Moreover, if positioned as something totally new, pragmatist consumers will not be able to compare products because they don't know what to compare it to. Firms may need to work with their rivals to overcome the prior technology successfully.

As the market for the new technology develops, the firms should then reference their rivals (i.e., selective demand). Finally, in late stages of the market, the market leader needs to reference its own products as competition; it should create new products that will cannibalize its old products.[28]

The final topic in this section on the decision-making process and concerns of customers is the issue of customer strategies to avoid obsolescence. Customers' desires to avoid obsolescence require that high-tech marketers proactively manage upgrade options for customers.

CUSTOMER STRATEGIES TO AVOID OBSOLESCENCE

High-tech markets are blessed (cursed?) with fast and significant (revolutionary) improvements, which result in "inflection points" or technological discontinuities in the marketplace. The steady stream of improved and overlapping product generations typically makes obsolete the customers' investments in prior generations, even while those investments are still perfectly functional in use.[29] For example, computer microchips show a rapid pace of constantly improved generations available to the marketplace, even while customers are using prior generations. Indeed, as noted in Chapter 2's discussion of technology life cycles, successive generations tend to arrive when the current generation's sales curve is still rising and may continue to rise for some time.[30]

In high-tech markets, customers must make important decisions about if and when to adopt a new generation of technology. In the extreme, customers may "leapfrog," or pass entirely on purchasing, a current generation of technology in anticipation of a new, better innovation coming down the pike in the near future. This **leapfrogging** behavior, based on customer expectations of imminent improvement, can have a chilling effect on sales of current products.[31] The customer says, "If I wait to buy tomorrow, the product will not only be cheaper, it will also be better."

In essence, the realities of customer decision making create a tension for the firm in providing state-of-the-art technology through the introduction of new-product generations and customers' expectations and fears of obsolescence. Customer investments in equipment from a prior generation creates a "footprint of the past." Hence, high-tech marketers must manage interfaces between these **legacy systems** and newer generations. Moreover, marketers' decisions regarding both the launch of a new generation and the withdrawal of the old become equally significant with overlapping generations. Marketers must also consider how to help customers migrate from one generation to another.

Customer Migration Decisions

What affects a customer's decision to adopt the new generation of technology? *Customers' expectations about the pace and magnitude of improvements* in the marketplace play a big role in their adoption decisions. More specifically, customers form expectations of the pace and magnitude of performance improvements and price decreases. The customer must balance the value of the existing products against the value of new offerings and even future arrivals. When products improve rapidly and significantly, the old adage about starting with a high price (to "skim" those who buy early) and then lowering price to entice later purchasers may not hold.[32] In general, the greater the anticipated product improvement or expected price decline, the greater the customer's propensity to delay purchase. Moreover, if the customer has already purchased, then the greater the product improvements and price decrements of successive generations, the greater will be the customer's regret factor—especially for early adopters.

The need to manage upgrade options can be especially sensitive for business customers, who often face a gap between a product's useful technological life (shorter than three years, in many cases) and its "accounting" life (for depreciation purposes, usually five years for durable assets). The race to market accelerates customer demand for low-cost solutions that provide benefits of "new and improved" without scrapping the old version entirely. Upgrades allow business customers to protect their investments in technology in these circumstances.

Upgrades for businesses are particularly important as the economic expansion ages. Some companies have shifted their information technology dollars to other organizational priorities, such as improving plant and manufacturing equipment. Others have spent so much on information technology that they are questioning why they need any more anytime soon.[33] These are vital issues for personal computer hardware and software makers, because the corporate market allows them to survive the razor-thin margins in the high-volume home PC market. But some corporate buyers have decided that the price/performance calculations don't warrant buying next-generation computers just for minute speed improvements. Because most firms can make the case that the technology in place is pretty workable, what is needed to motivate another buying round for new technology is a real technological breakthrough that convinces buyers their dollars are worth it.

Additional insights regarding the decision-making behaviors of organizational customers are found in Box 6-2 on high-tech organizational buyer behavior. It is based on the notion that a particularly useful way to understand business buyer behavior is to understand the time sensitivity of information in making technology-related purchasing decisions. Rapid and uncertain changes in the environment make information time sensitive, which leads organizational buyers to use information differently than in more traditional contexts.

Marketers' Migration Options

Marketers must help customers to manage the transitions between generations. One way they do this is to offer a **migration path,** or a series of upgrades to help the customer's transition between generations.[34] The various options along the migration path are based on the *degree to which the customer's options in the transition are more constrained versus enlarged.*

1. *Withdraw the older generation as soon as the new one is launched, with no assistance to the installed base.* Lack of parts and service for these customers forces them into a decision about migration sooner than they might like.
2. *Withdraw the older generation when the new one is launched, but offer migration assistance,* which can be in the form of technical help, trade-ins, backward compatibility with gateways, and the like. Customers can upgrade and maintain the old version or move to the new version later.
3. *Sell old and new generations together for a period of time,* after which the old generation is withdrawn. Customers can continue with installed version A, migrate to next generation B, or skip B entirely (leapfrog) and go to C.
4. *Sell both generations as long as the market desires them,* and provide migration assistance to the installed base.

BOX 6-2

Organizational Buyer Behavior in High-Tech Markets

ALLEN WEISS
Marshall School of Business, University of Southern California,
Los Angeles, California

One defining feature of a high-technology market is the fast pace of technological change. Such change creates high levels of uncertainties for buyers. The uncertainties that buyers face in high-technology markets is really about the *information* in these markets.

Unlike in slower-paced markets, the information in high-technology markets is time sensitive.[a] Time-sensitive information quickly loses its value. For example, computers and the microprocessors on which they are based have been rapidly improving in terms of speed, capabilities, and so forth. Consequently, knowledge associated with a given generation of computer quickly diminishes, and both customers and engineers are finding it difficult to maintain up-to-date knowledge. There are two broad implications for buyers in these markets.

First, as it relates to their purchase behavior, customers who perceive a rapid pace of technological improvements in computer workstations do tend to recognize the short shelf life of the received information. As a result, they tend to search for shorter periods of time because the information they receive is time bound.[b] In low-technology markets, uncertainties are typically resolved by longer periods of information search.

The short shelf life of information also affects buyers who have an existing relationship with a current (incumbent) vendor, but who decide to consider other vendors for a subsequent purchase. Paradoxically, this causes buyers both to expand their information collection effort and at the same time to restrict the tendency to switch vendors.[c]

For incumbent vendors, these information search characteristics of buyers pose an apparent dilemma. On the one hand, it would appear important for incumbent vendors to convince buyers that they are remaining technologically active. On the other hand, to the extent that such efforts contribute to increasing buyers' perception of technological change, it may create an incentive for buyers to consider the products of competitors. Interestingly, it appears that buyers end up staying with existing vendors. As such, rapid technological change actually buffers incumbent vendors from competition.

Rapid technological change also generates expectations in prospective customers that they may purchase a soon-to-be-obsolete technology. These expectations have been shown to induce prospective customers to leapfrog current generations of high-technology products.[d] Presumably, these expectations reduce the perceived benefits of owning a current product generation.

When information is time sensitive and customers anticipate rapid improvements, marketers of high-technology products face several other challenging product decisions. In particular, they must decide when to introduce new generations of a product and whether older generations should be sold concurrently. Although the pressures of producing leading-edge products are high, managers who quickly introduce new generations may both cannibalize their existing products and increase buyers' perceptions that their technology is changing rapidly. This may reduce the benefits of owning a current generation and ultimately encourage customers to leapfrog.

[a] Glazer, R. and A. M. Weiss (1993), "Marketing in Turbulent Environments: Decision Processes and the Time-Sensitivity of Information," *Journal of Marketing Research,* 30 (November), pp. 509–521.

[b] Weiss, A. M. and J. Heide (1993), "The Nature of Organizational Search in High-Technology Markets," *Journal of Marketing Research,* 30 (May), pp. 220–233.

[c] Heide, J. and A. M. Weiss (1995), "Vendor Consideration and Switching Behavior for Buyers in High-Technology Markets," *Journal of Marketing,* 59 (July), pp. 30–43.

[d] Grenadier, S. and A. M. Weiss (1997), "Investments in Technological Innovations: An Options Pricing Approach," *Journal of Financial Economics,* 44, pp. 397–416; and Weiss, A. M. (1994), "The Effects of Expectations on Technology Adoption: Some Empirical Evidence," *Journal of Industrial Economics,* 42 (December), pp. 1–19.

Based on an options model developed by Grenadier and Weiss,[35] the firm's choice of which migration path to offer to customers is affected by the following factors, shown in Table 6-3.

Expectations of Pace of Advancements   When customers expect rapid advances, albeit small ones, it pays for a firm to increase their options. Customers who anticipate a rapid pace of change tend to wait for price declines or bug fixes in the newly-launched version. These customers can also bypass completely, waiting for some yet-to-be-launched future version.[36] Both stalling and leapfrogging are mitigated by migration assistance. Without such assistance, firms will find their revenues swinging wildly.

Expectations of Magnitude of Advancements   In contrast to the pace of advancements, customers who expect significant advances in technology recognize that smooth upgrades are simply not possible. In such a situation, few customers are willing to wait to purchase an older generation of the product at a reduced price, which will be made

TABLE 6-3   Migration Considerations and Options

Customer Perceptions	*Implication for Customer Behavior*	*Implication for Migration Path*
Customers expect rapid pace in technology advancements	Willing to wait for price declines	Marketer should provide migration assistance
Customers expect large magnitude of change in technology advancements	Recognize smooth upgrading is unlikely; therefore, waiting to purchase an older model at a lower price may result in obsolescence	Migration path less crucial, because the latest technology effectively obsoletes any path that was available
Customers have anxiety about making a decision	Need to feel that their decisions are safe	Marketer should provide migration path, possibly selling old and new models together for a period of time

obsolete. In essence, there is less to be gained by keeping the customers' options open. As a result, where customers anticipate large discontinuities between generations, the firm may choose not to offer migration assistance. Even if the firm did, the reality is that the customers' existing investments have been destroyed.

Customer Uncertainty   When customers have uncertainty about their expectations, fear, and doubt, such a situation warrants migration assistance. A firm can choose to sell both the old and new versions to encourage customers with even older installed versions to migrate to the next step.

Any decision to offer upgrades must also account for complexities in managing relationships across the supply chain:

$$\text{Supplier} \rightarrow \text{Manufacturer/OEM} \rightarrow \text{Channel Members} \rightarrow \text{Customers}$$

Revenue from upgrades often flows to other members of the channel (e.g., the supplier in the case of chip upgrades, or manufacturers in the case of add-on components) and is smaller in size than that from selling entirely new units. Upgrades can also cannibalize sales of new products. So, the revenue implications and possible conflicts with other members of the supply chain must be monitored carefully with any decision.

Summary

This chapter has provided an in-depth look at issues related to customer purchase decisions: what affects their purchase decisions, different categories of adopters, segmenting markets and selecting an attractive target, and customer strategies to avoid obsolescence. The closing box takes the idea of a market orientation and ties it to many of the underlying concepts in both this section on understanding customers (Chapters 5 and 6) and the prior section on internal considerations in successful high-tech marketing (Chapters 2 through 4). In that sense, Box 6-3 offers an integrative summary of much of the material covered thus far.

Discussion Questions

1. What factors influence a customer's potential adoption of a new innovation? What are the implications of each of the factors for high-tech marketers?
2. What are the categories of adopters and their characteristics? What are the appropriate marketing strategies for each of the categories?
3. What is the chasm? Compare and contrast the marketing strategies that are necessary in the early market versus the mainstream market. For the conservatives?
4. What are the three phases of the pragmatist market (from *Inside the Tornado*)?
5. What are the four steps in segmenting markets?
6. What insights about market segmentation does the Technographics study offer?
7. What makes a good beachhead?
8. What is product positioning and how should a new innovation be positioned?
9. What are the issues in understanding customer strategies to avoid obsolescence? When should a migration path be offered?
10. How does knowledge of customer behavior in technology markets lead to insight in marketing? Provide examples.

BOX 6-3

*Putting It All Together: Market Orientation,
Innovation, Research, and Customers*

STANLEY F. SLATER
University of Washington, Bothell, Washington

A market orientation has been criticized for contributing to many things including incremental and trivial product development efforts, myopic R&D programs, confused business processes, and even a decline in America's industrial competitiveness. However, these views are seemingly at odds with the marketing concept that is the foundation of modern marketing.

The marketing concept says that an organization's purpose is to discover needs and wants in its target markets and to satisfy those needs more effectively and efficiently than do competitors. Since 1990, the theory behind market orientation—which is really the implementation of the marketing concept—has been developed and refined, valid measures of market orientation developed, and a strong relationship demonstrated between market orientation and specific measures of business performance including profitability, sales growth, and new-product success. This research supports the conclusion of many experts on the innovation process that a market orientation is essential to success in rapidly changing environments.

THE MARKET-ORIENTED BUSINESS

Market-oriented businesses are committed to understanding both the expressed and latent needs of their customers and the capabilities and plans of their competitors through the processes of acquiring and evaluating market information in a systematic and proactive manner. They continuously create superior customer value by sharing the knowledge broadly throughout the organization and by acting in a coordinated and focused manner.

Compared to less externally focused businesses, market-oriented businesses scan the market more broadly, have a longer-term focus, and are much more likely to have breakthrough insights.

No information "is more important to a technology-based firm than information flowing in from the market, as this information shapes science into commercial product or service."[a] Although market-oriented businesses use many of the same market research techniques as do traditional businesses, they combine these with other techniques to discover customers' latent needs and to drive breakthrough learning. For example, they observe customers' use of products or services in normal settings. By observing in context, they acquire information about customer needs that is not available from traditional market research.

They also work closely with lead users. A lead user is a customer, or potential customer, who has needs that are advanced compared to other market members and who expects to benefit significantly from a solution to those needs. Exploration with lead users often leads to the discovery of unexpressed needs and their solutions.

Thus, a true lead user should be a window into the future.

Of course, the future can never be fully known in a turbulent environment. Therefore, market-oriented businesses conduct market experiments, learn from the results of those experiments, and modify their offerings based on the new knowledge and insights. Companies such as Motorola, General Electric, and Corning maintain strong market positions by utilizing the "probe and learn process."[b] In this process, the initial product is only the first step in the development process, not its culmination. The initial product is a prototype that becomes the foundation for subsequent, more-refined generations that follow. Refinement is based on learning from customer experiences and reactions.

Market-oriented businesses also escape the "tyranny of the served market" by searching for unserved markets. The unserved market represents potential—those who might become customers. New products and unserved markets are the catalysts for organizational renewal in the market-oriented business.

A final point is that a market orientation is not a *marketing* orientation. Marketing is one functional area of the business. A business is market oriented only when the entire organization embraces the philosophy and when all business processes are directed at creating superior customer value.

IMPLICATIONS FOR COMPETITIVE ADVANTAGE

In a turbulent environment, competitive advantage is based on an ability to anticipate evolving customer needs and to generate new customer value based on that knowledge. Successful technology-based innovations must be accepted first by early adopters who tend to be market visionar-

ies. Their expectation is to exploit the new technology to achieve advantage over their competitors who use the old solution. The ability of the market-oriented business to work effectively with the market visionaries is key, because a "market orientation is more strongly related to new product performance at the early stage of the product life cycle than at the late stage."[c]

This is a critical stage in the commercialization of the technology as the solution embraced by the visionaries becomes the core of the product that will be adopted by early majority buyers.[d] The early majority are pragmatists in that they require a clear understanding of how adoption of the new technology will create economic value for them. The market-oriented seller also must work effectively with the pragmatists to demonstrate economic value because the pragmatists represent the larger, mainstream market. The research shows that a market orientation is associated with superior performance, and thus a position of competitive advantage, in turbulent environments and is particularly important to businesses that emphasize new product development.

CONCLUSION

Peter Drucker[e] suggested that the two essential activities of business are "innovation" and "marketing." Without the other, neither is sufficient for long-term success. A market orientation enables businesses to develop innovative solutions to both expressed and latent customer needs and to communicate the value of those solutions. Market-oriented businesses listen closely to the voices of their customers. They recognize that different types of customers provide different types of information. Moreover, those voices are only one source of information on which plans and strategies should be based. Their commitment to continuous market learning, to discovering latent needs and unserved markets, and to organization-wide mobilization of resources enables them to achieve market-focused innovation and to sustain competitive advantage in turbulent environments.

[a] Leonard-Barton, Dorothy (1995), *Wellsprings of Knowledge,* Boston: Harvard Business School Press, p. 177.

[b] Lynn, G., J. Morone, and A. Paulson (1996), "Marketing and Discontinuous Innovation: The Probe and Learn Process," *California Management Review,* 38 (3), pp. 8–37.

[c] Atuahene-Gima, K. (1995), "An Exploratory Analysis of the Impact of Market Orientation on New Product Performance," *Journal of Product Innovation Management,* 12, pp. 275–293.

[d] Moore, Geoffrey (1995), *Inside the Tornado,* New York: Harper Business.

[e] Drucker, P. (1974), *Management: Tasks, Responsibilities, Practices,* New York: Harper & Row.

Glossary

Beachhead.   A single target market from which to pursue the mainstream market. A good beachhead requires that customers have a single compelling, "must have" reason to buy.

Chasm.   The large gap between the early market (innovators and early adopters) and the mainstream market (early majority, late majority, and laggards) in the adoption and diffusion process.

Installed base.   Customers who have bought prior generations of a particular technology.

Leapfrogging.   Passing entirely on purchasing a current generation of technology in anticipation of a new, better innovation coming down the pike in the near future. Leapfrogging behavior, based on customer expectations of imminent improvement, can have a chilling effect on sales of current products.

Legacy systems.   Investments in prior technology.

Migration path.   Marketing tools (upgrades, pricing strategies, etc.) to help customers move from a prior generation of technology to a new generation.

Whole product.   A *complete solution* of what it takes to fulfill the reasons the customer is buying. For example, in the computer industry, the whole product includes hardware, software, peripherals, interfaces and connectivity, installation and training, and service and support.

Endnotes

1. Judge, Paul (1998), "Are Tech Buyers Different?" *Business Week,* January 26, pp. 64–66.

2. Kirkpatrick, David (1998), "The E-Ware War," *Fortune,* December 7, pp. 102–112.

3. Judge, Paul (1998), "Are Tech Buyers Different?" *Business Week,* January 26, pp. 64–66.

4. Interested readers may also want to review the book by Allan Reddy (1997), *The Emerging High-Tech Consumer: A Market Profile and Marketing Strategy Implications,* Westport, CT: Quorum Books.

5. It is also important to note that some believe there is no such thing as a high-tech consumer and that consumers approach the buying decision for technology products in the same way they would any product. See Cahill, Dennis and Robert Warshawsky (1993), "The Marketing Concept: A Forgotten Aid for Marketing High-Technology Products," *Journal of Consumer Marketing,* 10 (Winter), pp. 17–22; and Cahill, Dennis, Sharon Thach, and Robert Warshawsky (1994), "The Marketing Concept and New High-Tech Products: Is There a Fit?" *Journal of Product Innovation Management,* 11 (September), pp. 336–343.

6. Rogers, Everett (1983), *Diffusion of Innovations,* New York: Free Press.

7. Wildstrom, Stephen (1999), "Pentium III: Enough Already?" *Business Week*, March 22, p. 23.

8. Waite, Thomas, Allan Cohen, and Robert Buday (1999), "Marketing Breakthrough Products: The Secret Is to Educate Before You Sell," reprint #F99606, Harvard Business School.

9. Hof, Robert (1998), "The Click Here Economy," *Business Week*, June 22, pp. 122–128.

10. Byrnes, Nanette and Paul Judge (1999), "Internet Anxiety," *Business Week*, June 28, pp. 79–88.

11. Much of the material in this section is derived from Moore, Geoffrey (1991), *Crossing the Chasm, Marketing and Selling Technology Products to Mainstream Customers*, New York: HarperCollins.

12. McKim, Jenifer (1998), "Recharging Ahead," *Missoulian*, October 25, p. G1.

13. Moore, Geoffrey (1995), *Inside the Tornado*, New York: Harper Business.

14. Mahajan, Vijay and Etian Muller (1998), "When Is It Worthwhile Targeting the Majority Instead of the Innovators in a New Product Launch?" *Journal of Marketing Research*, 34 (February), pp. 488–495.

15. The majority of the information in this section is derived from Moore, Geoffrey (1991), *Crossing the Chasm, Marketing and Selling Technology Products to Mainstream Customers*, New York: HarperCollins.

16. Byrnes, Nanette and Paul Judge (1999), "Internet Anxiety," *Business Week*, June 28, pp. 79–88.

17. Mossbert, Walter (1999), "New Microsoft Browser Adds Some Nice Details for Simpler Use of Web," *Wall Street Journal*, March 18, p. B1.

18. Wildstrom, Stephen (1998), "The PalmPilot Flies Higher," *Business Week*, March 23, p. 20.

19. Himowitz, Michael (1998), "The Palm Pilot Sequel Is a Hit," *Fortune*, April 13, pp. 154–156.

20. Wildstrom, Stephen (1999), "Pentium III: Enough Already?" *Business Week*, March 22, p. 23.

21. Moore, Geoffrey (1995), *Inside the Tornado*, New York: Harper Business.

22. Moore, Geoffrey (1995), *Inside the Tornado*, New York: Harper Business.

23. Gross, Neil and Peter Coy with Otis Port (1995), "The Technology Paradox," *Business Week*, March 6, pp. 76–84.

24. Judge, Paul (1998), "Are Tech Buyers Different?" *Business Week*, January 26, pp. 64–66.

25. Judge, Paul (1998), "Are Tech Buyers Different?" *Business Week*, January 26, pp. 64–66.

26. Moore, Geoffrey (1991), *Crossing the Chasm, Marketing and Selling Technology Products to Mainstream Customers*, New York: HarperCollins.

27. Moore, Geoffrey (1995), *Inside the Tornado*, New York: Harper Business.

28. Moore, Geoffrey (1995), *Inside the Tornado*, New York: Harper Business.

29. John, George, Allen Weiss, and Shantanu Dutta (1999), "Marketing in Technology Intensive Markets: Towards a Conceptual Framework," *Journal of Marketing*, 63 (Special Issue), pp. 78–91.

30. Norton, John A. and Frank Bass (1987), "Diffusion Theory Model of Adoption and Substitution for Successive Generations of Technology Intensive Products," *Management Science*, 33 (September), pp. 1069–1086.

31. Weiss, Allen (1994), "The Effects of Expectations on Technology Adoption: Some Empirical Evidence," *Journal of Industrial Economics*, 42 (December), pp. 1–19.

32. Dhebar, Anirudh (1996), "Speeding High-Tech Producer, Meet the Balking Consumer," *Sloan Management Review*, Winter, pp. 37–49.

33. Ziegler, Bart and Thomas Weber (1996), "PC Sales Growth Slows As Corporate Ardor for New Models Cools," *Wall Street Journal*, March 25, pp. A1, A6.

34. John, George, Allen Weiss, and Shantanu Dutta (1999), "Marketing in Technology Intensive Markets: Towards a Conceptual Framework," *Journal of Marketing*, 63 (Special Issue), pp. 78–91.

35. Grenadier, S. and Allen Weiss (1997), "Investments in Technological Innovations: An Options Pricing Approach," *Journal of Financial Economics*, 44, pp. 397–416.

36. Weiss, Allen (1994), "The Effects of Expectations on Technology Adoption: Some Empirical Evidence," *Journal of Industrial Economics*, 42 (December), pp. 1–19.

CHAPTER 7

Product Development and Management Issues in High-Tech Markets

The product development process in high-technology environments relies on many of the same concepts used in product planning in more traditional environments. For example, firms must be concerned with different ways of categorizing products. The most common classification for high-tech products (from Chapter 1) classifies innovations on a continuum ranging from incremental to radical innovations. Recall that incremental innovations are continuations of existing methods or practices, and may involve extensions of products already on the market; they are evolutionary as opposed to revolutionary. Radical, or breakthrough, innovations employ new technologies to solve problems and, in doing so, often create totally new markets. Breakthrough innovations represent new ways of doing things. For success in commercializing innovations, the different types of innovations must be managed differently. Chapter 1 identified this notion as the contingency model for high-tech marketing.

Product managers also rely on the notion of product life cycles, which is modified in a high-tech environment. A technology life cycle (see Chapter 2) is the relationship between investments in improving the underlying technology of a product and its price–performance ratio. Typically, this relationship is S-shaped: Initial investments in a new technology may show modest improvements in the product's price–performance ratio, but after some threshold, additional investments show a drastic improvement in price–performance, which then levels off at some point. Importantly, technology life cycles help managers to understand that when a new technology enters the market, the new and the former technologies will compete with each other for a period of time, until the new technology eventually supercedes the former. Technology life cycles allow a product manager in a high-tech environment to anticipate when new technologies may supercede existing technologies and highlight the need to always be on the cutting edge. For example, when Microsoft introduced Windows 95 into the marketplace, many people continued to use DOS 3.1 for a period of time. However, eventually, the price–performance ratio of Windows was so compelling that even hard-core DOS users switched to the new software platform. Similarly, many users will continue to use Windows 95 rather than immediately migrating to Windows 2000.

Adoption and diffusion of innovation (from Chapter 6) are other concepts useful in managing both high- and low-tech products. Classifications of innovations, technology life cycles, and adoption and diffusion of innovation are but three of the product management concepts on which high-tech marketers rely. With what other issues do product managers in high-tech environments need to be concerned? In this chapter, we delve much more specifically into other product development and management tools used in a high-tech environment. One critical issue is the development of a technology map to guide investments and resource allocations within the firm. Another is the decision about how to approach the product development process. Firms face several routes to new-product development. They may choose to develop new products in-house, with their own resources and skills. Alternatively, high-tech firms may choose to partner with others in the new-product development process. Partnering allows firms access to others' skills and resources, which can both hasten product development time and lower costs.

High-tech marketers must also consider how far to develop the technology prior to offering it for sale in the marketplace. For example, a firm may decide to market and sell basic know-how (say, through a technology transfer or licensing arrangement) or develop a whole product (from Chapter 6), marketing and selling a ready-to-use product. The decision about how close to final form the product should be developed in the product development process is not a clear-cut decision but one that warrants consideration.

Other product development/management issues in a high-tech environment include the following:

- Should the firm use an underlying product platform strategy, in which derivative products can be made in a modular fashion and "dropped in" to the underlying technological platform?
- How does a firm know what level of functionality to include in the product?
- When or how should a firm halt investments and development in a new product whose success looks questionable?
- How should intellectual property rights be controlled?

These and related topics are explored in this chapter. To get us started, the Technology Expert's View from the Trenches provides a perspective on product development from an R&D manager in a high-tech company.

DEVELOPMENT OF A TECHNOLOGY MAP

The systematic evaluation and management of a firm's technological resources are critical to long-term product strategy. A **technology map** defines the stream of new products, including both breakthroughs and derivatives (incremental improvements based on the new technology) that the company is committed to developing over some future time period. Companies that are most successful in defining next-generation products use the map to force decisions about new projects amid the technological and market uncertainty found in high-tech markets.[1] The use of a technology map can promote cohesion and commitment to new-product development plans and can be used to clarify possible sources of confusion, to allocate resources, and to make trade-offs among various projects. Importantly, technology maps are not cast in stone but are updated and revisited regularly. Hence, rather than being a tool that inhibits innovation and creates blinders for a firm, a technology map should serve as a flexible blueprint for the future, updated and revised regularly.

Creating New Products

HANS WIJMANS
Director of Research and Development, Membrane Technology
and Research, Inc., Menlo Park, California

If I were to ask you to give me some examples of new inventions, chances are you would mention high-tech products from the computer, communications, or biotechnology industries. Easily overlooked are the less eye-catching inventions that nevertheless have a major impact on our lives. For example, the tremendous innovations that make your current car safer and more environmentally friendly and a better value all around than your previous one are important innovations in the automotive industry. Another less flashy category of innovations are the novel systems that are able to separate chemicals from each other and which reduce waste and increase energy efficiency in chemical processes, which is the business I am in.

The development of new products and/or technologies is a very costly process with no guarantee of success. So why do companies make the investment? New products are a company's lifeline, and their successful development is essential to the long-term viability of the company. How does a company maximize its chances in this high-stakes game of poker? There are two different strategies to choose from.

The first strategy is *market-driven,* in which a company conceives of a new product that it believes will fill a need in the marketplace. The company makes the product a reality using whatever technology is appropriate; if it does not have access to the technology required, the company develops the technology or acquires it. The risk of the market-driven approach is that one can be blind-sided by a radical new technology that changes the market as one knows it.

The second strategy is *technology-driven,* in which a company creates and develops a new technology with the expectation that new products will be generated along the way. Most start-up companies are technology-driven, and these companies dominate the development of truly new products that revolutionize the world. But it is equally true that the success rate of these companies is very low. The risk is that the technology does not work or that the company finds out that nobody has a need for it. So technology developers need to be mindful that success is not a nifty new technology, but rather, a useful product based on that technology. That means that the developers have to venture outside the laboratory and talk to potential users.

I believe that the two approaches are not exclusive and are best combined. The "best case" scenario that I have in mind starts with a technology-driven start-up that finds, through hard work and luck, the first winning application for its novel technology. The hurdle to market entry for a new technology is high, so this first product must be clearly superior and not just marginally better than the existing product. The company now has its first customer base and develops the infrastructure required to sell to these customers. Better understanding of these customers' needs leads to product diversification, yet all products are still based on the original technology developed. Selling these additional products is relatively easy, because the company and its technology are now known to the customers. The company is doing well and identifies potential applications for its technology in other industries. This leads to diversification of its customer base and to further growth of the company. The company realizes that other products, not based on its core technology, could be sold through its existing marketing and sales organization and the company decides to either develop or acquire the technology required to do so. The end result is a successful company, technology-driven and market-driven at the same time.

Not surprisingly, the above scenario is the one we at MTR are using. As a small R&D company, we pioneered a new way to separate organic vapors from gas streams based on a selective membrane permeation process. Membrane permeation is somewhat like filtration except that molecules, rather than particles, are separated. Based on this new technology, we have developed applications in the petrochemical industry and we sell to major petrochemical companies worldwide. As mentioned previously, our separation systems reduce waste and increase energy efficiency in chemical processes. Our revenues have tripled over the last three years and we have made the transition to selling products (separation systems), not just generating ideas. We are doing well in the petrochemical industry, and are currently looking to diversify our customer base into the refinery and oil and gas industries and will rely on our R&D capacity to generate additional products.

Capon and Glazer offer the following steps in developing and managing technology resources[2] (See Figure 7-1.).

1. *Technology identification.* Technology identification requires taking an inventory of the firm's know-how to find those ideas having the most value. Technology know-how can be found in products, in processes, and in management practices. Although most firms can easily identify the technology that forms the basis of their products, it is more difficult to identify process technology that might have value outside the firm itself. And organizational and managerial know-how can be equally difficult to identify. However, as "best practices" routines are becoming more common—for example, superior skills in total quality management, electronic commerce, customer service, and the like—such organizational and managerial know-how has also become a revenue-generating asset. Essentially, this first step in development—a map—requires taking stock of what a firm has.

2. *Make decisions about technology additions.* The technology identification from step 1 may highlight areas of weakness in the firm's strategy, identifying areas where it needs additional technologies in its platform and suggesting decisions about how to add them. Technology additions arise when the firm, through its technology identification process,

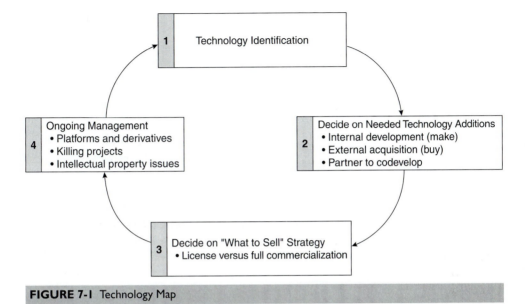

FIGURE 7-1 Technology Map

has recognized technology arenas in which the firm would like to have skills or products to round out its offering.

It can choose to add these skills or products through either internal development, external acquisition (buying another firm that has the requisite technology or licensing), or partnering. The decision about how to add needed skills and products is sometimes referred to as a "make versus buy" decision. "Make" refers to the decision to rely on internal development to develop new products, whereas "buy" refers to the decision to acquire externally the rights to a new product developed by another firm.

The key issue in the decision about how to add technology is *development risk.* It is sometimes best to pursue *internal development* (i.e., to make the product) if

    a. The R&D area is close to current corporate skills.
    b. The firm wishes to keep its technological thrust confidential.
    c. The firm's culture fosters the belief that the only good technology is developed internally.

In some cases, internal R&D may be cheaper than external acquisition. Issues pertinent to internal development were discussed earlier; for example, the ideas of R&D–marketing interaction, product champions, and so forth.

On the other hand, *external acquisition* (i.e., to buy the product) makes sense if

    a. Someone else has already developed the technology, and acquisition can save the firm time and effort.
    b. The firm does not have all the necessary skills to develop the desired technology.
    c. The firm wants to let others take big risks before participating.
    d. The firm needs to keep up with a competitor whose new technology is potentially threatening.
    e. The firm wants to obtain technology for products that can use present brand names, distribution channels, and so forth.

As a middle ground, a firm may choose to form a collaborative relationship for new-product development. Alliances between either competing firms or firms that provide complementary pieces to the product solution are frequently used. The unique issues associated with managing those alliances were discussed previously (in Chapter 3).

3. *Make decisions about commercializing, licensing, and so forth.* After acquiring or developing the desired technological know-how, the firm faces the commercialization decision. Here, *marketing risk* is the critical issue. The firm must decide exactly how far in the development process to proceed before marketing and selling the product. This decision is explored in the next section as the "what to sell" decision. If a firm chooses to commercialize its technology, issues related to timing the entry into a new market arise.

4. *Ongoing management.* Finally, the firm will need to actively manage its technology asset base, including the development of derivatives, whether to use product platforms in the strategy, when to "kill" new-product development projects, intellectual property management, and so forth. These issues are also discussed later in this chapter.

THE "WHAT TO SELL" DECISION

In a high-tech firm, technology itself either *is* the product (e.g., in a firm that licenses proprietary technology) or *gives rise to* the product (e.g., in a firm that chooses to commercialize products based on a new technology).[3] Firms that innovate technological know-how face a unique decision: Should they sell the knowledge itself or possibly license it? Should firms fully commercialize the idea—marketing, distributing, and selling a full solution including service and support? Or, given that final products can be "decomposed" into subsystems and components, should firms manufacture and sell some subsystem or component on an original equipment manufacturer (OEM) basis? Essentially, the decision about what to sell boils down to the basic issue of how to transform know-how into revenues.

Possible Options

As discussed next, firms can choose to sell know-how only; "proof-of-concept"; commercial-ready components to OEMs; ready-to-use final products or systems; or service bureaus that supply complete, end-to-end solutions for the customers' needs.

The decision is based on an underlying dimension: the required expenditures by customers to derive the intended benefits, above and beyond their acquisition costs of the focal purchase.[4] For example, funds can be spent for the core product, to purchase complementary items, services, and training, all of which can be necessary components to derive the intended benefit of the product. Customers who buy at the low end of the continuum (purchasing know-how only) must expend greater resources to realize the benefits of using the product, whereas customers who buy at the upper end of the continuum (purchasing the complete product and all ancillary support services) can fully realize the benefits of the product with their purchase price.

Sell or license know-how only. The sale of know-how requires the greatest additional expenditures of funds by the customer after the transaction to realize the intended benefit. For example, chemical firms may sell (or license) the rights to a specific molecule to downstream producers.

Sell "proof-of-concept."   The sale may include a prototype or pilot plant to establish that the know-how can indeed be made to work. Selling at this point on the continuum decreases the technological uncertainty for the buyer.

Sell commercial-grade components to OEMs.   Firms may manufacture and sell components that are ready to use in another firm's manufactured product. For example, Intel develops, makes, and sells computer chips to computer manufacturers (OEMs) that are ready to be inserted into the computer.

Sell final products or systems with all essential components, ready for use "out-of-the-box," to customers.   For example, computer manufacturers sell computers that are ready to be used by the customer.

Sell a complete, end-to-end solution.   This whole product solution delivers the intended benefits directly to customers with no need for them to incur additional expenditures on complementary items. For example, IBM has moved into the Web-hosting business, in which it will provide servers, software, and requisite services for any company that would like to have a Web site as part of its business solution.

Additional insights about the distinction between focusing on products and focusing on services is explored in the Technology Expert's View from the Trenches by Denice Gibson, senior vice president of marketing at Wam!Net.

What Decision Makes Sense?

The factors that affect a firm's decision about where along the continuum to generate revenues are shown in Figure 7-2 and discussed next.

In general, firms should lean toward the *selling know-how* end of the continuum when[5]

- The technology does not fit with the firm's corporate mission.
- The firm has insufficient financial resources to exploit the technology.
- The window of opportunity is tight and the firm cannot move quickly enough.
- The market potential is smaller than expected.
- The business cannot be made profitable by the firm.
- Allowing other firms access to the technology is the most appropriate action.[6]
- The range of technologies in a market is very diverse.

In this latter case, it is difficult for firms to keep up with all the relevant technologies across all the components or subsystems of a final product. As a result, firms may find it desirable to compete closer to the know-how end of the continuum rather than the end-product level.[7] This means that high-tech industries experience a pull toward "componentization." For example, the Technology Tidbit focuses on the wide range of technologies used in NASA's Earth Observing System.

Allowing other firms access to technology (e.g., via licensing agreements) makes sense when the market is characterized by network externalities. Recall from Chapter 1 that many high-tech markets are characterized by a situation in which the more customers that adopt and use a particular innovation, the greater its value for all users. For example, the value of an Internet portal (to both customers and companies linked to the portal) increases as more and more customers use that portal. Known as "demand-side increasing

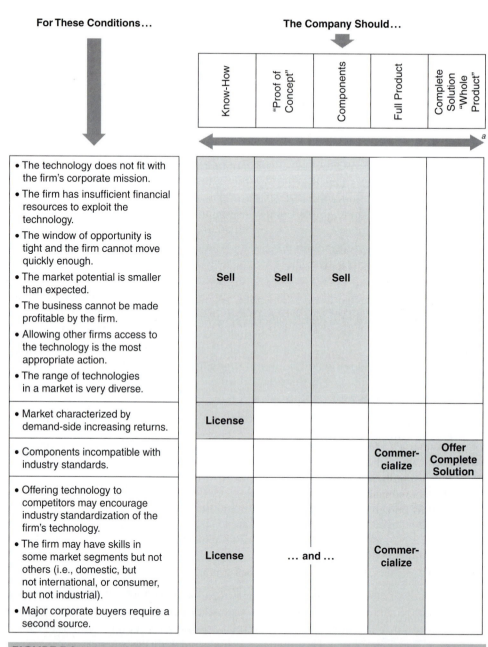

FIGURE 7-2 What to Sell

[a] Underlying continuum is based on customer expenditures needed beyond the initial acquisition cost to derive benefits of their purchase.

returns," this type of network externality tends, on the one hand, to favor a position on the continuum closer to selling know-how.[8] But, on the other hand, know-how often involves tacit knowledge, making it difficult to valuate and trade. (If a firm decides to sell its technology, a critical issue is pricing, which is explored in a later chapter.) Hence, this latter tendency pushes firms to a position closer to the end product.

Product versus Services—What Does That Mean?

DENICE Y. GIBSON
Senior Vice President of Marketing, Development,
Support, and Operations, Wam!Net, Minneapolis, Minnesota

In the world of technology, companies often define themselves in terms of the products they make. But, more and more, technology companies are going to find that defining themselves in terms of the services they provide offers a more viable strategy for long-term success. Services companies like Wam!Net assist their customers in maintaining their competitive advantage by focusing on our core-competency, providing e-business services to our customers. Services at Wam!Net include e-services for the Internet, training, professional services, data storage, data transport, applications through an API, and workflow. Making the decision to become a services company will be a natural outgrowth of the changes in the market as competition increases between companies and globalization occurs. And the Internet provides a level playing field from which to conduct business.

PRODUCT COMPANIES

In a product-focused company, the products themselves typically have a higher profile and a higher internal value than the company's customers. In communications about the company, the focus is all too often internal—on the product and its neat features—rather than on the external vision of how the product can benefit customers. The cultural mind-set of a "product" company mirrors that of the traditional engineer: deliberate, planned, very detailed. Quality is measured using engineering standards, which test whether the specifications of the products match the company's standards 100% of the time. Accuracy, precision, and excellence are significant and are often defined by the "creator" of the product, as opposed to the purchaser and user of the product. While just-in-time production processes have grown in importance, the "go faster" mentality in a product-driven company differs from a service-driven company. In a services environment, a service can be altered quickly to meet the needs of the customers.

SERVICES COMPANIES

Companies that understand that a focus on the product and its technology can be limiting to future success differentiate their product based on the services that accompany their products. Companies with this broader vision differ in three key ways from product-focused companies.

1. **The level of focus on the customer**   In a company that defines itself as a services company, the customer becomes King.

   - Customer-focused activities include the creation of a customer hotline (either e-mail or 1-800) and inclusion of reports from that hotline into management meetings and employee communications to assure continuous feedback and meaningful action.

- A high level of "visibility" on customers and their successes throughout the company (such as letters and pictures in the cafeteria, customer logos and lists in the lobby, customer testimonials on the walls).
- In media relations initiatives, more emphasis on case studies and "solutions" than on product specifications, trade shows, management and executive speeches, and corporate communications activities.
- Active, and well-known, customer satisfaction measurement systems are utilized such as: service audits, regional focus groups, formal annual customer surveys, management–customer calls, and user groups.

2. **The approaches to and structures surrounding work processes/activities** In a company that defines itself as a services company, the way the company works—its structure, systems, and processes—changes continuously:

- The formal and informal structures (organizational patterns, meeting participants, even assignment of department locations in the buildings) of the company are modified to drive increased collaboration and connections, especially between operations and marketing. There is a conscious movement from functional initiatives toward team initiatives. Typically, marketing communications leads this initiative as facilitator.
- The service delivery and quality systems are more precisely defined and managed. There are more rigorous measurement systems for business operations and for personnel. Formal metrics are put into place and very aggressively communicated.

The internal culture of a services company is:

- *Relationship-driven.* Caring for the customers' needs is visible in daily behav-

ior patterns, in communications, and in all aspects of the business's operations. The mental mindset of every company employee focuses daily on this question: "What have I done to win, grow, or satisfy a customer today?"
- *Focused outside-in.* The customer's needs are always considered before what the company wants, and this focus is based in service, not servitude. People's behavior is steeped in aggressive advocacy for what is in the customers' best interests *and* is consistent with the business's mission, vision, and values.
- *Positively motivated* by awareness, knowledge, understanding, and appreciation for the customers' businesses.

The *values* of the services-oriented company are:

- *Trust-based.* There is a profound belief in the company's mission, commitment to its vision, and support of its values.
- *Active, not passive.* There is a sense of ownership in the future of the business that drives hard work and attentiveness to excellence.
- *Collaborative.* People at a company committed to service excellence understand how significant, yet interdependent, their role is. They take pride in seeing all sides of an issue before acting.
- *Tolerant of ambiguity,* yet demanding of those answers that can be provided.

Attitudes of all employees, including management, are tolerant of differences, receptive to constructive criticism, open to change if it can be demonstrated to add value—to the organization and to them, collectively and individually. Progressive employees are interested in learning, in growing, in trying new approaches, in learning more from someone whose background and experience base are different. They are flexible, innovative, and risk tolerant.

3. **The content, frequency, and format of employee communications and evaluations**
In a company that defines itself as a services company, the internal communications and personnel evaluations are revolutionized.

- Employees play a more active and more publicly visible role, acting as ambassadors and advocates for the company.
- Internal communications are more frequent and more systematic, yet more informal and more human. They are also "consistent" with the company's business. So, technology-based companies use technology for their own internal communications (including audio and video teleconferences, intranet chat lines, on-line management presentations and Q&As, electronic clippings of news releases, etc.).
- Senior management is perceived to be more active in their communications, simply by being more visible and accessible.
- Training on service, interpersonal communications, and active listening receives at least as high a level of emphasis as technical skills training.
- Performance appraisals (and often incentive compensation plans) are directly linked to the new service metrics.
- Outside service experts become matched with internal technical experts to produce new systems and approaches to communications, training, and evaluation.

THE TRANSITION FROM PRODUCT TO SERVICES AT WAM!NET

When both products and services exist in a single company, there is confusion about what takes priority and how to best get things accomplished. While a product company grows its product with the philosophy that "you must have this new feature mentality," a service company services the customer to meet all of their needs. A service company asks the question, "What can we do differently today to make your life easier?" This difference is subtle yet extraordinary.

Moreover, as noted in the discussion above, the concept of product versus services can often cause confusion and conflict among employees. Most product companies have service departments that support their customers. These are normally based around service levels to the customers that support the product in its key functions. If Wam!Net continued on its product strategy while trying to deliver service, the relative weight of the two components might not be clear. Our sales force would be trying to sell products and not necessarily services. Our development staff would be focused on the next release of the product.

Leading Wam!Net to move from products to services was a revolutionary plan to grow the company. Switching to a services focus allows us to support many different types of products, while providing a transport and storage infrastructure to our customers. If we had proprietary products as well as services, we likely would service customers only if they also used our products. By focusing more exclusively on providing service, we can stay neutral with respect to the products we support, much like Switzerland's neutrality in global politics. This allows our customers to select the product that best fits their needs, and it allows us to have customers in all industries around the world. We don't have a specific product that competes with their selections.

NASA's Earth Observing System (EOS)

THOMAS LUNDELL

NASA launched the "flagship" of its Earth Observing System (EOS) series of satellites in December 1999. The first satellite, named *Terra,* is part of a precedent-setting program designed to provide daily information on the health of the planet. The launch is the start of a new generation of earth science approaches.

Source: Barbara Summey, NASA GSFC.

The effort is a cooperative venture. Various institutions around the country worked on EOS, designing hardware and software. Moreover, labs in Canada and Japan each provided one of *Terra*'s instruments. Researchers from the University of Montana's Numerical Terradynamic Simulation Group developed the software for *Terra,* which will use five different sensors to study the Earth's land, oceans, air, ice, and life as a total global system—each part impacting the others. The sensors provide images by contrasting the data from each sensor against others.

The first images from the satellite were beamed to the world headquarters in the University of Montana Science Complex on April 19, 2000. Clients are lining up to use information coming from *Terra,* especially in the fire community. The data can be used to detect and trace fires from space for the U.S. Forest Service. *Terra* and the other satellites (approximately 20 satellites will be part of this research) will monitor changes in rates of deforestation, glacial retreat, wildfires, urbanization, global warming, and so forth.

Sources: Mahan, John (2000), "UM, NASA Satellite Collaboration Begins to Pay Off," *Montana Kaimin,* April 20, p. 1; and Shimek, Cary (2000), "Launching Dreams," *Vision 2000,* pp. 4–7, University of Montana.

The best strategy may be to seek wide application and standardization of a technology (via licensing arrangements) in order to discourage other companies from producing substitute technologies. Sales of technology know-how are critical to such a strategy.[9]

As an aside, many firms that sell toward the know-how end of the continuum may be selling high-tech services (consulting, engineering, etc.). Essentially, they sell know-how in the form of their expertise.[10] Who is the most likely buyer for this highly tacit knowledge? Interestingly, rather than being a naïve customer who has a complete lack of knowledge about the service in question, it is more likely to be a customer who is close in range to the know-how the service provider offers.[11] The reason? The absorptive capacity, or the ability to understand and use information, of the unsophisticated buyer is lower, despite their greater need. This makes the sale to the naïve customer more difficult to close.

Firms tend to sell more toward the end-product level when they offer components that are incompatible with general industry standards. In general, customers want to be able to mix and match compatible components. Poor compatibility across the range of relevant technologies raises the customer's costs of putting together an acceptable system. In such a situation, selling know-how or individual components is difficult and selling new, improved components is even more difficult. For example, imagine a maker of computer disks with a new innovation in disks. If existing disk drives are incompatible with new disks, the innovator somehow has to persuade drive manufacturers to produce and market compatible drives. So firms that market incompatible products rather than industry standards may favor positions closer to the end user, in order to offer a complete package for customers.[12]

A firm that chooses to compete close to the end-user/system level of the continuum with a system or product that is incompatible with existing standards faces serious consequences.[13] Witness Apple Computer's ongoing travails in attempting to compete with the "Wintel" (Windows–Intel) duopoly. Apple's emphasis on its own proprietary standards over *de facto* open standards built around the Wintel platform made it extremely difficult to compete for third-party hardware and software developers.

Finally, firms may both commercialize and license technology when

- Offering technology to competitors may encourage industry standardization of the firm's technology.
- The firm may have skills in some market segments but not others (i.e., domestic, but not international, or consumer, but not industrial).
- Major corporate buyers require a second source.[14]

Rather than selling or licensing know-how, most firms have historically tended to sell close to the final user level. For example, royalty revenues (from licensing rights to know-how) have historically *not* been a major source of income compared to aggregate product sales revenue. Indeed, in many industries, royalty revenues are less than even the R&D expenditure itself.[15] But more and more high-tech firms are realizing revenues from different ranges along the what-to-sell continuum, say, by commercializing its technology in some markets and selling or licensing it in others.[16]

One of the reasons high-tech firms are moving to sell more than just the products or components themselves is that, in a high-tech environment, sustainable long-term corporate growth depends on the continual development and leverage of a firm's technology. To maximize the rate of return on technology investment, a firm must plan for full market exploitation of all its technologies. These technologies may, but need not necessarily, be incorporated into that company's own products and services. Thus, a company's marketing strategy may—and probably should—provide for the sale of technologies for a lump sum or a royalty.[17]

For example, Texas Instruments, which previously relied on selling components and final products, has recently received more in licensing fees than its entire operating income.[18] As another example of a firm realizing revenues from different points on the continuum, Canon simultaneously sells printer subsystems on an OEM basis to both Hewlett-Packard and Apple, and ready-to-use laser printers to end customers.

In many industries, the majority of the profits are captured by firms located at one or two favored locations, and these locations shift over time.[19] For example, in the personal computer industry, most profits currently flow to firms that compete at the component and subsystems levels. Intel and Microsoft capture a majority of these profits.

Intel's profitable component branding effort is an example of the fundamental importance and significance of "upstream" positions in high-tech markets. Suppliers of high-tech components and subsystems are not just anonymous suppliers anymore.

A final issue related to this what-to-sell decision pertains to *international markets.* In many cases, technology transfers to other countries may take place on the basis of standard turnkey deals.[20] Decisions to transfer technology to potentially low-cost producers must account for the effect on the company's own manufacturing plans. Many developing countries want to add value to their natural resources by buying sophisticated process technologies. Brazil, for example, wants to sell steel, not iron ore, and may be able to export steel relatively cheaply because it possesses key raw materials. The long-term effects of such a decision should not be ignored. Additional issues in licensing and technology transfer are addressed in the Technology Expert's View from the Trenches.

Regardless of where on the continuum a firm chooses to sell, the development of high-technology products and innovations necessitates enormous R&D investments. Because of this, firms often rely on a *technology platform* that allows them to design a common underlying technological core and then, rather than designing completely different products for each distinct market segment, develop several variants of the product for different segments, all based on the common core design. The issue of developing product platforms and subsequent versions is addressed in the next section.

PRODUCT PLATFORMS AND DERIVATIVES

What Are Platforms and Derivatives?

A **product platform** strategy is the development of a set of subsystems and interfaces that form a common structure; from this common structure, a stream of **derivatives** can be efficiently developed and produced.[21] The strategy creates a single design and components that are shared by a set of products. For example, Intel's Pentium chips are used across a variety of applications but share the same underlying technology. Commonly used in manufacturing consumer durables and industrial goods such as cars and aircraft in the early period of the industrial revolution,[22] platform strategies are now making a comeback.

Product platforms are typically designed with the idea of **modularity** in mind. Modularity relies on standardized component interfaces that allow users to mix and match (or "plug and play") the desired components and functions. In the design process, modularity allows the development of individual components to be isolated from one another. Designs that do not incorporate modularity have tightly coupled components, such that when any one component is changed, changes ripple through the entire system.

Modularity is a necessity with a diversity of technologies in a given market. Advances in one aspect of the product, say, software, can be accommodated without scrapping the entire system.[23] Designed around a common platform and system interface, both designers and customers gain flexibility. Rather than differentiating the product to heighten its uniqueness, and hence, its value, modular design directly invites potential competitors to "drop in" their components.

Robust, standard interfaces for both developing and using specific programs are central to the platform design strategy. The platform notion also allows for rapid development of market share and revenues. Speed and flexibility combine to allow tailoring

Technology Transfer Considerations

JON A. (TONY) RUDBACH, Ph.D., MBA
Director of Technology Transfer,
University of Montana, Missoula, Montana

Successful *technology transfer* is much like ballroom dancing: Both partners must be knowledgeable and willing to cooperate to make it work well. The partners in technology transfer are research institutions (universities, hospitals, and institutes) and commercial entities. From the commercial side, companies are seeking to expand or enhance their technology or product bases by acquiring intellectual property developed (mostly) in the public sector. They wish to do this at a reasonable cost, under conditions that will give the transfer the greatest opportunity for success. From the other side, universities (and other institutions) wish to exploit developments of their faculty and/or staff, in a manner consistent with laws and policies, that will result in a tangible return to them and their employees.

Undoubtedly, the greatest stimulus for technology transfer was the Bayh-Dole Act of 1980. This act gave, for the asking, to nonprofit institutions and small businesses the rights to inventions made with federal funds. If certain notifications are made in a timely fashion to the appropriate federal agency, the intellectual property rights are given to the institutions, which then are responsible for transferring the technology for commercial exploitation and revenue generation. These notifications include informing the federal granting agency that an invention has been made, requesting that title to the invention be granted to the requestor, and notifying the agency that a patent has been filed before the mandated deadline. Details on reporting requirements can be found in 37CFR ¶401.

Most research in universities and other nonprofit institutions in the United States is supported by taxpayers. Support is in the form of grants and contracts. It is the belief of many people that the taxpayers who support the research have a right to enjoy benefits from the products of the research. The way that this can best be facilitated is through transfer of the resultant technologies to a company that can develop and market the products or services, making them available to the public. Associated with this is a mechanism to share some of the profits from sales of the products or services with the inventor and the inventor's institution. This has dual benefits:

1. It rewards and encourages the inventors.
2. The funds paid back to the institution help support certain activities and, thus, reduce the taxpayers' burden.

Transfer of technology, leading to development of new products and services, is important and valuable to research institutions, commercial companies, and to the general population that supports research through taxes, donations, or investments. Technology transfer has emerged as a specialized field, which requires the merger and interaction of legal, scientific, and business/marketing disciplines. Its practice is proving to be one of the driving forces in economies of the United States and other parts of the world.

In the technology transfer process, certain principles apply to both *in-licensing* activities of companies that want to acquire new technologies or products and *out-licensing* activities of institutions that have developed the new technologies or products:

- The conditions and terms involved in the transfer process should be reasonable and equitable to both sides. As covered below, placing value on a technology, a product, or a patent is probably the most daunting task in technology transfer. Many methods have been developed for this process, and they are referenced in publications from the Association of University Technology Managers (AUTM) (e-mail autm@ix.netcom.com).

- Specific individuals responsible for the cooperative effort must be identified and given appropriate responsibility and authority.

- The agreement should contain a component of enforceable "diligence" to ensure performance (or provide remedies) if circumstances change for one of the entities. *Enforceable diligence* refers to financial penalties or other clauses that allow termination of a license agreement if product development or sales do not meet certain minimum levels or deadlines. On the licensor's side, timely filing of patents and reports, with appropriate penalties for nonperformance, are commonly included in the "diligence" portions of license agreements.

There is no substitute for experience in negotiating license agreements and in resolving the differences that inevitably arise. Frequently, both sides can benefit from discussing terms under negotiation in an agreement with an uninvolved, unbiased third party. Participation in the AUTM organization (see above) provides a network of colleagues that may be consulted about their opinions on contentious terms in an agreement under negotiation.

One of the major hurdles in the technology transfer process is establishing a realistic and accurate value on the technology to be transferred. Having worked on both sides of the negotiating table, first representing companies and then a university, I can say with some confidence that the inventors usually overvalue their contributions. Most do not appreciate, for example, that over $200 million and 7 to 10 years may be spent in developing a drug or a vaccine with no assurance that it will get marketing approval or that it will be a commercial success if approved. Thus, one of the more difficult jobs of a university technology transfer officer is to diplomatically negotiate an internal understanding of "sharing risks" with a corporate licensee. This can be accomplished through the use of specific hurdle or milestone payments, along with establishing a realistic and equitable running-royalty rate for a marketed product or service. Sometimes this can be dealt with most easily if the financial motives of the inventor are discussed (confidentially) and are understood by the negotiator. For example, if continuing research support rather than personal income is desired by the inventor, this may be negotiated more easily than license fees due to involvement of different corporate budgets and tax implications.

Another potential impediment in the technology transfer process, from the university side, is locating suitable companies to license specific technologies. In the past, our university has accomplished this, partially, through nonconfidential disclosures. However, recently we received a legal opinion that such disclosures may be interpreted as an "offer to sell," in light of the United States Supreme Court *Pfaff v. Wells Electronics, Inc.* decision. An "offer to sell" could bar an inventor from obtaining U.S. patent protection if the patent application is filed more than one year after the invention has been offered for sale. Thus, in the face of the *Pfaff* decision, institutions advertising technologies available for licensing must exercise extreme caution that they do not destroy the "novelty" of an invention and, thus, its patentability. A low-cost way to prevent this is to file a "Provisional Patent Application" before any attempt is made to attract licensees. This will protect U.S. and foreign patent rights for one year, during which the patent must be filed for continuing protection.

As presented in another section of this chapter, a patent does not allow practicing of an invention; it only prevents others from doing so. It is a common misconception that the act of patenting an invention limits application of the technology to benefit humankind. For example, the statement is often heard in academic institutions that "I will not patent this because I want to make it freely available to everyone." To the contrary, there are classic examples wherein a decision *not* to file a patent delayed introduction of new technology that could have benefited society.

Upon closer examination, the reason for this becomes obvious. During the practice of out-licensing, one of the most frequently asked questions is "What protection do you have or might you obtain

on the technology?" If the answer is "none," most prospective licensees lose interest in the opportunity. A company is unlikely to make the enormous investments required to develop a product for market unless it has some period of exclusivity during which it can recoup its investment and earn a fair return. Not patenting an invention greatly reduces the incentive for a company to invest in its development and, thus, may delay or prevent application of the technology for public use.

OUTLINE OF A TYPICAL TECHNOLOGY TRANSFER SEQUENCE FROM AN OUT-LICENSING PERSPECTIVE

1. Discover opportunities for technology transfer, both actively and passively.
2. Advise on maintaining a proprietary position while honoring "academic freedom."
3. Evaluate the technology for novelty, maturity, and utility.
4. Value the technology for both risk and market potential.
5. Establish an understanding of the innovator's goals for exploitation of the technology.
6. Plan a strategy to exploit the innovation that is acceptable both to the inventor and the institution.
7. Proceed with the strategic plan, continually updating participants.

For additional information, see Steele, Thomas, W. Lee Schwendig, and George Johnson (1990), "The Technology Innovation Act of 1980, Ancillary Legislation, Public Policy, and Marketing: The Interfaces," *Journal of Public Policy and Marketing*, 9, pp. 167–182.

for particular niches. The solution-specific modules can be "plugged" into a larger, more generalized foundation of common underlying technology that provides the baseline functionality for all specific solutions. The richness of the resulting product family can be a barrier to entry to other competitors.

Indeed, based on this approach, the platform should not be a monolithic entity that must be used in its entirety to create a derivative product. Rather, the platform is a collection of subsystems, composed of modules or components, that a single company can control and use.[24]

Each company needs an internal definition of its own platform and must create or derive the platform architecture for its own products. The platform is the base technology and derivative products are the add-in modules that can be seamlessly plugged into the underlying platform.

Why Use a Platform and Derivative Strategy?

At least two underlying reasons exist for using a platform and derivative strategy in high-tech markets. First, recall one of the common characteristics underlying high-tech markets—unit-one costs. High-tech marketers typically face a situation in which the cost of producing the first unit is very high relative to the costs of reproduction.[25] For example, the cost of burning an additional CD-ROM is trivial compared to the cost of hiring programmers and other specialists to develop the software code in the first place. This underlying feature of technology markets makes a product platform strategy very attractive. If the incremental costs of the resulting derivative products are relatively small, compared to the core design, then proliferating versions of a common design to reach various segments adds incremental revenue. Trying to reach various segments with tailored products is very expensive in markets with unit-one cost structures.

As shown in Figure 7-3, a second reason for using a platform and derivative strategy is that, when a firm introduces a breakthrough product, it will inevitably create "gaps" in the marketplace.[26] These gaps, or holes, exist in the customer's migration path from the old technology to the new technology. Importantly, a firm should not overlook these gaps, which would, in essence, allow competitors to come in with gap-filling strategies and possibly even dislodge a firm from the very market it creates.

It is vital that a firm understand who is buying current products and why they are buying, in order to make informed judgments about gaps in the market that a new product platform will create. Then, a firm must fill the holes with derivative products, which

FIGURE 7-3 Product Platforms and Derivatives

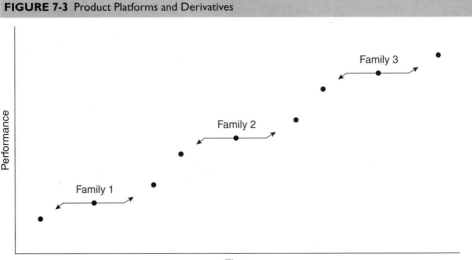

might include adding new features to the former model or scaling down versions of new products. The strategy addresses the needs of future customers while providing a migration path for current customers from the older to the newer product[27] (see also Chapter 6 on upgrade decisions from the customer's perspective).

Intel is a master at filling in the holes it creates by introducing new-platform products.[28] As shown in Figure 7-4, Intel has introduced derivatives to "gap fill" both the high and low end of its products. For example, with respect to the Pentium family only, Intel introduced the Pentium chip at 60 to 66 MHz speeds in March 1993; over time, it released successively faster versions that reached beyond 600 MHz. Each release involved a price cut that was made possible by cost reductions. The company also brought out compact versions of the chip for the laptop and notebook markets. Thus, Intel quickly filled all the performance, price, and applications gaps caused by the Pentium and so preempted the competition. Similarly, when the company introduced its new-platform Pentium Pro chip, it filled the market niches created by that chip. And the Pentium Pro chip worked with software applications designed for previous Pentium chips, providing a migration path for existing customers. In 1997, the company plugged the gap in the multimedia market by introducing MMX technology for audio, video, and graphics.

The use of a product platform strategy, which invites other players in the industry to develop derivatives running on the same platform, puts the issue of industry standards front and center in the product development process. The issue of government and industry standards is often vital to the success of new technologies.[29] This topic was discussed in Chapter 3.

FIGURE 7-4 Product Platforms and Derivatives in the Case of Intel[a]

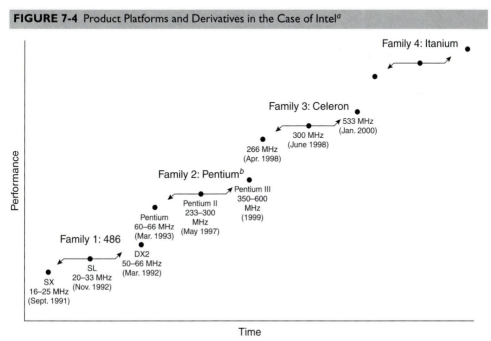

[a] Simplified summary of information from www.intel.com/pressroom/kits/processors/quickreffam.htm.
[b] Not shown: MMX & XEON series.

Making Decisions about Platforms and Derivatives

So how does one know what an appropriate common platform will be, so it can be "versioned" into multiple derivatives inexpensively and lucratively?[30] Rather than designing it to maximize its appeal to a specific segment, the platform should be designed for the high end of the user market and should incorporate as many of the desired features as needed for this segment.[31] Although the high end is not likely to be representative of the market as a whole, the large fixed development costs are more likely to be recovered from developing a design with the attributes desired by the highest willingness-to-pay segment. Then, subsequent versions can be sold at much lower prices with only modest incremental cost. It is the *subtraction* of features that is a lower incremental cost activity, rather than the addition of new, higher-end features.

This recommendation is consistent with both the notion of crossing the chasm and the lead user process. In crossing the chasm, products developed for innovators and enthusiasts will typically incorporate more technologically-advanced features than those versions desired by conservatives. Similarly, because lead users tend to be more sophisticated users, developing products with input from lead users may result in more technologically-advanced products. Regardless, before delving into the development of these subsystems, designers must first engage in a careful study of the users' requirements and incorporate these discoveries into engineering initiatives.[32] Conjoint analysis can be a useful tool in assessing desired features in the platform.[33]

The determination of how much better each new version should be, the time intervals between versions, and the positioning of versions relative to each other are complex issues that must be considered. Moreover, how to help OEMs and end users manage their migration choices (as covered in Chapter 6) must be part of these decisions.

Example of Product Platforms and Derivatives

The software industry offers a good example of designing product platforms and derivatives in the product development process.[34] The subsystems for most software programs include the file access, editing, graphics formatting, and printing subsystems, all with internal subsystem interfaces and a Windows-style user interface. In the software world, the interfaces are particularly important, and their design and evolution can lead to long-lived systems and market domination.

For example, Microsoft effectively guides the innovation of thousands of independent software companies by having developed and promoted as a standard the interface mechanisms that allow different programs to communicate with one another in a distributed computing environment. They also leverage the common software platform into market power, based on a common user interface, common methods of accessing data, and common approaches to communicating over networks and the Internet. The resulting compatibility, or *interoperability,* for customers reduces learning time from package to package and allows sharing of data. Moreover, by establishing the *de facto* platform for an industry, Microsoft enabled other companies to build modules that operate in or on the underlying platform. The development of these derivative products reinforces the standard, yet the company does not have to bear the direct cost of programming for each individual market niche. This transforms the company from merely a producer into a distribution channel, in which the independent developers become channel members for the original platform.

As another software example, Visio Corporation's graphics-sharing software is based on a platform strategy.[35] Scores of plug-in modules are available for Visio software, and all types of industry-specific diagrams are made by many other companies. The underlying platform is open (meaning not proprietary) and *scalable,* meaning it can be scaled up or down depending upon the needs of the customer for larger or smaller applications. The vision of the company was to create a major software industry platform onto which other companies or customers could incorporate add-in shapes and sharing scripts to draw charts and diagrams. The shapes and scripts are "intelligent" in that they automatically adjust connections between different shapes when moved or resized. The major components of the platform are the core graphics engine, the shapes management subsystem to incorporate and manipulate graphic objects, and an applications interface that provides scripting language so developers can create and integrate their own plug-in programs into Visio. Derivative products have been developed for home, business, and technical users.

A CAUTIONARY NOTE ON ISSUES RELATED TO "KILLING" NEW-PRODUCT DEVELOPMENT[36]

The decision about when to pull the plug on a new product that is not doing well in the market is extremely difficult. Managers often remain committed to a losing course of action in the context of new-product introductions; such a scenario is often referred to as "good money chasing after bad." Decision makers have strong biases that affect "stopping" decisions. Product champions and technology enthusiasts are perennial optimists about the future viability of their pet projects. Furthermore, because they have a personal stake in these projects, they tend to persevere at all costs. This escalation of commitment is a major problem in new-product introductions. Why does this happen?

Managers who tend to believe they can control uncertainties in their favor continue to escalate commitment to such projects. To justify their decisions, managers try to make data fit their desired expectations about the new product. So, if the decision maker is highly positive about the new product, then he or she will attempt to confirm this hypothesis by seeking out supporting data. For example, managers are much more likely to recall information that is consistent with prior (positive) beliefs, they tend to interpret neutral information as positive, and they will even ignore or distort negative information to support their desire to see their new pet project succeed. Indeed, they may interpret negative information as positive! In recent research, distorting negative information as positive occurs more than twice as often as distortions in the other direction (distorting positive information as negative).

These biases are one reason that improving the information affecting a decision to withdraw a new product from the market does not result in an actual withdrawal. Indeed, asking managers to set and commit to a stopping rule simply is ineffective. In light of these complications, managers should attempt to do the following.

1. It is clear that a change in direction will not be made unless managers are aware there is a problem in the first place. So, problem recognition requires that managers attend to possible negative feedback. However, in light of the confirmation bias noted previously, such recognition can be extremely difficult.[37]
2. Managers must also reexamine the previously chosen strategy, both clarifying the magnitude of the problem and possibly redefining the problem. This is equally difficult because of conflicting information and differences of opinion. Some stakeholders have a vested interest in maintaining the status quo, whereas others exert pressure to change direction.[38]

3. Managers should search for an alternative course of action, attempting to obtain independent evidence of problems and identifying new courses of action. Creativity is vital in identifying a wide range of options, and the firm should foster a culture that encourages open questioning.[39]

4. Managers should prepare key stakeholders for an impending change and attempt to manage impressions. Active attempts to remove the project from the core of the firm will help in this step.[40]

5. Boulding, Morgan, and Staelin suggest that managers should attempt to decouple the withdrawal decision from previous investments in the project. Ideally, this decision decoupling requires the use of a different decision maker for the withdrawal decision.[41]

6. Alternatively, a firm can try to use a stopping rule that was developed early on, based upon information available at the time of the project's inception or product launch decision. However, if a firm attempts to update this stopping rule based on new, factual information available at the time the withdrawal decision is to be made, this decision will likely not be effective because it will suffer from the biases already noted. A decision procedure that is most effective at reducing the escalation of commitment "takes out of play" information closely tied to those with a vested interest in the project and renders a decision based on benchmarks established prior to incremental commitments to the project.[42]

PROTECTION OF INTELLECTUAL PROPERTY

High-technology firms face an environment characterized by frequent innovation, high mortality rates, a high priority on research and development, stiff competition in a race to the marketplace, and partnerships with firms that may be potential competitors. In such an environment, the management of sensitive information is particularly critical.[43] One manager at a high-technology firm summarized the issue:

> Product life cycles are very short and development times are very long. That sets up a situation where having knowledge is extremely valuable. If one of our competitors were to acquire information, it would give them an edge. They could respond with their offerings in a stronger fashion than they might have.[44]

Information is vital to the success and vitality of an organization, but the potential of seepage from strategic alliances, employee turnover, and poor information-security procedures poses a real threat. Concerns about intellectual property and protection of trade secrets are important in many industries, but they are paramount in high-technology industries, in which the basis for competitive advantage is most likely to be superior technological know-how. In 1997, a conservative estimate put losses of intellectual property from U.S. corporations at approximately $25 billion.[45] Thefts of intellectual property are especially common in today's high-tech industries, in which the most prized assets can be stored on a disk.

So, information presents something of a double-edged sword to high-technology firms. On the one hand, as noted in previous chapters, high-tech companies want to be skilled in gathering and utilizing information—which includes information about their competitors—to gain advantage. On the other hand, each company wants its information to remain proprietary and its firm's boundaries to be impenetrable to the competitive intelligence-gathering efforts of its competitors. Protection of information can be particularly crucial when strategic alliances fail.[46] So, how is a company to manage this situation, which requires that it be both open and restrictive in information sharing at the same time? Knowledge of the various strategies to protect intellectual property is vital.

Intellectual Property

The high-tech industry is littered with the sagas of many companies who have sued for infringement of intellectual property rights. In 1997, Digital and Intel filed a series of suits against each other. Digital first sued Intel, accusing Intel of violating patents on a Digital chip called Alpha. Intel filed a countersuit demanding that Digital return confidential information about upcoming chips, such as its Merced chip being jointly developed with Hewlett-Packard, that it had received as a major customer. Intel alleged that Digital was misusing confidential information.[47] So then, Digital filed yet another suit, accusing the chip maker of using monopoly power to harm Digital by demanding the return of Intel's technical documents. Digital argued that Intel's recall of the confidential data about its chips could leave the company stranded in the technology race in its ability to develop products for the next-generation chips.[48] Digital did return the Merced information, because it decided not to pursue products for that chip's design, but said it wouldn't return other documents that Intel also supplied to other computer makers.

Intellectual property rights are also increasingly important in an era of e-commerce. The Internet makes it possible to distribute, worldwide, perfect digital copies of words, sounds, and images to anyone. This ability affects many industries, including the music, print, and advertising industries, among others.

Intellectual property refers to original works that are essentially creations of the mind. The U.S. legal system has protected a creator's right to enjoy due economic returns from his or her creations since the inception of the Constitution in 1789 (Article 1, Section 8). Intellectual property is an expansive term, referring broadly to a collection of rights for many types of information, including inventions, designs, material, and so forth. In the business arena, intellectual property may include not only creations from research and development but also general business information that a firm has developed in the course of running its business and that it needs to maintain as proprietary in order to remain competitive.

Companies have several options available to them in protecting the proprietary information that forms the basis of their competitive advantage.[49] As shown in Table 7-1, protection of intellectual property can be divided into four categories: patents, copyrights, trademarks, and trade secrets. Each of these is briefly reviewed in turn.

Patents

Grant of a **patent** confers to the owner(s) the right to exclude others from making, using, or selling the product or process described and claimed in the patent for a specific time period, usually 20 years from the date of filing an application for patent with the U.S. Patent and Trademark Office (PTO). Patentable subject matter includes any new and useful article of manufacture, composition of matter, or process. An invention is patentable only if it meets three requirements: It must be *useful, novel,* and *nonobvious.*

How are these three requirements met? To meet the *utility requirement,* the invention must be useful. That is, the invention must be capable of satisfying some function or benefit to humanity. Examples of inventions lacking utility include those that conflict with known scientific principles, such as a perpetual motion machine, or those that are

TABLE 7-1	Forms of Intellectual Property Protection
Patent	Exclusive right conferred on an invention by a government for a specified time period, authorizing the inventor to make, use, transfer, or withhold whatever may be patented. Grants the inventor the right to exclude others from making, using, or selling the invention.
Copyright	Legal protection of an author's writings or original creative works; grants the owner exclusive rights to reproduce, distribute, and adapt the copyrighted work. Protects the tangible medium of expression (i.e., the *form or manner* in which the idea is expressed, *not the idea itself*). Useful for artistic creations (music, literature) and products such as software that are mass marketed (which makes the protection of the information difficult).
Trademark	Words, names, symbols, or devices used by manufacturers to identify their goods and to distinguish them from others. Exists to protect consumers from being misled as to the identity of the producer of a product.
Trade Secret	Information that derives value from not being generally known to, and not being readily ascertainable by proper means by, other persons who might obtain value from its disclosure or use; is the subject of efforts that are reasonable under the circumstances to maintain its secrecy.

Source: Stern, Louis and Thomas Eovaldi (1984), *Legal Aspects of Marketing Strategy,* Upper Saddle River, NJ: Prentice Hall.

unreasonably dangerous, such as nuclear weapons. The *novelty requirement* is met when no single prior literature document—for example, patent, journal article, meeting abstract, or other public disclosure—describes, explicitly or inherently, each aspect of the claimed invention. If even a single reference is found that describes the invention, it is not novel. The *nonobviousness requirement* means that there is no implicit or explicit suggestion in prior literature of the subject matter claimed as the invention. In determining if an invention meets the nonobviousness requirement, the teachings in multiple literature references may be combined. If the teachings, when collectively considered, show or suggest the invention, then the invention is not patentable.

In the United States, there are two types of patent applications: provisional applications and utility applications. A *provisional application* is filed with the PTO with a filing fee of $150 and by definition has a lifetime of only one year. During that one-year life, the application remains in the PTO unexamined by a patent examiner. One year after filing, the application, to avoid abandonment, must be refiled as a utility application for examination. The benefit of the provisional application is that the inventor has that one-year period to do further research on the invention or to obtain investor monies to develop the idea. Filing of a provisional application provides a date of filing, establishing a "priority date."

Alternatively, if an inventor does not need time to do further research, time to obtain monies for development, or is anxious to obtain a patent, the application can be filed with the PTO as a *utility application,* along with the filing fee of $790. The application will be assigned to an examiner, who will render an initial decision regarding patentability. If that initial decision is unfavorable, the applicant can amend the claims or submit remarks in writing to the examiner addressing the unfavorable decision. The examiner will then issue a final decision. If the decision is favorable, a patent is granted, and the PTO will publish a patent (Figure 7-5). If the examiner's final decision is unfavorable and the patent application is denied, it is possible to appeal the situation. Alternatively, the application

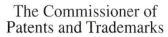

The Commissioner of Patents and Trademarks

Has received an application for a patent for a new and useful invention. The title and description of the invention are enclosed. The requirements of law have been complied with, and it has been determined that a patent on the invention shall be granted under the law.

Therefore, this

United States Patent

Grants to the person(s) having title to this patent the right to exclude others from making, using, offering for sale, or selling the invention throughout the United States of America or importing the invention into the United States of America for the term set forth below, subject to the payment of maintenance fees as provided by law.

If this application was filed prior to June 8, 1995, the term of this patent is the longer of seventeen years from the date of grant of this patent or twenty years from the earliest effective U.S. filing date of the application, subject to any statutory extension.

If this application was filed on or after June 8, 1995, the term of this patent is twenty years from the U.S. filing date, subject to any statutory extension. If the application contains a specific reference to an earlier filed application or applications under 35 U.S.C. 120, 121 or 365(c), the term of the patent is twenty years from the date on which the earliest application was filed, subject to any statutory extension.

Bruce Lehman

Commissioner of Patents and Trademarks

Amitra Manley

Attest

FIGURE 7-5 Sample of Patent

US005770789A

United States Patent [19]

Mitchell-Olds et al.

[11] Patent Number: 5,770,789

[45] Date of Patent: Jun. 23, 1998

[54] **HERITABLE REDUCTION IN INSECT FEEDING ON BRASSICACEAE PLANTS**

[75] Inventors: **Storrs Thomas Mitchell-Olds; David Henry Siemens**, both of Missoula, Mont.

[73] Assignee: **University of Montana**, Missoula, Mont.

[21] Appl. No.: **496,016**

[22] Filed: **Jun. 28, 1995**

[51] **Int. Cl.**[6] **A01H 5/00**; A01H 1/04; A01H 1/06; C12N 15/01

[52] **U.S. Cl.** **800/200**; 800/230; 800/DIG. 15; 800/DIG. 17; 435/6; 435/172.1; 47/58; 47/DIG. 1

[58] **Field of Search** .... 435/172.1, 6; 47/58, 47/DIG. 1; 800/200, 230, DIG. 17, DIG. 15

[56] **References Cited**

PUBLICATIONS

Berenbaum et al., *Plant Resistance to Herbivores and Pathogens Ecology, Evolution, and Genetics*, Chapter 4:69–87 (1987), Univ. Chicago Press, Chicago.
James et al., *Physiologia Plantarium*, 82:163–170, (1991).
Koritsas et al., *Ann. Appl. Biol.*, 118:209–221, (1991).
Lister et al., *Plant J.*, 4:745–750, (1993) No. 4.
Magrath et al., *Heredity*, 72:290–299, (1994) No. 3 Mar.
Magrath et al., *Plant Breeding*, 111:55–72, (1993).
Richard Mithen, *Euphytica*, 63:71–83, (1992).
Mithen et al., *Plant Breeding*, 108:60–68, (1992) No. 1.
Parkin et al., *Heredity*, 72:594–598, (1994).
Thangstad et al., *Plant Molecular Biol.*, 23:511–524, (1993).
Giamoustaris et al., Ann. appl. Biol. 126:347–363, 1995.
F.S. Chew, "Searching for Defensive Chemistry in the Cruciferae, or, do Glucosinolates Always Control with Their Potential Herbivores and Symbionts? No!," *Chemical Mediation and Coevolution*, Ed., Kevin C. Spencer, Academic Press, Inc., Ch. 4, pp. 81–112 (1988).

Lenman et al., "Differential Expression of Myrosinase Gene Families," *Plant Physiol.*, 103:703–7111 (1993).
Xue et al., "The glucosinolate–degrading enzyme myrosinase in Brassicaceae is encoded by a gene family," *Plant Molecular Biology*, 18: 387–398 (1992).
Höglund et al., "Distribution of Myrosinase in Rapeseed Tissues," *Plant Physiol.*, 95: 213–221 (1991).
Ibrahim et al., "Engineering Altered Glucosinolate Biosynthesis by Two Alternative Strategies," *Genetic Enginering of Plant Secondary Metabolism*, Ed., Ellis et al., Plenum Press, New York, pp. 125–152 (1994).
Hicks, "Mustard Oil Glucosides: Feeding Stimulants for Adult Cabbage Flea Bettles, *Phyllotreta cruciferae* (Coleoptera: Chrysomelidae)," *Ann. Ent. Soc. Am*, 67: 261–264 (1974).
Reed et al. 1989 Entomol. exp. appl. 53(3):277–286.
Bartlet et al. 1994. Entomol. exp. appl. 73(1):77–83.
Butts et al. 1990. J. Econ. Entomol. 83(6):2258–2262.
Bodnaryk et al. 1990. J. Chem. Ecol. 16(9):2735–46.
Haughn et al. 1991. Plant Physiol. 97(1):217–226.
Mithen et al. 1987. Phytochemistry 26(7): 1969–1973.
Jarvis et al. 1994. Plant Mol. Biol. 24(4):685–687.

Primary Examiner—David T. Fox
Attorney, Agent, or Firm—Fish & Richardson, P.C.

[57] **ABSTRACT**

A method for producing plants of the Brassicaceae family that have reduced feeding by cruciferous insects is disclosed. The method comprises selecting for the heritable trait of altered total non-seed glucosinolate levels or for the heritable trait of increased myrosinase activity. Selection may be performed on Brassicaceae cultivars, mutagenized populations or wild populations, including the species *Brassica napus, B. campestris* and *Arabidopsis thaliana*. Plants having such altered levels show reduced feeding by cruciferous insects, including flea beetle, diamond back moth and cabbage butterfly. Plants selected for altered levels of both glucosinolates and myrosinase also show reduced feeding by cruciferous insects.

25 Claims, 5 Drawing Sheets

FIGURE 7-5 Continued

can be refiled (for another $790 fee) with amended claims. Representative costs for filing are shown in Table 7-2 on patenting fees.

Most inventors use a patent attorney to do the filing and to act as their representative during examination of the application. Appendix A to this chapter details the steps in obtaining patent protection for both U.S. and international patents. The Technology Expert's View from the Trenches provides the perspective of a patent agent and details hidden pitfalls in the patenting process.

Disadvantages in Using Patents Although a patent provides the obvious benefit of giving the patent owner or licensee the exclusive right to practice the invention, there are some disadvantages in using patents as a means to protect intellectual property. One potential disadvantage is that, in order to obtain a patent, a full description of the invention

TABLE 7-2   Patenting Fees

U.S. Patent Costs		Foreign Patent Costs	
Application preparation	$8,000–$15,000	PCT filing fee[a]	$3,000–$5,000
Searching/patentability	$1,000–$2,000	Attorney's time to	$300–$1,200
Drafting application	$3,000–$8,000	prepare application	
Filing fees	$790	(per country)	
Examination/prosecution		Prosecution per country	
Attorney's time		Attorney's time	$1,000–$2,000
(per response)	$1,500–$3,000	Foreign associate's time	$600–$1,000
PTO fees for		Entry into each	
"late" responses	$110–$950	national country	$1,500–$10,000
Issue fee	$1,320	Examination in country	
Typical Total Range	**$18,000–$25,000**	Translation	
		Attorney's time	
Maintenance fees		Foreign associate's time	
3½ years	$1,050	**Typical Total Range**	**$37,000–$102,000**
7½ years	$2,100	(for 10 selected countries)[b]	
11½ years	$3,160		

[a] For application of average length (25 to 30 pages) that designates more than 10 countries (for flat fee to PCT of $1,050). PCT: Patent Cooperation Treaty. See Appendix A.

[b] Total range based on selecting 10 European countries; however, the total range will vary considerably if other countries are selected, due to additional translation costs and costs in each country.

must be given in the application at the time of filing with the PTO. In the United States, that application describing a company's proprietary information is not available to the public until the patent is actually granted and published by the PTO. However, in foreign countries, patent applications are published, making the proprietary information available to the public prior to grant of the patent. This provides a way for competitors to know about a company's intellectual property prior to grant of a patent. Regardless, because patents are public information, risks exist with this form of protection. One study found that 60% of patented innovations were "invented around" by other firms within four years.[50] Competitors may be able to design around the claimed invention by modifying a minor aspect of the invention in order to avoid infringing the patent.

Another disadvantage is that it is the patent owner's burden to enforce the patent—that is, to keep watch that competitors and others are not "infringing" the patent. Enforcement can and often does lead to lawsuits, an expensive undertaking. Moreover, a patent in such a lawsuit may be found to be invalid by the court, because grant of a patent does not guarantee validity of the patent.

Changes in Patent Law   Patent law, like copyright and trademark law, is concerned with fostering creativity by securing for the inventors, or authors in the case of copyright law, the exclusive right to their discovery. The law seeks to balance the right of the general public to useful information in a new discovery with the right of the inventors to benefit from their work. Recently, the balance has been shifting in favor of property owners, in part because of pressure from companies with valuable intellectual property portfolios.[51]

Until quite recently, business information and other business know-how were *not* patentable: Patents for business methods were prohibited. However, on July 23, 1998, the

---

TECHNOLOGY EXPERT'S VIEW FROM THE TRENCHES

Issues in the Patenting Process

JUDY MOHR
Patent Agent, Ph.D. (Chemical Engineering)
Dehlinger and Associates, Palo Alto, California

Patent attorneys or agents function at the crossroad between a company's research and development effort and its business and marketing goals. Patent agents operate from a very privileged vantage point, hearing firsthand from scientists about their budding inventions and early results. From computer disk drives with more storage capacity to gene sequences that express a protein for treatment of multiple sclerosis, patent attorneys are part of the forefront of science, working with corporations to develop a strategic patent portfolio. And for many products—for example, therapeutic products derived from gene sequences discovered from the ever-expanding research and development effort in biotechnology—early patent protection is crucial due to the competitive nature of the field.

In many companies, scientists find numerous potentially patentable inventions each year. Because of the expense involved in procuring patent protection, careful thought must be given to discern which of those inventions best fit with the business strategy. Knowing with certainty what will be the best fit, however, is a bit like predicting the future. It is entirely possible that a seemingly unimportant invention becomes a cornerstone product for a company. Further complicating the decision is the fact that in today's highly competitive, fast-paced world, filing for patent protection before a competitor is crucial. This means filing an application as soon as possible, and the luxury of doing a few more experiments to resolve one or two questions is often not possible. Decisions on whether or not to file for patent protection are often made prior to a full understanding of the commercial viability of the invention.

With the right decisions and a bit of luck, the result is amazing. For example, one small company started with a handful of people working on administering drugs for the treatment of various cancers. They worked with their patent agent to file patent applications on the scientists' findings. With time, the early findings grew into prototype products and, ultimately, into marketed products for cancer therapy in humans. That small handful of people grew to over 200 people—research scientists, product development people, and marketing representatives working together. The core patent position of the company effectively excluded the larger corporations from producing copycat products. With a patent-protected product on the market and several more in the pipeline, this young company was purchased for over $500 million by a major pharmaceutical firm. All that from just a seed of an idea described in an early patent. Amazing.

What are some common trouble spots with obtaining a patent? One, typically uncovered early in the preparation process, is that the inventor has previously "disclosed" (either orally or in writing) the invention prior to filing the patent application. For example, it's not uncommon for an inventor to give a talk at a conference or to publish an abstract or even a paper on the research before the patent application is filed. This is a fatal mistake for obtaining foreign patent protection, since disclosing the invention to the public prior to filing for a patent is an absolute bar in most cases to obtaining a patent in most foreign countries. The United States allows for a one-year grace period, in which the disclosure is not considered "prior art" if the application for patent is filed within one year of the disclosure. Be sure your company has a disclosure control program that watches over the scientists' publications.

A second common trouble spot is the misconception that, upon issuance of a patent, the patent owner is free to practice the invention. Grant of a patent confers to the patent owner the exclusive right to prevent others from making, using, or selling the claimed invention for 20 years. However, there are instances where a patent owner is unable to practice the invention because of a patent granted to another. That is, the patent owner is free to exercise his or her right to exclude others from practicing his or her invention; however,

the patent owner him- or herself is not able to practice the invention because doing so would infringe another patent. For example, suppose Company A has a patent that sets forth a claim to the chemotherapeutic drug paclitaxel, including derivatives of paclitaxel, for treatment of cancer. Company B has found that paclitaxel, when derivatized in a particular way, is significantly more effective in fighting colon cancer. So, Company B applies for and obtains a patent that claims this new derivatized paclitaxel for treating colon cancer. In this case, the patent issued to Company B falls within the broad claim to paclitaxel obtained by Company A, and hence, if Company B practices the invention, they would infringe Company A's patent. In this case, Company B can practice their invention only if a license to Company A's patent is obtained. Likewise, Company A is not free to practice the invention claimed in the patent to Company B. Although Company A has a broad claim to paclitaxel and its derivatives, Company A is excluded from using the paclitaxel derivative of Company B for treatment of colon cancer. Company A would need a license from Company B to practice the invention claimed in Company B's patent.

Federal Circuit Court of Appeals held that a business method that uses a mathematical formula can be patented, as long as it meets the three traditional criteria for legal protection (useful, novel, and nonobvious). In particular, the Boston-based Signature Financial Group was granted a patent for a unique data-processing software program that cut down on the cost of crunching numbers.[52]

This decision reflects an important shift in legal thinking and has been quite controversial. Critics contend that those few who hold a patent to a business method will slow the spread of valuable commercial innovations. Although processes are patentable, ideas, for the most part, are not. It is the fine line between processes and ideas that has allowed such business methods to be patented.

Patent Protection for Internet Business Models   With the change in legal precedent that now suggests business methods are patentable, the PTO has been flooded in recent years with applications for business method patents on e-commerce methods with the hope that such methods will lock in competitive advantage for a few firms. Recent e-commerce patents include that of CyberGold Inc. for a system of giving awards to people who click on an advertising message. Another is Priceline's patent for being the first to innovate a buyer-driven e-commerce system. It was granted a broad patent on a method of auctioning goods and services on the Internet.[53] Amazon.com was granted a patent for its one-click shopping cart, and Barnes & Noble was excluded from using a one-click shopping cart on its Web site. Some suspect that the field of medicine may see a surge of new patents, not only in methods of treatment but also in the management of patient and claims processing.

Critics say that because these methods are so common, they should not be eligible for patents. Patented processes are required to be novel, but some believe that the recently awarded Internet patents are not novel. These critics argue that merely transferring a marketing technique to the Web does not necessarily constitute novelty.[54] Patents are also supposed to be nonobvious, but with so many people using similar strategies on the Internet, these critics also say they cannot be considered nonobvious.

Moreover, patents have historically been granted to protect the common good by providing an incentive to innovate. However, some believe that patents granted for broadly defined Internet business models do not protect the common good; rather, they create protected profits for the few to the detriment of many,[55] resulting in burdening with inefficiency an area with so much potential to realize economic efficiencies. Do these patents act as an incentive to innovate? In many industries, the costs to develop and bring a new product to market are enormous and warrant protection. However, Internet ventures have not historically suffered from a lack of funding incentive.

The biggest issue in deciding whether to patent business methods on the Internet may be the financial value of such protection. With technology changing so quickly, some patents may be obsolete by the time they are awarded (usually two to three years after application).

Other Considerations Regarding Patents and Competition Outside the Internet domain, although some recent court decisions suggest that big businesses are getting the benefit of the doubt when it comes to intellectual property, other decisions suggest that consumer welfare and fair trade practices are more important.[56] For example, Intel's settlement with the Federal Trade Commission in the spring of 1999 forced Intel to make a key concession: It will no longer withhold vital data about its products from customers with whom it has patent disputes. Rulings with respect to both Intel and Microsoft indicate that the government can set conditions on how a company can use its intellectual property. To defuse government scrutiny, Intel has now licensed its interface technology to other companies. Microsoft has allowed Dell Computer to delete the icon for Microsoft's browser from some PCs.

Some experts warn that if patent holders can't fully control their property, it might chill innovation. However, others believe that more open information about intellectual property and preventing monopolists from abusing their power arising from intellectual property will actually enable inventors to experiment and innovate even better inventions.

Copyrights
Copyrights are similar to patents in granting protection of one's creations and in granting the owner exclusive rights to reproduce and distribute the copyrighted work. However, copyrights protect the *form or manner* in which the idea is expressed, *not the idea itself.* Copyrights are particularly useful not only for artistic creations (music, liter-

ature) but also for products such as software that are mass marketed (which makes the protection of the information difficult). For these types of products, although it is the underlying concept or generic capability that gives rise to its expression in the product, only the tangible representation of the idea is copyrightable.

Hence, because copyright laws do not offer protection of the idea itself, the ideas embodied in the creative work can be freely used by others. For example, the idea of a computer program that manages finances is not subject to copyright protection; however, the program code of Quicken, a particular software program, is protected by copyright. Therefore, although copying the Quicken program without permission constitutes copyright infringement, prior law suggests that writing another program that accomplishes all the same tasks would not be an infringement[57]—unless the business method is patented.

Copyright infringement occurs when someone other than the copyright owner performs one of the exclusive rights afforded the copyright owner, most typically unauthorized reproduction or distribution of the copyrighted work. The term for copyrighted works is either the life of the author plus 50 years or the shorter of 75 years from publication or 100 years from creation of the work, depending on the circumstances surrounding the creation of the work.[58]

Obtaining copyright protection is really quite easy. A copyright exists from the moment a work is created, without any formal action on the part of the author. Although there is a copyright registration procedure, registration is not required to obtain copyright protection. However, registration with the U.S. Copyright Office in Washington, DC, provides benefits should ownership of the copyright ever be challenged. Unless a copyright is registered, a copyright infringement suit cannot be filed should a firm need to file suit against an infringer.

Although information on the Internet is in the public domain, owners have not given up copyrights. Copyright owners should identify their materials subject to copyright protection by using a copyright notice with either the word *copyright* or © followed by the year in which the work was first published, followed by the name of the copyright owner. In addition, an explicit warning not to copy, or explaining the limits of permissible copying, is advisable.[59] There are digital systems to help owners find stolen material in use on the Net. Fingerprinting Binary Images (or FBI for short) embeds unique identifiers in on-line images. The Web can be searched for the use of these identifiers, and violators identified. Net crawlers can also search for protected material on the Internet.[60]

Trademarks

Often serving as an index of quality, **trademarks** are words, names, symbols, or devices used by manufacturers to identify their goods and to distinguish them from others. Trademarks provide protection against unscrupulous competitors who would attempt to trade on the firm's previously established goodwill and reputation by engaging in actions that confuse, deceive, or mislead the customer as to the identity of the producer of the goods.[61] If a product has *not* been patented, another firm can still copy and sell a similar product as long as consumers are not confused about who is producing the product. Hence, trademarks do not offer protection against such situations.

Trade Secrets

Trade secret protection in the United States evolved as common law in each of the 50 states and was standardized in 1979 in the Uniform Trade Secrets Act. This law establishes rules for fair competition among businesses with respect to proprietary information. **Trade secrets** are generally defined as any concrete information that

- Is useful in the company's business (i.e., provides an economic advantage or has commercial value)
- Is generally unknown (secret)
- Is not easily ascertainable by proper means
- Provides an advantage over competitors who do not know or use that information

The company must have a precise description of its trade secrets in order for the courts to recognize them as valid. The definition of a trade secret does not mean that other people or competitors do not possess the information or have not "discovered" the same information independently, but that such information is not commonly known. In addition, to be protected as a trade secret, the information must have been developed at some expense by the owner, and the company must maintain a rigorous program to protect the information that forms the basis of its success. Issues related to such a program are covered in Appendix B on **proprietary information programs.**

Hence, trade secrets are broadly defined and mean all forms and types of financial, business, scientific, technical, economic, or engineering information including patterns, plans, compilations, program devices, formulas, designs, prototypes, methods, techniques, procedures, programs, or codes; whether tangible or intangible; and whether stored physically, electronically, photographically, or in writing.[62] Examples of trade secrets might include product formulas, designs, manufacturing processes, customer lists, new-product plans, advertising plans, cost and pricing data, financial statements, employee information, and analyses of competitors.

Trade secret protection is premised on the notion that proprietary information is generally shared only by parties who have been held in confidence by one another. Violations of that trusting relationship would indicate a breach of, and the basis for intervention by, the law. Hence, many companies protect themselves and signal to the courts their confidential relationships through a series of contractual obligations with business partners.

Contractual Obligations with Respect to Proprietary Information *Nondisclosure agreements* (also referred to as confidentiality or proprietary rights agreements) set forth the nature of the secret and indicate that the firm both owns the information and expects the signer not to use or disclose the information described without permission. Employees, customers, and suppliers may be asked to sign such agreements that define ownership of the information and responsibilities to protect it.

Noncompetition agreements specify the rights of an employee who leaves the firm's employ with respect to future employment opportunities. Such contracts often specify time and territorial limits that prohibit the employee from joining or establishing a firm that competes directly with the former employer. Hence, noncompetition agreements prevent the signer from competing with the firm for a given period of time in a given territory. (The courts have found many of these agreements to be restrictive, and hence, care must be taken in their wording.)

Invention assignment clauses (and ownership of copyright notices) are signed by employees and assign the company rights to all inventions that the employee makes during the term of employment and often for a period thereafter. Again, these agreements specify the employee's role and rights to information relative to the employer. It is important that the firm realize that the employee can keep and freely use general knowledge or skills acquired on the job.

These three types of legal agreements are designed to protect against the loss of trade information. Indeed, in this information age, companies are trying harder to tie down their most important assets: knowledge in the employees' brains. The issue of who owns the knowledge in a person's head is an increasingly important one. As knowledge and intellectual property become more important than physical capital, businesses feel compelled to protect that intellectual capital by taking extraordinary steps.

Who Owns the Knowledge: The Employer or the Employee?[63]   Almost anything a person creates, develops, or builds while on the employer's payroll can be considered the employer's property. Unless a person can prove the idea or list was developed personally and not as part of the company's work product, it belongs to the company. Because it can include important information on customers, even an employee's Rolodex may belong as much to the employer as to the person.

The *doctrine of inevitable disclosure* recognizes that people who possess sensitive competitive information may, in the course of doing a new job, use information from their former employers. Hence, courts have been willing to ask a person to sit out of the industry for a time until the information they know is no longer as sensitive. For example, the president of DoubleClick, a company that has been selling advertising space on the Internet since 1996, found that two of his key employees were planning to set up their own company, Alliance Interactive Network. Because they possessed highly sensitive information about pricing and product strategies, databases, and plans for future projects, he was able to obtain an injunction that prohibited the two employees from selling or placing advertising on the Internet in any capacity for six months.

Companies can protect against departing employees taking trade information with them by following these steps:

- Have the employee sign a noncompete agreement and a nonsolicitation statement. These must be narrowly drawn with respect to geography and length of time.
- Have the departing employee sign a release document protecting the employer from postemployment lawsuits about alleged mistreatment during the course of his employment.
- Pay severance in installments, which can keep former employees on a tighter rein.
- Insist employees return all company documents and disks before leaving.
- Conduct a thorough exit interview to ask the employee if he or she learned or developed trade secrets at the company. Have the employee confirm the obligations of confidentiality. There should be another person to attend the interview and serve as a witness.

The employee's perspective is covered in Box 7-1, "Employee Considerations in Signing Noncompete Agreements."[64]

Patents or Trade Secrets?

Many types of business information do not qualify for patent protection (i.e., because they are not novel or are obvious). Even when such information does qualify for patent or copyright protection, trade secret status may be preferred. For example, a trade

BOX 7-1

Employee Considerations in Signing Noncompete Agreements

Departing employees may want to consider the following issues in loosening the grip of a noncompete pact.

1. It is important to negotiate acceptable terms before ever signing one, say, by shortening the duration of the agreement or the territory covered. It is also possible to negotiate carve outs, or specific jobs and places for which the clause doesn't apply.

2. It is important to manage the departure so that the former employer is less likely to accuse the departing employee of unfair competition. Even if the departing employee is innocent, it might not seem that way for people who have signaled their intent to depart to be in the office after hours or to take files home.

3. Both employers and employees should be aware that some states may void such clauses. For example, Florida didn't recognize the validity of noncompete agreements for independent contractors.

Even if a person cannot loosen the noncompete, there are things to do in the interim. Finding employment in a related field can provide new and useful knowledge, keep skill levels current, and add to personal networks. For example, one person left a company and faced a year in which he couldn't work for a competitor and would have to relinquish any software he invented in the meantime. Violating the agreement would have cost him his severance package (several million dollars). So, in the year he faced out of work, he contacted possible customers for his new business idea and asked them to share their requirements and future needs. When his noncompete expired, these contacts helped fund his firm's new product.

Source: Lancaster, Hal (1998), "How to Loosen Grip of a Noncompete Pact After Breakup," *Wall Street Journal,* February 17, p. B1.

secret can be protected as long as the company successfully prevents the secret from becoming widely known. In contrast, a patent has a lifetime of 20 years from the date of filing the application, after which time the information is available for public use. Given this, for many companies, classifying and treating intellectual property as trade secrets are the preferred ways to manage these assets. The comparison between trade secret and patent law is shown in Table 7-3 and summarized next.

When is trade secret protection preferred over patent protection?

- When the secret is not eligible for patent protection—for example, a way of doing business (although with the July 1998 ruling, this may be changed)
- When the product life cycle is short: say, a computer chip with a life of one to two years
- When the patent would be hard to enforce or would offer only narrow protection. For example, a process or method of making a computer chip—can it be known from inspection of the end product (chip) that a particular method was used for its preparation?

TABLE 7-3	Trade Secret versus Patent Protection	
	Trade Secret	***Patent***
Protects	A secret	A public disclosure
Lifetime	As long as information is secret	20 years from date of filing
Property Rights	Prevents unauthorized use by a person who acquired secret improperly	Excludes others from making, using, or selling
Scope	No protection for reverse engineering or someone else having same idea	Protects invention and equivalents thereof

Makes Sense When	Secret is not eligible for patent protection
	   e.g., a way of doing business
	Product life cycle is short
	   e.g., a computer chip with a life of 1½ to 2 years
	Patent protection difficult to enforce or would be narrow
	   e.g., a process or method of making a computer chip
	Secret is not detectable in product
	   e.g., Coca-Cola composition
		Product has long market lifetime
		   e.g., a drug or pharmaceutical composition
		Product can be reverse engineered
		Corporate policy is to "patent it" for reasons including:
		   Importance of patent portfolio to financial backers
		   Employee mobility
		   Professional growth of employees via publication, conference presentation of research
		Patent protection is enforceable

- When the trade secret is not detectable in the product (i.e., a secret component, ingredient, or process of making cannot be discerned via reverse engineering of the end product, the notorious example being Coca-Cola)

On the other hand, there are times when patents are preferred over trade secrets:

- When the product will have a long market lifetime, such as a drug or pharmaceutical composition
- When the product can be reverse engineered
- When it makes sense as a matter of corporate policy (i.e., as an indicator of financial viability, to enhance employee mobility, or for the professional growth of employees via publication of research)
- When protection is enforceable

Finally, because of the value of trade secrets, they are often targeted for theft by other countries and other companies. Information about the Economic Espionage Act of 1996 is covered in Box 7-2.

Managing Intellectual Property[65]

In today's successful high-tech companies, the management of intellectual property has become a core competence. Because intellectual assets rather than physical assets are

BOX 7-2

The Economic Espionage Act of 1996

Companies spend billions of dollars every year developing proprietary information to gain competitive advantage. Such information is a prime target for theft. Intellectual property losses by U.S. companies could amount to $63 billion annually.

Arising from Congress's recognition of the need to protect U.S. technology and know-how from theft by foreign business interests and foreign government agents, the Economic Espionage Act of 1996 makes stealing of trade secrets a federal criminal offense. The law bars stealing and using, in any fashion, another's trade secrets and makes it illegal to receive or possess trade secrets with the knowledge that they were stolen or misappropriated. The act applies to conduct occurring in the United States by a U.S. citizen or company or by foreigners. The act also applies to conduct occurring outside of the United States if the offender is a U.S. citizen, resident alien, or organization substantially owned or controlled by a U.S. citizen or company.

Anyone caught stealing business secrets for a foreign government, company, or agent could get 25 years in prison and a $250,000 to $10 million fine. The bill, advocated by the Justice Department, was designed to help federal law enforcement officials better combat economic espionage crimes. In addition to foreign economic espionage, the bill also targeted Americans who steal secret information from one business for the benefit of another. The maximum punishment for an individual would be 15 years in prison, or a fine of $250,000, and for an organization, a fine of $5 million.

The law is a useful extension of intellectual property rights, covering the protection of proprietary economic information. It has been particularly helpful to the FBI in bringing to court cases that deal with information rather than physical property. Moreover, it should make most businesses take appropriate steps to ensure that they minimize the likelihood of receiving stolen trade secrets to avoid being charged with violation of the act.

Companies who file a complaint under this act must be certain that they have taken all reasonable measures to protect their trade secrets, as discussed in Appendix B, "Proprietary Information Programs." One risk for companies that pursue a case under this act is disclosure of their trade secrets in a criminal investigation and trial. Although the courts try to limit such disclosure, it is a risk.

Although the law is not intended to apply to individuals seeking to capitalize on the personal knowledge, skill, or abilities they developed while working for a company, some worry that it may create problems for people switching jobs. Employees who change employers, or who start their own companies using general knowledge and skills they had previously developed, should be immune from prosecution. Yet care must be taken that employees who leave past employers do not use their knowledge about specific products or processes to duplicate them for a new employer.

Source: Shapiro, Barry (1998), "Economic Espionage," *Marketing Management,* Spring, pp. 56–58.

the principal source of competitive advantage, unlocking the hidden power of these assets is often a key source of success. One study reported that 67% of U.S. companies failed to exploit technology assets, and these companies let more than 35% of their patented technologies go to waste because they had no immediate use in products. Yet, active management of intellectual property assets is vital because

- Patents can be tapped as a revenue source (via licensing, for example).
- Costs can be reduced by cutting maintenance fees on unneeded patents (that could be donated to universities or nonprofits for a tax write-off).
- Patents can be repackaged to attract new capital and communicate an asset picture in a more attractive way to investors.

In addition to helping companies in the market by protecting their core technologies and business methods, patents can help a firm manage its product line. The potential strength of patents can help a firm establish R&D priorities. For example, Hitachi tries to develop only those products for which patents can help it establish market dominance. Similarly, in the biotech arena, Genetics Institutes says the strength of the potential patent position is a leading factor in deciding which research to pursue. Moreover, a patent strategy can help companies respond to shifts in the marketplace in an effective manner, by acquiring or partnering with firms that own patent rights to important developments.

Each of these issues points to the reality that intellectual property rights must be considered strategically in the product management process and not relegated solely to the realm of corporate attorneys.

Summary

This chapter has covered a wide range of topics that must be understood in order to effectively develop and manage high-tech products and services. Organized around the framework of steps in the technology development/management process, the chapter has addressed ways to manage a firm's products to maximize success. Ranging from deciding how close to final form the technology should be commercialized, to managing product platforms and derivatives, to killing new products, to protection of intellectual property, this chapter has presented insights about the development and management of high-tech products and services.

Discussion Questions

1. What is a technology map? What four steps does managing technology resources involve?
2. What are the various routes to product development that a firm can take? Why would a firm choose to partner?
3. What is the underlying dimension of the what-to-sell continuum? What factors affect a firm's decision about what to sell?
4. What is a product platform? What are the advantages to developers? To users?
5. What issues does a high-tech firm face in the decision to stop or kill a particular project?
6. What is intellectual property?

7. What are the three criteria for a patentable innovation? What are the steps in the patenting process? What are the pros and cons of using patent protection?
8. What are your thoughts on the use of patents in highly innovative markets? Do they encourage or stifle innovation?
9. What is a copyright? A trademark?
10. What are trade secrets?
11. What are the three ways to signal a confidential relationship?
12. What factors affect a firm's ability to maintain the integrity of its proprietary information?

Glossary

Copyright.   Copyrights protect the *form or manner* in which the idea is expressed, *not the idea itself;* they are similar to patents in granting protection of one's creations and in granting the owner exclusive rights to reproduce and distribute the copyrighted work.

Derivatives.   Spin-off products from a common underlying technology platform that include either fewer or additional features, to appeal to different market segments.

Intellectual property.   An expansive term, referring broadly to a collection of rights for many types of information, including inventions, designs, material, and so forth. In the business arena, intellectual property may include not only creations from research and development but also general business information that a firm has developed in the course of running its business and that it needs to maintain as proprietary in order to remain competitive. Simply, intellectual property is original works that are essentially creations of the mind.

Modularity.   Having standardized component interfaces that allow users to mix and match ("plug and play") the desired components and functions.

Patent.   A form of protection for intellectual property; grant of a patent confers to the owner(s) the right to exclude others from making, using, or selling the product or process described and claimed in the patent for a specific time period, usually 20 years from the date of filing an application for patent with the U.S. Patent and Trademark Office (PTO). Patentable subject matter includes any new and useful article of manufacture, composition of matter, or process. An invention is patentable only if it meets three requirements: It must be useful, novel, and nonobvious.

Product platform.   A company's strategy to develop a set of subsystems and interfaces that form a common structure from which a stream of derivative products can be efficiently developed and produced, as measured by cost and time required to generate incremental products from underlying platforms. The strategy creates a single design and components that are shared by a set of products.

Proprietary information program.   A company's policies and procedures regarding steps to protect proprietary information, including marking of sensitive documents, copying, distributing, securing, mailing, and storing. Must be in place in order to prove trade secret protection.

Technology map.   Defines the stream of new products, including both breakthroughs and derivatives (incremental improvements based on the new technology) that the company is committed to developing over some future time period. Companies that are most successful in defining next-generation products use the map to force decisions about new projects amid the technological and market uncertainty found in high-tech markets.

Trade secret.   Any information that is useful in the company's business (i.e., provides an economic advantage), is generally unknown, is not easily ascertainable by proper means, and provides an advantage over competitors who do not know or use that information. Trade secrets are broadly defined and mean all forms and types of financial, business, scientific, technical, economic, or engineering information including patterns, plans, compilations, program devices, formulas, designs, prototypes, methods, techniques, procedures, programs, or codes; whether tangible or intangible; and whether stored physically, electronically, photographically, or in writing.

Trademarks. Words, names, symbols, or devices used by manufacturers to identify their goods and to distinguish them from others; often serve as an index of quality; provide protection against

unscrupulous competitors who would attempt to trade on the firm's previously established goodwill and reputation by engaging in actions that confuse, deceive, or mislead the customer as to the identity of the producer of the goods. Trademarks do not offer protection against copying and selling a product that has not been patented, as long as consumers are not confused about who is producing the product.

Endnotes

1. Tabrizi, Behnam and Rick Walleigh (1997), "Defining Next-Generation Products: An Inside Look," *Harvard Business Review,* November–December, pp. 116–124.

2. Capon, Noel and Rashi Glazer (1987), "Marketing and Technology: A Strategic Coalignment," *Journal of Marketing,* 51 (July), pp. 1–14.

3. Capon, Noel and Rashi Glazer (1987), "Marketing and Technology: A Strategic Coalignment," *Journal of Marketing,* 51 (July), pp. 1–14.

4. John, George, Allen Weiss, and Shantanu Dutta (1999), "Marketing in Technology Intensive Markets: Towards a Conceptual Framework," *Journal of Marketing,* 63 (Special Issue), pp. 78–91.

5. Capon, Noel and Rashi Glazer (1987), "Marketing and Technology: A Strategic Coalignment," *Journal of Marketing,* 51 (July), pp. 1–14.

6. Capon, Noel and Rashi Glazer (1987), "Marketing and Technology: A Strategic Coalignment," *Journal of Marketing,* 51 (July), pp. 1–14.

7. John, George, Allen Weiss, and Shantanu Dutta (1999), "Marketing in Technology Intensive Markets: Towards a Conceptual Framework," *Journal of Marketing,* 63 (Special Issue), pp. 78–91.

8. John, George, Allen Weiss, and Shantanu Dutta (1999), "Marketing in Technology Intensive Markets: Towards a Conceptual Framework," *Journal of Marketing,* 63 (Special Issue), pp. 78–91.

9. Ford, David and Chris Ryan (1981), "Taking Technology to Market," *Harvard Business Review,* 59 (March–April), pp. 117–126.

10. John, George, Allen Weiss, and Shantanu Dutta (1999), "Marketing in Technology Intensive Markets: Towards a Conceptual

Framework," *Journal of Marketing,* 63 (Special Issue), pp. 78–91.

11. John, George, Allen Weiss, and Shantanu Dutta (1999), "Marketing in Technology Intensive Markets: Towards a Conceptual Framework," *Journal of Marketing,* 63 (Special Issue), pp. 78–91.

12. John, George, Allen Weiss, and Shantanu Dutta (1999), "Marketing in Technology Intensive Markets: Towards a Conceptual Framework," *Journal of Marketing,* 63 (Special Issue), pp. 78–91.

13. John, George, Allen Weiss, and Shantanu Dutta (1999), "Marketing in Technology Intensive Markets: Towards a Conceptual Framework," *Journal of Marketing,* 63 (Special Issue), pp. 78–91.

14. Capon, Noel and Rashi Glazer (1987), "Marketing and Technology: A Strategic Coalignment," *Journal of Marketing,* 51 (July), pp. 1–14.

15. Thurow, Lester (1997), "Needed: A New System of Intellectual Property Rights," *Harvard Business Review,* September–October, pp. 95–103.

16. Capon, Noel and Rashi Glazer (1987), "Marketing and Technology: A Strategic Coalignment," *Journal of Marketing,* 51 (July), pp. 1–14.

17. Ford, David and Chris Ryan (1981), "Taking Technology to Market," *Harvard Business Review,* 59 (March–April), pp. 117–126.

18. Capon, Noel and Rashi Glazer (1987), "Marketing and Technology: A Strategic Coalignment," *Journal of Marketing,* 51 (July), pp. 1–14.

19. John, George, Allen Weiss, and Shantanu Dutta (1999), "Marketing in Technology

Intensive Markets: Towards a Conceptual Framework," *Journal of Marketing,* 63 (Special Issue), pp. 78–91.

20. Ford, David and Chris Ryan (1981), "Taking Technology to Market," *Harvard Business Review,* 59 (March–April), pp. 117–126.

21. Meyer, Marc and Robert Seliger (1998), "Product Platforms in Software Development," *Sloan Management Review,* 40 (1), pp. 61–75.

22. For example, in the 1930s, a small team of aerospace engineers designed the DCI platform as a series of innovations to major aircraft subsystems. The new platform subsystems included designs for a welded frame, new engines from suppliers, new navigation systems, stronger landing gear, and a passenger-friendly interior. Later versions led to the DC3, and from it a passenger version, a cargo version, a troop-carrying version, and so on, all derivative products based on the same product platform. The underlying platform is credited with allowing commercial passenger traffic to be profitable for fledgling airlines (see footnote 21, Meyer and Seliger).

23. Grenadier, S. and A. Weiss (1997), "Investments in Technological Innovations: An Options Pricing Approach," *Journal of Financial Economics,* 44, pp. 397–416.

24. Meyer, Marc and Robert Seliger (1998), "Product Platforms in Software Development," *Sloan Management Review,* 40 (1), pp. 61–75.

25. John, George, Allen Weiss, and Shantanu Dutta (1999), "Marketing in Technology Intensive Markets: Towards a Conceptual Framework," *Journal of Marketing,* 63 (Special Issue), pp. 78–91.

26. Tabrizi, Behnam and Rick Walleigh (1997), "Defining Next-Generation Products: An Inside Look," *Harvard Business Review,* November–December, pp. 116–124.

27. Tabrizi, Behnam and Rick Walleigh (1997), "Defining Next-Generation Products: An Inside Look," *Harvard Business Review,* November–December, pp. 116–124.

28. Tabrizi, Behnam and Rick Walleigh (1997), "Defining Next-Generation Products: An Inside Look," *Harvard Business Review,* November–December, pp. 116–124.

29. Ford, David and Chris Ryan (1981), "Taking Technology to Market," *Harvard Business Review,* 59 (March–April), pp. 117–126.

30. Shapiro, Carl and Hal Varian (1998), "Versioning: The Smart Way to Sell Information," *Harvard Business Review,* November–December, pp. 106–114.

31. John, George, Allen Weiss, and Shantanu Dutta (1999), "Marketing in Technology Intensive Markets: Towards a Conceptual Framework," *Journal of Marketing,* 63 (Special Issue), pp. 78–91.

32. Meyer, Marc and Robert Seliger (1998), "Product Platforms in Software Development," *Sloan Management Review,* 40 (1), pp. 61–75.

33. Moore, William L., Jordan J. Louviere, and Rohit Verma (1999), "Using Conjoint Analysis to Help Design Product Platforms," *Journal of Product Innovation Management,* 16 (January), pp. 27–39.

34. Meyer, Marc and Robert Seliger (1998), "Product Platforms in Software Development," *Sloan Management Review,* 40 (1), pp. 61–75.

35. Meyer, Marc and Robert Seliger (1998), "Product Platforms in Software Development," *Sloan Management Review,* 40 (1), pp. 61–75.

36. Except where noted, this section is drawn from Boulding, William, Ruskin Morgan, and Richard Staelin (1997), "Pulling the Plug to Stop the New Product Drain," *Journal of Marketing Research,* 34 (February), pp. 164–176.

37. Keil, Mark and Ramiro Montealegre (2000), "Cutting Your Losses: Extricating Your Organization When a Big Project Goes Awry," *Sloan Management Review,* Spring, pp. 55–68.

38. Keil, Mark and Ramiro Montealegre (2000), "Cutting Your Losses: Extricating Your Organization When a Big Project Goes Awry," *Sloan Management Review,* Spring, pp. 55–68.

39. Keil, Mark and Ramiro Montealegre (2000), "Cutting Your Losses: Extricating Your Organization When a Big Project Goes Awry," *Sloan Management Review,* Spring, pp. 55–68.

40. Keil, Mark and Ramiro Montealegre (2000), "Cutting Your Losses: Extricating Your Organization When a Big Project Goes Awry," *Sloan Management Review,* Spring, pp. 55–68.

41. Boulding, William, Ruskin Morgan, and Richard Staelin (1997), "Pulling the Plug to Stop the New Product Drain," *Journal of Marketing Research,* 34 (February), pp. 164–176.

42. Boulding, William, Ruskin Morgan, and Richard Staelin (1997), "Pulling the Plug to Stop the New Product Drain," *Journal of Marketing Research,* 34 (February), pp. 164–176.

43. Mohr, Jakki (1996), "The Management and Control of Information in High-Technology Firms," *Journal of High-Technology Management Research,* 7 (Fall), pp. 245–268.

44. Mohr, Jakki (1996), "The Management and Control of Information in High-Technology Firms," *Journal of High-Technology Management Research,* 7 (Fall), p. 246.

45. "Eyeing the Competition" (1999), *Time,* March 22, pp. 58–60.

46. MacDonald, Elizabeth and Joann Lublin (1998), "In the Debris of a Failed Merger: Trade Secrets," *Wall Street Journal,* March 10, p. B1.

47. "You Sank My Battle Chip!" (1997), *Time,* June 9, p. 47.

48. Takahashi, Dean and Jon Auerbach (1997), "Digital Files Antitrust Suit Against Intel," *Wall Street Journal,* July 24, p. B5.

49. My thanks to Judy Mohr, Ph.D., for providing much of the information, tables, and graphs for this section.

50. Mansfield, E., M. Schwartz, and S. Wagner (1981), "Imitation Costs and Patents: An Empirical Study," *Economic Journal,* 91, pp. 907–918.

51. Updike, Edith (1998), "What's Next—A Patent for the 401(k)?" *Business Week,* October 26, pp. 104–106.

52. Updike, Edith (1998), "What's Next—A Patent for the 401(k)?" *Business Week,* October 26, pp. 104–106.

53. Updike, Edith (1998), "What's Next—A Patent for the 401(k)?" *Business Week,* October 26, pp. 104–106.

54. France, Mike (1999), "A Net Monopoly No Longer?" *Business Week,* September 27, p. 47.

55. Gurley, J. William (1999), "The Trouble with Internet Patents," *Fortune,* July 19, pp. 118–119.

56. Garland, Susan and Andy Reinhardt (1999), "Uncle Sam's Balancing Act: Patent Rights vs. Competition, *Business Week,* March 22, pp. 34–35.

57. Stavish, Sabrina (1997), "Copyrights on the Internet . . . Protecting Yourself," *Advertising and Marketing Review,* January, p. 6.

58. Stavish, Sabrina (1997), "Copyrights on the Internet . . . Protecting Yourself," *Advertising and Marketing Review,* January, p. 6.

59. Stavish, Sabrina (1997), "Copyrights on the Internet . . . Protecting Yourself," *Advertising and Marketing Review,* January, p. 6.

60. Morris, Glen Emerson (1997), "Protecting Intellectual Property on the Internet," *Advertising and Marketing Review,* January, p. 24.

61. Stern, Louis and Thomas Eovaldi (1984), *Legal Aspects of Marketing Strategy,* Upper Saddle River, NJ: Prentice Hall.

62. Shapiro, Barry (1998), "Economic Espionage," *Marketing Management,* Spring, pp. 56–58.

63. The information in this section is drawn from Lenzner, Robert and Carrie Shook (1998), "Whose Rolodex Is It, Anyway?" *Forbes,* February 23, pp. 100–104.

64. Lancaster, Hal (1998), "How to Loosen Grip of a Noncompete Pact After Breakup," *Wall Street Journal,* February 17, p. B1.

65. Rivette, Kevin and David Kline (2000), "Discovering New Value in Intellectual Property," *Harvard Business Review,* January–February, pp. 54–66.

Recommended Readings

Clark, Kim and Steve Wheelright (1993), *Managing New Product and Process Development,* New York: Free Press.

Farrell, J. and G. Saloner (1985), "Standardization, Compatibility, and Innovation," *Rand Journal of Economics,* 16, pp. 70–83.

Jolly, Vijay (1997), *Commercializing New Technologies,* Boston: Harvard Business School Press.

McGonagle, John and Carolyn Vella (1998), *Protecting Your Company Against Competitive Intelligence,* Westport, CT: Quorum Books.

Meyer, M. H. and A. P. Lehnerd (1997), *The Power of Product Platforms,* New York: Free Press.

Pooley, James (1987), *Trade Secrets: A Guide to Protecting Proprietary Business Information,* New York: American Management Association.

On-line Resources
for Intellectual Property

IP Worldwide, the Magazine of Law and Policy for High Tech (www.ipmag.com)

PIPERS Virtual Intellectual Property Library (www.piperpat.co.nz)

The following documents can be found free at www.oecd.org/dsti/sti/s_t/inte/prod/online.htm.

Facilitating International Technology Cooperation [DSTI/STP/TIP(97)14/FINAL]

Fiscal Measures to Promote R&D and Innovation [OCDE/GD(96)165]

Foreign Access to Technology Programmes [OCDE/GD(97)209]

Globalisation of Industrial R&D: Policy Issues

Government Venture Capital for Technology-based Firms [OCDE/GD(97)201]

Industry Productivity: International Comparison and Measurement Issues

The Knowledge-based Economy

National Innovation Systems

Patents and Innovation in the International Context [OCDE/GD(97)210]

Policy Evaluation in Innovation and Technology: Towards Best Practices

Regulatory Reform and Innovation

Technology Diffusion Policies and Programmes [OCDE/GD(97)60]

Technology and Environment: Towards Policy Integration

Technology Foresight and Sustainable Development: Proceedings of the Budapest Workshop, December 11, 1998

Technology Incubators: Nurturing Small Firms [OCDE/GD(97)202]

Venture Capital and Innovation [OCDE/GD(96)168]

APPENDIX A

Steps in Obtaining U.S. Patent Protection

To obtain a patent for any new and useful process, machine, article of manufacture, composition of matter, or any new and useful improvement thereof, an inventor must file, in a timely fashion, an application with the U.S. Patent and Trademark Office (PTO). The application must include a specification describing and precisely claiming the invention. The PTO assigns each application to an examiner with technical training in the pertinent technology; the examiner conducts a search of the prior art and determines whether the applicant's invention meets the three legal requirements of patentability (utility, novelty, and nonobviousness), as well as the requirements that the specification provide a full, enabling disclosure of the invention and that the claims be precise and clear. If the examiner reaches a favorable decision, the claims are allowed and a patent will issue in due course.

Patent procurement is expensive and procedurally complex. Often a preliminary assessment of patentability is done prior to preparing or filing an application (by either the inventor or a patent attorney on behalf of the inventor) in order to determine—to the extent possible—that the idea is new and nonobvious. An assessment of patentability is made by searching in a variety of databases, including patent databases such as those available at www.uspto.gov/patft/index.html and at www.patents.ibm.com, and literature databases relevant to the field of the invention.[1] An assessment of patentability can be made by determining if there is an absence of any reference or combination of references that teaches or suggests the invention. It is also important, prior to preparing or filing an application, to confirm with the inventors that the idea has not been disclosed to anyone. If the inventor has previously disclosed the

Source: Judy Mohr, Patent Agent, Dehlinger and Associates, Palo Alto, California.

idea, either orally or in writing, then it might no longer be considered novel, and as a result, a patent may not be granted.

After ascertaining that the idea is likely new and nonobvious, an application for patent can be prepared. Specific issues in preparing the patent application are addressed in Table 7A-1.

International Patent Protection   Under the auspices of the World Intellectual Property Organization (WIPO), an international application can be filed under the Patent Coopera-

tion Treaty (PCT). Although WIPO had 175 member countries, as of Fall 2000, not all members have ratified the PCT. Member countries of the PCT are shown in Table 7A-2. Under the PCT, an applicant can file an international application within one year of the filing date of a national application for patent (e.g., a U.S. provisional or utility application) and claim priority back to the filing date of the national application. The PCT enables an applicant to file one application in his or her home language and have that application acknowledged as a filing for patent in as many member

---

TABLE 7A-1   Preparation of a Patent Application

A patent application is prepared in a series of steps; someone from the inventing company ideally approves each step before the patent agent proceeds to the next. This approval process ensures that the patent application, which can easily cost more than $10,000 just for a U.S. filing, is on target. Preparation of an application typically includes these steps:

1. The inventor must be confident that the patent agent has a thorough and accurate technical understanding of the invention.

2. Based on information from the patent agent, the inventor assesses the closest "prior art" (any public information, such as a journal article, a conference abstract, a patent) in order to be aware of *what* the closest prior art document discloses and *how* that disclosure impacts the current invention. Sometimes there are no prior art concerns—no literature references or patents that describe anything similar to the invention. On the other hand, sometimes a prior art reference results in a decision not to pursue the idea (e.g., because the reference found is too similar to the invention). Most often, the prior art is between these two extremes, with one or two documents the patent agent and inventor must keep in mind throughout the process.

3. The claims are the heart of the patent application. They require the utmost care as they legally define the boundaries of the invention and are the basis for determining the breadth of protection. Drafting of the claims is a field unto itself, and a host of unique phrases and terms are used that at first can seem like a foreign language—but this language must be learned in order to maximize the odds of success with the application. So, the inventor must understand the claims well enough to create a physical picture in his or her mind of the product or process described. Does the product or process described in the claims agree with what the company envisions is the heart of the invention? Is anything in the product or process described in the claims something that a competitor can easily change to get around the claim? The claims should include several backup positions that are acceptable to the company in the event the patent office does not allow the broadest claim possible. It is critical that the patent agent and the inventor spend sufficient time scrutinizing claims.

4. The final step is the drafting of the drawings and of the application. Both should be checked to ensure that everything set forth in the claims is described so clearly that any person of skill in the art could read the application and be able to practice the invention. An examiner at the U.S. Patent and Trademark office will read the claims, as well as some of the application. That examiner likely knows little about the invention, yet must be able to understand what is written. If it's not written clearly enough for the inventor to understand, it definitely won't be clear to the examiner.

TABLE 7A-2 Countries from the World Intellectual Property Organization

Box No. V Designation of States

The following designations are hereby made under Rule 4.9(a) (*mark the applicable check-boxes; at least one must be marked*):

Regional patent

❑ **AP   ARIPO Patent: GH** Ghana, **GM** Gambia, **KE** Kenya, **LS** Lesotho, **MW** Malawi, **SD** Sudan, **SL** Sierra Leone, **SZ** Swaziland, **UG** Uganda, **ZW** Zimbabwe, and any other State which is a Contracting State of the Harare Protocol and of the PCT

❑ **EA   Eurasian Patent: AM** Armenia, **AZ** Azerbaijan, **BY** Belarus, **KG** Kyrgyzstan, **KZ** Kazakhstan, **MD** Republic of Moldova, **RU** Russian Federation, **TJ** Tajikistan, **TM** Turkmenistan, and any other State which is a Contracting State of the Eurasian Patent Convention and of the PCT

❑ **EP   European Patent: AT** Austria, **BE** Belgium, **CH and LI** Switzerland and Liechtenstein, **CY** Cyprus, **DE** Germany, **DK** Denmark, **ES** Spain, **FI** Finland, **FR** France, **GB** United Kingdom, **GR** Greece, **IE** Ireland, **IT** Italy, **LU** Luxembourg, **MC** Monaco, **NL** Netherlands, **PT** Portugal, **SE** Sweden, and any other State which is a Contracting State of the European Patent Convention and of the PCT

❑ **OA   OAPI Patent: BF** Burkina Faso, **BJ** Benin, **CF** Central African Republic, **CG** Congo, **CI** Cote d'Ivoire, **CM** Cameroon, **GA** Gabon, **GN** Guinea, **GW** Guinea-Bissau, **ML** Mali, **MR** Mauritania, **NE** Niger, **SN** Senegal, **TD** Chad, **TG** Togo, and any other State which is a member State of OAPI and a Contracting State of the PCT (*if other kind of protection or treatment desired, specify on dotted line*) ....

National patent (*if other kind of protection or treatment desired, specify on dotted line*):

❑	**AE**	United Arab Emirates		❑	**IL**	Israel ....
❑	**AL**	Albania		❑	**IN**	India ....
❑	**AM**	Armenia...		❑	**IS**	Iceland ....
❑	**AT**	Austria		❑	**JP**	Japan ....
❑	**AU**	Australia		❑	**KE**	Kenya ....
❑	**AZ**	Azerbaijan...		❑	**KG**	Kyrgyzstan ....
❑	**BA**	Bosnia and Herzegovina.........................		❑	**KP**	Democratic People's Republic of Korea.....
❑	**BB**	Barbados..		❑	**KR**	Republic of Korea ....
❑	**BG**	Bulgaria		❑	**KZ**	Kazakhstan ....
❑	**BR**	Brazil..		❑	**LC**	Saint Lucia...............................
❑	**BY**	Belarus...		❑	**LK**	Sri Lanka ....
❑	**CA**	Canada		❑	**LR**	Liberia ....
❑	**CH and LI** Switzerland and Liechtenstein			❑	**LS**	Lesotho ....
❑	**CN**	China		❑	**LT**	Lithuania ....
❑	**CR**	Costa Rica		❑	**LU**	Luxembourg ....
❑	**CU**	Cuba		❑	**LV**	Latvia ....
❑	**CZ**	Czech Republic......................................		❑	**MA**	Morocco ....
❑	**DE**	Germany...		❑	**MD**	Republic of Moldova ....
❑	**DK**	Denmark...		❑	**MG**	Madagascar ....
❑	**DM**	Dominica		❑	**MK**	The former Yugoslav Republic of Macedonia ....
❑	**EE**	Estonia...				
❑	**ES**	Spain		❑	**MN**	Mongolia..................................
❑	**FI**	Finland		❑	**MW**	Malawi ....
❑	**GB**	United Kingdom.....................................		❑	**MX**	Mexico ....
❑	**GD**	Grenada		❑	**NO**	Norway ....
❑	**GE**	Georgia..		❑	**NZ**	New Zealand ....
❑	**GH**	Ghana		❑	**PL**	Poland ....
❑	**GM**	Gambia		❑	**PT**	Portugal....................................
❑	**HR**	Croatia		❑	**RO**	Romania ....
❑	**HU**	Hungary...		❑	**RU**	Russian Federation...................
❑	**ID**	Indonesia		❑	**SD**	Sudan ....

TABLE 7A-2 *Continued*		
❏ **SE** Sweden..	❏ **UG** Uganda	
❏ **SG** Singapore...	❏ **US** United States of America.......................	
❏ **SI** Slovenia	❏ **UZ** Uzbekistan	
❏ **SK** Slovakia	❏ **VN** Viet Nam	
❏ **SL** Sierra Leone..	❏ **YU** Yugoslavia	
❏ **TJ** Tajikistan	❏ **ZA** South Africa	
❏ **TM** Turkmenistan	❏ **ZW** Zimbabwe..	
❏ **TR** Turkey..	Check-boxes reserved for designating States	
❏ **TT** Trinidad and Tobago	(for the purposes of a national patent) which	
❏ **TZ** Tanzania...	have become party to the PCT after issuance	
❏ **UA** Ukraine..	of this sheet:..	

Source: A current version of this form can be downloaded in PDF format from www.wipo.int/eng/pct/forms/index.htm.

countries as the applicant designates or elects. The country designations must be elected at the time of filing the PCT application.

An application filed under the PCT is published 18 months from the priority date. For example, suppose an application, either a provisional application or a utility application, is filed in the United States, establishing a "priority date." One year from the filing date of that U.S. application, a PCT application must be filed in order to preserve the right to claim back to priority date. The PCT application is then published 18 months from the priority date. However, prior to publication, at the option of the applicant, either an examiner in Europe or in the United States will review the application and conduct a search of the prior art and issue an international search report. Copies of the search report and of the cited art are sent to the applicant. No judgments or statements as to patentability are made at this point.

The fees for filing the application depend on the number of pages of the application, the country elected to conduct the prior art search to assess patentability, and the number of countries designated, with a $105 per country fee for each country designated up to 10 countries. More than 10 countries designated incurs a flat fee of $1,050 regardless of the number of designations. A typical range for filing fees for a PCT application of average length (25 to 35 pages) and designating more than 10 countries is about $3,000–$5,000 (see Table 7-2, p. 199).

If the applicant desires, a preliminary judgment of patentability on the application can be performed upon request and payment of the necessary fee. Typically, the examiner who conducted the international search will render a written, nonbinding judgment as to patentabilty. The applicant can respond in writing to the examiner's judgment and amend the claims if desired.

Upon completion of this preliminary examination phase, the PCT application enters, if the applicant so desires, each of the national countries designated at the time of filing the PCT application. The application then goes before an examiner in each national country. A translation of the application into the home language of each country is required, along with the national filing fee for each country. Costs to prepare multiple translations and to pay for the national filing fees, as well as the attorney fees for handling the application before each national PTO, quickly escalate to a range of $1,500 to $10,000 per country. The examiner in each country will consider the preliminary examination performed during the PCT phase; in some countries the PCT examiner's recommendation is merely "rubber-stamped," whereas in others the examiner's review yields a different outcome. International patent applications can also be filed directly in the patent office of those countries where patent protection is desired. This is the only way to obtain patent protection in countries that are not members of the PCT, such as Taiwan or Argentina.

Considerations in filing for international patents include the differing standards of enforceability in each country and the expensive translation costs. For example, it may be difficult to enforce patent rights in China or elsewhere. Translation costs, particularly for China, Japan, and so forth, account for the rapid escalation in international patent costs for a U.S. firm. In contrast, Canada and Australia are relatively inexpensive because no translation is needed. It is also important to recognize that international patent applications are published prior to examination and, hopefully, granted. Obviously, the risk here is that if the patent is denied, others still have access to the information.

Note

1. Two useful search sites are www.ncbi.nlm.nih.gov/PubMed and http://igm-01.nlm.nih.gov.

APPENDIX B
Proprietary Information Programs[1]

What factors affect a firm's ability to manage and control the proprietary information that forms the basis of its competitive advantage?

1. *Employees.* Possibly the single biggest danger to effective information management is a firm's own employees. Close to two-thirds of all U.S. intellectual property losses can be traced to insiders.[2] Unique management practices in high-technology industries, including efforts at team building (which include open information sharing and decentralized decision making), professional associations and ties, handling of new employees (many of whom may have been hired from a competitor), potential job dislocations, and so forth, greatly complicate the firm's ability to manage and control employees. Having a healthy organizational climate, with positive employee morale, results in employees motivated to see their organization succeed. Disgruntled employees are more likely to divulge information recklessly than are more satisfied employees. Moreover, a corporate culture that values information and tacitly understands the need to be circumspect in sharing information can be a strong tool in managing information.

2. *Senior managers.* Senior managers must send appropriate signals regarding the control of information. Information security can be viewed as just another nuisance, unless corporate officers stand behind the security program.

3. *Team-building efforts.* The use of team-building efforts and open information sharing can make it difficult to signal the sensitivity of information. Indeed, as access to information is more diffused, information is more likely to seep out of the organization. And generalized access to sensitive information can jeopardize the company's ability to successfully prosecute or defend a firm's claims to trade secrets. As a result, many firms attempt to share information on a *need-to-know* basis only.

4. *Internal politics.* All organizations are subject to the dynamics of power and politics. Access to information and knowledge is a signal used to convey power. As people try to gain access to information to boost their sense of power in the organization or to use it politically, they may ferret out information that is considered sensitive, but may not understand that it is.

5. *Proprietary information policy.* Most firms have a policy on handling of proprietary information (for one such policy, see the example in Figure 7B-1). Typically, the

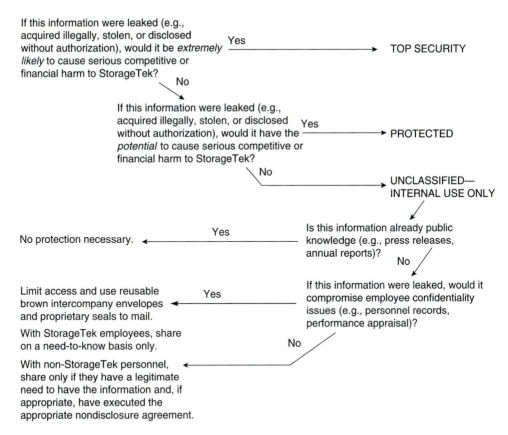

If this information were leaked (e.g., acquired illegally, stolen, or disclosed without authorization), would it be *extremely likely* to cause serious competitive or financial harm to StorageTek? **Yes** → TOP SECURITY

No

If this information were leaked (e.g., acquired illegally, stolen, or disclosed without authorization), would it have the *potential* to cause serious competitive or financial harm to StorageTek? **Yes** → PROTECTED

No

UNCLASSIFIED— INTERNAL USE ONLY

No protection necessary. ← **Yes** — Is this information already public knowledge (e.g., press releases, annual reports)?

No

Limit access and use reusable brown intercompany envelopes and proprietary seals to mail. ← **Yes** — If this information were leaked, would it compromise employee confidentiality issues (e.g., personnel records, performance appraisal)?

With StorageTek employees, share on a need-to-know basis only.

No

With non-StorageTek personnel, share only if they have a legitimate need to have the information and, if appropriate, have executed the appropriate nondisclosure agreement.

Proprietary Information Pyramid

The percentages listed below are current industry standards. As you move higher in the pyramid, fewer documents are affected, but more protection is required.

It is undesirable—and unnecessary—to classify too much information at the highest level of protection.

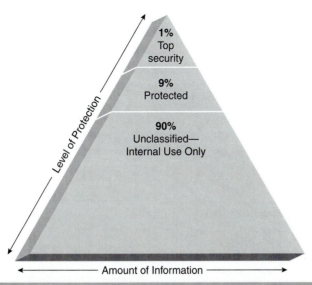

FIGURE 7B-1 Sample of Proprietary Information Policy

FIGURE 7B-1 *Continued*

Handling Strategies	Top Security	Protected	Unclassified— Internal Use Only
Marking	A Top Security cover sheet must be used on appropriate documents. (Copies of the cover sheet may be used.)	A Protected cover sheet must be used with appropriate documents. (Copies of the cover sheet may be used.)	No markings are required.
	Every document containing Top Security information must have every page marked Top Security. (Stamps are available for this purpose. Headers or footers may also be used.)	Internal page markings are optional, but recommended.	
	The automatic Declassification Date/Event must be marked on the document.	The automatic Declassification Date/Event must be marked on the document.	
Disclosure	It is the responsibility of the person making the disclosure to determine the need to know and to make the recipient aware of the information's classification.	Same as Top Security.	Take reasonable precautions against disclosure to outside parties or employees without a need to know.
Distribution List	Must be maintained. Serialization is recommended.	Employees are strongly encouraged to maintain a distribution list. At management's discretion, distribution lists may be required.	Distribution list is not required to be maintained.
Storage	When not in use or under the direct supervision of authorized personnel, all Top Security documents must be locked in a desk, file cabinet, or office.	Protected documents must be placed out of sight in a desk or file cabinet when not in use.	No special requirements. Judgment should be used to prevent casual disclosure when it is appropriate.
Reproduction	When copies are made of Top Security documentation and distributed to those with a need to know, a distribution list must be developed, accurately maintained, and periodically reviewed to reconfirm need to know. Cover sheets must be affixed to the copies. When, in the judgment of the originator, a Top Security document should not be copied, it is recommended that every page be printed on "DO NOT COPY" background paper before it is distributed.	Employees should use discretion and minimize the number of Protected documents that are reproduced. Cover sheets must be affixed to the copies. Employees are strongly encouraged to maintain a distribution list. At management's discretion, distribution lists may be required.	This material has no special restrictions; however, unnecessary copies should not be made.

FIGURE 7B-1 *Continued*			
	Top Security	*Protected*	*Unclassified—Internal Use Only*
Disposal/Destruction	Holders of Top Security documents must either destroy them or dispose of them in a proprietary information container. Contact the manager, corporate information security, for guidance on purchasing destruction devices (e.g., shredder) or proprietary information containers.	Same as Top Security.	Recycle or place in regular trash. Place confidential employee information in proprietary information containers.
Mailing	**Interoffice Mail–Pouch** Hand deliver when possible. When transmitted within the company, place in a red proprietary envelope. The red security envelope is for one time use only and should be opened only by the addressee. Pouch mail service is not recommended for Top Security material.	**Interoffice Mail–Pouch** Use brown interoffice envelope and proprietary information seal.	**Interoffice Mail–Pouch** Use regular interoffice mail envelopes. For confidential employee information, use brown envelope and proprietary information seal.
	External Postal–Delivery Services Must have appropriate markings (e.g., cover sheet or tag) and must be enclosed in an opaque, security StorageTek letterhead envelope. Certified mail must be used. Return receipt is required.	**External Postal–Delivery Services** Same as Top Security, except that pouch or regular mail may be used.	**External Postal–Delivery Services** Use pouch or regular mail.

Source: Storage Technology Corporation, Louisville, Colorado. Reprinted with permission.

security department identifies breaches of security. Monitoring can help find leaks of information and may deter information abuses. And some level of monitoring is required to gain trade secret status in legal proceedings. Excessive monitoring can demotivate employees and cause them to sabotage or circumvent the system.

6. *Geographic, professional, and friendship ties.* It can be difficult to manage information in high-tech industries given the close geographic ties (say, of Silicon Valley or the Boston Corridor), professional ties, and friendship ties that develop. People who switch employers may often maintain friendships with those at the former employer, and

communication with these people may be viewed as less risky because of the nature of the relationship. Moreover, engineers traditionally have had a culture of trading trade secrets on a reciprocity basis.[3] Engineers may view information sharing as either their right (because they "invented" the information) or their obligation (to disseminate research results at a professional meeting).

7. *Partnering relationships.* Partnering relationships with other firms also affect the ability to manage proprietary information. Preferred customers may be beta-test sites for new products. Suppliers may be provided with proprietary information to aid them in tailoring their processes to better meet the buyer's needs. Codevelopers also need access to product plans. Although partners may be asked to sign nondisclosure agreements, the extent to which they observe such agreements is questionable. In fact, some companies actually rely on the fact that customers will *not* observe nondisclosure agreements, scheduling customer visits so that their firm is the last one that a customer will visit in order to hear customers' comments regarding competitors' strategies.

A lot of our customers [on customer visits] are under nondisclosure, but they'll make comments in these briefings that just blow your mind. [You think,] "I don't know why you said that. . . ." They violate nondisclosures constantly—unwittingly, I might add.[4]

With respect to suppliers, similar issues may arise.

8. *Competitive intelligence gathering efforts by other firms.* Further, control of proprietary information is affected by the efforts of other firms to gain access to the information. For example, although many tools can be used legitimately to gather competitive intelligence, as advocated by the Society for Competitive Intelligence Professionals, many more nefarious and insidious tactics can be used as well. Industrial espionage by foreign governments has been on the rise and warrants careful security procedures, both at home and when employees travel abroad. Even hiring away employees with the express aim to access strategic information is common in high-tech fields, in which relationships sometimes characterized as "incestuous" are commonly used.

Awareness of these factors can help a firm to design proprietary information programs for success.

Notes

1. Mohr, Jakki (1996), "The Management and Control of Information in High-Technology Firms," *Journal of High-Technology Management Research,* 7 (Fall), pp. 245–268.
2. "Eyeing the Competition" (1999), *Time,* March 22, pp. 58–60.
3. von Hippel, Eric (1988), "Trading Trade Secrets," *Technology Review,* 91 (February–March), pp. 58–64.
4. Mohr, Jakki (1996), "The Management and Control of Information in High-Technology Firms," *Journal of High-Technology Management Research,* 7 (Fall), pp. 245–268.

CHAPTER 8

Distribution Channels and Supply Chain Management in High-Tech Markets

Representing the various firms and players involved in the flow of product from producer to customer, distribution channels are an important tool in high-tech markets. Manufacturers must manage both the flow of product between production and consumption and the different relationships between firms at the various stages. Figure 8-1 shows a sampling of the various supply chain and distribution options that might be used for high-tech products.

Distribution channel activities include traditional *logistics and physical distribution functions*—such as inventory, transportation, order processing, warehousing, and materials handling decisions—as well as the *activities used to structure and manage distribution channel relationships* (e.g., the selection and management of distribution channel structure and players).

FIGURE 8-1 High-Tech Supply Chain Options

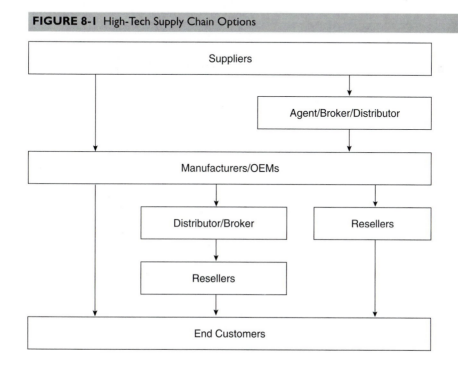

Distribution channels can be inefficient because suppliers and manufacturers, as well as manufacturers and distributors, often work at odds with each other; they may have conflicting goals and objectives and often don't think in terms of solving joint problems. Effective distribution channels allow a firm to identify redundancies and inefficiencies in the system, to develop relationships and alliances with key players, and to achieve both cost advantages and improved customer satisfaction. Some members of the channel may perform the functions more efficiently than others; a good distribution channel meets customer needs for channel functions in the most effective and efficient mode possible. The goal of channel management is to manage all the various logistics and distribution processes to provide value to the end customer effectively and efficiently.

New technologies are a major impetus today in redesigning supply chains and distribution channels. For example, in a logistical partnership with UPS based on proprietary software, Motorola radically redesigned its distribution process, eliminating multiple hand-offs and cutting delivery time by 75%. It consolidated products from eight Asian semiconductor plants and delivered directly to its U.S. customers' doors in a processing time of just seven days from order placement to delivery. The logistical partnership allowed Motorola's OEM customers to receive a higher level of quality, cost controls, and delivery.[1]

Channel members may also be used as marketing partners, playing a role in branding the product for the user, and providing services to the customer. A study by the Gartner Group[2] found that when customers go to dealers for assistance, 77% do not have a specific brand in mind. Of those customers who are not "prebranded," resellers report that nearly 90% of the customers purchase a brand recommended by the reseller. And, even if the customer is prebranded, resellers report that they switch the customer to an alternative brand 53% of the time. Hence, distribution channels are not only an order fulfillment mechanism but also an important tool used to establish brand identity and preference in the marketplace. Channel partners are used to assess customer needs, develop solutions, consult with the customer, and provide service.

To a large extent, high-tech marketers face distribution issues similar to those faced by marketers in more conventional contexts. Although this chapter will provide a brief review of basic channels strategy, it will focus primarily on managing some of the complexities in high-tech distribution channels. These complexities arise from the high value of many technologically sophisticated products, the rapid pace of market evolution, the need to maintain sales and service support, and the ease with which some high-tech products can be pirated. Other complexities arise from the addition of the Internet as a new distribution channel.

This chapter begins with a brief review of the basic issues in distribution channel design and management. It then addresses issues specific to high-tech marketplaces. The third section of the chapter addresses the addition of the Internet as a new distribution channel. The chapter concludes with an expanded view of distribution to include supply chain management issues and resources.

ISSUES IN DISTRIBUTION CHANNEL DESIGN AND MANAGEMENT

Distribution channels exist to perform vital functions in making marketing exchanges complete. From providing assortments for customers in the amount and variety they desire, providing service and other facilitating functions (credit terms, training, installation, etc.), to communicating with end users, and so forth, these functions are necessary for a successful exchange between buyer and seller. In designing a distribution channel, firms face the following decisions or issues, shown in Table 8-1:[3]

1. Consideration of Channel Objectives, Constraints, and External Environment Firms have a variety of needs to consider in structuring and designing a distribution channel. Customer needs and buying habits are some of the most important considerations. Purchase quantity, location convenience, delivery speed, product variety, and service needs must be considered. The channel structure used by competitors and product characteristics must also be examined.

2. Choice of Channel Structure: Direct versus Indirect A *direct* channel structure is one in which a manufacturer sells directly to the customer, say with its own sales force or via the Internet. Of course, the Internet is a major force leading to more direct channels across a variety of industries, and its revolutionary role is examined in detail later in this chapter. An *indirect* channel is one in which a manufacturer uses some type of intermediary(ies) to market, sell, and deliver products to customers. Direct and indirect channels are not mutually exclusive, as a firm may use some combination of them to get its products to customers. The combination of direct and indirect channels is known as a **hybrid channel,** or a **dual channel.**

The reality is that most firms typically juggle both direct and indirect channels in reaching their customer base. They may use a direct sales force for some customers, use channel intermediaries for others, and offer a Web page too. Especially when a firm uses a hybrid channel, channel management is quite complex. Some of these complexities include the facts that indirect channels are subject to less management authority than are direct channels, posing a control issue, and as more units compete for customers and revenue, conflict between various members in the channel can increase. These complexities are addressed in the section on adding new channels.

Some people argue that by using a direct channel, the intermediary can be eliminated and the price of the product lowered. However, a careful examination of the underlying role of a distribution channel shows the fallacy of this thought. Although intermediaries can be eliminated, the functions they perform—providing assortments for customers in the amount and variety they desire, providing service and other facilitating functions, communicating with end users, and so forth—cannot. If a firm were to use a direct channel, either the manufacturer or the customer must assume responsibility for those functions.

TABLE 8-1 Issues in Distribution Channel Design and Management

1. Consideration of channel objectives, constraints, and external environment
2. Choice of channel structure: direct versus indirect
3. Choice of type of intermediary
4. Penetration/coverage: number of intermediaries
5. Channel management
   a. Selection and recruitment of channel intermediaries
   b. Control and coordination
   c. Consideration of legal issues
6. Evaluation of performance

And, in either case, although the price of the product may be lower, the costs for one or the other channel members have increased because of the additional functions performed.

3. Choice of Type of Intermediary If a firm chooses an indirect channel, it can use different types of intermediaries. Computer products resellers occupy a place in the channel between distributors and end users. Distributors usually operate nationally, buying directly from the manufacturers and often bundling products for resale. Resellers, who typically operate locally, have a closer relationship with end users and customize computers, networks, or software for clients.[4] Many resellers of high-tech products are referred to as **value-added resellers (VARs)** or **value-added dealers (VADs),** which purchase products from one or several high-tech companies and add value to them to meet their target market's needs. For example, a value-added reseller in the computer industry may purchase computer hardware and an operating system and then bundle with that a proprietary software program for managing health and dental records for physicians' offices. VARs and VADs commonly integrate products from a variety of companies, adding their own expertise and knowledge; they then market this bundled solution to a particular vertical (i.e., industry-specific) market. These firms tend to be smaller resellers and they target specific market niches. **Systems integrators** typically manage very large or complex computer projects and typically create customized solutions for their customers. To create these solutions, they bundle and resell different brands of equipment.

Inbound versus outbound dealer organizations are other terms used to identify channel members in the high-tech setting. **Inbound dealers** typically have a retail storefront, and their primary customers are walk-in traffic generated through traditional advertising and promotion means. **Outbound dealers** have a sales force that makes calls on customers, typically at the customer location (the dealer may or may not have a storefront).

Depending upon the type of high-tech product being sold, many traditional channel intermediaries found in the retail sector may also play a channel role. Mass merchandisers, "category killers," small mom-and-pop stores, and franchises (such as ComputerLand or Radio Shack) may all be members of a firm's distribution strategy.

4. Penetration/Coverage: Number of Intermediaries If a firm uses an indirect channel, it must decide how many intermediaries to use within each region or territory. An important trade-off is that between the *degree of coverage* and the *degree of intrabrand competition.* Firms typically want as much market coverage as possible and, as a result, may sell through as many intermediaries as they can. Although such a decision may provide additional market penetration, this penetration comes at a cost. When a firm has many dealers in any area, each dealer competes with other dealers in its territory. To the extent that competition between different brands or makes in the marketplace, or **interbrand competition,** is fostered, it can be healthy. However, when such competition occurs between dealers on the same manufacturer's brand, or **intrabrand competition,** it can cause problems.

Dealers competing against each other to sell the same brand of product often rely on price competition. Not only can this be damaging to the manufacturer's reputation and perceived quality in the market, but the dealers themselves often end up making a lower margin on those manufacturer's sales. As a result, it is difficult for them to support the level of service and training that the high-tech products often require. So, too much penetration can actually lead to problems over the long term, in which the product is neither supported nor valued by channel intermediaries and end-user customers, in the way a firm might desire. Hence, in deciding on the degree of coverage in a market, a firm must maintain a balance between too limited coverage and too much coverage (which invites intrabrand competition). Vertical, or territorial restrictions, in which a select distributor is granted exclusive rights to a particular territory, can be used to inhibit intrabrand competition.

5. Channel Management   Channel management includes the ongoing activities that a firm uses to maintain channel relationships and effective channel performance over time.

a. Selection and recruitment of channel intermediaries   Once a channel structure is decided upon, a firm must attract and recruit intermediaries for the firm's product. Attending trade shows can be a useful strategy for doing so, as can using a targeted direct-mail campaign, effective publicity and public relations, or personal selling.

b. Control and coordination   Depending upon the particular type of intermediary, many channel members are interested in creating an identity and position for their store in a local market. Manufacturers generally have less preference over where a particular customer buys its goods, so long as the customer chooses its brand over competing brands. Given this discrepancy between manufacturers' and channel members' goals and objectives, manufacturers must use coordination mechanisms to manage, guide, and monitor its resellers' activities.

A variety of tools and mechanisms can be used to guide and manage the behavior of intermediaries.[5] **Authoritative control** tools reside in one channel member's ability to develop rules, give instructions and, in effect, impose decisions on the other. Such control might arise from ownership (via vertical integration) of the channel member or the authority arising from formal, centralized decision making (say, as in franchising). Formal controls and monitoring focus attention on desired behaviors and outcomes and, where coupled with a basis in authority, realign a partner's interests and activities to ensure desired ends. Authoritative control might also arise from one party's power over another. Importantly, power arising from unilateral authority does not necessarily imply an exploitative relationship; power can be used in a benevolent fashion as well. As a governance tool, power provides a basis for administering and managing exchange relationships.

Bilateral control mechanisms originate in the activities, interests, or joint input of *both* channel members. An important form of bilateral control involves relational norms or shared expectations concerning channel members' attitudes and behaviors in working together to achieve mutual goals. The spirit of such sentiments is reflected by a commitment to flexibility and adaptation to market uncertainty, mutual sharing of benefits and burdens, information sharing, collaborative communication, and so forth. These norms establish a social environment in which individually-oriented attitudes and behaviors are discouraged in favor of mutual interest seeking.

Joint interdependence and commitment can also serve as an effective basis for bilateral channel control. Interdependence creates incentives that regulate and motivate each party's conduct. Jointly shared (high symmetric) dependence is conducive to more flexible, long-term channel relationships. In such relationships, the need for (and power over) one another tempers inclinations toward self-interest seeking and motivates mutually beneficial behaviors.

Trust, or the extent to which partners jointly believe that each will act in the best interest of the partnership, can also provide effective bilateral coordination. Mutual trust can provide the basis for conflict reduction, higher performance effectiveness, and satisfaction in ongoing exchange. Mutual trust alleviates the fear that either party will act opportunistically toward the other. If both parties trust one another, each possesses confidence in the other's integrity and reliability and expects the other to act responsibly toward it in the furtherance of their exchange relationship.

Legal tools can also be used to control the relationship. Vertical restrictions, exclusive distribution, and similar tools can be used to motivate and align channel members' behavior.

c. Consideration of legal issues Two legal issues have recently received increased attention in high-tech distribution channels. **Tying** occurs when a manufacturer makes the sale of a product in high demand conditional on the purchase of a second product. Among other things, the Justice Department accused Microsoft of tying its operating system to its Internet browser. Tying may also come in the form of bundled rebates that give buyers discounts for hot products if they bundle the purchase with the company's other products.[6]

Exclusive dealing arrangements restrict a dealer to carrying only one manufacturer's product. Ostensibly, such arrangements are put into place to ensure adequate service, but antitrust implications arise if large companies use their dominance to restrict customers' access to competitors' products.

6. Evaluation of Performance It is important to assess the performance of the various channels and channel members. Questions about efficiency typically guide the selection of one type of channel structure over another. According to Dataquest,[7] the cost of selling through channels ranges from 10% of a firm's selling, general, and administrative expenses for a VAR channel to 11.5% for a VAD channel to 18% for a retail channel (which requires market development funds for advertising, returns, etc.).

In terms of selection and evaluation of particular intermediaries, issues related to both quantitative and qualitative performance indicators are pertinent.[8] Quantitative indicators might include sales volume moving through a particular intermediary or the manufacturer's market share in the intermediary's relevant territory. Qualitative indicators might include the dealer's satisfaction with and commitment to the manufacturer and the dealer's willing coordination of activities with the manufacturer's national programs. Table 8-2 identifies a variety of channel performance indicators.

TABLE 8-2 Channel Performance Indicators

Reseller's contribution to supplier profits

Reseller's contribution to supplier sales

Reseller's contribution to growth

Reseller's competence

Reseller's compliance

Reseller's adaptability

Reseller's loyalty

Customer satisfaction with reseller

Source: Kumar, Nirmalya, Louis Stern, and Ravi Achrol (1992), "Assessing Reseller Performance from the Perspective of the Supplier," *Journal of Marketing Research,* 29 (May), pp. 238–253.

CHANNEL CONSIDERATIONS IN HIGH-TECH MARKETS

How do these issues in channel design and management play themselves out in high-tech markets? Because of the high value of many technologically sophisticated products, and because of the rapid pace of market evolution, high-tech marketers face serious incentives to minimize the number of products held in inventory in the channel. The average selling price for information technology products has declined, placing pressure on vendor profitability. So, manufacturers look for the most cost-efficient channel to take their products to market. As mentioned previously, different types of indirect channels have different costs. Moreover, the advent of the Internet as a distribution channel for high-tech products has changed the nature of the relationship between channel members and manufacturers. Channel design and management must address the characteristics in the external environment for high-tech products shown in Figure 8-2. The implications of these characteristics for distribution channels are addressed here.

Blurring of Distinctions Between Members in the Supply Chain

One of the key channel implications of the characteristics of the high-tech environment is that the line between suppliers and channel members is blurring. For example, one of the largest computer retailers, CompUSA, announced in 1997 that it would offer build-to-order kiosks in its stores, allowing customers to design and receive computers to their specifications.[9] These build-to-order models offered higher profit margins for the company and effectively put CompUSA in the position of competing with its vendors. Although CompUSA said that the build-to-order kiosks would draw incremental business from customers who were likely to buy from value-added resellers and integrators, there is likely to be some degree of cannibalization from customers of name-brand products. In this new capacity, CompUSA no longer is merely a computer reseller; it has begun to

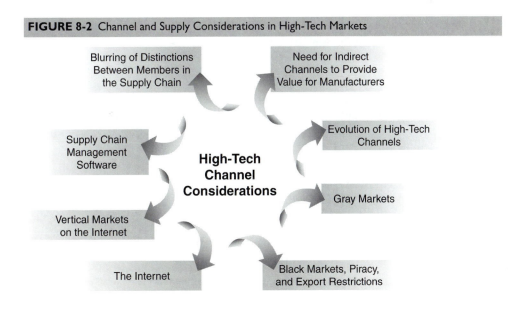

FIGURE 8-2 Channel and Supply Considerations in High-Tech Markets

assemble computers also and in that sense has blurred the boundaries between manufacturing and distribution.

At a different level in the supply chain (that between a supplier and its OEM customers), a similar phenomenon is occurring. Relationships between Intel and computer OEMs have been somewhat fractious due to OEMs' legitimate concerns that Intel would one day no longer be content with being a chip supplier and enter the computer market. The fact that Intel is making and selling complete motherboards gives some credence to this fear. These two firms—Intel and CompUSA—now potentially have increased ability to enter the computer manufacturing business.[10]

Need for Indirect Channels to Provide Value for Manufacturers

Traditionally, costly and complicated high-tech products were sold from manufacturer to distributor to reseller to end user. But now, many firms are moving to a direct model. For example, one estimate is that Compaq has shifted from a ratio of traditional channel sales to direct sales of 98–2 in 1998 to 80–20 in 1999.[11] With the direct-sales model becoming increasingly popular for computer and network products, distribution partners who played a key role in the early stages of the industry are scrambling for ways to add value to their position in the supply chain.[12] As noted previously, some channel members are reaching into functions traditionally provided by other channel partners, such as manufacturers and resellers. Two new strategies are channel assembly and colocation.

In **channel assembly,** manufacturers ship semifinished products to distributors that configure them to client specifications and complete production before shipping the products. The advantages are customization and speedy turnaround for customers. Although resellers also do assembly, the function is increasingly shifting to distributors who have warehouse space to tailor products to order more efficiently, cutting down on time and expense.

> Rather than trying to anticipate demand by stocking huge amounts of inventory that can become obsolete, the strategies are evolving to building products once true demand is known. Channel partners now deliver exactly what is needed at the time it's needed.[13]

As another example, Pinacor Inc., a distributor in Arizona, partnered with Lucent Technologies to perform final configuration, testing, and distribution of a telecommunications system. The partnership reduced lead time from 30 to 45 days down to 10 days, and the enhanced speed increased the odds the distributor competed successfully for the sale. Some believe that channel assembly is still too complex to have multiple partners assemble products in multiple locations and that, ultimately, the direct model will be more efficient, with one assembly point for each region.

In another strategy to bolster the value of indirect channels, **colocation** has the distributor's employees work from a vendor's manufacturing site to ship completed, high-demand models to either resellers or end users. Colocation can shave 7 to 10 days from the delivery cycle. Major distributors, such as Ingram Micro and Merisel, and Tech Data, Inc., Florida, partnered with IBM, have begun colocation efforts. Both colocation and channel assembly put customization all under one roof.

Although buying, bundling, and selling hardware and software are important for re-sellers, the shrinking profit margins on product sales are forcing them to *shift into services.* Hardware margins average only 1% to 8%, but service margins are 17% to 35%.[14] Services to help clients keep up with rapidly changing technology is vital. Customers want solutions to their problems, and as a result, more and more resellers are moving into territory typically held by consultants. Resellers are providing more client services, such as technical support, product maintenance, designing and installing networks, and implementing complex software solutions.

Evolution of High-Tech Channels

The type of channel a firm uses typically changes over the course of a technology's life cycle,[15] shown in Figure 8-3. When new technologies first appear in the market, sales strategies are naturally focused on original equipment manufacturers, independent software vendors, and integrators as the products struggle to gain support and a presence in the industry. Once the technology gains a toehold in the market and the target moves to the early adopters, technically astute value-added resellers join integrators as a key sales channel. VARs and early adopters determine whether a new technology establishes a presence in the market. And to leverage full efficiencies of the indirect channel, vendors work with distributors to expand their reach and grow their base of VARs.

FIGURE 8-3 Evolution of High-Tech Channels

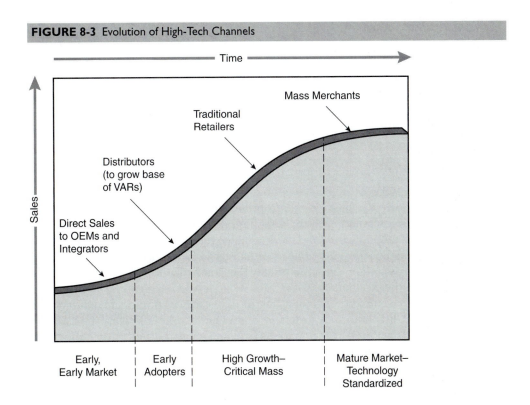

As the technology approaches critical mass and enters a high-growth phase, a fairly traditional dealer channel is necessary. National distributors, value-added dealers, and traditional retailers (such as computer superstores) each serve to add coverage in a growing market. At this point in the technology life cycle, the earlier channel members (such as the value-added resellers) may transition to newer technologies and opportunities, even while maintaining their presence in the current technology as a convenience to their customer base.

Once technology reaches maturity as a standardized technology, the distribution cycle shifts again and mass-market channels become increasingly important. As the technology reaches maturity, increased use of mass merchants, consumer electronics, and office products stores may be seen.

Of course, there are exceptions to the model depicted here. Some products' first success might be with a retail channel. For example, if the product has an application in a home environment, then vendors must sell where this customer buys, which is typically at a retail store or via the Internet. Or, if the market is comprised of business customers with an installed base of existing technology, customers face headaches in migrating to a new technology and so may be more conservative and require more personal selling.

Geoffrey Moore believes that a direct sales channel is the most effective one to create demand for a new product and to cross the chasm.[16] But he argues that volume and predictability of revenues determine whether a direct-sales model is even viable. To support a single consultative salesperson requires a revenue stream of anywhere from $500,000 to several million dollars, depending on the amount of pre- and post-sales support needed. For a quota of $1.2 million per year, the salesperson must close $100,000 per month. If the sales cycle is six to nine months, and if the close rate is one of every two opportunities, then twelve to eighteen $100,000 prospects must be in the pipeline at all times, or some smaller number of significantly larger deals.[17]

A retail channel model may also be successful for a mainstream market, but it is not ideally suited for crossing the chasm. A retail channel does not create demand (rather, it is suited for situations in which customers are looking for a channel to fulfill demand), and it does not help develop the whole product.[18]

Understanding Gray Markets

In managing and controlling distribution channels, manufacturers want to ensure that the channels they use reach the appropriate customer segments with the combination of products and services each segment desires. In some cases, however, some channel members, rather than selling and marketing the firm's products to legitimate customers, may sell to unauthorized distributors or markets. For example, if a manufacturer offers large volume discounts, a distributor may feel compelled to buy a large quantity to take advantage of the discount; however, rather than inventorying those goods to be sold at a later date to legitimate customers and resellers, the distributors may "divert" them to unauthorized distributors, exporters, or other markets. Alternatively, if a large price differential exists between export markets (say, due to tariffs or other conditions), channel intermediaries in one market may try to take advantage of the price differential and sell to unauthorized distributors in those markets.

Known as the **gray market,** such unauthorized distribution refers to the selling of goods at discounted prices through resellers not franchised or sanctioned by the producer[19] and results in a lack of control over the product, distribution, and services. It is considered a legal violation for firms to sell trademarked goods without the manufacturer's approval. In the case of international markets, the appropriate customs service can levy cease and desist orders or prevent the import of offending goods.[20]

Although some may believe that the gray market offers another way to move product through another channel—and indeed, it may be only a small amount of total sales that is being diverted—it can cause serious problems. Legitimate channel members and resellers may become confused and angry over the unfair advantage the unauthorized distributors gain in buying and selling at a lower price point. Both the legitimate outlets and the firm's own sales force may lose business to the gray marketers. Gray marketers typically don't provide the sales and service that authorized distributors do. In turn, legitimate channel members become less motivated to push the firm's products. In some cases, the company's products may wind up competing across different channels, lowering the price point. Ultimately, the negative backlash can end up hurting the firm's brand and position in the marketplace.

Causes   In order to understand and address the issue of gray markets, a firm must have a solid understanding of its root causes. As shown in Table 8-3, the most commonly cited cause of gray markets is a *firm's pricing policies.*[21] Manufacturers tend to structure discount schedules in favor of large orders, which causes distributors and other customers to buy more than they can sell or use (known as "forward buying") and then to resell the rest to unauthorized resellers. This problem can be exacerbated if distributors and customers must commit to purchases far in advance, with penalty clauses for canceling orders. Although manufacturers may have strong production reasons for such conditions, it contributes to the gray market problem.

A second cause is the price arbitrage opportunity that arises from *differentials in exchange rates in international markets.* Termed "parallel importing,"[22] this type of gray market activity occurs when goods intended for one country are diverted into an unauthorized distribution network, which then imports the goods into another country. Globalization has increased this type of gray market opportunity.

A third cause arises from the *cost differences between different resellers' cost structures.*[23] For example, full-service resellers have a higher cost structure than do discounters. Full-service resellers tend to provide functions including advertising, product demonstrations, postsales service support, and so forth. Gray marketers can free ride on these functions. Resellers may also use some products as loss leaders, selling products at or below cost in order to attract traffic. Loss-leader tactics are common among gray marketers of popular brand-name products. Full-service resellers look to brand-name products to

TABLE 8-3   Causes and Solutions for Gray Markets

Causes	*Solutions*
Volume discount price policies	Eliminate sales to the source of the gray market
Differentials in exchange rates	Eliminate the arbitrage problem: one-price policy
Different resellers' cost structures	Increase market penetration
Highly selective distribution	Gather information on gray market problem
Producers performing many marketing functions	Institute consistent performance measures internally
Inconsistent internal policies	

perform a very different role in their businesses; the product is expected to generate sufficient profit to cover the costs associated with providing full service.

Fourth, gray markets may be fostered *when suppliers practice highly selective distribution.* Territorial restrictions, exclusive dealing, and so forth may lessen intrabrand competition, but can draw nonfranchised dealers into the market if demand is strong.[24]

Fifth, gray markets can also develop *when producers assume a range of marketing functions* that might otherwise be provided by full-service dealers. When such services are available from the manufacturer, the buyer's risk in buying from minimal-service dealers is reduced. Moreover, heavy advertising by the producers may build total demand and brand image and decrease buyers' dependency on resellers' reputations.[25]

Sixth, *inconsistent and incompatible policies* regarding a manufacturer's own departments can contribute to the gray market problem.[26] Plant managers may view gray markets positively when they contribute to the ability to operate plants at full capacity. Sales personnel may overlook gray market activity if the volume contributes to the quota in their territory. Such problems make it difficult to establish a clear solution to the gray market problem.

Solutions In light of the causes, the solutions are many and varied. First, a firm may *use serial numbers on products* to track the source of units sold to gray marketers. Then, the firm can cut off the offender and is legally justified in doing so. Although the firm may lose some sales in the short term, it may sell more units through remaining authorized distributors and mitigate price erosion. Such a move sends a strong signal of commitment to the authorized distribution channel. However, this solution can be costly in terms of the time and administrative burden of identifying the offending dealers. Moreover, cutting off a distribution network may be satisfying to the authorized dealers but may actually cut off a market where the firm may have some competitive advantage.[27]

A second solution is to eliminate the source of the arbitrage and *offer a one-price policy with no quantity discounts.*[28] This strategy, although useful in eliminating one of the root causes of the problem, forecloses valid price–differentiation opportunities among different types of customers that have different transaction costs and receive different benefits from the product. It doesn't reward the larger, full-service dealers in the network, which may have other options available to them.

A third solution is to *move toward increased penetration in the market,*[29] balancing the potential of attracting unauthorized distributors with restrictive distribution against the increased intrabrand competition from too intensive distribution. Above all, it is important to have *information on the extent to which gray markets exist* in the distribution system, coordinated pricing brackets, and *consistent performance measures.*

Black Markets, Piracy, and Restricted Exports

Counterfeit, high-quality knockoffs pose yet another problem that is endemic to high-tech industries. Given the unit-one cost structure, in which the cost of producing the very first unit is high (due to R&D investments) relative to the reproduction costs of subsequent units, pirated copies of software and related items can be relatively cheap and easy to make. The sales lost due to software piracy amounted to $3.2 billion in North America, $3.4 billion in Eastern and Western Europe, and $2.9 billion in Asia in 1998.[30] One estimate says that most of the stolen sales—perhaps two-thirds—come from Microsoft products.[31] Indeed, software counterfeiting in Europe is very sophisticated, and companies have found it difficult to ferret out such operations. And in Argentina, lax copyright laws lead to large problems with piracy, with about 62% of all computer software being from illegal copies.[32]

In addition to being aware of potential counterfeit problems, firms selling strategic high-tech products, such as satellites, must also be aware of export controls. For example, chip makers must submit applications to sell microprocessors to certain countries, such as the former Soviet Union states or China. Sales of "dual use" products—nonmilitary items with military applications—are restricted to some countries. Even when restricted items are sold legally, problems can arise.

For example, in 1994, McDonnell Douglas sold China machine tools for a civilian machine center in Beijing and subsequently found the tools had been diverted to a military complex. Other items sold to China legally have included computers sold to the Chinese Academy of Sciences, which could be used in nuclear-fusion projects. The U.S. satellite company Loral hired China to propel its communications satellite into orbit using the Chinese-made Long March rocket. However, upon liftoff in the Sichuan province in February 1996, the rocket exploded. A committee of Western aerospace experts investigated the explosion and faxed its report to the Chinese government. A subsequent federal investigation concluded that this technical feedback may have helped China improve the accuracy of its rocket and missile program and that Loral and Hughes, another satellite company, had engaged in serious export control violations.[33]

The purpose for rules against technology sales are to protect U.S. security interests abroad. But the policy is fraught with problems. Some industry experts say that it is impossible to prevent the goods sold to friendly countries from ending up in restricted-access countries. Intel spokesperson Bill Calder says, "We ship chips to thousands of distributors all over the world, who aren't prevented from selling to these countries. There's a disconnect there."[34] Moreover, some believe that the controls actually undermine the United States' position as the leader in technology. For example, the U.S. share of the international satellite market dropped from 73% to 53% during the 1999 to 2000 time frame; and French, Canadian, and German firms picked up the satellite contracts that the U.S. firms couldn't fill due to export restrictions.[35] Others believe that, rather than restricting access to such products, it may actually serve U.S. strategic interests to have countries such as China use U.S. technology. The United States will understand the technology being used. Moreover, strict restrictions could drive these countries to other suppliers, which might put even more information in the hands of other countries.

Manufacturers of high-tech goods must be aware of issues surrounding export controls in order to ensure that their distribution channel operates legally. And manufacturers must take proactive steps to protect their goods against counterfeiting.

ADDING NEW CHANNELS: THE INTERNET

Probably one of the most compelling challenges firms face in their distribution channels is managing the changes brought about with the Internet. Hewlett-Packard's medical-products unit provides a case in point. This division uses 500 sales representatives and dozens of distributors to sell more than $1 billion of equipment per year worldwide.[36] The sales model used by these people has been face-to-face interactions to build customer relationships and demonstrate products. However, changes in the health care field are forcing hospital chains to gain efficiencies. One way they are doing so is to demand one-stop shopping on the Internet, allowing the chains to buy ultrasound machines to electrodes without ever seeing a salesperson. So, HP finds itself in a quandary: Should it offer customers the sales channel that they want and, in doing so, risk mutiny from the traditional sales force and distributors? Or should it keep its existing channel members happy but risk losing customers to competitors who do deliver what they want? A middle ground option might use some combination of traditional channels and Web-based sales. But this also invites conflict between the manufacturers and traditional retailers.

Companies adding an Internet sales channel to their existing distribution channels have found that, inevitably, with multiple channels pursuing customers, conflicts arise as different channels simultaneously pursue the same customers. In addition, customers may become confused and angry as both the manufacturer and its channel members pitch the same account, often with wildly different terms and conditions.

The situation is another example of co-opetition. Manufacturers want to cooperate with their channel partners in reaching the segment(s) of the market the partners serve, but they also will compete with those partners when they go directly on-line. Strong retailers can strong-arm their suppliers to avoid the Web, letting them know that a supplier who chooses to sell products is ultimately viewed as a competitor rather than a partner. Even in cases when a firm agrees to avoid the Web, its products may still wind up there if gray market activity exists.

Ultimately, however, the synergies that can be found in offering products both in traditional channels and on the Internet (a "click-and-brick" model) may be superior to either pure brick-and-mortar channels or Internet pure plays. Customers can use physical stores for return centers, for example, and on-line sales can attract a new customer segment.

Regardless, rather than adding new channels incrementally, without a clear vision of an ultimate go-to-market architecture—which can create conflict and morale problems internally and confuse customers externally—managers must design and manage channel systems strategically to achieve advantage.[37] The objectives of a hybrid channel are to increase market coverage while maintaining cost efficiency. Increased coverage and lower costs can create a competitive advantage for firms that understand how to implement and manage a hybrid channel effectively.

Steps in Managing Hybrid Channels

The key steps in effectively implementing and managing hybrid channels follow.[38]

1. *Identify customer target segments.* Customers can be targeted on the basis of size of customer, geographic region, products purchased, or buying behavior/needs.
2. *Delineate the tasks or functions that must be performed in selling to those segments.* Tasks include activities such as lead generation, sales prospect qualification, presales activities, closing the sale activities, postsales service and support, and ongoing account management.
3. *Allocate the best (i.e., efficient and effective) channels–tools to those tasks.* The various channels/tools/methods that can be used include national account management, direct sales, telemarketing, direct mail, retail stores, distributors, dealers/VARs, Internet, and so on. Not all channels must perform all tasks. Rather, channels should be combined to optimize costs and coverage relative to the tasks they are performing for various customer segments.

This model is the familiar contingency model, depicted in Figure 8-4. The idea is that no one channel can be used for optimum performance. Rather, the type of channel used

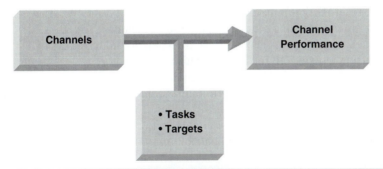

FIGURE 8-4 Contingency Approach to Developing Hybrid Channels

must be matched to the tasks needed by particular customer segments (or target markets). Only by effectively matching the appropriate channel tasks to the channel used to perform the tasks will optimum channel performance occur.

Another way to look at this model is as a grid that aligns the various tasks performed by the different channels across customer segments.[39] For example, the grid in Figure 8-5 shows that for one particular company, direct mail was desirable to generate leads for three customer segments based on size (small, medium, and big). Once leads are generated,

FIGURE 8-5 Grid: Allocating Tasks to Channels

Channels \ Tasks	Lead Generation	Quality Sales	Presales	Close Sales	Postsales Service	Account Management
National Account Management						B
Direct Sales			B	B		B
Telemarketing		B M	M	M	B M	M
Direct Mail	B M S					S
Retail Sales		S	S	S		
Distributors						
Dealers/VARS						

S Small customers   **M** Medium customers   **B** Big customers

Source: Moriarty, Rowland and Ursula Moran (1990), "Managing Hybrid Marketing Systems," *Harvard Business Review,* November–December, pp. 146–155. Copyright © 1990 by the President and Fellows of Harvard College; all rights reserved. Reprinted by permission of *Harvard Business Review.*

telemarketers perform the lead qualification task for medium and big customers, but smaller customers are directed to a retail channel for the remainder of the tasks. Presales and sales closing activities for large accounts are then performed by a direct sales force, whereas telemarketers perform those tasks for medium accounts. Ongoing account management is similarly allocated based on customer size.

As an example of this system at work, a major manufacturer of computer-aided manufacturing systems (CAD/CAM) sells its offerings in the United States and Europe through a direct sales force; in Japan, it uses an exclusive distributor. Because the channels and customers are physically separated, little conflict occurs (except in global accounts). Similarly, Xerox used product boundaries when it entered the personal copier market. It sold mid-range and high-end machines through a combination of direct sales and dealer distribution and low-end machines exclusively through retail channels (electronics and appliance stores, mass merchants, etc.).

In taking this hybrid model to the on-line world, the basic issues are

- How can a firm manage the addition of an Internet channel to its existing distribution system?
- When will an on-line channel lead to incremental sales versus displacement of existing sales through an existing channel?

These issues are addressed in the next section.

Application to the Internet

Compaq's Experience[40] In 1998, Compaq decided it had to launch a Web site to compete with Dell Computer. Compaq attempted to balance the needs of traditional computer dealers with the competitive urgency to provide products to Internet buyers. It appeared to follow the hybrid channel strategy very carefully. To avoid conflict with its distribution channel, it created a unique set of business-oriented Prosignia computers for Internet-only sales. It targeted only small and medium-size businesses, which weren't the dealers' primary sales focus. And it created a way for dealers to profit from Internet referrals. So, what went wrong?

Resellers saw Compaq's embrace of the Internet not as a way to take business from rival Dell, but as a sign of Compaq's indifference toward their role. The fact that Compaq also slashed the number of distributors in North America from 39 to 4 contributed to this perception. Its reason given for doing so was to cut the costs of maintaining inventories at resellers—costs that direct-model competitors such as Dell never incur. The fact that Compaq also started to deal in a more rigid fashion with its on-line resellers was little consolation to its traditional dealers. For example, Compaq's Internet-only resellers that sell the home-PC line had to adhere to minimum-advertised-price rules *and* provide repair services. And its five corporate dealers who were approved for on-line sales also had to follow specified rules when selling PCs from their own Internet sites. Regardless, dealers and other resellers felt left out by the direct-sales Internet strategy and competing business line, and they shunned selling *any* Compaq PCs.

Predicting the Effects of Disintermediation Compaq's lesson shows some of the potential issues that must be addressed in **disintermediation,** or the adding of an on-line distribution channel that bypasses existing intermediaries in favor of a direct-sales model. Although Compaq attempted to clearly delineate the channel used by the type of product sold, the strategy still invited conflict.

The question is whether the new Internet channel creates a new value proposition for end users, or whether it merely creates a more efficient distribution structure on-line.[41] Channels with clearly delineated value propositions are likely to attract different segments of customers and, hence, will invite less cannibalization. For example, some firms are finding that an Internet presence extends the brand to shoppers they were not reaching with traditional retail stores. Yet, in other cases, the Internet channel merely cannibalizes an existing sales channel. This is why, for example, the Internet has displaced sales of airline tickets from traditional travel agents to the Internet: Merely buying over the Internet is not going to increase the number of vacations or trips purchased. On the other hand, the Internet has empowered and encouraged more individual investors to buy and sell stocks and mutual funds than was ever done through investment houses or brokers. The ease of access and ability to transact on-line created a new value proposition. This is why both the frequency and number of transactions have increased.

What factors predict whether an Internet channel will lead to incremental sales or instead cannibalize or displace existing sales? The flowchart in Figure 8-6 provides an assessment of critical factors that must be considered.

Making the Transition to the Internet

Ultimately, regardless of whether sales are cannibalistic or incremental, firms must balance the transition from existing channels to the channel strategies that create the most value for the customer (in terms of efficient services, convenient ordering, etc.). As shown in Table 8-4, some companies have handled this transition in different ways, each with its own pros and cons.

Avoiding Conflict

1. *Use Web sites to disseminate product information only.*   For example, 3M lists hundreds of products on its Web site but generally doesn't provide any way to order them directly. This is deliberately done out of concern for channel members. This solution uses the Internet to perform an information dissemination function only and relies on other channels for the sales functions.
2. *Use the Web only to generate leads; direct potential buyers to the nearest dealers.*   For example, the automakers initially handled their Web sites this way. They couldn't afford to alienate the established dealers. IBM has also used this option on its Web site. Unfortunately, this approach doesn't take full advantage of the Internet's ability to wring costs out of the system.
3. *Use Web sites only for limited merchandise offerings.*   For example, the Sharper Image tends to sell merchandise that is excess or out-of-season inventory. Similarly, Compaq attempted to sell only one line of products dedicated solely for Internet sales.
4. *Take on-line orders for small customers only; direct larger sales to dealers.*   For example, Jackson Products, a St. Louis company that makes safety goggles and welding gear, will sell products over the Web, but any on-line shoppers who need to purchase over $1,000 in merchandise are directed to a distributor.[42] Another variation of this strategy is to pursue on-line sales in geographic areas retailers don't cover.[43]
5. *Launch a Web site with no publicity.*   A company that markets software for handling digital photos, Radius Inc. (Mountain View, California), began offering Internet sales on-line with no promotion of its Web site (because it didn't want to alienate its traditional distributors). Within three months, nearly 10% of its sales were coming from

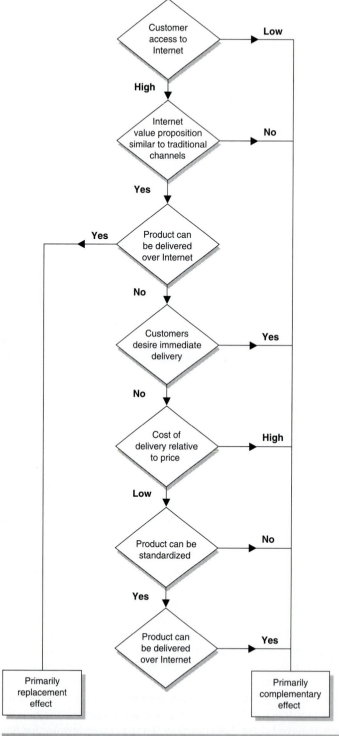

FIGURE 8-6 Complementary versus Replacement Effect of the Internet

Source: Kumar, Nirmalya (1999), "Internet Distribution Strategies: Dilemmas for the Incumbent," *Mastering Information Management,* March 15, pp. 6–7.

TABLE 8-4   Managing the Transition to the Internet

Avoid Conflict with Existing Channel

1. Use Web sites to disseminate product information only.
2. Use the Web only to generate leads; direct potential buyers to the nearest dealers.
3. Use Web sites only for limited merchandise offerings.
4. Take on-line orders for small customers only; direct larger sales to dealers.
5. Launch a Web site with no publicity.

Manage Conflict with Existing Channel

1. Assess the magnitude of conflict.
2. Establish boundaries for channels and customers.
3. Keep prices on the manufacturer's Web site aligned with traditional channels.
4. Give a cut of each Internet sale to dealers.
5. Improve the flow of information.

the Internet. The executives at this company recognize that despite this modest success, roughly 90% of their sales still come from distribution, and they can't afford to risk losing that channel.

Although these strategies take advantage of the tasks the Web can perform and attempt to match them to channels to minimize conflict, the reality is that they don't take full advantage of what the Internet has to offer—and a firm's competitors are surely likely to do so.

The dilemma of the Internet is that a firm must be willing to overturn long-successful distribution strategies—even if it means eroding the very revenue streams the company was founded upon—in order to remain competitive in a digital world.[44] This is why Compaq rolled out its own Web site, selling computers at low prices directly to small business customers and individuals. Although its traditional personal computer dealers were very unhappy about this new channel, Compaq justified the strategy by saying that it had to use the Internet in order to stay competitive.

Managing Conflict in Hybrid Channels   Capitalizing more fully on the distribution efficiencies the Web has to offer will invite conflict, but it may be the only viable option. Not to capitalize on the Web in order to avoid conflict with distribution channels may threaten long-term business survival. Actively cannibalizing one's own distribution channel, although traditionally considered an evil to be avoided, is consistent with the notion of creative destruction. Indeed, the radical innovations that the Internet has fostered threaten the very foundation of many businesses—and not just in distribution. For example, for Eastman Kodak, embracing digital imaging means undermining its specialized investments in production, processing, and distribution of silver-halide film. General Electric's Internet business units are referred to as "destroy-your-business.com."[45] Creative destruction in the on-line world essentially means survival by suicide. In order to compete with the pure-play Internet start-ups, firms must turn from brick-and-mortar to click-and-mortar (or click-and-brick). Companies that try to manage the health of their existing distribution channel will likely not succeed in the new world. As the experts say, cannibalize before there is nothing of value left to cannibalize.[46]

As an initial step in managing conflict, *assessing the magnitude of potential conflict* is vital (see Table 8-4). With no revenue in conflict, channel members may become complacent and not pursue their tasks effectively enough. On the other hand, with too much conflict, dysfunctional effects distract channel members from performing their jobs with clarity and enthusiasm. One guideline is that having more than roughly 10% to 30% of a firm's revenue in conflict between multiple channels provides a dysfunctional amount of conflict and can result in angry feedback from both customers and marketing personnel.[47]

After assessing the magnitude of conflict, *clear boundaries and guidelines for managing the conflict,* based on who owns which customer, must be established.[48] As indicated in the hybrid channel model, customers can be delineated on the basis of size, order size, decision process, industry, or geography; alternatively, firms can bound the conflict based on product line (low end, mid-range, or high end). Using such heuristics to identify which channels can pursue which customers will keep the level of conflict in a manageable, functional range.

Other strategies that might be used include the following. First, firms can *keep their own on-line prices high,* so traditional dealers can lead the way in offering discounts. For example, Hewlett-Packard rolled out a Web site to let major hospitals buy on-line. On-line prices were carefully aligned with those in other sales channels. Intuit offers Quicken and TurboTax on its Web site only at list price. (Firms that have significantly lower on-line prices are inviting a gray market situation.)

Second, firms can also *give a cut of each Internet sale to dealers and salespeople,* regardless of whether they played a role in generating it. At Hewlett-Packard, on-line orders generate commissions for the sales reps who typically handled the account. Compaq paid resellers an "agent fee" for steering business on-line. Although this strategy may seem counterintuitive, it actually weights the compensation structure in favor of the success of the new channel.[49] Although new channels are added to gain cost efficiencies in coverage, the new channel is unlikely to contribute a large percentage of revenues in the short term. Rather, as customers are migrated to the new channel, it is important to alleviate concerns of channel members whose customers are migrating. Without concern for these issues, channel members may sabotage the success of the new channel.

Finally, *improving the flow of information* is another way to manage potential channel conflicts. Channel management software products are available that allow customized information to specific resellers. In such a way, pricing, leads, and promotions can be more effectively and efficiently communicated. Moreover, forecast accuracy can be improved by improving communication flows from the channel members to the manufacturer.

Additional Considerations

Additional considerations in adding an on-line channel include the following:[50]

- Does the company currently sell products through a catalog?
- Are the company's products simple in nature (no configuration required, not integrated with products from other manufacturers)?
- Is the sales process clear-cut and nonconsultative?
- Are the products easy to install and maintain?
- Does the company have an existing infrastructure to support direct sales (order fulfillment, returns, customer service, etc.)?
- Do customers usually know what they want when they are ready to buy, or do they need information about competitors' products and product benefits from a third party?
- Is the company willing to promote the Web site enough to attract sufficient prospects?

Smart Fuel Pumps

The term *disintermediation* may soon take on new meaning in the realm of gas stations, where filling up your gas tank is becoming more and more like an episode of the Jetsons. Motorists in Indianapolis can fill up from the comfort of their driver's seat while a robotic gas pump does the work.

The SmartPump is a robotic mechanism that first reads a transponder placed on the windshield of the car to identify its make and model. The arm has a suction cup that opens the fuel tank door, and the unit engages the nozzle through a spring-loaded gas cap. The process works on nearly any car made since 1987 (unless the gas tank is underneath the license plate). The technology was developed by a combination of companies including H. R. Textron, which manufactures the service robot; a pump manufacturer; a fuel-cap manufacturer; Texas Instruments, which developed the windshield transponder; and Canada's International Submarine Engineering, which helped with motion sensor technology.

A similar technology, Autofill, has been used in Sweden for several years al-

Photograph reprinted with the permission of Shell Oil Company, Houston, Texas.

ready. Shell conducted a test market in Sacramento, California, with 500 customers in 1997, and the project has gone live in a suburb of Indianapolis. Other companies are also developing different versions of the robotic system.

What are reactions in the United States so far? Some drivers are worried about damage to their vehicles. Others don't like the $1 transaction fee that accompanies each fill-up. Ultimately, the convenience could be worth it, though.

Source: Rowell, Erica (2000), "Pumping It Up with Robotics," ABC News.com (www.abcnews.go.com/sections/tech/DailyNews/smartpump000310.html), March 10.

Kirsner argues that if a company can answer "yes" to all seven of these questions, then a Web direct-sales model does make sense. If, however, the answer to any of the questions is "no," then a Web direct-sales model may be problematic. (Note, however, that some companies, such as Dell Computer, have been successful, despite the product complexity, need for bundling, and a moderate level of installation complexity.)

As with most marketing issues, however, it is vitally important to keep the customer in mind. What benefits does the channel deliver to customers? How can the Web be used to enhance customer value, either through the channel or with a direct-sales model? Going direct on the Web may work for some companies, but the inherent complexities can mean that a middle-ground approach may also be part of the answer. One company's struggle with these issues is detailed in the Technology Expert's View from the Trenches.

Distribution Channel Strategy and Management

MICHAEL McDONOUGH
Senior Vice President of Sales and Marketing,
GTE Wireless, Atlanta, Georgia

Distribution channel productivity is often a critical success factor for many businesses. The importance of distribution channel strategy development and effective management of the channels is growing, as many businesses move to a more complex channel design with multiple direct and indirect traditional channels as well as rapid expansion of electronic channels. For example, here at GTE Wireless, we have a direct marketing channel with direct mail and telemarketing, an Internet-direct channel, and a sales force for business accounts, as well as retail, wholesale, and mass merchandisers, and traditional agents. How well a company manages these changes to more complex channels will be the difference between winning and losing in the marketplace.

We at GTE Wireless have learned steps that can be taken to improve the probability of success so one won't have to deal with the questions: "Why aren't we getting the results?" "Was the strategy flawed or was it poor execution?"

First, the channel strategy must be integrated with the total company strategy of what products go to what markets. Even the best distribution strategy will fail without well-founded product and target decisions.

Second, analytical rigor is important. The assessment of market opportunity, coverage models, channel-specific benefit/cost analysis, etc., is needed to determine channel resource allocation. But, more importantly, logic and quantification are needed so you can communicate to the organization what you are doing and why, and what you are asking them to do. It is the numbers and facts behind the logic that make the changes compelling and understandable.

Third, the channel strategy should include not only the "front-end" of sales and sales support, but also the "back-end" of order processing, inventory fulfillment, and customer care. One cannot make channel decisions in isolation of these back-office functions.

Finally, the changes must be led by sales management, including first-line sales managers. This is the key leverage point. If the salespeople do not buy into the changes, they may sabotage or undermine the changes. One of the key ways to get buy-in is consistent reinforcement of the strategy delivered by sales leadership and a compensation structure supportive of that strategy.

We at GTE Wireless have found that this four-pronged approach to making channel decisions and channel changes enhances the odds of success.

EXPANDING THE VIEW:
FROM DISTRIBUTION CHANNELS
TO SUPPLY CHAINS

Distribution channels trace the flow of product after it leaves the manufacturer, through the various intermediaries and institutions that add value along the way, to the end user. Supply chain considerations broaden the focus to include not only the distribution of the product but also the logistical management of all of the incoming components and pieces used in the manufacturing process of a particular product. Whereas distribution channels are concerned about inventory levels and customer service in the channel, supply chain management is concerned about inventory on the production floor, managing both the inflow and outflow of product.

Again, given the characteristics of high-tech products, firms are very concerned about efficient supply chain management. For example, when Intel saw the life of its microprocessors going from about eight years for the 386 series (introduced in 1985) to less than a year and a half in 1998, it realized it needed smaller inventory.

> When the product is being devalued so fast, I want to ship it at today's price, not tomorrow's, and I want to know the right amount of new stuff to build on the right day. Our product, ounce for ounce, is more valuable than platinum, and the cost of inventory is a number beyond anything you can imagine.[51]

So, Intel adopted SAP's enterprise resource planning (ERP) software to handle what had previously been managed by four separate systems, that handled orders from the United States, Japan, Asia, and Europe, to track them all together. The system allowed Intel to understand where its inventory was on a given day and to track orders and shipping costs. The system was integrated to handle parts and materials coming in from suppliers as well as goods outbound on the way to customers. It reshuffled Intel's global logistics, focusing on three new warehouses next to critical airports. Routing international shipping through these three points allowed Intel to guarantee that contractors' plants operated at full capacity, or close to it.

The new supply chain reduced finished goods inventory from eight weeks' worth in 1995 to four weeks' worth in 1998. Now Intel can see its inventory anywhere in the world, commit it to a customer, and deliver it in three days. It reduced the chip-making cycle time and used electronic links to customers to reduce their chip inventories. For example, the system is hooked electronically to five leading personal computer makers. The software automatically triggers a new shipment when customers' inventory falls to about four days' worth. The customer's inventory might get as low as one day's supply before a new shipment arrives. This halves the time customers hold valuable inventory. In essence, the system has traded information for inventory. And links to the retail chains that are the PC makers' biggest customers get the system one layer closer to the end customer in its market-sensing capacity.[52]

Effective Supply Chain Management[53]

Again, following the contingency model for effective high-tech marketing, an effective supply chain strategy matches the type of innovation (incremental versus breakthrough) to the type of supply chain needed. A supply chain can serve two functions:

- *Physical functions* convert raw materials, transport goods, and so forth.
- *Market mediation functions* ensure the variety of products reaching the marketplace matches what customers want.

Costs arise when supply exceeds demand or when supply is less than demand (the opportunity cost of lost sales or unhappy customers). As the matrix in Figure 8-7 shows, the appropriate match between the supply chain focus and the type of innovation is imperative.

For incremental, more functional products—or those with stable, predictable attributes, long life cycles, and fairly low margins—market mediation is fairly easy. Because the products have a long history and don't change significantly, matching products to customer needs can be straightforward. Instead of focusing efforts on flexibility and reading market signals, companies can focus on managing physical costs. They can manage the flow of information within the chain between players to coordinate activities. Close coordination between suppliers and distributors offers the greatest opportunities to slash lead times and inventory.

For innovative products (unpredictable demand, short life cycle), however, firms must read early-market signals to react quickly and get crucial information from the market to the players in the chain. A firm must know where to position inventory and production capacity in order to hedge against uncertain demand. For these innovative products, critical issues are speed and flexibility more than low cost. The primary challenge is responding to uncertainty. Uncertainty can be reduced with data and information systems, with a produce-to-order model, or by manufacturing closer in time to when

FIGURE 8-7 Matching Type of Innovation to Supply Chain Functions

	Incremental	Breakthrough
Physical Function	☆	– 0 –
Market Mediation Functions	– 0 –	☆

Supply Chain Functions (vertical axis)

Type of Innovation (horizontal axis)

☆ Appropriate match of type of product to supply chain functions

– 0 – Inappropriate match

Source: Fisher, Marshall (1997), "What Is the Right Supply Chain for Your Product?" *Harvard Business Review,* March–April, pp. 105–116. Copyright © 1997 by the President and Fellows of Harvard College; all rights reserved. Reprinted by permission of *Harvard Business Review.*

demand materializes. *For innovative products, rewards from investments in supply chain responsiveness are greater than rewards from efficiency investments.* Improvements in responsiveness result in savings from fewer stock-outs and markdowns.

For example, consider a typical innovative product with a contribution margin of 40% and an average stock-out rate of 25%. The lost contribution to profit and overhead resulting from stock-outs alone is huge: 40% * 25% = 10% of sales—an amount that usually exceeds profits before taxes. Consequently, the economic gain from reducing stock-outs and excess inventory is so great that intelligent investments in supply chain responsiveness will nearly always pay for themselves. This is why, for example, Compaq chose to produce high-variety, short life cycle circuits in-house rather than outsource them to a low-cost Asian producer; local production gave the company increased flexibility and lead times. Note that this logic doesn't apply to functional products. With a contribution margin of 10% and an average stock-out rate of 1%, the lost contribution to profit and overhead amounts to only 0.1%.

The changes in the distribution channel for computer products, including channel assembly and colocation, provide other good examples of changing from a physically efficient supply chain to one more usefully focused on market mediation. Although inventory turns are a familiar measure, the market increasingly demands responsiveness.

Trends in Supply Chain Management

Two important trends in supply chain management that high-tech firms rely on to gain efficiencies are the movement toward vertical markets on the Internet and the use of sophisticated supply chain management software to manage the supply chain function.

Vertical Markets on the Internet   **Vertical markets,** or **vertical communities,** are industry-specific Web sites that provide electronic business solutions ranging from e-commerce (sales of products) to document sharing, bill presentment, order tracking, contract negotiations, and credit services. These hubs use e-business solutions at many points along the supply chain to build links between suppliers, customers, manufacturers, and even competitors. For example, VerticalNet.com is a company whose strategy is to create a multitude of vertical infomediaries or industry portals, including communities in advanced technologies and communications. The business solutions offered can add or create value by streamlining and eliminating redundancy of current or traditional processes being used within an industry. Because of the Web's value in simplifying many business-to-business transactions, the forecasts for electronic commerce show B-to-B transactions being three to four times larger than consumer transactions.

These electronic marketplaces are typically owned and operated by a new class of intermediaries on the Web: **cybermediaries,** or **infomediaries.**[54] One study estimated that some 100,000 cybermediaries had cropped up by 1998.[55] Digital intermediaries function as brokers, helping people gather and decipher the vast quantity of information on the Web, bringing together buyers and sellers, and providing value by offering advice, personal service, or other benefits. This new class of intermediaries provides a more direct and inexpensive conduit between producers and buyers than do traditional distributors.[56] And these infomediaries typically serve the buyer rather than the producers.[57]

The value created by bringing a number of buyers and suppliers together onto a neutral and secure Web site is much greater than that obtained by the prior generation of technology, electronic data interchange (EDI), or by Web sites run by a single player.

Infomediaries aimed at trade between businesses pool buying power to extract deals from vendors. Many of these cybermediaries function as portals that draw buyers or direct them to manufacturers and service providers. For example, FastParts.com links buyers and sellers of surplus electronic parts. These digital intermediaries gather a critical mass of buyers and sellers, which, in turn, makes the site self-renewing: People continue to come because that's where the action is. Given this drawing power, some predict that these cybermediaries will soon extract more revenue from advertisers and sponsors.

E-marketplaces are currently being used for many low-tech products, such as steel, plastics, energy, and surplus parts. The change to hubs is likely to be particularly intensified in industries in which products don't need to be tried on, tested, tasted, or touched. However, it is important that high-tech manufacturers be aware of this trend, because it will likely be used for high-tech goods and components as well. And even high-tech companies must purchase things such as maintenance, repair, and operating (MRO) items; ad space; and other goods for which electronic marketplaces may be the preferred purchasing route. Awareness of the use of on-line communities for supply chain relationships is vital for high-tech marketers; these communities are explored further in Chapter 11.

Supply Chain Management Software   With the advent of ever-increasingly sophisticated information technology, companies are using new software programs to redesign their business processes. Known as **enterprise resource planning (ERP),** enterprise software refers to the roughly $23 billion a year subindustry of software for companies looking to use technology to improve virtually every key corporate function, including manufacturing, finance, sales, marketing, human resources, supply chain management, and the data juggling behind the e-commerce scenes. The industry for ERP software is anticipating predicted sales of $84 billion by 2002.[58] ERP programs were originally focused on automating business processes, rather than on the strategic use of information. Now, they function as an electronic nervous system for the business operation, tracking orders, receivables, products, warehousing, inventory, accounting, suppliers, customers, anything of interest to the increased efficiency and effectiveness of the business process.

A subset of ERP software, supply chain management programs—$2 billion in 1997, expected to grow to $14 billion in 2002—bring data from manufacturing, inventory, and suppliers to create a unified picture of the elements that go into building a product. For example, one vendor's products, i2 Technologies, can help a firm decide if it makes more sense to build just one factory or three separate ones that are closer to its customers. Tracking the manufacturing of products and the various business processes as the product moves from order entry to order fulfillment can help in managing facilities, vendors, subcontractors, and so forth. Other back-office programs help companies analyze their operations to unearth ways to cut costs in areas such as order processing, customer service and returns, and order fulfillment.

Supply chain management used to be handled with proprietary EDI links between suppliers and OEM customers. But with the increased velocity and unpredictability in the high-tech environment, accurate predictions have increased in importance.[59]

Although supply chain management software that forecasts and mediates supply and demand provides important efficiencies, it could wreak havoc on traditional supply chain relationships. For example, traditional parts brokers may become obsolete in an era of on-line virtual communities and vertical networks. Former single-source suppliers may be pitted against each other in auction bids. These issues have yet to be reconciled in the still-emerging world of on-line supply chain management.

Summary

This chapter has provided an overview and understanding of some of the issues pertinent to designing and managing distribution and supply chain relationships in the high-tech environment. Given the characteristics of the high-tech environment, firms are seeing a blurring of distinctions between members in the supply chain, and indirect channels are changing to provide more value. This chapter also addressed the way in which high-tech channels evolve as an innovation becomes more mainstream, the causes and solutions to gray market problems, piracy concerns, and export restrictions.

The Internet is having a significant impact on distribution channels; therefore, the chapter provided a framework, based on a contingency theory of managing hybrid channels, to integrate the Internet into existing distribution channels. Moreover, contingency theory was also used to provide insights into supply chain management in high-tech markets. Radical changes arising from the introduction of the Internet as a distribution channel, vertical communities for supply chain relationships, and sophisticated software programs for supply chain planning will likely continue to affect distribution channels in the future.

Discussion Questions

1. What are the six basic issues in designing and managing a distribution channel?
2. What are the various types of intermediaries commonly used in high-tech channels?
3. What is the nature of the trade-off between the *degree of coverage* and the *degree of intrabrand competition?*
4. What tools can be used for control and coordination of channel members?
5. What is tying? What are its legal implications?
6. What is an exclusive dealing arrangement? What are its legal implications?
7. How can channel performance be measured?
8. How and why is the line between suppliers and channel members blurring?
9. What are channel assembly and colocation? Why are they being used in high-tech channels?
10. What is the typical evolution pattern for channels in high-tech markets?
11. What is the gray market? Why is it a problem? What are its causes and solutions?
12. What is the purpose of export restrictions?
13. What are the objectives of a hybrid channel? What are the key steps in effectively implementing and managing hybrid channels?
14. What factors are used to assess whether an Internet channel will cannibalize existing sales or lead to incremental sales?
15. What are some of the intermediate steps in managing the transition to an Internet channel?
16. What is the source of conflict in a hybrid channel? How can it best be managed?
17. What is supply chain management? How should supply chain functions be matched to the type of innovation?
18. What are vertical communities? What is the role of the cyber- or infomediary? How are these communities used in supply chain management?
19. What is ERP? How do supply chain management programs work?

Glossary

Authoritative controls. Reside in one channel member's ability to develop rules, give instructions, and in effect, impose decisions on the other; include ownership (via vertical integration), formal, centralized decision making (say, as in franchising), formal controls and monitoring, or one party's power over another.

Bilateral controls. Originate in the activities, interests, or joint input of *both* channel members and include relational norms (shared expectations concerning channel members' attitudes and behaviors in working together to achieve mutual goals) such as flexibility, mutual sharing of benefits and burdens, information sharing, and so forth; joint interdependence, commitment, and mutual trust.

Channel assembly. Manufacturers ship semi-finished products to distributors that configure them to client specifications and complete production before shipping the products. The advantages are customization and speedy turnaround for customers.

Colocation. When the distributor's employees work from a vendor's manufacturing sites to ship completed, high-demand models to either resellers or end users.

Cybermediaries (infomediaries). A new class of intermediaries on the Web that brings together buyers and sellers.

Disintermediation. The adding of an on-line distribution channel that bypasses existing intermediaries in favor of a direct-sales model.

Enterprise resource planning (ERP). The redesign of business processes and functions, including manufacturing, finance, sales, marketing, human resources, supply chain management, and the data analysis used to support e-commerce, to improve effectiveness and efficiency; typically based on ERP software and the Internet.

Exclusive dealing arrangements. Restrict a dealer to carrying only one manufacturer's product; antitrust implications arise if large companies use their dominance to restrict customers' access to competitors' products.

Gray market. Unauthorized distribution of goods at discounted prices through resellers not franchised or sanctioned by the producer; results in a lack of control over the product, distribution, and services.

Hybrid channel or **dual channel.** When a firm uses a combination of direct and indirect channels.

Inbound dealers. Typically have a retail storefront, and their primary customers are walk-in traffic generated through traditional advertising and promotion means.

Interbrand competition. Competition between different brands or makes in the marketplace.

Intrabrand competition. Competition between dealers on the same manufacturer's brand.

Outbound dealers. Have a sales force that makes calls on customers, typically at the customer location (the dealer may or may not have a storefront).

Systems integrator. A type of dealer who manages very large or complex computer projects, typically creating customized solutions for customers by bundling and reselling different brands of equipment.

Tying. When a manufacturer makes the sale of a product in high demand conditional to the purchase of a second product.

Value-added reseller (VAR) or **value-added dealer (VAD).** Smaller channel intermediaries that purchase products from one or several high-tech companies and add value to them, via integrating with proprietary expertise, to meet their target market's (often a vertical market) needs.

Vertical markets or **vertical communities.** Industry-specific Web sites that provide electronic business solutions ranging from e-commerce (sales of products) to document sharing, bill presentment, order tracking, contract negotiations, and credit services. These hubs use e-business solutions at many points along the supply chain to build links between suppliers, customers, manufacturers, and even competitors.

Endnotes

1. "Managing Customers As Assets" (1995), *Fortune,* May 29, Special Advertising Section, p. S4.

2. "How Technology Sells" (1997), Dataquest, Gartner Group, and CMP Channel Group, CMP Publications, Jericho, NY.

3. Stern, Louis and Frederick Sturdivant (1987), "Customer-Driven Distribution Systems," *Harvard Business Review,* July–August, pp. 34–41. This section introduces the basic elements of channel design and management; the intent is not to provide all the decision tools and trade-offs faced in designing a distribution channel, but rather to provide a foundation for the subsequent development of particular issues faced in distribution channels for high-tech products.

4. Briones, Maricris (1999), "Resellers Hike Profits Through Service," *Marketing News,* 33 (February 15), pp. 1, 14.

5. Mohr, Jakki, Christine Page, and Greg Gundlach (1999), "The Governance of Inter-Organizational Exchange Relationships: Review and State-of-the-Art Assessment," Working paper, University of Montana, Missoula, MT.

6. France, Mike (1998), "Are Corporate Predators on the Loose?" *Business Week,* February 23, pp. 124–126.

7. "How Technology Sells" (1997), Dataquest, Gartner Group, and CMP Channel Group, CMP Publications, Jericho, NY.

8. Kumar, Nirmalya, Louis Stern, and Ravi Achrol (1992), "Assessing Reseller Performance from the Perspective of the Supplier," *Journal of Marketing Research,* 29 (May), pp. 238–253.

9. "Line Blurs Between Supplier and Supplied" (1997), *Computer Retail Week,* October 6, www.techweb.com/se/directlink.cgi?crw1997 1006s0048.

10. "Line Blurs Between Supplier and Supplied" (1997), *Computer Retail Week,* October 6, www.techweb.com/se/directlink.cgi?crw1997 1006s0048.

11. Briones, Maricris (1999), "What Technology Wrought: Distribution Channel in Flux," *Marketing News,* 33 (February 1), pp. 1, 15.

12. Briones, Maricris (1999), "What Technology Wrought: Distribution Channel in Flux," *Marketing News,* 33 (February 1), pp. 1, 15.

13. Briones, Maricris (1999), "What Technology Wrought: Distribution Channel in Flux," *Marketing News,* 33 (February 1), p. 15.

14. Briones, Maricris (1999), "Resellers Hike Profits Through Service," *Marketing News,* 33 (February 15), pp. 1, 14.

15. "How Technology Sells" (1997), Dataquest, Gartner Group, and CMP Channel Group, CMP Publications, Jericho, NY.

16. Moore, Geoffrey (1991), *Crossing the Chasm, Marketing and Selling Technology Products to Mainstream Customers,* New York: Harper-Collins, chapter 7.

17. Moore, Geoffrey (1991), *Crossing the Chasm, Marketing and Selling Technology Products to Mainstream Customers,* New York: Harper-Collins, chapter 7, p. 173.

18. Moore, Geoffrey (1991), *Crossing the Chasm, Marketing and Selling Technology Products to Mainstream Customers,* New York: Harper-Collins.

19. Duhan, Dale and Mary Jane Sheffet (1988), "Gray Markets and the Legal Status of Parallel Importation," *Journal of Marketing,* 52 (July), pp. 75–83; Corey, E. Raymond, Frank V. Cespedes, and V. Kasturi Rangan (1989), *Going to Market: Distribution Systems for Industrial Products,* Boston: Harvard Business School Press, chapter 9 (The Gray Market Dilemma).

20. Myers, Matthew and David Griffith (1999), "Strategies for Combating Gray Market Activity," *Business Horizons,* November–December, pp. 2–8.

21. Corey, E. Raymond, Frank V. Cespedes, and V. Kasturi Rangan (1989), *Going to Market: Distribution Systems for Industrial Products,* Boston: Harvard Business School Press, chapter 9 (The Gray Market Dilemma).

22. Duhan, Dale and Mary Jane Sheffet (1988), "Gray Markets and the Legal Status of Parallel Importation," *Journal of Marketing,* 52 (July), pp. 75–83.

23. Corey, E. Raymond, Frank V. Cespedes, and V. Kasturi Rangan (1989), *Going to Market: Distribution Systems for Industrial Products,* Boston: Harvard Business School Press, chapter 9 (The Gray Market Dilemma).

24. Corey, E. Raymond, Frank V. Cespedes, and V. Kasturi Rangan (1989), *Going to Market: Distribution Systems for Industrial Products,* Boston: Harvard Business School Press, chapter 9 (The Gray Market Dilemma).

25. Corey, E. Raymond, Frank V. Cespedes, and V. Kasturi Rangan (1989), *Going to Market: Distribution Systems for Industrial Products,* Boston: Harvard Business School Press, chapter 9 (The Gray Market Dilemma).

26. Corey, E. Raymond, Frank V. Cespedes, and V. Kasturi Rangan (1989), *Going to Market: Distribution Systems for Industrial Products,* Boston: Harvard Business School Press, chapter 9 (The Gray Market Dilemma).

27. Corey, E. Raymond, Frank V. Cespedes, and V. Kasturi Rangan (1989), *Going to Market: Distribution Systems for Industrial Products,* Boston: Harvard Business School Press, chapter 9 (The Gray Market Dilemma).

28. Corey, E. Raymond, Frank V. Cespedes, and V. Kasturi Rangan (1989), *Going to Market: Distribution Systems for Industrial Products,* Boston: Harvard Business School Press, chapter 9 (The Gray Market Dilemma).

29. Corey, E. Raymond, Frank V. Cespedes, and V. Kasturi Rangan (1989), *Going to Market: Distribution Systems for Industrial Products,* Boston: Harvard Business School Press, chapter 9 (The Gray Market Dilemma).

30. Baker, Stephen and Inka Resch (1999), "Piracy!" *Business Week,* July 26, pp. 90–94.

31. Baker, Stephen and Inka Resch (1999), "Piracy!" *Business Week,* July 26, pp. 90–94.

32. South American Business Information (1999), "Argentina: Decreasing Software Piracy," September 2, p. 1008244u5629.

33. Cohen, Adam (1999), "When Companies Leak," *Time,* June 7, p. 44.

34. Cohen, Adam (1999), "When Companies Leak," *Time,* June 7, p. 44.

35. Gay, Lance (2000), "U.S. Satellite Controls Have Backfired," *Missoulian,* June 1, p. A7.

36. Anders, George (1998), "Some Big Companies Long to Embrace Web, but Settle for Flirta-tion," *Wall Street Journal,* November 4, pp. A1, A13.

37. Moriarty, Rowland and Ursula Moran (1990), "Managing Hybrid Marketing Systems," *Harvard Business Review,* November–December, pp. 146–155.

38. Moriarty, Rowland and Ursula Moran (1990), "Managing Hybrid Marketing Systems," *Harvard Business Review,* November–December, pp. 146–155.

39. Moriarty, Rowland and Ursula Moran (1990), "Managing Hybrid Marketing Systems," *Harvard Business Review,* November–December, pp. 146–155.

40. McWilliams, Gary (1999), "Dealer Loses?" *Wall Street Journal,* July 12, p. R20; Useem, Jerry (1999), "Internet Defense Strategy: Cannibalize Yourself," *Fortune,* September 6, pp. 121–134.

41. Kumar, Nirmalya (1999), "Internet Distribution Strategies: Dilemmas for the Incumbent," *Mastering Information Management,* March 15, pp. 6–7.

42. Kirsner, Scott (1998), "Channel Concord: The Web Isn't Just for Alienating Partners Anymore," *CIO Web Business,* November 1, pp. 32–34.

43. Kirsner, Scott (1998), "Channel Concord: The Web Isn't Just for Alienating Partners Anymore," *CIO Web Business,* November 1, pp. 32–34.

44. Useem, Jerry (1999), "Internet Defense Strategy: Cannibalize Yourself," *Fortune,* September 6, pp. 121–134.

45. Useem, Jerry (1999), "Internet Defense Strategy: Cannibalize Yourself," *Fortune,* September 6, pp. 121–134.

46. Useem, Jerry (1999), "Internet Defense Strategy: Cannibalize Yourself," *Fortune,* September 6, pp. 121–134.

47. Moriarty, Rowland and Ursula Moran (1990), "Managing Hybrid Marketing Systems," *Harvard Business Review,* November–December, pp. 146–155.

48. Moriarty, Rowland and Ursula Moran (1990), "Managing Hybrid Marketing Systems," *Harvard Business Review,* November–December, pp. 146–155.

49. Moriarty, Rowland and Ursula Moran (1990), "Managing Hybrid Marketing Systems," *Har-*

vard Business Review, November–December, pp. 146–155.

50. Kirsner, Scott (1998), "Channel Concord: The Web Isn't Just for Alienating Partners Anymore," *CIO Web Business,* November 1, pp. 32–34.

51. Brown, Stuart (1998), "Wresting New Wealth from the Supply Chain," *Fortune,* November 9, p. 204X.

52. Brown, Stuart (1998), "Wresting New Wealth from the Supply Chain," *Fortune,* November 9, pp. 204C–204Z.

53. Except where noted, this section is drawn from Fisher, Marshall (1997), "What Is the Right Supply Chain for Your Product?" *Harvard Business Review,* March–April, pp. 105–116.

54. Hof, Robert (1998), "The Click Here Economy," *Business Week,* June 22, pp. 122–128.

55. Stapanek, Marcia (1998), "Rebirth of the Salesman," *Business Week,* June 22, pp. 146–147.

56. Hof, Robert (1999), "The Buyer Always Wins," *Business Week e.biz,* March 22, pp. EB26–EB28.

57. Hagel, John III and Marc Singer (1999), *Net Worth,* Boston: Harvard Business School Press.

58. Kirkpatrick, David (1998), "The E-Ware War: Competition Comes to Enterprise Software," *Fortune,* December 7, pp. 102–112.

59. Gross, Neil (1998), "Leapfrogging a Few Links," *Business Week,* June 22, pp. 140–142.

Recommended Reading

Coughlan, Anne, Erin Anderson, Louis Stern, and Adel El-Ansary (2001), *Marketing Channels,* Upper Saddle River, NJ: Prentice Hall.

CHAPTER 9

Pricing Considerations in High-Tech Markets

THE HIGH-TECH PRICING ENVIRONMENT

What forces impinge on high-tech pricing decisions? As shown in Figure 9-1, the forces are varied and strong. Many high-tech firms might find it desirable to price at a high level, in order to recoup investments in R&D and to signal high product quality. However, many factors conspire to push prices down.

High-tech firms face an environment characterized by ever-shortening product life cycles, with the inevitable rapid pace of change and potential obsolescence of products. Moore's Law[1] operates unforgivingly: Every 18 months or so, improvements in technology double product performance at no increase in price. Stated a different way, every 18 months or so, improvements in technology cut price in half for the same level of performance. So introductions of product versions with better price/performance ratios are a given, creating downward pressure on prices.

Moreover, as identified in Chapter 1, network externalities and unit-one costs operate in the market. Recall that network externalities exist when the value of the product increases as more users adopt it; examples include the telephone, portals on the

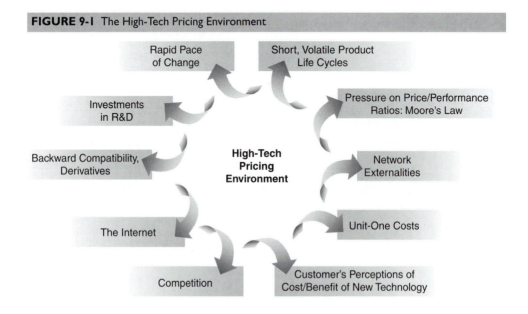

FIGURE 9-1 The High-Tech Pricing Environment

Internet, and so forth. Unit-one costs refer to the situation in which the cost of producing the first unit is very high relative to the costs of reproduction for subsequent units. For example, the costs of pressing and distributing a CD-ROM are trivial compared to the cost of hiring programmers and content specialists to develop the code recorded on it. Both of these factors create pressure to acquire a critical mass of users through lower price structures.[2]

Furthermore, customer perceptions of the cost/benefit of the new technology affect pricing strategy. Customer anxiety may cause delays in adoption. For example, as firms introduce one new-and-improved version after another, consumers are "balky"; they postpone purchases in the hope (fear?) that prices eventually will come down and performance will improve substantially.[3] For example, the remarkable improvements in the speed of modems, critical for fast Internet connections, caused consumer anxiety about their 14.4K modems passing into obsolescence with the 56K units. In such a situation, marketers may need to lower the prices of newer versions aggressively to reduce possible switching costs, to offer special deals for upgrades, or to entice customers switching from a competing application.[4]

The effect of customer anxiety on purchase considerations is further complicated by the upgrading considerations covered in Chapter 6: The customer's perceptions of the degree of change between the old and new generations relative to the cost to upgrade have a strong influence on purchase behavior. Because of this anxiety, marketers may have to lower prices for future generations to encourage upgrades.

Other complicating factors include the fact that high-tech firms must ward off penetration by competitors. Moreover, the Internet has allowed both consumers and organizational customers the ability to compare prices and negotiate for lower prices to a much greater degree than in the past. Issues of backward compatibility, support for existing products, changing operating standards, maintenance pricing for product derivatives, and so forth, all must be considered in pricing strategy.

Pricing even in conventional marketing contexts is a very complex decision; this overview of the high-tech pricing environment shows that it is doubly complex for high-tech products and services. As in prior chapters, this chapter does not go over pricing basics (such as calculating payback periods, return on investment, break-even points, experience curves, leasing, competitive bidding, price elasticity, penetration versus skimming strategies, etc.); interested readers should consult other resources to learn the basics. Rather, this chapter addresses how pricing decisions can be made that incorporate and address many of the environmental considerations mentioned previously. We start by examining the three major factors that all marketers must systematically consider when setting prices: costs, competition, and customers.

THE THREE Cs OF PRICING

The three Cs of pricing—costs, competition, and customers—are analogous to a three-legged stool, shown in Figure 9-2. Stools with only two legs are unbalanced and likely to topple over. Similarly, setting price on the basis of considering only one or two of the three Cs results in an unstable situation. Solid pricing strategy must be based on a systematic consideration of all three factors.

Competition

Costs   Customers

FIGURE 9-2 The 3 Cs of Pricing

Costs

Costs provide a floor, generally below which marketers ought not price. Companies that position on a low-price basis should not do so unless they have a strong, nonimitable cost advantage in the industry that is unlikely to disappear with future generations of technology. For example, a cost advantage based on economies of scale arising from large volume sales based on existing technology may not translate to a cost advantage when a new generation of technology comes down the pike.

A firm that bases prices primarily on its own cost structure (i.e., on a markup, cost-plus, or target-return basis) often fails to recognize the impact that market factors have on profitability. Overlooking the impact of the market on pricing and profitability can be a fatal mistake in high-tech markets, in which market considerations are so important.

Competition

Competition provides a benchmark against which to evaluate prices. A firm might let competitors set prices and then establish its price below, equal to, or above those of competitors, depending upon its position in the market.

In the high-tech arena, a firm that introduces a radical innovation to the marketplace often (wrongly) believes that, because its innovation is so new, there is "no" competition. However, this belief is not necessarily the case from the customer's perspective. A customer can always choose not to adopt new technology, but to solve problems based on former solutions (which provide the competitive benchmark for radical innovations). Indeed, one executive from Motorola said: "Our biggest competitor isn't IBM or Sony. It's the way in which people currently do things."[5]

Customers

Customers provide a ceiling above which marketers should not price. This ceiling is based on the perceived value of the product to the customer. Simply, customers balance the benefits of a purchase against its costs. High-tech marketers often find it difficult to understand fully the customer's perceptions of benefits and costs. The innovating firm may find the new technology so compelling, so sophisticated, or so "innovative," that it assumes the benefits are obvious to users. Similarly, the innovating firm may not fully appreciate the customer's perceptions of costs.

Product benefits might include the following:[6]

- *Functional benefits.*   The utilitarian aspects that might be attractive to engineers or technology enthusiasts
- *Operational benefits.*   The product's reliability and durability

- *Financial benefits.*   Credit terms, leasing options, and so on
- *Personal benefits.*   The psychosocial satisfaction from being an early adopter, purchasing a well-known brand to avoid risk, and the like

The costs a customer perceives are similarly diverse and might include the following:[7]

- *Monetary costs.*   The price paid, transportation, installation, and so forth.
- *Nonmonetary costs.*   The risk of product failure, risk of obsolescence, obsoleting of a prior piece of equipment, obsoleting of prior investments in related products (i.e., VHS tapes that won't play on the new DVD player), risk of late delivery, and the like. For business-to-business goods, nonmonetary costs might include factory downtime for repair and maintenance of machinery.

The **total cost of ownership** (or **life cycle costing**) is one way to look at customers' costs; it reflects the total amount a customer expends in order to own and use a product or service. Total cost of ownership includes the price paid for the good (including financing fees), as well as delivery or installation costs, service costs to maintain and repair the good, power costs to run the equipment, supplies, and other operating costs *over the life of the equipment.* Statistics show that in 1995, the initial purchase price of a corporate personal computer accounted for only 10% of its lifetime cost of $42,000. The rest is comprised of troubleshooting, administration, software, and training.[8] Using the total cost of ownership in pricing strategy can help a firm position its products, relative to those of competitors. Showing that the total cost of ownership of a product is lower than the competitor's can be a compelling benefit to a customer—despite an initially higher outlay for the product. Firms such as Microsoft use this approach when selling to corporate customers.

The Technology Tidbit provides information regarding pricing for a two-hour flight into space.

In summary, solid consideration of costs, competitors, and customers is vital in establishing a successful pricing strategy. Focusing on costs alone can be myopic and can cause problems. Similarly, focusing on competition can be hard in high-tech markets, when the competition for a radical innovation might be the customer's behavior pattern. Both of the drawbacks in focusing solely on costs or competition point to the value in taking a customer perspective in pricing. Taking a customer perspective in pricing forces the marketer to realize that the firm's costs to manufacture a product and its investments in R&D are relatively unimportant to the customer's perceived value. Moreover, the customer tends not to care about the firm's costs so much as his or her own costs in buying and using the product.

Because of the importance of a customer orientation in pricing, this leg of the stool deserves additional consideration.

CUSTOMER-ORIENTED PRICING

A customer-oriented perspective on pricing is provided in the Technology Expert's View from the Trenches by Keith Flaugh, director of pricing strategy at IBM.

Steps in Customer-Oriented Pricing[9]

In order to price products based on the value that customers perceive, marketers can use the steps shown in Table 9-1.

TECHNOLOGY TIDBIT

Space Tourism

According to preliminary market surveys, 10,000 would-be space tourists are willing to spend $1 million each for a two-hour flight into space. Indeed, more than 130 people have already paid a deposit to Space Adventures in Arlington, Virginia, to hold their spots, tentatively slated for flight in 2005.

The costs involved are astronomical: It costs $10,000 per pound to launch a simple satellite into orbit, with no oxygen, life support, or return trip necessary—not to mention the liability insurance!

Because NASA has no interest in this market, a host of smaller companies are working to design a reusable launch system that's inexpensive, safe, and reliable. Kelly Space (San Bernardino, California) has a prototype that looks like a plane with rocket engines. Rotary Rocket in Redwood City, California, has a booster with rotors to make a helicopter-style return to Earth. Kistler Aerospace in Kirkland, Washing-

Rotary Rocket
Photograph reprinted with the permission of Rotary Rocket, Redwood City, California.

ton, has an elaborate parachute system. Indeed, the market for space tourism is heating up. Hilton and Budget are planning to build space hotels, and some are talking about using *Mir* as a hotel. Bigelow Aerospace (Nevada) was founded solely for the purpose of designing and building space hotels, and Shimizu, a construction company in Japan, has done a large amount of research on space hotels.

My thanks to Richard Stockmans, Rotary Rocket, for insights into this market.
Source: Cray, Dan (2000), "Will We Take Vacations in Space?" *Time,* April 10, p. 63; Boudette, Neal (2000), "U.S. Space Buffs See Otherworldly Profit in Russia's Rickety Mir," *Wall Street Journal,* June 16, p. A1.

TABLE 9-1 Steps in Customer-Oriented Pricing

1 Understand exactly how the customer will use a firm's products.
2 Focus on the benefits customers receive from using the products.
3 Calculate all relevant customer costs, and understand how a customer trades off costs versus benefits in the purchase decision.

---

1. *A firm must understand exactly how the customer will use its products.* Customer-oriented pricing requires that a marketer completely understand how customers apply and use the products they buy from the firm. Each end use of a product may have a different cost/benefit analysis. For example, a customer who purchases a Quicken tax program to run a small business doing tax preparation and consulting would place a different value on the product than a person who purchases the same program to do his or her individual taxes.

Pricing Insights from the Field:
The Power of Customer Financing and Leasing

KEITH O. FLAUGH
Director of Pricing Strategy,
Sales and Distribution, IBM Corporation,
White Plains, New York

It's true! The challenges of implementing and realizing an effective pricing strategy in today's high-technology environment can be nerve-racking at best, and if you deal with these changes at only the product level (on just the tactical price/performance improvement basis), you significantly increase your company's vulnerability to poor results and lower profitability. With 20+ years experience in pricing within IBM, I offer a couple of lessons learned beyond the classic product techniques to, hopefully, help you think through your strategy in today's rapidly changing Information Technology (IT) world.

Don't get me wrong: It is imperative to understand and manage very closely the elements of costs, expenses, warranty, etc., and, of course to the extent possible, the technology cycle. Without a maniacal focus on these things, you won't survive long enough to worry about a long-term pricing strategy. And much has been written recently about profit maximization models where companies are unwilling or too slow to cannibalize a successful but aging technology model for quarterly profit pressures, so I won't belabor the critical importance of this aspect to an effective pricing strategy.

My first suggestion is simple enough but, in my experience, not frequently enough practiced: Think about how the target customer set will *use your product and/or services*; really try to *understand the risks they have to deal with* in using your technology product; figure out how to *help them manage these risks*! Specific examples of risks include

- The risk of technology obsolescence, particularly with shorter and shorter product life cycles

- The dramatic shift from hardware-dominant IT solutions to complex business solutions driven by software and services

- The financial risks of budget management, timing project cash inflows and outflows to match business results

- Planning for scalability as the customer grows

There are a powerful set of tools, if integrated into marketing offerings and pricing strategy, that IT provider companies often either overlook or choose (for internal structural reasons) to offer as a "separate service." I'm referring to *customer financing and leasing*. Think about the customer risks you can help manage with the integration of financing and leasing terms into the marketing offering. This integration

- Provides the customer underlying technology upgrades or even replacement flexibility

- Creates stepped, increasing payment streams that allow the customer to match results to cash outflows

- Provides a capitalization or even off–balance sheet way of managing assets
- Allows for the customer's need for scalability

From the customer view, consider two examples. The first is a customer who needs to implement a new data imaging system for more efficient invoicing and billing. The customer needs a processor (15% of solution cost), storage (20%), digital imaging and database management software (50%), and ongoing maintenance and support (15%). If successful, the project will scale to 8–10 times start-up cost in two years. If your game is to sell a single—or even several—component of this solution, your company marketing representatives are most often selling an up-front investment of $100,000+; yet, the customer is left to manage the technology integration risk, new technology changes, multivendor negotiations and future "glue" problems getting the components to work together, financial budgeting, cash flow timing, etc.

Now, instead of offering your "widget" for sale, *provide an integrated marketing solution and an equivalent monthly payment as a package deal.* This deal can range from a full payout (or near full payout) deal to a leased deal where your company may choose to take a residual value investment in elements of the deal. You can leverage your company's market position with other key vendors to economically package the pieces, offer technology obsolescence protection at customer-predefined flexibility points in the future for your content, and even offer technology flexibility for the other vendors (if you set up the economics with them), step payments to lower the outflows in first year, and, most importantly, build in capacity upgrades for customer scalability. Your company now has the long-term relationship for this business

solution with the customer and is providing value on a broader front than the "widget approach." Your ability to make profit and manage a sustainable customer relationship goes up dramatically.

A second example is prevalent in today's environment of personal computers (PCs). Many medium- and large-scale companies, educational institutions, and government agencies have hundreds or thousands of PCs, no standards for managing software applications or hardware replacement cycles, totally decentralized buying approaches, and, most importantly, no way to leverage the mission-critical data and intellectual assets across the PC assets of the enterprise. Here, an integrated financing and marketing approach by a manufacturer or service provider can dramatically enhance the customer's ability to manage his or her inherent risks.

Consider an asset management deal that buys out the old PCs (environmental concerns won't allow a large company to junk them easily; the average cost of disposal is about $200 each). Moreover, such a deal lets the customer establish some preset basic standards and multiple vendor(s), and provides an asset management tool that lets the customer track assets, pay local sales and use taxes, etc. Many customers have saved 20, 30, or even 40% of their total cost of computing and have leveraged their utilization of key assets with dramatically improved productivity.

The customer assessment of risks and value provides the basis for enhanced profitability. But the benefits to your company also include your ability to get out of the "commodity vendor" game. By broadening the value of your marketing offering through an integrated pricing strategy, you can also often reduce the component discounting so prevalent in the industry today. Take a page from the automobile companies to package "below market" interest rates with solution deals. This can be an extraordinary marketing tool!

One word of caution—when you take on the role of managing a broader and different set of customer risks and value components, you must develop the ex-

pertise to understand these different risks and manage them effectively (i.e., credit risk, technology inflection points, etc.), but they are not rocket science and are very manageable through an integrated financing organization or an outsource partnership.

Because of the varying ways in which customers use products, marketers may need to segment on an end-use (usage occasion) basis.

Moreover, customers evaluate costs and benefits in terms of a complete usage system, and not just in terms of an isolated part of that system. For example, if a firm has decided to use an e-business, Web-based solution for its business processes (e.g., customer relationship management, supply chain management, customer service and billing, etc.), it must also have an Internet service provider, a Web-hosting service, and technical support (whether in-house or outsourced). Evaluating the costs/benefits of, say, the Web-hosting service, really cannot be considered in isolation of the total value to be gained from performing the business processes in the digital arena. And, obviously, for critical product applications, customers will perceive greater value.

2. *A firm must focus on the benefits customers receive from using its products.* The various types of benefits a customer can obtain were previously discussed and include functional, operational, financial, and personal benefits. In analyzing benefits, firms must not fall into the trap of focusing on product features at the expense of benefits. A familiar example is that the person who buys the quarter-inch drill bit does not want the drill bit, but wants the *capability* to drill quarter-inch holes. Customers buy benefits, not features. High-tech firms often mistakenly stress the cool technical wizardry of their inventions and are hard-pressed to identify the real benefits customers receive. Focusing on customer needs is a good way to overcome this problem.

For example, in marketing computers, ads frequently discuss terms such as *megahertz, megabytes, pixel resolution,* and so forth. Although customers might know that greater numbers on each of these categories are presumably better, they might not know what the "improved performance" really delivers. Speaking in terms of processing speed (less wait time for functions to be performed), greater storage capacity (for the ever-increasing size of software programs), and greater clarity of the screen can help customers understand what they are getting.

3. *A firm must calculate customer costs,* including product purchase, and other relevant costs (discussed previously) including transportation, installation, maintenance, training, and nonmonetary costs, and *understand how a customer trades off costs versus benefits in the purchase decision.*

For example, in considering the purchase of a high-definition TV, typically priced upward of a couple thousand dollars, marketers have focused quite heavily on the aspect ratio and greater resolution of the picture. A customer-oriented perspective on pricing would ask:

- How or why will customers be using the product?
- What are the tangible benefits a customer receives from the features of aspect ratio and greater resolution?
- What are the costs that a customer perceives, in addition to the purchase price?

Customers who buy the product to watch TV at home for personal enjoyment will likely assign different value to the attributes than will sports bars and other businesses whose competitive advantage is wrapped around viewing programs. For at-home customers, the tangible benefits of greater resolution might not be all that clear (pun intended). In addition to the purchase-price outlay, customers might have to consider the costs of obsolescence of their existing TV sets, and the "cost" that not many programs are broadcast in digital format in the early stages of this product's life cycle. Hence, in terms of a trade-off of costs/benefits, many at-home customers may find it difficult to justify the high price tag.

The implications of these steps in customer-oriented pricing should help marketers in the following ways. First, this analysis helps marketers to realize that *pricing considerations should not be made* after *a product is developed and ready for commercialization, but* early *in the design process.* Treating price as a design variable helps the firm to understand the relevant cost/benefit trade-offs involved for the customer.[10] Many firms take a customer-oriented perspective on pricing early in the design process, and then develop the product around the relevant price point. For example, Hewlett-Packard, in its foray into the digital photography market, had research showing that a $1,000 price point was the maximum a consumer would be willing to pay for a scanner and printer for digital photography needs. As a result, HP worked its price analysis backward from the customer value point, through the retail channel, subtracting out the margin that retailers would take, ending with a figure that HP had to meet in product design and manufacturing. It then built its componentry and manufacturing around this price point. Similarly, in the high-definition TV example, working more diligently early in the design process on the whole product, which would include programming considerations, might help tip the balance more positively toward higher benefits versus costs.

Second, this analysis shows that *different customers in different segments will value the same product differently.* Moreover, different customer segments will require varying levels of service and support. Rather than setting price on the cost to serve a particular account, prices must be set on the basis of product value to customers. Understanding that different customers value the product dissimilarly, and that different customers require distinct levels of service, means that the profitability of different customer accounts can vary widely—and differentially affect the profitability to the firm. Hence, *firms should track the profitability of different customer accounts.*

Customer-oriented pricing requires that companies manage their customers based on profits, not just sales.[11] High-tech firms must be attuned to the costs of serving customers and filling orders, which can vary significantly by customer, depending upon the sales support, design or applications engineering, and systems integration required. Costs to serve customers can include presales costs (sales calls, applications engineering, etc.), production costs, distribution costs, and postsales service costs. Unfortunately, the price paid by a particular customer often does not correlate with the costs to serve that customer. A customer-oriented approach to pricing focuses not just on sales, but on profits. In order to facilitate this view on customer profitability, Benson Shapiro and his colleagues have developed a customer classification matrix to analyze customers.

Analyzing Customers for Profitability

Customers can be classified into different profitability categories, based on the net price they pay for a product and the cost to serve a particular customer account.[12] These are shown in the matrix of Figure 9-3. Customers classified as *carriage trade* cost a great deal for a firm to serve, but are willing to pay top dollar for its products. This category might include customers who want customized products and a high service level and are willing to pay for them. Cost-plus pricing may offer a rather simple pricing strategy that is successful with these customers.

Bargain basement customers are price sensitive and do not demand many services. *Aggressive* customers demand a high level of services and low prices simultaneously. They tend to be powerful, because they are large and important to the marketer's firm. Companies with a large number of customers in either of these quadrants may find it advantageous to have a centralized office to price large orders and to screen customer needs for services. Financial implications, products, and customers' needs must be balanced to ensure profitability. Volume alone may not be worth it.

Passive customers are willing to accept high prices but don't require many services; these accounts generate very profitable orders. Customers may fall into this category if they are insensitive to price because the product is crucial to operations, or if they face switching costs in moving from one vendor to another. Pricing in this quadrant must be based squarely on the value the customer places on the product.

A particular customer can migrate between categories over time. A customer might begin in the carriage trade category, in which new customers need extensive sales and service support, and are willing to pay for functionality. Over time, however, as customers gain experience and grow more confident in dealing with the product, the cost of serving them may decline and they may become more price sensitive. For commodities, customers may migrate to the bargain basement category. But if the product is quite important and complex, the buyer may continue to need a high level of service.

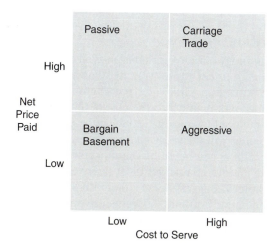

FIGURE 9-3 Customer Classification Matrix

Source: Shapiro, Benson, V. Rangan, R. Moriarty, and Elliot Ross (1987), "Manage Customers for Profits (Not Just Sales)," *Harvard Business Review,* 65 (September–October) pp. 101–108. Copyright © 1987 by the President and Fellows of Harvard Business College; all rights reserved. Reprinted by permission of *Harvard Business Review.*

Setting prices based on the customer's profitability to the firm requires tracking of costs incurred by key customers. Activity-based accounting, which allows a sophisticated cost accounting analysis on a customer-by-customer basis, is a necessity. Moreover, firms must know the net price paid by customers.

In analyzing the profitability of customer accounts, one implication that can arise is that *companies may actually decide* not *to serve some customers*[13]—unless there are mitigating reasons for doing so. Despite the sales volume gained, accounts that result in lost profits may simply not be worth it. Mitigating factors might include situations in which the lifetime value of a particular account is likely to be positive, or in which ancillary products and services might be sold at a profitable level. These and other mitigating factors are discussed in the next section on the technology paradox.

THE TECHNOLOGY PARADOX

Probably one of the most significant factors high-tech marketers face is the rapid pace of price declines. Competition is beating down prices in products ranging from semiconductor chips to finished personal computers; the pace of declines has reached 20% or more annually.[14] This situation requires huge gains in volume if a firm is to maintain sales totals, let alone profitability. Falling prices can help a firm or an industry sell more units—some believe that the demand for digital resources is almost infinitely elastic[15]—and increasing volumes can allow for more price cuts. But the cycle is spinning ever faster, and companies have to keep up.[16]

Known as the **technology paradox,**[17] businesses can thrive at the very moment when their prices are falling the fastest—if they understand how to thrive in such an environment. At a minimum, the situation requires exponential growth in the marketplace, such that volume grows faster than prices decline. However, at its extreme, technology is virtually free, and companies cannot count on volume to provide profits when they are literally giving the products away. Witness the advent of free PCs (discussed later). Extremely low-price or even free offers are attractive to the late majority adopters who can be difficult to acquire. For example, for those who are still not on-line and don't have a PC, it will take a really good offer to get them to adopt. But, the cost to obtain these sales has a serious effect on the bottom line.

What can companies do to thrive when prices are falling so quickly?

Solutions to the Technology (Pricing) Paradox

Obviously, one implication of the technology paradox is that high-tech companies must know how to *keep costs falling faster than prices.* Moreover, the question of how to be competitive when technology is free requires a whole new paradigm for profitability. Companies must redefine value in an economy in which the cost of technology is free. In such an environment, there is no single set of rules, as value can be found in several solutions.[18] For example, some companies will thrive by charging a premium for their products (e.g., Intel and Microsoft). Others can make money in selling products like commodities (disk drives). But, in the middle, companies must be inventive with their pricing strategies, as the solutions in Table 9-2 suggest. As so eloquently stated in *Fortune* magazine, "as lower prices undermine already crummy margins, anyone who wants to be top dog in computers must master some new tricks—and the initiatives have little to do with selling PC's."[19]

TABLE 9-2 Solutions to the Technology Paradox
1. Squeeze out cost inefficiencies.
2. Avoid commodity markets.
3. Have agility and speed in getting products to market.
4. Find new uses for products.
5. Develop long-term relationships with customers.

First, *technology companies must make every effort to avoid getting stuck making commodity goods.* Commodity markets compel companies to follow supply/demand dynamics, and pricing power dissolves altogether. For example, Lucent Technologies no longer makes telephone handsets, which had become a commodity; rather it sells network solutions.[20] When products become near-commodities, firms must focus on giving customers something that provides value, above and beyond the competition's offerings. This might include customization (the Dell model), 24-hour technical support or maintenance agreements, or a strong brand name (see Chapter 10). Mass customization, or serving mass markets with products that are tailored to individuals, can be a compelling source of competitive advantage, and provides knowledge of individual customer tastes and preferences. Amazon.com has taken this strategy into the Internet world.

Second, as discussed in Chapter 2, *firms must have agility and speed.* If a firm can't get to market on time, it might have missed its chance for profitability, because the price point will have moved.[21] Relatedly, engineers must focus less on the *best possible solution* and more on the *best solution possible* in the fastest time frame.[22] Efficient design and systems are probably less important in a market in which prices decline rapidly than getting the product to market quickly. As noted in Chapter 5, Guy Kawasaki refers to this as rule number 2 for revolutionaries: "Don't worry, be crappy."[23] His inflammatory rhetoric means that it is sometimes acceptable to strive not for perfection, but for the minimum level of market acceptability with the first generation of a radical new product.

Third, *companies can strive to find new uses for their products.* For example, Intel has actively been cultivating partnerships with a wide variety of companies, including toy companies, car companies, appliance manufacturers, and so forth, to expand the markets and uses for its chips.

Fourth, rather than being found in selling hardware or software, *a real source of value is found in developing long-term relationships with customers.* When the cost of manufacturing one more unit is negligible (unit-one costs), the goal of the firm changes from making a high margin on each product sold to building relationships with customers. The telecommunications companies are recognizing this as they use sophisticated database marketing to sell customers their whole range of telecommunications product needs in a one-stop shopping model. Partly, their strategy is driven by the reality that optical fiber is making the cost of carrying one more additional phone call practically zero. (This is also why some long-distance carriers have adopted "postal pricing," in which the cost of a three-minute call is the same anywhere in the continental United States.)[24]

Companies can justify extremely low product pricing, or at the extreme, giving away products for free, when it allows them to build strong customer relationships that establish the following:

- *A market hold.* Establishing a market hold with a large volume of customers is a viable strategy when customer attention is the most valuable commodity. Grabs for "mind share" are part of a high-tech, attention-driven economy, based on the scarcity of customer time.[25] In an **attention-based economy,** the consumer's attention is considered to be more valuable than the money paid for the product. Getting big fast, gathering enough consumer eyeballs, and acquiring knowledge about those consumers' shopping habits are the goals. Because customer time is scarce, and because technology keeps getting more costly in terms of the time required to master it, firms can grab attention by making products easy to use, exciting, or both.

Establishing a market hold with a large volume of customers was one justification Amazon gave for its strategies. It strives to develop personalized knowledge of each individual's tastes and preferences, and then capitalize on that knowledge by being the provider of choice for related products and services.

- *An installed customer base that will buy additional products and services.* One form of establishing an installed customer base is known in traditional marketing as **captive product pricing.** The basic idea is that a firm can be highly profitable by giving away the base or foundation product and making money on the complementary goods required to make the product useful. For example, Nintendo charted a business model in which the game consoles would be given away to consumers at or below cost, in order to boost sales of its game software. Virtually all of Nintendo's profits flow from sales, license fees, and manufacturing charges on the game software.[26] Cell-phone companies subsidize the price of handsets and make money with monthly service bills.

Another form of this strategy (establishing a customer base that will buy additional products) is to *focus on the whole product,* or the entire set of items needed by a customer for a smoothly functioning system. For example, Gateway Computers recognized that the personal computer is only the "enabler" of all the activities that go on around the box itself.[27] And a typical 5% margin on a $1,500 PC yields only $75 in profit. So, Gateway made a major move to expand into marketing a whole product; it bundles software, maintenance, services, peripherals (printers and scanners), and Internet service. Customers can pay for this package over time with credit and can trade in for a new machine in the future.

Yet another form of this strategy can be found in *relying on advertising and marketing revenue for income.* Firms that establish solid relationships with customers can then sell their "eyeballs" to advertisers. For example, Free-PC offers a free computer in exchange for a constant ad presence on the consumer's desktop.

Whether these strategies will continue to be viable in the future remains to be seen.

Drawbacks to Low-Price Strategies

One drawback to giving away products for free is that the strategy can create the perception that the product being given away for free (e.g., the base unit or the hardware) is simply not worth much. This can be a problem for manufacturers and put additional downward pressure on prices. Additional considerations in the trend toward "free" are explored in Box 9-1.

In addition to being aware of the negative impact on perceived value, firms must also be aware of potential antitrust considerations in low-price or free offers. Given the existence of network externalities, there is a tremendous incentive to give away high-tech products, such as software, to build an installed base. And, because there is a strong tendency for consumers to band around one standard, once a company gains a decisive lead in an industry such as computing, it is almost impossible for rivals to unseat it. In such a

BOX 9-1

"Free" Products

It seems as if "free" is the new high-tech bandwagon. There are at least five companies giving away free PCs; five offering Internet access; two promising long-distance calls at zero cents a minute; three passing out voice mail boxes; a dozen providing no-cost e-mail; and one that will do free stock trades for accounts over $100,000; one offers a free network operating system; another offers a complimentary suite of office software.[a] Some believe that the trend toward free became popular when Microsoft purchased the free e-mail provider Hotmail for $400 million in 1997, or $44 per user. Hotmail's business model was attractive, because once a customer has an e-mail address, he or she visits the site regularly. This allows a firm to make additional revenues in advertising and other offers.

The trend toward free is based on at least two factors:

1. The reality that the consumer's attention is often more valuable than the money paid for the product, a truism in today's attention-based economy

2. The fact that the real money can be made in the ancillary services that the initial product supports[b]

For example, people buy computers to hook up to the Internet. The real money is in being an Internet service provider. This is why AOL was willing to pay a $400 rebate to consumers who bought a computer from eMachines, Inc. In return, the consumer had to sign up for three years of unlimited Internet access at $21.95 per month. Despite the acquisition cost of $400, AOL says that a guaranteed three-year customer was a good deal.[c]

Although the free phenomenon is popular for consumers, it is also used in the corporate market. For example, the most popular program for running Internet servers in 1998 was Apache, developed by a coalition of volunteer programmers who worked and distributed it for free across the Internet.[d] In 1998, Apache ran on roughly half of all servers connected to the Net. IBM threw its weight behind the Apache "freeware" program for many reasons. It gave credibility to a product that companies felt uneasy about relying on. IBM's support created a strong competitor to Netscape, which was trying to rebuild its strategy around corporate server programs. IBM's support also allowed Apache to compete more directly with Microsoft, which also gave away free a basic Web server with Windows NT. IBM's support of Apache allowed it to focus on selling higher value-added products that run on top of the basic server.

From a customer's perspective, the free offers must be scrutinized carefully.[e] With free PC offers, the PCs themselves are typically not well-known, brand-name units. Although some of the offers promise replacement machines, allaying consumer fears of obsolescence, customers must typically sign up for a particular Internet service, often for a two- to three-year contract. They may be asked to divulge sensitive data about themselves for marketing purposes and have to view ads on their PC screens. There may be hefty cancellation fees and deposits. However, customers who never thought they could afford a PC are simply and easily able to get on the Internet.

---

[a] Greenfeld, Karl Taro (1999), "Giving Away the e-Store," *Time,* November 22, pp. 58–60.

[b] Hamilton, David (1999), "Micron Electronics Is Planning Offer of 'Free' Computer," *Wall Street Journal,* July 9, p. B1.

[c] Weber, Thomas (1999), "New Hard Sell on the Internet: Buy Our Service, Get a Free PC," *Wall Street Journal,* July 1, p. B1.

[d] Cortese, Amy (1998), "A Feather in Apache's Cap," *Business Week,* June 29, p. 42.

[e] Hamilton, David P. (1999), "With Free PCs, You Get What You Pay For," *Wall Street Journal,* April 14, p. B1.

situation, there is likely to be a high payoff from predatory pricing. Moreover, by scaring off potential competitors, firms with a strong reputation for predatory pricing find it cheaper to conquer new markets.[28] This is particularly effective in high-tech markets, because there's a continuous stream of new products. Because of these issues, some experts believe that software is the perfect market for predatory pricing.[29]

Where is the line drawn between effective high-tech pricing strategy and predatory pricing?

Antitrust Considerations in Free Pricing: The Microsoft Case   Large firms must be aware that when they give products or services away for free, they may be more closely scrutinized for anticompetitive practices than are smaller players. For example, like others, Microsoft has frequently used the strategy of giving away its products in order to steal market share away from competitors. It has bundled free giveaways, such as its Internet browser and many parts of its lucrative corporate software (disk compression, firewalls, Web site management, and database analysis), into existing products.[30] Is Microsoft merely responding to customer needs? And is the software industry so dynamic that any dominant position is inherently short lived?

One test that is used in an assessment of the anticompetitive impact of business practices is the effect on prices. In the Microsoft case, one issue was whether Microsoft ended up raising prices to above-market levels to reap the benefits of being a predator. Some believe the answer to that question was "yes": The price it charged PC manufacturers for its Windows operating system doubled from 1991 to 1998. And Microsoft also tightened the terms of its user licenses for corporate clients.[31]

The Justice Department found in November 1999 that Microsoft used its dominant position in the market to "bludgeon the competition."[32] The court found that it bundled its Internet Explorer browser into Windows just to beat out Netscape and, in bullying its competition, caused the demise of innovations that would have "truly benefited consumers." And, its bundling actually came at the expense of its own product's performance; bundling a Web browser into Windows 98 actually slowed down the operating system, increased the likelihood of a crash, and made it easier for viruses to find their way from the Internet onto computers.[33]

The lesson from the Microsoft case is that firms must consider their market position (in terms of potential monopoly power) prior to using any marketing strategy, and particularly pricing.

THE EFFECT OF THE INTERNET ON PRICING DECISIONS[34]

Another factor that is exerting downward pressure on prices is the Internet. The Internet creates **cost transparency,** which allows buyers to find more easily information about manufacturers' costs and prices, providing them more leverage in making product choices. For example, through the Internet, customers are better armed with information about features and benefits. More knowledgeable customers know more about how to gauge value. The Internet makes a buyer's search more efficient. Reverse auctions allow customers to identify manufacturers' price floors, or the lowest price at which they are willing to sell a product or service. Moreover, the Internet makes it more difficult for a firm to engage in different pricing strategies in different markets—something that was commonly done in international markets in the past. And the increasing frequency of low-priced or free offers on the Net makes customers more sensitive to prices.

In light of these challenges, how can firms work to overcome these downward pressures? *Pricing lining,* or versioning, follows the practice of offering different products and services at various price points to meet different customers' needs. For example, America Online offers its U.S. members five options with rates that vary according to the level of subscriber usage. Alternatively, *bundling* can make it more difficult for buyers to discern a manufacturer's costs. For example, the bundling of Internet service with low-priced computers is a way to mitigate cost transparency.

Probably, the optimal way to mitigate the Internet's downward pressure on price is through *innovation.* AOL's ongoing innovation in services such as parental controls over children's access and novel ways to share photographs, combined with its bundling of related products (such as using 3Com's PalmPilot to read AOL e-mail), gives customers a reason to pay higher prices.

The final section of this chapter explores other pricing issues germane to high-tech markets.

ADDITIONAL PRICING CONSIDERATIONS

The role of pricing in any market is to transfer rights of the product to the buyer, in exchange for some form of payment. High-tech products are valuable because of the know-how embedded in them. Recall from Chapter 7 that revenues can be generated by selling the know-how in multiple forms; firms can sell the know-how itself, they can sell components to OEMs, they can sell complete systems in a ready-to-use form, or they can operate a service bureau, providing complete, hassle-free solutions to customers (as IBM does with its e-business and Web-hosting solutions).

Because of the embedded nature of know-how, it can be difficult to price high-tech products at different levels on the continuum. A firm can price for a complete transfer of rights, whereby the buyer owns the product and related know-how completely and can do with it whatever he or she pleases, or it can use highly restrictive licensing arrangements that specify volume, timing, and purpose of usage.[35] The issue for a firm is how to maximize profits by choosing the "right" amount of property rights to transfer. In this section, the following options are briefly examined: outright sale versus licensing agreements; licensing restrictions for a single use versus multiple users; pay-per-use versus subscription pricing; and leasing.

Outright Sale of Know-How versus Licensing Agreements[36]

An outright sale of know-how requires that the net present value of the technology over the relevant time horizon be estimated. However, with technological uncertainty, it is hard to assess the value of the technology at the time of transfer, so outright sales of know-how can be difficult to consummate. On the other hand, short-term licenses require an estimation of value over specific fields of use, which can be more readily estimated. When compared to an outright transfer of rights—for which buyers will presumably pay more—short-term licenses may reduce the revenue stream. However, given the high levels of technological uncertainty in high-tech markets which make it difficult to valuate know-how, firms might be more willing to use short-term licenses. Although short-term licenses generally yield lower revenue than outright sales of know-how, they are easier to valuate and execute. Rather than undervaluing the know-how, they get a guaranteed stream of revenue for a specified time and use.

Licensing Restrictions: One-Time Use versus Multiple Users[37]

In considering licensing terms, firms can either restrict or allow the customer rights to transfer the product to subsequent uses or users. For example, digital videodiscs are available in two formats: DIVx or DVD. DIVx has an encryption device for pricing on a pay-per-view basis, which grants the right for only a single use. On the other hand, DVDs are either bought outright by the user or rented from a video store. In general, should a firm price lower for individual use or charge a higher price for multiple uses (with possibility of re-leasing, etc.)?

Whether a firm charges a higher price and allows sharing among multiple users (via site licenses or, equivalently, renting a product to multiple users) or charges a lower price and restricts usage to an individual depends upon the customer's cost of distribution/sharing the product, relative to the manufacturer's cost. For example, because network computing has made it easier for customers to "share" software, firms have moved to site licenses with rights to copy, rather than individual shrink-wrap licenses. In essence, unit-one costs favor multiple-use formats rather than restricting usage to a specific individual.

On the other hand, when tacit know-how limits exchangeability (i.e., the customer would have inherent difficulty in sharing the product/knowledge), then pricing for an individual use makes more sense than pricing to encourage multiple uses.

Pay-Per-Use versus Subscription Pricing[38]

An additional consideration is whether a pricing strategy should be based on subscription plans or micropayment schemes. Subscription plans charge one fee, regardless of usage; such a plan can increase customer usage volume. Micropayment schemes, on the other hand, charge on a pay-per-use basis, as might be found with some Java applets that self-destruct after the paid-for usage expires. In general, due to the network externalities found in some high-tech markets, pricing schemes that encourage customer usage are desirable; per-use pricing might inhibit growth of the network. Moreover, technological uncertainty can impose steep learning curves on customers, which creates uncertainty about the value of a product over time. Customers may act in a risk-averse fashion and "pay" for insurance in the form of a one-time fee. Customers tend to prefer flat rates as more uncertainties are introduced.

Although micropayments enable the sale and delivery of small units of information, at the opposite end of the continuum, one could envision bundling digital information. For example, cable television sells a product with nearly zero marginal costs of reproduction. Bundling-oriented pricing schemes are common, including a basic bundle that excludes certain goods and more "deluxe" bundles. Similarly, Lotus is competing by bundling its products with applications that previously were sold separately.[39]

Leasing

Another option for pricing in high-tech markets is to offer leasing to customers. This issue is explored by an expert at Babcock and Brown, one of the premier lease brokers, in the Technology Expert's View from the Trenches.

Leasing Considerations in the High-Tech Arena

LEONARD SHAVEL
Partner, Babcock and Brown, Greenwich, Connecticut

My firm is an investment bank specializing in long-term financing of large-scale capital assets. We are typically hired by an equipment purchaser, say, a telecommunications company looking to arrange financing in connection with major capital purchases, for instance, satellites. In that sense, the basic leasing issue is how customers can finance their purchases of high-tech equipment from vendors. Less frequently, we are hired by vendors (say, of aircraft engines) looking to use attractive financing as an inducement to customers to purchase their equipment; these vendors may also hire us simply to assist their customers so that they, as vendors, will not have to supply their own funding.

Whether hired by the customer or the vendor, our roles are to

- Identify and evaluate for the client the various financing alternatives that may apply to their equipment
- Execute the transaction by placing the respective components of debt and/or equity with investors
- Facilitate the entire process through negotiation of terms and documentation

Given this background, we do not participate directly in the purchase decisions of our clients.

Our view of high technology in the marketplace is narrowly focused on the kinds of equipment our clients own or elect to purchase for their basic business. An example would be the recent build-out of PCS networks by several of the major "Baby Bell" telecommunications companies. In two separate series of transactions,

we were hired to arrange low-cost lease financing of the major network components (specifically, transmission, switching equipment, and peripheral devices). Although the form of financing (cross-border leases) was the same, the clients had chosen different technologies for their data transmission systems (technically: TDMA, or time division multiplexing, and CDMA, code division multiple access). Our responsibility was to obtain attractive funding without regard to the relative merits of the chosen technology.

In most cases our involvement begins after the selection of the vendor has occurred. Exceptions would be (a) where the client's decision to purchase a given asset hinges on the availability of attractive financing, or (b) where we are representing a bidding vendor who is seeking to create a competitive advantage by means of the financing element. These situations arise from the fact that a purchasing company often can extract favorable financing from its vendor(s) as an inducement to make a large or precedent-setting order. For a vendor, financing can be used as a means to differentiate itself from other manufacturers of similar equipment, or as a way to maintain its desired price level in the face of competition, or both.

As a proxy for the high-tech sector, our experience with telecommunications companies may be instructive. Given the pace of modernization and expansion in the telecommunications industries (media, voice, data), there has been tremendous growth in the purchase of new (mostly digital) equipment by these companies, precipitating, in turn, increasing demands on the financial sector—and our firm—to provide innovative funding. In general, one can divide the types of telecommunications companies we work with into two categories:

1. Well-established companies with strong balance sheets and high credit ratings who use their newly acquired, high-valued assets to get the most advantageous financing (in terms of cost, efficient use of tax benefits, and/or favorable accounting treatment)

2. Start-up companies, who need to raise money any way they can and for whom an asset-based structure might be a means of attracting investors who otherwise would not want to take their company's business risk

Examples of our clients that fit into the first group are companies like Inmarsat (satellites), Telenor (telephone switching equipment), and TCI (digital set-top boxes), all investment-grade rated entities that could have financed their equipment purchases in a number of different ways (including out of operating cash flow) but were able to lower the cost of acquiring and owning the respective assets by means of domestic or cross-border leases. Such well-heeled companies often share the following objectives:

- To generate savings through the use of tax benefits
- To minimize balance sheet impact and indemnification risks associated with the investor's participation
- To maintain operating flexibility, including the ability to substitute and/or replace equipment over time

These companies also view their asset-based financings as a means to develop relationships with new capital sources.

The second category (start-ups in need of financing) has grown exponentially in the last decade, given the creation of new telecommunications technologies and the types of companies involved. In the United States alone, there are many examples of early stage projects that were the first to commercialize new technologies: Echostar and USSB (direct broadcast satellite television), Sprint PCS and PrimeCo. (wireless telephony), and Sirius (digital radio). By using structured financing, companies like these have been able to obtain earlier stage funding (in most cases, prior to the start of commercial operations) than they would have otherwise. The typical form has been either long-term debt secured by their "crown jewels" equipment, or "venture leases" wherein a lessor obtains warrants in the lessee company in exchange for assuming an unrated credit exposure. The key consideration for the investors is often: Will I have a valuable asset to sell, and hopefully recover a good share of my investment, even if the management of this company does not succeed? Satellites and wireless telephone networks, while not as fungible as aircraft and railcars, are now recognized to have such value, independent of the specific business plan.

Perhaps the greatest risk associated with arranging structured financings is failure to close. These are complex transactions involving two or more parties, sometimes in different jurisdictions, each seeking to achieve results that may be in direct conflict with the other's. A lessee (i.e., the equipment purchaser) may want to obtain a very low lease rate as the result of the lessor (investor) making certain favorable assumptions. The allocation of risks associated with these assumptions can be the most time-consuming aspect of a transaction, sometimes leading to impasse. With this in mind, we advise companies to approach these transactions on an opportunistic basis, wherever possible having alternatives "just in case."

Summary

This chapter has addressed some of the salient issues in pricing in high-tech environments. After examining the many factors that create a complex pricing environment, the chapter then presented an overview of the "3 Cs of pricing" (cost, competition, and customers), a framework for the issues that must be simultaneously considered prior to setting prices. Because of the vital importance of a customer orientation in the high-tech arena, the chapter delved more deeply into customer-oriented pricing concerns.

One of the most significant factors high-tech marketers face is the inexorable decline in prices over time; therefore, special attention was given to strategies to generate revenue in light of price declines. Known as the "technology paradox," businesses who understand these strategies can be profitable despite falling prices. The strategies and solutions offered for the technology paradox are not without their disadvantages, however, and astute marketers balance antitrust concerns and brand reputation with their pricing strategies.

As with other chapters in this book, focused attention was also given to the effect of the Internet on pricing strategies. Because the Internet provides what is known as "cost transparency" for buyers, in which buyers have a better understanding of manufacturers' costs of doing business, tools to handle pricing strategies in light of cost transparency were addressed.

Finally, special pricing considerations, such as sales of know-how, licensing, pay-per-use, subscription pricing, and leasing, were addressed. For the many reasons outlined, pricing decisions are very difficult; despite this difficulty, marketers must systematically address the issues presented here in order to minimize the odds of making a mistake. Importantly, success is difficult to guarantee.

Discussion Questions

1. What are some of the complicating factors in the high-tech pricing environment? What is the impact of these factors on price?
2. What are the 3 Cs of pricing strategy? Describe the importance of each.
3. What are the relative costs and benefits of the purchase of a high-tech product from the customer's perspective?
4. What is the total cost of ownership? What is its pricing implication?
5. What is customer-oriented pricing? What are the steps in customer-oriented pricing? What are the implications of understanding this approach to pricing?
6. How can customers be classified according to their profitability to the selling firm? What are the implications for price of each quadrant?
7. What is the technology paradox in pricing? What five strategies can a firm use to stay profitable, despite the downward pressures on price, or even free products?
8. How can a company justify giving away products for free? What are the various strategies to make a profit in such a situation?
9. What are the potential drawbacks of the solution to price low to gain customer relationships? What is the lesson to be learned from the Microsoft case on low pricing?
10. What is cost transparency? How can firms address it in their pricing strategies?

11. When should a firm use the following pricing strategies?
    - Outright sale of know-how versus licensing
    - Single-use licenses versus multiple-use licenses
    - Subscription pricing versus micropayment (per-use) scheme
12. What strategies from the chapter can be seen in the views of the pricing experts?

Glossary

Attention-based economy. The consumer's attention is often more valuable than the money paid for the product.

Captive product pricing. A strategy of giving away a base or foundation product that is required to use a corollary product, and making money on the complementary goods required to make the base product useful.

Cost transparency. Buyers have information about manufacturers' costs and prices, providing leverage in purchase decisions.

Technology paradox. Businesses can thrive at the very moment their prices are falling the fastest.

Total cost of ownership (or life cycle costing). The total amount of money expended by a customer in order to own a product or use a service; includes the price paid for the good (including financing fees), as well as delivery or installation costs, service costs to maintain and repair the good, power costs to run the equipment, supplies, and other operating costs over the life of the equipment.

Endnotes

1. This phrase was coined by Gordon Moore, co-founder of Intel, in the semiconductor industry.
2. Smith, Michael F., Indrajit Sinha, Richard Lancioni, and Howard Forman (1999), "Role of Market Turbulence in Shaping Pricing Strategy," *Industrial Marketing Management,* 28 (November), pp. 637–649.
3. Dhebar, Anirudh (1996), "Speeding High-Tech Producer, Meet the Balking Consumer," *Sloan Management Review,* 37 (2), pp. 37–49.
4. Smith, Michael F., Indrajit Sinha, Richard Lancioni, and Howard Forman (1999), "Role of Market Turbulence in Shaping Pricing Strategy," *Industrial Marketing Management,* 28 (November), pp. 637–649.
5. Martin, Justin (1995), "Ignore Your Customer," *Fortune,* May 1, p. 122.
6. Shapiro, Benson and Barbara Jackson (1978), "Industrial Pricing to Meet Customer Needs," *Harvard Business Review,* 56 (November–December), pp. 119–127.
7. Shapiro, Benson and Barbara Jackson (1978), "Industrial Pricing to Meet Customer Needs," *Harvard Business Review,* 56 (November–December), pp. 119–127.
8. Gross, Neil and Peter Coy with Otis Port (1995), "The Technology Paradox," *Business Week,* March 6, pp. 76–84.
9. Shapiro, Benson and Barbara Jackson (1978), "Industrial Pricing to Meet Customer Needs," *Harvard Business Review,* 56 (November–December), pp. 119–127.
10. Shapiro, Benson and Barbara Jackson (1978), "Industrial Pricing to Meet Customer Needs," *Harvard Business Review,* 56 (November–December), pp. 119–127.
11. Shapiro, Benson, V. Rangan, R. Moriarty, and Elliot Ross (1987), "Manage Customers for Profits (Not Just Sales)," *Harvard Business Review,* 65 (September–October), pp. 101–108; Myer, Randy (1989), "Suppliers—Manage Your Customers," *Harvard Business Review,* (November–December), pp. 160–168.
12. Shapiro, Benson, V. Rangan, R. Moriarty, and Elliot Ross (1987), "Manage Customers for Profits (Not Just Sales)," *Harvard Business Review,* 65 (September–October), pp. 101–108.
13. Bishop, Susan (1999), "The Strategic Power of Saying No," *Harvard Business Review,* (November–December), pp. 50–61.

14. Wysocki, Bernard (1998), "Even High-Tech Faces Problems with Pricing," *Wall Street Journal,* April 13, p. A1.

15. Gross, Neil and Peter Coy with Otis Port (1995), "The Technology Paradox," *Business Week,* March 6, pp. 76–84.

16. McDermott, Darren (1999), "Cost-Consciousness Beats Pricing Power," *Wall Street Journal,* May 3, p. A1.

17. Gross, Neil and Peter Coy with Otis Port (1995), "The Technology Paradox," *Business Week,* March 6, pp. 76–84.

18. Gross, Neil and Peter Coy with Otis Port (1995), "The Technology Paradox," *Business Week,* March 6, pp. 76–84.

19. Kirkpatrick, David (1998), "Old PC Dogs Try New Tricks," *Fortune,* July 6, pp. 186–187.

20. McDermott, Darren (1999), "Cost-Consciousness Beats Pricing Power," *Wall Street Journal,* May 3, p. A1.

21. McDermott, Darren (1999), "Cost-Consciousness Beats Pricing Power," *Wall Street Journal,* May 3, p. A1.

22. Gross, Neil and Peter Coy with Otis Port (1995), "The Technology Paradox," *Business Week,* March 6, pp. 76–84.

23. Kawasaki, Guy and Michele Moreno (1999), *Rules for Revolutionaries,* New York: Harper Business.

24. Gross, Neil and Peter Coy with Otis Port (1995), "The Technology Paradox," *Business Week,* March 6, pp. 76–84.

25. Gross, Neil and Peter Coy with Otis Port (1995), "The Technology Paradox," *Business Week,* March 6, pp. 76–84.

26. Gross, Neil and Peter Coy with Otis Port (1995), "The Technology Paradox," *Business Week,* March 6, pp. 76–84.

27. Kirkpatrick, David (1998), "Old PC Dogs Try New Tricks," *Fortune,* July 6, pp. 186–187.

28. France, Mike and Steve Hamm (1998), "Does Predatory Pricing Make Microsoft a Predator?" *Business Week,* November 23, pp. 130, 132.

29. France, Mike and Steve Hamm (1998), "Does Predatory Pricing Make Microsoft a Predator?" *Business Week,* November 23, pp. 130, 132.

30. France, Mike and Steve Hamm (1998), "Does Predatory Pricing Make Microsoft a Predator?" *Business Week,* November 23, pp. 130, 132.

31. France, Mike and Steve Hamm (1998), "Does Predatory Pricing Make Microsoft a Predator?" *Business Week,* November 23, pp. 130, 132.

32. Cohen, Adam (1999), " 'Microsoft Enjoys Monopoly Power . . . ,' " *Business Week,* November 15, pp. 61–69.

33. France, Mike and Steve Hamm (1998), "Does Predatory Pricing Make Microsoft a Predator?" *Business Week,* November 23, pp. 130, 132.

34. This section is drawn from Sinha, Indrajit (2000), "Cost Transparency: The Net's Real Threat to Prices and Brands," *Harvard Business Review,* (March–April), pp. 3–8.

35. John, George, Allen Weiss, and Shantanu Dutta (1999), "Marketing in Technology Intensive Markets: Towards a Conceptual Framework," *Journal of Marketing,* 63 (Special Issue), pp. 78–91.

36. John, George, Allen Weiss, and Shantanu Dutta (1999), "Marketing in Technology Intensive Markets: Towards a Conceptual Framework," *Journal of Marketing,* 63 (Special Issue), pp. 78–91.

37. John, George, Allen Weiss, and Shantanu Dutta (1999), "Marketing in Technology Intensive Markets: Towards a Conceptual Framework," *Journal of Marketing,* 63 (Special Issue), pp. 78–91.

38. John, George, Allen Weiss, and Shantanu Dutta (1999), "Marketing in Technology Intensive Markets: Towards a Conceptual Framework," *Journal of Marketing,* 63 (Special Issue), pp. 78–91.

39. Bakos, Yannis and Erik Brynjolfsson (1999), "Bundling Information Goods: Pricing, Profits, and Efficiency," *Management Science,* 45 (December), pp. 1613–1630.

Recommended Reading

Nagle, Thomas T. and Reed K. Holden (1994), *The Strategy and Tactics of Pricing: A Guide to Profitable Decision Making,* London: Pearson.

CHAPTER 10

Advertising and Promotion in High-Tech Markets: Tools to Build and Maintain Customer Relationships

Asolid advertising and promotion mix is as important in high-tech markets as in traditional markets. Some of the key tools that can be relied upon include traditional advertising (in both mass media as well as trade journals), trade shows, sales promotions (contests, incentives, etc.), public relations (event sponsorships, etc.), publicity (articles in the news media), the Internet, direct marketing (mail, telemarketing), and personal selling. High-tech marketers should avail themselves of a useful handbook that covers the basic advertising and promotion (A&P) tools and issues. Rather than covering A&P basics, this chapter delves into issues to which high-tech marketers must pay particular attention—tools that are often overlooked or not used to the extent that would be useful.

For example, engineers and technical personnel often disparage the important role advertising can play in developing brand awareness and brand equity. Yet fear, uncertainty, and doubt often plague the customer's buying decision. In such a situation, customers rely on heuristics to help them make safer, easier decisions, and a solid brand name is one such heuristic. Web portals and communities have realized this and rely heavily on traditional advertising to develop, reinforce, and sustain brand equity.

Moreover, the timing of new-product announcements can be vitally important in high-tech markets. Preannouncements help customers know what new products are coming down the pike and can delay them from buying a competitor's product in anticipation of another one coming in the near future. However, the pros and cons of preannouncing new products must be considered carefully. Finally, high-tech marketers need to understand how to use marketing communication to build and sustain relationships with customers.

Before delving into the specifics of this chapter, a useful device for planning and coordinating advertising and promotion tools is presented, the advertising and promotion pyramid.

ADVERTISING AND PROMOTION MIX: AN OVERVIEW

The advertising and promotion (A&P) pyramid,[1] shown in Figure 10-1, positions advertising and promotion tools based on two dimensions:

- The degree of coverage, or reach, of the target audience.
- Cost efficiency. One useful way to compute cost efficiency is based on cost per thousand (CPM).

$$CPM = \frac{\text{\$ Cost of the advertising and promotion tool (say, an ad in a particular trade journal)}}{\text{Number of people the tool reaches}} * 1,000$$

At the base of the pyramid are tools that have wider coverage of the target audience and lower cost on a per-contact basis. Tools at the top of the pyramid generally have narrower coverage and higher cost on a per-contact basis. Of course, the Internet can be used for a variety of advertising and promotion tasks along the pyramid and can prove to be very cost efficient, regardless of the breadth of coverage of the target market.

The idea behind using the pyramid as a coordinating device for the advertising and promotional tools is that a firm should not use the tools at the highest level of the pyramid in isolation of the tools at lower levels. The role of the tools at the lower levels of the pyramid is to create product and brand awareness, and to "warm up" prospects prior to using the more expensive, narrower tools.

For example, a new product may be announced with free product announcements in trade journals. Leads from that announcement that come in (either via a Web site or an 800 number) can be sent a direct-mail piece, possibly consisting of a brochure or other

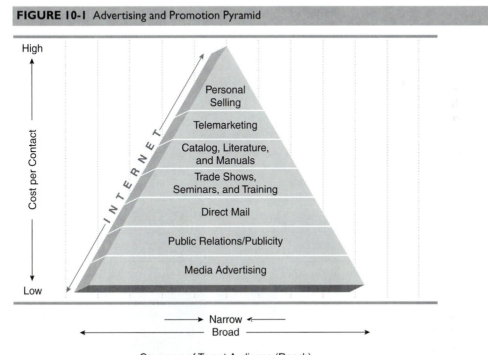

FIGURE 10-1 Advertising and Promotion Pyramid

Coverage of Target Audience (Reach)

Source: Adapted from Ames, B. Charles and James D. Hlavacek (1984), *Managerial Marketing for Industrial Firms,* New York: Random House, p. 253.

collateral material. As prospects continue to express their interest, they can be contacted more personally via either telephone, e-mail, or a salesperson's visit. Importantly, the use of higher-level tools is leveraged on the efficiency and effectiveness of the lower-level tools, and is geared to the prospect's continuing interest.

The notion of matching the advertising and promotion tools to the appropriate task is also consistent with the hybrid channel model presented in Chapter 8. The idea is to understand the strengths and weaknesses of each of the tools, relative to the objectives each tool is to perform. The tool used must be matched (based on effectiveness and efficiency considerations) to the task at hand. A brief discussion of pertinent issues for each of the tools follows.

Brief Overview of A&P Tools

Media Advertising   Starting at the base of the pyramid, high-tech companies can use media advertising in both mainstream (mass) media and trade journals. Critical issues are the degree to which the audience of the media vehicle overlaps with the firm's target market, the cost efficiency (CPM) of the vehicle, the fit of the editorial content of the media vehicle with the brand message, and the size and frequency of the ads that will be run.

How can high-tech firms identify appropriate media outlets? An advertising agency is a good start. If a firm does not utilize the services of an ad agency, the Standard Rate and Data Service (www.SRDS.com) is a useful resource to search by industry, audience, and so forth for appropriate media vehicles. Moreover, CMP Media Inc. (www.cmp.com), as a high-tech media company, prints trade publications serving a wide technology spectrum including the builders, sellers, and users of technology worldwide. Some of its publications are highlighted in Figure 10-2. Finally, it is possible to get a media kit from the ad sales rep of any media outlet, which will provide useful information about not only

FIGURE 10-2 CMP Media Inc. Publications

Source: Screen shot used with permission of CMP Media Inc., Manhasset, New York. All rights reserved, no further duplication authorized.

the specific media vehicle but also its audience, ad rates, editorial calendar with upcoming special issues, other publications in the industry, and pertinent industry statistics.

Identifying appropriate media options is only half of the equation in using media advertising. A firm also must decide on an effective message that breaks through the competitive clutter of the many competing ads vying for the viewer's attention, while simultaneously reinforcing a brand message in a quick and easy manner. Striking a balance between gaining attention and reinforcing a brand message can be tough. Some firms err on the "gaining attention" side, using cute techniques (humor, sex, babies, etc.) to gain attention in a way that actually has little to do with the brand message, and so may even distract the viewer from the brand message. Other firms err on the side of delivering a brand message, providing so much technical detail—in jargon, which is, at best, uninteresting to the audience, and, at worst, unintelligible—that attention is quickly lost.[2] The best ads will both break through the clutter and use an attention-getting device that quickly and effectively delivers the key benefit without being lost in details—details that would be better provided in the next contact with a customer.

Public Relations/Publicity   Public relations (PR) includes the activities a firm undertakes to develop goodwill with its customers, the community in which it does business, stockholders, and other key stakeholders (i.e., government regulators, etc.). These activities might include sponsoring events, such as sporting events or charitable causes, cause-related marketing (aligning with a nonprofit organization), corporate advertising regarding the firm's position on critical issues or its philosophy of doing business, or other outreach activities (speeches by company executives, tours, etc.). Publicity refers to any coverage the company receives in the news media (print or broadcast) regarding its products or activities. Firms can attempt to gain favorable news coverage by holding press conferences, sending press releases, or staging events.

High-tech firms should not ignore the value that comes from maintaining a positive image. In watching the beating that Microsoft took with its approach to the Justice Department's investigation, Intel decided to take a very different approach. In settling the Federal Trade Commission's charges of abuse of monopoly power outside of court, Intel wanted to avoid a public relations fiasco at a time when it was in the midst of a $300 million ad campaign for its new Pentium III processors.[3]

One of the most important types of publicity for smaller high-tech firms is the use of product announcements that many trade journals feature. By sending information about a firm's products to the appropriate contact, information will be printed, typically for free, by that trade journal. This initial publicity can prove to be a valuable source of sales leads.

Although PR and publicity are shown at a higher level in the pyramid in Figure 10-1 than is media advertising, it is important to note that publicity can often be less expensive than media advertising. Furthermore, media advertising can also reach a narrower audience than can PR efforts, and so, the relative position of these two tools in the pyramid may be juxtaposed depending upon the specific media vehicle or public relations tool.

Direct Mail   Because direct mail can generally be more precisely targeted than can advertising or public relations, it is placed higher in the pyramid than those two tools. Lists can be obtained from a number of list brokers, including the mailing lists of many trade publications, or Dun and Bradstreet, to name just two sources. Additional information on possible lists can also be found in the Standard Rate and Data Service. Costs are usually determined on a per-name basis, with more targeted lists that are frequently updated costing more. Firms must decide how many pieces to mail, as a function of the potential size of the target market, as well as the frequency of mailings. One mailing is typically insufficient to achieve results.

Trade Shows, Seminars, and Training Trade shows, seminars, and training reach yet a narrower group of customers at a proportionately higher cost than tools lower in the pyramid. In the computer industry, Comdex–Fall remains the industry launchpad for new products and innovative technologies, as well as a key environment to compare, contrast, and test-drive them. At Comdex–Fall 1999, more than 2,100 vendors showed thousands of new products to more than 200,000 attendees, including possible business customers, trade channel members, and OEM partners who pay between $800 and $2,000 for Comdex registration.

Trade shows can be quite expensive for exhibitors, including expenses for exhibitor fees, design and setup of a booth, personnel to staff the show (with the attendant travel, meals, and entertainment costs), and so forth. Estimates of trade show costs vary widely by show, industry, and location. On the low end, *Business Week Frontier* cites one example of a small cost-conscious exhibitor who spent roughly $10,000 for a three-day show with two other people to staff the booth.[4] On the other end of the spectrum, large companies spend $2 million to $4 million for huge exhibits at Comdex (over 20,000 square feet) at a cost of $50 per square foot.[5]

Especially in such a large show as Comdex, one must trade off the large exposure potential from exhibiting at the show against the investment needed to break through the competitive clutter in such an environment. Large players tend to dominate the space, and unless attendees have a compelling reason to visit a particular booth, a firm may not realize a return on its costs of attending the show. For example, Parker Manufacturing attended the A/E/C Systems show, a show for technology companies that serve the architecture, engineering, and construction industries, in Los Angeles in May 1999, hoping to talk to structural engineers about their pneumatic button punch, a tool used to crimp steel building seams tight. Linda McPherson and Jim Parker set up a 10-by-10-foot booth, and $8,000 later, languished with little traffic and no sales to show for their investment. They had no attention-getting device to compete with larger machines and had poor booth position (people were focused on bypassing them in favor of the food court).[6]

At a minimum, a company must absolutely plan on an accompanying advertising and promotion campaign just to generate traffic at its booth. Additionally, some attention-getting device can be helpful, to the extent it ties in with the product's message. Follow-up on the leads generated and a postshow evaluation are also critical. Additional information on generating publicity and marketing at a show can be found on Key3Media's Web site at www.key3media.com. This chapter's Technology Expert's View from the Trenches shares the insights gained from one company's trade show experiences.

Despite the costs and risks of attending trade shows, the trade show statistics are compelling. A national survey done by Data & Strategies Group Inc. in Framingham, Massachusetts, showed that closing a sale from a lead generated at a trade show costs an average of $625 and takes 1.3 follow-up calls, compared to the average $1,117 and 3.7 calls for other leads.[7]

Catalogs, Literature, and Manuals Companies must have brochures or other collateral material of some sort to provide customers with additional information. The material must

TECHNOLOGY EXPERT'S VIEW FROM THE TRENCHES

Maximizing the Value of Trade Shows—On a Shoestring

WILLIAM MARTENS
Co-President, Computer Friendly Stuff, Inc., Chicago, Illinois

One visit to the Electronic Entertainment Expo in Los Angeles or the Comdex show in Las Vegas will illustrate just how important trade shows are to manufacturers of high-technology products. The dominant manufacturers spare no expense on the development, design, and manufacture of their trade show exhibits. They do this for several reasons.

First, every significant member of the trade and consumer press attends these events. The magazines sometimes produce special issues almost exclusively devoted to these shows, not to mention that the major television networks assign correspondents who file special daily reports for the morning and evening newscasts. Those manufacturers who create the most excitement over their exhibits will be the ones who receive the most media attention.

Secondly, the distributor buyers and retail chain buyers are not oblivious to which manufacturers are receiving the most media attention. Sometimes a buyer, despite whatever friendly relationship he or she may have with a particular manufacturer, will choose to make a more significant purchase from another manufacturer simply because of the buzz that manufacturer generated at the show. Often it doesn't mean that manufacturer number 2 is making a better product but rather is doing a better job of marketing a product of equal or even lesser quality. More often than not, retail buyers make their decisions based on what they believe the public will purchase rather than based on their impressions of a product's quality or how well they are treated during a visit to a manufacturer's exhibit.

In the high-tech field, virtually all product launches take place at major trade shows. The first impression is usually the lasting one, so, for the major manufacturers, maximizing the value of a trade show usually boils down to "how deep are your pockets?"

For the smaller manufacturer who can afford only a 10′ × 10′ or 10′ × 20′ booth space and who is not on the main floor with the major manufacturers (who take booths that are often 50′ × 50′ or even 100′ by 100′), visual impact can sometimes take second place to booth location. The smaller manufacturers look for corner booth locations on heavily trafficked aisles. A lot of buyers don't like to go to the part of the show floor where the smaller manufacturers are exhibiting simply because it's a lot of work stopping to look at every 10′ × 10′ booth. Sometimes they'll make a quick pass through the show floor by traveling down the main aisle, which is usually wide and fairly easy to navigate. If something immediately catches their eye, most buyers will stop and take a look.

How have we at Computer Friendly Stuff been able to gain visibility at trade shows? Probably one of our most successful launches was for our second product, Monitor Morphs (cute poseable arms that stick to the side of a computer monitor and that come with a CD-ROM containing funny screensaver faces), at the Electronic Entertainment Expo (E^3) in May of 1998. We paid our booth fee very early, about 10 months prior to the show, and were able to secure a fantastic corner booth location on the main aisle. We had very limited financial resources at the time, so we built our own booth out of PVC piping and stretch fabric. Using wood and very good house paint, we built a gigantic, artificial computer keyboard and computer monitor casing and, using my big screen television, created a huge fake computer onto which we attached giant Monitor Morph arms. (You wouldn't believe how many people thought our giant fake computer was real!) We converted our Morph screensavers to video and demonstrated the product on a huge scale. In other words, with three other regular size computers demonstrating our other product, we had a lot going on in our small 10′ × 10′ booth. We ended up landing a spot on CBS's *Saturday Morning* and on Fox's morning show. We also got write-ups in *Gameweek* magazine and appeared on French television as well. This exposure led to sales of Monitor Morphs, Computer Bugs, and our follow-up product, the Computer Rear View Mirror, in places like CompUSA, Electronics Boutique, Fry's Electronics, Babbages, and on-line through eToys.com and ComputerGear.com. Our products are also available at many of the major chains throughout Europe.

Comdex is a show for serious, high-tech items rather than entertaining computer novelties or computer gaming, so we decided to focus our energy on shows like E^3 and the New York Toy Fair. Had we not discovered the right show for us, we may not have succeeded. So, if you are a new or small manufacturer, be sure you've identified your audience and that you find a trade show that caters specifically to them. The Internet is your least expensive research tool. Otherwise, there's nothing like actually purchasing a ticket and attending a show yourself. If you don't begin your search early and secure booth space very early in the game, you may end up with a mediocre exhibit space. A poor booth location even at a great show may do you no better than a great booth location at a fair show.

build on earlier communications with customers and showcase the key benefits of the products in terms customers can understand. Supporting technical detail is appropriate in these later follow-ups with customers. Issues such as relative advantage (costs/benefits), compatibility/interoperability, scalability, service, and warranties should be addressed. Especially for new technologies that may cost more than existing solutions, communicating benefits in terms of total cost of ownership can be effective.

Telemarketing   Telemarketing can be done on an outbound or inbound basis. *Outbound* calls are made by a company's personnel to existing customer accounts or on a cold-call basis. *Inbound* calls are made by customers or prospects calling into the company's call center, typically via a toll-free number. Having the opportunity to maintain customer relationships with a person dedicated to particular accounts can be an efficient use of resources. Telemarketers can help provide support to the field salespeople, answering questions, maintaining contact with accounts, and staying abreast of account changes in between visits from field sales personnel.

Personal Selling   At the highest level in the pyramid is the use of personal selling, where each salesperson can generally reach just one customer at a time. One implication of the use of the advertising and promotion pyramid is that small high-tech companies that are resource constrained generally should *not* use their company founders and salespeople to call on prospects *unless the prospects have first been contacted using less expensive, broader-reach tools.* Although small firms may say that they lack the resources to fund public relations or a direct-mail campaign, the real issue is whether they can afford to use their existing resources in an inefficient manner. By leveraging the tools at lower levels in the pyramid, firms ensure that the value of their high-expense tools is maximized.

Do not misunderstand this message. It is *not* meant to imply that personal selling and wooing customer accounts with top executives is unimportant. For example, EMC Corporation, maker of computer storage devices, hears from its customers that sending its top sales executive to its customers' headquarters has been a key tactic in winning customers' business away from companies such as IBM.[8] The lesson to be learned is that the value of such resource-intensive tools is maximized by ensuring that customers are appropriately primed to receive the company's message.

The Internet   The Internet is being used to support and, in the extreme, replace, many traditional advertising and promotion tools. Advertising on the Internet (i.e., banner ads), targeted permission-based e-mail advertising, delivery of "brochure-ware" via the Web, and personalized customer contact all can be achieved with the cost efficiency the Internet offers. The importance of the Internet in effective high-technology marketing warrants dedicated attention, and is addressed in the next chapter.

This chapter continues with a discussion of topics to which high-tech marketers must pay particular attention but that are sometimes overlooked.

THE IMPORTANCE OF BRANDING IN HIGH-TECH MARKETS

The importance of strong brands built by efforts to establish and nurture a corporate identity can be seen in many examples. Microsoft, Intel, Hewlett-Packard, 3Com, AOL, and Yahoo! are names that come to mind. The importance of **branding** is one reason that technology companies decided in 1998 to begin making a big play at the Super Bowl.[9] Nokia, Qualcomm, Oracle, and other companies use the mass media to reach a large number of customers in order to define their brands.

In addition to being a marketing concern, branding is also a financial concern. In 1998, AOL's brand-name recognition dwarfed that of Yahoo!, Netscape, or even the Microsoft Network. As the AOL brand built strength, it was able to spend less on marketing. In a two-year time frame (1996 to 1998), AOL's cost of acquiring a new subscriber dropped from $375 to $90. AOL's marketing director, Brad Pittman, likes to remind people that Coca-Cola does not win the taste test, and Microsoft is not the best operating system: Brands win.[10]

Strong brands possess important advantages in a competitive marketplace. Well-known brands generally are priced at a premium, resulting in higher margins to the companies that sell them. Strong brands are used as a badge or emblem that bestows credibility and attracts attention in new markets, be it a new country, a new category, or a new industry.[11] Hence, a strong brand can reduce risks a company faces in introducing new products, because customers may be less vigilant about examining the specifics.

From a customer's perspective, strong brands stand out as a beacon to the harried customer, a safe haven from the daily cacophony of technologies, new products, and media clutter around them.[12] Strong brands help customers to simplify their choice, providing a safe shortcut in their decision making. A sizable segment of customers tends to migrate to the familiar in a cluttered and confusing world. Some believe that in high-tech markets, in which products change rapidly, a strong brand name is even more important than in the consumer packaged goods industry[13]—which wrote the book on developing strong brands. Because customers may lack the ability to judge the quality of high-tech products, they may use brand reputation as a means to reduce risk.

For example, Cisco Systems makes routers, computers that sort the streams of information packets that travel the Internet. It is the third-largest company in the world, behind General Electric and Microsoft, and controls 50% of the $21 billion business-network market, dwarfing rivals such as 3Com, Cabletron, and BayNetworks.[14] Its online sales for business-to-business e-commerce in 1999 were about $9.5 billion, compared to Amazon's $1.5 billion. Now, Cisco is turning its focus to the consumer-network market, which is growing as people are wiring their homes electronically—everything from refrigerators to furnaces may be Web enabled, which is why Cisco is partnering with Whirlpool and Samsung. In order to leverage its success in the behind-the-scenes B-to-B (business-to-business) market to this new market, Cisco believes it has to let customers know who and what it is. It believes that creating a stronger brand will help the company enter a whole new business—telecommunications—in which many strong competitors exist. In order to compete there, customers must trust the Cisco brand and actually exert pressure on their telephone companies to run Cisco networks, which stand for performance and reliability. So Cisco spent $60 million airing its "Are You Ready?" television commercials and is emulating Intel's successful "Intel Inside" campaign.

Kevin Keller, one of the premier experts on brand equity, notes that the short product life cycle for high-tech products has several significant branding implications. First, it puts a premium on creating a corporate or family brand with strong credibility associations. Because of the often-complex nature of high-tech products and the continual introduction of new products or modifications of existing products, consumer perceptions of the expertise and trustworthiness of the firm are particularly important. In a high-tech setting, trustworthiness implies longevity and "staying power."[15]

In addition to having a solid understanding of traditional brand-building activities such as advertising, building brands in the high-tech arena, with its rapid change and ambiguity, requires additional considerations.

Developing a Strong Brand

So, how does a firm develop a strong brand? At a minimum, *customers expect marketers of strong brands to supply a steady stream of innovations* in exchange for their loyalty. And it is important that strong brands deliver the value they promise. The price/performance ratio must not be perceived as inequitable for the exchange, be the customer an OEM, an enterprise (business) user, or a consumer. Additional issues in branding in the high-tech environment are shown in Table 10-1 and discussed next.

Traditional Media Advertising and PR Tools   Advertising with strong brand messages that focus on brand equity (versus price) is a vital ingredient in the branding mix. On the other hand, traditional sales promotions, with their focus on price, tend to erode brand equity. For example, when Northern Telecom decided to launch a corporate-branding campaign, to move beyond its roots as a maker of telephone switches, it developed ads to suggest a hip, cool image—one that was not associated with Nortel in the past. Linking its

TABLE 10-1   Strategies for Branding in the High-Tech Environment
Create a steady stream of innovations with strong value proposition
Emphasize traditional media advertising and PR rather than sales promotion
Influence the influencers and stimulate word of mouth
Brand the company, platform, or idea
Rely on symbols or imagery to create brand personality
Manage all points of contact
Work with partners (cobranding and ingredient branding)
Use the Internet effectively

products with the ability to bring the power of the Internet to the corporate networking market, the new tag line was "How the world shares ideas." Northern Telecom believes that mass-market advertising has created value for its technology-based company, both in terms of selling more product and in identifying the company as a good investment.[16]

Because real-world brand building helps customers become familiar with the brand even before they go on-line, Internet companies also rely heavily on mass-media advertising to create brand awareness and familiarity,[17] including some that are willing to spend millions of dollars for one ad on the Super Bowl.[18] They are increasing their on-line advertising budgets only modestly, but their spending on television, print, and billboards was up by almost 300% in 1999.[19] For example, AOL is famous for its use of traditional direct marketing of sample disks.[20] Yahoo! runs an aggressive brand-marketing campaign on TV and in print media, and also has licensing agreements with Visa cards and T-shirts. Furthermore, successful and well-known Internet companies have sought significant publicity off-line. Autobytel.com stages events such as car giveaways to gain press coverage. Although the magnitude of spending by dot.coms to build their brands may be excessive, the basic principle is sound.

Influence the Influencers and Word of Mouth[21]   Many high-tech companies rely on an "influence the influencers" program to generate publicity and favorable word-of-mouth endorsements. Public relations personnel must work hard to court the experts that influence the masses. For example, both Palm and Sony gave products away for free or at substantially reduced prices to technology experts, enthusiasts, and opinion leaders. As a result, these people became a type of emissary for the products, with corresponding credibility greater than advertising. Third-party endorsements from top companies, leading industry or consumer magazines, or industry experts may help to achieve the necessary perceptions of product quality.[22] To gain such endorsements requires demonstrable differences in product performance, suggesting the importance of innovative product development over time.

Because brands in the high-tech arena are not built up over decades but over months, the frequent use of product giveaways helps to stimulate word of mouth, public relations and publicity, and brand familiarity.

Brand the Company, Platform, or Idea[23]   Given the rapid obsolescence of high-tech products, it would not only be prohibitively expensive to brand new products with new names; it would be equally difficult for customers to develop product or brand loyalty. Therefore, firms should rely on *family names* taken from either *the company* or *the underlying technology platform*. Typically, names for new products are given modifiers from existing products—Windows 2000, for example, or Microsoft Word, Microsoft Works, Microsoft

Explorer, and so forth. Alternatively, the company might choose to *brand the idea* behind the product, as in "Powered by Cisco" or Apple's "Think Different" campaign.

When a company does use a new name for a new product, it should be done to signal to customers that this new generation is a major departure and significantly different from prior versions of the product. Regardless, high-tech firms should not introduce new sub-brands too frequently.[24]

Rely on Symbols   Associations related to brand personality or other imagery may help establish a brand identity, especially in near-parity products.[25] For example, Kinetix, a multimedia company owned by AutoDesk, developed an animation software package. Part of the demo package was a funky dancing baby character, which become indelibly linked to the Kinetix brand.[26]

Manage All Points of Contact   Customer service is equally important in building strong relationships to the brand. If customers cannot get the service they need, it negatively affects the brand.

Work with Partners   Moreover, high-tech brands are targeted not only to consumers and the financial community but also to partnerships and alliances. **Cobranding** is based on the idea of synergy: The value of two companies' brands, when used together, is stronger than that of one brand alone. Intel has relied on a variation of this strategy extensively, based on the idea of creating a brand identity for a component or ingredient used in the customer's end product, or **ingredient branding,**[27] discussed subsequently.

Use the Internet   High-tech companies must also consider the role of the Internet in their branding strategies. The notion of on-line branding seems to make sense for companies whose value proposition is intimately linked to the Web, as it is for Dell Computer. At a minimum, an effective branding strategy needs coordinated on- and off-line campaigns.

Rather than being a passive viewing experience (as in the media in which traditional branding has been most successful), the Internet shifts power and choice of viewing to the customer. Hence, branding tactics that work in the physical realm don't always translate on-line. The Internet is as powerful an embodiment of the company as is the product or a store. The Web must be more than brochure-ware, or gratuitous digitization,[28] and used to create customer value. Communicating with and helping a customer at the same time build brands on-line.

Indeed, on the Internet, the *customer's experience* at a particular Web site communicates brand meaning.[29] A traditional television ad might drive customers to the Web, and the Web then turns that into an experience. This dual strategy, of first driving traffic to the Web site and then ensuring that the technological creation and delivery of value at the Web site create a meaningful customer experience, creates on-line brand messages. Hence, a new idea called **rational branding**[30] (coined by Jupiter Communications) marries the emotional sell of traditional brand marketing with a concrete service offered on-line. Box 10-1 further explores branding strategies for on-line companies.

Despite these guides for on-line branding strategies, some believe that the use of the Internet to create brand meaning is a misguided venture. Rather than using it as a venue to help create a brand identity, some believe that the Internet is best used as a direct-marketing medium.[31]

BOX 10-1

Branding Strategies for On-line Companies

The growth of popular Internet companies shows that a brand can grow and secure customer loyalty on the Net.[a] Although information about competing brands is easily obtained on the Internet, and, to a certain extent, Web sites might be easily commoditized, a well-known name is a shortcut to information, a connection between a company and its customers. Brands are what people can rely on, and hence, become even more important in an environment that has low switching costs. A brand that matters to the targeted on-line community can get Web surfers to a site and keep them coming back.

Although branding is important for on-line companies, harnessing the reach and interactivity of the Internet to build and maintain brands has become the Holy Grail of marketing.[b] The Internet is a new marketing frontier, in which tried-and-true models of advertising and marketing may not work in the same way as in traditional media. Some companies are using a "spray and pray" strategy, or throwing money at the Web in hopes of reaching a mass audience and building a brand, just as they did before in the broadcast world.[c] However, the reality is that the emotional, fuzzy branding components that can be powerfully conveyed through television are not so easily conveyed in an on-line environment.

The common thread running through the successful on-line technology sellers, such as Yahoo!, Amazon, and America Online, is that they help the Web-surfing customer do something.[d] The Web site itself is the crucial building block for the brand. The senior vice president for product development at Amazon, David Risher, says that 70% to 80% of the feeling people have about the brand is from the experience they have at the site.[e] Customers in a physical world can touch or feel products, but on-line customers do not enjoy the same level of sensory intake. Therefore, things such as speed and response time also play an important role. Branding on-line requires a credible and relevant promise to the market and delivering on that promise with every interaction.[f] Web surfers must have a clear idea of what the Web site is about. So, for example, Yahoo! built an identity from the very beginning.[g] On-line brand-building successes rely on having millions of people use their service every day and expanding that service to keep getting better.

[a] *The Economist* (1999), "Advertising That Clicks," October 9, p. 71.

[b] Neuborne, Ellen and Robert Hof (1998), "Branding on the Net," *Business Week,* November 9, http:// businessweek.com/datedtoc/1998/981109.htm.

[c] *The Economist* (1999), "Advertising That Clicks," October 9, p. 71.

[d] Neuborne, Ellen and Robert Hof (1998), "Branding on the Net," *Business Week,* November 9, http:// businessweek.com/datedtoc/1998/981109.htm.

[e] Neuborne, Ellen and Robert Hof (1998), "Branding on the Net," *Business Week,* November 9, http:// businessweek.com/datedtoc/1998/981109.htm.

[f] Siegel, Alan, and Andrew Zolli (1999), "Portal Envy: Internet Portals Lack Strong Branding, Risking Audience and Ad Dollars," *Advertising Age,* May 10, p. 50.

[g] Brown, Eryn (1999), "9 Ways to Win on the Web," *Fortune,* May 24, pp. 112–124.

Source: Revolution.com (2000), "E-Brands: Brand-Building in the New Economy," April 1.

Ingredient Branding (Cobranding)

An ingredient branding strategy pulls demand up the supply chain from end users through the distribution channel to the OEMs, which feel pressure to use the branded ingredient in the goods they make. Business-to-business marketers will recognize this strategy as one designed to stimulate **derived demand:** Demand for the component, or ingredient, is derived from the end customers' demand for the products in which the components are used.

Supplier of ingredient or component →	OEM/manufacturer →	Retail →	Customers
Intel	Compaq, Acer	CompUSA	You

The way these strategies typically work is that the ingredient supplier provides cooperative advertising dollars[32] to the OEM/manufacturers, which when they advertise, feature the ingredient in their own (OEM's) ads. Using this campaign, Intel's awareness level increased from 22% in 1992 to 80% in 1994.[33]

Advantages and Disadvantages of Ingredient Branding   As shown in Table 10-2, ingredient branding does have its advantages and disadvantages. On the upside, the brand awareness created by the strategy creates a competitive advantage in the marketplace for the ingredient supplier. It establishes brand preference among end users, allowing the firm to fend off growing competition and stake out its own turf or identity. However, it is a costly proposition to develop a strong brand name for an ingredient and to provide the necessary cooperative advertising dollars to make it work. Moreover, if one of the OEMs that is participating in the branding program experiences product/performance problems, a halo effect occurs in which the supplier's reputation is tarnished also. (Note that this halo effect can work both ways: If it is the supplier's ingredient that has performance problems, the OEM's image will be tarnished as well.) And, as discussed subsequently, this strategy can create conflict with a supplier's large OEM customers.

From a small OEM's perspective, using a cobranding strategy can lend credibility to its brand, making it more competitive with stronger brands in the market. Smaller

TABLE 10-2   Pros and Cons of Ingredient Branding

	Pros	*Cons*
Supplier	Creates competitive advantage	Costly
		Possible risk if OEM has product problem
		Conflict with large OEMs
Large OEM		Erodes ability to differentiate
		Risk if supplier's product has performance problems
		If doesn't cobrand, consumers might question product
		Worry about supplier forward integrating
Small OEM	Lends credibility to its product	Risk if supplier's product has performance problems
	Gets advertising support	

companies can benefit from the sharing of advertising expenses through the cooperative advertising funds.

However, for large OEMs, the strategy can erode the ability of top-end brands in the market, say, IBM, for example, to differentiate its products. Customers in the marketplace often assume that industry leaders have something special in their products, but, with a cobranding strategy, customers begin to realize that the industry leader's product has the same ingredients as do lesser-known brands. This can cause conflict between the ingredient supplier and key OEMs in the marketplace, making the strategic relationship difficult to manage.

An ingredient branding strategy can also cause problems when the ingredient supplier and the OEM have different goals in the marketplace.[34] For example, the ingredient supplier, say, Intel, would like end users to demand the latest chips—those that sell at the highest margin. To drive this engine, ingredient suppliers typically invest huge expenditures in research and development. And the best scenario from the ingredient supplier's perspective is to have a large number of OEMs all competing on the basis of price.

But the OEM may have a very different strategy. For example, Compaq in the early- to mid-1990s wanted to develop a large mass market for relatively inexpensive PCs, which could best be done by using inexpensive rather than cutting-edge semiconductor chips. (The price that the OEM pays for the chip from the chip supplier, say, Intel, accounts for 20% to 25% of the cost of the personal computer.) An OEM with this strategy is less interested in working with a supplier that has developed a strong brand for its ingredient and charges a premium price for that brand. So large OEMs may actively try to cultivate ties with other suppliers, to try to avoid being so dependent on the branded-ingredient supplier only.

And, if an OEM sells products without relying on the cobranding arrangement, products without the ingredient's logo (say, "Intel Inside") might arouse suspicion among consumers in the marketplace. Lastly, if OEMs fear that the ingredient supplier will attempt to enter their marketplace in the future (say, if Compaq fears that Intel will try to develop its own line of personal computers), they don't want to participate in the cobranding strategy, which will only serve to develop a strong brand for a company that may become a future competitor.

Reconciling these tensions may be next to impossible, but at least being aware of them helps firms to make more educated choices.

NEW-PRODUCT PREANNOUNCEMENTS

Gamespot's Vaporware Hall of Shame (www.gamespot.com/features/vaporware) reads something like this:

> How would you feel if you'd seen dozens of ads for a new product, but when you went to buy it, you discovered that the product wouldn't be out for another couple months? Or, what if you read a glowing review of another new product, but were told by the salesperson at the store that it hadn't yet been shipped—and, in fact, would be months before it did?

Scenarios such as these happen regularly in the world of PC games, and in that industry, it is called **vaporware:** products that are announced before they are ready for market.[35]

More formally referred to as **preannouncements**[36]—or formal, deliberate communication before a firm actually undertakes a particular marketing action (say, shipping a new product)—they are a form of market signaling that conveys information to competitors, customers, shareholders, employees, channel members, firms that make complementary products, industry experts, and observers of the firm's future intentions. Because of their versatility, preannouncements are a very appealing tool for strategic marketing communications.

High-tech firms routinely preannounce new products. For example, 3Com's Palm Computing preannounced in December 1998 that it would produce a connected organizer in 1999 with built-in wireless connection to the Internet and corporate intranets. The preannouncement was made to maintain its market position at a time when Microsoft and its hardware partners were pushing Windows CE2.0-based handheld PCs.

Advantages and Objectives of Preannouncements

Firms choose to preannounce new products for many reasons. In order to maximize their value, firms must have a clear intent for their preannouncements. As shown in Table 10-3, by preannouncing, firms can potentially reap a *pioneering advantage,* creating barriers to entry to later entrants. By announcing products before they are fully available, a firm can preempt competitive behaviors. For example, networking equipment maker Alteon Web-Systems Inc. leaked news of its new product a full year early to "freeze" the market for comparable gear from competitors. Its CEO Selina Lo says this is one more bullet she uses to gain competitive advantage.[37]

Preannouncements can also *stimulate demand.* By helping develop word of mouth and opinion leader support, preannouncements can accelerate the adoption and diffusion of innovation when the product does hit the market. In addition to building interest for the product among channel members and customers, another factor related to consumer behavior is to *encourage customers to delay purchasing* until the announcing firm's new product is available. This latter reason is primarily used for big-ticket items that are purchased rather infrequently.

TABLE 10-3 Pros and Cons of Preannouncements

Pros	*Cons*
Pioneering advantage: Preempt competitors	Cue competitors
Stimulate demand	Delays damage to reputation or survival of firm
Encourage customers to delay purchase	Cannibalize current products
Help customers plan	Confuse customers
Gain customer feedback	Create internal conflict
Stimulate development of complementary products	Generate antitrust concerns
Provide access to distribution	
Pursuit of leadership position	

Businesspeople say that announcing products before they are ready for market is a "valuable tradition" in the software industry, divulging future-product plans to customers. Such preannouncements can be beneficial when they *help customers to plan for their future needs,* or when they *allow customers to have input* in order to develop a more useful product. Users often need to know a software maker's plans early, because the software is so critical for their own businesses. So, alpha and beta versions, prototypes used to test and refine a program, may be sent to lead users months before the program appears on the market.[38] This gives customers, channel members, and OEMs time to prepare their operations for the new product and gives the manufacturer valuable market feedback.

Other advantages of and reasons for using preannouncements might include to *stimulate the development and marketing of complementary products* and to *provide access to distribution.* For example, Barco Projection Systems used preannouncements to keep its dealer channel interested in the vitality of its product line. Ultimately, one of the key drivers of a firm's propensity to preannounce is its *pursuit of a high-profile leadership position* within its industry.[39]

Disadvantages of Preannouncements

The benefits of a preannouncement strategy must be balanced against the costs of preannouncing. Preannouncements can *cue competitors* to what is coming down the pike, allowing them the opportunity to react to the new product.[40] For example, Storage Technology Corporation took a proactive strategy in preannouncing a new innovation in massive disk-storage systems used by large corporate clients. However, delays in its development turned into an advantage for its competitors, which were able to beat it to market. For example, EMC Corporation and IBM were both able to bring out similar systems and capitalize on Storage Technology's preannouncements. Indeed (and despite the desire to use preannouncements to reap a pioneering advantage), the risk of cuing competitors is one reason why a firm's propensity to be a pioneer is *negatively* related to a firm's use of preannouncements.[41] Concerns about competitive retaliation and the risk of delays combine in such a way that firms seeking a pioneering advantage may actually avoid preannouncements.

Indeed, preannounced products may turn into vaporware and never materialize. Because the development process of high-tech products is so complex, *delays* are sometimes inevitable. For example, boo.com hyped the launch of its fashion and shopping Web site for June 1999. However, the launch didn't actually happen until mid-November. (Moreover, when the site was finally launched, many technical glitches, including slow-loading graphics and consumers being bumped off the site, prevented users from buying anything.)[42] Such difficulties in delivering the preannounced product can be *damaging to the firm's reputation.*

Preannouncements can result in *cannibalization* of the firm's current product line, caused when customers delay purchases of current products in anticipation of the new ones. At the extreme, the combination of cannibalization and delays in meeting delivery can prove to be *catastrophic to a firm,* as Storage Technology found out in the early 1990s. Its new product, code named "Iceberg," was formally preannounced in January 1992, with anticipated deliveries in one year's time. However, due to development problems and "buggy" software, beta testing did not begin until early 1994, and shipments didn't occur until later that year. In the ensuing time period, irate customers canceled orders, the firm lost approximately $189 million, and its stock dropped 76% from $78.00 to $18.50 a share.[43] Other disadvantages include the risk that preannouncements might also *confuse customers* who try to buy the product thinking that it is already available. Preannouncements might also *cause internal conflict* between departments, frustrating the efforts and objectives of another group. For example, engineering might want secrecy, but financial officers may want to send signals to the market early.

Finally, *antitrust concerns* can lead a firm to avoid preannouncing strategies, particularly for dominant firms. Vaporware can have detrimental effects in the marketplace when a firm has no intention of following through on its announcements, which are used merely as a competitive tactic in the marketplace to harm competitors. In an early investigation of Microsoft, the Justice Department decried the frequent use of vaporware, which businesspeople know is deceitful.[44] When the preannouncement is for the sole purpose of causing consumers not to purchase a competitor's product, then the predatory intent is inferred to be anticompetitive and subject to regulation under antitrust laws. Some believe that dominant players in a market—such as Microsoft—must be held to a higher legal standard because of the likely harm of their preannouncements to competitiveness in a marketplace.[45]

Tactical Considerations in the Preannouncement Decision

In making decisions about new-product announcements, firms must consider several tactical factors, shown in Figure 10-3. These include the timing of the announcement, the nature and amount of information, the communication vehicles used, and the target audience(s).[46]

Timing The timing of preannouncements must consider many factors, including the advantages and disadvantages of preannouncing relative to the

- Innovativeness and complexity of the new product
- Nature of customer switching costs and the length of the buying process
- Timing of final determination of the product's attributes

Earlier preannouncements (farther away from the actual product launch) are particularly useful when complements to the new product are necessary to its success, for highly novel or complex products that will engender buyer uncertainty, for products

FIGURE 10-3 Tactical Considerations in Preannouncement Decisions

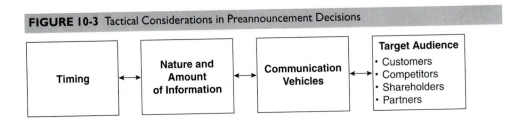

that have a long buying process, or for those in which buyer switching costs are high. *Later preannouncements* (closer to the actual product launch) make more sense when the firm needs to keep information about the new product from potential competitors, when product features are frozen late in the process, and when the firm seeks to minimize risks of cannibalization. Regardless, preannouncements must be *timed to coincide with the purchase cycle of customers.* For example, if customers take approximately six months to decide on a new purchase, a preannouncement with a six-month lead time would be acceptable.[47]

Nature and Amount of Information   Firms must consider how much and what kinds of information to include in the preannouncement. Some new-product preannouncements contain information on the attributes of the new product, how the product works, and how it compares to existing products in the market, whereas others contain very limited information. Information about pricing and delivery date are other content considerations.

Communication Vehicles   Communication vehicles might include trade shows, advertisements, press releases, or press conferences.

Target Audiences   These might include customers, competitors, shareholders, or partners.

Other Considerations   In their study of new-product preannouncing behavior, Eliashberg and Robertson found that preannouncements are useful under the following conditions:[48]

- When a firm has low market dominance, it faces lower cannibalization risks.
- For smaller firms, which face fewer antitrust concerns
- When a firm believes that competitors are not likely to respond preemptively to the preannouncement. This might be likely in an industry in which R&D and technology are specialized (e.g., the pharmaceutical industry in which specialization around therapeutic category reduces the number of competitors who can react). Reliance on patents may also reduce competitive response.
- If a product requires substantial customer learning or if customers face switching costs, preannouncing can be advantageous to advance the learning process. Preannouncements can encourage advance planning for customers to switch to the new technology and can help them standardize around key specifications and operating systems.

On the other hand, firms may not benefit from preannouncing when

- A firm has a strong portfolio of products, and preannouncing may encourage customers to postpone purchases. (As an aside, strong brands may also be used to counter competitive preannouncements.)
- Large firms have more risk due to inferences of predatory behavior.

The Technology Tidbit focuses on a product whose applications were preannounced three years ago. Regardless of whether a firm chooses to preannounce its products, it must consider its use of marketing communications tools in building relationships with customers.

Electronic Noses

A new device has been developed which mimics the human olfactory process. Cyrano Sciences is developing an electronic nose that will enable machines to "smell." In contrast to other chemical-detection technologies, Cyrano Sciences' technology is inexpensive ($8,000), portable, and adaptable to practically any odor-detecting task. The initial product is a lightweight, portable electronic nose for use in the field to detect volatile compounds, and can be used in a variety of applications ranging from disease detection to disaster prevention. For example, it can sniff some of the types of bacteria responsible for urinary tract and respiratory infections, spoiling food, and chemical solvents.

Image reprinted with the permission of Cyrano Sciences, Pasadena, California.

Odorous vapors enter the sensor through an antenna-like probe. The chemical constituents of the odors pass to a circuit board with 32 sensors made of polymers that expand on contact with vapors, increasing their electrical resistance.

The pattern of electrical resistance is compared with a database of stored profiles to identify the odor. The sniffing detection is so fine that the device can sniff a variety of rice and tell which one it is and even where it was grown.

It is likely that electronic noses using polymer composite sensors will be found in a broad range of applications in the near future. Application areas include quality control, process measurement, hazardous materials identification, leak detection, bacterial identification, and aroma identification. Arranged by industry, the application areas include food and beverage, packaging, petrochemical, industrial chemicals, and hygiene products. A succession of products will lead to NoseChips that will enable a variety of high-volume consumer applications, from medical diagnostic breath analyzers to smart room-air monitors to appliances able to detect food preparedness and spoilage.

Source: Izarek, Stephanie (2000), "The Nose Knows," *Foxnews.com*, April 20.

THE ROLE OF MARKETING COMMUNICATIONS IN CUSTOMER RELATIONSHIPS

Another important role for advertising and promotion tools is to develop and maintain relationships with customers. *Customer relationship marketing* allows a firm to create long-term mutually beneficial relationships with customers that result in greater loyalty and improved sales.

As noted in Chapters 3 and 9, although customer relationship marketing is an important tool, not all customers warrant the cost- and time-intensive efforts that relationship marketing entails. As a result, many firms rate their customers based on customer volume and profitability to the firm.[49] Identifying, recognizing, and rewarding the best customers to sustain their profitable behavior make sense.

For example, using a customer database, a telecommunications company can identify which customers ("the good") buy many services at a high level of profitability (i.e., proportionately fewer services and marketing investments) compared to those who spend just as much but cost more to keep ("the bad"). Customers who spend little and likely won't spend more in the future ("the ugly") don't receive as high a level of service or marketing attention, which brings the firm's costs down.[50] By sifting through information about each customer's calling patterns, demographic profiles, the mix of products and services used, and related data, a company can identify the less profitable customers who have the potential to be more profitable in the future. The company can also determine a maximum amount to spend on marketing to a particular customer before it becomes an unprofitable venture.

Discussed subsequently, sophisticated customer relationship management software is used to this end. Firms are using customer databases to compare the mix of marketing and services that go into capturing and retaining each individual customer to the revenue that customer is likely to bring in. Also referred to as **database marketing,** or **one-to-one marketing,** these efforts allow marketers to target individual customers with pinpoint accuracy.

Categories of Customers

As shown in Figure 10-4, at a minimum, a company can identify four segments of customers, based on the company's share of customer purchases in a category and the customer's relative consumption level of the category.[51]

1. *Low share–low consumption.* These are low-consumption customers with which the firm has a low share of their purchases. Given some compelling reason to invest in these customers (Are they opinion leaders? Might their buying status change in the near future,

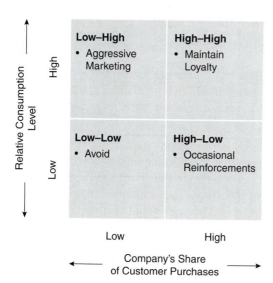

FIGURE 10-4 Categories of Customers

Source: Barlow, Richard (1999), "Reap What You Reward," *The DMA Insider,* Fall, pp. 35–38.

for example, a college student?), a firm should avoid these customers by providing a low base of reinforcing communications and services.

At the extreme, a firm may decide to weed them out of the customer base entirely, for example, if these customers consume more resources than they return. Although such a notion is anathema to many new high-tech start-ups, with their salaries to pay, rent that is due, and infrastructure investments to make, a firm must shepherd its resources wisely. Indeed, the hardest part of being an entrepreneur can be learning to turn down business. However, it may be the only way to survive and grow, if customers take a firm away from its mission, values, and areas of expertise. In addition, saying yes to the wrong business can damage employee morale.[52]

How does a firm say no? It can politely recommend a competitor whose value proposition and capabilities more closely match the customer's needs. Or, based on the pricing principles discussed in Chapter 9, it can charge a sufficiently high price that turns the account into a more profitable one—assuming the customer doesn't defect.

Of course, there are risks to this strategy. If done incorrectly, alienating customers can cost a company negative word of mouth. Moreover, if a company rejects the wrong customers, who prove to be major spenders in the future, it may be a nonrecoupable decision. Despite these risks, serving unprofitable customers does not make good business sense.

2. *High share–low consumption.* These customers are relatively loyal to the firm, but spend relatively little in the category. Although they can be reasonably profitable, if they have little growth potential, the firm should attempt to maintain them with a minimum level of marketing investment. Communicating often enough to sustain a sense of specialness and giving occasional bonuses should be sufficient to sustain their current level of activity.

3. *Low share–high consumption.* Although the firm has a low share of these customers' purchases, they represent a major opportunity, given their high consumption in the category. Many firms lack an understanding of how much their customers spend in a category. For example, if a company knew that 15% of its best customers purchased nearly twice as many products from a competitor, think of how it would change the way it markets to them. Once these high-opportunity customers have been identified, the goal is to grow the firm's share of their business aggressively by convincing them to switch and cementing their loyalty. This may require significant value-added services to overcome their current loyalties.

4. *High share–high consumption.* These customers are a company's bread and butter and represent, to a competitor, the customers whom it would like to lure away. The goal is to maintain these customers' current spending levels while increasing their commitment to the firm.

How can a company make the ideas in this section actionable? Let's take a hypothetical situation. Say a wireless telecommunications company knows, for example, that it costs, on average, $350 to acquire a new customer and about $35 per month to service a customer. Given average revenues of $60 a month per customer, customers must be retained for at least 14 months to be profitable. Moving beyond averages into the customer tiering advocated here, this company may discover that a specific customer is using wireless technology for personal safety needs, is susceptible to churn (competitive switching based on price offers), and frequently calls the customer service department with questions. With additional data, this company may discover that this customer is in the low–low category and decide not to engage in the typical telemarketing or direct-mail campaigns used with its customer base. On the other hand, another customer may be using wireless technology in place of landline phones for both personal and business use and relying on the Internet for customer service needs. The greater types of usage make switching costs higher for this customer. Depending upon its relative consumption in the category, this customer would be in either the third or fourth category. Such a customer definitely warrants specialized attention and intelligent marketing to cross sell other products.

The vital message here is that it is entirely appropriate—indeed, it is imperative—that a company segment its customers on the basis of profitability. Different strategies are required to be successful with different types of customer accounts. Moreover, as explored in the next section, in fast-paced environments with a rapid pace of innovation, strategies for customer relationship management can include more than the standard focus on capturing lifetime customer value.

Strategies for Customer Relationship Management

Strategies to manage customer relationships proactively go beyond mere data mining and database marketing. As shown in Table 10-4, Rashi Glazer identifies six strategies that are useful in turbulent market environments.[53]

Capture the customer is based on the objective of realizing as high a share as possible of the customer's total purchases over time (lifetime customer value). Using interactive communications, a firm can use information gained during previous encounters and transactions to cross sell and up sell customers appropriate products. In this case, once a company has acquired the customer, any acquisition costs can be amortized over many different product/service transactions. For example, Oracle Software's telemarketing sales effort is driven by (what else?) a sophisticated relational database from which an Oracle representative interacting with a prospect can call up all relevant information on

TABLE 10-4 Strategies for Customer Relationship Management	
Capture the Customer	Similar to database marketing. Uses information from past interactions with a customer to tailor future offers to their particular needs. Objective is to capture as high a share as possible of the customer's total purchases over time (lifetime customer value).
Event-Oriented Prospecting	Based on information about customers that might trigger a purchase, marketing is tailored to a particular life cycle event (graduation, first job, etc.).
Extended Organization	Dissolves functional boundaries between firms, allowing one firm to manage the activities of another in its value chain. Creates high switching costs for customers.
Manage by Wire	Guides interactions with customers based on a combination of human decision making and expert computer systems (a type of artificial intelligence).
Mass Customization	Flexible manufacturing that tailors products to individual customer needs.
Yield Management	Tailors pricing to different customers' price sensitivities in order to maximize returns.

Source: Glazer, Rashi (1999), "Winning in Smart Markets," *Sloan Management Review,* Summer, pp. 59–69.

the product in question, competitors' offerings, and all previous interactions with the caller (including other people at the prospect's firm who have interacted with Oracle). The system has documented success rates of over 90%, prospects who after a single call have either purchased a product or been converted into highly qualified sales leads.[54]

Event-oriented prospecting is based on a firm's ability to store information about customers that might trigger a purchase. For example, when a child graduates from high school, a computer firm might send an ad to the family with an offer to purchase a computer as a graduation gift for the child to take to college.

Extended organization strategies dissolve functional boundaries between firms and allow one firm to manage the activities of another in its value chain. For example, Federal Express has developed sophisticated software systems that allow it to manage the shipping and logistics functions for its customers. This creates high switching costs for customers.

Manage by wire strategies guide customer interactions, based on a combination of human decision making and expert computer systems (a type of artificial intelligence). For example, the health care industry is moving to a model in which, when customers call a health maintenance organization for questions, the person on the phone is guided by an elaborate computer script, updated continuously based on hundreds of customer records, about how to treat a specific problem.

Mass customization, or flexible manufacturing, tailors products to individual customer needs. For example, Dell Computer has based its business model around mass customization. Although this model typically requires a significant initial investment in fixed costs, customized units can be made with little marginal cost. The firm can also typically avoid heavy inventory carrying costs under this model.

Yield management is based on tailoring pricing to different customers' price sensitivities. Pioneered in the airline industry, which uses sophisticated pricing algorithms to determine seat pricing that will maximize returns, the conditions under which this technique is appropriate are similar to those for mass customization: high fixed-cost assets, low marginal cost of providing an additional unit, and the product cannot be inventoried.

Customer Relationship Management Software

The primary tool used to implement the sophisticated strategies used in customer relationship marketing, which are premised on gathering and using detailed information about each customer's interaction with a company, is customer relationship management software. This was a $4.45 billion industry in 1999, anticipated to grow to $21.8 billion by 2003, according to data from AMR. This growth rate is nearly five times that of the overall software market.[55]

At a broad level, these software programs are used to capture data about customers from any contact within the enterprise. These one-to-one marketing applications provide the ability to track profitability per customer; to detect customers' dissatisfaction before they leave; or to improve product selling and retention, loyalty, and revenue. More specifically, customer relationship management software includes the following:

- Sales force automation, which allows sales reps to track accounts and prospects
- Call-center automation, used to create customer profiles, provide scripts to help service reps answer customer questions or suggest new purchases, and to coordinate phone calls and messages on Web sites
- Marketing automation, helping marketers to analyze customer purchasing histories and demographics, design targeted marketing campaigns, and measure results

- Web sales, to manage product catalogs, shopping carts, and credit card purchases
- Web configurators, to walk a customer through the process of ordering custom-assembled products
- Web analysis and marketing, used to track on-line activities of individual shoppers, and offer them merchandise they're likely to buy based on past behavior and special, on-the-spot prices for specific customers, and to target marketing via e-mails to individual customers

For example, salespeople can use CRM software for many things, such as to figure out how much a prospect is probably authorized to spend, profile a product against competition, or find an advocate within a customer's organization. Customer service reps can use the data in these programs; the knowledge enables a meaningful, intelligent dialogue with the individual customer. These programs provide a strong value proposition not only for businesses but also for their customers.

Summary

This chapter has provided four frameworks to help high-tech managers make decisions about advertising and promotion strategies. Beginning with the idea of the advertising and promotion pyramid, this chapter initially addressed how a firm can leverage a variety of advertising and promotion tools in a cost-efficient manner. Second, the chapter provided coverage of why and how a high-tech firm can develop a strong brand name, including ingredient advertising and Internet strategies. Third, the chapter addressed the strategic issues in making product preannouncements, with explicit coverage of the objectives, risks, and tactical considerations. Finally, the chapter concluded with a discussion of the role of marketing communications in managing customer relationships. In addition to discussing the categories of customers and strategies to manage customer relationships, an overview of customer relationship management software was provided.

Advertising and promotion issues are particularly salient in the high-tech marketing environment. Although high-tech marketers may be either unfamiliar or uncomfortable with these strategies, the importance of a strong brand, the use and timing of new-product preannouncements, and the development and maintenance of strong customer relationships, through the leveraging of the tools in the advertising and promotion pyramid, are vital.

Discussion Questions

1. What is the logic behind using the advertising and promotion pyramid as a coordinating device?
2. What are some of the critical issues in each of the tools in the advertising and promotion mix?
3. What are the advantages of a strong brand—to firms? To customers?
4. How does a firm develop a strong brand?
5. What is the role of the Internet in branding strategies? How does the Internet change the branding environment? What are the major implications?
6. What is the logic behind ingredient advertising (also known as cobranding and derived demand advertising)?
7. What are the advantages and disadvantages of ingredient advertising? Be sure to consider the viewpoints both of the supplier as well as the OEM.

8. Under what conditions might ingredient advertising be most useful or most likely?
9. What are preannouncements? What are the pros and cons?
10. What is vaporware? What are the ethics involved? (Be sure to consider the perspectives of the various constituencies involved, including customers, competitors, and the firm.)
11. What factors affect the timing (early or late) of preannouncements?
12. When is preannouncing most likely to be effective (from the company's perspective)? When is it most likely to cause problems?
13. What is database, or one-to-one, marketing?
14. On what basis should companies identify customers who are good prospects for customer relationship management? What are the resulting categories?
15. What six strategies can be used for customer relationship management?
16. What functions can customer relationship management software perform?

Glossary

Branding. The strategy of creating a strong, recognizable, familiar brand name in a target market.

Cobranding. When the value of two companies' brands, when used together, is stronger than one brand alone, synergy is created in developing ties between the two companies' brands.

Database (one-to-one) marketing. Using a customer database to capture data on which to rate customers, based on customer volume and profitability to the firm. Allows a firm to compare the mix of marketing and services that go into capturing and retaining each individual customer to the revenue that customer is likely to bring in. Allows marketers to target individual customers with marketing programs geared to their profitability and volume level.

Derived demand. Demand for the component, or ingredient, is derived from the end customers' demand for the products in which the components are used. For example, the demand for chips is derived from end users' demand for computers, which is pulled up the distribution channel to retailers, then to computer manufacturers, and finally, to chip suppliers.

Ingredient branding. The strategy of creating a brand identity for a component or ingredient used in the customer's product.

Preannouncement. Formal, deliberate communication before a firm actually undertakes a particular marketing action (say, shipping a new product); a form of market signaling that conveys information to competitors, customers, shareholders, and firms that make complementary products.

Rational branding. The idea in an Internet environment that customers expect more than a brand message; they expect a useful service or information. Rational branding marries the emotional sell of traditional brand marketing with a concrete service offered on-line. Communicating with and helping a customer at the same time builds brands on-line.

Vaporware. Products that are announced before they are ready for market and which may never materialize.

Endnotes

1. Ames, B. Charles and James D. Hlavacek (1984), *Managerial Marketing for Industrial Firms,* New York: Random House.
2. Bellizzi, Joe and Jakki Mohr (1984), "Technical Versus Nontechnical Wording of Industrial Print Advertising," in R. Belk et al. (eds.), *AMA Educators' Conference Proceedings,* pp. 171–175, Chicago: American Marketing Association.
3. Wilke, John, Dean Takahashi, and Keith Perine (1999), "Accord Lets Intel Avoid Trial and a Beating Such as Microsoft Is Taking," *Wall Street Journal,* March 9, pp. A1, A10.

4. Klein, Karen (1999), "Show and Sell," *Business Week Frontier,* August 16, pp. F.26–F.30.

5. "Comdex Loses Appeal to Industry Players," (1998), *Wall Street Journal,* November 16, p. B6.

6. Klein, Karen (1999), "Show and Sell," *Business Week Frontier,* August 16, pp. F.26–F.30.

7. Klein, Karen (1999), "Trade Shows Are Indispensable . . . but You've Got to Prepare Ahead," *Business Week Frontier,* August 16, pp. F.21–F.24.

8. Auerbach, Jon (1996), "Cutting-Edge EMC Sells the Old-Fashioned Way: Hard," *Wall Street Journal,* December 19, p. B4.

9. Richtel, Matt (1998), "Technology Companies Making Big Play at Super Bowl," *New York Times,* January 23.

10. Gunther, Marc (1998), "The Internet Is Mr. Case's Neighborhood," *Fortune,* March 30, pp. 69–80.

11. Morris, Betsy (1996), "The Brand's the Thing," *Fortune,* March 4, pp. 73–86.

12. Morris, Betsy (1996), "The Brand's the Thing," *Fortune,* March 4, pp. 73–86.

13. Morris, Betsy (1996), "The Brand's the Thing," *Fortune,* March 4, pp. 73–86.

14. Greenfeld, Karl Taro (2000), "Do You Know Cisco?" *Time,* January 17, pp. 72–74.

15. Keller, Kevin Lane (1998), *Strategic Brand Management,* Upper Saddle River, NJ: Prentice Hall, p. 610.

16. Mehta, Stephanie N. (1999), "Northern Telecom Plays Down Phone Roots, Embraces 'I' Word," *Wall Street Journal,* April 14.

17. Freeman, Laurie (1999), "Why Internet Brands Take Offline Avenues," *Marketing News,* July 19, p. 4.

18. Hyman, Mark (2000), "Now That's a Hail Mary Play," *Business Week,* January 31, pp. 100–102.

19. "Advertising That Clicks," (1999), *The Economist,* October 9, p. 71.

20. "Branding," (1998), *Business 2.0,* November, pp. 69–84.

21. Winkler, Agnieszka (1999), "The Six Myths of Branding," *Brandweek,* September 20, p. 28.

22. Keller, Kevin Lane (1998), *Strategic Brand Management,* Upper Saddle River, NJ: Prentice Hall.

23. Winkler, Agnieszka (1999), "The Six Myths of Branding," *Brandweek,* September 20, p. 28.

24. Keller, Kevin Lane (1998), *Strategic Brand Management,* Upper Saddle River, NJ: Prentice Hall.

25. Keller, Kevin Lane (1998), *Strategic Brand Management,* Upper Saddle River, NJ: Prentice Hall.

26. Winkler, Agnieszka (1999), "The Six Myths of Branding," *Brandweek,* September 20, p. 28.

27. Arnott, Nancy (1994), "Inside Intel's Marketing Coup," *Sales and Marketing Management,* February, pp. 78–81.

28. Used by Tim Smith, Red Sky Interactive, San Francisco.

29. "Branding," (1998), *Business 2.0,* November, pp. 69–84.

30. Neuborne, Ellen and Robert Hof (1998), "Branding on the Net," *Business Week,* November 9, http://businessweek.com/datedtoc/1998/981109.htm.

31. "Branding," (1998), *Business 2.0,* November, pp. 69–84, and *The Economist* (1999), "Advertising That Clicks," October 9, p. 71.

32. Cooperative advertising dollars are typically provided as a percentage of product purchased. For example, at one time, Hewlett-Packard's cooperative advertising strategy was to set aside 3% of a dealer's purchases of HP product into a cooperative advertising account. Then, when the dealer ran an ad for his or her store that also featured HP product, the dealer would submit to HP a copy of the ad along with the invoice from the media in which the ad was run, and HP would then cut the dealer a check from his or her co-op account.

33. Morris, Betsy (1996), "The Brand's the Thing," *Fortune,* March 4, pp. 73–86.

34. Kirkpatrick, David (1994), "Why Compaq Is Mad at Intel," *Fortune,* October 31, pp. 171–176.

35. Yoder, Stephen Kreider (1995), "Computer Makers Defend 'Vaporware,'" *Wall Street Journal,* February 16, pp. B1, B6.

36. Except as noted, this section is drawn from Eliashberg, J. and T. Robertson (1988), "New Product Preannouncing Behavior: A Market Signaling Study," *Journal of Marketing Research,* 25 (August), pp. 282–292; Lilly, Bryan and Rockney Walters (1997), "Toward a Model of New Product Preannouncement Timing," *Journal of Product Innovation Management,* 14, pp. 4–20; and Calantone, Roger and Kim Schatzel (2000), "Strategic

Foretelling: Communication-Based Antecedents of a Firm's Propensity to Preannounce," *Journal of Marketing,* 64 (January), pp. 17–30.

37. Reinhardt, Andy (2000), "'I've Left a Few Dead Bodies,'" *Business Week,* January 31, pp. 69–70.

38. Yoder, Stephen Kreider (1995), "Computer Makers Defend 'Vaporware,'" *Wall Street Journal,* February 16, pp. B1, B6.

39. Calantone, Roger and Kim Schatzel (2000), "Strategic Foretelling: Communication-Based Antecedents of a Firm's Propensity to Preannounce," *Journal of Marketing,* 64 (January), pp. 17–30.

40. Additional detail about incumbent competitors' reactions to new product preannouncements can be found in Robertson, Thomas, Jehoshua Eliashberg, and Talio Rymon (1995), "New Product Announcement Signals and Incumbent Reactions," *Journal of Marketing,* 59 (July), pp. 1–15.

41. Calantone, Roger and Kim Schatzel (2000), "Strategic Foretelling: Communication-Based Antecedents of a Firm's Propensity to Preannounce," *Journal of Marketing,* 64 (January), pp. 17–30.

42. "Boo Who," (2000), *Business 2.0,* February, p. 105.

43. Schifrin, Matthew (1993), "No Product, No Sale," *Forbes,* June 7, pp. 50–52; Ambrosio, Johanna (1993), "Users Cooling to Oft-Delayed Iceberg," *ComputerWorld,* November 1, p. 4.

44. Yoder, Stephen Kreider (1995), "Computer Makers Defend 'Vaporware,'" *Wall Street Journal,* February 16, pp. B1, B6.

45. Yoder, Stephen Kreider (1995), "Computer Makers Defend 'Vaporware,'" *Wall Street Journal,* February 16, pp. B1, B6.

46. Lilly, Bryan and Rockney Walters (1997), "Toward a Model of New Product Preannouncement Timing," *Journal of Product Innovation Management,* 14, pp. 4–20; Calantone, Roger and Kim Schatzel (2000), "Strategic Foretelling: Communication-Based Antecedents of a Firm's Propensity to Preannounce," *Journal of Marketing,* 64 (January), pp. 17–30.

47. Eliashberg, J. and T. Robertson (1988), "New Product Preannouncing Behavior: A Market Signaling Study," *Journal of Marketing Research,* 25 (August), pp. 282–292.

48. Eliashberg, J. and T. Robertson (1988), "New Product Preannouncing Behavior: A Market Signaling Study," *Journal of Marketing Research,* 25, pp. 282–292.

49. Judge, Paul (1998), "Do You Know Who Your Most Profitable Customers Are?" *Business Week,* September 14.

50. Judge, Paul (1998), "Do You Know Who Your Most Profitable Customers Are?" *Business Week,* September 14.

51. Barlow, Richard (1999), "Reap What You Reward," *The DMA Insider,* Fall, pp. 35–38.

52. Bishop, Susan (1999), "The Strategic Power of Saying No," *Harvard Business Review,* (November–December), pp. 50–64; and Davids, Meryl (1999), "How to Avoid the 10 Biggest Mistakes in CRM," *Journal of Business Strategy,* November–December, pp. 22–26.

53. Glazer, Rashi (1999), "Winning in Smart Markets," *Sloan Management Review,* Summer, pp. 59–69.

54. Glazer, Rashi (1999), "Winning in Smart Markets," *Sloan Management Review,* Summer, pp. 59–69.

55. Hamm, Steve and Robert Hof (2000), "An Eagle Eye on Customers," *Business Week,* February 21, pp. 67–76.

Recommended Readings

Ries, Al and Laura Ries (2000), *The 11 Immutable Laws of Internet Branding,* New York: Harper-Business.

Seybold, Patricia (1998), *Customers.com: How to Create a Profitable Business Strategy for the Internet and Beyond,* New York: Times Books/Random House.

Winkler, Agnieszka (1999), *Warp-Speed Branding: The Impact of Technology on Marketing,* New York: John Wiley.

CHAPTER 11

E-Business and Internet Marketing

INTRODUCTION: PERSPECTIVES ON THE INTERNET

No book on high-technology marketing would be complete in today's environment without a detailed discussion of the Internet. In just five years (1995 to 2000), the Internet went from a tool used primarily by technology sophisticates (used by just 4% of the U.S. population every day)[1] to one used by 110 million people—30% of the U.S. population uses the Internet everyday.[2] Indeed, growth forecasts that some thought were too aggressive have turned out to underestimate the speed with which American consumers and corporations have moved business on-line. By comparison, it took radio 30 years to reach 60 million people, and TV, 15 years.[3] Worldwide, the United States accounts for nearly 43% of the total 259 million Internet users (although this percentage is expected to decline as international usage increases).

The Internet fundamentally changes the economics of transactions, in ways that benefit both consumers and producers, by lowering transaction costs. Consumers gain convenience; timely access to products, service, and information; and a variety of choices not available in more traditional contexts. The Internet matches buyers and sellers so that buyers can become better informed without ever talking face-to-face. For businesses, on-line connections squeeze out costs, minimize inventory, and shorten reaction times, all of which are helping to streamline supply chains.

When people think of doing business on the Net, they think of either selling products and services to consumers for their personal consumption and enjoyment, or sites providing information for customers. However, it is the world of business-to-business (B-to-B) commerce that has provided much of the impetus for on-line commerce. In 1998, B-to-B transactions accounted for 78% of revenue generated on the Internet.[4] Forrester Research estimated Internet sales of about $118 billion for the year 2000, $100 billion of which were B-to-B sales, and $18 billion of which were business-to-consumer (B-to-C) sales.[5] (Despite the magnitude of these numbers, it is important to keep them in context. By the year 2003, on-line consumer retail purchases are forecast to be just 6% of total retail purchases.[6])

Lou Gerstner, chairman of IBM, said in the spring of 1999 that "the Internet has become the ultimate medium for business," and that consumers and investors will be dazzled by the ingenious ways that bedrock U.S. companies will harness the Internet to their advantage. IBM is getting 25% of its revenue from areas related to electronic business. The Internet presents a gigantic service opportunity for established computer companies such as IBM.[7] The Web presents a business revolution comparable to the effect of Japan's quality and just-in-time movement in the 1980s.

Electronic commerce is not only generating revenue and saving money for businesses, but also creating new wealth by creating a new class of business entrepreneurs.[8]

One study estimated that some 100,000 cybermediaries had cropped up by 1998.[9] This new class of Web-savvy intermediaries provides a more direct and inexpensive conduit between producers and buyers than do traditional distributors.[10]

When one combines the revenue generated by B-to-B and B-to-C transactions with the cost savings such transactions allow, the Internet is calculated to add $10 billion to $20 billion to the U.S. gross domestic product during the four-year period of 1998 to 2002. By 2003, B-to-B sales could reach $1.3 trillion in the United States alone.

The purpose of this chapter is to address the ways in which the Internet impacts customers and businesses (from a variety of perspectives). Regardless of whether one is selling traditional consumer products or high-technology products, the use of the Internet for marketing and business purposes can itself be considered a high-tech proposition. Hence, this chapter uses examples from a variety of industry contexts and is not constrained only to the marketing and selling of high-tech products and innovations—although it is logical that a technology-oriented marketing tool can be especially useful for high-technology products.

Three primary perspectives are addressed in this chapter, as shown in Figure 11-1, the triangle of Internet perspectives. First and foremost, no business phenomenon can be ad-

FIGURE II-I Internet Perspectives

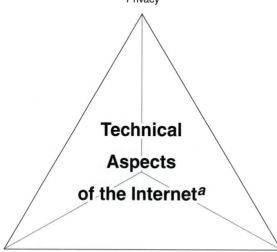

Customers
- Customer control
- Privacy

Technical

Aspects

of the Internet[a]

Businesses
- Changing rules of the game
- Threats to traditional businesses
- Coping with threats
- Functions other than sales
  (e.g., supply chain management)

Content Sites
- Portals
- Cybermediaries
- On-line communities
- Electronic marketplaces
  for B-to-B e-commerce

[a] Technical aspects of the Internet, such as broadband connections, provide the foundation for links among customers, business, and content sites.

equately understood without an in-depth understanding of how it relates to *consumers* and their behavior.

Second, many people gravitate to the Web because of the variety of useful information, or *content,* that can be gleaned in a fast, efficient, and thorough manner. Content sites include the portals, communities, and information areas that people go to participate in the Internet environment.

Businesses, the third leg of the triangle, use the Web for a variety of reasons, ranging from display of product information, managing customer service, and selling of products, to advertising and partnering to gain marketing efficiencies.

Finally, some additional detail about the *technical aspects* of how the Internet functions is provided, because the technical side affects the ability of the Internet to meet the needs of the three groups described using the Web for their different purposes. Box 11-1 provides a layperson's overview of some of the infrastructure issues underlying the Web. Readers are also referred to the special February 2000 issue of *Business 2.0,* which provides a detailed description of the various technologies needed for a business to implement electronic-enabled sales, or e-commerce.

Although each of the three perspectives affects, and is affected by, the other two, this chapter, for convenience, is divided into five distinct sections. The first section examines consumer behavior issues on the Web. The next two sections examine business perspectives on the Web. The fourth section examines two types of content sites, on-line communities and electronic business-to-business marketplaces. The fifth section examines keys to success in an on-line world.

SECTION I: BUYER BEHAVIOR ISSUES AND THE WEB

Two of the largest effects of the Internet with respect to buyer behavior relate to the empowerment of customers relative to suppliers and customer concerns about privacy.

Customer Control

At its broadest level, the Internet changes the dynamic between buyer and seller. Gary Hamel, an expert in business strategy and competitive dynamics, refers to the Internet as a foundation for a new industrial order based on customer control.[11] Compared to traditional buyer–seller relationships, the Internet may come to represent the ultimate triumph of consumerism, radically transforming buyer–seller dynamics. The Internet empowers customers in at least six ways, relative to the companies they purchase from (see Table 11-1).

TABLE 11-1   Bases of Customer Control
1   Choice of information
2   Web site product customization
3   On-line auctions
4   Freedom from geographic constraints
5   Access 24 hours a day, 7 days a week
6   Word of mouth

BOX 11-1

How Does the Internet Work?

The Internet is a global mesh of computer networks sharing a common software standard called "TCP/IP." The backbones of the Internet are high-speed fiber trunk lines owned by telephone companies. National service providers, such as UUNET, aggregate data traffic and zip it over the backbones. They work with local service providers that connect to customers via their PC modems or digital (T1) connections.[a] Increasingly, information appliances are offering wireless connections to the Internet. The Web site http://boardwatch. internet.com/isp/summer99/internetarch. htm provides more technical information in the eight chapters there.

WHAT DOES THE INTERNET DISTRIBUTION CHAIN LOOK LIKE?[b]

Customer ➜ PC maker ➜ Operating system ➜ Browsers ➜ ISPs ➜ Hosts ➜ Portals

Each player in the Internet distribution chain wants a piece of the possible revenues to be gained from the value provided at each step of the chain. Most are looking for compensation for referring customers to possible sites.

Those players closest to the customer are the *device manufacturers*, which control the customer's first point of interaction with the Net. These firms are trying to wrest control of start-up screens from Microsoft. If they succeed, their power will grow. Ideally, they'd like to control channels, bookmarks, and Web points a customer sees when setting up his or her personal computer, so they can demand payment for that placement. As technology improves, the device manufacturers

could include TVs, set-top boxes, cell phones, and even kitchen appliances.

Next in line are the *operating system vendors*. Microsoft controls over 90% of this market and wants to claim a cut of the Internet money flow. It is working on making Internet service providers (ISPs) pay for choice placement inside the Windows program that runs to set up Internet access, in order to receive a bounty for each customer that signs on with one of these ISPs. And content providers (of the Web site/service) have agreements with Microsoft to ensure they are on the customer's desktop channels. (Microsoft is looking beyond the personal computer and is now seeing the use of Windows CE in set-top boxes and wireless phones; it is also into media with its MSN portal.)

Then come the *browsers,* or *access-software vendors*, including Microsoft, Netscape, and AOL, to name a few that link customers to the Net. Embedding the browser with links to favored Web sites clearly influences traffic flow. So, these vendors negotiate with content providers for premier placement within bookmark lists or channels. AOL wants to maintain its leadership with more video and entertainment (over TVs as well as PCs), a contributing factor in its merger with Time-Warner. It also needs faster speed than is available over phone lines.

Internet service providers control the capital-intensive infrastructure, known as broadband, the high-speed system for transmitting data. Phone, cable, and satellite companies are racing to provide broadband connections for Internet access and other digital services to guarantee influence and power. Although one might assume the capital-intensive nature of the infrastructure is a barrier to entry, ISPs have not established control in the Internet environment. However, this might change with the following:

- ISPs are entering marketing arrangements with search sites to leverage their physical distribution; an example is the partnership between AT&T and Yahoo!
- The ISP market is consolidating: Larger players translate to greater influence.
- ISPs may sell Web sites the right to priority queuing.

Many ISPs are communication companies, which want big, fat, digital pipes to sell all sorts of services: phone calls, digital television, Web surfing, on-line shopping.

- *Cable* companies have been the most aggressive to date in developing broadband, although AT&T is building cable because it believes cable pipes will develop sooner. Cable modems (via fat coaxial cables that carry TV signals) permit data transfer 500 times faster than 56K personal computers, and their Web connection is always active (like TV), so surfers don't have to dial in to the Net. Cable companies may even get into cable phone service and will need technology (Cisco, Lucent) to make voice-over-Internet calls possible.
- *Phone companies* use copper wire, so they are moving to digital subscriber lines (DSL) to move data faster. Although DSL costs about the same as cable modem service ($30 to $60 a month), it hasn't spread as quickly due to lack of aggressive marketing.
- *Satellites* can relay data at superfast speeds, but consumers can't beam up at the same speed when using their conventional modems at 56K. So not many subscribers currently use satellites. However, two-way systems are coming, backed by Bill Gates and McCaw Cellular.

Cable is theoretically the fastest, but because scores of customers share the connection, this makes it slower in practice. In light of this, DSL tops out in speed with its dedicated connection; however, its bandwidth is not guaranteed. The cheapest DSL services are not fast enough for TV-quality movies, and they won't work beyond a three-mile range from a phone-switching office. Satellite is still in nascent form. Because of the rapid technological changes in this arena, by the time you read this, more issues and opportunities may exist.

Hosts are used by many popular Web sites to help manage and run their Internet servers (i.e., an outsourcing arrangement). If such hosts offer higher-quality access than Web sites can get on their own, they may gain strength. Web hosting arrangements with companies such as Power-Surge.net and HostPro.net are among the thousands available (www. hostindex.com). Hosts are frequently used by businesses who outsource their technology needs.

Finally, the *search sites,* or **portals,** offer an array of services and information.[c] These businesses have gone further in exploiting their position in the Internet infrastructure than any other point in the chain. They have signed multimillion-dollar deals with Web sites to increase traffic. There are specialty portals, or single-subject sites, such as ESPN or E*Trade. Specialty portals are adding e-mail, search, and e-commerce in order to become the hub of choice for specific content. For example, E*Trade's goal is to become the hub for all things financial on the Web and not just a low-cost trading site. As a result, it now includes financial news reports, stock quotes, chat, insurance, and mortgage information, and—importantly— its traffic more than doubled in two months. Adding services and content attracts more visitors and more ad dollars.

The megaportals are the sites such as Yahoo! and Excite, which have expanded their turf to include single-subject sites such as finance, health, women's issues, and so forth. These big sites hope to attract more visitors and more ad dollars. For example, iVillage.com is the most popular women's site. Megaportals received 67% of North American ad dollars on the Internet in 1998. They use distribution deals, whereby they collect a fee for directing consumers to a partner's Web site. For example, MSN.com's portal received $60 million from various search engines to be listed there, and SportLine USA charges companies to be listed on its site. As traditional TV audiences drift onto the Net, traditional media companies want to follow. As Web audiences gravitate to portals—which combine search services, content, and handy links to other sites in a single place—this is where some broadcasters want to be.

A central irony of this Internet distribution chain is that in most businesses, the firms closest to the customer tend to be better off than the firms farthest from the customer. However, on the Net (with the exception of Microsoft), the companies farthest from the consumer are extracting the most value; the portals have made the best deals. Being closest to the **clickstream** of customers provides the greatest ability to learn about their on-line habits. Because the battle is fought with information, not inventory, customer learning is the *sine qua non* of success in e-commerce,[d] and daily customer information is the gold mine.

Importantly, the positions along the chain are not fixed, and many partnerships are occurring. Historically, the ISPs have paid to have personal computer companies bundle their dial-up software with the computers. But now, Microsoft is trying to aggregate this function into its operating system, wresting revenue away from the personal computer manufacturers.

----

[a] Reinhardt, Andy (1998), "Log On, Link Up, Save Big," *Business Week,* June 22, pp. 132–138.

[b] Gurley, William (1998), "Getting in the Way on the Net," *Fortune,* July 6, pp. 188–190.

[c] Green, Heather (1998), "The Skinny on Niche Portals," *Business Week,* October 26, pp. 66–68.

[d] Stewart, Thomas (1999), "Larry Bossidy's New Role Model: Michael Dell," *Fortune,* April 12, pp. 166–168.

Source: Reinhardt, Andy (1999), "As the Web Spins," *Business Week,* May 24, pp. 30–31.

Consumers Can Choose What Information They Want from the Internet Web users want to learn about products on their own terms. On-line consumers can "suck" out of cyberspace whatever interests them and leave behind whatever doesn't. By doing so, consumers can escape the incessant interruptions of vendors. This newfound control is the antithesis of how mass marketers typically operate and, instead, allows customers to be in control of the information they get. In addition, consumers want unbiased information on the Internet (versus the hype and "fluff-and-bluff" tactics of traditional advertising). How does this affect marketing strategy? Probably most important is moving to a **permission-based marketing** model, which asks the customer to opt in to receive marketing messages based on his or her interests in a particular topic.

In the past, retailers and vendors realized that consumers didn't have the time and patience to shop for the best deals. In essence, customer ignorance had been a profit center. But now, with better-informed consumers, prices will probably trend downward. Although some vendors may view this as a drawback, they will see indirect benefits, including the ability to cut inventory carrying costs, and, because the market-clearing price is known, it may become possible to maximize revenue on every sale through yield management strategies. In addition, vendors will know whether it will pay to add more capacity.

For example, the Internet makes it relatively easy to make on-line comparisons. The use of electronic agents, or **bots,** to cruise the Internet and come back with a list of items, prices, and merchants is increasing (see Box 11-2). Moreover, through the use of information brokers and search engines—such as Junglee and C2B, which search products and bargains all across the Net—consumers can comparison shop in one stop. And consumer **cybermediaries,** on-line intermediaries that provide information for buyers and sellers, could save an average household $1,110 a year by searching for the best deals on its behalf. Infomediaries aimed at trade between businesses will save even more. They will pool buying power to extract deals from vendors.

Consumers Want to Configure Products to Their Own Requirements   Internet technology allows customers to easily and economically customize products to their own needs. This customization can be with respect to the products the customer is purchasing—for example, N2K.com allows consumers to specify what tracks they want on a compact disc, and configurator technology in customer relationship management software allows mass customization of physical product orders—or with respect to the Web site the customer frequents. **Personalization** refers to the ability to tailor a Web site or e-mail to a consumer based on past behavior, tastes shared with others, age, or location.[12] This is an important advantage of the Internet to customers and, because of its role in forming and maintaining long-term customer relationships on the Web, is discussed in some detail subsequently. Personalized on-line advice for services is also made economical with Net technology.

Consumers Will Have Producers Bid Against Each Other in Real-Time Auctions for Their Business   Sites such as Onsale, Webauction.com, eBay, and PriceLine.com offer buyers the ability to bid on the items in which they are interested. Consumer and business auctions will account for 29% of electronic commerce, or $129 billion, by 2002, up from $3.8 billion at the end of 1998. In 1999, 35% of on-line buyers purchased through auctions.[13] Most auctions (70%) in 1999 were of the person-to-person variety on sites such as eBay. By 2003, 66% of on-line auctions will be businesses selling to consumers. For example, Amazon.com and the Sharper Image have added auction sites.

Cyberauctions could usher in an era of dynamic pricing, in which a wide range of goods would be priced according to what the market will bear, instantly, constantly—much like stocks are priced. Indirect effects of on-line auctions are that consumers gain access to data about products and pricing, and sellers learn more about buyers and can tailor products and prices to individual customers. However, despite these benefits, retailers fear that buyers might eventually demand price concessions on products not listed on auction sites. If so, the real possibility exists that the reduced sales and marketing costs may not outweigh the lower profit margins. Despite this, by 2003, airline tickets, hotel rooms, car sales, and apparel sales will see increased action on auction sites.

The use of auctions in a commercial environment—especially for perishable wares, such as advertising space—is also transforming commercial (B-to-B) markets. Adauction. com sells on-line ad space that once went unsold. It has also moved into print publications

---

BOX 11-2

Bots

Shopping robots (**bots**) are computer programs that scan the Internet for bargains. The theory is that they can enhance consumer power by giving perfect information, bypassing intermediaries, and cutting markups. They home in on specific pieces of information, such as model numbers and prices, and can sift the needed data from the software code itself.

Although many consumers think that they can use the bots to get the best deals, some caution is warranted. Because retailers are frightened that shopping bots could spark a pricing war, they try to stymie the bots. Some on-line retailers block the bots to prevent them from using price as the only basis for comparison. As CDNow's founder says, "It's too expensive to try and serve a customer who's only going to shop with us one out of three times because of a 50-cent savings."[a] Its site has many expensive features, including music reviews, commentaries, and personalized recommendations. Shopping on price alone devalues these features.

Moreover, because on-line retailers can see the address of a visitor, retailers can also refuse to answer requests that come from known bot sites. Or they can confuse the bots by changing the site's format so the bot doesn't know where to look for pricing information. Some retailers resort to lowering the product's base price, but then charge higher fees for shipping and handling. Apparently, some retailers seem to feel that the risks outweigh the possible benefits of the traffic that can be directed to a retailer's site. However, if consumers rely more and more heavily on bots, retailers may have to cooperate.

It is also important to know that some bots charge merchants for listing their products and, hence, those merchants who refuse to pay are excluded from the comparisons. For example, Barnes & Noble has not paid to list its site with Junglee and, hence, is not searched. Moreover, some on-line merchants themselves offer shopping bots, which are programmed to ignore competitors' products. For example, Amazon.com owns Junglee Corporation. This creates a conflict of interest, if in fact the bot directs traffic to competitors' sites.

Other types of bots do exist. Some bots may be used to influence customers' buying habits without their knowing it.[b] For example, a company might program a bot to go into a chat room to talk up a particular product while masquerading as an ordinary person. Andrew Leonard refers to these as "lying, no-good propagandabots."[c] And bots and electronic agents can be used to hone a Web advertiser's ability to cumulatively fine-tune customer profiles much more thoroughly than the technology currently being used. This again raises issues of abuse of customer information. For more on bots, see www.botspot.com.

---

[a] Quick, Rebecca (1998), "Web's Robot Shoppers Don't Roam Free," *Wall Street Journal,* September 13, p. B1.
[b] Buskin, John (1999), "Online Persuaders," *Wall Street Journal,* July 12, pp. R12, R26.
[c] Leonard, Andrew (1997), *Bots: The Origin of New Species,* New York: Penguin Books.
Source: Quick, Rebecca (1998), "Web's Robot Shoppers Don't Roam Free," *Wall Street Journal,* September 13, pp. B1, B8.

and plans to go into broadcast. Commercial auctions, such as FreeMarkets Online Inc., show that business auctions are growing even faster than B-to-C auctions.

Consumers Will Be Able to Break Free of Geographically Constrained Purchasing Physical retailers typically had a defined geographic scope, but with the Internet, consumers will be able to escape the shackles of geography to buy from anyone, anywhere. Indeed, in the past, some companies might have wrongly assumed that captive customers were loyal customers. In the Internet environment, loyalty will have to be honestly earned.

Net Shopping Is More Efficient, Convenient, and Timely   Internet shoppers can save time via on-line searches, and they can shop when they want to—24 hours a day, 7 days a week. They can minimize the hassle of finding a needed item (search economies) and getting the item (order fulfillment). More and more, the distribution chain will go directly to the customer. The desirability of these aspects of Internet shopping were initially lost on grocery store executives. Their response to on-line shopping? "Too expensive." However, these executives are now realizing that personalized delivery ("my place, my time") is something for which consumers will pay.

Consumer Word of Mouth Is More Powerful in an On-Line World   Because it can travel with mouse clicks, both the upside potential and downside risks of consumer word of mouth are intensified in an on-line environment. Intel saw this with the initial problems in its Pentium chip's math processing abilities. Hotmail saw this in the amount of on-line buzz it received from its offer of free e-mail services. Marketers must recognize that word of mouth travels very quickly on-line and harness this potential ability to their advantage, including the use of **viral marketing,** which relies on users to pass along catchy messages to friends. As Amazon.com's CEO Jeff Bezos says, because of the far-reaching impact of word of mouth on the Internet, a company should devote 70% of its resources to creating a great customer experience, and only 30% to "shout" about it (versus the off-lines' reverse allocation).[14]

Ultimately, each of these characteristics of the Internet will allow customers to gain control vis-à-vis the firms with which they conduct business. A second factor affecting buyer behavior on the Web relates to concerns about privacy.

Privacy Concerns

Forty-one percent of on-line shoppers were very concerned about Web sites' use of their personal information to send them unwanted information, and 92% of Net users expressed discomfort about Web sites sharing personal information with other sites.[15]

Although many Web shoppers have these concerns, many may not realize just how insidious the technology is that can potentially pose privacy violations. Through the use of electronic trails called **cookies** (also known as "client-side persistent data"), or software downloaded into a browser's personal computer hard drive by a Web site that records the browser's Web habits, merchants can collect reams of data about a particular person. For example, by uploading cookies from the browser's hard drive, and combining cookie data with information that browsers provide by filling out registration forms as well as data available from secondary databases, marketers can glean credit ratings, salary, vehicle registrations, and lifestyle information. Ultimately, sites can use this data to build profiles about what customers do or don't buy, what they look at, how much time they spend in different areas, what ads they click on, how much time elapsed between visits, and whether the user looked at the same pages, in the same order, and so forth. Cookie data can also be sold to advertisers to help them target more likely prospects.

The arguments in favor of collecting and sharing such information come from businesses that believe that through improved information about customers, they can get closer to their customers, gaining business efficiencies and improving the effectiveness of their marketing efforts. Customers are more likely to receive information in which they are genuinely interested. And companies who misuse customer data will be ferreted out and punished by market forces.

However, many people are not convinced of the merits of these arguments. They note that companies often don't limit how they or their business partners use customer information, and that they transfer information to partners without telling their customers, practices that ultimately erode consumer trust. *Business Week* has gone so far as to call self-regulation a sham.[16] Ninety percent of on-line companies collect personal information on their customers, but only 10% follow the guidelines of the Fair Information Practices Act, which require the following:

- Companies clearly disclose how they collect and use information.
- Consumers have control over whether information about them is collected and used via *opt-in* procedures.
- Consumers have the ability to inspect their data and correct any errors.
- The government has the power to impose penalties when companies break the rules.

The current default on gathering information is "*opt out*"; in other words, if a person does not want a company to collect information about him or her, the customer must take an action to specify that. On the other hand, an opt-in procedure would have as the default that no information is collected unless the consumer has first given consent. Such procedures would require effort on both businesses' and consumers' parts, but may ultimately create a more trusting environment.[17]

As an initial step toward regulation, the federal government passed the Children's Online Privacy Protection Act in 1998, which limits the collection of information about children under age 13. This act requires parents to opt in, by letter or fax to the site, before their children can use online chat rooms and message boards.

Because many on-line merchants see regulation as the "wolf at their door," many believe more stringent self-regulation is the way to proceed. As one expert says, "Privacy is good business."[18] Along these lines, many commercial sites can receive a "trust label," through www.truste.org, which independently evaluates the privacy policies of registered sites. It was founded on the principles of disclosure and informed consent, and functions as a "Good Housekeeping seal of approval," so to speak, with respect to on-line privacy policies. However, it is important to recognize that even with a privacy policy, such pledges may not be consistently enforced.

Ultimately, the success of electronic commerce depends on the ability to keep personal data safe from abuse. Privacy policies that are strictly adhered to, in which users can see how different sites will use their personal information, are vital. More information about how browsers can protect their privacy can be found in Box 11-3.

BOX 11-3

Protecting Against Cookies

The use of cookies, which many browsers know nothing about, invites concerns about privacy. How can browsers protect their privacy?

First, users can set the security preferences on their browser software to require browser approval before accepting any cookies. (Browsers can see which cookies are on their hard drive by checking their temporary Internet files, or cookie files, using their file directory system, such as Windows Explorer.) It is important to know that when the security preferences are set either to not accept cookies or to require browser approval first, surfing on the Web is negatively affected. Some sites will not open without the ability to set a cookie. And constantly having to click "yes" or "no" to accept a cookie every time a dialog box pops up prior to a window opening can be very cumbersome.

Alternatively, browsers can download software that lets the browser list the sites from which he or she will accept cookies (Kookaburra Software at www.kburra.com). Another site (www.anonymizer.com) allows customers to surf the Web anonymously by blocking the browser's identity. Enonymous.com offers free downloadable software that ranks the privacy policies of 10,000 Web sites. Zero-Knowledge Systems Inc.'s Freedom software is another option.

The Platform for Privacy Preferences (www.w3.org/P3P) has a standard to let surfers choose how much information they will disclose (e.g., zip code and gender only) by setting browser preferences. P3P offers a privacy assistant that allows users to be informed and in control of their information, based on their individual privacy preferences. Sites with practices that fall within the range of a user's preference could, at the option of the user, be accessed "seamlessly"; otherwise, users will be notified of a site's practices and have the opportunity to agree to those terms or other terms and continue browsing if they wish.

This platform is supported by the World Wide Web Consortium, an international industry-supported consortium jointly hosted by three institutions: the Massachusetts Institute of Technology's Laboratory for Computer Science (MIT–LCS [Americas]); the National Institute for Research in Computer Science and Control (INRIA [Europe]); and Keio University Shonan Fujisawa Campus (Asia). All three hosts work together to form the "W3C Team," providing vendor-neutral leadership in the evolution of the Web.

At the minimum, before people buy on-line, they should check the privacy policy of the on-line merchant.

Source: Baig, Edward, Marcia Stepanek, and Neil Gross (1999), "Privacy," *Business Week,* April 5, pp. 84–90.

SECTION II: A BUSINESS PERSPECTIVE ON THE INTERNET

The Internet can be viewed either as an incremental or a radical innovation, depending upon its impact on a particular business or industry. When the Internet is used by a business to manage the flow of information internally—say, to improve an existing product in order to better serve an existing client base—it might be viewed as an incremental innovation. Alternatively, when the Internet is used to completely reinvent a business in terms of how it serves its customers, it would be viewed as a more disruptive, or radical, innovation.[19] This section of the chapter explores some of the ways in which the Internet is radically changing the face of many business industries, some of the reasons for that change, and some of the new ways of operating to be successful in a digital world. Charles Schwab Corporation's successful transition into on-line stock trading provides a case in point for many of the concepts.

Charles Schwab's Successful Foray into the World of On-line Brokering[20]

In 1995, the Charles Schwab Corporation developed an experimental application of Web-based stock trades to demonstrate how different computer systems could talk to one another. However, the unintended outcome of this demonstration was that the Schwab people viewing the demo instantly recognized the implications from a business perspective. Says Schwab, "I fell off my chair."[21] The company immediately put together an independent project team that worked in secrecy in a separate electronic unit, bypassing Schwab's normal hierarchy and reporting directly to one of the two co-CEOs. The reason that Schwab gave for using this type of skunkworks operation was that the group needed to feel unshackled from the larger bureaucracy and to react in a nimble way to a handful of deep-discount brokerages, such as E*Trade, that were also racing to perfect Web trading. The team describes the early days as intense, freewheeling meetings in which everyone could shout ideas back and forth. Another reason for e.Schwab's quarantine from the rest of the company: caution. Said Dan Leemon, head of strategy, "We created e.Schwab because we wanted to learn. But we did not want to risk the whole company."[22]

The upshot of this early development was that e.Schwab began trading in the middle of 1996 on a radically new basis. Rather than the usual sliding scale of commissions, customers paid only a flat fee for any stock trade. The initial volume of trades on this site catapulted e.Schwab to number one in the marketplace, at 10 times the assets of E*Trade. But the downside was that customers could not call regular branch offices for service (they had to address all questions via e-mail), and the dual-pricing structure for on-line versus assisted trades both confused and annoyed clients. One solution was to eliminate the dual-pricing structure; offer the low-priced, flat-fee trades for everyone; and allow clients to still use their brokers for questions. The resistance to this solution was high. Switching to one low on-line commission, which made up nearly half the company's revenues, would reduce revenues by $125 million, even allowing for the heavier trading volume the lower commission might induce. The negative impact on the firm's stock price would hit employees particularly hard, because they owned 40% of the stock.

Whereas many firms might try to adopt a hybrid business model to remedy this situation, Charles Schwab was quite aggressive. It realized that customers had indicated very clearly that Web trading was the cheapest, fastest way to meet their needs. Charles Schwab said, "This isn't that hard a decision, because we really have no choice. It's just a question of when, and it will be harder later."[23] So the radical solution Schwab implemented in 1997 was to integrate the electronic trades within the existing business structure.

This integration was easier said than done, of course. When one attempts to merge a fiercely independent technology-driven team into the rest of a large bureaucratic organization, resistance comes from multiple quarters. The tech team wanted a relaxed dress code, which created tension with the buttoned-down culture. The branch people thought the tech team was given preference in picking offices. Despite these concerns, the technology team was able to convey to the existing personnel that it had no interest in or intent to "bulldoze" the traditional bricks-and-mortar branches in favor of the Web.

In January 1998, Schwab stepped into its future. Both revenues and profits initially declined. Revenues dipped 3% in the first quarter, earnings were $6 million short of expectations, and stock prices fell 9% on the day of the earnings announcement. However, after the initial negative impact, the positive implications began to be felt. Schwab realized efficiencies from its Web-based trading. The number of trades Schwab handled per day doubled in two years, but the number of telephone calls stayed flat. So, the Web handled five times as many trades as the call centers. Switching business from the phones to the Web resulted in lower costs and productivity gains. The company refers to this improvement as the "Web dividend." Revenues and the stock price went up.

Shortly after going on-line with $39.95 trades, Schwab decided to lower its price. Under its former business model, Schwab would have advertised the low price commissions aggressively. However, the Web price cut (which went from $39.95 to $29.95 per trade) was not advertised. Under the new business model, people realized that focusing too heavily on price would implicate price as the most important factor in on-line trading, which might invite a price war. Although price did matter to the active traders who were the early adopters of Web trading, what makes on-line trading work is service. People care less about fast, cheap, and cool than about simple, reliable, and informative. The distribution of investment information, the ability to customize the homepage to see personal account information when a customer logs on, and an asset allocation model with automatic e-mails that alert customers when portfolios are not in balance are key features that drive Schwab's success. Additions of content sharing with retirement, mortgages, taxes, and insurance further cemented Schwab's position in the market.

How On-line Business Changes the Rules of the Game[24]

In addition to changing the dynamic between buyer and seller, based on customer control, the Internet is having other profound effects on business, as shown in Figure 11-2.

Traditional businesses are based in a brick-and-mortar world that has high fixed assets. Many are shackled with a corporate hierarchy, in which decision making and implementation can be slow and deliberate. Traditional businesses' return on investment is tied to the size of their margins on sales. They must show steadily increasing earnings growth, quarter to quarter, for favorable reviews from Wall Street. On-line businesses operate in a virtual world where fixed assets are fewer in nature. On-line businesses are far from hierarchical and can move very quickly. The Internet world does not tolerate caution or deliberation. Losing the first-mover advantage can be a liability that is never overcome. For example, Barnes & Noble was blindsided by Amazon.com. And despite its huge expenditures and massive advertising since its on-line debut, Barnes & Noble's on-line sales are barely more than one-tenth of Amazon.com's. On-line companies' return on investment is tied to total dollars taken in relative to the amount of capital needed. "If Amazon.com has 5% gross margin versus a 30% margin for a traditional book seller, both firms might have an equal return on investment."[25] In the Internet world of the past several years, companies have been rewarded for plowing every cent

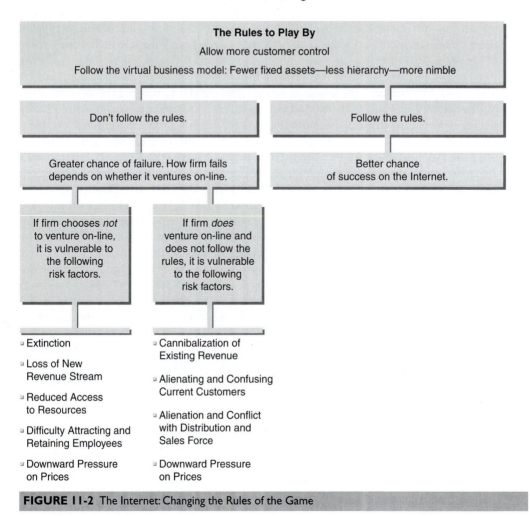

FIGURE 11-2 The Internet: Changing the Rules of the Game

into development, even if it meant huge losses. That model is coming under scrutiny, however.

Threats to Traditional Businesses from On-line Competitors

These new rules of the game pose serious threats for incumbents in established industries. As shown in Figure 11-2, the changing rules of the game, with fewer requirements for working capital, inherent speed and efficiency, and direct access to customers and suppliers, provide a radical new business model. Many of these threats were previously covered in Chapter 2 and are just quickly reiterated here.

Extinction   "Companies that don't move fast to get in on the game risk having their lunch eaten by tiny rivals who may have barely existed just a few years ago. In industry after industry, fledgling Net companies have transformed the way business is done and snatched market share from their much bigger, established rivals."[26]

Loss of a Potential New Revenue Stream   The Net is a huge part of the economy. From 1995 to 1998, the Internet economy grew at an astonishing annual 174.5% rate. At $300 billion in 1999, that rivals sectors such as telecommunications and autos.[27]

Reduced Access to Resources   Net-based initial public offerings (IPOs) are restructuring the corporate landscape. Sixty-six Internet companies raised $5.5 billion in the first six months of 1999, or 25% of the total dollars raised by U.S. public offerings (versus 6% of the total raised by all IPOs in 1998). In June 1999, the average price/earnings ratio of the stocks on the Goldman Sachs Internet index (GIN) was 674 versus 34 by the S&P 500.[28] Although the devaluation of tech stocks in early 2000 modified this situation somewhat, the reality is that the disparity between pumped-up valuations of Net stocks and valuations of more traditional stocks allows Net businesses to buy rivals with real-world assets, making Net companies a threat to more established players.[29] For example, Monster.com (an on-line job search resource) consolidated its foray into head-hunting by buying LAI Worldwide Inc. and is becoming a serious competitor of established rivals such as Korn/Ferry.

Difficulty in Attracting and Retaining Talented Employees   The ability to offer stocks and big options gains gives Internet-based companies an advantage in hiring. Good employees are the heart of any company's ability to prosper. But traditional companies are losing key players to the lucrative world of the Internet. Indeed, some executives are leaving traditional companies simply in order to survive. They see the handwriting on the wall and realize that the Net transformation of the economy is the growth industry of the future.

Cannibalization of a Company's Revenue Stream   Going on-line requires that companies be willing to **cannibalize** their own core franchise. The Charles Schwab example highlights the fact that the initial impact of moving to an on-line environment was a decrease in revenues, earnings, and stock prices.

Alienating and Confusing Current Customers   The Charles Schwab example demonstrated that when on-line customers are treated differently than other customers are, neither group is particularly happy. On-line customers liked the prices of their trades but resented the limits on customer service. Regular brokerage customers liked the service but not the higher commissions. Lessons in *crossing the chasm* from Chapter 6 indicate that a company's best customers are typically the last to embrace a disruptive technology because it doesn't provide the service and performance they prefer. The people who embrace the new technology first are the ones a company typically pays least attention to. This situation makes an established company particularly vulnerable to being blindsided by the innovation.[30]

Alienation and Conflict with the Company's Distribution Channel and Sales Force
Cutting out channel intermediaries, or **disintermediation,** allows companies potentially to reach buyers faster and cheaper. This has happened most extensively to date in the travel industry, in which airlines are bypassing travel agents entirely and allowing customers to buy their tickets directly from the airlines' Web sites. Although customers have always been able to buy directly from the airlines, the Web now makes this so convenient for customers, and so efficient for airlines, that it is radically changing the role of the travel agent. Airlines have taken advantage of the situation by cutting travel agent commissions, because agents have less power in the channel than they used to. The impact of the Internet on distribution relationships was covered in Chapter 8. Box 11-4 offers additional insight regarding possible benefits of adding an on-line channel.

BOX 11-4

Possible Benefits in Adding an On-line Channel

Taking advantage of the potential efficiencies arising from disintermediation can mean going into direct competition with the company's own sales force or its distributors. The potential intractability and severity of consequences that can arise from this risk lead some Internet experts to identify conflict with existing sales channels as the single biggest impediment to selling on-line. Many firms believe that it is hard to justify such conflict when the current revenues to be gained through electronic commerce may represent only a small portion of overall revenues.[a]

A flip-side perspective on this issue comes from examining the extent to which demand goes unfulfilled by traditional channels.[b] For example, when Peapod groceries began accepting on-line orders and filling them in traditional retail stores for customer delivery, it found that out of stocks were three to four times more prevalent than grocery executives realized. Macy's Internet presence has extended its brand to shoppers it wasn't reaching in its stores.[c]

In addition, addressing the issue of conflict with existing channels entails recognizing the reality that not all customers are going to do all their buying on-line (but few will do all their buying off-line either). The development of hybrid (brick-and-click) models, as described in Chapter 8, will likely capture the best of both worlds. Some companies, such as Gap, for example, have done so, and are capitalizing on the potential synergies that such a model can offer.[d]

---

[a] Hof, Robert (1998), "The Click Here Economy," *Business Week,* June 22, pp. 122–128.

[b] Hamel, Gary and Jeff Sampler (1998), "The e-Corporation," *Fortune,* December 7, pp. 80–92.

[c] Neuborne, Ellen and Robert Hof (1998), "Branding on the Net," *Business Week,* November 9.

[d] Hamel, Gary and Jeff Sampler (1998), "The e-Corporation," *Fortune,* December 7, pp. 80–92; Lee, Louise (1999), "'Clicks and Mortar' at Gap.com," *Business Week,* October 18, pp. 150–152.

Downward Pressure on Prices   A final threat to established businesses from the Internet comes in the pricing arena. The most common thinking regarding the impact of the Internet on pricing strategy is that electronic commerce is killing prices.[31] Many goods and services are cheaper on the Web than off it. It's cheaper to buy and sell stocks, books, and computer equipment, to name a few.

However, others believe that on-line prices are not lower than their real-world counterparts.[32] Many manufacturers won't let cybersellers undercut their retailers. Similarly, many retailers with e-commerce sites don't want to undercut store prices. A study in 1998 found that only 12% of electronic merchants offered lower prices on the Web than off-line.[33] And shipping costs typically ate away much of the savings.[34] So, although the Web may offer shoppers convenience and selection, the price advantage is less certain.

Some believe that the downward pressure on prices is overstated. For example, although the current effect is that buyers are using the Internet to widen their choices—and an increase in supply invariably has a negative effect on price—the future impact may be quite different. Some predict that the Internet will bring along a new wave of dynamic pricing models. In an electronic world, merchants will know what the hot items are and will be able to raise their prices more quickly. Already, the airlines use sophisticated algorithms to maximize profitability of their various routes by adjusting seat prices. Moreover, by studying a customer's cookie clickstream, or the way a person navigates through the Web, companies can easily use price discrimination. For example, Amazon.com can follow every move a surfer makes on its site using software called Personify. This means that if a surfer browses the site casually, he or she may be offered lower prices. Alternatively, if one searches specifically for books on, say, yachting, golf, and personal investment, one may not get as great a deal. Finally, some customers can be invited to become "preferred customers," and given special log-ins and a discount when they check out. Or e-mails could be sent to targeted customers with hyperlinks to special sites where prices are lower or shipping is free.[35] (Recall that the pricing chapter—Chapter 9—addressed other ways firms can overcome the downward pressure on prices.[36])

Even if prices do continue to fall on-line, the efficiencies to be gained in on-line commerce may allow merchants to maintain or even increase profit margins. Many believe that these efficiencies are the basis of the New Economy described in Chapter 1. Over time, however, the Internet may turn out to be more of a price leveler than a price cutter.[37] Economic theory predicts that improving the flow of market information tends to make prices converge. Hence, airline customers may, over time, be more likely to narrow the gap between seat prices found on the same flight. By the same logic, the markup that many businesses enjoy outside their home markets may also be leveled. However, for this logic to hold, more sales will need to come from a non-U.S. base.

Coping with Threats Through Organizational Structure and Reintermediation

For each of the threats discussed in the prior section, the reality is that if an established company chooses not to serve either existing or potential customers in ways that provide superior value, then competitors surely will. This is the nature of *creative destruction:* the willingness constantly to reinvent one's business in order to utilize the benefits of new technology, despite the sunk investments in prior business models. If an established company isn't willing to cannibalize its existing business, then it will lose sales to other competitors. This is one reason why some companies such as CompUSA and Staples are not overly worried about cannibalization. On the other hand, Compaq's and Merrill Lynch's concerns about cannibalization and conflict have meant that they've ultimately lost sales to on-line competitors.

On this basis, this section of the chapter continues with different issues in coping with these threats. First, the organizational structure of an on-line unit relative to the existing organizational structure must be carefully considered. Second, with the new opportunities for doing business on the Web, people can find their jobs changed in a fairly radical fashion—possibly even eliminated. Probably those most directly affected are traditional distributors and retailers.

Organization   How should an on-line unit be integrated within an established company? Some argue that a completely *separate entity* allows the on-line unit the ability to capitalize on the huge stock advantages available with Internet offerings. This allows a firm to offer employees the best options, investors the highest return, and capitalization of the new start-up. One expert[38] believes that there must be a completely independent organization that is allowed to flourish and even attack the parent. Having a separate organization allows the parent to maintain a primary focus on an existing client base that may be uncomfortable with the Internet, while not burdening the Internet business with serving those customers. The reality is that the new unit will have to compete against other firms without those types of customers and should be given free rein.

Other companies believe that separating the on-line unit from the rest of the company is not advantageous. Rather, *integrating the Net unit* within a firm's existing structure allows for synergies between the on-line business and the firm's core business. For example, Microsoft has kept its MSN portal in-house. And Sabre, American Airlines' on-line reservation system, has kept Travelocity.com in-house also.

These two views (separate or integrated) are consistent with the information presented in Chapter 2 about incubators and skunkworks. Charles Schwab's situation shows the potential advantages of using a skunkworks-type operation initially. The original unit worked in secrecy and bypassed Schwab's normal hierarchy. These decisions unshackled the unit from the larger bureaucracy and allowed it to act in a nimble fashion. Once it was clear that the unit needed to be more a part of the existing organizational structure and that the very nature of Schwab's core business would be changing, the group was integrated.

Yet another *middle-ground approach* can be found in companies that hold a minority interest in on-line ventures, with the option to increase stakes later on, depending on the venture's success. For example, Fingerhut, an expert in database marketing, has a 20% stake in several on-line companies. This organizational strategy allows the firm to operate fairly independently, with the advantages such independence offers, but allows the stakeholder future options.

The Changing Role of the Intermediary   Traditional value-added activities of distributors included aggregating information (e.g., the names of buyers/sellers, product specifications, knowledge of supply and demand), assuming quality and credit risk for both buyer and seller, aggregating inventory, and assuring prompt delivery. Now, the Internet allows the manufacturer to do all three activities without distributors.[39] So the Net challenges intermediaries, such as travel agents, insurance brokers, real estate agents, and retailers, to consider carefully how they add value to the customer. One travel agent referred to e-commerce as "a two-by-four hitting [us] over the head, getting our attention, and making us do things differently."[40] Similarly, "Any dealer is dead if his only claim to a share of the money in the value chain is a window in front and a warehouse out back. The Web gives the manufacturer a window in the customer's home."[41] In essence, e-commerce will devalue a lot of what intermediaries were paid for. What are some of their coping strategies?

- *Do nothing.*   Despite the powerful force for change, not all intermediaries are trying to figure out how to change their role in a Net-based world. Some stores will still focus on individualized customer attention and intimate knowledge of products. For example, a children's bookstore in suburban Detroit, Reading in the Park, knows the Net is cutting into its business, but doesn't choose to participate in that kind of a depersonalized environment.
- *Reinvention.*   Others will try to reinvent themselves. For traditional intermediaries to compete, they will likely consolidate and offer improved services of their own. For example, in a digital world, it will be more cost effective to send cars to homes for a

test-drive than to have three hundred cars sitting in a car lot in Des Moines, Iowa. And resellers may have an advantage on-line, because manufacturers' sites often do not offer a complete solution that includes products from competing vendors.

- *New types of intermediaries.* While some intermediaries are being disintermediated, the Internet has created, or *reintermediated* with, a whole new class of **cybermediaries.**[42] These new players are needed because the unintermediated Internet is as unwieldy and inefficient as a marketplace without retailers. Digital intermediaries function as brokers, helping people gather and decipher the vast quantity of information on the Web, bringing together buyers and sellers, and providing value by offering trusted advice, personal service, or other benefits. Infomediaries typically claim allegiance to the buyer, instead of the producer.[43] The greatest opportunities for new intermediaries may be those in which information is the product. For example, FastParts.com links buyers and sellers of surplus electronic parts. The change is likely to be particularly intensified in industries whose products are commodities that don't need to be tried on, tested, tasted, or touched.

As more people go on-line and a new generation who grew up with the Net comes of age, it may be hard for intermediaries to ignore the digital world. For intermediaries to survive, they will have to reinvent themselves, too. "If you're not part of the rubber, you're the road" (in other words, you'll get run over).

SECTION III: OTHER BUSINESS FUNCTIONS PERFORMED USING THE INTERNET

In addition to generating revenues with on-line transactions (both B-to-C and B-to-B), a business can use the Internet to enhance its operations in many other ways. For example, establishing links with suppliers, factories, distributors, and customers to automate time-consuming, tedious tasks is a function ideally suited to the Internet. Some ways in which a firm can use the Web to manage its business are explored in this section and shown in Figure 11-3. These uses of the Web are not mutually exclusive and do have some degree of overlap.

Streamline Supply Chain Management

Many companies are using the Internet as a way to manage their supply chain, or the flow of products from suppliers to the factory and, ultimately, to channel intermediaries and customers. This allows a company to track sales on a timely basis, get instant feedback from customers, keep inventories to a minimum, and simplify complex, costly transactions. E-commerce is making huge changes in the supply chain, facilitated by powerful software tools that automate the flow of information. These software programs sharpen a company's view of parts and products moving through the supply chain so it can better grasp what stocks are available and how demand may be shifting. In a fast-changing market, profits depend on accurate predictions.[44] For example, by streamlining inefficient buying processes, Adaptec, a computer storage products firm, has used the Internet to speed up communications with its Taiwanese chip suppliers and improved profitability. It has reduced its time from order to delivery by more than half, and saved $1 million in costs.[45]

The sharing of information over the Internet with selected business partners via authorized access turns the Internet into an **extranet.** Extranets allow suppliers, distributors,

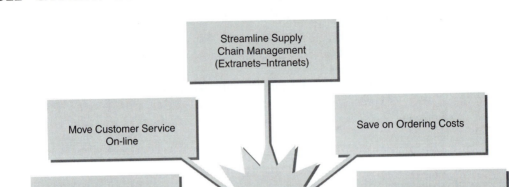

FIGURE 11-3 Business Functions (in Addition to On-line Selling) on the Web

and customers the ability to view company data on a restricted secure basis.[46] One important issue in extranets is the potential security risk. Many companies hooking partners into an extranet specify the types of routers, firewalls, and security procedures each partner must employ to safeguard the extranet connection before turning it on.[47]

One example of a company realizing supply chain efficiencies on the Internet is Dell. Dell Computer has always relied on a direct-to-customer sales model, but the real advantage with on-line sales has come from supply chain efficiencies. Messages are sent out every two hours over the Internet to manage the supply chain. Suppliers are given access to internal inventory levels and manufacturing plans, and are given explicit feedback on their performance. Hence, Dell's speed in customizing and delivering products remains unmatched in the industry. For example, Dell's on-hand inventory is 8 days, compared to Compaq's 26 days.[48] By letting the Web take care of tedious, repetitive tasks, employees can focus more on customer needs.[49] Although other competitors have tried to copy Dell's business model, they've been unable to duplicate Dell's supply chain and distribution efficiencies. Competitors have either been unwilling or unable to overhaul their business process, and given that they still rely heavily on dealers, their on-line personal computer prices continue to be higher than Dell's.

The Technology Expert's View from the Trenches is provided by Chris Couture, vice president and chief information officer of Dell Computer.

TECHNOLOGY EXPERT'S VIEW FROM THE TRENCHES

Developing an E-Business Strategy

CHRIS COUTURE
Vice President and Chief Information Officer, Dell Computer,
Round Rock, Texas

In developing an e-business strategy, companies must first define their strategic objective for creating an Internet presence. In today's highly competitive business world, where direct interactions with the customer are rewarded and middlemen find it harder and harder to define their value proposition, "the Internet could be considered the ultimate extension of a direct business approach."[a] It is the ability to leverage the Internet in order to conduct business directly with customers and suppliers that will separate the average company from the truly exceptional company.

In order to implement an e-business strategy, companies may choose one of three primary courses of action:

- Incremental changes in their current business model
- Replacement of their current business model
- Innovation/incubation of a completely new business model

Those companies who choose an *incremental strategy* will take the best parts of their current business and simply "Internet enable" them in order to take advantage of new opportunities. This is the lowest risk approach to developing an e-business model and allows a company to leverage its existing strengths in order to take advantage of new Internet opportu-

nities. The downside is that it may take companies a long time to migrate their traditional business to the Web as they are forced to migrate old business rules as well. Additionally, companies may have a business model that does not necessarily lend itself to the transition to an e-business model. These two issues offset the low risk of an incremental business strategy with potential low rewards.

With a *replacement strategy,* companies decide to throw away their current business model in favor of a completely new one. This strategy is extremely high risk and can be presumed to fail in all but a very few circumstances. Companies that abandon their existing business structures may also abandon their existing customers. Customers have different speeds at which they are willing and able to adjust to a new way of doing business. A complete replacement strategy, without a migration path for existing customers, will open up a huge window of opportunity for the competition to gain market share.

The last e-business strategy is referred to as *innovation or incubation.* This occurs when a completely new Internet-enabled business opportunity is discovered, and a company allows a team of innovators to develop and pursue the opportunity without being encumbered by existing business rules and thought processes. This methodology allows businesses to develop breakthrough products and services that can take advantage of all that the Internet has to offer, while still maintaining the existing business structure in order to serve the current set of customers. A company that follows this methodology can attract new customers to its new e-business model, while giving current customers a migration path from the traditional model to the new.

Regardless of which e-business strategy (incremental, replacement, or incubation) that a company chooses, there are really only three key success factors:

- Velocity
- Efficiency
- Customer experience

Velocity simply means reducing both the time and distance between a business and its customers and suppliers. In the case of supply chain management, allowing a company's suppliers instant access to inventory levels, without having to physically visit a warehouse, will dramatically aid in the supplier's ability to meet demand in an accurate and timely manner. Old business thinking meant that companies would protect their internal business data. E-business thinking requires companies to open up their vaults of corporate data and share it with customers and suppliers in order to make everyone in the value chain more effective.

In an e-business world, *efficiency* is more than internal cost savings to a company. It means finding ways to make it easier and more cost-effective for your customers to do business, which in turn translates into internal cost savings for the company. For example, in the case of a typical procurement function, purchase orders are filled out and sent to a supplier. The supplier then enters these purchase orders into its fulfillment system. Companies that leverage the Internet are able to offer direct links that identify a customer's standards and specific pricing, allow customers to build their own quote, automate the purchase approval process, and submit a paperless purchase order. By focusing on the customers to eliminate the expense of purchase order processes on their end, the supplier is able to eliminate the expense of an order-processing step on its end.

The final success factor of an e-business, *customer experience,* is the most important. The Internet allows consumers to comparison shop between many different companies in a matter of seconds. This has had the effect of turning many products and services into simple commodities. Ultimately then, the success of any e-business is based on its ability to retain its customer base and ensure repeat business. The creation of an experience that is unique and customized for each customer is the differentiator between those e-business models that will survive and those that will fail. Quality of customer service (62%) is three times more important to repeat online sales than the price of the product (19%).[b] Those companies who are focused on mass customer segments, and compete on products and prices offered, will be most vulnerable to the competition. Those e-businesses that offer customers personalized access to their own account information can make the Internet site better for the customer with each visit and can personalize services to every customer. These are the companies that will be around for the long-term and will be the true leaders of the Internet economy.

[a] Dell Computer Corporation CEO Michael Dell (1997), *Austin-American Statesman,* February 26.

[b] Hanrahan, Timothy (1999), "Price Isn't Everything," *Wall Street Journal,* July 12, p. R20.

Save on Ordering Costs

Some companies are saving on costs by consolidating corporate purchases in one centralized area. By doing so, they are able to get better deals from suppliers. For example, General Electric bought $1 billion worth of supplies on the Net in 1997 and saved 20% on its costs.[50] Boeing booked on-line $100 million in orders from airlines for spare parts in 1997. National Semiconductor has distributors order products on-line, which saved it $20 million.

An earlier generation of technology used to automate business ordering was electronic data interchange (EDI). However, to implement EDI in business relationships required proprietary systems between business partners, which, while secure, can be expensive to set up and inflexible in their use and number of users. Moreover, using EDI is slower in that the technology is not oriented toward a fast, build-to-order production model.

In 1998, the number of EDI transactions was 14 times larger than Internet transactions; however, given the benefits of using extranets to automate ordering systems, the ratio of EDI to Internet transactions is expected to be 50–50 by the year 2003. It is predicted that beyond 2003, the number of Internet-based ordering transactions will be greater than those using EDI.[51] This change will be stimulated by improvements in **HTML** (hypertext markup language, which is the software language used to develop Web sites). Called **XML** (extensible markup language), the improvements will allow users to compare products and services more easily by standardizing what data on a Web page mean. For example, when XML sees $3.99, it will recognize such data as a price.

One use of the Internet to save on ordering costs is to set up connections with prequalified vendors, from whom employees can order supplies within specified jurisdictions. GE Information Systems has set up such a system called Trading Partner Network Register to order office supplies. Gary M. Reiner, GE's chief information officer, estimates that office supply orders off-line cost between $50 and $200 each to process, because of all the paperwork, whereas on-line purchases cost only about $1 apiece to process. Some manufacturers are customizing Web pages for retailers to feed data to their manufacturers.

Another use of the Internet to save on ordering costs is to use a reverse auction, or a process in which suppliers bid to be the supplier of choice for a customer's business. For example, rather than spending hours calling construction outfits in a bidding process that would take days to complete, Herman Ricker, an assistant contract manager at Norfolk Southern Railway, solicits bids on a reverse auction site, RailNet-USA.com, a Web site set up exclusively for rail contractors. According to Ricker, this yields more competitive bids and frees up his time for other projects.[52]

Using the Web in this fashion offers a virtually unlimited number of users, is not as costly to set up as EDI, and the potential cost savings are greater. It allows automated programs to interpret communication between manufacturers and suppliers, to assess accurately what parts are available across many suppliers at what price. Using the Internet to automate such ordering procedures is cheap and based on open standards. Hence, the Internet makes electronic ordering available to even small companies.

These changes in supply chain management and order routines are blurring the roles between suppliers, manufacturers, distributors, and retailers, changes that can create tension. In the extreme, software that forecasts and mediates supply and demand can cause problems in traditional supply chain relationships. The use of on-line auctions, for example, makes it difficult to rely on long-term customer relationships and puts the focus instead on short-term price advantages as the basis for doing business.[53]

Speed Product Development

Some companies are using the Web as a corporate **intranet** to speedily distribute information among internal departments. Intranets have secure firewalls so that only authorized users have access to the information.[54] For example, the Ford Motor Company uses its corporate intranet to share strategic information about product designs. Its intranet connects 120,000 computers around the world, letting engineers, designers, and suppliers carefully document and share in real time the thousands of steps in product development, including testing and design. Sharing such information has helped Ford reduce the time it takes to turn new car models into full products from about 36 months to 24 months.[55]

A corporate intranet can enhance organizational effectiveness when[56]

- Senior managers are committed to it, they communicate its importance very clearly, and they provide sufficient investments to maximize its functionality.
- The intranet is designed around ways to make employees do their jobs better.
- It is based on up-to-date information and is indexed accurately.

Get Feedback from Customers

In addition to taking orders from customers, the Internet can be used to solicit input from customers. The Internet is being used to collect marketing research, get more rapid feedback, both solicited and unsolicited, and in the process, improve marketing strategy.

On-line Recruiting

Some companies are finding that using the Web as a recruiting tool is improving both the effectiveness and efficiency of their recruiting efforts. For example, Sun Microsystems uses its corporate intranet to solicit referrals for possible applicants from current employees. It uses an on-line matchmaker on its Web site, which e-mails prospects about jobs that match their skills and interests. Moreover, by using ads on strategic sites on the Internet that engineers are likely to visit, Sun is getting a more measurable response than from traditional classified ads.

Reach International Markets[57]

Another way the Internet is being used is to make goods available to customers that a company couldn't otherwise reach. For example, Neoforma Inc. (Santa Clara, California), a medical-supplies distributor, has used its Web site to reach the government of Oman.

Coordinate Finance[58]

Financial data that once took weeks to gather and verify can now be collected automatically as part of doing business. This allows a company to stay in tight control, shorten the time needed to close books at the end of each quarter, and cut spending on finance. Transparency between the financial aspects of a business and its marketing data allows people to make decisions quickly and in a responsive manner to the marketplace.

Improve Business Relationships

Companies are also using the Web to improve the flow of information with business partners. For example, Prudential Healthcare uses the Web to link to corporate networks of large subscribers, allowing new employees to enroll themselves. This saves paperwork and customer service staffers.

Extranets can also be used to forge better links among business partners, allowing collaboration on product design, and sharing business data. For example, Hewlett-Packard and Procter & Gamble both use the Web to link to their advertising agencies, swapping marketing plans and reviewing ad campaigns.

Move Customer Service On-line

Companies are using the Web to automate existing customer service routines that are currently handled in an off-line manner. For example, many companies are using the Internet to answer customer questions in a timely, cost-efficient manner. E-service savings can be huge: Web service costs companies just $.04 per customer on average for a simple Web page query versus $1.44 per live phone call. Shifting service to the Net lets companies handle up to one-third more service inquiries at 43% the cost.[59] Companies using the Internet for customer service can see cost savings of 30% or more.[60]

Businesses operating on the Net handle 13% of their customer inquiries electronically.[61] For example, Cisco Systems booked $4 billion on the Web in 1998. It saves $363 million in technical support, marketing, and distribution costs, one-third of which is saved by hiring fewer people to assist customers.[62] Indeed, the most progressive companies using the Internet for customer service are using it proactively, to communicate with customers about potential problems even before they arise.[63] For example, Federal Express used its Web site to deliver news to 30,000 customers about the implications of a possible pilot strike, allaying concerns before they even arose.

The ultimate money saver, though, is automating service so thoroughly that few reps are needed at all. For example, using software from Motive Communications Inc., companies such as Dell can take a digital snapshot of a customer's troubled computer system, pinpoint the problem, and send repairs over the Web—all without human intervention. Wells Fargo has found that its 450,000 customers with electronic accounts place 40% fewer calls to the bank than do other customers.

The third perspective in the triangle of Internet perspectives comes from on-line sites that host content in some manner—the search engines, portals, and communities of the on-line world.

SECTION IV: CONTENT SITES

Content sites provide information to customers in some fashion. Many cybermediaries function as **portals,** consumer magnets that draw buyers or direct them to manufacturers and service providers. General portals such as Yahoo!, America Online, Lycos, and Netscape provide the browser with entrance onto the Net. Specialty portals do the same, but are based on some underlying interest base or on customized screens customers can set up. On-line communities (e.g., BabyCenter.com) exist to link people with common interests. Vertical hubs and other e-marketplaces are a type of on-line community that facilitates business-to-business transactions.

These digital sites gather a critical mass of people, which is both very attractive to advertisers and makes the site self-renewing: People continue to come because that's where the action is. Ad revenues among the top 10 sites expanded from 64% in 1998 to 75% in 1999.[64] Given this drawing power, some predict that these types of sites will soon extract even more revenue from advertisers and sponsors. The two types of content sites explored in this chapter are on-line communities and electronic marketplaces, portals for business-to-business e-commerce.

On-line Communities[65]

Internet communities are sites that people migrate to because of common interests and common concerns. At these content sites, people can join chats, find useful information that meets their needs, and participate in a comfortable and reassuring setting. Sites such as Tripod, GeoCities, Parent Soup, and iVillage are popular consumer communities. Such communities are also an important part of the B-to-B world. Sites such as @griculture and the Electronic Coffee Shop offer visitors technical insights necessary for their respective professions.

On-line communities have become more popular over the years because the on-line population, more and more, is mirroring the mass population. From a surfer's perspective, on-line communities offer both useful information and an emotional connection, which sometimes is lacking in an increasingly depersonalized world.

From a marketer's perspective, on-line communities are attractive for several reasons. First, visitors to well-established communities tend to stay at the site much longer than at other sites. This allows more time for viewing of ad messages. In addition, members of Net neighborhoods tend to spend a greater amount of money at the site than do nonmembers. Although on-line communities are important to marketers, they must respect the nature of the community, which tends to be averse to crass commercialism. For example, stick a Coca-Cola ad in a chat room and participants will quickly start *flaming* Coke, or sending angry, emotional e-mail in response to violation of Netiquette. On-line communities can also help marketers build stronger brands.[66] The best communities take advantage of interactivity to help the members feel connected and committed to the site.

Hubs for Business-to-Business Electronic Commerce

Electronic marketplaces are portals for business-to-business e-commerce. These communities are being created as B-to-B transactions make a paradigm shift from a traditional business environment to an Internet environment. These new e-business models are referred to as hubs or communities because they gather a critical mass of buyers and sellers to form a global Internet presence for conducting business transactions. The Gartner Group estimates growth from 500 hubs today to nearly 7,500 by the year 2002. Ninety-five percent of the hubs will be vertical, industry-specific sites.

These electronic marketplaces are the real engines behind B-to-B e-commerce.[67] The Precursor Group estimates a $50 billion to $100 billion transaction value will flow through these hubs. The Gartner Group also estimates 80% of the Global 1,000 companies will participate in hubs by 2002. They expand the choices available to buyers, give sellers access to new customers, and reduce transaction costs for all the players. By extracting fees for the transactions occurring within the B-to-B marketplaces, these hubs can earn vast revenues. Unlike consumer commerce ventures, B-to-B hubs tend to be two-way networks that mediate between buyers and sellers, and create value for both sides. Synergy is the greatest benefit of these communities. Links to individual Web sites deplete the e-marketplace or portal by sending Internet users to other places. In addition, the cost of maintaining individual Web sites and reinventing the wheel for various solutions is costly. If all the industry players need the solution, providing it in one place creates synergy. Such synergies are the reason that predictions for the on-line auto exchange (run by General Motors, Ford, and DaimlerChrysler) include the possibility of efficiencies equal to 25% of the retail price of the car, savings to Ford alone of $8 billion in procurement prices and nearly $1 billion more from reduced overhead, paperwork, and other transaction efficiencies.[68]

Two types of hubs are vertical hubs and horizontal hubs. Industry-specific or *vertical hubs,* such as PlasticsNet.com, e-Steel, and PaperExchange.com, offer industry-specific solutions. For example, Verticalnet.com hosts on-line marketplaces for a wide array of industries. Vertical communities provide e-business solutions ranging from auctions, e-commerce, document sharing, document creation, bill presentment, tracking, contract negotiations, credit services, and so forth. They use e-business solutions along the value chain to integrate the suppliers, customers, manufacturers, and competitors through strategic partnerships. Box 11-5 provides a more detailed look at vertical hubs. *Horizontal* or functional hubs are focused on operating inputs, such as maintenance, repair, and operating goods (e.g., office supplies) that are needed across multiple industries; examples include MRO.com, iMark.com (for used capital equipment), and Employease.com.

The popularity of electronic marketplaces is based on their ability to offer efficiencies to buyers. These efficiencies arise not only in *transaction costs* savings (e.g., from automating orders, payments, and product information, and eliminating the myriad faxes and invoices that conventional purchases generate), but also in their ability to cut *purchase prices* through on-line auctions. For the parts one buyer bought recently in five auctions, it estimated it would have had to pay $6.8 million using the traditional RFQ (request for quote) system. However, when the auctions were over, it paid just $4.6 million.

Unlike traditional purchasing, in which an RFQ is sent to various suppliers, who in turn submit (typically closed) bids, from which the buyer selects one, an on-line auction turns the RFQ process into open bidding. As an example, on-line auctions at FreeMarkets.com are run for a set time period, typically between 20 and 30 minutes. Based on a Dutch reverse auction model, the price starts high and moves downward; sellers can see competitors' bids in real time. In a recent auction, twenty-five suppliers participated; the client started with most recent price paid, $745,000, as a benchmark. At the opening, the lowest supplier bid was $738,000. Then, just 10 minutes into the auction, a rapid sequence of bids sent the low bid to $612,000, where it plateaued for a brief period. Then, just before the official 20-minute deadline, another frenzy of bids sent the low bid to $585,000. Finally, after 13 minutes of overtime bidding (each bid that comes during the last minute of the regular auction extends it into a minute of overtime; each overtime bid extends it 60 seconds more), the final bid was $518,000, which gave the buyer a savings of 31%.[69]

Many electronic marketplaces are maintained by an independent, *neutral* infomediary, who hosts the Web site and collects a transaction fee from each transaction consummated on the site. These infomediaries provide the infrastructure and solutions, sponsor relevant content for the industry or function, and host e-business solutions such as an e-marketplace.

Other electronic marketplaces are run not by a neutral infomediary but by buyer groups or seller groups. Those run by sellers work forward in the supply chain to negotiate with buyers, as in the case of TradeOut.com, which hosts auctions for buyers. Those

BOX 11-5

Vertical Hubs

BRUMBY McLEOD, MBA, University of Montana,
President, e-railroad, Inc.

THE CHEMICAL INDUSTRY

Four e-marketplaces in the chemical industry are Chemconnect.com, Chemdex.com, Chematch.com, and E-Chemicals. Their strategies are diverse, but their purpose is to gain a share of the chemical industry market. The chemical industry is a multi-trillion-dollar industry. More specifically, the petrochemical industry is a $1.3 trillion industry. Forrester Research predicts e-commerce within the U.S. petrochemical industry will jump from $4.7 billion in 1998 to $178.3 billion in 2003. The purchases are made in bulk and average around $200,000 per transaction.

One of these hubs, Chemconnect.com, was founded in 1995. It is a global chemical and plastics exchange for chemical and plastic manufacturers. Their exchange is called the World Chemical Exchange. The exchange allows buyers to make product requests, and it allows suppliers to make product offerings. The technology links the offering and requests via online accounts that are managed like e-mail accounts summarizing bids and offers from other members. Buyers have two methods of buying: a search of offers and a product request. Sellers have two options also: a search of product requests and a product offering. The largest transaction as of December 3, 1999, was $3,660,000, and the average transaction is around $194,638. The hub earns a percentage of each transaction and charges membership fees for participating in the e-marketplace.

Chematch.com is a direct competitor of Chemconnect.com. It provides an exchange for the buying and selling of bulk commodity chemicals, plastics, and fuel products. It recently merged with PetroChem.net, a professional community for the petrochemical industry. PetroChem.net had over 7,600 users prior to the merger. Chematch.com "promises to redefine the way the chemical industry conducts business" with this merger.

VERTICALNET.COM

VerticalNet.com is a company whose strategy is to create a multitude of vertical infomediaries or industry portals. It holds a portfolio of over 41 vertical communities from 10 different industries, including advanced technologies, communications, environmental, food and packaging, food service/hospitality, healthcare industries, manufacturing and metals, process, science, and service. These 10 different industries have been further subdivided. For example, the communications industry is divided into digital broadcasting, fiber optics, photonics, and wireless.

VerticalNet acts as an industry portal for relevant electronic storefronts. One example of an online infomediary owned by VerticalNet is www.solidwasteonline.com. It provides news stories, product reviews and recommendations, and access to storefronts from hundreds of vendors.

The streamlining of purchasing and ordering routines requires seamless integration of the various players' technology infrastructures. For example, the integration between the hub and the supplier's back-office operations, the interface with the customers' front-office ordering systems, and the ability to integrate software applications, including accounting and finance, is key. *Enterprise resource planning (ERP) software* is used to achieve this integration. The need for such integration makes hubs costly to create—the e-commerce application itself runs nearly $500,000.

run by buyers, such as the auto exchange network run by the Big Three automakers, work backward in the supply chain to negotiate with suppliers.

When hubs are biased in favor of buyers or sellers, they can raise concerns over violations of antitrust policy. For example, because first mover advantages in exchanges are strong, those hubs that achieve scale first will take on monopoly-like economic power. The Federal Trade Commission's concern is that the exchanges could deter competition by controlling pricing.[70] Moreover, issues about coercion and free trade arise.[71] For example, what if the Big Three automakers refused to do business with suppliers that did not use their marketplace? Even if they didn't demand that they do so, would any supplier risk not going to the Big Three site?

Electronic marketplaces clearly offer much promise in the B-to-B realm. However, a critical concern is the *long-term impact on buyer-supplier relationships*. To what extent will the use of auction market-making mechanisms undermine such relationships? Even more seriously, will on-line auctions squeeze vendors to the breaking point? Squeezing out inefficiencies is one thing; cost-shifting to smaller members of the supply chain is another. The long-term impact on suppliers remains to be seen.

SECTION V: KEYS TO SUCCESS IN AN ON-LINE WORLD

If a firm is to be successful with a business model on the Internet, several critical factors come into play, as shown in Figure 11-4. This is true for both content providers and portals, as well as businesses selling products on the Web.

Create a Well-Designed, Effective Web Site

First and foremost, for success in the on-line world, a company must have an effective site that provides the right information and is easy to navigate. For example, Amazon.com

FIGURE 11-4 Steps to On-line Success

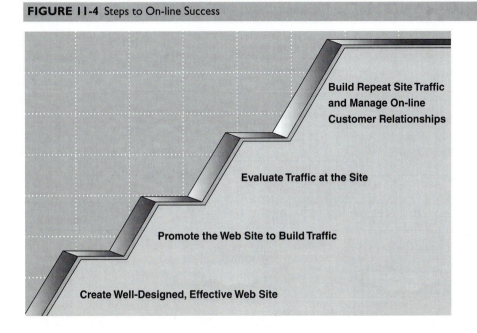

Build Repeat Site Traffic and Manage On-line Customer Relationships

Evaluate Traffic at the Site

Promote the Web Site to Build Traffic

Create Well-Designed, Effective Web Site

built its site with the visitor experience in mind. Although its site characteristics—such as wide selection, easy-to-navigate features, use of e-mail, and recommendations—are easily copied, Amazon's ability to identify novel ways to deal with customers and leapfrog its competitors is how it succeeds.[72] For example, by asking customers what they want, sorting through purchase histories to identify customer preferences, conducting focus groups, and collecting information in ways that don't impose on customers, it is convincingly able to offer customer care as its defining value.

Martin Roth offers the four Cs for designing effective Web sites, shown in Figure 11-5.[73]

Content.   People come to a certain Web site to find something in particular. Many sites suffer from the philosophy that more is better, which is not always the case. Having the right content, in the right format, in the right functionality is what's important. Understanding the customers and creating a great experience is absolutely critical.

Commerce.   If a company sells products or services on-line, it must do so in a way that adds value over other types of distribution.

Customization.   Web sites should be designed to deliver a personalized experience for the individual customer, or one-to-one marketing, as discussed subsequently.

Community.   The most effective Web sites create a sense of community that involves people interacting with one another.

Effective Web sites that build on these four Cs have a "sticky" quality to them, which means they have the ability to get on-line visitors to register with the site, to spend time at the site, and ultimately, to return repeatedly to the site.[74] Because of the importance of using the Web to manage customer relationships, a later section addresses this issue. Some of the best Web sites receive the CASIE Award (www.CASIE.com—Coalition for Advertising Supported Information and Entertainment). Winners in 1999 included Kraft Foods, Star Media, Procter & Gamble, and Continental Airlines. The following Technology Expert's View from the Trenches provides additional insight about Web site design.

FIGURE 11-5 Web Site Design

Two Common Pitfalls in Developing a Web Site

MARK HAIR
President, BaseCamp Interactive, Inc., Seattle, Washington,
www.compellingwebsites.com

A Web site is a company's window into the Internet economy. How well the site represents that company or fulfills the functionality intended defines that company's prospects in the New Economy. There are two mistakes I see happening consistently for those hoping to develop a well-designed Web site.

- Underestimating the cost
- Failing to align the site properly with business plans

MISTAKE NUMBER ONE

The number one mistake people make is to underestimate when planning for the cost. Though it is still possible for a little firm to put up a site alongside the big firm, the bar has been raised dramatically in terms of content quality (also known as production values), site interactivity, and application functionality, in addition to the major cost and effort in getting customers to view a site.

Many people seem to believe that with a few thousand dollars, they can throw up a respectable Web site and people will come flocking to it. This mistaken belief arises in part due to the industry's low barriers to entry—like desktop publishing, it started as a cottage industry with some practitioners of dubious skills.

Suffice it to say, even small sites can require substantial budgets. The reason for this is that all sites must follow a well-established process known by many names, but for clarity, let's call it the software and content development life cycle. Many tasks in this life cycle, such as concepting the site, don't scale with the size of the site. Therefore, such overhead tasks (meaning any tasks that are not directly involved in physically creating the site) will add the same cost to a small site as to a large one. In addition, it is well established in software engineering that mistakes caught and corrected in the first tasks of development, such as requirements gathering, can cost up to 100 times less to fix than those caught in the latter phases. These and other factors must be conveyed to clients in explaining why a small site often is not that much less expensive to build than a medium-size site.

To avoid the mistake of under-funding a site, start by choosing a quality developer. The developer should be able to articulate the life cycle of Web development to your satisfaction, and should insist that you follow this life cycle. I've worked with a number of clients who wanted to shortcut the process and jump straight into producing the site. This would be the equivalent of throwing up a building before it was conceived, analyzed, and designed by an architect. No one would think of doing that for a building, so why would they for a Web site? With a little education on the importance of these tried-and-true software engineering principles, clients understand how following the process can actually enable the realization of their vision for their Web site most efficiently.

Further concerning cost, consider two words—intellectual capital. Not only is the Internet economy a new business paradigm, it's a constantly changing sea of technological innovation. It draws from a workforce whose knowledge of their industry is made obsolete annually or sooner, requiring them to constantly re-educate themselves. This demands driven, academically-minded, creative, and technical talent. They must be bent on re-inventing the future of interactive media technology, and be willing to spend their free time studying new programming languages and developing leading-edge techniques. Rates can be quite high. How a developer attracts this talent can vary dramatically. BaseCamp Interactive employs the concept of collaborative virtual teaming, meaning we maintain a core team for creative and technology direction and management, and subcontract other expertise project-by-project as needed. The advantages of such a model are low overhead and the utilization of experts who are self-employed, and highly skilled and motivated in their craft. Moreover, we work via the Net (surprise!), which allows people to create in their most productive environments—their own studios or offices. Collaborative virtual teaming is a business model whose time has come.

What can a company do when the estimate for the Web site is substantially higher than its budget? It must either find the necessary funding or narrow the project scope to meet a pre-established budget. Which course is more prudent depends on their expectations for the site, and how well those expectations align with the business plan, which will be discussed below in mistake number two. The bottom line is: To attract the eyeballs of a target audience, the bar is now very high. That bar can range from $50,000 for a very small "static" site with nice production values to $2,000,000 for a large, database-driven e-commerce site, utilizing a content management system for production.

MISTAKE NUMBER TWO

The second most common mistake, in my opinion, is not putting one's Web site in proper perspective—that is to say, treating the Web site as if it is either

a. An afterthought, a necessary evil for being in business these days, or
b. The only truly important aspect of the business where, say, 80% of newly acquired capital should be invested

Generally, a Web site should be neither.

To be more specific, taking approach *a* above means not fully understanding the significance of a Web presence. How a company is perceived directly alongside its competitors on the Web will make a huge impact on how it is perceived overall. In fact, the Web site will often be a customer's first impression, especially for the most motivated "pull" customers who seek out a company even before it seeks them out. Don't underestimate the value of the Web site in forming your company ethos.

In approach *b* above, the naive company puts the majority of resources into its site, but underestimates the cost and complexity of its fulfillment systems, distribution systems, and marketing. The lesson here is that whether or not a company is a Web-oriented business, it still has the same challenges businesses have been solving for decades.

The Internet economy is not a rewrite of traditional economics. It is only an extension, and one should neither expect it to bring fabulous wealth just because the Web site "is there," nor give it the "quick treatment" with a skeptical eye. Don't leave business fundamentals at the door!

In today's Internet economy, a Web site must be fully integrated with the business plan. Make the Web site spending and emphasis realistic and congruent with the business plan. That is not to say it should include the kitchen sink. The site should fulfill the goals and requirements targeted during the initial phase of the development life cycle, and utilize a bit of Internet-economy savvy.

FINAL THOUGHTS: CHOOSING A WEB SITE DEVELOPER

Choose a developer based on reputation, not based on the bid, unless the bid seems to be outside industry norms. A good source for price comparison is the Web Price Index, at www.netb2b.com/webPriceIndex/index.html. Be sure to compare apples to apples in terms of the quality of developers you're soliciting, or their bid range will vary wildly and seem confusing. Once chosen, make that developer a partner in meeting your goals, a much more positive approach than working as an adversary.

Promote the Web Site to Build Traffic

Companies that establish a Web site must not follow the tenet "Build it and they will come." Rather, companies must work diligently to build traffic for their Web sites. Figure 11-6 shows the most popular means consumers use to find Web sites.

To drive traffic to their sites, companies have many options including using both traditional and on-line advertising media, sponsorships, promotional offers, and e-mail messages (see Table 11-2). In addition to using the tools presented here, it is vital that a firm have a strong brand name as part of its drawing ability.[75]

Use Traditional and On-line Advertising Media   Although on-line ads and sponsorships can help to generate Web traffic, traditional media, including TV, is vital for building broad consumer awareness. E*Trade, Yahoo!, AOL, and Priceline, for example, spend large amounts on both radio and TV spots.[76] Amazon.com spent $133 million on marketing and sales in 1998.

With respect to on-line advertising in particular, Figure 11-7 shows that advertising spending on the Web more than doubled in 1997 and 1998, going from $917 million in 1997 to $1.9 billion in 1998[77] to $4.62 billion in 1999.[78] Despite these numbers, on-line advertising represents only 2.8% of corporate advertising budgets.[79] And when companies ad-

---

TABLE 11-2   Ways to Promote the Web Site to Build Site Traffic

1 Traditional and on-line advertising (banners, live banners/rich media)
2 List with search engines
3 Traditional promotions
4 Use of affiliates
5 Viral marketing
6 Permission marketing

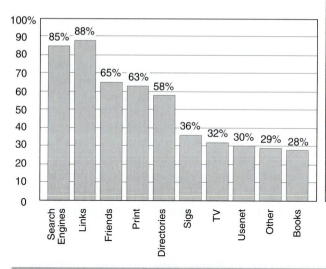

Key

Search engines: Internet search engines (e.g., Alta Vista, Lycos, etc.)
Links: Follow hyperlinks from other Web pages
Friends: Friends
Print: Magazines–newspapers
Directories: Internet directories (e.g., Yahoo!, McKinley, etc.)
Sigs: Signatures at end of e-mail messages
TV: Television advertisements
Usenet: Usenet newsgroups
Other: Other sources
Books: Books

FIGURE 11-6 How Consumers Find New Web Pages and Sites

Source: Graphic, Visualization, and Usability Center (GVU), Georgia Institute of Technology (1999), *10th WWW User Survey,* October–December.

vertise on-line, they need to make sure they aren't simply engaging in "gratuitous digitization," or simply putting on-line what would be better put in traditional media.

What these ad dollars deliver depends on the model of advertising one uses. The differing models depend upon whether Internet users are active or passive acquirers of information. Passive information seekers are similar to viewers of broadcast TV shows or radio. Broadcast users typically watch or listen to a channel and receive information passively. They typically have little control over their exposure to ad images (except by chan-

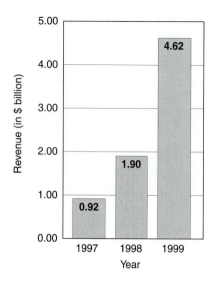

FIGURE 11-7 On-line Advertising Revenues

Source: "Online Ad Revenues Surged in 1999," www.nua.ie/surveys/index.cgi?f=VS&art_id=905355730&rel=true, downloaded June 9, 2000.

nel surfing or going to the refrigerator). To get a viewer's attention in such an environment, advertisers must use clever attention-getting devices and repetition in order to make an impact. On the other hand, *active information seekers* are searching for certain information to meet particular needs. Under this model, companies must offer meaningful information while at the same time attempting to market their products.

This section covers the different types of Internet ads, the issues in on-line advertising (see Figure 11-8), and the pricing of Internet ads.

Types of on-line advertising.   As shown in Figure 11-9, *banner ads* remained the most popular form of on-line advertising in 1999, accounting for 56% of all Internet ads.[80,81]

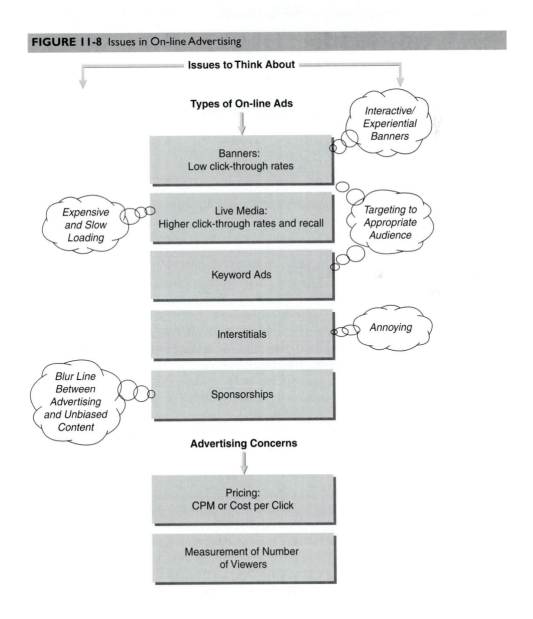

FIGURE 11-8 Issues in On-line Advertising

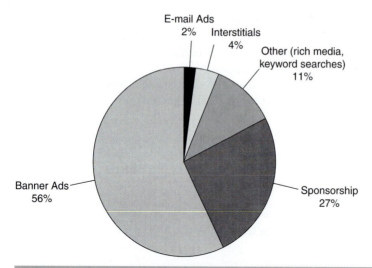

E-mail Ads
2%   Interstitials
4%

Other (rich media,
keyword searches)
11%

Banner Ads
56%

Sponsorship
27%

FIGURE II-9 Types and Usage of On-line Advertisements

Source: "Online Ad Revenues Surged in 1999," www.nua.ie/surveys/index.
cgi?f=VS&art_id=905355730&rel=true, downloaded June 9, 2000.

Despite their popularity, banner ads are also the most controversial of Internet ads.[82] Banners are easy to ignore and most surfers may not want to leave the site they are viewing to check out an ad. Indeed, the click-through rate (the number of surfers who visit a page by clicking on the banner ad) on banner ads in 1999 was .36%,[83] far less than the 2% click-through rate of 1997. Those who subscribe to the active model of Internet usage say that banner ads are easy to tune out because surfers don't "watch" the Internet, they "use" it. Because Web users can control the amount of time they spend on a page, they can decide what they want to pay attention to. And browsers can access technology to block banners.

However, those who subscribe to the passive model of Internet usage say the ads are cheap and help distinguish broad-based brands whose products are similar to the competition's. And such ads fit the traditional approach to advertising: With enough creativity and repetition, an impact will be made.

Different avenues are being used to improve the click-through rate on banners. Banner ads that include tiny questionnaires to promote interactivity have had some success for John Hancock Mutual Life Insurance. Almost 5% of Web surfers have clicked on their banners offering a quick calculation about how much money one will need to retire.[84] (Surfers fill in their age and annual income.) These *experiential* on-line ads provide interactive services for customers and are predicted to grow from $1.1 billion in 1998 to $11.2 billion by 2002.[85]

And, as in any media buying decision, *the degree to which the ad is appropriately targeted to a receptive audience has a positive effect on its impact.* Using cookie data, or information about which sites users have visited, some software can sort cookies into different categories of users, say, those interested in entertainment, business, or sports. Then an advertiser can direct its ads to users in a particular category. The response rate to banner ads targeted in this way has been shown to exceed response to traditional banner ad placement (8% to 12% versus 1.5% for banners on targeted sites). The issue is not how many people the ad reaches, but how many of the right people.

Another innovation in banner ads designed to address their drawbacks are *live banners* that use video and sound.[86] Such forms of rich media move, talk, flash, or play music to "interact" with the Web surfer. These ads let the viewers click on a banner and get its message without departing from a site,[87] allowing Web users to order merchandise, play video games, and interact without leaving the site hosting the ad. These ads were developed by companies such as Narrative Communications Corporation and Thinking Media Corporation. These are categorized in the "Other" category of on-line advertising.

The drawbacks are that live banners require sufficient processing speed and bandwidth to deliver streaming video and sound and, hence, typically work slowly with modems. And they are four to five times more expensive than animated banners that require click-throughs to another page. A typical banner might cost between $250 and $7,500 to develop, but rich banners can run up to 20 times that amount.

The cost may be worth it, because advertisers say that they get higher responses from live banners than from the standard click-through variety. Click-on rates (versus click-through, which implies leaving the host page) for these banners can be four to five times that of regular banners, and as high as 10%. Moreover, @Home Network, a rich media company, says that recall of rich media ads is 34% higher than for regular banners, and of those who clicked on rich media ads, more than half spent 30 seconds engaged with the ad information and the brand.[88]

Although rich media ads now account for less than 10% of Internet ads, some predict that they may comprise 60% of all banners by 2002.[89] The real advantage of the interactive banners is that they provide immediate direct-selling capabilities. In that sense, they are less like a bumper sticker, which a browser either clicks on or doesn't, and more like direct marketing, which is user driven. The point of sale is closer to the initial encounter with customers.

Another category of on-line advertising is called an **interstitial ad,** or "in your face" ad, which pops up a separate window when users click through to another site; the interstitial pops up before the Web page that was called up appears.[90] An example is shown in Figure 11-10. These types of on-line ads account for about 4% of on-line advertising expenditures. Some surfers find them annoying because one must actively click to remove them from the screen.

Another type of on-line ad is a *keyword ad* (also included in the "Other" category). Featured primarily on Web search engine sites, advertisers can link a specific ad to text or subject matter that an information seeker enters. Miller Brewing, for example, bought the word *beer* on Yahoo. Every time someone conducted a search using that term, a banner ad for Miller Genuine Draft popped up.[91] Some creative companies have even bought their competitor's name. These ads present a way to improve the targeting of banner ads. An example of a keyword ad appears in Figure 11-11.

Another way to advertise a Web site is through a *cobranding* or *"sponsorship" arrangement,* which accounts for approximately 27% of on-line advertising expenditures. In these arrangements, advertisers typically form a partnership with a site that provides content. The advertiser gets to offer information about its own products along with the other, ostensibly objective, information on the site. For example, as shown in Figure 11-12, EPT sponsors part of BabyCenter.com, a site for parents who are expecting or have young children. (Also note its banner at the top of the page, probably not coincidental.)

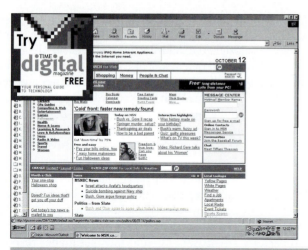

FIGURE 11-10 Example of an Interstitial

Interstitial screen: © 2000 Time Inc. Used with permission.

FIGURE 11-11 Example of a Keyword Ad

Unlike clicking on a banner ad that takes one to the advertiser's site, clicking on a sponsor's icon typically keeps the browser within the original site.

Some worry that cobranding crosses the line that separates editorial content (ostensibly objective information) and advertising (in which the information's purpose is based on a financial stake in making a sale). Content sites must be aware of this issue so

FIGURE 11-12 Example of a Sponsorship

Reprinted with the permission of BabyCenter.com.

that people who come to their sites for the presumably unbiased information don't doubt their objectivity. Clearly identifying sponsors, as in the BabyCenter.com example, is vital to keeping content unbiased.

Pricing of on-line advertising: CPM or cost per click?   How is Internet advertising priced?[92] As with traditional media, the price is a function of the number of viewers (in this case, the number of eyeballs) and the desirability of and ability to focus on specific demographic profiles. The more targeted a population a site offers, and the more desirable its demographics, the higher the rates that can be charged.

There are two specific formats for Internet advertising charges. *Cost per thousand* (or *CPM—M* is the Roman numeral for 1,000) is the cost to display a particular ad one thousand times. It is computed as follows:

$$\frac{\$ \text{ Cost of ad}}{\text{Number of people reached}} * 1,000$$

Web advertisers generally pay a fee for every 1,000 times their ads are displayed. As one would expect, the CPM is higher for Web sites that offer a tighter, more targeted population. For example, whereas the average CPM for Internet advertising is $35, the CPM for the *Wall Street Journal* site is $65. Selling on-line ads on a CPM basis is akin to the more passive view of advertising: Simply exposing people to banners is assumed to have some impact over time.

Some are highly critical of paying for Internet ads on a CPM basis, likening such a model to "I-Way robbery."[93] In traditional media, CPM is computed on the basis of reach, or the number of individuals exposed to an ad. However, in an on-line environment, CPM is computed on the basis of impressions, or the number of times the ad is viewed, regardless of whether it is viewed multiple times by the same person. Moreover, comparing click-through rates on banner ads to responses to direct marketing campaigns is equally deceiving. A .5% response to a direct-mail campaign typically means the ad was redeemed or an offer accepted; however, a .5% click-through rate on a banner ad simply means the surfer viewed the complete offer. Based on this logic, these critics argue that paying for Internet ads should be done on a cost-per-click basis.

Cost per click refers to the ad rate charged only if the surfer responds to a displayed ad. This requires measuring how many surfers click through from the site of the ad. Selling ad space on a cost-per-click basis takes a more active view of Internet surfers and assumes that click-throughs will tie directly to moving customers along the consumer decision-making process.

Whether an advertiser is willing to pay on a CPM or cost-per-click basis likely depends upon its on-line advertising goals. If the advertising is designed to support broad-based awareness and brand familiarity, a CPM pricing model might make sense. On the other hand, if the goals of the campaign are to develop a database of possible customers and move toward a direct sale, then paying on a cost-per-click basis might make more sense.

Regardless of which approach one uses to price on-line ads, a critical issue is how the number of viewers is measured. Several companies measure the number of viewers of on-line ads, such as Internet Advertising Bureau (www.iab.net), www.ipro.com, and BPA International (www.BPAI.com). Each of their Web sites describes the methods and reports available, similar to what advertisers of more traditional media expect in terms of reporting. Moreover, a number of new companies specialize in placement of on-line ads, including Mediatwo.net and Doubleclick.com, to name just two.

Theoretically, the on-line supply of ad space is infinite, whereas traditional media such as radio and TV have only a finite spectrum and airtime. Because advertisers have countless choices on-line, the rates that sites charge for ads are coming down. Even while the CPM is dropping, ad revenues on-line continue to grow. However, the top 10 portal sites are capturing this growth, taking the lion's share (75%) of the ad revenue in 1999.[94] Many Internet sites are surviving because they count on ad revenue more than on selling goods.

Having explored the topic of on-line advertising in detail, the chapter continues with ways to generate Web site traffic.

List with Search Engines   Another way to build Web site traffic is to register with the various search engines so that when browsers are looking for specific content, the engine can access the companies' Web sites. This is an especially important tool because 85% of people use search engines to find new Web sites.[95] Using automated software, search engines send out "spiders," or crawlers, that make copies of the pages they find on the Web. The search engine automatically stores copies of these pages and indexes some or all of the words on the page. Then, when a Web surfer types in a search, the engine looks up the words in its index and calls up the appropriate Web addresses. The engine doesn't actually go out on the Web each time a search is requested. There are a variety of different types of search engines, and each uses a different algorithm for determining how different pages are ranked. Even if a company doesn't register with any search engines or directories, Web crawlers will still visit sites and find pages to list. Circulating fresh content through a site is one way of triggering a crawler's, or spider's, indexing reflexes.[96]

However, registering the pages in a Web site is very important, given that even the most thorough search engines manage to find only about one-third of the relevant Web sites in a search; others cover 10% or less of the relevant sites.[97] For example, in a 1998 study, HotBot covered 34% of the estimated 320 million Web pages, AltaVista covered 28%, Northern Light 20%, Excite 14%, Infoseek 10%, and Lycos, a mere 3%. (For a browser, the best thing one can do is to use multiple search engines, which will yield 3.5 times more results, covering about 60% of available pages.) Yahoo! was not covered in this study, because it is technically a directory, based on human classification and categorization, rather than an automated search engine.

Because of the importance of this topic, combined with its technical nature, additional detail on search engine registration and placement appears in the Appendix to this chapter.

Traditional Promotions   Many companies use traditional promotions and rebates to entice customers to visit their sites. Some banner ads entice customers with the chance to enter sweepstakes and contests. Traditional media can also be used to communicate such offers.

Use of Affiliates   **Affiliates** are Web sites that are cross linked to another Web site. For example, Amazon.com enlists Web site owners that offer Amazon's books, music, and videos on their own sites. The company pays affiliates a commission of 5% to 15% for any sales on their sites, but pays nothing for the added exposure.[98]

Viral Marketing   **Viral marketing,** or referral marketing, refers to making offers so compelling that people voluntarily pass them around to their friends. It takes advantage of the power of contacts and shared interests to stimulate word of mouth via e-mail. For example, Nike and Absolut vodka both allowed visitors to their sites to create videos and music messages to e-mail to their friends. E-mail is the primary tool in this technique. When people respond to the offer via e-mail, it enables the company to capture names and e-mail addresses of possible customers.

Permission Marketing[99]   The idea behind **permission-based marketing** is to ask the customers to opt in to receive marketing messages based on their interests in a particular topic. This is very different from nearly all conventional advertising and promotion, which might be characterized as "interruption marketing." Furthermore, permission marketing takes a very direct approach in marketing to customers, rather than the more veiled persuasion inherent in most traditional marketing attempts. The Internet is a natural environment for permission marketing because of e-mail communication and its growing ability to close sales and, in the case of purchasing informational or digital products, to fulfill sales.

Once a company has received the customer's permission to receive e-mail information and product offers, a business should follow **relationship marketing** strategies. Rather than pouring marketing dollars into prospecting for new customers, a business should try to up sell and cross sell to existing customers. Customers who trust the vendor to give them reliable products and services at a fair price will stay loyal. In relationship marketing, the true value of any customer is based on the value of his or her future purchases across all the product lines, brands, and services offered by a firm. So, although companies spend anywhere from $10 to $200 to acquire a new customer, their belief is that the lifetime value of a customers is so great that all-out marketing and low initial prices may pay off.[100]

Importantly, permission-based marketing avoids the use of its antithesis, spamming. **Spamming** is sending unsolicited, undesired e-mail to people. Its real-world analogy is junk mail and cold-call telemarketing. "Netiquette," or the informal rules of the Internet in terms of etiquette and decorum, is fiercely opposed to the use of the Internet in such a manner. A host of unscrupulous Web sites can inform possible Web marketers about how to engage in spamming, but doing so invites the ire of the very clientele a firm is trying to reach. Avoid spamming at all costs.

Evaluate Traffic at the Web Site

It is important to evaluate the number of visitors coming to a particular Web site and where they are coming from. Many software programs available on the market can do this, and firms such as Media Metrix Inc. provide independent traffic counts. For example, WebStat.com is a free Web-based program for analyzing traffic to a particular Web site. Other software packages are WebTrends or HitBox. Through a series of convenient and easy-to-read graphs and tables, people can track the performance of their Web site over time, tracking data such as

- Hourly, daily, weekly, and monthly hits and unique visitors
- Top referring URLs (sites with a link to the site)
- Traffic from various search engines (i.e., Infoseek, Yahoo!, AltaVista, etc.)
- Top keywords used per search engine
- Traffic from different geographic areas, including other countries

In evaluating site traffic, it is important to understand the different ways of counting visitors. *"Hits"* are counted any time a Web page is accessed. So, for example, hits can come from Web spiders, or from someone who may log on twice in one day from different computers, or from someone who goes back and forth between elements of a Web site—each time a particular page is accessed, it counts as a hit. *"Unique visitors"* counts the number of individual visitors who have come to a Web site over a specified time period. So, for example, if a person accesses a Web site many times on various days, he or she would be counted only once. More importantly, if a person goes back and forth between pages at a Web site, that person would be counted only once. Indeed, the number of hits a site generates does not correlate highly with the actual number of site visitors. Unique visitors rather than hits is generally the preferred number to use when measuring Web site traffic.

Build Repeat Site Traffic and Manage On-line Customer Relationships

For Web sites based on a direct-sales model or on a portal basis to be profitable, they must focus on building repeat site traffic. To build repeat traffic, sites must have a very clear (and accurate) understanding of what customers value about the site. This section explores two strategies to build repeat site traffic and manage on-line customer relationships: personalization and providing high-quality customer service. Customer service has been identified as the top factor in determining whether a customer returns to a particular merchant; customer service was more important than on-time delivery, price, and other concerns.[101]

Personalization   The ability to personalize the customer's browsing experience can be a very powerful glue in building repeat site traffic and cementing customer relationships. Sites that are able to collect data on customers and details about what they do on-line are better able to identify and target the best customers, and to better tailor the browsing experience to that specific customer's characteristics and preferences.[102,103] Personalization can boost new customers by 47% in one year and revenues up to 52%.[104] Moreover, people who use personalization come back at least five times as often as those who don't (and possibly up to 20 times as often[105]) and view double the number of pages. In addition, the site N2K found that the recommendations from personalization prompted people to buy 10% to 30% of the time, compared to the average 2% to 4% on the rest of the site. Ralston-Purina's breed selector allows visitors to go through a series of questions about their pet preferences (e.g., size of dog, temperament, etc.) to suggest pet breeds that match the person's desires. This new feature increased the number of visitors to the site by 25%, and the visitors stayed twice as long.[106]

In the early days of the Internet, the ability to customize the browsing experience was referred to as "push" technology, filters,[107] or "Web casting."[108] Although the technology to offer a personalized browsing experience was available earlier, few merchants took full advantage of this capability until recently. Indeed, now the formation and management of customer relationships in an on-line environment may prove to be the ultimate tool in one-to-one marketing, enabling interactive, customized interactions with customers in a cost-efficient way.

Information used to personalize the browsing experience can be given voluntarily by a surfer to the Web site. Customization involves choices that Web site visitors make to specify what they want to see. Even when browsers do not voluntarily provide such data, merchants can glean such information indirectly by the surfer's movements or purchases on the site by monitoring cookies. Ultimately, by using mathematical formulas that match people's likely interests, given their existing profile as compared to other buyers who have similar profiles and clickstreams, a personalized experience can be offered to browsers.

Pros and cons of personalization.   What are the relative benefits and costs of using a personalization strategy with customers (see Table 11-3)? One of the key benefits from a customer's perspective is that better matching marketing offers to customers' interests allows browsers to see offers that are genuinely interesting to them. And personalization can save a browser time.

From a business's perspective, Web sites earn more revenue by understanding the buying and browsing habits of their customers. Second, personalized sites have *stickiness,* meaning people stay at the site longer.[109] Length of time spent on a site is important,

TABLE 11-3   Pros and Cons of Personalization

	Pros	*Cons*
Customers	Tailored offers based on interests Efficiency in browsing/on-line shopping	Technology not precise Privacy concerns Weblining
Businesses	Increased ad revenues "Stickiness" Aid in research and design of products; optimize manufacturing	Expensive

because viewing time equates to more opportunity to view marketing messages. Third, when ads are targeted more accurately to potential customers, based on data available from personalization, merchants can charge more for ads that deliver results. For example, when Peapod, the on-line grocer, targeted its banner ads on sites by Kraft and Kellogg, it saw a 27% increase in sales. And Web coupons targeted to shoppers' preferences are redeemed more than 20% of the time (10 times more than conventional coupons).[110] Also, these sites can earn commissions for routing customers to their advertisers' sites.

Not only can personalization transform a company's contact with its customers; it can also affect its operations, including research and design of products and manufacturing.[111] For example, rather than relying on inexact forecasts of future demand, actual customer demand using mass customization will be the primary driver of production. Customers can also influence product research and design via the Web. For example, Sapient Health Network collects information on patient symptoms and compiles such information into studies, which are then sold to drug companies. Both of these uses of personalization also provide additional evidence of the shifting of control to the customer.

One downside for businesses: The software can be expensive (between $50,000 and $3 million), but with these results, it can reach payback within one year. The downside may be larger from a customer's perspective. The technology is still somewhat cumbersome. For example, if a person buys a gift for someone with different tastes, the future recommendations may never be well matched again. Moreover, sometimes the separate databases from within a single site may never be pieced together. For example, Amazon.com might recommend books that a customer has already purchased there.

Probably the largest concern is the potential alienation of customers due to privacy abuses.[112] For personalization to work, browsers must fill out lengthy forms about themselves that reveal personal information. Even when browsers do not voluntarily provide such data, merchants can use cookie data that are then sold to advertisers. For example, a life insurance company might search potential customers' disk drives to weed out individuals who have visited the sites of tobacco or alcohol companies, or sites devoted to specific diseases or pharmaceuticals.[113] When such information is collected and used without the customer's knowledge, he or she may feel abused. Because of these concerns, some consumers may feel a need to shield their identify and personal facts; if such shielding happens to a large degree, e-commerce may never reach the full potential that personalization can provide.

Related to the use of browsers' information is the fact that, when merchants sell such information to advertisers, they are making money from information that rightfully belongs to the customers themselves. Some believe that rather than the merchant being compensated for providing such data to advertisers, the browsers themselves should be compensated.[114]

Another downside of personalization is called **Weblining.**[115] Weblining refers to the classification of customers into tiers based on volume and profitability. Top tier, or A, customers will get the best treatment in terms of service and deals, whereas bottom tier, or C, customers might be the ones who wait on help lines, do not get deal offers, or are cut off as customers. Some refer to Weblining as an insidious form of discrimination.[116] Priority customers at MCI get help within three rings, whereas those who switch carriers frequently wait until after priority customers are treated.[117]

It is important to note, however, that such practices are not limited to the on-line world. Indeed, the segmenting of customers into categories based on business and profitability is a common aspect of relationship marketing strategies, as discussed in previous chapters. By using database marketing techniques, which collect personal information about customers, including customer habits and purchase histories, customers can be segmented into categories. At FedEx, for example, customers are rated as the good, the bad, and the ugly. Says the managing director for marketing analysis at FedEx:[118] "We want to keep the good, grow the bad, and the ugly we want nothing to do with." The downside of such a strategy in its risk of alienating customers not receiving top treatment has been identified by experts in relationship marketing.[119]

Companies will want to be aware of the drawbacks of personalization in order to ensure that they use it effectively and wisely. Used effectively, personalization can help build repeat traffic. Note, however, that while repeat business is a necessary condition for having a profitable Web site, it alone is insufficient for success. For example, although repeat buyers accounted for more than 60% of Amazon.com's sales in 1998,[120] it was not profitable in 2000. On-line businesses must also have a winning financial model that delivers a sales margin sufficient to cover their costs of doing business (including cost of goods sold, and customer acquisition and other marketing costs).

Customer Service   In addition to using personalization strategies, high-quality customer service is paramount to getting customers to return. BizRate.com studied the factors affecting on-line shoppers' likelihood of buying again from the same site.[121] Its results, shown in Table 11-4, show that the level and quality of customer service are the most important factors related to repeat buying; price was rated as the least important factor.

Customers lured on-line with low prices and one-click ordering still demand the same level of customer service as they do in the real world. They expect orders to be filled on time, complaints to be addressed, and people to help them with questions. Because

TABLE 11-4   Predicting Repeat Sales

Correlations Between On-line Shoppers' Ratings of a Variety of Factors and Their Likelihood to Buy Again from the Same Site

Level and quality of customer service	62%
On-time delivery	55
Product representation	47
Product shipping and handling	47
Privacy policies	41
Ease of ordering	22
Product selection	22
Product information	22
Web site navigation and looks	21
Product price	19

Source: Hanrahan, Timothy (1999), "Price Isn't Everything," *Wall Street Journal,* July 12, p. R20.

cybershoppers can easily go to a competitor's site, good customer service is no longer just a nice thing to do: It's mandatory.[122]

Despite the importance of customer service, the Internet has many sites with inadequate customer service that make a mockery of vendors' claims that on-line buying will be safe, easy, and fun.[123] The increase in on-line revenues is not being matched with investments in infrastructure and service. Studies show that on-line customer satisfaction slipped to 74% in January 1999 from 88% in July 1998. Although many sites offer e-mail and phone support, phone numbers can be hard to find on a site, and reaching a real person can mean a long wait. E-mails can go unanswered for days.

Customer service can cut into the thin margins of on-line sellers. As a result, many companies use a tiered customer service process that begins with low-cost, automated customer service, providing real-time, person-to-person service only as a last resort. For example, a customer with a question might first be guided to a Frequently Asked Questions page on the site. If that doesn't handle the situation, the customer is given the chance to send an e-mail. If the e-mail reply doesn't satisfy the customer, then he or she is given a phone number to talk to a real person.

Others are experimenting with smart software that automates responses to customer inquiries.[124] For example, on-line mortgage broker American Finance & Investments answers 65% of its questions, such as "What are your current rates?," in seconds. To determine the proper response to more complex questions, the automated technology guides customers through a series of pop-up on-line forms. For inquiries that are beyond the software's ability, tele-Web technologies allow customers to start an interactive chat with a service representative.[125]

By following these guidelines for success in an on-line world, companies may find success beyond their wildest dreams, as is highlighted in Box 11-6.

SUMMARY: REALIZING THE INTERNET'S POTENTIAL

The Net is deconstructing the fundamental nature of business transactions. Traditional distinctions between manufacturers, distributors, and suppliers are blurring.[126] Although buyers ostensibly will be the winners—by comparing products and prices from a wide range of suppliers faster and more easily than ever before, and by sharing information among themselves—the process will not prove to be painless. Shifts in the balance of power mean that relentless innovation, unparalleled service, and an attitude of genuine helpfulness, delivered in new ways, will allow a firm to capitalize on the potential the Internet has to offer.[127] Says Andy Grove, chairperson of Intel Corporation: "Today, we are preoccupied with Internet companies. In five years, that label will be meaningless because all companies will be Internet companies."[128]

This convergence might best be seen in the increasing use of a *bricks-and-clicks* business model, in which a business blends physical and digital assets. In some cases, a physical store might play a critical role in gaining initial sales, and salespeople can effectively sell many add-ons. In other cases, a physical store for e-tailers can help to create brand image, providing a "physical canvas upon which to create a customer experience."[129]

BOX 11-6

On-line Success?

THOMAS LUNDELL

For some businesses, the Internet can be boon, but to most it is neither savior nor magic potion. Managing an on-line operation requires substantial technical expenses and many working hours—hours that might be better spent managing existing customers.

For example, Chris J. Klemm co-owns and operates Great Lake Fabrics with his two sisters. The company wholesales 10,000 items to professional upholsterers. Klemm was eager to capitalize on Internet opportunities and decided to get help in creating a Web site. He got an estimate of $50,000 from an outside firm, but since this was more than Klemm's $1,000,000 business could afford, he hired a freelancer to do the job. The freelancer paid little attention to detail and frequently misspelled "upholstery" on the site. After being billed for 300 hours, Klemm decided to relieve the free-lancer from his duties and to take on the project himself. He spent five hours a day battling for top positions on search engines to make sure that everyone looking for fabrics was steered to Great Lake Fabrics site.

It turned out that Klemm was a tad too successful in his quest for additional sales. Queries poured in at the rate of 2,000 per day, but the cost of sending out catalogs to potential customers exceeded the additional income generated by the Web site. Klemm began to charge $15 per catalog, and was just about to make ends meet when AltaVista changed the look of its homepage and in the process unintentionally wiped Great Lakes Fabrics from its directory.

For Klemm and many other small vendors on the Internet, the "e" in e-commerce doesn't stand for electronic, expedient, or excellent. It is simply short for exasperation.

Source: Weinberg, Neil (2000), "Net Losses," *Forbes,* January 10, p. 176.

Obviously, despite its many complexities, the Web offers many opportunities for businesses. Firms must use the Web to learn about customers, adapt their offerings, and gain more customers. They must offer convenience, selection, community, service, personalization, and effective pricing. Firms that are successful on the Net recognize that they must constantly reinvent themselves. For example, Yahoo! started out as a search engine, designed to provide a list of Web sites to help people navigate the Net. Now, it has transformed itself into a portal, and customers can place stock trades, check personalized information, and tailor the portal to their own individual needs.[130]

Firms want the efficiencies that the Internet can provide, which in many cases requires dumping or modifying old business practices. For example, some manufacturers require the manual checking of documents to ensure accuracy and reliability (to preclude fraud or unintentional errors), but such redundancy is costly. The use of bad business practices in a Net-based environment limits the efficiencies that can be gained.

Firms must rethink their deepest loyalties.[131] When it comes to the issue of whether they should protect their traditional distribution and sales channel, the real issue is the ultimate customer's preferences and habits. Although protecting traditional channels may have some value in the short run, in the long run companies that do so will be denying their customers true value.

In order for the Internet to achieve its potential, a series of hurdles remain and must be addressed:[132]

- *Congestion.*   The Internet feels jammed at times. However, this congestion can be handled by improved technology and by routing some traffic at off-peak hours.
- *Security.*   The Internet was designed to enhance open access to information, but the need for security, and its attendant restrictions in access, implies just the opposite. Hackers can be sealed off with firewalls, but ad hoc security measures make systems incompatible and communications cumbersome.

  The fear about a lack of security is having a negative effect on the rate people are adopting the Web for business-to-business transactions. Fewer than one in seven companies is willing to link its critical applications to the Net.[133]

  Many companies have made this problem a research priority, based on the military doctrine of deterrence. They make it expensive for hackers to gain access, hoping it won't be worth the cost. Companies build firewalls by constructing concentric layers of encryption and adopting electronic passports that strictly limit entry to different areas of the network. These technologies are expensive, and companies are protecting themselves against a risk they can't quantify specifically.
- *Privacy.*   The success of electronic commerce depends on the ability to keep personal data safe from abuse. Privacy policies that are strictly adhered to, in which users can see how different sites will use their personal information, are vital.
- *Technical standards/protocols.*   The lack of common standards with respect to business activities makes it hard for businesses to swap data. For example, the supply chain management programs offered by the top vendors (such as Oracle, SAP, and PeopleSoft) are not compatible. Corporate pressures for efficiency in sharing data may help to bring about such standards.
- *Quality.*   Obviously, doing business in a digital world requires higher quality in software and hardware. An environment with no crashes is imperative. But the profusion of companies with on-line ambitions means that skilled programmers are in short supply, leaving many companies with Web sites that crash annoyingly frequently.[134]
- *Cultural questions.*   Legitimate questions remain about how many hours people will spend shopping on-line. To the extent that other needs (social needs, tangible goods to inspect or try on, etc.) are important, the extent of on-line sales will be limited.
- *Internet taxes.*   Businesses continue to worry and wonder when the government will begin to tax on-line sales. If this happens, people worry that it will have a negative backlash on e-businesses.[135]

Even if these problems are addressed, many are predicting a huge shakeout in the dot.com world.[136] The survivors will be those that have (1) a solid business model based on the number of customers a business can connect with, (2) depth and detail of information that the business can give to and responsibly collect about the customer, and (3) affiliations to customers.[137] In addition to having a solid business model, successful on-line businesses also must be effective at implementation. Because of the changing nature of this phenomenon, Box 11-7 offers Web resources to readers. In closing, in lieu of a Technology Tidbit for this chapter, see Box 11-8, "Proverbs for the Millennium."

BOX 11-7

*Additional Web Resources on Internet
Marketing and E-Business*

A variety of useful resources and Web sites are available to those wanting to learn more about Internet marketing. The following sites offer just a beginning.

Understanding the digital economy

Digitaleconomy.gov

Ecommerce.gov

Thestandard.net (the newsmagazine of the Internet economy)

www.Internet.com

Compendium of Internet surveys, including international data

www.nua.ie/surveys

www.cyberatlas.internet.com

www.bcg.com (The Boston Consulting Group has reports on e-commerce.)

On-line journals dealing with e-business

www.redherring.com

www.wired.com

www.business2.com

www.emarketer.com

www.ecommercetimes.com

www.WebSiteJournal.com

www.revolution.com

www.upside.com

www.clickz.com

www.websitegarage.com

www.cmp.com (CMP.net; the Technology Network)

www.ipmag.com (the magazine of law and policy for high-technology industries)

On-line resources for database marketing

www.cyberdialogue.com

Reports on a variety of high-tech industries

www.datamonitor.com

www.idcresearch.com

www.wolfBayne.com/lists/ (marketing lists on the Internet)

www.hightechmktg.com (high-tech marketing ideas)

Advertising

www.Internetadvertising.org

www.admedia.org/internet/management.html (Internet advertising resource guide)

CASIE.com (Coalition for Advertising Supported Information and Entertainment, specializes in Internet advertising)

Search engines

searchenginewatch.com

Domain name registration

www.internic.net

www.icann.org

www.ntia.doc.gov/ntiahome/domainname/domainhome.htm

BOX 11-8

Proverbs for the Millennium

1. Home is where you hang your @.
2. The e-mail of the species is more deadly than the mail.
3. A journey of a thousand sites begins with a single click.
4. You can't teach a new mouse old clicks.
5. Great groups from little icons grow.
6. Speak softly and carry a cell phone.
7. C:\ is the root of all directories.
8. Oh, what a tangled Web site we weave when first we practice.
9. Pentium wise, pen and paper foolish.
10. The modem is the message.
11. Too many clicks spoil the browse.
12. The geek shall inherit the earth.
13. There's no place like home(page).
14. Don't byte off more than you can view.
15. Fax is stranger than fiction.
16. What boots up must come down.
17. Windows will never cease.
18. Virtual reality is its own reward.
19. Modulation in all things.
20. Give a man a fish and you feed him for a day; teach him to use the Net and he won't bother you for weeks.

Author unknown.

Discussion Questions

1. What are the strengths, weaknesses, and issues associated with each point of the Internet's "distribution chain" in connecting to the customer?
2. In what ways have customers gained control via the Internet?
3. What are the important issues as regulators frame the debate over on-line privacy?
4. In what ways is the Internet changing the rules of the game?
5. What are threats that on-line start-ups pose for traditional businesses? What is the major implication of these threats?
6. What are the pros and cons of integrating an on-line unit with the existing business versus keeping it separate?
7. How is the role of the intermediary changing? How should intermediaries "reinvent" themselves?
8. In addition to selling products over the Web, what are the other ways in which the Web is used to support business? Be sure to elaborate and provide supporting detail on each way.
9. What are on-line communities? What are their advantages to marketers?
10. What are electronic hubs? Describe the two types and their advantages.
11. What are the keys to being successful in an on-line world?
12. What are the four Cs of Web site design?
13. What are the tools a firm uses to build traffic for its Web site?
14. What are the two models of how Web surfers acquire information? How does that affect the relative views of using Internet advertising (i.e., banners)?

15. What are the major types of Internet ads? What are the ways to improve click-through rates on banners?
16. How is Internet advertising priced? What are the pros and cons of the two pricing models?
17. How can a firm evaluate site traffic?
18. What are at least two tools used to build repeat site traffic?
19. Do the pros of personalization outweigh the cons?
20. What are the hurdles the Net faces in realizing its potential?
21. The chapter offers two apparently conflicting views of how the Internet relates to customer control. On the one hand, customers seemingly have more control because of their increased freedom and choices regarding information and products. On the other hand, the collection of cookies and other information indicates that customers may not control the information about themselves, and are giving marketers more control because of the information collected. How is this paradox to be reconciled? Do customers really have power in the on-line world?

Glossary[138]

Affiliates.   Partner companies who sell the products from another's Web site, in exchange for a portion of the revenues from purchases by the referred customers. For example, Amazon.com enlists Web site owners who offer Amazon's books, music, and videos on their own sites. The company pays affiliates a commission of 5% to 15% for any sales on their sites.

Bots.   Shopping robots, or knowbots, are computer programs that scan the Internet for specific types of information to report back to their owners. The most common types of bots gather price comparisons, looking for bargains.

Cannibalization.   The loss of sales from an existing distribution or sales channel that are taken over by an on-line channel. Although cannibalization is generally considered to be something that should be avoided, in the Internet world, if companies are not willing to cannibalize their own core franchise, they may find themselves playing catch-up to more aggressive competitors.

Clickstream.   The sequence of mouse clicks as a Web user navigates from one page to another.

Cookies.   Software downloaded into a PC's hard drive by a Web site to record the browser's Web habits. Used to match marketing pitches to customers' interests. Customers can change their browser's security preferences to block cookies; the default mode for browser software is to accept cookies. Customers can view the cookies on their computer's hard drive by checking their "cookie" file or their temporary Internet files.

Cybermediaries.   A new class of digital intermediaries that function as brokers, helping people gather and decipher the vast quantity of information on the Web, bringing together buyers (both consumer and business) and sellers, and providing value by offering trusted advice, personal service, or other benefits. They provide a more direct and inexpensive conduit between producers and buyers than do traditional distributors, and typically claim allegiance to the buyer, instead of the producers whose wares they offer.

Disintermediation.   Bypassing of channel intermediaries in favor of going directly to customers.

Extranet.   Business network that extends a company's internal network (intranet) to key partners over the Internet.

HTML.   Hypertext Markup Language, the authoring language used to create documents on the World Wide Web.

Interstitial ads.   Live banner, or "in your face" banner, ad that pops up a separate window when users click through to a site; the interstitial pops up in the dead time before the Web page that was called up appears.

Intranet.   A company's internal network, protected by firewalls from the outside world, based on Internet technology and programming.

Permission-based marketing. Marketing based on the idea of getting people's permission to send them information (often on a regular basis via e-mail) about a company's products and services (in contrast to conventional advertising and promotion, which might be characterized as interruption marketing, which occurs regardless of whether a consumer has given permission).

Personalization. The use of sophisticated software to tailor a Web site or e-mails to a consumer based on that customer's past behavior, tastes shared with others, age, or location. Customer information is given by surfer to site operators or gleaned from customers' movements or purchases on the site.

Portals. Web sites that draw buyers with information and services such as content, search engines, and so forth; a type of digital intermediary.

Relationship marketing. Cultivating close, customized relationships with customers based on their purchase histories and customer characteristics.

Spamming. (1) Stuffing Meta Tags with countless or unrelated keywords; will cause the site to be demoted or banned from most search engines; (2) sending unsolicited, undesired e-mail to people; real-world analogy is junk mail and cold-call telemarketing. Netiquette, or the informal rules of the Internet in terms of etiquette and decorum, is fiercely opposed to the use of the Internet in such a manner.

Viral marketing. The use of compelling, catchy aspects on a Web site that are voluntarily passed on to one's friends via e-mail.

Weblining. Classifications of customers based on purchase volume and profitability. Customers classified in less desirable segments may not receive best offers or service.

XML. Extensible Markup Language, a variation of the programming language used to create Web documents. Use of customized tags allows the definition, transmission, validation, and interpretation of data between applications.

Endnotes

1. Hamel, Gary and Jeff Sampler (1998), "The e-Corporation," *Fortune,* December 7, pp. 80–92; Hof, Robert (1998), "The Click Here Economy," *Business Week,* June 22, pp. 122–128.

2. "The World's Online Populations," (2000), http://cyberatlas.internet.com/big_picture/geographics/article/0,1323,5911_151151,00.html, June 8.

3. Hof, Robert (1998), "The Click Here Economy," *Business Week,* June 22, pp. 122–128.

4. Hof, Robert (1998), "The Click Here Economy," *Business Week,* June 22, pp. 122–128.

5. "Golden Opportunity," (2000), www.pccomputing.com, February, p. 102.

6. Hamel, Gary and Jeff Sampler (1998), "The e-Corporation," *Fortune,* December 7, pp. 80–92.

7. Anders, George (1999), "Buying Frenzy," *Wall Street Journal,* July 12, pp. R6, R10.

8. Hof, Robert (1998), "The Click Here Economy," *Business Week,* June 22, pp. 122–128.

9. Stepanek, Marcia (1998), "Rebirth of the Salesman," *Business Week,* June 22, pp. 146–147.

10. Hof, Robert (1999), "The Buyer Always Wins," *Business Week e.biz,* March 22, pp. EB26–EB28.

11. Hamel, Gary and Jeff Sampler (1998), "The e-Corporation," *Fortune,* December 7, pp. 80–92.

12. Hof, Robert (1998), "Now It's Your Web," *Business Week,* October 5, pp. 164–178.

13. Hof, Robert, Heather Green, and Paul Judge (1999), "Going, Going, Gone," *Business Week,* April 12, pp. 30–32.

14. Stepanek, Marcia (1999), "You'll Wanna Hold Their Hands," *Business Week e.biz,* March 22, pp. EB30–EB31.

15. Green, Heather, Mike France, Marcia Stepanek, and Amy Borrus (2000), "It's Time for Rules in Wonderland," *Business Week,* March 20, pp. 83–96.

16. Green, Heather, Mike France, Marcia Stepanek, and Amy Borrus (2000), "It's Time for Rules in Wonderland," *Business Week,* March 20, pp. 83–96.

17. Hoffman, Donna, Thomas Novak, and Marcos Peralta (1999), "Building Consumer

Trust Online," *Communications of the ACM,* 42 (April), pp. 80–85.

18. Baig, Edward, Marcia Stepanek, and Neil Gross (1999), "Privacy," *Business Week,* April 5, pp. 84–90.

19. Christensen, Clayton (1999), *The Innovator's Dilemma,* Cambridge, MA: Harvard Business School Press.

20. The bulk of the information in this section is taken from three articles: Byrnes, Nanette (1999), "How Schwab Grabbed the Lion's Share," *Business Week,* June 28, p. 88; Schonfeld, Erick (1998), "Schwab Puts It All Online," *Fortune,* December 7, pp. 94–100; and Useem, Jerry (1999), "Internet Defense Strategy: Cannibalize Yourself," *Fortune,* September 6, pp. 121–134.

21. Schonfeld, Erick (1998), "Schwab Puts It All On-line," *Fortune,* December 7, p. 95.

22. Schonfeld, Erick (1998), "Schwab Puts It All On-line," *Fortune,* December 7, p. 96.

23. Schonfield, Erick (1998), "Schwab Puts It All On-line," *Fortune,* December 7, p. 98.

24. Much of the information in this section is taken from the following articles: Byrnes, Nanette and Paul Judge (1999), "Internet Anxiety," *Business Week,* June 28, pp. 79–88; Hof, Robert (1998), "The Click Here Economy," *Business Week,* June 22, pp. 122–128; Kerwin, Kathleen, Peter Burrows, and Diane Brady (1999), "A New Era of Bright Hopes and Terrible Fears," *Business Week,* October 4, pp. 84–98.

25. Byrnes, Nanette and Paul Judge (1999), "Internet Anxiety," *Business Week,* June 28, p. 84.

26. Byrnes, Nanette and Paul Judge (1999), "Internet Anxiety," *Business Week,* June 28, p. 84.

27. Byrnes, Nanette and Paul Judge (1999), "Internet Anxiety," *Business Week,* June 28, p. 84.

28. Byrnes, Nanette and Paul Judge (1999), "Internet Anxiety," *Business Week,* June 28, p. 84.

29. Byrnes, Nanette and Paul Judge (1999), "Internet Anxiety," *Business Week,* June 28, p. 84.

30. See also Christensen, Clayton (1999), *The Innovator's Dilemma,* Cambridge, MA: Harvard Business School Press.

31. Wysocki, Bernard Jr. (1998), "Internet Is Opening Up a New Era of Pricing," *Wall Street Journal,* June 8, p. A1.

32. Green, Heather (1998), "Cyberspace Winners: How They Did It," *Business Week,* June 22, pp. 154–160.

33. Green, Heather (1998), "Cyberspace Winners: How They Did It," *Business Week,* June 22, pp. 154–160.

34. Wysocki, Bernard Jr. (1998), "Internet Is Opening Up a New Era of Pricing," *Wall Street Journal,* June 8, p. A1; Sager, Ira and Heather Green (1998), "So Where Are All the Bargains?" *Business Week,* June 22, pp. 162–164; Green, Heather (1998), "Cyberspace Winners: How They Did It," *Business Week,* June 22, pp. 154–160.

35. Woolley, Scott (1998), "I Got It Cheaper Than You," *Forbes,* November 2, www.forbes.com/Forbes/98/1102/6210082a.htm.

36. Sinha, Indrajit (2000), "Cost Tranparency: The Net's Real Threat to Prices and Brands," *Harvard Business Review,* March–April, pp. 3–8.

37. Wysocki, Bernard Jr. (1998), "Internet Is Opening Up a New Era of Pricing," *Wall Street Journal,* June 8, p. A1.

38. Christensen, Clayton (1999), *The Innovator's Dilemma,* Cambridge, MA: Harvard Business School Press.

39. Stewart, Thomas (1999), "Larry Bossidy's New Role Model: Michael Dell," *Fortune,* April 12, pp. 166–168.

40. Stapanek, Marcia (1998), "Rebirth of the Salesman," *Business Week,* June 22, pp. 146–147.

41. Stewart, Thomas (1999), "Larry Bossidy's New Role Model: Michael Dell," *Fortune,* April 12, pp. 166–168.

42. Hof, Robert (1998), "The Click Here Economy," *Business Week,* June 22, pp. 122–128.

43. Hagel, John III and Marc Singer, (1999), *Net Worth,* Boston, MA: Harvard Business School Press.

44. Gross, Neil (1998), "Leapfrogging a Few Links," *Business Week,* June 22, pp. 140–142.

45. Hof, Robert (1998), "The Click Here Economy," *Business Week,* June 22, pp. 122–128.

46. Reinhardt, Andy (1998), "Log On, Link Up, Save Big," *Business Week,* June 22, pp. 132–138.

47. Judge, Paul (1998), "How Safe Is the Net?" *Business Week,* June 22, pp. 148, 152.

48. Hof, Robert (1998), "The Click Here Economy," *Business Week,* June 22, pp. 122–128.

49. Brown, Eryn (1999), "9 Ways to Win on the Web," *Fortune,* May 24, pp. 112–124.

50. Hof, Robert (1998), "The Click Here Economy," *Business Week,* June 22, pp. 122–128; Reinhardt, Andy (1998), "Log On, Link Up, Save Big," *Business Week,* June 22, pp. 132–138.

51. Reinhardt, Andy (1998), "Log On, Link Up, Save Big," *Business Week,* June 22, pp. 132–138.

52. Cohn, Laura, Diane Brady, and David Welch (2000), "B2B: The Hottest Net Bet Yet?" *Business Week,* January 17, p. 36.

53. Gross, Neil (1998), "Leapfrogging a Few Links," *Business Week,* June 22, pp. 140–142.

54. Reinhardt, Andy (1998), "Log On, Link Up, Save Big," *Business Week,* June 22, pp. 132–138.

55. Cronin, Mary (1998), "Ford's Intranet Success," *Fortune,* March 30, p. 158.

56. Brown, Eryn (1999), "9 Ways to Win on the Web," *Fortune,* May 24, pp. 112–124.

57. Anders, George (1999), "Buying Frenzy," *Wall Street Journal,* July 12, pp. R6, R10.

58. Jeffery, Steve (1999), "The Power of B2B e-Commerce," *Strategic Finance,* September, pp. 22–26.

59. Stepanek, Marcia (1999), "You'll Wanna Hold Their Hands," *Business Week e.biz,* March 22, pp. EB30–EB31.

60. Burrows, Peter (1998), "Instant Info Is Not Enough," *Business Week,* June 22, p. 144.

61. Burrows, Peter (1998), "Instant Info Is Not Enough," *Business Week,* June 22, p. 144.

62. Reinhardt, Andy (1998), "Log On, Link Up, Save Big," *Business Week,* June 22, pp. 132–138.

63. Brown, Eryn (1999), "9 Ways to Win on the Web," *Fortune,* May 24, pp. 112–124.

64. Green, Heather and Linda Himelstein (1999), "To the Victors Belong the Ads," *Business Week,* October 4, p. 39.

65. Hof, Robert (1997), "Internet Communities," *Business Week,* May 5, pp. 64–80.

66. McWilliam, Gil (2000), "Building Stronger Brands Through Online Communities," *Sloan Management Review,* Spring, pp. 43–54.

67. Kaplan, Steven and Mohanbir Sawhney (2000), "E-Hubs: The New B2B Market-places," *Harvard Business Review,* May–June, pp. 97–103; and Sawhney, Mohanbir and Steve Kaplan (1999), "Let's Get Vertical," *Business 2.0,* September.

68. Kerwin, Kathleen and Marcia Stepanek (2000), "At Ford, E-commerce Is Job 1," *Business Week,* February 28, pp. 74–78.

69. Tully, Shawn (2000), "The B2B Tool That Is Changing the World," *Fortune,* March 20, pp. 132–145.

70. Greenbert, Paul (2000), "B2B Marketplaces Face FTC Scrutiny," *E-Commerce Times,* March 29, downloaded June 26, 2000 from www.ecommercetimes.com.

71. E-Commerce Times Staff (2000), "And Now, B2B Cartels?" *E-Commerce Times,* March 8, downloaded June 26, 2000 from www.ecommercetimes.com.

72. Brown, Eryn (1999), "9 Ways to Win on the Web," *Fortune,* May 24, pp. 112–124.

73. Roth, Martin (1998), "Differentiating Your Presence on the Web with the 4Cs," *Marketing Management,* Winter, p. 24.

74. Brown, Eryn (1999), "9 Ways to Win on the Web," *Fortune,* May 24, pp. 112–124.

75. Brown, Eryn (1999), "9 Ways to Win on the Web," *Fortune,* May 24, pp. 112–124.

76. Petersen, Andrea (1999), "Getting Noticed," *Wall Street Journal,* July 12, pp. R16, R26.

77. Buskin, John (1999), "Online Persuaders," *Wall Street Journal,* July 12, pp. R12, R26.

78. "Online Ad Revenues Surged in 1999," www.nua.ie/surveys/index.cgi?f=VS&art_id=905355730&rel=true, downloaded June 9, 2000.

79. "Two Thirds of Major U.S. Companies Advertise Online," www.nua.ie/surveys/?f=VS&art_id=905355770&rel=true, downloaded June 9, 2000.

80. Estimates of banner ad spending vary widely. Forrester Research predicted spending on banners to top out in 1999 and begin to decline (see Neuborne and Hof [1998], for example). Others estimate that spending on banner ads is still growing, based on the sizable estimate of $2.6 billion spent in 1999 (see Petersen [1999], for example).

81. Petersen, Andrea (1999), "Getting Noticed," *Wall Street Journal,* July 12, pp. R16, R26.

82. Buskin, John (1999), "Online Persuaders," *Wall Street Journal,* July 12, pp. R12, R26.

83. *San Francisco Chronicle* (2000), "Click-Through Rates Down, Ad Spending Up," April 3, downloaded from www.nua.ie.surveys, June 9, 2000.

84. Petersen, Andrea (1999), "Getting Noticed," *Wall Street Journal,* July 12, pp. R16, R26.

85. Neuborne, Ellen and Robert Hof (1998), "Branding on the Net," *Business Week,* November 9.

86. Briones, Maricris (1999), "Rich Media May Be Too Rich for Your Blood," *Marketing News,* March 29, p. 4.

87. Bulkeley, William (1998), "New Method for Web Ads Stirs Attention," *Wall Street Journal,* October 22, pp. B1, B15.

88. Briones, Maricris (1999), "Rich Media May Be Too Rich for Your Blood," *Marketing News,* March 29, p. 4.

89. Briones, Maricris (1999), "Rich Media May Be Too Rich for Your Blood," *Marketing News,* March 29, p. 4.

90. Himelstein, Linda (1997), "Web Ads Start to Click," *Business Week,* October 6, pp. 128–136.

91. Himelstein, Linda (1997), "Web Ads Start to Click," *Business Week,* October 6, pp. 128–136.

92. Gunther, Marc (1999), "The Trouble with Web Advertising," *Fortune,* April 12, pp. 147–148.

93. www.pawluk.com/pages/mktg/marketing_banners.html, downloaded September 4, 2000.

94. Green, Heather and Linda Himelstein (1999), "To the Victor Belong the Ads," *Business Week,* October 4, p. 39.

95. Graphic, Visualization, and Usability Center (GVU) at the Georgia Institute of Technology (1999), *10th WWW User Survey,* October–December.

96. Pollock, Heidi (1999), "Strengthening Your Search Engine Showing," *Web Site Journal* (websitejournal.com), 2 (17), April 28.

97. Weber, Thomas (1998), "Web's Vastness Foils Even Best Search Engines," *Wall Street Journal,* April 13, p. B1, B5.

98. Petersen, Andrea (1999), "Getting Noticed," *Wall Street Journal,* July 12, pp. R16, R26.

99. Godin, Seth (1999), *Permission Marketing: Turning Strangers into Friends, and Friends into Customers,* New York: Simon & Schuster.

100. Anders, George (1999), "Buying Frenzy," *Wall Street Journal,* July 12, pp. R6, R10.

101. Hanrahan, Timothy (1999), "Price Isn't Everything," *Wall Street Journal,* July 12, p. R20.

102. Baig, Edward, Marcia Stepanek, and Neil Gross (1999), "Privacy," *Business Week,* April 5, pp. 84–90.

103. Brown, Eryn (1999), "9 Ways to Win on the Web," *Fortune,* May 24, pp. 112–124.

104. Hof, Robert (1998), "Now It's Your Web," *Business Week,* October 5, pp. 164–178.

105. Baig, Edward, Marcia Stepanek, and Neil Gross (1999), "Privacy," *Business Week,* April 5, pp. 84–90.

106. Hof, Robert (1998), "Now It's Your Web," *Business Week,* October 5, pp. 164–178.

107. Quick, Rebecca (1997), "Finding What You Want on the Web May Get Easier," *Wall Street Journal,* November 6, pp. B6–B7.

108. Cortese, Amy (1997), "A Way Out of the Web Maze," *Business Week,* February 24, pp. 94–104.

109. Anders, George (1999), "The Race for 'Sticky' Websites," *Wall Street Journal,* February 11.

110. Hof, Robert (1998), "Now It's Your Web," *Business Week,* October 5, pp. 164–178.

111. Hof, Robert (1998), "Now It's Your Web," *Business Week,* October 5, pp. 164–178.

112. Baig, Edward, Marcia Stepanek, and Neil Gross (1999), "Privacy," *Business Week,* April 5, pp. 84–90.

113. Roth, Martin (1998), "Customization and Privacy," *Marketing Management,* Winter, p. 22.

114. Baig, Edward, Marcia Stepanek, and Neil Gross (1999), "Privacy," *Business Week,* April 5, pp. 84–90.

115. Baig, Edward, Marcia Stepanek, and Neil Gross (1999), "Privacy," *Business Week,* April 5, pp. 84–90; Stepanek, Marcia (2000), "Weblining," *Business Week e.biz,* April 3, pp. EB26–EB34.

116. Baig, Edward, Marcia Stepanek, and Neil Gross (1999), "Privacy," *Business Week,* April 5, pp. 84–90.

117. Burrows, Peter (1998), "Instant Info Is Not Enough," *Business Week,* June 22, p. 144.

118. Judge, Paul (1998), "Do You Know Who Your Most Profitable Customers Are?" *Business Week,* September 14.

119. Fournier, Susan, Susan Dobscha, and David Glen Mick (1998), "Preventing the Premature Death of Relationship Marketing," *Harvard Business Review,* 76 (January–February), pp. 42–51.

120. Hof, Robert (1998), "Now It's Your Web," *Business Week,* October 5, pp. 164–178.
121. Hanrahan, Timothy (1999), "Price Isn't Everything," *Wall Street Journal,* July 12, p. R20.
122. Stepanek, Marcia (1999), "You'll Wanna Hold Their Hands," *Business Week e.biz,* March 22, pp. EB30–EB31.
123. Anders, George (1999), "Buying Frenzy," *Wall Street Journal,* July 12, pp. R6, R10.
124. Stepanek, Marcia (1999), "You'll Wanna Hold Their Hands," *Business Week e.biz,* March 22, pp. EB30–EB31.
125. Burrows, Peter (1998), "Instant Info Is Not Enough," *Business Week,* June 22, p. 144.
126. Wysocki, Bernard Jr. (1998), "Internet Is Opening Up a New Era of Pricing," *Wall Street Journal,* June 8, p. A1.
127. Hamel, Gary and Jeff Sampler (1998), "The e-Corporation," *Fortune,* December 7, pp. 80–92.
128. Anders, George (1999), "Buying Frenzy," *Wall Street Journal,* July 12, pp. R6, R10.
129. Hodges, Jane (2000), "Bricks for Branding," *Business 2.0,* February, pp. 95–98; Wise, Richard and Richard Christner (2000), "On Again, Off Again," *Business 2.0,* February, pp. 257–258; and Yang, Catherine (1999),

"No Web Site Is an Island," *Business Week e.biz,* March 22, p. EB38.
130. Green, Heather (1998), "Cyberspace Winners: How They Did It," *Business Week,* June 22, pp. 154–160.
131. Hamel, Gary and Jeff Sampler (1998), "The e-Corporation," *Fortune,* December 7, pp. 80–92.
132. Gross, Neil and Ira Sager (1998), "Caution Signs Along the Road," *Business Week,* June 22, pp. 166–168.
133. Judge, Paul (1998), "How Safe Is the Net?" *Business Week,* June 22, pp. 148, 152.
134. Anders, George (1999), "Buying Frenzy," *Wall Street Journal,* July 12, pp. R6, R10.
135. Gleckman, Howard (2000), "The Tempest over Taxes," *Business Week e.biz,* February 7, pp. EB32–EB36.
136. Greenwald, John (2000), "Doom Stalks the DotComs," *Time,* April 17, pp. 38–42.
137. Evans, Philip and Thomas Wurster (1999), "Getting Real About Virtual Commerce," *Harvard Business Review,* 77 (November–December), pp. 85–94.
138. For additional detail on many Web-based terms, see Webopedia.com.

Recommended Readings

Agre, Philip and Marc Rotenberg (1998), *Technology and Privacy: The New Landscape,* Cambridge, MA: MIT Press.

Bishop, Bill (1998), *Global Marketing for the Digital Age: Globalize Your Business with Digital and Online Technology,* New York: HarperCollins.

Bronson, Po (1999), *Nudist on the Late Shift: And Other True Tales of Silicon Valley,* New York: Random House.

Davis, Stan (1999), *Blur: The Speed of Change in the Connected Economy,* New York: Warner Books.

Downes, Larry and Chunka Mui (2000), *Unleashing the Killer App: Digital Strategies for Market Dominance,* Cambridge, MA: Harvard Business School Press.

Easton, Jaclyn and Jeff Bezos (1998), *Strikingitrich.com (Striking It Rich.com): Profiles of 23 Incredibly Successful Websites You've Probably Never Heard Of,* New York: McGraw-Hill.

Evans, Philip and Thomas Wurster (1999), *Blown to Bits: How the New Economics of Information Transforms Strategy,* Cambridge, MA: Harvard Business School Press.

Gates, Bill (with Collins Hemingway, contributor) (1999), *Business @ the Speed of Thought: Using a Digital Nervous System,* New York: Warner Books.

Murphy, Tom (2000), *Web Rules: How The Internet Is Changing the Way Consumers Make Choices,* Dearborn, IL: Dearborn Trade.

Schumann, David and Esther Thorson (1999), *Advertising and the World Wide Web,* Mahwah, NJ: Lawrence Erlbaum Associates.

Schwartz, Evan (1999), *Digital Darwinism: 7 Breakthrough Business Strategies for Surviving in the Cutthroat Web Economy,* New York: Broadway Books.

Strauss, Judy and Raymond Frost, (2001) *E-Marketing,* Upper Saddle River, NJ: Prentice Hall.

APPENDIX

Search Engine Placement

DALLAS NEIL, MBA, University of Montana,
President, Kinetic Sports Interactive

Search engines change rapidly. Their algorithms change. They form and dissolve partnerships and alliances daily. How can a business know how a search engine is going to rank a Web site? The first step is to understand how search engines work. The following explanation relies on an example of a specific company, snapApps.com.

HOW SEARCH ENGINES WORK

The term *search engine* is often used generically to describe both search engines and directories. They both contain a wealth of information gathered from billions of Web pages throughout the Internet. Directories and search engines differ mainly in how each compiles its database of information.

Directories

A directory such as the Open Directory, www.dmoz.org, *depends on people for compiling its information.* People from around the world submit their Web site URLs, such as www.mywebsite.com, to the Open Directory Add URL text box with a brief description of the content. Volunteer editors view the Web site and decide whether it is appropriate for the Open Directory and then place it in a category. Web surfers who visit the Open Directory can either browse through the categories to find what they want or conduct a keyword search.

Search Engines

A search engine such as Altavista.com *compiles its information automatically.* No human interaction takes place with the Web sites submitted. Search engines have three major elements.

1. *The Spider (also called the crawler).* The spider visits a Web page, reads it, and then follows links to other pages within the site. This is what it means when someone refers to a site being "spidered" or "crawled." The spider returns to the site on a regular basis, such as every month or two, to look for changes.

2. *The Index (also called a catalog).* Everything the spider finds goes into the second part of a search engine, the index. The index is like a giant digital book containing a copy of every Web page that the spider finds. If a Web page changes, then this book is updated with new information. Sometimes there is a time lag for new Web pages to enter the index; a Web page may have been "spidered" but not yet "indexed." Until a Web page is added to the index, it is not available to those searching with the search engine.

3. *The Software.* Search engine software is the third part of a search engine. This is the program that sifts through the millions of pages recorded in the index to find matches to a search and ranks them in an order the specific search engine deems most relevant.

Hybrid Search Engines

Many search engines maintain a directory *and* have search engine results for keywords that are not in the directory. This may seem confusing, but think of typing the term *nuclear missile* into a hybrid search engine. First, the hybrid search engine will look in its directory for the page under one of the many categories. If no page is found in the listing, then the hybrid search engine will default to the index (catalog) of a large search engine.

One of the most popular default search engines is the Inktomi database. Inktomi is a technology-based company; one of its main products is the Inktomi search engine. The Inktomi database does not have a Web page that someone can search; instead it sells the use of its index to other search engines, such as Yahoo! Inktomi licenses its search engine out to other companies that want their own search engines without having to build them from scratch. HotBot, launched in May 1996 and owned by Wired Ventures at the time, was Inktomi's first customer. Inktomi now also powers MSN Search and other search engines, and it provides supplementary results to Yahoo!, Snap, GoTo.com and other search services.[1]

As an example of a hybrid search engine, Go (Infoseek) lists sites primarily in two ways. It has a directory, in which human editors have organized sites into categories. It also has a search engine component, in which its spider crawls the Web to build an index of Web pages. Formerly known as Infoseek, the service was officially rebranded Go in May 1999. Other examples of hybrid search engines are Yahoo.com, snap.com, lycos.com, and America Online.

Specialty Search Engines

In general, search engines, directories, and hybrid search engines generate the majority of the search engine traffic. New models for search engines are being continually developed. Many Web sites have the ability to search through just the information located on their Web site. One example is www.microsoft.com, which offers search capabilities of just Microsoft information. Community portals are also becoming popular. Portals are Web sites tailored to a specific theme or target market. For example, the search capabilities for these Web sites are tailored to specific topics of interest.

Another unique model for a directory is GoTo.com. To develop its index, companies submit URLs* to GoTo.com and associate a specific page (URL) to a keyword along with a particular price bid. Then, when a consumer enters a search for a particular keyword/ phrase, say "digital camera software," if the consumer actually clicks through to that company's URL, the company is charged on a cost-per-click basis for that listing. Under this model, the pages in the index are ranked not by page content, but by the highest cost-per-click bid by the companies who submitted their URLs. This can be an effective tool in driving targeted customers to specific pages in a Web site. GoTo.com is one of the highest revenue-generating directories due to this cost-per-click model.

What "Spiders" Look for When They Crawl a Web Site

Imagine typing "digital camera" into a search engine. The search engine will check its index of pages and find the Web page with the highest relevance. How does the spider decide which page is the most relevant? This is a very important step in the success of search engine positioning.

When a spider searches a page, it generally looks for items referred to as HTML** tags; refer to Figures 11A-1 and 11A-2. The relationship between what the user actually sees (Figure 11A-1, the Web page) and the HTML code that creates it (Figure 11A-2, the HTML code) is explained here.

1. **Title Tag**—<title>Inexpensive Digital Camera Software</title>
   a. This tag is often used as the title in the search engine results. Often the text is transparent to the user viewing the page. It is highlighted in boldface in the HTML Code in Figure 11A-2 and denoted by the <title> tag.
2. **Meta Tags**—Meta Tags are invisible to those who view the Web page. They are

---

*URL (universal resource locator) is another term used for a Web address.

**Hypertext markup language (HTML)*—the authoring language used to create documents on the World Wide Web. HTML defines the structure and layout of a Web document by using a variety of tags and attributes. The correct structure for an HTML document starts with <HTML><HEAD>(enter here what document is about)</HEAD><BODY> and ends with </BODY></HTML>(Webopedia.internet.com).

written in the HTML code right after the title and are used for providing keywords and a description of the page contents. Search engines often use Meta Tags to sort and rank Web pages according to the keywords entered into the HTML code.

a. **Keyword Meta Tags—<META NAME = "keywords" content =**
   i. These keywords are chosen to replicate what a user would enter into a search engine to find that particular site.

b. **Description Meta Tags—<META NAME = "description" content =**
   i. Usually this description is located below the title on search engine results and offers an explanation of what the Web site contains.

3. **Link Tags—href="http://www.snapapps.com"**
   a. Link Tags are URL addresses to other Web sites. One of the Link Tags on this page is to www.snapapps.com, snapApps' homepage. Many search engines follow the links to other pages and find out how many times the key-word comes up on the corresponding Web pages. By following the hyperlinks to other pages, search engines can ensure that the Web site's content is devoted to the specific keyword that is entered into the search engine.

4. **ALT Tags—ALT="Digital Cameras"**
   a. An ALT Tag is the description of an image. Each image on the Web page can have one ALT Tag. The ALT Tag tells browser software to show specified text (ALT Tag) while the images are loading, or the text will be used as an alternative to the image if a person's browser has "Graphics turned off."

5. **Comment Tags—<!—This is a comment and cannot be seen by users—>**
   a. Denoted by an exclamation mark in the HTML code, the Comment Tag consists of HTML notes that the developer can see, but are not shown to the user viewing the HTML page.

6. **Heading Tags—<H1 align="center">**
   a. Web pages can have different-size text. These are referred to as Heading Tags. Most search engines give a

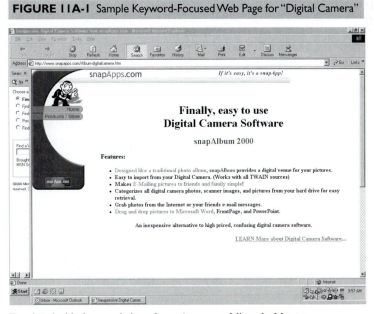

FIGURE 11A-1 Sample Keyword-Focused Web Page for "Digital Camera"

Reprinted with the permission of snapApps.com, Missoula, Montana.

```
<!DOCTYPE HTML PUBLIC "-//W3C//DTD HTML 4.0 Transitional//EN">
<html>
<head>
<title>Inexpensive Digital Camera Software</title>
<META NAME = "keywords" content = "digital cameras, DIGITAL CAMERA, cameras,
digital photos, digital camera software">
<META NAME="description" content="snapAlbum 2000 works like a digital photo Album
and stores pictures from any digital camera.">
</head>
<body leftmargin=0 topmargin=0>
<map name="buttons">
<area shape="rect" coords="2,3,141,16" href="http://www.snapapps.com">
<area shape="rect" coords="2,23,141,36"
href="https://commerce.snapapps.com/index.cfm?page=store</map>
<table cellspacing="0" cellpadding="0" border="0">
<img src="images/snap_left_options2.gif" width=158 height=141 ALT="Digital Cameras"
border="0"
usemap="#buttons"><br>
<!—This is where the body text goes—>
<!—This is a comment and cannot be seen by users: note the exclamation mark—>
<h1 align="center"> This is a heading tag and carries the most weight compared to h2, h3
<br>Finally, easy to use Digital Camera Software</center></h1>
<h2 align="center"><font color="#000080">snapAlbum 2000</font></h2>
<!—More content for the page and then the final link at the bottom—>
href="https://commerce.snapapps.com/index.cfm?page=detail&amp;ProductID=16&amp;x=45
&amp;y=30" target="_top">LEARN More about snapAlbum</a> . . . </b></p>
</body>
</html>
```

FIGURE IIA-2 The HTML Code for the Web Page Shown in Figure IIA-I

Reprinted with the permission of snapApps.com, Missoula, Montana.

higher relevance to larger headings. H1 is the largest heading and the size decreases with H2, H3, and H4.

i. Example (H1)—Refer to the Web page in Figure 11A-1 and the text "Finally, easy to use Digital Camera Software." This can be found in the corresponding HTML code in Figure 11A-2 as **<h1 align="center"> Finally, easy to use Digital Camera Software</center></h1>**

Determining Ranking

When a consumer enters a word or phrase into the search engine, he or she wants only relevant information. For a Web page to show up at the top of the search results, the specific Web page must rank highly on that keyword entered into the search engine. The quest for keyword-focused pages is the common denominator that all search engines look for.

Keyword density is one way search engines decide which Web pages are most relevant to a particular keyword search. The keyword density is calculated by dividing the total number of words on the page by the number of keywords on the page ("digital camera" in this case). The total words for the Web page shown on Figure 11A-1 is 320; "digital camera" is used 14 times in the page. By dividing these numbers, a keyword density of 22.9 is calculated for the search.

The search engine then uses a specific algorithm that takes the keyword density for each HTML tag (the six HTML tags were just explained in detail) and gives the page an overall *percentage of relevance* for "digital camera." The higher the percentage of rele-

vance for the page, the higher the ranking on the search engine. All search engines use a different, secret algorithm to weight each HTML tag. These various weighting techniques are the main reason why the same page may be ranked differently by various search engines.

Figure 11A-3 summarizes the most popular search engine scoring strategies as of February 2, 2000.

FIGURE 11A-3 Search Engine Scoring Strategies

www.SearchEngineWatch.com		
Indexing	*Yes*	*No*
Full Body Text	All	None
Meta Description	All but . . .	FAST, Google, Lycos, NLight
Meta Keywords	All but . . .	Excite, FAST, Google, Lycos, NLight
ALT text	AltaVista, Go, Lycos	Excite, FAST, Google, Inktomi, NLight
Comments	Inktomi	ALL Others
Ranking	*Yes*	*No*
Meta Tags Boost Ranking	Go, Inktomi	AltaVista, Excite, FAST, Google, Lycos, NLight
Link Popularity Boosts Ranking	AltaVista, Excite, FAST, Google, Go, Inktomi, NLight	Lycos

Key

This exhibit covers the crawler-based portions (index not directory) of AltaVista, Excite, FAST Search, Go (Infoseek), Google, Lycos, and Northern Light. It also covers the Inktomi results that form portions of AOL Search, HotBot, and MSN Search. Excite covers portions of Excite-owned Magellan and WebCrawler.

Full Body Text All major search engines say they index the full visible body text of a Web page.

Meta description and Keywords These engines in the "No" column use other criteria (HTML tags) than Meta Tags for relevancy.

ALT Text and Comments These engines in the "Yes" column use ALT Tags and Comment Tags in determining ranking.

Meta Tags Boost Rankings These engines in the "Yes" column put a large amount of weight on the Meta Tags.

Link Popularity Boosts Rankings These engines in the "Yes" column put more relevance on pages that have many other Web pages linking to them.

This chart displays general knowledge about what type of HTML tags are important to each search engine. The exact weight of each of these tags is unknown.

HOW TO MAKE A SITE SEARCH-ENGINE FRIENDLY

Once a company is armed with the knowledge of what spiders are looking for and how people search the Web, a company can decide what keywords are crucial to driving traffic to its Web site. As discussed in the previous sections, the main factors for search engine ranking are the frequency and relevance of the HTML tags in reference to the keyword searched. The first step in preparing a site for high search engine positioning is to find the appropriate keywords upon which to focus the Web page description. Once this list of keywords is compiled and refined, a Web developer can implement these words into the various HTML tags in the Web page.

Choosing the keywords for the Web page focus takes research. It is similar to conducting a target market study before the start of a new marketing campaign. If a Web site developer does not appropriately pick the right keywords, the customers who find the Web site through search engines will likely not be targeted customers.

Prior to choosing the keywords for Web pages, the company should realize that some keywords, because of their common usage, are less useful for ranking than are others. A company can boost its success in search engine positioning by focusing on more distinctive words. For a company to appear at the top of the search engine results for the word *screensaver* is much more difficult than using the phrase *Montana Screensavers*. By choosing more specific words and phrases, companies will increase the likelihood of success at search engine positioning.

How to Generate Keywords and Meta Tag Keywords

Generating keywords can be accomplished by, but is not limited to, the following:

1. *Analyze competitors' source code.* Generate a list of all known competitors in the on-line environment. See which of their sites continually show up high in search engine positioning. As shown in Figure 11A-4, go to the Web pages of the highest ranked competitor sites and click View Source in the menu bar of your Web browser (Internet Explorer or Netscape). Viewing the source code shows the HTML code for that homepage. Check all the keywords in the Title Tag and Meta Tag portions of the document. (Refer to Figure 11A-2 for a sample of where the tags are located.) Make note of these words and phrases for use as possible keywords. View the source code for each product or product line also.

2. *Survey the consumers' perspective.* Generate a customer profile of how the target market searches the Web. For example, if consumers are children, then the keywords in the HTML pages will be much different than if the market is comprised of brain surgeons. Try to anticipate what the user is going to type in the search engine. Use these five tips as a starting point.

   - Features of the product or information they are looking for
   - Benefits gained from the product or information
   - Phrases and questions possibly asked
   - Common misspellings of popular words
   - Trade name and common name

3. *Use search engines.* Many of the search engines offer helpful hints to narrow people's searches. When a person searches by keyword on Excite, the search engine provides the user with suggestions of other words to refine the search. For example, in a search for "digital camera," Excite offered 10 other words to narrow the search (such as *megapixel, handycam,* and *Nikon*). Make note of these keywords, but only if the information is relevant to the Web site being developed.

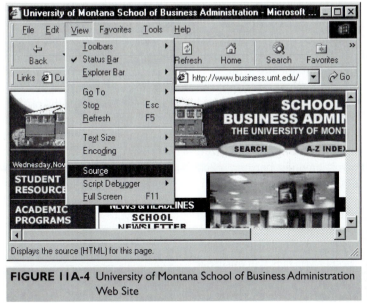

FIGURE 11A-4 University of Montana School of Business Administration Web Site

Reprinted with the permission of the University of Montana School of Business Administration.

CREATING A SEARCH-ENGINE-FRIENDLY PAGE

Once a list of keywords has been developed, the general design of the site can be established. Even if a company already has a Web site, these keywords should be added into those existing pages. However, for the Web pages to be consistently at the top of search engines, the company must deliver valuable content based on the keyword that was added to the pages. For example, simply placing the keyword *parrot* in the HTML tags may boost search engine rankings for people searching for parrots. However, if the page is about pornography or a topic other than parrots, this is considered to be *search engine spamming* or *spamdexing.** These unethical Web pages are

not detected electronically by crawlers or spiders; instead when Web surfers notice an unusual listing in a search engine results list, they can e-mail the Web master of the search engine, who will then remove the page from the index indefinitely. Many businesses competing for a top position on search engine results will e-mail Web masters to complain about irrelevant pages and unethical behaviors.

Many Web developers believe that placing a large variety of keywords on a specific page increases its odds of being ranked highly. On the contrary, each keyword should be focused on the topic of an individual Web page. If a Web page is using many different keywords throughout the same page, the percentage of relevance for one individual keyword is diluted by the other words. If a company has 20 different keywords on the same page, it simply cannot score well with the search engines. This is why each Web page needs to have keywords focused on relevant content.

Some Web developers try to hide hundreds of the same keywords on the same Web page. This is also considered to be spamdexing

*The alteration or creation of a document with intent to deceive an electronic catalog or filing system. Any technique that increases the potential position of a site at the expense of the quality of the search engine's database can also be regarded as spamdexing—also known as *spamming* or *spoofing* (www.cadenza.org/search_engine_terms/srchsz.htm#set_spamdexing).

and is considered unethical by all search engines. Furthermore, a specific keyword may be overused on a Web page. Search engines test pages for reasonable length and reasonable speech, which essentially means if the keyword density for the page is too high, the search engine will know that it is not a normal page and give it a lower ranking.

So what is an engine-optimized page? No one can really create an engine-optimized page for all search engines because each search engine has different criteria. The criteria are kept secret by each search engine. The solution to this problem is to understand the HTML tags that the spiders are looking for. The majority of the time, distributing the keywords into the HTML tags will ensure a fairly high ranking. The key to getting to the number-one ranking is tweaking various HTML tags and adjusting the frequency of keywords.

Software programs are one tool that can be used to assist in optimizing pages for improved search engine positioning. For example, WebPosition Gold (www.webposition. com), based on its understanding of what the various search engines look for, offers software called the Page Critic. The Page Critic knows each search engine's unique personality and how to optimize pages for a top ranking without spamming or abusing the search engines. WebPosition Gold's Page Critic accomplishes this task by critically analyzing the top pages of thousands of different keywords at each search engine. From this data, the Page Critic generates the tendencies of each search engine and explains why the pages ranked highly. Based on this analysis, modifications to the page can be made to improve search engine ranking. For example, the Page Critic found that highly ranked pages at AltaVista had an average keyword frequency of one. The sample Web page shown in Figure 11A-1 has a keyword frequency of three in the Meta Tag for keywords. Although the page in Figure 11A-1 was keyword focused for *digital camera,* it would not have ranked highly on the

AltaVista search engine due to AltaVista's preference for the keyword frequency of one.

For many companies, simply understanding what keywords the pages will be focused on is sufficient. Firms that specialize in search engine positioning can be hired to take those keywords and make the proper modifications for the Web pages to receive a higher ranking. Incorporating these words into the Web page is the first step to higher search engine ranking. After making the site search-engine friendly, the next step is to submit these Web pages to the appropriate search engines and directories.

SUBMITTING WEB PAGES TO SEARCH ENGINES

Search engines and directories do not automatically know that a new page has been created on the Web. The Web pages must be submitted before they can be spidered and indexed. Submitting the appropriate pages to search engines and directories is a time-consuming, yet essential, part of search engine positioning. Thousands of search engines and directories on the Web allow Web page submissions. Individually submitting each page in a Web site to thousands of search engines is a daunting task. Instead, most developers focus on the search engines and directories that are the most popular.

To identify the most popular search engines and directories, firms can access reports on monthly statistics on Internet usage from a variety of sources. For example, Media Metrix publishes a variety of monthly statistics on Internet usage, including the monthly traffic of the top ten portals. Figure 11A-5 shows the 10 most popular search sites as of January 4, 2000, compiled by Media Metrix.

Web marketers estimate that the majority of all search engine traffic originates from the top 10 search engines and directories. Focusing one's time submitting Web pages to these popular search engines is much more effective than trying to rank high on the multi-

Rank	Top 10 Search Sites	Unique Visitors Per Month (000s)
1	Yahoo.com	43,338
2	Go.com	20,334
3	Lycos.com	17,926
4	Excite	14,060
5	AltaVista Search Services	12,697
6	Snap.com Search & Services	10,719
7	Looksmart.com	8,920
8	Goto.com	6,899
9	Iwon.com	6,330
10	AskJeeves.com	6,264

FIGURE 11A-5 Top Ten Search Sites, January 2000

Source: www.mediametrix.com, January 4, 2000.

tude of other search engines. However, if a company finds that a specialty search engine fits the consumer's needs better and attracts targeted customers, then it should be included.

To submit a Web page, go to the desired search engine or directory where the page is to be submitted. Each search engine and directory has a link from its homepage that is characterized as "Add URL" or something very similar. This link will lead the user to a page on which the information can be submitted. A sample directory submission at www.msn.com, the Microsoft Network, is shown in Figure 11A-6. For most search engines, the only information needed to make a submission is a URL. However, many directories and a few search engines require various other types of information. For example, the MSN submission in Figure 11A-6 required not only the URL but also a category, an e-mail address, a title, and a description of the Web page being submitted.

How Often to Submit Pages

A very important issue in search engine positioning is the frequency of submission. Some search engines consider more than one submission per day unethical, whereas others have no limits on the number of page submissions. Figure 11A-7 shows general submission guidelines for the different search engines and directories. Two caveats apply to relying on the guidelines shown in Figure 11A-7: (1) Submission guidelines are likely to change in the future, and (2) not all of the search engines and directories are listed in the table.

FIGURE 11A-6 Sample Web Page Submission to MSN (Microsoft)

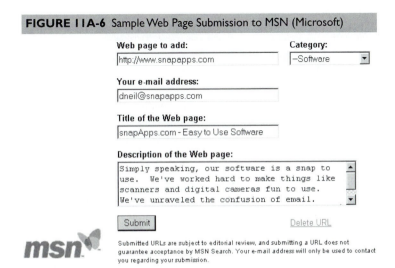

Source: http://search.msn.com/addurl.asp?q=&RS=CHECKED&co=20.

Search Engine	Submit More Than Homepage	Submit Limit	Submitted Pages Appear In	Nonsubmitted Pages Appear In	Overall Freshness[a]
AltaVista	Yes	About 5 pages per day	1 to 2 days	About 1 month	1 day to 1 month
Excite	No	25 pages per week	Within 2 weeks	Up to 6 weeks	1 day to 3 weeks
Google	No	No limit, but only sub a few pages per site	4 to 6 weeks	4 to 6 weeks	1 day to 6 weeks
HotBot	Yes	50 pages per day	Within 2 months	Within 2 months	1 day to 2 months
Go (Infoseek)	No	1 page per day	Within 6 weeks	Within 6 weeks	1 day to 6 weeks
Lycos (Web index)	Yes	No limit, but stay below 50 a day to be safe	3 to 6 weeks	3 to 6 weeks	1 day to 6 weeks
Northern Light	No	No limit, but sub only a few pages per site	2 to 4 weeks	2 to 4 weeks	1 day to 1 month

FIGURE 11A-7 General Submission Guidelines, as of December 4, 1999

[a] Spiders look for new and updated content and give higher rankings to pages with "fresher," newer content.
Source: www.searchenginewatch.com.

A solution to the complexity of the submission process is through a Web site submission tool. One effective tool that automates search engine submission is AddWeb. Instead of entering submission information many times at each search engine and directory, AddWeb creates the ability to enter the information into AddWeb only once. Once the information is gathered by AddWeb, it automates the process of submitting to almost 2,500 search engines through what is called *browser emulation.* Some search engines cannot receive submissions unless they can recognize the Web browser that is doing the submission. So, for example, if they don't see that Internet Explorer or Netscape Navigator submitted the page, they won't receive the submission. AddWeb and other tools have the ability to emulate these browsers when they submit Web pages so that the search engine recognizes the submission as being browser generated. Furthermore, AddWeb and similar tools automatically check to see how often the pages can be submitted to each search engine.

This process of checks and balances helps to avoid search engine spamming.

The drawback of using AddWeb to submit to many search engines is that the pages cannot be tailored to each search engine. Moreover, although a firm might have first used the Page Critic software by WebPosition Gold prior to using AddWeb, the software analyzes the Web page according to only the top 10 or so search engines. Finally, check the pages meticulously before submitting to the search engines because there is no opportunity to (un)submit them.

TRACKING THE SUCCESS OF WEB PAGE SUBMISSIONS

The two easiest ways to track the success of the Web site submissions is through checking the submission status at each of the search engines or generating Web site statistics through log files.

Checking Submission Status

The search engines and directories offer a simple way for checking the status of the Web site. For example, at Altavista.com, one types the URL, or Web address, of the page to be checked into the search box. If the Web page shows on the search results, the page has been indexed. Many people expect that the Web pages will appear within a few days. However, as shown in Figure 11A-7, some search engines may take as long as six weeks to index pages. Furthermore, some of the submissions at the search engines and directories never are indexed. This is due to the overwhelming number of Web pages submitted daily. Search engines have been known to shut down the submissions area of the Web site for periods of time due to the overload of pages to be processed.

Checking the status of all the pages on all the search engines can be an overwhelming task. Many third-party tools on the Web make this process easier. These various tools save a considerable amount of time.

Using Log Files to Generate Statistics

Many companies want to know the actual traffic that these search engine rankings generate for their Web sites. Web servers, the computers that host Web sites, maintain log files that catalog every request made to the server by people surfing the Web. The log files catalog hundreds of Web site statistics, but the data are stored in a format that is difficult for people to understand. Log file analyzers take the raw log file data and transform it into useful marketing information. With log file analysis software, it's possible to generate a good idea of where visitors are coming from, what term they used in the search engine, how often they return to the Web site, and hundreds of other useful statistics.

Often, the Internet service provider (ISP) that hosts the Web site will generate these statistics from the log files for a small fee. If the Internet service provider does not provide comprehensive statistics, firms can either download or purchase software, log file analyzers, that is extremely easy to use and accessible on the Web for all authenticated employees to see.

LIMITATIONS OF SEARCH ENGINE POSITIONING

Even though search engine positioning offers many advantages, there are some limitations. The first and foremost limitation is understanding that attracting consumers to a Web site does not necessarily mean they are going to purchase anything. The traditional tools of advertising and promotion and a convincing message are still very important. An excellent source for understanding on-line selling can be found at www.sitesell.com. This digital book outlines the key essentials on how to not only increase the number of visitors but also increase sales.

The second limitation of search engine positioning relates to the nature of consumer search. How does a company target a person who doesn't know the correct word to type in to find the appropriate Web site? For example, snapApps.com sells a product that organizes user names and passwords in a simple computer software application. Although it offers a useful service, this product, called snapSafe, has been very difficult to sell through search engine positioning. People don't generally search for a product to organize their passwords. Finding interested customers means using keywords that are not directly associated with the product, such as the keyword *Web surfer.* Web surfers generally access many different Web sites and therefore would need to store many user names and passwords. If on one hand, snapApp.com focuses its Web page on generating traffic from the keyword *Web surfers,* and if on the other hand, its Web page is about organizing passwords, that could be characterized as spamdexing. Search engine positioning is generally limited to consumers that are informed rather than uninformed about the product offering. Uninformed consumers need to be reached in other environments and advertising media.

Third, the whole process of (re)designing the Web site and (re)engineering the pages so that they are keyword focused is a time-consuming process. Furthermore, Web page submissions take a significant amount of time. After the pages have been submitted to an engine, the pages must be frequently checked to see if they have been indexed. One option for search engine positioning is to use the services of a third-party vendor. Outsourcing search engine positioning can save a significant amount of time and money. For example, third parties, such as Morevisibility.com or Positionsolutions.com, can usually deliver rankings in the top 10 for each keyword and are accustomed to understanding how the on-line environment for search engines is changing. In January 2000, Morevisibility.com offered search engine positioning for $1,200 per keyword per year. In June 2000, Positionsolutions offered search engine positioning for $199 per month for 30 keywords.

The potential value of high rankings on search engines makes engaging in search engine positioning difficult to ignore. The value of successful search engine positioning is hard to dispute, but the process to get to the top of search engine rankings is not a simple one. The various techniques used to perform effective search engine positioning were explored in detail in this Appendix to help marketers and business decision makers understand the concepts and processes associated with search engine positioning that will aid in making an educated and informed decision.

Note

1. Searchenginewatch.com, *How Inktomi Works,* January 4, 2000.

CHAPTER 12

Realizing the Promise of Technology

> *If the automobile industry had made as much progress as the computer industry in the past 50 years, a car today would cost a hundredth of a cent and go faster than the speed of light.*
> —RAY KURZWEIL,
> *The Age of Spiritual Machines,* 1999

Technological developments offer so many promises of a better life, from making us more efficient, to entertaining us, to keeping us in touch with each other, to making us healthier. At the same time, however, technological advances not only have proven to fall far short of their promises; they've also created problems and unforeseen hazards. For example, air bags were touted as a space-age fail-safe measure to protect people who refused to wear seat belts. But the early air bags, which deployed at speeds approaching 200 miles per hour, ended up killing 141 people, mostly children or small adults.[1] Similarly, breakthroughs in antibiotics early last century inspired predictions about the eradication of disease, but now we are faced with drug-resistant microbes, and we are running out of antibiotics.[2] This chapter addresses some of these issues, issues that can pose obstacles to realizing the promise of technology, such as unintended consequences of technology, ethical controversies over technological developments, concerns over some high-tech firms' apparent lack of and disregard for social issues, and market forces which may stymie innovation and access (see Figure 12-1).

THE PARADOXES OF TECHNOLOGY[3] AND UNINTENDED CONSEQUENCES

In the 1930s, the fierce, biting South American fire ant entered the United States as a ship stowaway. Although it was targeted for eradication with DDT and superpesticides, after three decades, the pesticides had done more damage to the ants' predators than to the invaders. The chemicals actually ended up helping to increase the ant population rather than to eradicate it.[4]

As this example shows, the best-laid technological plans often go awry. Many people are susceptible to overinflated enthusiasm about the possible benefits of high-tech solutions. Yet technology is inherently paradoxical, with every positive quality potentially countered by an opposing negative quality. Although we find ourselves in an environment that promises adventure, power, joy, growth, and transformation of both ourselves and our world, the pace, complexity, and unintended consequences of technological development are threatening, too. Not only has technology provided people freedom, control, and efficiency; it has degraded the environment, usurped human competence, encouraged human dependence and passivity, and at the extreme, put us on the brink of obliteration.

371

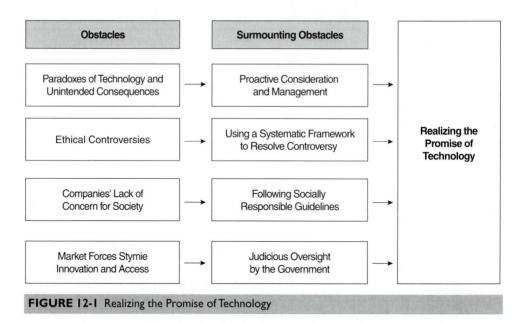

FIGURE 12-1 Realizing the Promise of Technology

Research conducted by David Mick and Susan Fournier identified eight paradoxes regarding consumers' views of technology.

Technology Paradoxes

As Figure 12-2 shows, eight paradoxes can be identified that characterize the relationship between consumers and technology.

1. *Control–chaos.* Technology is supposed to help bring order to our lives and businesses. However, once purchased, technology can disrupt our everyday routines. For example, as a society, we have become so dependent on computers that if they fail, we can no longer do our work. Indeed, in this wired world, we are more susceptible than ever to crashes from viruses that bring work to a standstill, as witnessed by both the Melissa and LoveBug computer viruses.

2. *Assimilation–isolation.* Many technologies help us connect with other people, either by facilitating communication or by providing shared experiences. But these technologies have also become a substitute for face-to-face and personal contact, and other social activities. Ultimately, when we log on to virtual communities, we sit alone at our computers. For example, research shows the more hours people spend on the Internet, the more depressed, stressed, and alienated they feel, even if most of their time is spent sending messages or "interacting" in chat rooms. "We've become so removed from reality that we don't even know how to feed our increasing hunger for intimacy."[5] Moreover, 6% of Internet users suffer from some form of addiction to it, such as compulsive Internet use, on-line gambling, porn/sex sites, consumerism, stock trading, surfing, or chat rooms.[6] False feelings of intimacy, timelessness, and lack of inhibition contribute to the addictive force of the Internet.

3. *Intelligence–stupidity.* Sophisticated products are supposed to help us be smarter by allowing us to perform complex tasks. But if the products are difficult to master

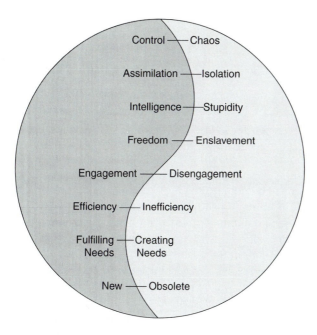

FIGURE 12-2 The Yin and Yang of Technology

or cause us to lose old skills, we actually feel inadequate or inferior in mastering new technologies.

4. ***Freedom–enslavement.***   Products that offer freedom can end up creating new restrictions. For example, voice mail gets us away from our offices, but makes us feel obligated to check our messages constantly. Cell phones give us freedom, but now we are always available.

5. ***Engagement–disengagement.***   Although some technologies are designed to make participating in activities easier, they may detract from the quality of the experience. For example, instead of smelling and squeezing lemons for ripeness, we can now order them from a computer checklist. We watch food heat under plastic wrap behind glass microwave doors instead of carefully stirring pots and inhaling aromas that have filled the house with comforting smells.[7] The very things that are supposed to simplify our lives and allow us to stay in touch with each other are putting us further out of reach with sense-dulling "conveniences."

6. ***Efficiency–inefficiency.***   New technology can help us perform tasks faster, but also creates time-consuming new chores. For example, the average number of e-mail messages received each week by U.S. office workers in 1998 was 179, according to eMarketer.com. For those in Internet firms, the number rises to 233.[8] Additionally, many companies invested in information technology with the expectation that such investments would make their businesses more productive. Although most statistics do suggest that the increases in economic productivity are, in large part, due to investments in information technology, at the personal level, inefficiencies arising from such things as continued efforts to keep current with software upgrades, the use of computers for personal activities (such as e-mail and Internet surfing), and so forth, cause frustration.[9]

7. ***Fulfilling needs–creating needs.***   Many technology products create new needs even as they fulfill others. For example, although we might be able to use software to do

more sophisticated tasks, we also now need to attend training programs to learn how to use the software to do those tasks.

8. *New–obsolete.* Although people are excited by owning cutting-edge products, their excitement is chronically undermined by a fear of falling behind.

These paradoxes highlight the fact that technological developments do have unintended consequences. Of course, the unintended consequences are not always negative, as is highlighted in Box 12-1.

How do these paradoxes affect the way people view technology and, ultimately, their purchase strategies and behaviors? Potential purchasers of technology create coping strategies to lessen the presence of the paradoxes. Understanding such coping strategies can give marketers insight into segments of technology consumers and the differing types of marketing messages that may be useful, given consumers' concerns. For example, buyers of computers may place limits on how often they use them so that they don't take over their lives. Indeed, some Silicon Valley executives decidedly reject the use of technology during their personal time, refusing to own computers and other electronic gadgets.[10] For others, the response to the presence of the paradoxes of technology is to lessen the impact of technology by engaging in activities such as yoga, massage, and Tai Chi.

At its extreme, the backlash against technology can be seen in the Luddite movement.[11] **Luddites** are people opposed to technology and changes brought about by technology. (The etymology of the word possibly comes from Ned Ludd, an eighteenth-century Leicestershire worker who destroyed machinery [circa 1811],[12] or from a boy named Ludlam, who, to spite his father, broke a knitting frame.[13]) Regardless, to protest unemployment caused by the industrial revolution in the early nineteenth century, English workers known as Luddites resorted to a campaign of breaking machinery, especially knitting machines. The Luddites signed their destruction "General Ludd," "King Ludd," or "Ned Ludd." The government dealt harshly with the Luddites—fourteen were hanged in January 1813 in York. Although sporadic outbreaks of violence continued until 1816, the movement soon died out.

Unfortunately, technology marketers, with their enthusiasm for the products they market, are sometimes blind to the dual impacts of technology from a customer's perspective. At a minimum, marketers must be alert to the presence of the paradoxes, try to actively consider what the unintended consequences of a new technology might be, and develop contingency plans for their marketing efforts. Ultimately, firms must be aware that blind pursuit of the technological imperative can potentially be viewed as threatening and interfering with sociological needs for safety and human dignity. Because customers will ultimately make the decision whether to buy, firms must pay attention to the tension these paradoxes pose. The controversy surrounding genetically modified food provides an example.

Example of Backlash Due to Fears Arising from Technology: Protests over Genetically Modified Foods

What are genetically modified foods? To answer this question, one must understand the function of DNA. The code of all life-forms is written in deoxyribonucleic acid (DNA), which takes the form of a double helix (long spiral staircase). The rungs linking the two sides of the staircase are composed of pairs of nucleotides: adenine and thymine, or

BOX 12-1

Unintended Consequences of the Internet

The Internet is having a profound impact on the environment. While the economy grew more than 9% in 1997 and 1998, energy demand stayed almost flat. The Internet has allowed people and businesses to use energy and resources more efficiently. For example, on-line retailers with warehouses have eight times the number of sales per square foot as a physical store. If, as predicted by the Organization for Economic Cooperation and Development, the Internet makes 12.5% of retail space superfluous, it would save $5 billion worth of energy every year.[a] Similarly, a book purchased on-line costs about one-sixteenth the energy of one bought in the store. And, one minute spent driving uses the same amount of energy as 20 minutes of shopping from home. By putting reading materials on-line, the Internet is predicted to reduce worldwide demand for paper by about 2.7 million tons by 2003.[b]

[a] Cox, Beth (2000), "E-commerce Said to Be Eco-Friendly," *InternetNews.com,* January 11.
[b] Taylor, Chris (2000), "Why Mother Nature Should Love Cyberspace," *Time,* April–May, p. 82.

cytosine and guanine. Importantly, these base pairs contain the complete set of instructions for an organism's biological processes required to live and reproduce, its "genome." As an example, there are three billion base pairs for the human genome.[14]

So, genetically modified (GM) foods are grown from seeds that reweave the strands of DNA to alter the instruction set. For example, modifications have rewoven genes to make crops withstand frost, herbicides, and even produce their own pesticides. Monsanto includes DNA from a common bacterium in its seeds that makes plants toxic to insects, but not to humans. These modifications have proven popular with farmers: Increases in crop yields mean an increase in profits.

Sales of genetically modified seeds rose from $75 million in 1995 to $1.5 billion in 1998. Figure 12-3 shows the percentages of corn and soybeans that are grown from genetically modified seeds. The use of corn and soy grown from genetically modified seeds is prevalent in many products, including soy baby formula, vegetable spreads, and McDonald's milkshakes.[15]

In the United States, genetically modified components are viewed as additives and do not require Food and Drug Administration (FDA) approval. The FDA says foods with GM ingredients are perfectly safe. However, others argue that there are profound differences between GM and traditional crops, and that problems have arisen in the past. For example, pollen from some strains of corn with built-in pesticides kills the larva of the Monarch butterfly. There is passionate concern over modifying the genetic code of other species. For example, genetic modifications to salmon have produced fish that grow twice as fast, resist disease, and outmate competitors.[16] Critics worry that this is a biological time bomb that could destroy the remaining natural salmon populations.

The rise of companies marketing products guaranteed to be free from genetic alterations, and selling such foods at premium price, is evidence of the backlash against this technological advance. Firms that have invested hundreds of thousands of research

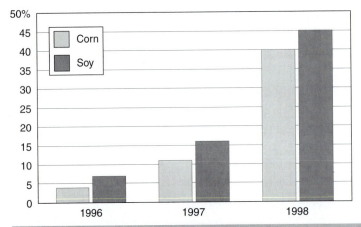

FIGURE 12-3 Percentage of Corn and Soy Grown with Genetically Modified Seeds

Source: Kluger, Jeffrey (1999), "Food Fight," *Time,* September 13, pp. 42–44.

dollars into GM foods inevitably question its value when the resulting products sell at a lower rather than higher price.

Public fears about GM food are very acute in Europe. Whereas 90% of Americans believe the U.S. Department of Agriculture's statements on biotechnology, only 12% of Europeans trust their national food regulators. The European Union has approved the sale of 18 GM products, but banned importation of nonapproved GM corn. Because GM strains in the past were mixed with ordinary strains in the United States, the entire U.S. corn export to Europe was banned in 1998. Moreover, since 1997 the EU has required that foods with engineered DNA be labeled as such. Major protests have been staged in France, such that U.S. agribusiness giants are now segregating their genetically modified crops from conventional ones, so as not to ship GM products overseas.

Marketing and Business Implications What are some of the marketing and business lessons that can be learned from this controversy? Probably the biggest lesson—and challenge—is to *manage the public's misgivings* about the altered products. People's instincts often are to concentrate not on potential benefits, but on potential accidents and abuses. These instincts are particularly pronounced in the case of GM foods because, rather than making food better tasting, cheaper, or safer, these technological discoveries have helped primarily with the production and distribution of food.[17] Because the benefits are not obvious to consumers, it is natural that fears about the technology supercede desires for it.

Another implication comes in the area of *labeling.* Research by Konstantinos Giannakas and Murray Fulton shows that if consumers are averse to genetic modification and don't see the benefits of genetic modification (say, in lower prices), to the extent that they trust the regulatory system, labeling makes sense. However, if consumers don't trust the regulatory system, an outright ban may occur. Because consumer awareness about GM products and their preferences or aversion for them affect purchase decisions, public policy makers must consider the effects of labeling on consumer demand.[18]

In terms of other business implications, these scientific discoveries are *erasing boundaries between businesses.* Agricultural seed companies compete with chemical companies—

the new seeds are direct threats to pesticides and herbicides—and with pharmaceuticals (when the foods are designed with medicinal value). Future discoveries with important implications for human health may now come from agricultural and chemical labs. This convergence of industries arising from developments in the life sciences is just beginning to take effect. Ripple effects are predicted to be felt in health care, consumer products, and cosmetics companies. For example, the ratio of doctor bills to pharmaceutical costs, which is now 9–1, is predicted to shift to 1–1 in the next 25 years.[19] Other implications will be felt in the energy business, which will use renewable plant sources for energy, textiles, mining, and environmental remediation. The Technology Expert's View from the Trenches provides insights on challenges to realizing the promise of biotechnology.

The Technology Tidbit focuses on nanotechnology. Nanotechnology, as it is expected to develop during the next 30 years, offers the potential to cure all physical diseases, reverse aging and prolong or restore vital youth, provide abundant and almost limitless wealth, open the frontiers of space, and in general empower individuals to seek fulfillment of their wildest dreams, within, of course, the limits imposed by the laws of physics. It also offers the potential to produce our worst nightmares. The transition from our current world to the world of nanotechnology will be a time of immense danger, instability, and uncertainty, as well as a time of great opportunities.[20] Concerns over unintended consequences also highlight the fact that many technological breakthroughs can create ethical dilemmas.

ETHICAL CONTROVERSIES SURROUNDING TECHNOLOGICAL ADVANCES

Many technological breakthroughs are outpacing society's capacity to deal with the ethical dilemmas that arise. For example, scientists have identified a gene that enhances memory in mice. The gene, NMDA receptor 2B, or NR2B, directs production of a nerve protein that helps the brain recognize when two things are linked. The gene normally becomes less active in middle age, as memory declines. But when an extra copy of the gene programmed to remain active in old age is inserted into mouse embryos, the enhancement is permanent and is passed on to offspring.[21] Such discoveries raise many ethical concerns. Who will have access to the genes that improve cognitive performance? Only those who can afford to pay for the procedures? Can families now order "designer babies," specifying the gene enhancements that go beyond simply correcting abnormalities to increasing human capacities above those currently deemed normal?

Similarly, in 1995, scientists discovered that women of Ashkenazi Jewish descent (of Central or Eastern European ancestry) whose close relatives had breast and ovarian cancers and who had inherited a particular mutated gene called BRCA1 had as much as a 90% risk of developing breast cancer and a 40% to 50% risk of developing ovarian cancer. Further study revealed that as many as 1% of Jewish women carried this mutation.[22] Scientists and labs decided *not* to offer the test for the mutation to the general public, because questions remained about the risk posed by the gene (it was not clear if a woman with the mutated gene would get cancer), about what could be done to lessen the risk of getting cancer, and about whether testing would do more harm than good (concern over insurance coverage for these women). However, at least one lab found these reasons patronizing, saying that women have right to know, and offered the test.

Controversies in other technology arenas also arise. Technologies for sharing music files, such as those developed by MP3.com and Napster, allow for the violation of

Biotechnology: Promises and Challenges

RALPH E. CHRISTOFFERSEN, Ph.D.
CEO and President, Ribozyme Pharmaceuticals, Inc.,
Boulder, Colorado

The last thirty years have been described by many as the "age of biology." Cloning, from proteins to sheep, has provided unprecedented opportunities for understanding and treating diseases. Sequencing of the human genome has expanded the possibilities dramatically, and allows for the long-term possibility of diagnosing and treating diseases with specificity previously unimagined. Indeed, many diseases thought to be untreatable now have treatments thanks to biotechnology advances, and many others are being studied with the potential for treatment in the future. With such significant advances and future potential, it has been thought by many that the decades ahead will bring major advances in therapeutic design and development, and the practice of medicine will be changed dramatically. Not surprisingly, this potential has spawned a new industry, the "biotechnology industry," led by entrepreneurs who believe that not only scientific advances but new business paradigms are possible that can accelerate the process.

At the same time, these significant promises have been mitigated by a number of serious challenges. Historically, development of a new therapeutic agent has been highly risky. Depending somewhat on the nature of the disease, development of a new therapeutic agent has taken approximately 10 years, required approxi-mately $100 million or more in cash, and had an overall probability of success of ap-proximately 10%. Given these odds, many potential investors passed on the biotech-nology opportunity, claiming that "the odds of success were probably better in Las Vegas." However, entrepreneurs be-lieved that new business models along with new scientific paradigms that would improve the probability of success sub-stantially were possible.

The result has been, in large part, an enormously successful experiment. Several very successful companies have been built with products meeting critical medical needs, including Amgen, Genentech, Bio-gen, and Chiron. Furthermore, the next generation of companies is developing rapidly, and promises to continue both the business and scientific revolution that has begun. The result has been creation of thousands of new, high-paying jobs along with a competitive advantage for the United States, in which the environment has been nurtured. At the same time, tra-ditional pharmaceutical companies have discovered the power of the new technolo-gies and nontraditional business models, and have embraced them through partner-ships, internal efforts, and acquisitions to improve their traditional record of success.

With such successes, it would be ex-pected that the biotechnology industry would be burgeoning with new entries, each following the paradigm for success set down by the leaders. In some ways this has happened, since more than 1,500 biotechnology companies now exist in the

United States, of which approximately 300 have successfully become public companies. On the other hand, a number of significant challenges to development of the industry remain, that make starting or developing a biotechnology company a very risky business.

Among the challenges and barriers are the product development time and life cycle. While patent protection can, in principle, provide more than 15 years of proprietary commercial sales for a successfully developed product, regulatory requirements for product approval can use up ten or more years of the patent protection time. When compared with other product development times and commercial opportunities (e.g., information technology products and services), investors frequently choose other options. In addition, the amount of money needed to develop each product presents a daunting challenge. No single person or group of investors is likely to invest $100 million in a ten-year development program at the outset. The result typically has been initial investment by venture capital investors in the $10 million to $15 million range, with the hope that an IPO and successive public investments will fund the remainder of product development costs. This means that a biotechnology company is almost always on the verge of running out of money, which has been exacerbated further by both venture capital and public investor expectations of results sooner than science or funding could reasonably be expected

to produce. This makes recruitment and retention, as well as maintenance of morale, of employees a significant challenge. Furthermore, with the specter of price controls on the horizons in the United States, the potential for increased investor reluctance due to decreased potential profit is very real.

More subtly, a number of other internal challenges exist within individual companies. One of the most important is having a technology that has broad therapeutic application. All too often, companies have been formed based on development of a single product, which raises the potential for failure significantly. Another challenge relates to finding appropriate personnel. The need for persons with drug discovery, development, and commercial experience from large pharmaceutical companies is evident, but finding such persons who also possess entrepreneurial skills and risk tolerance is frequently a very difficult task. Adding to these challenges are uncertainties associated with patents (will they issue, will they have broad claims, will they be challenged, etc.?), political and ethical issues (price controls, fears of "eugenics," treatment of human genetic information, etc.), and the status of competitors.

As a result, biotechnology is not for the faint of heart. The benefits, both to mankind and individuals in the field, can be enormous, but the risks and frustrations can make success quite challenging to achieve.

intellectual property rights and copyright laws. The parties whose rights are violated have taken their fight to the courts, but at its heart, such developments can also boil down to one of ethics.

In addition to such controversies, charges have been leveled at the new Silicon Valley business model that it is one based on greed and a lack of ethics.[23] This is somewhat surprising, because the young businesspeople who run them are often Generation Xers and Yers—generations that data suggest have been critical of the hypocrisy of prior business

---

TECHNOLOGY TIDBIT

Nanotechnology, Molecular Biology, and Molecular Computing

Technological breakthroughs are endowing people with machine-like attributes, and machines with human-like attributes. Within one hundred years, some predict that our descendants will be more machine-like than human! For example, the MIT Media Lab is designing wearable computers to enhance memory and interactive virtual systems to augment reality. British Telecommunication has an R&D effort called "Soul Catcher" aimed at developing a computer to implant in the brain to expand memory and computational capacity. Some predict that notebooks and palmtops will disappear, with their displays built into contact lenses or painted on the retina.

At its extreme, the exponential development of nanotechnology, biotechnology, and computing technology will converge to launch ultra-intelligent machines, and the world will enter a posthuman era, in which new, smarter, faster generations roll over in years, then months, then days. Educated guesses are that this technology will arrive sometime in the next 15 to 30 years.

What is nanotechnology?[a] *Nano-* is a prefix used in science meaning "a billionth of," and in technology, it means building things based on atomic and molecular structures. Its components are single devices that are a fraction of the size of DNA molecules; they work at the individual atomic or molecular level, with devices ranging in size from 1 nanometer

(one-billionth of a meter) to 100 nanometers. Predicted to have as significant an impact in the twenty-first century as antibiotics, the integrated circuit (chips), and man-made polymers did in the twentieth century, the U.S. government is investing hundreds of millions of dollars into nanotechnology research (through the White House Science and Technology Council, the Interagency Working Group, and the National Science Foundation). Among the applications:

> Molecular manufacturing is the anticipated ability to inexpensively fabricate complex devices, both large and small, with precise control over the arrangement of the individual atoms that constitute the device. For example, nanotechnology may allow bricks to be built with molecules instructed to repair themselves when cracks appear.

> Molecular computing is predicted to be the next generation of computing, bringing a giant leap in computing beyond the current generation of transistors (currently based on electric impulses), based on molecular reactions.

> Another use will be based on biomolecular reactions. Medical nanomachines will operate at the cellular level, say, to identify and attach to individual cancer cells. Nanoparticles will also help prevent immune reactions against implants with prosthetic limbs and artificial organs. Medical diagnostics can also use DNA detection based on small amounts of blood, which can be screened for numerous diseases.[b]

---

[a] Westphal, Sylvia Pagan (2000), "Remaking the World One Atom at a Time," *LATimes.com,* downloaded June 19, 2000.

[b] Licking, Ellen (1999), "The Great DNA Chip Derby," *Business Week,* October 25, pp. 90–92.

Source: Bryan, Rebecca (2000), "Two-Timing the Clock: Trying to Slow the Raging River of Progress? Take a Step Back and Disconnect from the World," *Business 2.0,* February, pp. 227–230.

models and skeptical of businesses. Is the problem due to lack of understanding of how to address ethical dilemmas responsibly?

Controversy inevitably surrounds many technological developments, and high-tech firms cannot simply ignore these issues when they arise. The risk of possible negative publicity and antitechnology backlash can have a very detrimental effect on the commercialization and success of new technologies. Because of the many ethical dilemmas presented by the development and marketing of high-technology products and innovations, this chapter offers a framework for addressing such dilemmas, as shown in Table 12-1. The use of this framework will be demonstrated in the context of the pharmaceutical industry with the situation faced by Merck Pharmaceutical in the 1980s.

Merck, Ivermectin, and River Blindness[24]

In 1978, a disease called river blindness plagued at least 85 million people throughout Africa and parts of the Middle East and Latin America. The cause of the disease is a parasitic worm carried by a tiny black fly that lives and thrives along fast-moving rivers. When the flies bite people, the larva of the parasitic worm enters the human body, eventually growing to more than two feet in length and causing grotesque but relatively innocuous nodules in the skin. The health problems caused by the worms begin when the adult worm reproduces, releasing millions of microscopic offspring, which swarm through the body tissue causing terrible itching, so terrible that some past victims committed suicide. After several years, the microfilariae cause lesions and depigmentation of the skin. Eventually, they invade the eyes, often causing blindness.

Indeed, the disease was so prevalent in some areas that the children assumed blindness was simply part of growing up. The World Health Organization labeled river blindness as a public health and socioeconomic problem, because of the burdens of the illness coupled with attempts of people to avoid flies, in which they abandoned fertile ground near rivers, moving to poorer land with decreased food production.

In Merck's labs, a scientist stumbled upon the possibility that one of its drugs used to eliminate insect-borne parasites in cows, ivermectin, might actually have properties that would enable it to eliminate the parasite that caused river blindness. However, from Merck's perspective, this was not necessarily good news. For starters, the process to identify which discoveries to pursue was difficult. For every pharmaceutical compound that became a "product" candidate, thousands of others fell by the wayside. Moreover, if Merck did make the decision to invest in further research for this drug, including conducting field trials in remote areas of the world, it was plagued by many critical issues. First, the population that would benefit from this discovery was relatively small. Second, the population lacked the means to pay for the medication. Third, there was no infrastructure in place to deliver the medication and oversee the administration of the treatments over

---

TABLE 12-1   Framework for Addressing Ethical Dilemmas

1 Identify all stakeholders who are affected by the decision.
2 For each stakeholder group, identify its needs and concerns, both if the decision *is* implemented and if the decision is *not* implemented.
3 Prioritize the stakeholder groups and perspectives.
4 Make a decision.

the series that was required. Fourth, if a human derivative of ivermectin proved to have any adverse health effects when used on humans, it might taint its reputation as a veterinary drug. Fifth, there was concern that a human version of the drug distributed to the Third World might be diverted to the black market, undercutting sales of its veterinary product. Clearly, Merck faced an ethical dilemma in how to proceed with this scientist's discovery. How would the use of the framework help in resolving this dilemma?

Step 1: Identify All Stakeholders Who Are Affected by the Decision   In Merck's case, the stakeholders might include the following:

- Shareholders
- The public at large
- The Third World population affected
- The government
- Employees

Step 2: For Each Stakeholder Group, Identify Its Needs and Concerns   This requires identifying the results both if the decision is implemented and if the decision is *not* implemented. What were each stakeholder group's needs and concerns if the decision to explore the drug further were to proceed, and if the decision to explore the drug further were curtailed?

From the *shareholders' perspective,* shareholders were concerned about the likely negative impact if this discovery were pursued. Studies showed that, on average, it took 12 years and $200 million to bring a new drug to market. So, if the company pursued this development, it would be costly, regardless of the outcome. And, even in the most positive scenario, the costly development and drug trials, coupled with the lack of a target market's ability to pay for the drugs, indicated that the company might lose money in proceeding further with this discovery.

On the other hand, the company might face negative publicity if it withheld useful medications from people. Possible repercussions from such negative publicity might include competition gaining a stronghold.

From the *public at large's perspective,* if the drug were further pursued, the company might be viewed favorably for its efforts, and gain more loyal customers. If the drug were shelved, the public might begin to question Merck's motives in developing drugs to address human suffering. In choosing not to develop drugs that have the potential to enhance significantly the quality of life for people, the resulting skepticism could cause problems in managing customer relationships. Moreover, given the presence of knowledge spillovers in high-tech markets, in which innovations and developments in one area have the potential to lead to new innovations in other areas, there was a legitimate question related to what other human diseases this discovery might ultimately lead to, discoveries that might never be made if the drug were not pursued.

From the *perspective of people afflicted with the disease,* if the drug were developed, and if it proved to be effective in combating river blindness, the quality of life of this population would be greatly enhanced. This could lead to other improvements, in that any support currently provided by relief agencies or local governments to assist this population with ongoing sustenance and survival could be redirected to other needy populations. There was also the risk that if the drug were developed, some unknown side effects might occur (which hopefully would be uncovered during additional development and prior to administration of the drug to this population). One would have to weigh (as with any drug) the benefits the drug could deliver relative to possible side effects.

If the drug were not developed, not only would this population continue with the grim situation, but the placement of profits over people could lead to a general backlash against corporations in developing countries, with, at a minimum, ensuing negative publicity or possibly even local protests with resulting violence.

From the *government's perspective,* if the drug were further pursued, the U.S. government might choose to expedite the lengthy approval process in order to hasten Merck's ability to relieve human pain and suffering. If the drug were not pursued, although the U.S. government typically does not legislate drug development, a sufficient outcry might cause intervention, requiring Merck to make its formularies for the bovine medicine available on a licensing basis to other competitors so they could pursue its development for river blindness. Issues related to infrastructure and drug administration would also ultimately be government concerns.

From the *employees' perspective,* if the drug were developed, Merck employees might feel negative revenue implications with possible belt tightening and layoffs. Still, the scientists and people involved would feel confident that their work had purpose and meaning. If the drug weren't developed, employees might not face negative revenue implications, although the decision not to pursue potentially lifesaving discoveries might be demoralizing.

Step 3: Prioritize the Stakeholder Groups and Perspectives   How did Merck prioritize the various stakeholders? It is vital that this step not be considered simply a debate over people versus profits (which is frequently what happens with many ethical business dilemmas). Framed in such a manner, the discussion typically becomes one based on whose view is "right" or which views come from more powerful people in the firm, rather than leading to insights about priorities. Instead, priorities should be based on a company's mission and a long-term perspective. A real benefit of this step comes in the clarification of values and the explication of implicit assumptions that underlie decision making in a company.

In the Merck case, Merck had, over the years, deliberately fashioned a corporate culture to nurture the most creative, fruitful research. Its scientists were among the best paid in the industry and were given great latitude to pursue intriguing leads. Moreover, they were inspired to view their work as a quest to alleviate human disease and suffering worldwide. Employees found inspiration in the words of George W. Merck, son of the company's founder and its former chairman:

> We try never to forget that medicine is for the people. It is not for the profits. The profits follow, and if we have remembered that, they have never failed to appear. The better we have remembered it, the larger they have been.[25]

These words formed the basis of Merck's overall corporate philosophy.

Step 4: Make and Implement a Decision   In wrestling with the dilemma, Merck explicitly recognized that its success in the pharmaceutical market was, in large part, due to the efforts of its scientists in making discoveries just like this one. If its scientists did not believe that their discoveries would be used to their fullest capabilities, then not only would they possibly become demoralized, Merck might also have difficulties recruiting, attracting, and retaining the best scientists. On this basis, it decided to proceed with further study on the drug, which was eventually released for human purposes in 1987.

Box 12-2 on the Merck case provides additional information.

BOX 12-2

Additional Information on the Merck Case

After a seven-year clinical research program, Merck & Company, Inc., in collaboration with the World Health Organization (WHO), demonstrated that a single oral dose of Mectizan, taken once per year, could prevent blindness and alleviate skin disease. In 1987, Merck decided to donate Mectizan free of charge to all people affected by river blindness, for as long as necessary. Merck approached William Foege, M.D., then executive director of the Carter Center, for assistance with the global distribution of Mectizan. Together, they created the Mectizan Donation Program (MDP) and housed it at the Task Force for Child Survival and Development, an independent partner of the Carter Center. MDP acted as the liaison between Merck, nongovernmental development organizations (NGDOs), affected countries' ministries of health, and United Nations organizations such as WHO.

The Mectizan Donation Program is currently advised by the Mectizan Expert Committee, an independent body established by Merck, which is comprised of public health and parasitic disease experts. These experts must approve all applications for the drug that are submitted by river blindness treatment programs worldwide. Applicants must demonstrate effectiveness in addressing such issues as storage and transport of Mectizan, dosage and administration of the drug, medical support personnel, and patient selection.

The statue of a boy leading a blind man has become recognized as a symbol of the fight to eliminate river blindness. The statue commemorates the success of three WHO–Pan-American Health Organization–led programs: the Onchocerciasis Control Programme in West Africa (OCP), operating in 11 countries; the African Programme for Onchocerciasis Control (APOC), covering 19 countries outside West Africa; and the Onchocerciasis Elimination Program for the Americas (OEPA), present in 6 countries. OCP, after 25 years, has practically eradicated the disease in West Africa and the program will cease operations in 2002. APOC became operational in 1996 and will continue its support to national control until 2007 and OEPA aims at eliminating the disease in the Americas by 2007.

Photograph reprinted with the permission of Merck & Co., Inc.

THE GIFT OF SIGHT

As of October 1999, the transmission of the disease was on the verge of elimination in West Africa. An estimated 12 million children have grown up without the risk of being blinded by onchocerciasis. On the 25 million hectares of land now reclaimed for cultivation near river areas, enough food is produced to feed 17 million people per year.

Source: www.who.int/ocp/ (Onchocerciasis Control Programme of West Africa); www.merck.com/overview/ philanthropy/mectizan/; www.cartercenter.org/rblindprogram.html, September 5, 2000.

Benefits of the Framework

The benefits of using this framework to guide the resolution of ethical dilemmas are three-fold. First, the framework makes explicit the various issues that the company will need to wrestle with, regardless of the resulting outcome. For example, in the Merck case, the framework makes explicit the need to manage possible shareholder concerns about a loss of profitability against the need to manage scientists' incentives for discovery. Second, the framework brings into stark relief the various perspectives of the affected stakeholders. By highlighting the various perspectives and their respective "stakes," a firm gets a better sense of the magnitude of the controversy it will encounter, regardless of the decision it makes. Third, the framework leads to a heightened sense of commitment to the resulting outcome. In an ethical dilemma, a company is exposed to criticism, regardless of which side of the dilemma the resulting decision supports. By using the framework, company spokespeople can feel greater confidence in their decisions that come under attack. The systematic approach to considering all stakeholders involved, their relative stakes in the decisions, and using some solid basis to prioritize their relative needs leads to a sense that the decision is not a knee-jerk tendency about "people over profits" (or vice versa as the case may be), but rather, is one that is well grounded in explicit consideration of all parties' perspectives. In communicating the issues to concerned third parties (i.e., the media or boards of directors), the thoroughness of the process used to make the decision becomes clearer.

Some may say that Merck's decision, based on its desire to keep talented, driven scientists, was fundamentally based on profits and self-serving; therefore, Merck could be criticized for a lack of altruism. However, it is important to recognize that the most obvious decision to support profitability in this case would have been for Merck to forego the drug, rather than to proceed. Indeed, given the lack of a profitable market opportunity, a decision based solely on profits would have led to a very different outcome.

The unfortunate reality faced by companies wrestling with such ethical dilemmas is that they often find themselves in a catch-22: They are "damned if they do and damned if they don't." Even if a company engages in an action that ultimately reflects some level of social responsibility, it can be criticized by those who believe that "people above profits" should have been the underlying basis for the decision.

In order to explore the issue of socially responsible corporate behavior further, additional information on social responsibility and business is provided.

SOCIAL RESPONSIBILITY AND BUSINESS DECISIONS

Seventy-eight percent of American adults say they are more likely to buy a product from a company associated with important social causes, and 84% say that such "cause marketing" creates a positive image of a company.[26] As a result, an increase in corporate social responsibility investments has followed, with spending of $2.5 billion in 1997 predicted to double over three years.[27] To guide socially responsible decision making, companies should examine their goals, mission, and potential liabilities.

In certain cases, a company may decide to engage in socially responsible behavior either because its corporate values suggest such behavior, because key personnel believe that it is the right thing to do, or for a host of other reasons. When based on a corporate mandate, a company may worry less about the profit impact of the decision and more about convincing other company personnel or stakeholders about the merits of the decision. In other cases, the potential motives for and benefits of ties to nonprofit causes, charitable giving, or socially responsible practices are less clear.

How can technology companies address the need for and opportunities associated with social responsibility? One is to identify areas in which proactive giving will benefit not only society but also the company. For example, should a telecommunications company work to build access to broadband technologies in rural areas, despite the expense relative to the potential revenues earned? A company can use three criteria to help it trade off the benefits versus the costs of social responsibility or, more broadly, sponsorship of events in general (see Table 12-2).

Does the Mission of the Company Match the Mission of the Cause?   To the extent that the mission of the company has an explicit tie to the social cause, the investment of corporate monies makes sense. For example, a telecommunications company's investments in broadband access to rural communities makes sense, because it is part and parcel of the company's raison d'être. However, based on this factor, such a company's sponsorship of environmental reclamation in these communities would make less sense; environmental reclamation is unrelated to its mission.

Does the Target Market of the Company Have Some Vested Interest in the Cause?   This consideration requires that the company explicitly address whom it is targeting with its products and services, and whether that target market has a vested interest in the cause. In this case, if a telecommunications company's primary target market was new users of telecommunications services, such as women-owned small businesses, then sponsorship of a breast-cancer awareness campaign or support of educational programs for young girls in math and sciences would match this criterion. Note that in this case, attempting to connect to the target market and to build competitive advantage via causes in which the target is interested may take the company into socially responsible activities somewhat removed from its primary business.

Will the Socially Responsible Behavior Yield Goodwill Among Key Stakeholder Groups, and Will the Company Benefit from Positive Exposure the Behavior Generates?   This consideration is based on the fact that socially responsible behavior is ultimately one way to maintain a positive image among key stakeholder groups. For example, a telecommunications company might donate money to a local food bank in some of its primary communities. In this case, the cause is not directly tied to its mission, nor specifically targeted to its primary customers. Even though the direct link to possible sales is not explicit, such an activity can create goodwill in its local communities.

Further, the likelihood of benefiting from socially responsible behaviors is increased to the extent that the company will benefit from publicity. To what extent will the company's behaviors be known to the broader public? If the event will be marketed and televised, or if the company plans on advertising its affiliation to the cause, then

---

TABLE 12-2   Considerations in Social Responsibility

Does the mission of the company match the mission of the cause?

Does the target market of the company have some vested interest in the cause?

Will the socially responsible behavior yield goodwill among key stakeholder groups, and will the company benefit from positive exposure the behavior generates?

some exposure will be generated. Such exposure can be used to generate brand-name awareness. If, however, the event is small and will not be marketed or televised, then the exposure will be more limited.

Companies that operate at only this third level of social responsibility run great risk if they are merely engaging in socially responsible behaviors in one area to compensate for socially irresponsible behaviors in others. As in the ethics section, socially responsible behaviors can be viewed skeptically when people question the motives behind business behavior; this is more likely to be the case if companies' actions are not perceived as genuine. Companies that exhibit social responsibility in areas more closely related to their businesses, and that are genuine in their efforts, are less likely to be accused of hypocrisy. (Again, however, this criticism obscures the fact that in the end, if businesses are acting in socially responsible ways, regardless of the reason, it benefits people and society.)

Ultimately, the business of innovation, and the decisions of innovative businesses, are human endeavors very much shaped by human forces. Ethics and values do underlie the push to innovate, as Greg Simon speaks to so eloquently in the Technology Expert's View from the Trenches.

What is the role of the government in realizing the promise of technology?

THE ROLE OF THE GOVERNMENT

What is the role of government in this time of technological turbulence? Depending upon one's perspective, the government can play a vital role in helping to realize the promise of technology. For example, it can support science and education through research and outreach programs to maintain innovativeness. In the 1980s and 1990s, the United States was ranked at the top on an overall innovation index based on R&D funding and other factors. By 2005, because of their spending on basic research and education and percentage of technical workers, Japan, Finland, Denmark, and Sweden are expected to be at the top.[28]

Typically, government legislation is directed at efforts that enhance competition and consumer welfare. It can fund research and development initiatives; it can help with dialogues over standards (or legislate them if the industry players cannot agree among themselves, as in the case of digital TV standards);[29] it can pass legislation designed to encourage competition, as in the Telecommunications Act of 1996, or to protect consumers, as in the Children's On-Line Privacy Protection Act. In order to help realize the promise of technology, the government can continue efforts to update its regulatory models on antitrust and intellectual property to reflect changes in the economy, and to facilitate the public's access to technology.

Update Regulatory Models

Antitrust Models   Many of the guiding principles used for economic thinking were formed in the late eighteenth century, in an era of physical goods. This not only meant that firms were concerned with the factors of production and limitations on supply; it also implied that a good could be consumed by only one individual.[30] However, in the New Economy, information can be consumed by many people at once. Indeed, due to network externalities, the more people that consume a good, the more valuable it becomes. For example, consumers want to buy what everyone else is using, so their equipment is compatible. At its extreme, the most popular products are widely used, creating monopoly-like economic power, as in the case of Microsoft.

TECHNOLOGY EXPERT'S VIEW FROM THE TRENCHES

Realizing the Promise of Technology

GREG SIMON
President and CEO, Simon Strategies, LLC, Washington, DC

Over five hundred years ago in Germany, a goldsmith who had bungled a surefire money-making venture by getting a crucial date wrong was looking for a way to mollify his business partners. He decided to use his goldsmithing skills to mold what became known as moveable type, and he used the type to print the one book he knew would sell, the Bible, in this case, the Gutenberg Bible. About a hundred years later in Antwerp, another entrepreneur began to print Bibles with maps of the Holy Land in the back, leading to the development of printed cartography that could be updated with each new voyage. The first fanatics who used these new and improved maps for their ventures, the Dutch, soon began returning from voyages with profits of 500% or more.

This got everybody's attention, to say the least, and led to a demand for cash to invest that was so great that new ways were needed to allow for borrowing against land, which was the source of wealth at the time. The result was land registers and secured mortgages, the bulk of which went into paying for ships. These new ventures needed some protection, referred to as insurance, and limited joint stock companies sprang up to pool resources for both investing and insurance, leading to the creation of the stock market. Naturally something was needed to coordinate all this; national banks were the answer, and they brought along credit (and, unfortunately, credit agencies). With further refinement of the printing press, institutions arose to manage specialized information in standardized formats. Because of this standard, more reliable data, individuals and companies could take more risks, leading to massive economic expansion and development.

The only management system capable of holding all this together turned out to be the business contract, which eventually made its way into social theory and then, with the help of those like John Locke, into political theory. The best example of the social contract is the contract between state and citizen contained in the Constitution of the United States. All this, thanks to a goldsmith's mistake.

The history of the United States shows how the forces that shape communication shape our economic, social, and political well-being. The history of our democracy is closely entwined with the history of communication. Our revolutionary battle cry reflected the failure of our communication with our mother country. "No taxation without representation" was a colonial protest against one-way, centralized communication from England that did not provide for any response or interactivity. And it is no accident that our First Amendment to the Constitution is the right of free speech, the right to communicate.

Thomas Jefferson put very well why information is a peculiar resource, one that grows as people share it. He said, "He who receives an idea from me receives instruction himself without lessening mine.

He who lights his taper with mine receives light without darkening me."

Throughout our history, our desire to improve our means of communication has helped us grow and prosper. Our earliest laws regarding radio frequencies and communications spectrum were provoked by the tragedy of the *Titanic,* in which the failure of radio operators to man their stations and the inability of the *Titanic* to communicate its SOS signal on a clear frequency led to the death of thousands.

Morse was also a famous portrait artist in the United States. His portrait of President James Monroe hangs today in the White House. While Morse was working on a portrait of General Lafayette in Washington, his wife, who lived about 500 kilometers away, grew ill and died. But it took seven days for the news to reach him. In his grief and remorse, he began to wonder if it were possible to erase barriers of time and space, so that no one would be unable to reach a loved one in time of need. Pursuing this thought, he came to discover how to use electricity to convey messages, and so he invented the telegraph.

The transcontinental railroad, the telephone, Marconi's wireless radio, the television, the interstate highway, and now the information superhighway both fulfilled our dreams and set us to dreaming anew.

But today's dream is not about technology. It is about breaking the barriers of how we know our world, our neighbors, and ourselves. It is about millions of individual journeys to explore the frontiers of knowledge, whether it is a child's e-mail conversation with a scientist at the South Pole or a tour of the Louvre from one's living room.

Some things have to be seen in order to be believed. But some things have to be *believed* in order to be seen. The revolution that sprang from the development of the Gutenberg press was not simply the result of the innovation by a goldsmith with a need to raise money. It succeeded because the world was ready to receive and nurture the idea Gutenberg set forth. After all, moveable metal type had been invented in Korea two hundred years before Gutenberg invented it again. But conditions conspired to keep that first moveable typeface from spreading. Confucianism prohibited the commercialization of books, and the Korean royal presses would print only classical Chinese literature, not the more popular Korean literature.

By Gutenberg's time, there were better conditions: better paper, better metals, and eyeglasses. And Europeans were ready for a cheaper way to copy books than using scribes who charged for one copy what a printing press would charge for a thousand.

We have a similar challenge today to create the commercial, technical, legal, and social conditions that will produce the foundation for a global information infrastructure. We have, each of us and each nation, a job to do to bring the world to the next generation. The work we do to cross our common oceans to build a global information infrastructure is not in the service of wires or satellites but is in the service of a global vision that can be realized in every neighborhood of the world.

The technology that so fascinates and occasionally dominates us is a mute guest in our lives. It cannot, left alone, speak of values or a vision. It cannot yet tell the difference between the bricks of a church and the bricks of a prison. But we can and must speak of values and we can and must recognize the moral choices in our lives. We cannot choose to delay or deny the future; we must make ready for it. But there is no better way to predict the future than to create it.

The question is whether the characteristics of a high-tech environment, with emphasis on unit-one cost structures, network externalities, and knowledge spillovers, render traditional economic models moot. Technology enthusiasts say "yes." In favor of relaxed antitrust restraints, they argue that while the New Economy may lead to more monopoly-like economic power, such concentrations will be temporary and quickly overthrown by new innovations that are superior. Reliance on the invisible hand of the market will allow new innovations to curtail monopoly-like economic power.

Others say "no." Traditional economic models are not moot and society still needs traditional antitrust protections. For example, once a technology standard is set, consumers feel a need to buy that product, even if it's not the best. Temporary monopolies can stifle innovation, competition can decline, and the pace of innovations can slow. Monopoly-like economic power in technology markets can be problematic. For example, Microsoft's control of the operating system that is crucial to running 99% of the world's computers can create issues of access to the market, which, if limited, can stifle competition and innovation[31] (see Box 12-3). Similarly, the merger of Time Warner and AOL may also, by controlling the cable into the home and the first screen seen on a TV or computer, create a critical bottleneck in broadband access into the home. The findings of the Justice Department in the Microsoft case suggest that these areas require oversight to ensure access and competition to stimulate ongoing innovation.

The concerns over competition and innovation highlight that, although technology might have changed the rules for antitrust enforcement, it has not necessarily changed the need.[32]

Intellectual Property Models   Technological developments are also affected by governmental regulation in the area of intellectual property. The New Economy is based on ideas and information. Knowledge does not operate in the economy in the way that tangible goods do. It is neither finite nor depleted by use. Indeed, knowledge becomes less valuable when it is not used or shared.

In light of this, some worry that the patents being granted for New Economy breakthroughs such as genes, prime numbers, and even lab animals (a Harvard mouse) will lead to excessive control of information that will stymie possible knowledge spillovers that could build on these developments in profound, but unknown, ways.

The Internet and the human genome are two such breakthroughs. The earlier chapter on intellectual property protection provided a summary of the debate with respect to patenting Internet business models. With respect to the life sciences, a single company, Human Genome Sciences, has received patents on 106 complete human genes, including some that are crucial to treating osteoporosis and arthritis, and it has patents pending on more than 7,500 genes.[33] The rush to patent genes raises profound ethical and social questions. Will such patenting allow breakthroughs to be shared with the broad scientific community? Will advances that could improve consumer welfare be restricted? For example, in the genetically modified foods area, five U.S. farmers and one French farmer filed an antitrust lawsuit against Monsanto, accusing the company of conspiring to control markets for corn and soybean seeds; Novartis, DuPont, and seven other companies were named as coconspirators.[34]

Although costly research and development does merit recompense, some middle ground between the right to exclude others from using the innovations and sharing that knowledge may be desirable.[35] Lobbying by industry players does affect the government's decisions. For example, the entertainment industry's recent attempts to use

BOX 12-3

Microsoft versus the Justice Department and 19 State Attorneys General

What were the basic issues at the heart of the Microsoft case? U.S. District Judge Thomas Penfield Jackson ruled that the software giant illegally protected its Windows monopoly against competitors and that Microsoft attempted to monopolize the market for browsers used to navigate the World Wide Web. He ruled that Microsoft illegally tied Windows to its Internet Explorer software. For example, to use Microsoft Exchange, the most popular corporate e-mail system, one must use Windows NT or Windows 2000 for an operating system. Similarly, the new Pocket PC handhelds synchronize only with Windows desktops and work with Exchange as the mail service. Microsoft was found to use its monopoly power to induce other companies to abandon projects that threatened Microsoft, and punished those companies that resisted, say, by refusing them technical support in integrating Microsoft products with their own or by refusing them access to important computer code.

On the side of the government, the Justice Department believes that the company's dominance in operating systems matters, and that Microsoft is using the same tactics it used to overpower Netscape in Web browsers in other markets, such as software used to provide audio and video over the Web, as well as Internet servers and security software.

On Microsoft's side, many believe that the rapid rise of the Internet has already shifted power away from Microsoft and its desktop monopoly. New innovation is happening on the Web more so than in the area of operating systems. Moreover, Microsoft argued that its business practices helped consumers by improving products and lowering costs, and that no one forced consumers to use Microsoft's products.

Of the various remedies considered, the basic issues were to prevent Microsoft from further violations of the law, without hampering innovation. To do so, Microsoft must be prevented from illegally using the monopoly of the Windows operating system to "bully its way" into new software markets using its "embrace, extend, and extinguish" approach to new markets.

With the recommendation to break the company into two separate entities, one company would handle the operating system, and the other would handle new software application products. This would force Microsoft to offer versions of the Windows operating system that aren't illegally tied to other software applications such as e-mail and Internet browsing. And it will give Microsoft's customers, the computer manufacturers, the flexibility to choose their own partners in new markets such as online payments or communications services.

The underlying motive is to allow the market to be competitive enough to foster innovation, rather than to necessarily have to rely on one company's products as the *de facto* standard.

Sources: Wilke, John and David Bank (1999), "Microsoft Is Found to Be Predatory Monopolist," *Wall Street Journal,* November 8, pp. A3, A30; Wilke, John, Rebecca Buckman, and David Hamilton (2000), "Microsoft Judge Faces Demands of Market and of Monopoly Law," *Wall Street Journal,* April 4, pp. A1, A16; Wilke, John, Rebecca Buckman, and Michael Orey (2000), "Judge's Breakup Order Stands to Transform Microsoft, Its Industry," *Wall Street Journal,* June 8, pp. A1, A10; Cohen, Adam (1999), "'Microsoft Enjoys Monopoly Power . . . ,'" *Business Week,* November 15, pp. 61–69; France, Mike (1999), "Does a Breakup Make Sense?" *Business Week,* November 22, pp. 38–42; Wildstrom, Stephen (2000), "A Win–Win–Win Breakup?" *Business Week,* May 15, p. 31; Mandel, Michael (2000), "Antitrust for the Digital Age," *Business Week,* May 15, pp. 46–48.

technology-based restrictions on information sharing rather than new business models exhibit a desire to control intellectual property in ways that may be incompatible with the New Economy.[36] Although strong protections for intellectual property are essential for promoting continued innovativeness, such protections also shouldn't stifle competition and access.

Some high-tech firms worry that, rather than helping to realize the promise of technology, the government actually interferes with innovativeness. Clearly, there are two sides to each issue, and the government's task of balancing them is challenging, as shown in Figure 12-4. Yet another area in which the government is faced with a delicate balancing act is in the facilitating of access to technology.

Assist with Access to Technology

The government may also help to realize the promise of technology by assisting with consumer access to technology, particularly with respect to the technology "haves" and "have-nots," referring to the disparity in access to technology between different socio-economic and geographic groups. For example, Federal Communications Commission (FCC) Chairman William Kennard wants delivery of Internet access to wireless devices, such as cellular phones and handheld computers, to democratize the Internet, making it available to people who can't afford a PC in their home. To facilitate competition, he's willing to auction more airwaves for wireless technology.

Two discrepancies are highlighted here: (1) the Digital Divide, or the gap in on-line access between urban and rural areas, and (2) the Racial Ravine, or the gap in access to computing power between poorer inner-city populations and wealthier populations.

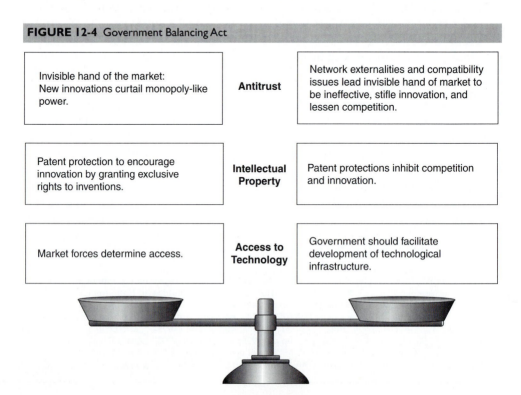

FIGURE 12-4 Government Balancing Act

Invisible hand of the market: New innovations curtail monopoly-like power.	**Antitrust**	Network externalities and compatibility issues lead invisible hand of market to be ineffective, stifle innovation, and lessen competition.
Patent protection to encourage innovation by granting exclusive rights to inventions.	**Intellectual Property**	Patent protections inhibit competition and innovation.
Market forces determine access.	**Access to Technology**	Government should facilitate development of technological infrastructure.

These issues are important, because "if the technology revolution leaves some Americans behind, all of America will suffer."[37]

Digital Divide   Unequal access to technology is apparent between rural versus urban and suburban areas. Small towns and rural areas, particularly in sparsely populated western states, simply do not have access to broadband technology that will allow Internet connections. Both the distance and the sparse population contribute to the problem. Consider that in New Jersey, the average distance between a customer and phone company's nearest switching facility is about 2.6 miles; in Wyoming, the distance is twice as far, making the cost to the phone company of reaching a customer twice as high. Moreover, parts of the rural West have as few as half a dozen households per square mile, compared with thousands in urban and suburban areas.[38] Some phone companies say they should not have to serve customers in those areas if that's where they choose to live. As stated by Garry Betty, president and CEO of Earthlink.net: "To tell me I've got to serve someone at a certain speed regardless of the cost because he chooses to live in the far reaches of Montana is not fair. Let them pay for it themselves."[39]

If the economics of the situation do not support businesses developing digital access for rural communities, the government believes it has a role to play in a manner similar to the role it played with the subsidies provided to develop the telephone and the interstate freeway infrastructures. FCC Chairman Kennard says that the United States should make a commitment to provide some level of Internet service to rural Americans, with cable and computer companies contributing to a universal service fund. Because the long-term health and survival of rural America is, to a large extent, dependent on its ability to attract and retain economic development and activity, which in turn, requires access to current technologies, this type of support is considered by many to be vital.

Another solution to the Digital Divide can also be found in new technological developments, such as satellite and other types of high-speed wireless access, that do not require wiring "the last mile." Although not specifically intended for rural markets, Motorola and Cisco jointly contributed $1 billion to create wireless, high-speed Internet networks, and AT&T is experimenting with cellular-like services that compress data and bring high-speed Web access into homes.

Racial Ravine   Whites are twice as likely as blacks to own a computer and three times as likely to have Internet access.[40] Some groups (such as the Initiative for a Competitive Inner City) and firms are actively trying to make access more available to all, by making a case for focusing marketing efforts on inner-city groups. For example, data provided by PricewaterhouseCoopers says that inner-city consumers account for 7% of all U.S. retail sales, or $85 billion annually,[41] a sizable market. Moreover, although only 24% of inner-city dwellers have access to the World Wide Web at home (versus 41% of United States at large), 30% of them have bought products on-line versus 27% overall. The number of African Americans going on-line is predicted to grow from 23% in 1999 to 40% in 2000. Densely populated inner cities spend more than six times as much per square mile as an average urban area ($344 million per square mile versus $53 million average throughout the New York area). Because congested city neighborhoods generate more sales volume, these groups argue that the inner cities can be profitable.

With respect to the Hispanic market, the Spanish-speaking population in the United States is in the top 10 markets worldwide, as big as the Canadian market. The number of Hispanics on-line will go from 36% in 1999 to 43% in 2000.[42] Gateway recognized this, and ran a $2.5 million campaign in November 1999 to sell PC and Internet service to Hispanics, targeting Latino communities in Miami and Phoenix.

What is the role of businesses in these situations vis-à-vis the government's mission to enhance consumer welfare? Do businesses have a moral obligation to worry about such issues as access? Can an economic argument be made for providing access to rural areas or inner cities? These are tough issues to be sorted out.

Summary

This chapter explored factors related to the ability to realize the promise of technology, including paradoxes and unintended consequences, ethical dilemmas and social responsibility, and the role of government. Although technology is not the panacea for society's ailments, nor the force that can solve all human problems—including food shortages, health problems, transportation snafus, and business inefficiencies—neither is it essentially incompatible with human values, the source of all woes in our society, including the spread of nuclear weapons and environmental degradation. Proactive consideration of the paradoxes technology poses for users, as well as its unintended consequences, will enable firms to better anticipate obstacles so that the promises of their innovations can be realized. Similarly, proactive consideration of ethical dilemmas can go a long way toward minimizing possible negative effects. Use of both the framework on wrestling with ethical dilemmas as well as explicit attention to the considerations in socially responsible business decisions will help a firm to navigate through potential controversies. The government's role is to balance carefully the need to foster a climate that promotes innovation while ensuring a competitive marketplace.

Many of the vital technologies in the world today were literally inconceivable two centuries ago. The steamship was not an evolutionary development of the sailing ship; the automobile is not an evolutionary development of the horse and buggy; the transistor did not evolve from improvements in vacuum tubes; and the personal computer did not evolve from the mechanical calculator.[43] Technological development requires creativity, serendipity, perseverance, and resources. Indeed, the time lag between an innovation and product development may be up to 40 years. The market may not be ready for it, government regulators may not know how to facilitate it, the costs may be too high, or some other development may come along that supersedes it. Innovators must be tireless crusaders regarding their inventions. Although they may not immediately find a viable commercial application, they must persevere, hoping that it one day may be useful.[44]

Ultimately, technology is a tool meant to serve human purposes. However, the promises that new technologies offer can be realized only if inventors take careful steps in the commercialization and marketing of their ideas. A good idea alone is insufficient. Smart marketing based on systematic consideration of critical issues is necessary to allow innovations to benefit society in the ways in which they are intended. Without effective marketing of high-technology products and innovations, the benefits such innovations can yield will remain elusive.

Discussion Questions

1. What are the eight paradoxes technology can pose from a user's perspective? Give an example of each one. What are the marketing implications?

2. Identify and describe one unintended consequence arising from technology (not from the chapter). What are the marketing implications (how should a marketing manager use knowledge of this unintended consequence)?
3. Identify and describe an ethical controversy arising from technological developments (not from the chapter). Use the framework presented in the chapter to make a decision about how to proceed, in light of the ethical controversy.
4. Pick a high-tech company and identify the nonprofit causes either with which it is affiliated or with which you believe it could usefully be affiliated. Evaluate that company's connection based on the three considerations for social responsibility presented in the chapter.
5. For each of the following three issues, summarize the pros and cons for government involvement:
   a. Active intervention in the market with respect to antitrust concerns
   b. Active intervention in the market with respect to intellectual property concerns
   c. Active intervention in the market with respect to access to technology concerns

Glossary

Luddites.   People who are opposed to technology and changes brought about by technology.

Endnotes

1. Ball, Jeffrey (1999), "High-Tech Air Bags Are Lacking in Grasp of Human Dimensions," *Wall Street Journal,* August 5, pp. A1, A6.
2. Dibbell, Julian (1996), "Everything That Could Go Wrong . . . ," *Time,* May 20, p. 56.
3. Except as noted, this section is drawn from Mick, David Glen and Susan Fournier (1998), "Paradoxes of Technology: Consumer Cognizance, Emotions, and Coping Strategies," *Journal of Consumer Research,* 25 (September), pp. 123–143.
4. Dibbell, Julian (1996), "Everything That Could Go Wrong . . . ," *Time,* May 20, p. 56.
5. Donato, Marla (1999), "Sense-Dulling Conveniences Creating Alienated World," *Missoulian,* January 12, p. A8, from *Chicago Tribune.*
6. Down, Jeff (1999), "Plugged in to Excess," *Missoulian,* August 23, p. A1, Associated Press.
7. Donato, Marla (1999), "Sense-Dulling Conveniences Creating Alienated World," *Missoulian,* January 12, p. A8, from *Chicago Tribune.*
8. Bryan, Rebecca (2000), "Two-Timing the Clock: Trying to Slow the Raging River of Progress? Take a Step Back and Disconnect from the World," *Business 2.0,* February, pp. 227–230.
9. Siegel, Matt (1998), "Do Computers Slow Us Down?" *Fortune,* March 30, pp. 34, 38; Landauer, Thomas (1995), *The Trouble with Computers: Usefulness, Usability, and Productivity,* Cambridge, MA: MIT Press.
10. Tam, Pui-Wing (2000), "Taking High Tech Home Is a Bit Much for an Internet Exec," *Wall Street Journal,* June 16, p. A1.
11. http://escape.com/~spyder/LUDDITE.HTML, downloaded September 5, 2000.
12. www.m-w.com/cgi-bin/dictionary, downloaded September 5, 2000.
13. http://escape.com/~spyder/LUDDITE.HTML, downloaded September 5, 2000.
14. Enriquez, Juan and Ray Goldberg (2000), "Transforming Life, Transforming Business: The Life-Science Revolution," *Harvard Business Review,* March–April, pp. 95–104.
15. Kluger, Jeffrey (1999), "Food Fight," *Time,* September 13, pp. 42–44.
16. Golden, Frederic (2000), "Make Way for Frankenfish," *Time,* March 6, p. 62.
17. Enriquez, Juan and Ray Goldberg (2000), "Transforming Life, Transforming Business: The Life-Science Revolution," *Harvard Business Review,* March–April, pp. 95–104.

18. Giannakas, Konstantinos and Murray Fulton (2000), "Consumption Effects of Genetic Modification: What if Consumers Are Right?" working paper, University of Nebraska, Department of Agricultural Economics, Lincoln, NE.

19. Enriquez, Juan and Ray Goldberg (2000), "Transforming Life, Transforming Business: The Life-Science Revolution," *Harvard Business Review,* March–April, pp. 95–104.

20. www.halcyon.com/nanojbl, September 5, 2000.

21. Weiss, Rick (1999), "Smarter Mice Run Ethical Maze," *Missoulian,* September 2, pp. A1, A9, from *Washington Post.*

22. Kolata, Gina (1996), "Breaking Ranks, Lab Offers Test Assessing Breast Cancer Risk," *Boulder Daily Camera,* April 1, p. A3.

23. Useem, Jerry (2000), "New Ethics . . . or No Ethics?" *Fortune,* March 20, pp. 83–120.

24. "Merck & Co., Inc." (1991) in David Held, *Property, Profit, and Justice,* The Business Enterprise Trust.

25. "Merck & Co., Inc." (1991) in *Property, Profit, and Justice,* The Business Enterprise Trust.

26. Kadlec, Daniel (1997), "The New World of Giving," *Time,* May 5, pp. 62–64.

27. Kadlec, Daniel (1997), "The New World of Giving," *Time,* May 5, pp. 62–64.

28. "U.S. Innovation Ain't What It Used to Be," (1999), *Business Week,* March 22, p. 6.

29. The reason that digital TV is considered an issue of consumer welfare is that the switch to digital signals allows broadcasters to squeeze more video and data into existing channel space, which can be used to provide more options for consumers.

30. Murray, Alan (1999), "Pushing Adam Smith Past the Millennium," *Wall Street Journal,* June 21, p. A1.

31. Murray, Alan (2000), "In the New Economy, You've Got Scale," *Wall Street Journal,* January 17, p. A1.

32. Murray, Alan (1997), "Antitrust Isn't Obsolete in an Era of High-Tech," *Wall Street Journal,* November 10, p. A1.

33. Enriquez, Juan and Ray Goldberg (2000), "Transforming Life, Transforming Business: The Life-Science Revolution," *Harvard Business Review,* March–April, pp. 95–104.

34. Enriquez, Juan and Ray Goldberg (2000), "Transforming Life, Transforming Business: The Life-Science Revolution," *Harvard Business Review,* March–April, pp. 95–104.

35. Shulman, Seth (1999), "We Need New Ways to Own and Share Knowledge," *The Chronicle of Higher Education,* 45 (24), p. A64.

36. Griffin, Jim (2000), "The Digital Delivery of Intellectual Property Is Our Generation's Nuclear Power," *Business 2.0,* February, p. 212.

37. Crocket, Roger (1999), "High Tech's Next Big Market? Try the Inner City," *Business Week,* December 20, p. 48.

38. O'Malley, Chris (1999), "The Digital Divide," *Time,* March 22, pp. 86–87.

39. O'Malley, Chris (1999), "The Digital Divide," *Time,* March 22, pp. 86–87.

40. O'Malley, Chris (1999), "The Digital Divide," *Time,* March 22, pp. 86–87.

41. Crocket, Roger (1999), "High Tech's Next Big Market? Try the Inner City," *Business Week,* December 20, p. 48.

42. Crocket, Roger (1999), "High Tech's Next Big Market? Try the Inner City," *Business Week,* December 20, p. 48.

43. Ayres, Robert (1994), "Technological Trends," *National Forum,* 74 (Spring), pp. 37–43.

44. Bronson, Gail (1987), "Technology: Songs the Sirens Sing." *Forbes,* July 13, pp. 234–237.

Recommended Readings

Nonfiction Readings Related to Chapter Content

Kaplan, Jerry (1994), *Startup: A Silicon Valley Adventure,* New York: Penguin Books.

Kurzweil, Ray (1999), *The Age of Spiritual Machines: When Computers Exceed Human Intelligence,* New York: Viking Press.

Ries, Al and Laura Ries (2000), *The 11 Immutable Laws of Internet Branding,* New York: Harper-Business.

Tenner, Edward (1996), *Why Things Bite Back: Technology and the Revenge of Unintended Consequences,* New York: Alfred A. Knopf.

Fiction Books with Premonitions of the Internet

Gibson, William (1995), *Neuromancer,* New York: Ace Books, Penguin Putnam Inc.

Stephenson, Neal (1993), *Snow Crash,* New York: Bantam Books.

Name Index

A

Abernathy, W., 34n. 35, 34n. 44, 34n. 49, 34n. 51
Achrol, Ravi, 228, 251n. 8
Agre, Philip, 358
Ahlstrom, Par, 71
Ames, B. Charles, 277, 300n. 1
Anderson, Erin, 253
Arnott, Nancy, 301n. 27
Atuahene-Gima, K., 171
Auerbach, Jon, 83
Ayers, Doug, 114n. 29, 114n. 37
Ayres, Robert, 396n. 43

B

Badaracco, J. L., Jr., 95n. 1, 95n. 6
Baig, Edward, 313
Bakos, Yannis, 275n. 39
Bank, David, 391
Barabba, Vincent, 145
Barclay, Donald, 40–43, 52
Barlow, Richard, 295, 302n. 51
Bartus, Kevin, 17, 18, 34n. 34, 34n. 41, 34n. 46–47, 34n. 52
Bass, Frank, 172n. 30
Bayus, Barry L., 53–54
Beamish, Paul W., 95n. 4
Belk, R., 300n. 2
Bellizzi, Joe, 300n. 2
Beyer, Janice M., 77, 92n. 6
Bezos, Jeff, 358
Binder, Gordon, 15
Bishop, Bill, 358
Bishop, Susan, 274n. 13, 302n. 52
Bloom, Paul, 83
Bohlman, Jonathan, 145n. 49

Borenstein, Seth, 46
Bort, Julie, 144n. 38
Boudette, Neal, 258
Boulding, William, 194, 212n. 36, 212–213n. 41–42
Bower, Joseph, 113n. 12, 113n. 17
Brandenburger, Adam, 92n. 4–5
Briones, Maricris, 251n. 4, 251n. 11–14, 357n. 86, 357n. 88–89
Brody, Herb, 140, 145n. 50–51
Bronson, Po, 358
Brown, Eryn, 287
Brown, Shona L., 68n. 1, 70, 71
Browning, Larry D., 77, 92n. 6
Bruce, Margaret, 93n. 12
Bryan, Rebecca, 380, 395n. 5
Brynjolfsson, Erik, 275n. 39
Bucklin, Louis P., 93n. 16
Buckman, Rebecca, 391
Buday, Robert, 172n. 8
Burgelman, Robert, 69n. 24
Buskin, John, 310
Byrnes, Nanette, 54

C

Cahill, Dennis, 171n. 5
Calantone, Roger, 301–302n. 36, 302n. 39, 302n. 41, 302n. 46
Calder, Bill, 235
Capon, Noel, 33n. 8, 176–178, 211n. 2–3, 211n. 5–7, 211n. 14, 211n. 16, 211n. 18
Capp, Al, 58

Carpenter, Gregory S., 54
Cespedes, Frank V., 251n. 19, 251n. 21, 252n. 23–29
Chandy, Rajesh K., 68n. 7, 68n. 11, 69n. 28–29, 113n. 16, 144n. 43
Chicos, Roberta, 145n. 49
Christensen, Clayton M., 70, 113n. 12, 113n. 17, 355n. 19, 355n. 30, 355n. 38
Christner, Richard, 358n. 29
Christoffersen, Ralph E., 378–379
Churchill, Gilbert, 143n. 5
Clark, Kim, 144n. 31, 213
Clausing, Don, 144n. 26, 144n. 30
Cohen, Adam, 391
Cohen, Allen, 172n. 8
Cooper, Arnold, 33n. 29, 68n. 14
Cooper, Lee, 68n. 1
Corey, E. Raymond, 251n. 19, 251n. 21, 252n. 23–29
Cortese, Amy, 267
Coughlan, Anne, 253
Couture, Chris, 322, 323–324
Cox, Beth, 375
Coy, Peter, 34n. 61
Cray, Dan, 258
Cusumano, Michael, 71

D

Dahlstrom, Robert, 114n. 29, 114n. 37
Datar, Srikant, 71
Davis, Stan, 358

Johnson, George, 189
Jolly, Vijay, 213
Judge, Paul, 54, 160

K

Kano, Noriaki, 131
Kao, John, 70
Kaplan, Jerry, 396
Kaplan, Steven, 356n. 67
Karlsson, C., 71
Kawasaki, Guy, 133, 144n. 33, 265, 275n. 23
Keil, Mark, 212n. 37–40
Keller, Kevin Lane, 284, 301n. 15, 301n. 22, 301n. 24–25
Kerin, Roger A., 54
Kirsner, Scott, 252n. 42–43, 253n. 50
Kleinschnitz, Don, 144n. 32
Kline, David, 213n. 65
Kluger, Jeffrey, 376
Kohli, Ajay K., 113n. 4, 114n. 34–35, 114–115
Kosnik, Thomas, 33n. 17, 33n. 19, 33n. 26, 34n. 53–54
Krajewski, J., 145n. 46
Kress, G., 145n. 45
Krishnamurthi, Lakshman, 54
Kumar, Nirmalya, 93n. 18, 228, 240, 251n. 8, 252n. 41
Kunda, Gideon, 114n. 27
Kurzweil, Ray, 396

L

Lambert, Denis, 71
Lancaster, Hal, 206
Lancioni, Richard, 274n. 2, 274n. 4
Landauer, Thomas, 33n. 28, 395n. 6
Larcker, David F., 71
Lee, S., 145n. 46
Lehnerd, A. P., 213
Lei, David T., 95n. 2
Leifer, Richard, 22
Lemonick, Michael, 74
Lenzner, Robert, 213n. 63
Leonard, Andrew, 310
Leonard-Barton, Dorothy, 68n. 5, 69n. 18, 70,

113n. 6–7, 113n. 11, 113n. 13–14, 114n. 26, 119, 120–121, 143n. 4, 143n. 6–8, 143n. 9, 143n. 11–12, 171
Levary, Reuven R., 145n. 44
Leverick, Fiona, 93n. 12
Levy, Nino, 70
Licking, Ellen, 380
Lilly, Bryan, 301–302n. 36, 302n. 46
Lipkin, Richard, 33n. 15
Littler, Dale, 93n. 12
Longstaff, Jennifer, 109–111
Louviere, Jordan J., 212n. 33
Luker, William, 29, 33n. 13–14, 33n. 16, 35n. 67
Lundell, Thomas, 14, 46, 69n. 46, 103, 141–142, 156, 184, 349
Lynn, G., 70, 171
Lyons, Donald, 29, 33n. 13–14, 33n. 16, 35n. 67

M

MacDonald, Scott, 28
Mahalan, Vijay, 172n. 14
Mahan, John, 184
Maidique, Modesto, 69n. 27
Makridakis, S., 145n. 45
Maltz, Elliot, 108, 114n. 34–35
Mandel, Michael, 3, 391
Mansfield, E., 213n. 50
Markides, Constantinos, 70
Markman, Arthur B., 54
Martens, William, 281–282
McCosh, Dan, 14
McDermott, Christopher M., 22
McDonough, Michael, 244
McGee, V. E., 145n. 45
McGonagle, John, 213
McKenna, Regis, 93, 115, 144n. 34
McLeod, Brumby, 330
McQuarrie, Edward, 124
McWilliam, Gil, 356n. 66
Meryl, David, 302n. 52
Meyer, Marc H., 212n. 21, 212n. 24, 212n. 32, 212n. 34–35, 213

Mick, David Glen, 357n. 119, 372, 395n. 3
Mohr, Jakki, 93n. 9, 93n. 13, 93n. 15, 96n. 8, 144n. 39–40, 213n. 43–44, 222n. 1, 222n. 4, 251n. 5, 300n. 2
Mohr, Judy, 200–201, 213n. 49, 214
Montealegre, Ramiro, 212n. 37–40
Moore, Geoffrey, 9, 25, 33n. 20, 33n. 22, 33n. 25, 34n. 58, 151–154, 157, 158–159, 162, 171, 172n. 11, 172n. 13, 172n. 15, 172n. 21–22, 172n. 26–28, 251n. 16–18
Moore, Gordon, 271n. 1
Moore, William, 144n. 28, 212n. 33
Moorman, Christine, 56–57
Moran, Ursula, 237, 252n. 37–39, 252–253n. 47–49
More, Roger A., 43, 52
Moreno, Michele, 144n. 33, 275n. 23
Morgan, Robert, 92n. 3
Morgan, Ruskin, 194, 212–213n. 41–42
Moriarty, Rowland, 33n. 17, 33n. 19, 33n. 26, 34n. 53–54, 237, 252n. 37–39, 252–253n. 47–48, 263, 274n. 11–12
Morone, J., 70, 171
Morris, Glen Emerson, 213n. 60
Moss, Rosabeth Kanter, 70
Mui, Chunka, 358
Muller, Etian, 172n. 14
Murphy, Tom, 358
Myer, Randy, 274n. 11
Myers, Matthew, 251n. 20

N

Nagle, Thomas T., 275
Nalebuff, Barry, 92n. 4–5
Narasimhan, Om, 113n. 1, 113–114n. 20
Narver, John C., 115

Stanton, Steven A., 70
Starkman, Dean, 3
Stavish, Sabrina, 213n. 57–59
Steele, Thomas, 189
Stepanek, Marcia, 3, 313
Stephenson, Neal, 396
Stern, Louis, 93n. 18, 196, 213n. 61, 228, 251n. 3, 251n. 8, 253
Stessa, Danielle, 3
Stevenson, Mirek, J., 145n. 52–53
Stewart, Thomas, 3, 308
Stockman, Richard, 258
Strauss, Judy, 358
Stuart, Elnora, 93n. 23
Sturdivant, Frederick, 145, 251n. 3
Sultan, Fareena, 33n. 23
Swap, Walter, 70
Syverson, Tami, 136, 137–138

T

Tabrizi, Behnam, 69n. 30, 211n. 1, 212n. 26–28
Takahashi, Dean, 83
Takerhashi, Fumio, 131
Tappen, David, 166–167
Tappen, Jeanne, 166–167
Taylor, Chris, 375
Tellis, Gerard J., 68n. 7, 68n. 11, 69n. 28–29, 113n. 16
Tenner, Edward, 396
Thach, Sharon, 171n. 5
Thomke, Stefan, 126, 131, 143n. 3, 143n. 14–15, 143–144n. 18–22, 144n. 24
Thorson, Esther, 358
Thurow, Lester, 211n. 15

Trautman, Jack, 100–101
Tsuji, Shinichi, 131

U

Urban, Glen L., 143n. 14, 145n. 49
Utterback, J., 34n. 35, 34n. 44, 34n. 49, 34n. 51

V

Varadarajan, P. Rajan, 54
Varian, Hal, 212n. 30
Vella, Carolyn, 213
Verma, Rohit, 212n. 33
Veryzer, Robert W., Jr., 22
Volcker, Paul, 3
von Hippel, Eric, 23, 34n. 50, 70, 125–128, 131, 143n. 3, 143–144n. 14–22, 144n. 24, 145, 222n. 3

W

Wagner, S., 213n. 50
Waite, Thomas, 172n. 8
Waldman, Peter, 14
Walker, Charlie, 64, 65–66
Walker, Orville C., Jr., 114n. 36, 115
Walleigh, Rick, 69n. 30, 211n. 1, 212n. 26–28
Walters, Rockney, 301–302n. 36, 302n. 46
Warshawsky, Robert, 171n. 5
Weber, Thomas, 267
Weinberg, Bruce, 145n. 49
Weinberg, Neil, 349
Weiss, Allen M., 33n. 32, 93n. 17, 95n. 5, 96n. 7, 145n. 45, 145n. 47,

166–167, 172n. 29, 172n. 31, 172n. 34–36, 211n. 4, 211n. 7–8, 211n. 10–13, 211–212n. 19, 212n. 23, 212n. 25, 212n. 31, 275n. 35–38
Westphal, Sylvia Pagan, 380
Wheelwright, Steven C., 144n. 31, 145n. 45, 213
Wijmans, Hans, 175–176
Wildstrom, Stephen, 145n. 54, 391
Wilemon, David L., 113–114n. 20, 114n. 33, 115
Wilke, John, 391
Wilson, Edith, 69n. 18, 113n. 7, 113n. 11, 113n. 13, 119, 143n. 4, 143n. 6–7
Winkler, Agnieszka, 301n. 21, 301n. 23, 301n. 26, 302
Wise, Richard, 358n. 29
Workman, John, 106, 114n. 21, 114n. 28, 114n. 30–32
Wurster, Thomas, 358, 358n. 137

X

Xuereb, Jean-Marc, 113n. 2

Y

Yoffle, David, 71
Yovivich, B. G., 144n. 38

Z

Zaltman, Gerald, 145
Zhang, Shi, 54
Zolli, Andrew, 287

Subject Index

407

Innovation *(continued)*
 liability of smallness in, 60–66
 marketing decisions and, 23–28
 market pioneering advantages and risks, 53–54
 matching research methods to, 117
 new sources of ideas for, 49
 perceptions of, 17–18
 radical, 15–16, 19–22, 102, 104–105
Innovators, 9–10, 18, 53, 151, 152, 154
Inside the Tornado (Moore), 157, 158–159
Installed base, 266
Integrated goals, 108
Intel, 25, 27, 39, 59–60, 77, 79, 83, 86–87, 121–122,
  155, 156, 185–186, 191, 195, 202, 230, 245,
  264, 279, 283
Intellectual capital, 334
Intellectual property, 194–209, 390–392
 copyright, 196, 202–203
 defined, 195
 international protection, 215–218
 managing, 207–209
 patents, 195–202, 205–207
 thefts of, 194
 trademark, 196, 203
 trade secrets, 84, 196, 203–207
Interactive conversations, 123
Interbrand competition, 226
Interdependence, 85
Intermediaries, 320–321
 cybermediaries, 247, 303–304, 309, 321
 distribution channel, 227
International markets, 186, 215–218, 326
International Submarine Engineering, 243
Internet, 228, 235–243, 303–370. *See also* Web sites
 as advertising and promotion tool, 283, 286,
  335–342
 in branding process, 286, 287
 business perspective on, 313–321
 business relationships and, 327
 buyer behavior and, 305–313
 chasm in use of, 155
 content sites, 305, 327–331
 creative destruction and, 46–47
 customer service via, 327, 347–348
 financial data and, 326
 in gathering competitive intelligence, 135
 hurdles for, 350
 as hybrid channel, 236–242
 innovation and, 59–60, 150–151
 international markets and, 326

keys to success on, 331–348
 nature of, 306–308
 on-line recruiting and, 326
 ordering costs and, 325–326
 patents for business models, 201–202
 pricing decisions and, 268–269, 318–319
 privacy and, 311–313, 387
 product development process and, 326
 resources on, 351
 search engines, 342–343, 359–370
 supply chain management and, 246–247,
  321–324
 tyranny of the served market, 49, 102, 170
 unintended consequences of, 375
Internet Advertising Bureau, 342
Internet Explorer, 155, 268, 391
Internet service providers (ISPs), 306–307
Interoperability, 192
Interpersonal relationships, 56–57
Interstitial ads, 339
Intrabrand competition, 226
Intranet, 326
Intuit, 120, 242
Invention assignment clauses, 204–205
Iomega, 52
i2 Technologies, 146, 248
Ivermectin, 381–384
iVillage, 328

J

Jackson, Thomas Penfield, 391
Jackson Products, 239
J. D. Edwards, 146
John Deere, 103
John Hancock Mutual Life Insurance, 338
Junglee Corporation, 310
Jupiter Communications, 286
Justice Department, U.S., 26, 27, 268, 279, 292,
  390, 391

K

Kano concept, 131–132
Kennard, William, 392, 393
Key3Media, 280
Keywords
 in advertising, 339
 search engines and, 362–363
Khan, Malik, 64
Killer apps, 158
Killer strategies, 52